With Assistance from the Archives of Maclean's

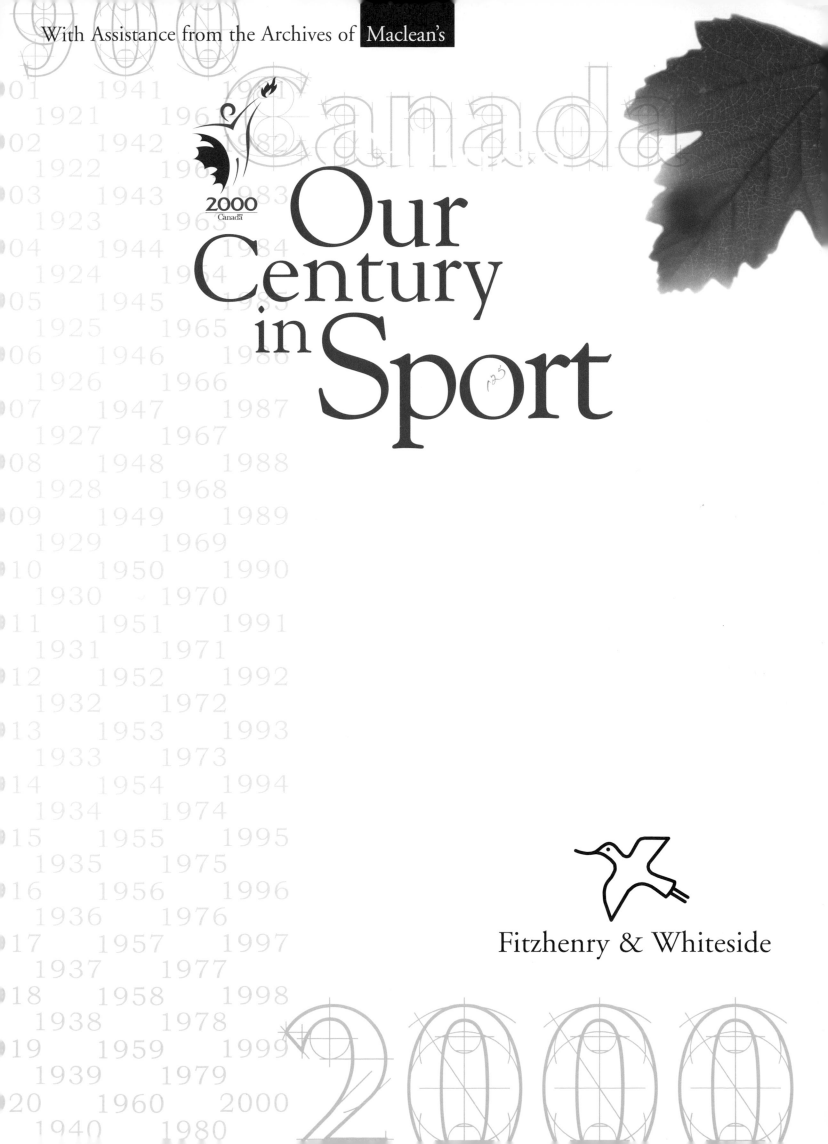

Our Century in Sport

Fitzhenry & Whiteside

Cover Photo Credits

Front Cover

Row 1, Left to Right: CSI/COA; CSI/COA; CSI/COA; CSI/COA; CSHOF; Toronto Star/Frank Lennon
Row 2, Left to Right: CSHOF; CSHOF; CSHOF; CSHOF; CSHOF; CSHOF
Row 3: CSI

Back Cover

Row 1, Left to Right: CSHOF/NSSHOF; CSI/COA; CPC; CSI/COA; OIB; CSI/COA
Row 2, Left to Right: CSHOF; CSHOF; CSHOF; CSHOF; CSHOF; CSHOF
Row 3: CSI/COA

Canada: Our Century in Sport
Copyright © 2002 Dave Best, Altis International Inc.

First Published in the United States in 2002

Fitzhenry and Whiteside Limited
195 Allstate Parkway
Markham, Ontario L3R 4T8

In the United States:
121 Harvard Avenue, Suite 2
Allston, Massachusetts 02134

www.fitzhenry.ca   godwit@fitzhenry.ca

Fitzhenry & Whiteside acknowledges with thanks the Canada Council for the Arts, the Government of Canada through its Book Publishing Industry Development Program, and the Ontario Arts Council for their support of our publishing program.

National Library of Canada Cataloguing in Publication Data

Main entry under title:
        Canada: our century in sport : 1900-2000
Includes index.
ISBN 1-55041-636-7
        1. Sports—Canada—History—20th century. I. Best, Dave

GV585.C24 2002   796'.0971'0904   C2002-900217-6

U.S. Cataloguing-in-Publication Data

Best, Dave.
        Canada our century in sport 1900 - 2000 / Dave Best. — 1st ed.
At head of title: With Assistance from the Archives of Maclean's
[608] p. : photos. (some col.) ;   cm.
Includes index.
Summary: Anthology of the most exciting and memorable moments in Canadian sport in the 20th century.
ISBN 1-55041-636-7
        1. Sports — Canada — History — Twentieth century. 2. Athletes — Canada — History — Twentieth century.   I. Maclean's. II. Title.

796/ .0971 21   CIP GV585.B47 2002

Printed and bound in Canada

The Producers gratefully acknowledge the financial support of the Government of Canada's Millennium Partnership Program in the development of this project.

2000
Canada

SHARING THE MEMORY   DES SOUVENIRS À PARTAGER
SHAPING THE DREAM   DES RÊVES À FAÇONNER

Preface/Acknowledgements

I love sport. I have loved it for as long as I can remember. I love all aspects of sport — playing, watching, reading about it, coaching, managing, and administering. I love the social dynamics sport provides — the coming together of people from different backgrounds for one thing — sport. I love the camaraderie between athletes, coaches, fans, and everyone else involved. I love to cheer on my team, and I love to applaud when the opponents do well. I know I'm not unique. Sport can provide so many positive attributes, countless thrills and endless excitement for so many people. There's an old definition of sport that includes the phrase "…a release from reality." I love that too, because regardless of how trivial it may sound, it's true. Sport provides that, plus character building, challenge, personal satisfaction … the list goes on.

Having read and dreamed about sport my whole life, I noticed that while there are countless books dedicated to specific sports, only a few multi-sport chronologies of Canadian sport have been published. So, after 15 years in sport administration that ranged from high school championships to Olympic competitions, I decided that since sport had given so much to so many for so long, it would be a good idea to collect a series of defining moments in Canadian sport. The collection turned into this book, this project, and became my way of life for three years.

Throughout the process I encountered many people to acknowledge and thank for helping the project come to fruition. There is not space to thank everyone, and those of you who helped know how grateful I truly am. Yet, I do need to single out a few: John Restivo for encouraging me to try and make a living with sport history; Allan Stewart at *Canada's Sports Hall of Fame* for taking so many calls and good-naturedly answering so many questions from me; Dr. Bob Hindmarch, for remaining my mentor and unquestioned supporter; Cathryn Jobling for helping out so much in the early part of the project, with little extrinsic benefit; John McCarney at the *Millennium Bureau of Canada* for directing me through the project's support with Government; Claude Parent for his countless hours of French research and translation, at minimum cost; the late Frank Ratcliffe, who would have loved being involved with this project and would no doubt have made it better; all the writers and researchers for working much harder than they were paid to; designers Les Stuart and Liette Guérin at ACR, for somehow managing to understand my vision when I was having trouble articulating it — the book "looks great" because of them; and a special thanks of gratitude and praise to my editor and colleague, Hans Posthuma, who in the end bought into the project as much as I did.

Finally, I need to give the biggest, sincerest, thanks to my sons Doug and Scott, whose budding athletic talents give me more pleasure watching sport than I ever had playing, and to my wife Carol, who has heard me talk of this project for more than 20 years. She accepted my passion for sport as a way of life, encouraged me along the way, and knows better than anyone what this project means to me and her role in helping it become a reality.

I hope you like the book.

Dave Best, Ottawa, October 1, 2001.

Canada

Our Century in Sport

1900-2000

Canada's Sports Hall of Fame

Member Name (Nickname)	Category	Inducted
Abate, Bob	Multi Sport	1976
Adams, Jack	Hockey / Builder	1975
Amyot, Frank	Canoeing	1955
Anakin, Douglas	Bobsleigh	1964
Anderson, George	Soccer	1973
Apps, Syl	Hockey	1975
Arnold, Don	Rowing	1957
Athans, George Jr.	Water Skiing	1974
Aubut, Marcel	Hockey / Builder	1999
Bain, Donald (Dan)	Multi Sport	1971
Baker, Norman	Basketball	1955
Balding, Al	Golf	1969
Baldwin, Matt	Curling	1973
Ball, James A. (Jimmy)	Track & Field	1959
Baptie, Norval	Speed Skating	1963
Batstone, Harry	Football	1975
Bauer, Rev. Father David	Hockey / Builder	1973
Baumann, Alex	Swimming	1987
Bédard, Myriam	Biathlon	1998
Bédard, Robert	Tennis	1996
Belanger, Albert (Frenchy)	Boxing	1956
Béliveau, Jean	Hockey	1975
Bell, Florence	Track & Field	1955
Bell, Marilyn	Swimming	1958
Ben, Big	Equestrian	1996
Bernier, Sylvie	Diving	1987
Bionda, Jack	Lacrosse	1982
Blake, Hector (Toe)	Hockey	1975
Bluenose, The	Yachting	1955
Boa, Gilmour	Shooting	1958
Boland, Martin	Rowing	1977
Boldt, Arnie	Track & Field	1977
Boucher, Frank	Hockey	1975
Boucher, Gaétan	Speed Skating	1984
Bowden, Norris	Figure Skating	1955
Bower, John William (Johnny)	Hockey	1999
Box, Ab	Football	1975
Boys, Bev	Diving	1979
Brasseur, Isabelle	Figure Skating	1996
Breen, Joseph	Football	1975
Bricker, Dr. Cal	Track & Field	1956
Brooks, Leila	Speed Skating	1972
Brosseau, Eugene	Boxing	1956
Brouillard, Lou	Boxing	1955
Browning, Kurt	Figure Skating	1994
Burka, Ellen	Figure Skating / Builder	1996
Burka, Petra	Figure Skating	1965
Burka, Sylvia	Speed Skating	1977
Burke, Lt. Col. Desmond	Shooting	1972
Burns, Tommy	Boxing	1955
Cain, Larry	Canoeing	1997
Callura, Jackie	Boxing	1969
Cameron, Michelle	Synchro Swimmimg	1991
Campbell, Clarence	Hockey / Builder	1975
Catherwood, Ethel	Track & Field	1955
Chenier, George	Snooker	1971
Chuvalo, George	Boxing	1990
Clancy, Francis M. (King)	Hockey	1975
Clapper, Aubrey Victor (Dit)	Hockey	1975
Cliff, Leslie	Swimming	1984
Clifford, Betsy	Skiing	1970
Coaffee, Cyril	Track & Field	1956
Coleman, Jim	Journalist	1985
Conacher, Charlie	Hockey	1975
Conacher, Lionel	Multi Sport	1955
Cook, Myrtle	Track & Field	1955
Cook, William (Bill)	Hockey	1975
Côté, Gerard	Track & Field	1956
Coulon, John (Johnny)	Boxing	1955
Cowan, Gary	Golf	1967
Cox, Ernest	Football	1975
Coy, Eric	Track & Field	1971
Craig, Ross B.	Football	1975
Cranston, Toller	Figure Skating	1977
Croke, Dennis	Rowing	1977
Crothers, Bill	Track & Field	1971
Cutler, Wes	Football	1975
D'Hondt, Walter	Rowing	1957
Dafoe, Frances	Figure Skating	1955
Davies, Col. Jack	Multi / Builder	1978
Davis, Victor	Swimming	1990
Day, James	Equestrian	1968
DeGruchy, John	Football	1975
Delamarre, Victor	Weightlifting	1973
Delaney, Jack	Boxing	1955
Dennett, Jack	Broadcaster	1975
Desmarteau, Etienne	Track & Field	1955
Dewar, Phyllis	Swimming	1971
Dexter, Glen	Yachting	1981
Dionne, Marcel Elphege	Hockey	1997
Dojack, Paul	Football / Builder	1995
Drake, Clare	Hockey / Builder	1989
Drayton, Jerome	Track & Field	1978
Drillon, Gordie	Hockey	1989
Dryden, Ken	Hockey	1984
Duguid, Don	Curling	1991
Dunnell, Milt	Journalist	1991

Member Name (Nickname)	Category	Inducted
Durelle, Yvon	Boxing	1975
Durnan, Bill	Hockey	1986
Duthie, George	Multi Sport	1969
Edwards, Dr. Phil	Track & Field	1997
Eisler, Lloyd	Figure Skating	1996
Elder, James	Equestrian	1968
Emerson, E.K. (Eddie)	Football	1975
Emery, Dr. John	Bobsleigh	1964
Emery, Victor	Bobsleigh	1964
Esaw, Johnny	Broadcaster	1991
Esposito, Phil	Hockey	1989
Ewing, Walter	Shooting	1958
Fabre, Edouard	Track & Field	1964
Faloney, Bernard James (Bernie)	Football	1999
Fear, A.H. (Cap)	Football	1975
Ferguson, Elmer	Journalist	1968
Filion, Herv	Harness Racing	1969
Firby, Howard	Swimming / Builder	1971
Fisher, Hugh	Canoeing	2000
Fitzgerald, William	Lacrosse	1961
Fletcher, Pat	Golf	1975
Fogh, Hans	Yachting	1985
Fortier, Sylvie	Synchro Swimmimg	1977
Foster, Harry E. (Red)	Multi Sport / Builder	1984
Fox, Terry	Track & Field	1981
Fréchette, Sylvie	Synchro Swimmimg	1999
Gabriel, Tony	Football	1985
Gainey, Robert (Bob)	Hockey	1995
Galbraith, Sheldon	Figure Skating / Builder	1980
Gall, Hugh	Football	1975
Gallivan, Danny	Broadcaster / Hockey Builder	1989
Gardiner, Charles Robert (Charlie)	Hockey	1975
Gate, George	Swimming / Builder	1983
Gaudaur, Jake Jr.	Football / Builder	1990
Gaudaur, Jake Sr	Rowing	1956
Gayford, Tom	Equestrian	1968
Genereux, George	Shooting	1955
Geoffrion, Bernard (Boom, Boom)	Hockey	1994
Gerard, Edward George (Eddie)	Hockey	1975
Gibson, George (Mooney)	Baseball	1958
Golab, Tony	Football	1975
Gomez, Avelino	Horse Racing	1990
Gorman, Charles	Speed Skating	1955
Goulding, George	Track & Field	1955
Graham, Laurie	Skiing	1993
Gray, George	Track & Field	1973
Greene, Nancy	Skiing	1967
Grenier, Dr. Jean	Speed Skating / Builder	1992
Gretzky, Wayne (The Great One)	Hockey	2000
Griffith, Harry	Football	1975
Guest, Jack Sr.	Rowing	1955
Gwynne, Horace (Lefty)	Boxing	1955
Hall, Glenn Henry	Hockey	1993
Halter, G. Sydney	Football / Builder	1975
Hamilton, Jack W.	Hockey / Builder	1972
Hanson, Fritz	Football	1987
Hartman, Barney	Shooting	1980
Harvey, Doug	Hockey	1975
Hayward, Robert	Speed Boating	1960
Heddle, Kathleen	Rowing	1997
Heggtveit, Anne	Skiing	1960
Henderson, Paul	Hockey	1995
Hepburn, Doug	Weightlifting	1955
Hewitt, Foster	Broadcaster	1975
Hildebrand, Ike	Lacrosse	1985
Hodgson, George	Swimming	1955
Howard, Richard (Kid)	Boxing	1972
Howe, Gordie (Mr. Hockey)	Hockey	1975
Hull, Robert Marvin (Bobby) (Golden Jet)	Hockey	1988
Hungerford, George W.	Rowing	1964
Huot, Jules	Golf	1978
Hutton, Ralph	Swimming	1977
Irvin, James Dickenson (Dick)	Hockey / Builder	1975
Isbister, Robert Sr.	Football	1975
Jackson, Donald	Figure Skating	1962
Jackson, Dr. Roger	Rowing	1964
Jackson, Harvey (Busher)	Hockey	1975
Jackson, Russ	Football	1975
James, Edward	Football	1975
Jelinek, Maria	Figure Skating	1962
Jelinek, Otto	Figure Skating	1962
Jenkins, Ferguson (Fergie)	Baseball	1987
Jerome, Harry	Track & Field	1971
Joliat, Aurèle (Little Giant)	Hockey	1975
Josenhans, Andreas	Sailing	1981
Juckes, Gordon	Hockey / Builder	1981
Kelly, Leonard Patrick (Red)	Hockey	1975
Kerr, Robert (Bobby)	Track & Field	1955
Kidd, Bruce	Track & Field	1968
Kirby, Peter	Bobsleigh	1964
Knox, Walter	Multi Sport	1955
Knudson, George	Golf	1969
Kreiner, Kathy	Skiing	1976
Krol, Joe	Football	1975
Kryczka, Joseph (Justice Joe)	Hockey / Builder	1990
Kwong, Norm	Football	1975
Lafleur, Guy Damien	Hockey	1996

Member Name (Nickname)	Category	Inducted
Lally, Patrick	Lacrosse / Builder	1965
Lalonde, Ed (Newsy)	Lacrosse	1955
Lancaster, Ron (The Little General)	Football	1985
Langford, Sam (Boston Tar Baby)	Boxing	1955
Laumann, Silken	Rowing	1998
Laviollette, Jack	Lacrosse	1960
Lawson, Smirle (Big Train)	Football	1975
Leadley, Frank (Pep)	Football	1975
Lecavalier, Rene	Broadcaster	1994
Lee-Gartner, Kerrin	Skiing	1995
Lemieux, Mario	Hockey	1998
Leonard, Stan	Golf	1964
Lessard, Lucille	Archery	1977
Levesque, Jean-Louis	Horse Racing	1986
Lidstone, Dorothy	Archery	1977
Loney, Don (Father of Maritime Football)	Football / Builder	1988
Longboat, Tom	Track & Field	1955
Longden, Johnny (The Pumper)	Horse Racing	1958
Loomer, Lorne	Rowing	1957
Lovell, Jocelyn	Cycling	1985
Luftspring, Sammy	Boxing	1985
Lumsdon, Cliff	Swimming	1976
Lyon, George	Golf	1955
MacDonald, Irene	Diving	1981
MacDonald, Noel	Basketball	1971
MacDougall, Hartland	Multi Sport / Builder	1976
Mackenzie, Ada	Golf	1955
MacKinnon, Lt. Col. Dan	Harness Racing	1957
MacMillan, Sandy	Sailing	1981
Magnussen, Karen	Figure Skating	1973
Mahovlich, Frank (The Big M)	Hockey	1990
Malone, Maurice Joseph (Joe)	Hockey	1975
Mara, George	Multi / Builder	1993
Marchildon, Phil	Baseball	1976
Martel, Wilbert (Marty) (Kingpin of Candles)	Bowling	1962
Martini, Paul	Figure Skating	1988
Mayer, Charles	Journalist	1971
McBean, Marnie	Rowing	1997
McBrien, Harry	Football	1978
McCarthy, Dennis	Rowing	1977
McCarthy, Dermot	Rowing	1977
McCready, Earl	Wrestling	1967
McCullough, Jack	Speed Skating	1960
McGill, Frank	Multi Sport	1959
McKinnon, Archie	Rowing	1957
McLarnin, Jimmy	Boxing	1963
McLaughlin, Col. R.S.	Horse Racing / Builder	1963
McNaughton, Duncan	Track & Field	1963
McPherson, Donald	Figure Skating	1963
Miles, John C. (Johnny)	Track & Field	1967
Millar, Ian	Equestrian	1996
Mitchell, Ray	Bowling	1975
Molson, Percy	Football / Builder	1975
Morenz, Howie (Statford Streak)	Hockey	1955
Morris, Alwyn	Canoeing	2000
Morris, Ted	Football	1975
Muir, Debbie	Synchro Swimmimg / Builder	1995
Murray, Ken	Multi Sport / Builder	1980
Murray, Mgr. Athol (Pere)	Hockey / Builder	1972
Nattrass, Susan	Shooting	1977
Nicholas, Cindy (Queen of the Channel)	Swimming	1993
Nighbor, Frank (Flying Dutchman)	Hockey	1975
Northcott, Ron (The Owl)	Curling	1970
Northern Dancer	Horse Racing	1965
Nugent, John	Rowing	1977
O'Brien, Andy	Journalist	1980
O'Brien, Joseph	Harness Racing	1965
O'Donnell, Bill (Magic Man)	Harness Racing	1992
O'Neill, John	Rowing	1966
Orr, Robert Gordon (Bobby)	Hockey	1982
Orser, Brian	Figure Skating	1991
Orton, George W.	Track & Field	1977
Ottenbrite, Anne	Swimming	1994
Ouellette, Gerard (Gerry)	Shooting	1957
Page, Percy	Basketball / Builder	1995
Parker, Jackie	Football	1987
Patrick, Frank, A.	Hockey / Builder	1975
Patrick, Lester	Hockey / Builder	1975
Paul, Robert	Figure Skating	1957
Pearce, Robert	Rowing	1975
Peden, Doug	Multi Sport	1979
Peden, William (Torchy)	Cycling	1955
Percival, Lloyd	Multi Sport / Builder	1976
Percy, Karen	Skiing	1994
Perry, Gordon	Football	1975
Perry, Norman	Football	1975
Plante, Jacques	Hockey	1981
Podborski, Steve	Skiing	1987
Pollock, Sam	Hockey / Builder	1982
Porter, R.A. (Bobby)	Multi Sport	1969
Poshby, Dr. Tom	Builder	2000
Post, Sandra	Golf	1988
Power, Walter	Rowing	1977
Presley, Gerald	Bobsleigh	1965
Price, Harry I	Multi Sport / Builder	1970
Primeau, Joe	Hockey	1975
Primrose, John	Shooting	1977
Purcell, Jack	Badminton	1955
Quilty, John (Silver)	Football	1975
Ramage, Pat	Skiing / Builder	1984
Rea, W. Harold	Multi Sport / Builder	1976
Read, Ken	Skiing	1986
Reed, George	Football	1984
Reeve, Ted	Multi Sport	1959

Member Name (Nickname)	Category	Inducted
Richard, Henri (Pocket Rocket)	Hockey	1992
Richard, Maurice (The Rocket)	Hockey	1975
Richardson, Arnold	Curling	1968
Richardson, Ernie	Curling	1968
Richardson, Garnet	Curling	1968
Richardson, Wes	Curling	1968
Riley, C.S.	Rowing	1974
Ritchie, Alvin	Football / Builder	1964
Robertson, Bruce	Swimming	1977
Robinson, Graydon (Blondie)	Bowling	1971
Robson, Fred J.	Speed Skating	1971
Rogers, Doug	Judo	1977
Rogers, Levi (Shotty)	Rowing / Builder	1973
Rosenfeld, Fanny (Bobbie)	Track & Field	1955
Ross, Arthur Howie (Art)	Hockey	1975
Roue, William J.	Yachting	1955
Rowe, Paul	Football	1975
Rubenstein, Louis	Figure Skating	1955
Russell, Jeff	Football	1975
Ryan, Joseph B.	Football	1975
Ryan, Thomas F.	Bowling	1971
Ryder, Gus	Swimming	1963
Saunders, Claude	Rowing / Builder	1982
Sawchuk, Terrance Gordon (Terry)	Hockey	1975
Schmidt, Milton Conrad (Milt)	Hockey	1975
Schmirler, Sandra	Curling	2000
Schneider, Bert	Boxing	1975
Scholes, Lou	Rowing	1955
Scott, Barbara Ann (Canada`s Sweetheart)	Figure Skating	1955
Secord, Bob	Multi Sport / Builder	1993
Selke, Frank Sr.	Hockey / Builder	1975
Sellar, Peggy	Synchro Swimmimg	1966
Shaughnessy, Frank	Multi Sport / Builder	1974
Shedd, Marjory	Badminton	1970
Sherring, William (Billy)	Track & Field	1955
Shore, Edward (Eddie)	Hockey	1975
Simpson, Ben	Football	1975
Simpson, Harold Joseph (Joe)	Hockey	1975
Simpson, William (Bill) (Mr. Soccer)	Soccer / Builder	1971
Smith, Ethel	Track & Field	1955
Smith, Graham	Swimming	1986
Smith-Johannsen, Herman (Jackrabbit)	Skiing	1982
Smythe, Conn	Hockey / Builder	1975
Somerville, Charles Ross (Sandy)	Golf	1955
Sorensen, Gerry	Skiing	1989
Speers, James R. (Mr. Racing)	Horse Racing / Breeder	1966
Sprague, David S.	Football	1975
St. Godard, Emile	Dogsled Racing	1956
Stack, Frank	Speed Skating	1974
Steen, Dave	Track & Field	1992
Stewart Streit, Marlene	Golf	1962
Stewart, Nelson Robert (Nels) (Old Poison)	Hockey	1975
Stewart, Ron	Football	1989
Stirling, Hugh (Bummer)	Football	1975
Storey, R.A. (Red)	Multi Sport	1986
Strike, Hilda	Track & Field	1972
Stukus, Annis	Football / Builder	1991
Sullivan, Jack	Journalist	1983
Supertest, Miss III	Speed Boating	1960
Tanner, Elaine (Mighty Mouse)	Swimming	1971
Taylor, Dr. Ron	Baseball	1993
Taylor, E.P.	Horse Racing / Builder	1974
Taylor, Fred (Cyclone)	Hockey	1975
Tewksbury, Mark	Swimming	1995
Thom, Linda	Shooting	1992
Thompson, James (Jim)	Speed Boating / Designer	1960
Thomson, Earl (Tommy)	Track & Field	1955
Timmis, Brian	Football	1975
Tommy, Andy	Football	1976
Townsend, Cathy	Bowling	1977
Trifunov, James	Wrestling	1960
Tubman, Joe	Football	1975
Turcotte, Ron	Horse Racing	1980
Turner, Dave	Soccer	1955
Underhill, Barbara	Figure Skating	1988
Vanderburg, Helen	Synchro Swimmimg	1983
Van Vliet, Dr. Maury	Builder	1997
Villeneuve, Gilles	Auto Racing	1983
Wagner, Barbara	Figure Skating	1957
Waldo, Carolyn	Synchro Swimmimg	1991
Wall, Nick	Horse Racing	1979
Walters, Cptn Angus	Yachting	1955
Walton, Dorothy	Badminton	1961
Waples, Keith	Harness Racing	1973
Watson, Ken J.	Curling	1969
Welch, Hawley (Huck)	Football	1975
Weslock, Nick	Golf	1971
Whalen, John	Rowing	1977
Wheeler, Lucile	Skiing	1958
Whitaker, Brig. Gen. Denis	Equestrian / Builder	1990
Williams, Percy	Track & Field	1955
Wilson, Bruce	Soccer	2000
Wilson, Harold A.	Speed Boating	1975
Wilson, Jean	Speed Skating	1955
Windeyer, Walter	Yachting	1972
Wood, Howard (Pappy)	Curling	1977
Woolf, George (The Iceman)	Horse Racing	1956
Worrall, Jim	Multi Sport / Builder	1987
Wright, Dr. Jack	Tennis	1955
Wright, Harold	Multi Sport / Builder	1987
Wright, Joe Jr.	Rowing	1955
Wright, Joe Sr.	Rowing	1955
Young, George (The Cat)	Swimming	1955
Young, Michael	Bobsleigh	1965

Credits

Production	Altis International Inc.	**Research**	Cathryn Jobling
			Jean Forrest
Producer, Managing Editor and Lead Writer	Dave Best		Claude Parent
			Shari Orders
Editing and Lead Writer	Hans Posthuma		Dave Golden
			Michael Cantalon
Writing Team	Henrietta Veerman		Elizabeth MacDonald
	Pat MacAdam		
	Bill Humber	**Photo Research**	Sandy Grant,
	Jim Kearney		*Canadian Sport Images*
	Ted Reynolds		
	Bob Hindmarch	**Design and Layout**	*ACR Communications Inc.*
	Eric Morse		Les Stuart
	Claude Parent		Liette Guérin
	Fred Hume		
		Special Thanks	*Millennium Bureau of Canada*
	Additional Feature Stories were adapted from the archives of *Maclean's*		*Canada's Sports Hall of Fame*
			Maclean's
			Hockey Hall of Fame
			VIA RAIL CANADA
			John Restivo
			Jean Forrest and Bob Hindmarch
			Claude Parent
			Allan Turowetz
			The athletes, their family members and friends for contributing stories

Photo Credits

The producers of *Canada: Our Century in Sport* made every effort to locate the owners of photos reproduced in the project. Where applicable, abbreviated photo credits are attached to the photo. The absence of a credit indicates that the photo was received from Canada's Sports Hall of Fame. If an accidental error has been made, please contact the producers at *Altis International Inc.*

Photo credit abbreviations and sources:

No credit — Canada's Sports Hall of Fame (CSHOF)
AP — Associated Press
BCSHOF — British Columbia Sports Hall of Fame
Brian Pickell
CFHOF — Canadian Football Hall of Fame
Canada Games Council
CGFC — Commonwealth Games Federation of Canada
CP — Canadian Press
CP/COA — Canadian Press / Canadian Olympic Association
CODA — Calgary Olympic Development Agency
COJO/OIB — Olympic Installations Board
CPC — Canadian Paralympic Committee

CSA — Canadian Soccer Association
CSI — Canadian Sport Images
CSI/COA — Canadian Sport Images / Canadian Olympic Association
CSO — Canadian Special Olympics
CSFAC — Canadian Sport and Fitness Administration Centre
Doug Sturrock
G&M — The Globe and Mail
HHOF — Hockey Hall of Fame
National Archives of Canada
NSSHOF — Nova Scotia Sports Hall of Fame
OIB — Olympic Installations Board
Personal Photograph by Name
Reuters
Toronto Star

Ⓜ Olympic words and symbols are official marks of the Canadian Olympic Association

Table of Contents

Chapter I

The Games of Our Lives

Sporting firsts, lifetime achievements, broken records and the importance of sport to Canadians

Canada at the Games

Canada's proud history at the Olympics,
Commonwealth Games and more

.... 171

Clouds and Silver Linings

Triumphal or disappointing second place
finishes, hardships, and even tragedy

C h a p t e r   I V

Victory

Canadians win!

. . . . 377

Introduction

"Henderson scores for Canada!" Where were you when Foster Hewitt shouted those immortal words as Paul Henderson scored his goal in the 1972 Canada-Russia series, a goal that would win a hockey game and preserve our national psyche? For people who were around in the 1970s, it was an easy question to answer — for them it was the defining sports moment of the decade, perhaps of their generation, and they could answer the question easily. Many of them would even consider it the top moment of the whole century.

That goal may top the opinion polls at the end of the century, but many other memorable moments in sport took place throughout the 20th century — moments that helped us define ourselves as a country, a province, a region, a city, or a community. Sport has been an integral thread in Canada's social fabric, and forms an important part of our collective lore and passion.

There are few aspects of Canadian society that are more popular, more dynamic, than sport. Yet, now that we have begun the new millennium and are starting to look back at the 20th century, how do we celebrate Canada's achievements in sport — the people, the myths, the stories, the joys of victory and the pains of defeat? How do we re-visit *an entire century* of sport at the end of a *millennium*? Our way was to develop a project that would celebrate 2000 moments in Canadian sport.

Trying to identify those 2000 moments was a monumental challenge, and given the subjective nature of the exercise, we were guaranteed to make some "wrong" choices regardless of how we went about it. No two people, let alone 30 million, could agree on even 10 top moments, and we wanted to pick 2000. In the end, many individual moments stood out clearly, but there were also many cases where a team or an athlete's stellar achievements over time had to be summarized as a "collective" moment, or one event selected as a "representative" moment among many.

The selection criteria were simple — the moment had to either involve a Canadian athlete, take place on Canadian soil, or have a clear Canadian connection, and it had to have been relatively widely reported in the media. From there the process quickly became more and more complicated, though. Were we giving fair representation to the Canadians who started their road to stardom here, but who shone even more brightly abroad? Were American football players who hailed from Mississippi but who played in Saskatchewan eligible? How could we ensure fair representation to all regions of the country, the various eras of the century, and as many sports as possible? And, how many moments should be allocated to the lifetime accomplishments of an athlete like Wayne Gretzky?

Then there was the decision of how much space to give each moment and how to present them. To do a feature story on each moment would take up volumes, so we chose some 200 of them to present in detail as *featured moments*. The remaining 1800 or so moments are included as short paragraphs, highlights, photo captions and entries in lists. Bearing in mind the impossibility of the task, there was no attempt to rank the moments in order of their importance. Nor did we organize the moments by sport or by strict chronology. The emphasis was rather on the story, recognizing that the nature of sport is such that a story told in the 1920s is no less riveting than one from the 1960s or the 1990s. In the end, this became simply a collection of great stories, organized into four separate themes.

Our first chapter, *The Games of Our Lives*, illustrates the important role of sport in Canadian culture, with stories of sporting firsts, records being broken or certain athletes' lifetime achievements. Next, *Canada at the Games* recounts Canada's proud history at multi-sport competitions like the Olympics or Commonwealth Games.

Canada
Our
Century
in Sport

1900–2000

To remind us that sport is not always about winning, *Clouds and Silver Linings* tells about those who finished just behind the leader, as well as stories of hardship or even tragedy. The final chapter, *Victory*, requires no explanation — Canadians have done their share of winning over the years.

There were many times when the flavour of an event was best captured by those who wrote about it at the time it happened. Accordingly, many of our *featured moments* come courtesy of our partnership with *Maclean's*, which has chronicled Canadian life for nearly a century. About 75 of our *featured moments* are adapted from articles originally published in *Maclean's*. A number of stories are also written by the athletes themselves (like Crazy Canuck Ken Read, or women's hockey star Hayley Wickenheiser), or someone close to the athlete (such as Lionel Conacher's son Brian).

It would be wrong to take it for granted that every Canadian's most memorable moment is Paul Henderson's goal. Therein lies the beauty of sport — while the passion and enthusiasm remain constant, the defining moments of each generation are different. Those born early in the century may know about Team Canada, but they might be more likely to recall the feats of athletes like the "Matchless Six" as the defining moment of their generation. Ardent sports fans born late in the century might be more apt to count an event involving Wayne Gretzky as their defining moment.

There are hundreds of moments that captured the country's attention in their day: Percy Williams' 1928 sweep of the Olympic sprints; Donovan Bailey's Olympic gold medal and world record performance in 1996; the shock at the sudden death of hockey star Howie Morenz in the 1930s; the Rocket scoring 50 goals in 50 games in 1945; young Marilyn Bell's triumphal first-ever crossing of Lake Ontario in 1954; Northern Dancer's triumph at the 1964 Kentucky Derby; Terry Fox's courageous "Marathon of Hope;" and Canada's women's hockey team winning all six world championships in the century, to name but a few. And it wouldn't take a die-hard sports fan to remember the 1988 day that sprinter Ben Johnson was disqualified for steroid use after winning the Olympic 100m title.

But those stories are only the tip of the iceberg. Canada has a rich and proud history of sporting achievements, and the 20th century was full of moments that inspired us, thrilled us, and sometimes even disappointed us. Some of the stories we collected are about athletes who have been household names at one point or another through the century — you'll read about Team Canada '72, Wayne Gretzky, Fanny Rosenfeld, Lionel Conacher, Nancy Greene and many more. You'll also read about people whose fame may have been more fleeting, but whose achievements remain extraordinary.

Just like sport is not just about winning, not all our stories are about gold medals and victories. Many sporting moments are memorable because of what they conveyed to us about the character of the participants or the passion of the moment rather than the end result.

Sport remains an important part of Canadian culture. The courage and determination that are essential ingredients of an athlete's success are equally necessary in other aspects of life, which probably explains why so many Canadians like to both watch and participate in sports. As Pierre de Coubertin, the founder of the modern Olympic movement said, "It is better to have fought well and lost than not to have fought at all." Throughout the 20th century, Canadians certainly fought well.

Canada
Our
Century
in Sport

1900-2000

Sport is an integral part of
Canada's social fabric
and touches almost all our lives.
It includes many dramatic elements
that spark our interest,
whether as participants or spectators —
conflict, emotion, struggle, character
development and even surprise endings.
In The Games of Our Lives, we have
collected stories that captured our
imagination over the years,
whether it was because they were about
records being broken,
an athlete's achievement over a lifetime,
or a sporting first.

1937 1991
1900 1962
1938 1992
1902 1967
1940 1993
1905 1971
1948 1994
1909 1973
1950 1999
1912 1976
1952 2000
1915 1978
1954
1928 1980
1955
1930 1984
1956
1935 1989
1957
1936 1990
1960

Canada
Our
Century
in Sport

1900-2000

Chapter 1

The
Games of
Our Lives

Canada's Athletes

Wayne Gretzky

HHOF — Dave Sandford

HHOF — Graphic Artists

of the Century

Female Athlete of the Century

Nancy Greene

Hockey

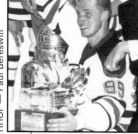

HHOF — Paul Bereswill

The Best in the World

By Peter Gzowski
January 25, 1988

You can play it over and over again in your mind's eye, and it is still just as pretty as it was last September.

With a minute and a half left on the clock, the Canadians line up for what could be the final face-off of the series. They are deep in their own end, tied 5-5, and the crowd in Copps Coliseum in Hamilton is throbbing. Gretzky coasts in to the red circle, but when the Russians send out their face-off specialist, he gives way to Dale Hawerchuk of the Winnipeg Jets and takes up a position on the far reaches of the right wing, like a sleeper in the old football play. The other Canadian skaters — Paul Coffey on the left, Hawerchuk, Larry Murphy and Mario Lemieux — are strung out in a single rank. The Russians are set three and two.

Hawerchuk wins the face-off. Lemieux pounces from his position on the right and slaps the puck outward and towards the boards at the left. Meantime, Gretzky has left his sleeper's position and crossed the ice. As Lemieux lifts his eyes, he sees the familiar 99 ahead of the play, sprinting along the boards. He shovels the puck forward. Gretzky scoops it up in full flight and heads across centre.

Now Larry Murphy breaks clear on Gretzky's right. As they cross the blue line, they are two on one against a retreating Soviet defenceman. For an instant, it looks as if the moment has passed — as if the rush has been diffused and the Soviets, flying back into their own zone, will have a chance to regroup. Gretzky veers left, still carrying the puck. The defenceman, now sure Murphy's momentum has carried him past the point where he can receive a pass, flings himself to the right.

And now comes the moment of magic. Gretzky gently wafts the puck into what at first appears to be the open ice behind the play. But only at first. Suddenly, there is Mario Lemieux, now in full control of his body and

skating at full steam into the Soviet zone. The puck clicks neatly onto his stick. He glides, aims, cocks the trigger and fires a classically perfect wrist shot into the top right corner of the net, shooting, as the scouting reports have suggested, high on Sergei Mylnikov's glove side. From face-off to the glow of the goal judge's light, four seconds have elapsed. The Canadians, for the time being at least, are back on top of the hockey world.

In the winter Wayne Gretzky turned three — he was born in January of 1961 — his father, Walter, made a rink in their backyard in Brantford, Ont. All through Wayne's childhood, the rink was a passion for both of them. In the daytime, the boy would skate on it and play hockey with the sticks Walter used to shave down for him. In the

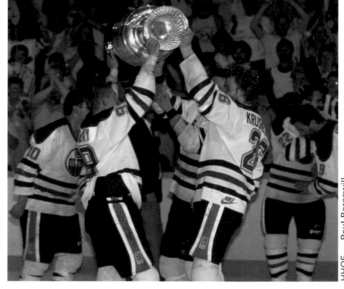

HHOF — Paul Bereswill

evenings, they would work together on the drills Walter had worked out. Wayne skated through networks of tin cans and practised leaping over sticks. Walter would water the rink every night using a lawn sprinkler, until the year his wife, Phyllis, refused to go to the hardware store to buy a replacement for the one that had broken. "They will think I'm crazy," Phyllis said, "buying a lawn sprinkler in February."

Wayne started in organized hockey when he was six, and Walter was his first coach. Walter had his own drills there, too. He would shoot the puck into a corner, for instance, and tell the kids to chase it. When they chugged doggedly into the corner, he would yell, "No, no." "Wait for it to come round," he would say. "Don't go where it is — go where it's going to be. Anticipate, anticipate." Watching Gretzky appear so quickly in front of Lemieux last fall, you could think about that.

The year Wayne turned eight, he scored 104 goals in 40 games. When he was 10 and stood four feet, four inches, he scored 378 in 68 games. I met him when he was 14. He had scored 988 goals by then. He came into *This Country in the Morning*, the CBC Radio program

I was hosting at the time. He was already, if you remember, quite a celebrity. Much later I came to know a couple of young men who had played against him, and they told me that they thought he was a little spoiled, set apart. But I liked him. He knew he was good, all right, but to my eye, at least, it hadn't gone to his head. He was polite and rather serious. He had a kind of buck-toothed look, partly from the three teeth that had to be pegged into his mouth to replace those he'd broken on the hockey rink. I remember asking him if he thought he'd ever make $100,000 a year playing hockey, and he just laughed.

In the summer of 1980, I decided to write a book about hockey. Although I hadn't figured out what shape to impose on it, I was toying with the idea of following one NHL team around through a season. I called Wayne, who was just coming into his own as the dominant player of his time — he had tied with Marcel Dionne for the scoring leadership the season before — and we arranged to play golf. He suggested that I choose the Edmonton Oilers. The result was what I called *The Game of Our Lives*. But most people who mention my treatise on hockey just describe it as "your book about Gretzky."

I know why, of course. He is hockey now. Although virtually every age of the game has had its pre-eminent players — Morenz, Richard, Howe, Hull, Orr — no one has ever transcended it as he has. An American magazine that once used to treat hockey with little more seriousness than steeplechasing has called him "the greatest athlete in the world." A newspaper piece I read last weekend on the news of his engagement made reference to Charles and Di. The little kid from Brantford is now the biggest star we have.

We spent a lot of time together in the season I followed the Oilers, and I'd like to think, became friends. Even then, though, it was hard to get time alone with him, away from the groupies and other hangers-on. I used to wonder at his patience. Everyone he talked to — including me, of course — wanted something from him; as best he could, he tried to give it.

He was always most comfortable talking hockey. He didn't read much about anything else, and on the rare evenings he had to watch television, he was happy with *The Love Boat*. But on the game, he was an encyclopedia — and nearly always serious. Though our relationship was an easy one, involving much banter, I could never tease him about his occasional lapses on the ice: the missed breakaways or the lost face-offs. His face would turn red, as I am sure you have seen it after a referee's call against him or after his team goes down a goal.

At one point in the season, I left the team and spent some time among academics, trying to figure out what gifts Wayne had that so set him apart from all the other boys who had started playing as he had and who at least seemed to have similar physical gifts. When I returned with the theory I eventually expounded in the book, which involved a lot of phrases like "short-and long-term memory" and "chunks of information," and drew analogies from everything from chess to jazz piano, he understood it instantly, and used to enjoy going over tapes of his goals with me and showing how it applied. I thought of those days again, too, when I contemplated his pass to Lemieux, for essentially my theory holds that where lesser players see the positions of other individuals in a game, Wayne sees situations. In reaction to any particular pattern of play, he simply summons up one of the chunks of information he has stored in his long-term memory, without having to go through the process of rational thought — having taken the pass from Lemieux behind him, he knew without thinking where Lemieux would next emerge.

I don't see him much these days. The television where I live shows too many less interesting teams than the Oilers, and with the hockey book behind me, I have returned to broadcasting and other interests. When I do call him, I am embarrassed to say, it is almost always because I, too, want something from him — an interview for the radio, an appearance at some event. When he can, still, he accommodates me, and it impresses me, as much now as it did in 1974, how little he has let his fame go to his head. ❧

The Great One

By James Deacon
April 26, 1999

Hollywood will no doubt make a movie about Wayne Gretzky some day, and it will have to include the scene where he plays his last game in Canada, in Ottawa against the Senators: Gretzky and his New York Rangers, who had already been eliminated from playoff contention, were playing the home team to a draw, thus denying the Senators a chance to boost their own playoff position. Yet with 4:45 left in the third period, during one of Gretzky's shifts, the crowd began to chant "One more year! One more year!" Then, minutes later during a stoppage in play, the big-screen scoreboard above the ice replayed highlights from Gretzky's career and the PA system played Carly Simon's *Nobody Does it Better*. The crowd rose in tribute and players on both benches stood, too, banging their sticks against the boards and on the ice in the quintessential hockey salute.

When the game finally ended in a 2-2 tie, the Senators lined up, one by one, to shake Gretzky's hand. As for the Corel Centre fans, they stood by their seats long after they would normally have scattered for the parking lots, cheering, whistling, clapping. This from the *opposing* teams' supporters.

A team player to the end, Gretzky holds every meaningful NHL goal-scoring record, yet his greatest hockey talent was his knack for setting up other players to score. ❦

"I remember when he got off that little jet I sent to get him. Here's this skinny little kid with peach fuzz. I thought, 'My God, I paid $750,000 for that?' Just kidding."

- Peter Pocklington, former Edmonton Oilers owner

"My fondest memory of Wayne is undoubtedly the Canada Cup. Practising with him and playing alongside Wayne for six weeks was the turning point in my career. He showed me how to win, and for that I am eternally grateful."

- Mario Lemieux, Pittsburgh Penguins

Nancy Greene, Olympic Champion

Canada's tiger of the slopes

Because of the utterly fearless fashion in which she raced down her home hill of Red Mountain at Rossland, BC, Canada's greatest alpine skier, Nancy Greene, was dubbed the "tiger of the slopes." Indeed, the sobriquet gained such currency that she wore a tiger head decal on her crash helmet while winning the World Cup of skiing in 1967 and, in 1968, a second World Cup, plus gold and silver Olympic medals.

Inasmuch as the World Cup competition lasts a full season and demands winning performances virtually every weekend, December through March, ski racers view it as the true world championship. Winning it just once is a tremendous feat. Winning it two consecutive years, and fitting in a couple of Olympic medals (gold in giant slalom, silver in slalom) at Grenoble along the way, was phenomenal.

Her coach, Verne Anderson, once pinpointed the two extras she had going for her, the two special qualities that made her the finest woman skier of her time: fearlessness and strength. He said she was the first woman skier he had ever encountered who kept going strong at certain danger points where the women of her era would put on the brakes just a little.

Just as importantly, she was the first woman skier to do extensive weight training to strengthen her legs. Routinely during fall training, she did 40 deep knee bends daily with a 170-pound barbell across her shoulders. She beat her opponents with much better times on the bottom half of the race courses. While their legs were beginning to tremble with fatigue, hers were still rock solid at the finish line.

Although hailed by many as an overnight success story, she could honestly reply that she spent more than 20 years becoming an "overnight success." In fact she started skiing when she was only three.

But she skied only for fun until she was 14, and only by accident did she start competitive skiing. Young skiers from all across Canada came to Rossland in 1958 for the Canadian junior championships. Several girls, including two from British Columbia, were injured in practice runs on Red Mountain's steep and icy slopes.

The BC coach, who already had Nancy's older (by two years) sister, Liz, on the team, asked her to substitute for one of the injured girls. She accepted the challenge and 12 hours later, in her first race beyond local high school competition, she finished third in the slalom.

In the downhill the next day she finished second. Liz, whom she was soon to eclipse, finished first in both races. The two oldest of six children, it might be said that they came by their talent naturally. Mom and dad were so much into the sport, they spent their honeymoon on a ski holiday.

Her good results changed Nancy's life. Suddenly she wanted to compete. At 14, she became a racer. She trained with her older sister and 18 months later was invited to join the Canadian Olympic program. She came along so quickly that she was chosen, at just 16, to the Canadian team for the 1960 Olympics at Squaw Valley, California.

While finishing well back in both slalom and giant slalom, she had the good luck to room with Ottawa's Anne Heggtveit, who won gold in the slalom. She said later that Anne taught her a lot about what it takes to be a winner.

Recovering from a broken leg in her final race of the 1960-61 season, she got into weight training on the advice of her coach, a move that was to lay much of the foundation for her eventual success. For various reasons, she also spent two years training with the men's ski team. But the breakthrough didn't come at the 1964 Olympics in Innsbruck.

There she discovered that strength and courage could not overcome a certain lack of technical excellence. She finished a disappointing — to her — seventh in the downhill. That was followed by a more disappointing 16th in the slalom and 15th in the giant slalom.

Her breakthrough year came in 1965 when she won the overall title, against a top international field, at the US Nationals at Mount Crystal, Washington. She was first in both slalom and giant slalom and fourth in the downhill.

At the world championships in Portillo, Chile, a year later, she was 50 yards from the downhill finish line and a certain winner when she caught an edge and went out of the race in three spectacular somersaults. Two days later, with a ski pole taped to one hand because it was so sore from the fall she couldn't grip it, she managed a fourth place finish in the giant slalom.

When World Cup competition started in the 1966-67 season, Nancy was still angry from her Chilean experience and translated her feelings into a controlled fury that saw her launch the nine-event competition with three consecutive victories, starting with the slalom and giant slalom at Oberstaufen, Germany. She followed that up with victories in the downhill at Grindewald, Switzerland, and, after catching a tip and failing to complete the slalom, the giant slalom. Four wins in her first five World Cup races.

She skipped three more events in Europe in order to return home with the Canadian team to meet non-World Cup obligations in Canada. Some people wondered about her jeopardizing her chances of winning the overall World Cup, but she felt that competing at some Canadian events would provide a needed boost to domestic racing. In first place when she left, she was third when the tour came to North America for its last three stops. It took a few races to get back into top racing shape, which meant she still needed to win two giant slaloms and a slalom in the final meet at Jackson Hole, Wyoming, in order to win the cup. She did just that, her 176 points putting her just above Marielle Goitschel of France, with 172.

With the victory, the Canadian public now paid as much attention to her as Europeans had already been doing. The federal government, which was in the early stages of funding the development of sport in Canada, asked her to sit on a committee to study sport. Despite her public commitments, she was able to stay focused and fit in preparation for the next season.

The 1968 World Cup season started slower than expected, putting her in third place after two events. To compound her problems, she injured her ankle in training just a few weeks before the Olympics in Grenoble.

Even though she was still recovering from the ankle sprain that had kept her off skis for two weeks, she remained a medal favourite, and was named the Canadian team's flag bearer in the Opening Ceremonies. Greene had built her reputation with her slalom and giant slalom victories, but her favourite race was the downhill. That's the one she really wanted to win at Grenoble.

It was not to be. She had the right wax, but some dirt that had been tracked across the starting area from the feet of various officials, stuck in the wax. It slowed her to the extent of a disappointing 10th place finish and brought her close to tears while being interviewed by the Canadian media.

But she made up for that finish in her next two races — a silver medal in the slalom, .2 seconds behind winner Marielle Goitschell, and gold in the giant slalom, nearly three seconds faster than the runner-up, France's Annie Famose.

Buoyed by the gold medal, she went on to win nine straight races, seven of them World Cup competitions, to win the cup for a second time. The second to last one, the first and only World Cup competition at Red Mountain, drew all of the world's top skiers — men and women — to Rossland, the little town of 5,000 where she learned to ski.

Fittingly, she won the giant slalom and clinched her second World Cup triumph. One more race in California and her 10-year racing career was over. With no more worlds to conquer, she retired a couple of months before her 25th birthday. In 1968 she was named, not only Canada's female athlete of the year, but also the best overall Canadian athlete of the year (Lou Marsh Trophy), and Canada's woman of the year. On top of that, she received the Order of Canada.

Away from the competitive arena, Greene was one of the earlier Canadian athletes to translate her success on the slopes into an endorsement contract, popularizing Mars chocolate bars with a generation of Canadians.

Both before and since the 1960s, Canadian women skiers have distinguished themselves in Olympic and World Cup competition, but in terms of world-wide impact and accomplishment she ranks number one. In 1969 she married Al Raine, later Canada's national alpine ski coach, and they became pioneers in the development of North America's premier ski area, Whistler-Blackcomb, just north of Vancouver.

The Nancy Greene Ski League, which she formed for the development of Canadian youngsters starting out in skiing, is her lasting legacy. More than 30 years after her retirement, her accomplishments stood the test of time, as Canadian Press named her the Canadian Female Athlete of the Century. ❧

Nancy Greene takes Olympic silver and gold

February 6, 1968 – Opening Ceremonies
In 1967 the International Ski Federation (FIS) initiated the World Cup to determine the best skiers. Nancy Greene won the inaugural overall World Cup, a feat she repeated in 1968. On this day, Nancy Greene led the Canadian team in the Opening Ceremonies of the 1968 Olympic Winter Games in Grenoble, France. At 24, she was the veteran of the Canadian women's ski team and the leader for the whole team.

February 10, 1968
The weather was awful – snowy and windy. When the day finally cleared enough, it was time for the first ski event, the downhill. After posting the fastest times in practice runs, Greene wound up a disappointing 10th. Greene blamed herself. Her coach blamed himself. Even though she was a world champion, she had lost her confidence.

February 13, 1968
In the two World Cup slaloms prior to the Games, Greene finished third in one and was disqualified from the other for missing a gate. Coupled with her downhill disappointment, she entered Olympic slalom in low spirits. However, a surprising fifth place finish in the first run gave her renewed hope, and new energy. In the second run she confidently wove her way through the course, surpassing the times of three skiers ahead of her and finishing just .29 seconds behind the gold-medal winner to claim the silver medal. She would take her renewed confidence into the final event, the giant slalom.

February 15, 1968
The giant slalom was Greene's specialty. On this day she was ready, confident and poised. She would attack the course. A few hundredths of a second, less time than it takes to blink, can make all the difference in the world between the top skiers, where winners are separated by mere fractions of a second. Greene exploded from the start gate, accelerating like none other. Keeping her momentum and her balance on the icy slopes, her time of 1:51.97 put her nearly three seconds ahead of France's Annie Famose who finished in 1:54.61 and Switzerland's Fernande Bochatey's 1:54.74.
Nancy Greene delivered a perfect race and won the Olympic gold medal.

On March 26, 1968 – Retirement
Nancy Greene, one of Canada's top athletes of the century, announced her retirement at 24 years of age. *"This year, I had set gold medals and world championships as my goals. With those behind me, it seems that to set these goals again would not be progress at all."*

December, 2000
The Canadian Press announced that Nancy Greene had been selected as Canada's Female Athlete of the Century in a nationwide poll.

Athletes of the First

Lionel Conacher

Canada's athlete of the first half-century

In 1950, Lionel Conacher had been retired from sports for 15 years. But there was no surprise, only nods of recognition when the Canadian Press announced he was voted in as the outstanding athlete of the half-century.

The oldest boy of a family of 10 raised on a teamster's salary, Lionel saw sports as the way out of poverty. All the children were athletic, but it was Lionel who set their collective sights on sports. He led the family to a better life and on the way, created a Canadian legend.

The "Big Train," as he was called, earned the name through hard work. He was a natural athlete in build – six feet, one inch and 200 pounds of muscle. But he was the first person in the family to play sports, and had to learn everything from scratch.

Hard work and talent more than made up for the lack of family tradition. The "Big Train" earned his nickname because he could do it all. Hockey, football, lacrosse, baseball, wrestling, boxing — Lionel was an all-round athlete who excelled at every sport he tried, the likes of which has not been seen since. Skill, grace, dexterity, smarts, athleticism, power, determination, fair play: every adjective in the book of sports applies to Lionel Conacher.

At 16, he won the Ontario 125-pound wrestling championship. At 20, he won the Canadian lightweight boxing championship in his first competitive bout. When Jack Dempsey came to town, it was Lionel they turned to for an exhibition match. He didn't win, but by his own admission, he got his punches in.

In one memorable day in 1922, he led his baseball team, Toronto Hillcrest, to the Ontario championship, hitting a triple in the final inning. Then he roared across town to play the Ontario lacrosse championship. His team, the Toronto Maitlands, was behind 3-0 when he arrived. Lionel scored four goals and assisted on another to pull his team to a 5-3 win.

Football was his favourite sport. In the 1921 Grey Cup, Lionel scored three touchdowns, almost single-handedly pulling the Toronto Argonauts ahead of the Edmonton Eskimos. US football coaches sang his praises, and he, a Canadian, was even called down to coach at Rutgers University.

Half Century

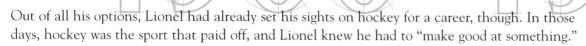

Out of all his options, Lionel had already set his sights on hockey for a career, though. In those days, hockey was the sport that paid off, and Lionel knew he had to "make good at something."

At the advanced age of 16, he learned to skate. And it was tough going from the start. "The average kid starts skating at the age of seven or younger," Lionel said later. "I laced on skates for the first time at the age of 16, and you'll never know the humiliation and utter weariness of the long hours which I spent on rinks with younger and much more skilled players before I won a post in junior circles."

But for Lionel Conacher, giving up was never an option. Compared to the other players, he was awkward on the ice, but he was smarter. A defenceman, Lionel figured out all the angles for covering the net — and so was able to foil any fast-moving forward from breaking around and getting a clear shot at the net. To cope with his slow feet, he'd drop to one knee, with split-second timing, and slide to block the shot. One Toronto sports writer, Ted Reeve, dubbed him the "Travelling Netminder" for that move.

His tactics worked. The boy Lionel played pro hockey for the Pittsburgh Pirates, New York Americans, Montreal Maroons and Chicago Blackhawks. He was on two Stanley Cup winning teams — Chicago in 1934 and Montreal in 1935.

At Lionel's urging, Charlie Conacher followed his big brother into hockey. He became one of Canada's most celebrated hockey players as part of the famous "Kid Line" on the Toronto Maple Leafs during the '30s. One night, Leafs boss Conn Smythe put right-winger Charlie together with center Joe Primeau and right-winger Harvey Jackson, aged 20, 22 and 18 respectively. The "kids" won that game, and the next, and so the Kid Line was born and went on to win three Stanley Cups in six years.

Basically, in those years, if one Conacher kid wasn't winning the Cup, the other was.

There was glory, yes, but there was also pain. Professional sports, then as today, is tough on the individual. Lionel had an estimated 600 stitches from hockey injuries, with 150 on his face and head alone. He broke his nose eight times. As a big defenceman, he looked after the smaller forwards on his team, once taking 17 minutes in penalties for fights with five different players.

In another game, with five minutes to go, he fell on someone's skate. It left an eight-inch long gash on his thigh that took the team doctor 14 stitches to pull together. But Lionel just got up and finished the game without a word.

Yet even as Lionel saw sports as means to an end for himself and his family, he was also driven by a love of the game. He went into politics in his retirement, but never stopped playing sports, literally until the day he died.

On May 26, 1954, Lionel drove from Toronto to Ottawa to play in the annual softball game between Members of Parliament and the press gallery. In the sixth inning, he hit a ball into left field, sent another player home and, breathing heavily, made it to third base.

A few seconds later, he toppled to the ground. Lionel Conacher, the Big Train, was dead, although his legend would live on. ♣

Brian Conacher talks about being the son of the greatest athlete of the first half-century

"When I was born in 1941, my father's sports career was long over. He retired in 1937. I didn't really know my father as an athlete," recounts Brian Conacher. *"I learned that as I grew up with the name Conacher.*

While my father was still alive, I can remember him coming to some of my games, but not with any regularity. There could be two reasons for that. He was an MP, having to drive to Ottawa, and he wasn't around a lot.

But it might have been his choice, because it would put a lot of pressure on us as children if he were always there. How could you ever play up to that? You'd be expected by the name to be better than good.

When Dad died in 1954, I was 12, turning 13. When he was named athlete of the half-century, I was 9. I don't really remember that event.

But what I remember vividly, is that after that, people to this day even, would come up to me and say, 'Who is your father, Charlie or Lionel?' And I answer, Lionel. Their next words are always, 'What a great athlete. I remember when...'

That is the most familiar phrase of my youth. They knew who my Dad was, and who Uncle Charlie was. And they always spoke of them with the greatest respect and told the greatest stories.

But for all that, we kids were never led to feel like sports was our only choice. We were taught to see education as important.

Dad's family was poor when he was growing up. He played sports to get to a better life. Dad never wanted us to have the feeling that we were only destined to be pro athletes. He did sports so we could have a choice.

Both my brother Lionel Jr. and I did play professional sports — he played football for the Alouettes, and I played hockey. But all three of us boys went to Upper Canada College, as did my son.

Having gone through the school of hard knocks, the injuries, and the competition, I think that Dad's goal was it was going to be a better life for his kids than for him. Even though he excelled at sports, it was and is a tough life."

Canada's female athlete of the first half-century

There is a park named after her in Toronto, right downtown between the SkyDome and the CN Tower. A stamp issued in 1996 has her picture on it. A street bears her name in her hometown of Barrie, Ontario. Every year, the Canadian Press hands out a trophy in her name to the top Canadian female athlete.

So, who is she?

Fanny "Bobbie" Rosenfeld is Canada's female athlete of the first half-century. She is celebrated for epitomizing women's sport in the 1920s, a decade famous for flapper girls and bobbed hair, a backlash against staid Victorian ideology. For women, part of that newfound emancipation and freedom was the rise of women's sports, with Bobbie Rosenfeld leading the way.

Historians have struggled to do full justice to Rosenfeld's abilities. Like her male counterpart, Lionel Conacher, Rosenfeld was the consummate, all-round athlete, who excelled in every sport available to girls and women at the time. Rather than list them off, many simply say, "Well, she wasn't good at swimming…"

Rosenfeld was born in Russia on December 28, 1903. While very young, she immigrated with her family to Canada. She got into sports through her older brother, who was an outstanding athlete himself and proud of his sister's prowess, especially her slapshot. Rosenfeld was soon playing baseball, basketball and hockey. She also played tennis, winning the Toronto Ladies Grass Court Championship in 1924.

But it was her accomplishments on the track that really brought her to national attention. She won her first trophy at a meet in Barrie in 1922 and she never looked back. In 1925, Rosenfeld entered the Ontario Ladies Track and Field championships in Toronto. She was the only entrant from the St. Pats Athletic Club — and she won enough points on her own to capture the team title.

Her greatest glory came during the 1928 Olympic Games in Amsterdam. Rosenfeld was one of the "Matchless Six," the team of six female athletes that led Canada to the overall team point title at the Amsterdam Olympic Games. Her single most celebrated feat is winning gold in the 4 x 100m relay at those Games — her first leg opened a lead that no other country could close and set an Olympic record.

It could have been her second gold of the Games, which would have matched "Peerless" Percy Williams' medal count. Earlier, she was awarded a silver medal in the 100m, losing to American Elizabeth Robinson in a controversial, split judging decision. Some observers felt the finish was either a dead heat or that Fanny won. Rounded off by a

Fanny Rosenfeld

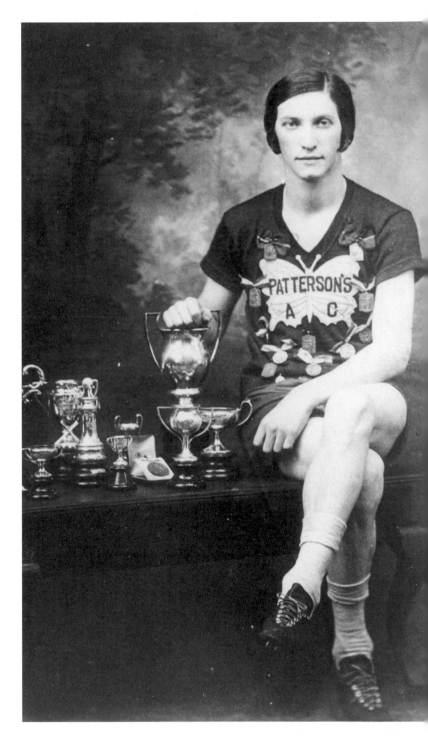

At the 1925 Ontario Ladies Track and Field meet in Toronto, Fanny Rosenfeld was the only entrant from the St. Pats Athletic Club to enter the meet. Nonetheless, she single-handedly earned enough points to win the overall team title for the Club. She won the discus, the 220-yard race, the 120-yard hurdles and the long jump events. She also came second in the 100-yard run and the javelin throw.

1928

Women's 100m Olympic Final

Canadian favourite Myrtle Cook, and the German champion, each had two false starts and were eliminated from the women's 100m final in Amsterdam, 1928. The fifth start was clean and Canadians Fanny Rosenfeld and Ethel Smith took off madly down the track. The duo hit the finish tape at apparently the same instant, joined by the American, Elizabeth Robinson. The Canadian team jumped with pride, sure that Fanny had edged out the other two. They were even hopeful that Ethel could have managed second place. It was not to be. When the official results were posted, the American was first, with Fanny second and Ethel third. The Canadians immediately launched a protest, which Canadian Amateur Athletic Union President, Dr. Lamb, refused to back for "gentlemanly reasons." Criticism from all corners of the official starter, American John Taylor, was so intense that he resigned his post and from the Olympic staff.

fifth in the 800m, her accomplishments have not been matched by any Canadian female track athlete since. In fact, she garnered more individual points than Percy Williams, who, with two gold medals, was publicly hailed as the hero of the Amsterdam Olympic Games.

Despite the success of Canada's women's team, there were still many naysayers who felt women did not belong in sport, including none other than Dr. A.S. Lamb, the president of the Amateur Athletic Union of Canada. Lamb's perspective was shared by the President of the International Olympic Committee, Compte de Baillet-Latour. Besides combating these negative attitudes, Rosenfeld was also Jewish, which in her day meant facing additional prejudice. Ultimately, this made her triumphs even more meaningful.

The forces that wanted to limit women's sport gained a partial victory. Although women's events continued to be held, races longer than 200 metres were banned by the International Amateur Athletic Federation until 1960.

Rosenfeld's athletic career was cut short at age 30 by the onset of a painful, debilitating arthritis. She was awarded the title of female athlete of the half-century in 1950, nudging out figure skater Barbara Ann Scott by one vote. ❧

Fanny Rosenfeld winning a race in Toronto, 1924.

Fanny Rosenfeld, far right, was the anchor for the famed Matchless Six, Canada's first women's Olympic track team, 1928.

1936-2000
Outstanding Athletes

The Lou Marsh Trophy

The Lou Marsh Trophy is awarded every year to the person judged to be Canada's best athlete, whether male or female, amateur or professional, regardless of sport. Awarded since 1936, it also serves as a memorial to a man considered the premier sports journalist of his time.

Lou Marsh toiled for the Toronto Star for 43 years, starting as a copy boy and eventually becoming a widely popular columnist and the newspaper's sports editor. After his untimely death from a stroke in 1936 at the age of 58, messages of condolence came from athletes, journalists, sports officials and ordinary people from all across North America. His column, "With Pick and Shovel," had been read by thousands of people as the authoritative word on sport happenings of the day.

Marsh was an athlete himself, and also an accomplished referee, and it was not unknown to find him writing about the very hockey game or boxing match he had just refereed. Blunt, authoritative and outspoken, people read what he wrote, even if they didn't agree with him.

It was testimony to his stature among his peers that within months of his death they established the trophy that bears his name. Some years the selection has been obvious, with one athlete's performance standing out clearly. Other years, the debate has been long and hard to choose the most deserving athlete from a long list of worthy contenders. Nonetheless, the list of winners reads like a Who's Who of Canadian sport. ❧

Lou Marsh trophy winners

1936 Dr. Phil Edwards Track & Field	**1958** Lucile Wheeler Alpine Skiing	**1979** Sandra Post Golf
1937 Lt. W. Marshall Cleland Horsemanship	**1959** Barbara Wagner/ Robert Paul Figure Skating	**1980** Terry Fox Track & Field
1938 Bobby Pearce Rowing	**1960** Anne Heggtveit Alpine Skiing	**1981** Susan Nattrass Shooting
1939 Robert Pirie Swimming	**1961** Bruce Kidd Track & Field	**1982** Wayne Gretzky/ Rick Hansen Hockey/Wheelchair
1940 Gérard Côté Track & Field	**1962** Donald Jackson Figure Skating	**1983** Wayne Gretzky Hockey
1941 Theo Dubois Rowing	**1963** Bill Crothers Track & Field	**1984** Gaétan Boucher Speed Skating
1942-1944 Awarded to the perpetual memory of All Canadian athletes who made the supreme sacrifice	**1964** George Hungerford/ Roger Jackson Rowing	**1985** Wayne Gretzky Hockey
	1965 Petra Burka Figure Skating	**1986** Ben Johnson Track & Field
1945 Barbara Ann Scott Figure Skating	**1966** Elaine Tanner Swimming	**1987** Ben Johnson Track & Field
1946 Joseph Krol Football	**1967** Nancy Greene Alpine Skiing	**1988** Carolyn Waldo Synchronized Swimming
1947 Barbara Ann Scott Figure Skating	**1968** Nancy Greene Alpine Skiing	**1989** Wayne Gretzky Hockey
1948 Barbara Ann Scott Figure Skating	**1969** Russ Jackson Football	**1990** Kurt Browning Figure Skating
1949 Clifford Lumsden Swimming	**1970** Bobby Orr Hockey	**1991** Silken Laumann Rowing
1950 Robert McFarlance Track & Field	**1971** Hervé Filion Harness Racing	**1992** Mark Tewksbury Swimming
1951 Marlene Stewart Golf	**1972** Phil Esposito Hockey	**1993** Mario Lemieux Hockey
1952 George Généreux Shooting	**1973** Sandy Hawley Horse Racing	**1994** Myriam Bédard Biathlon
1953 Doug Hepburn Weightlifting	**1974** Ferguson Jenkins Baseball	**1995** Jacques Villeneuve Motor Racing
1954 Marilyn Bell Swimming	**1975** Bobby Clarke Hockey	**1996** Donovan Bailey Track & Field
1955 Edith Elizabeth Whittal Swimming	**1976** Guy Lafleur Hockey	**1997** Jacques Villeneuve Motor Racing
1956 Marlene Stewart Golf	**1977** Sandy Hawley Horse Racing	**1998** Larry Walker Baseball
1957 Maurice Richard Hockey	**1978** Ken Read/ Graham Smith Alpine Skiing/ Swimming	**1999** Caroline Brunet Canoeing
		2000 Daniel Igali Wrestling

Velma Springstead Award

Year	Athlete	Sport
1934	Phyllis Dewar	Swimming
1935	Aileen McGregor	Track and Field
1936	Betty Taylor	Track and Field
1937	Robina Higgins	Track and Field
1938	Noel MacDonald	Basketball
1939	Jannette Dolson	Track and Field
1940	Dorothy Walton	Badminton
1941	Rose Mary Thacker	Figure Skating
1942	Joan Langdon	Swimming
1943	Joan Langdon	Swimming
1944	Rhoda & Rhona Wurtele	Skiing & Swimming
1945	Barbara Ann Scott	Figure Skating
1946	Irene Strong	Swimming
1947	Barbara Ann Scott	Figure Skating
1948	Viola Myers	Track and Field
1949	Eleanor McKenzie	Track and Field
1950	Rosella Thorne	Track and Field
1951	Betty Hamilton	Fencing
1952	Luella Law	Track and Field
1953	Ernestine Russell	Gymnastics
1954	Ernestine Russell	Gymnastics
1955	Ernestine Russell	Gymnastics
1956	Marlene Stewart	Golf
1957	Irene MacDonald	Diving
1958	Lucile Wheeler	Alpine Skiing
1959	Anne Heggtveit	Alpine Skiing
1960	Anne Heggtveit	Alpine Skiing
1961	Mary Stewart	Swimming
1962	Mary Stewart	Swimming
1963	Nancy McCreadie	Track and Field
1964	Gail Daley	Gymnastics
1965	Petra Burka	Figure Skating
1966	Elaine Tanner	Swimming
1967	Nancy Greene	Alpine Skiing
1968	Nancy Greene	Alpine Skiing

Year	Athlete	Sport
1969	Linda Crutchfield	Luge
1970	Angela Couglan	Swimming
1971	Karen Magnussen	Figure Skating
1972	Karen Magnussen	Figure Skating
1973	Karen Magnussen	Figure Skating
1974	Wendy Cook	Swimming
1975	Nancy Garapick & Diane Jones	Swimming & Track and Field
1976	Cheryl Gibson	Swimming
1977	Sylvia Burka & Susan Nattrass	Figure Skating & Shooting
1978	Diane Jones Konihowski & Cathy Sherk	Track & Field & Golf
1979	Helen Vanderburg	Synchronized Swimming
1980	Angella Taylor	Track & Field
1981	Susan Nattrass	Shooting
1982	Angella Taylor	Track & Field
1983	Lynn Chornobrywy	Modern Pentathlon
1984	Linda Thom	Shooting
1985	Caroyln Waldo	Synchronized Swimming
1986	Caroyln Waldo	Synchronized Swimming
1987	Caroyln Waldo	Synchronized Swimming
1988	Caroyln Waldo	Synchronized Swimming
1989	Heather Houston	Curling
1990	Sylvie Daigle	Speed Skating
1991	Silken Laumann	Rowing
1992	Kerrin Lee-Gartner	Alpine Skiing
1993	Kate Pace	Alpine Skiing
1994	Myriam Bédard	Biathlon
1995	Alison Sydor	Cycling
1996	Alison Sydor	Cycling
1997	Caroline Brunet	Canoeing/Kayaking
1998	Catriona Le May Doan	Speed Skating
1999	Caroline Brunet	Canoeing/Kayaking
2000	Lori Kane	Golf

CSI/COA

Caroline Brunet, 1997 & 1999 Velma Springstead Award winner.

Mary Stewart, 1961 & 1962 Velma Springstead Award winner.

1900

Lacrosse introduced two important rule changes: goal nets were to be used and the "baggy" stick was allowed in all official games.

1900

The new sport of badminton was first played at the Governor General's residence in Ottawa.

1901

Governor General Lord Minto donated a trophy for amateur lacrosse teams competing across the country. The first winners were the Ottawa Capitals. In three years the Minto Cup would become symbolic of the professional champions of Canada. By 1937 the Cup would become the prize for the top Junior team in the country.

1901

The first Canadian Ladies Golf Championship was held at the Royal Montreal Golf Club. The event was won by Lily Young.

1902

Canada's final *penny-farthing* bike race was held at the Brockton Oval in Vancouver's Stanley Park.

1902-03

The very first overseas rugby tour for Canadians took place in 1902-03 when a team consisting of players mostly from Nova Scotia, British Columbia, Ontario and Quebec played 23 matches in Ireland, Scotland, Wales and England over an eight-week period. Meeting some very strong club sides like Ulster, Glasgow, Llanelli, Swansea and Bristol, the Canadians established a creditable record of eight wins and two draws. H.L. Fenerty, one of the Nova Scotia players on the tour, wrote in 1967 that: " . . . We were always a bit tired. Playing in the afternoon with a large formal dinner in the evening and a train journey the next day did not make for good football."

1903

The St. Catharines Rowing Club was formed. Soon to be world famous, the Canadian Henley course made its permanent home on the Welland Canal outside St. Catharines.

1904

The first Canadian Open Golf Championship was held at the Royal Montreal Golf Club with a purse of $170, won by John H. Oke from the Royal Ottawa Golf Club (shooting 156 for 36 holes). The Canadian Open is the third oldest national open championship in the world. Only the British Open (1860) and the US Open (1895) have been around longer. Some of the biggest names in golf have won the Canadian Open — Sam Snead, Byron Nelson, Arnold Palmer and Greg Norman to name a few. The great Jack Nicklaus, who designed the Glen Abbey course that was home to many of the tournaments later in the century, never won, but was runner-up a record seven times. The last Canadian to win the tournament was Pat Fletcher, who carded a 280 in 1954 at Point Grey.

1904

Speed skater Fred Robson of Toronto set the world indoor mass-start record for the mile.

1906

The Federal Lord's Day Act, making commercial sport on Sunday illegal, was passed by the Canadian Parliament.

1906

The first university athletic association was formed — the Canadian Intercollegiate Athletic Union (CIAU).

1907

The Canadian Amateur Athletic Union created a specific committee for Canada's participation in the Olympic Games – the Central Olympic Committee. By 1909 this would become the Canadian Olympic Committee within the newly amalgamated AAU of C (Amateur Athletic Union of Canada). After many incarnations within the AAU of C it would become an independent body, the Canadian Olympic Association (COA) in 1949.

1908

Canada made its first international trip in curling, visiting Scotland. The Canadians won 23 of 26 matches, including three international contests for the Strathcona Cup.

1909

The Canadian Amateur Athletic Union and the Amateur Athletic Federation of Canada amalgamated to form the Amateur Athletic Union of Canada (the AAU of C), with a mandate to oversee sport development and participation in Canada.

1909

Five-pin bowling was invented by Thomas Ryan, originally from Guelph, Ontario. Ryan was operating a 10-pin bowling alley in Toronto when he came up with the idea of making the game more attractive to a larger audience. Finding the 10-pin balls too heavy for some, he reduced the size and weight of the ball, which also eliminated the need for the cumbersome finger holes. He then reduced the number of pins to five and simplified the scoring.

The Men of the Nine Thirteen

Heroes of St. John's annual Regatta

"Come all who love a manly sport and listen while we tell
Of a famous oldtime racing crew that in Outer Cove did dwell."

The annual St. John's rowing Regatta might be Canada's best-kept sporting secret but it is the stuff of legends and odd Newfoundland custom, particularly the famous race of 1901.

The event is held on St. John's Quidi Vidi Lake, or Kitty Vitty as those less versed in the romance language of Latin dub it. It had its origin in the sailing and rowing races in St. John's harbour at the start of the 19th century. Records suggest that the first race took place on Quidi Vidi as early as 1818 ranking it as one of the oldest organized sporting events in North America.

The race date is set by a committee of local citizens and is understood to be, "The first Wednesday in August, or the first fine day thereafter." The committee has unusual powers, among them the right to declare the day a commercial and bank holiday.

Much notoriety has been earned through the exploits of its participants whose boats were six-oared shells with fixed seats. They were required to row to the foot of the pond where they turned around buoys and returned to the starting line, a total of 1 2/3 miles.

Festive spectators gather along with local residents whose fishing cabins rim the lake, in a carnival atmosphere, featuring games of chance and refreshments. These have sometimes overshadowed the rowing itself.

Such was not the case in 1901, however, when the Outerbridge crew and their boat the Blue Peter took to the water.

> *"The gun was fired and yellow spray was seen on either hand*
> *As cheers broke out, the band struck up 'The Banks of Newfoundland'*
> *Twas nip and tuck right to the stakes, with muscles taut and lean*
> *Our heroes won by half a length in the time of the nine thirteen."*

Incredibly they had set a record that would last 80 years, gain them later recognition in Canada's Sports Hall of Fame, and entitle them to a reunion after World War I when their exploits were the subject of a popular serenade.

> *"Now of that crew from Outer Cove, John Whalen was the stroke,*
> *John Nugent, two McCarthy boys, Mart Boland and Din Croke,*
> *Walt Power was their coxswain bold and he knew his men, I ween*
> *When he drove her round the course that day in the time of the 9:13."* ♣

Highlights

General Highlights

1910
Parliament banned horse race betting by bookmakers.

1910
The Mann Cup, donated by Sir Donald Mann, became emblematic of Canadian lacrosse supremacy for senior amateurs. The challenge trophy was real gold and originally valued at $2500. (By the end of the century it was worth some $40,000 and the original trophy stayed in a showcase at the BC Sports Hall of Fame.) The first winners were from the young Toronto Club. Earlier in the century, the New Westminster Salmonbellies would win the trophy many years, set up a museum, and keep the original Cup in their vault.

July 23, 1910
In Victoria, more than 15,000 fans cheered the New Westminster Salmonbellies on to a successful defence of the Minto Cup against Montreal. The Salmonbellies were one of the most dominating Canadian lacrosse teams throughout the century, winning 29 Canadian Senior Lacrosse Championships.

1911
Pari-mutuel betting on horse races was introduced at Woodbine in Toronto and shortly thereafter at Calgary and Winnipeg tracks.

1911
A Canadian team attended the *Festival of the Empire Games*, a forerunner to the British Empire and Commonwealth Games.

1911
Fred Robson of Toronto again set the world indoor mass-start speed skating record for one-mile.

1911
The Canadian Professional Golfers Association (CPGA) was formed. Later that year, the first Canadian Professional Golfers Association Championship was held at the Mississauga Golf Club, won by Charles Murray of the Royal Montreal Golf Club.

1911
The Canadian Professional Baseball League was formed with teams from Ottawa, Peterborough, Brantford, Toronto, Guelph, St. Thomas and Hamilton.

1913
The Canadian Ladies Golf Union was formed.

Levi (Shotty) ROGERS
Rogers stood only five foot four and weighed 115 pounds but he did not lack stamina. He spent 58 consecutive years — five as an oarsman and 53 as a coxswain on St. John's Quidi Vidi Lake. In that period he steered more than 300 winning crews. Rogers' name is a legend in Newfoundland and his memory is revived each year at the St. John's Regatta, the oldest annual sporting event on record in North America. He is a member of Canada's Sports Hall of Fame.

C y c l i n g

The Little Boy from Canada

Archie McEachern, an early golden boy of Canadian sport, dazzled the world of cycling in late January, 1902 as he shattered the five-mile motor-paced (cycling behind a motorcycle as a wind break) bicycle record on the indoor track in Philadelphia's 2nd Regiment Armoury. His rivals, Jean Gaugoltz of France, and Americans Harold Freeman and Jimmy Michael watched in amazement as he lowered the world record by almost nine seconds to 7:52.4.

The brilliant McEachern from Woodville, Ontario had actually started his career as a boxer, winning an amateur welterweight championship in 1898, before turning to cycling the next year and winning several races in Toronto.

On the United States Memorial Day in 1900 he won his first major race, a four-cornered event, as it was described, near Boston. Before the year was finished he had set a record in Philadelphia, competed at Boston's Charles River Park, and along with a partner, finished second in Chicago's six-day race.

He opened Boston's indoor cycling season on December 29, 1900 at the Park Square Garden by entering the 25-mile championship. Racers from Germany, France and the United States exchanged the lead before McEachern, "the little boy from Canada" as the Boston press dubbed him (despite his 5 foot 9 inch 170 pound physique), took the lead with five miles to go and won the title with a time of 1:05:01.4.

In 1901 he had become one the sport's premier performers, and until Arthur Spencer's 1917 victory in the United States Professional Championship, was probably the best known Canadian in the sport. In 1902 he announced his engagement to a leading New York City actress and celebrated by teaming with Bobby Walthour to win the Chicago six-day event.

In May of that year he went to Atlantic City in New Jersey to pursue the one-mile motor-paced record. The omens were unkind, as first a dog crossed the track upsetting all, and then a young lad invaded the course, causing McEachern to swerve and fall, badly cutting his arm.

Unperturbed, he then asked his pacers to take him out on 15-mile circuit of the track. Nearing the end, however, disaster struck as the chain on the motorcycle broke, causing it to slow down abruptly. Riding close behind at a high rate of speed, McEachern was unable to avoid the motorcycle and slammed into the back. He was thrown violently onto the track.

Rising briefly and with blood covering the track he had only time to say, "I am done for," before collapsing and succumbing to his injuries.

His body was returned to Woodville for burial. Attending the funeral were members of Ontario's elite including Colonel Sam Hughes M.P., R.J. McLaughlin, and leading newsmen and lawyers.

The Globe closed its account by noting, "The most profound sorrow prevails at the loss of one who was by universal consent, the most generous hearted and popular favourite that ever carried our Canadian flag to victory on the wheel." ❦

Mickey MacIntyre – Not a Champion, but …

Mickey MacIntyre was one of the classiest lightweight or welterweight boxers Canada ever produced. He was a protégé of both Tommy Burns and Sam Langford. In July, 1912, he was awarded a decision over the great Battling Nelson in a 12-round match in Winnipeg and Mickey MacIntyre became the welterweight champion of Canada.

On May 1, 1913 he outpointed Billy Griffiths in a 12-round contest in Calgary, with the Calgary Herald reporting that: "Mickey MacIntyre has now one of the strongest claims in the ring for the welterweight championship of the world."

Former world heavyweight champion Tommy Burns said of the MacIntyre-Griffiths bout: "There is only one thing that can be said, in my opinion, it would be impossible to see a better contest anywhere. It was the best welterweight fight I have ever seen."

Mickey MacIntyre's last great fight was in 1914 when he was 24. In his hometown of Glace Bay, he scored a technical knockout over Johnny Connolly, the champion of Scotland. He came out of semi-retirement in 1917 for one last bout — a draw against Joe Rivers. After the bout he retired from the fight game permanently.

Mickey MacIntyre was born with a spirit his flesh could not contain and in 1922, still only 32 years old, he lost a decision to pneumonia.

During his brief career he commanded large box-office purses but the money went out faster than it came in. He was generous with his friends — to a fault.

"Mickey MacIntyre was undoubtedly the greatest boxer ever produced in Cape Breton and old-timers remember when he was knocking on the front door of the world welterweight champion." ❧

Mickey MacIntyre

NSSHOF

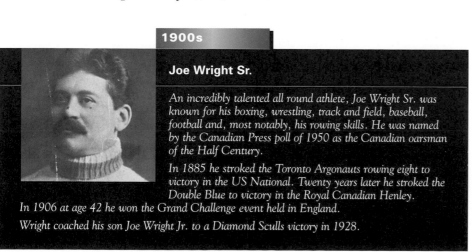

1900s

Joe Wright Sr.

An incredibly talented all round athlete, Joe Wright Sr. was known for his boxing, wrestling, track and field, baseball, football and, most notably, his rowing skills. He was named by the Canadian Press poll of 1950 as the Canadian oarsman of the Half Century.

In 1885 he stroked the Toronto Argonauts rowing eight to victory in the US National. Twenty years later he stroked the Double Blue to victory in the Royal Canadian Henley.

In 1906 at age 42 he won the Grand Challenge event held in England.

Wright coached his son Joe Wright Jr. to a Diamond Sculls victory in 1928.

Hockey

1893-1993

Our Game:

Canadians celebrate 100 years of the Stanley Cup – and their deep-seated love of hockey

by Bob Levin
April 26, 1993

1924 Olympic hockey action.

They can gussy it up all they want. They can add the designer uniforms, the canned chants and flashing message boards, as if Canadians need to be *told* when to cheer a hockey game. They can pay the combatants the kind of money bank presidents and fashion models make and build a new Hall of Fame full of whiz-bang computers and video screens. They can even add the Anaheim Mighty *Ducks* and that's all just fine.

The game is still the game.

A stick. A puck. A net. That's the game. Street hockey and backyard rinks. Sweat-stained socks and jocks and jerseys, and parents sipping bad coffee watching their kids skate around cold arenas before the sun is even up.

And that special, uneasy mix of finesse and fury, the breathtaking rush on goal and the brutal body check — that, too, is Canada's game. It is played for fun and sport and fame and, beginning in earnest with the National Hockey League

Charlie Gardner

playoffs this week, for the honour of having one's name inscribed on the gleaming silver Stanley Cup — hockey players' heaven, a century old this year.

One hundred years: the nation hasn't existed all that much longer. In 1893, the 4,000 people of Calgary incorporated themselves as Alberta's first city. The Manitoba Women's Christian Temperance Union was fighting for female suffrage. And Lord Stanley, the Governor General of the day, donated the first incarnation of the Cup to spur on a game that the new land had spawned, the woods echoing with the sounds of saws and hammers and slapshots. Rugged land, rugged game. "Canada has never had a major civil war," a baseball pitcher named Jim Brosnan once said. "After hockey, Canadians would probably have found it dull."

It is no longer *just* Canada's game. The world has caught the fever. With expansion next year, 18 of the 26 NHL teams will be based in the United States and six of those in the Sunbelt. The game that, as Hall of Famer Ken Dryden put it, "was weaned on long northern winters uncluttered by things to do," will even have two teams in Florida, where the thing to do is sunbathe and the only ice is in drinks.

Americans *play* the pro game, too, and so do Europeans. This was supposed to be the year of Eric Lindros, the Philadelphia Flyers' man-mountain rookie from Toronto. But the hottest new goal-getters are Teemu Selanne — the Finnish Flash and now the Winnipeg Wonder-boy — and Pavel Bure, the Russian Rocket of Vancouver. There are plenty of Czechs and Swedes, as well, adding new styles and excitement and making Don Cherry bust a gut. *Hockey Night in Canada*'s designated tough guy, who attacks foreigners and defends fighting with his barstool blasts of oratory, should note that more than 500 of the 700-plus

Frank Nighbor

players who saw action in the NHL this year were good Canadian boys from places like Sudbury and Swift Current and Trois-Rivières. And most are still known to throw the odd punch.

Hockey politics aside — and the NHL has enough internal troubles to exhaust an automaker — it's been an interesting year. Mario Lemieux has returned from cancer treatments to lead the Pittsburgh Penguins' drive for a third straight Stanley Cup. Wayne Gretzky is back from back troubles, lighting up Los Angeles, while Toronto's revitalized Maple Leafs are suddenly reminding their fans of former glories. The Quebec Nordiques, after trading the rights to Lindros who had scorned their money, are rivalling the mighty Montreal Canadiens for Quebec supremacy.

And new stars are in the pipeline. Parents drive ever-longer distances to transport their up-and-comers to top minor leagues, while the perennial search continues for the next homegrown superstar, the next Gretzky or Lemieux.

The new Hockey Hall of Fame looks promising, too. Located in downtown Toronto (the old one was on the remote Canadian National Exhibition grounds), the $25-million Hall, scheduled to open on June 18, will offer visitors the chance to broadcast a taped scoring play or take shots at a computer goalie. But all is not arcade gadgetry. Last week, amid the drop cloths and electrical wires and buzz of power tools, the tributes to many Hall-of-Famers were already in place. There was Gordie Howe and Howie Morenz and Jean Béliveau; there was Bobby Orr and Rocket Richard and Terry Sawchuck and Cyclone Taylor and King Clancy. There were old-time sweaters and wooden seats from Madison Square Garden and a smile-inducing re-creation of an early 1960s living room — dad, mom, daughter, son and dog — a scene complete with the requisite Slinky and Monopoly and, of course, hockey on the old TV.

But the best will lie upstairs. There, in the beautiful old Bank of Montreal building that is part of the Hall, with its wood-panelled walls and stained-glass dome, will sit the Stanley Cup, shining symbol of what is *still* Canada's game.

Happy birthday. ♦

Bernie Geoffrion

Bob Gainey

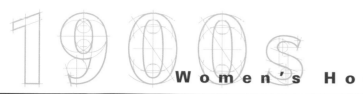

1900s Hockey

A woman's game

Lord Stanley, Canada's sixth Governor General, is forever renowned because of his gift of a trophy for Canadian hockey supremacy, but he was a pioneer in at least one other way. Encouraging his entire family to take up the new game, both Lady Stanley and the couple's two daughters joined the boys in raucous play at Rideau Hall as early as 1890.

By the turn of the 20th century women were playing hockey all over Canada. University women from Toronto, Queen's and McGill were enthusiastic players and the sport was enjoyed in places like Brandon, Manitoba and Barrie, Ontario. A newly formed Ladies' Hockey League in Quebec had teams from Montreal, Quebec City, and Trois-Rivières.

"It is as natural for Quebec girls to skate as it is for other women to walk," a local commentator noted.

One early match in Quebec advertised for paying customers as the women attempted to raise money for soldiers' wives. "People wanted to see how women would play and they got a most agreeable surprise. The players wore ordinary skirts and some of them, most notably Edith White, displayed much skill," a local scribe said.

As often as not, however, women's games around the turn of the century were played in covered rinks away from the prying eyes of spectators, better to avoid the embarrassment of skirts flying high.

Regular hockey garb had been adopted by the 1920s and at least until World War II, women continued to play a hockey unencumbered by commercialism and careerism. It became a staple of both small town working class females and university women, who were pioneers anyway by virtue of attending these elite institutions.

There were many small leagues that sprung up during the 1920s and 1930s. In a league in Bowmanville, Ontario, for example, it is recorded that the Goodyear Tire Ladies' Hockey Team lost 1-0 to the Thompson Knitting team during the 1922 regular season. This followed Goodyear's victory over the Ross Can Sextette. Goodyear then beat the Front Street Team 1-0 and advanced to the playoffs where they outscored Front Street again.

The final was played on soft ice and the game went back and forth before Goodyear in their snappy blue and white uniforms beat Thompson 2-1 to win the Mason Cup, donated by George Mason of the S.W Mason and Son dry goods store. The banquet featured speeches, dinner and dancing by the young women and their dates.

For university women, McGill, Queen's and Toronto played a lively series of games beginning in 1921. McGill withdrew from the university competition after 1925 and Queen's in 1934 and the series evaporated, but at their peak the teams featured players who would become some of Canada's most prominent women.

As far back as 1917, Charlotte Whitton from Renfrew, later elected Ottawa's first female mayor, had played for Queen's. Whitton's pugnacious political career included several near and actual physical tussles with political rivals, perhaps reminiscent of her time as a hockey player.

Maryon Moody, who managed a college team, later married a future Prime Minister, Lester Pearson.

The University of Toronto also played in the Toronto Ladies Hockey League in 1924-25 and eventually defeated the Ottawa Alerts to win the Ladies Ontario Hockey Association title. One of Toronto's star players, Marian Hilliard, went on to a distinguished medical career. In a memorable contest of the era, Hilliard once outplayed the best all-round female athlete of the day, Bobbie Rosenfeld, as the university women met the women of the City of Toronto.

By the 1950s however a women's place was decidedly not favoured on a hockey rink. In a celebrated case it was discovered that Abby Hoffman, a registered player in the juvenile Toronto Hockey league, was in fact an eight-year old girl. She was encouraged to play with other girls but such options were so limited she switched to track and field and became an Olympic runner.

Women's hockey slowly revived over the next several decades and eventually surpassed the golden age of the early 1900s as it organized its first World Championships and earned a spot on the Winter Olympic program. ❦

CSI/COA

The first Women's World Hockey Championships took place in Ottawa in March of 1990. The Canadian women, seen here in shocking pink, won.

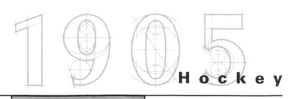

The Incredible Journey

Dawson City's 1905 Stanley Cup challenge

In its early years, the hunt for the Stanley Cup was an all-Canadian affair and challenges came in to the Cup's trustees from all over the country. The most incredible challenge in the history of the Cup was the brainchild of Joe Boyle. He was a Klondike gold seeker originally from Woodstock, Ontario, who struck it rich in the Yukon. Modern players who complain about jet lag might want to reflect on the 24-day, more than 6000 km odyssey that brought Boyle and his Dawson City hockey team to warmer climates in search of hockey's highest honour.

Boyle, who in his life crossed paths with kings, presidents, and, most famously, Queen Marie of Romania, saw no limits to the possibilities for the Yukon. He imagined things that others said were impossible, including a team from Dawson City playing for the Stanley Cup. Just making the long trek east was undertaking enough in those days, let alone taking on the greatest team of that era, the Ottawa Silver Seven and their star player, One-Eyed Frank McGee.

When Weldy Young, a civil servant and hockey player, wrote to Philip Ross, a Cup trustee, in July 1904 formally requesting the opportunity for a Yukon team to play the Silver Seven for the Stanley Cup, the folks in Dawson realized an all-star squad taken from their four-team league was their best hope.

Boyle, prominent in Yukon affairs through his control of timber and electrical resources, was conscripted to put the challenge together with authorities in Ottawa. He arranged the series and developed the team's travel plans for these games and those that would follow.

"If the players followed my schedule they'd arrive in Ottawa with plenty of time to get ready. Nothing could be left to chance. We had some good players. Albert Forrest, originally from Quebec wasn't even 20 but had great reflexes. J.K. Johnstone worked in the post office. And three of our guys, Norman Watt, George (Sureshot) Kennedy, and Hector Smith were still digging for gold.

"Of course they'd have to put up their own money, but the return was a share of the tour's profits. Win the Cup and they could set their price, but even a loss would be covered by their novelty and appeal to other communities."

Boyle tried in vain to keep the playing dates flexible in case anything went wrong but Ottawa wouldn't hear of it. Nor would they take into consideration the fact that their rink was 25 feet longer than Dawson City's, arguing that the size of the rink was their prerogative as home team. They did relent on the issue of having a non-partisan referee, by providing an official from Brockville.

The journey east was extraordinary. The first part of the trek was made partly by dogsled. A snowstorm followed in their wake, preventing them from getting to their boat in the port of Skagway, Alaska. By the time they got there, they had to wait three days for another boat to take them down the coast to Seattle in a sea of wretched weather and heaving stomachs.

They then backtracked to Vancouver, where they caught the CPR trans-continental. Hardly any time had been available for workouts and even though they had their skates there was no chance to use them. The team would get sticks and uniforms in Ottawa but only had two days to try them out.

Game day dawned on the hardly-propitious Friday the 13th of January, 1905.

1905 Stanley Cup Champions, The Ottawa "Silver Seven"

Boyle tried unsuccessfully to reschedule the game. "The 13th's no date to sail or play such an important series. But it was their cup and their rink and they expected 2,500 along with Governor General Earl Grey to pack Dey's Arena.

"For a few minutes I thought we might have a chance. Forrest made some great saves and we were only down 3-1 at half-time. But the ref, bless his soul, couldn't keep up with the play. The offside rule prevents forward passes unless the passer can catch up with the play and put his teammate onside. Now that didn't happen but the referee was too far behind to see and Ottawa got four illegal goals.

"We lost 9-2 but I was convinced we could catch them next game, especially since we'd have our skating legs. Some of us wondered why they made such a big thing about their supposed star Frank McGee. They say he has only one eye and I think it showed. We won one battle however, Watt got a stick in the mouth from Moore so he broke his over the Ottawa player's head and knocked him out for ten minutes."

Meanwhile plans were progressing for exhibition games beyond the series. Few seemed to care how Dawson did against Ottawa. There were teams in Atlantic Canada and northern Ontario who saw Dawson's plucky challenge as a basis for their own.

The final game against the Silver Seven, however, was a disaster and ultimately led to changing the rules for Stanley Cup challenges.

"We attacked early but their goalie Finnie was brilliant. Then they started scoring and our guys were all in, they just stopped skating and Ottawa scored at will. Our team was broken up and in no condition to play. It was one of the most painful things I've ever had to watch. McGee was a little better than we thought. He scored 14 times and we lost 23-2.

"From then on the trustees wouldn't allow a team like ours to ever play for the Cup again. Teams had to have proven themselves against worthy competitors."

The Dawson team's journey wasn't over yet, though. They went on to Nova Scotia and New Brunswick. At first they lost, but then, having gotten their legs and welcomed Weldy Young, who had finally made it east, they started winning. First they defeated a Cape Breton all-star team, then one from Pictou County, and others from Moncton and Fredericton.

Tired and possibly homesick they lost badly to Queen's and then crossed the US border where they won a three game series against Pittsburgh. Boyle and the team now turned homeward. They lost in Winnipeg but on the first day of spring beat Brandon. Then the thaw set in and in the era before artificial ice, games were cancelled across the prairies and in British Columbia.

Young Albert Forrest later recalled, "Boyle left us in Brandon and we made our own way home. It took me seven days to walk into Dawson from Whitehorse. I'd broken even on the series. If only those games in the west hadn't been cancelled we'd have made some money."

Dawson never again challenged for the Stanley Cup, which eventually became the exclusive property of the National Hockey League and its teams. ♦

Edouard "Newsy" Lalonde

At 5'9" and 165 pounds, Edouard "Newsy" Lalonde was not a big man, but in the annals of Canadian sport he stood very tall indeed. A native of Cornwall, Ontario, this son of a shoemaker acquired the "Newsy" moniker while working at the local newspaper during his teenage years. Soon, mention of his name would strike fear into goaltenders across the country — in both hockey and lacrosse.

In hockey, "Newsy" was simply one of the best, most dynamic, players of the first 50 years of the century, remembered for both his skill and his toughness. When Lalonde started pro hockey in 1905, teams still played seven-a-side and forward passing was not allowed. Yet, in any configuration of the rules, "Newsy" scored often — collecting 314 goals in the 220 professional games he played in from 1905 to 1925. He led the scoring in each league he played, and he played in a whole alphabet of leagues — NHL, NHA, PCHA, OPHL, OHL, WCHL, MHL, FAHL and the IPHL.

Following a stellar amateur career in Cornwall, "Newsy" began his professional pursuit of hockey with Sault Ste. Marie in 1905, playing in the first-ever pro hockey league — the International Professional Hockey League. Moving to Toronto with the Ontario Professional Hockey League for the 1907-08 season, he led the OPHL with 29 goals. That year "Newsy" played in his first Stanley Cup final, against Montreal — losing 6-4 in the one-game challenge, but scoring two goals and easily being the fastest player on the ice. After two seasons with Toronto, Lalonde moved to the Montreal Canadiens and the Renfrew Millionaires for the 1910 and 1911 seasons, scoring 59 goals in 32 games. He scored two goals in the Canadiens first ever game, January 5, 1910. It was interesting that in Montreal he was promoted locally as a "French hockey player," even though he described himself as more of a lacrosse player from Cornwall.

Lalonde became the definitive hockey traveller, often selling his skills to the highest bidder for a year at a time. In 1910-11 he was lured out of Montreal for cash, and on March 8 he scored six goals to lead the Renfrew Creamery Kings (also known as the "Millionaires") to a 17-2 win over Ottawa in an NHA game. Heading west for the 1911-12 season with the Vancouver Millionaires of the PCHA, "Newsy" led the new league in scoring — 27 goals in 15 games. He had been lured west after Millionaire owner and league-founder Frank Patrick, and his lacrosse-team owner friend Con Jones, offered him both hockey and lacrosse contracts. After spending the 1911-12 season playing hockey and lacrosse in the west, Lalonde was lured back east again for even bigger bucks. Playing for the Montreal Canadiens again, he joined famed netminder Georges Vezina in his debut game. He would stay with the Habs for the next 10 years, from 1913 until 1922, establishing himself as the first dominant player — the first "Flying Frenchman" — with the Montreal Canadiens, winning four scoring championships and captaining the team to a Stanley Cup in 1916.

In one of the century's earliest "big trades," Lalonde was traded from the NHL Canadiens to the Saskatoon Sheiks of the WCHL (Western Canada Hockey League) on September 18, 1922 — for the up-and-coming Ottawa-native Aurèle Joliat. Not even being a two-time scoring champ averaging 25 goals a season in the five-year-old NHL could keep Lalonde in Montreal, where he had been having recent squabbles with management. Besides, the Habs were about to launch the career of Howie Morenz in a big way and were in need of a playmaker to get him the puck. They found him in Aurèle Joliat.

At first, Montrealers were concerned the deal was a dud. Lalonde had been one of the Habs' most potent offensive weapons for 12 years. It was a trade which angered the loyal Hab fans and they initially booed the even-smaller Joliat during his first few games. One columnist stated the collective concerns quite succinctly: "To deport Lalonde to Saskatoon for an unknown player like Joliat is sheer madness. If Joliat can survive two years in the NHL it will be a miracle." The miracle came through — Joliat played for 16 seasons and helped Montreal to Stanley Cup victories in 1924, 1930 and 1931 and along the way won the NHL's new Hart Trophy as the league's most valuable player. Lalonde, meanwhile, proved he was not as washed up as they thought — becoming a huge fan favourite and leading the WCHL in scoring with 30 goals in the 28-game 1922-23 season. He would play three more years in the west before returning to the NHL for one season with the New York Americans, taking his final bow as a player on November 16, 1926 when he appeared briefly in a game.

As good as he was in scoring and playing for many teams throughout his storied career, Lalonde is also remembered for his tough, rough, play and his clashes with opponents such as Bad Joe Hall, Sprague Cleghorn and his brother Odie, and other contemporaries. In 1915-16, for example, when "Newsy" was leading the NHA in scoring with 31 goals for the Canadiens, he cemented his well-earned nasty reputation. "Newsy" slammed Odie Cleghorn of Ottawa so hard into the boards that brother Sprague Cleghorn skated straight to Lalonde and smashed his stick over Lalonde's head, just missing his eye. The incident was talked about for years to come.

"I wasn't very big, but I never backed up an inch," he is quoted as saying later in his life. "I didn't start much trouble, but if anyone did me dirt, he got it right back."

When his playing days ended in 1925, he had played for at least 11 teams in nine different leagues, including stints with Cornwall, Sault Ste. Marie, Renfrew, Toronto, Vancouver, Saskatoon, New York and 12 seasons with the Montreal Canadiens.

"Newsy" Lalonde hockey highlights and stories could fill their own lengthy book, and include:

- March 1, 1919 — Setting a Stanley Cup playoff record with five goals in a 6-3 Hab victory over Ottawa

- January 10, 1920 — Scoring six goals in a 14-7 win by Montreal over the Toronto St. Patricks, a record that would stand for 66 years

- 1919-20 — Scoring 17 playoff goals and getting 18 playoff points, a point total that stood until 1944 when Toe Blake tied it

- 1920-21 — Finishing third in goals with 33 and fourth in assists with eight, taking the scoring title with a combined 41 points in just 24 games for his last NHL scoring title

- 1922-23 — As player/coach during his first year in Saskatoon, leading the WCHL in scoring, even though his team finished dead last

As good as he was in hockey, Lalonde was perhaps even stronger and better in lacrosse. In the first few years of the century, the newly established hockey star had also for some time been a top lacrosse player. "Newsy" initially starred with the powerful Montreal Nationals, one of the key teams involved in Canada's "golden age" of field lacrosse. By 1911 his hockey and lacrosse talents were in demand country-wide, enabling him to become the first professional or "free agent" to travel the country playing for the team that most wanted his services and would pay the most money. Con Jones, the Vancouver promoter, along with the Patrick hockey family, brought Lalonde west to play hockey for Patricks' Millionaires and lacrosse for Jones' Vancouver Greenshirts in an attempt to wrest away the Canadian championship from the hated New Westminster Salmonbellies. Lalonde received $6500 just for the lacrosse season, almost four times what he and another star, Cyclone Taylor, were making in hockey. It proved to be a good investment, however, as Lalonde led Jones' 1911 Vancouver team to its first and only Minto Cup of the century and the Canadian professional lacrosse championship.

His ability as a hockey and lacrosse player is legendary. His followers turned out to cheer him while others bought their way in to scream "Get Lalonde." A cutup to the last, it is safe to say that they never "Got Lalonde."

"Newsy" Lalonde is the only player inducted into both the Lacrosse and Hockey Halls of Fame, with the Hockey Hall recognizing him as the dominant player of the first quarter century and the Lacrosse establishment honouring him as Canada's outstanding lacrosse player of the first half-century. In 1950, "Newsy" provided the strongest challenge to Lionel Conacher's selection as Canada's Athlete of the Half Century. ♣

1917-1918

Newsy Lalonde and Joe Malone – Top Guns

Joe Malone scored five goals in his first Montreal Canadiens and NHL game – a record for a Habs road game through the century. He had two more five-goal games that season, the only one to accomplish the feat in the century. This first year he scored 44 goals in 20 games for a 2.2 goal per game average — the highest ratio of the century by far.

Career Note: "Newsy" and Joe Malone were the only NHL players ever to score more than 100 goals and average more than a goal per game. They ended up with very similar career totals: Lalonde getting 124 goals in 99 games for a 1.25 average; Malone netting 143 goals in 125 games for a 1.14 average. In competition outside the NHL, they also were very similar over a 25-year span — Lalonde averaging 1.36 goals to Malone's 1.35 goals per game average. By contrast, even Wayne Gretzky's best season saw him average 1.18 goals per game.

"Newsy" Lalonde after his playing days.

Highlights

Hockey Highlights

1899-1900

The second season for the Canadian Amateur Hockey League (CAHL) featured netting between the goal posts for first time.

1901

At Almonte, Ontario, in a playoff game played on neutral ice between Smith's Falls and Pembroke of the NHA, a referee was used to drop the puck between opposing players for the first time.

1903

The goal line was adopted by the Federal Amateur League.

1903-1906

An Ottawa team won nine straight defences of the Stanley Cup — and each of the seven members received a silver nugget, resulting in the team's nickname — The Ottawa Silver Seven.

February 25, 1904

Ottawa's Frank McGee recorded the first five-goal game in Stanley Cup play in an 11-2 victory over Toronto.

January 16, 1905

Frank McGee of the Ottawa Silver Seven scored a record 14 goals in a 23-2 Stanley Cup romp over a team from the Yukon. In 1900, McGee lost an eye during a game, hence his nickname "One-eyed Frank McGee." Sadly, in 1916 McGee lost his life in WW I.

March 6, 1906

Cornwall's Owen McCourt became the first recorded hockey fatality, with his death occurring in a Federal Amateur League game, a result of a "blow from the hockey stick of Charles Masson."

December 26, 1907

The first professional team, the Montreal Wanderers, challenged for the Stanley Cup, and won.

January 1907

Even though they held it only for a short period, the smallest town to ever win the Stanley Cup was from Rat Portage, Ontario, featuring a team full of future hall-of-famers called the Kenora Thistles. They challenged the professional Montreal Wanderers to the Cup — and won it in January, only to lose the challenge again to Montreal two months later.

1907-1908

Canada's eventual lacrosse athlete of the first half century, "Newsy" Lalonde, played and starred in an alphabet soup of hockey leagues, including the OPHL, FAHL, MHL, OPHL, WCHL and eventually the NHL. In the 1907-08 season he led the OPHL with 29 goals.

December 2, 1909

The National Hockey Association was formed – and included a new team called the Montreal Canadiens.

1909-1910

Ottawa's Cyclone Taylor was paid $5,250 for a 12-game hockey season, by far the most lucrative salary in sport up to that time.

1910-1911

The NHA introduced three-20 minute periods for games, jersey numbers to identify players and dropped the rover position, leaving teams playing with six players per side for the remainder of the century.

December 31, 1910

Montreal Canadiens netminder Georges Vezina played his first of 367 consecutive regular season and playoff games covering the next 15 years.

1911

"Newsy" Lalonde and Cyclone Taylor went west to play for the Pacific Coast Hockey League (PCHL) started by the Patrick family in Vancouver. They were coaxed through money and the chance to play lacrosse at the same time. For the most part, Taylor stayed in the west, while Lalonde moved around to the highest bidder for the next 15 years.

1911

The first artificial ice surface was built in Vancouver by the Patrick family for PCHA hockey. Victoria, also owned by the Patricks, was next.

1912-1913

"Phantom" Joe Malone really kicked off his scoring exploits this season with the Quebec Bulldogs of the NHA. The 23-year old netted 43 goals in only 20 games, including seven goals in one game against Toronto. In the Stanley Cup Challenge against Sydney, "Phantom Joe" scored nine goals in one game.

1915-1916

Newsy Lalonde, now playing for the Montreal Canadiens, won the NHA scoring title with 31 goals.

March 30, 1916

The Montreal Canadiens won their first of 24 Stanley Cups in the century.

Joe Malone, Montreal Canadiens, 1918.

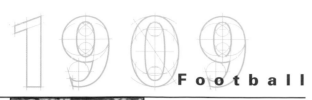

F o o t b a l l

Smirle Lawson

The First Grey Cup Game

Kicking for glory

December 4, 1909
Rosedale Field, Toronto

Football was a different game in 1909, more like the English sports of rugby and soccer. The centre scrimmage put the ball in play by heeling it back with his foot, and players provided their own equipment which as often as not was a canvas covering with bits of padding around the shoulder. There were five-minute penalties for rough play and 14 men aside.

Games were dominated by two runs into the line followed by a booming kick. Dribbling the ball was allowed but the forward pass was forbidden. Strategy consisted largely of getting favourable field position and kicking single points.

The modern fan would at least recognize the ultimate prize in the game, as on December 4 two teams met for the first ever Grey Cup. At Toronto's Rosedale Field, the University of Toronto played their cross-town rivals, the Parkdale Canoe Club, for the new trophy donated by the Governor General, Earl Grey, a keen enthusiast of the game.

Football in Canada goes back to at least 1845 when it was restricted as part of the Lord's Day Act prohibition of Sunday sports. It was a tangled affair in which two teams would swarm around the ball, not unlike that first Grey Cup game. Canadians can also take credit for having introduced Americans in 1874 to their more rugby-like version of the game in contrast to the soccer leaning sport played in the United States.

After that the gridiron game prospered south of the border while Canadians created their own interpretation. Its larger field, fewer downs and single-point rouges owed as much to English rugby as it did to American innovation.

That first Grey Cup game was played on a typically cold blustery day, attracting only 3,807 spectators. This should give pause to those who furrow their brows over the Canadian Football League's inability to draw over 50,000 for recent Grey Cups. There were no parades, no Miss Grey Cup, and no awards ceremony and, so far as we can tell, less drinking.

The Grey Cup, 1909.

Canada

The first Grey Cup Game, 1909.

Varsity were the heavy favourites, but the upstarts from Parkdale, representing the Ontario Rugby Football Union shocked the college boys with a late second quarter touchdown. Tom Meighan scored when Hughie Gall mishandled a Billy Foulds lateral and Parkdale ended the half down only 6-5 (touchdowns were worth five points at the time).

In the third quarter, however, a Parkdale fumble was followed by players wildly kicking at the spinning ball as it gradually made its way towards the Parkdale goal line. Eventually Varsity's Murray Thomson, the outside wing, scooped up the ball and raced into the end zone.

Hughie Gall, whose early miscue had made the game close, then took over. His mighty punts accounted for six straight singles in the University's favour and Smirle Lawson added a last second touchdown to clinch a 26-6 victory.

A national celebration had begun! ❦

1905

Canadian football took a number of years to evolve from Rugby Union football. In 1905, many clubs adapted various new rule recommendations by University of Toronto player Thrift Burnside, such as dropping the number of players from 14 to 12, and requiring the offensive team to make 10 yards on three downs. These became known, of course, as the Burnside Rules.

December 4, 1909

The first Grey Cup Game was played in Toronto, but the Cup was not ready to be presented. The University of Toronto defeated the Parkdale Canoe Club 26-6. The first Grey Cup presentation ended up taking place February 7, 1910.

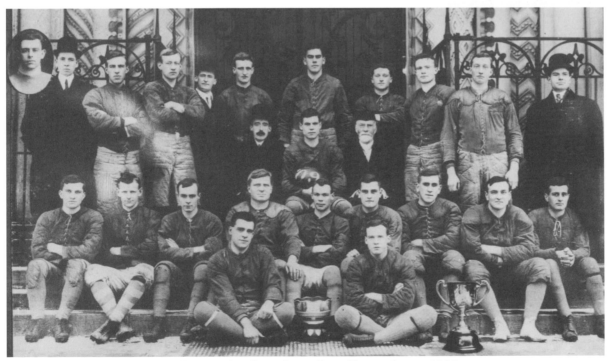

The University of Toronto Blues, the first Grey Cup Champions, 1909.

Football Highlights

1920

The Western Canada Rugby Union entered the Grey Cup competitions and joined the Canadian Rugby Union (CRU), making the Cup truly a national championship.

December 3, 1921

The "Big Train" Lionel Conacher led the Toronto Argonauts to a 23-0 Grey Cup victory over the Edmonton Eskimos at Varsity Stadium.

1920s

FRANK "PEP" LEADLEY

Leadley captained Queen's Golden Gaels and the Hamilton Tigers in a dynamic career. He helped bring five Intercollegiate championships to Kingston and three successive Grey Cups (1923-24-25) plus two more Grey Cups with the Tigers (1928 and 1929).

1908-1914

Smirle Lawson, above, was a great plunging halfback hailed as the "Original Big Train" when he starred for the University of Toronto's Grey Cup victories in 1909 and 1910 and the Argonaut win in 1914.

1908-1912

Hugh Gall could kick with either foot and from 1908 through 1912 the backfielder with the University of Toronto Blues became one of Canada's first football heroes. In the 1909 inaugural Grey Cup against Parkdale, he scored one touchdown and kicked eight singles.

1920s

HARRY BATSTONE

Weighing in at only 155 pounds, Harry Batstone was a 1920s triple threat halfback who could pass, run and kick. He and Lionel Conacher made the end run play a success, especially in winning the first East-West Grey Cup Game in 1921 when the Argonauts beat Edmonton. Later, playing at Queen's, Batstone was often the star through a string of 26 consecutive victories, which included three Grey Cups in a row.

1920s-1930s

TED REEVE

"The Moaner" was known to many fans and readers. A soldier in World War I, Reeve was an excellent football and lacrosse player as well as a winning football coach. He played at Queen's University, for the Argonauts and later for Balmy Beach, becoming famous for blocking kicks. He was also a standout reporter for the Toronto Star for many years, both during and following his football career. Nearing his retirement as a player, he wrote in the Star: "When I was younger and in my prime, I used to block punts all the time, but now I'm getting older and turning gray, I only block punts once a day."

1920s-1930s

BRIAN TIMMIS

It is said that Timmis often sacrificed his body to make the big play for the Hamilton Tigers. He played helmetless and with determination, three times helping the Tigers to Grey Cup wins (1928, 1929 and 1932). He made a comeback at age 38 for a playoff game in Ottawa and played 58 minutes despite a bad shoulder.

1915

After the Hamilton Tigers won their second Grey Cup, they decided to get even with their rivals from The University of Toronto club. The Tigers took the Cup, and had engraved their own name on it for a 1908 victory they had had over Toronto, even though the victory came before the official Grey Cup era of 1909.

Jeff Russell starred for the famous Montreal Winged Wheelers from 1922 to 1925. He was killed tragically in the 1926 off-season while repairing a power line in a driving rainstorm. The Jeff Russell Memorial Trophy was established to honour the Eastern player who shared the same gifts as an athlete and sportsman as Russell had.

Grey Cup

The first forward pass for a Grey Cup touchdown was thrown by Warren Stevens of the Montreal Winged Wheelers against the Regina Roughriders. Knowing the game would be played on a frozen field, the Regina coach decided to play the game in tennis shoes ordered just before the game. The shoes didn't turn up until halftime, and were delivered to the Montreal dressing room! The Winged Wheelers wore them instead, and ran around the Roughriders en route to a decisive 22-0 victory.

1928-1934

The Regina Roughriders made the trip east to play in the Grey Cup six times in seven years — and lost every time. The club would not win the Cup until 1966, by which time it was known as the Saskatchewan Roughriders.

1929

The Regina Roughriders used the forward pass successfully all season, but the new play was not accepted into the Grey Cup Game until 1931.

December 6, 1930

Foster Hewitt is mostly remembered for his countless hockey broadcasts, but in 1930 he called the play-by-play for the first radio broadcast of the Grey Cup as Toronto's Balmy Beach defeated Regina 11-6.

1931

Lionel Conacher organized the first fully professional football club, the Cross and Blackwell Chiefs, playing against mostly American-based teams out of Toronto.

1936 and 1942

The Eastern football clubs convinced the CRU to restrict the number of imports (i.e. American players) on teams and, as a result, the western club champions were banned from playing in the Grey Cup game.

World War II

Unlike WW I, the Grey Cup was played during World War II in the 1940s, mostly by armed force units stationed across the country.

1931-37 — St. Thomas, Ontario, native Hugh Stirling was one of the early century's finest triple-threat backfielders. Playing his entire career with the Sarnia Imperials of the old ORFU, Stirling was a six-time all-star and won the ORFU Most Valuable Player Award in 1936. He was one of the best, most accurate, punters of his generation, an agile runner of the ball, and a star receiver in the early days of the forward pass.

December 10, 1938, Grey Cup
Red Storey's football career lasted only three years, but in 15 minutes of the 4th quarter of the '38 Grey Cup he scored three touchdowns and missed a fourth by an inch in leading Toronto to a 30-7 victory over Winnipeg.

New Westminster Salmonbellies

Lacrosse, a game that originated with Canada's native people and grew to world-wide popularity, was widely played in Upper and Lower Canada during the late 1800s. It wasn't until the arrival of the CPR in BC, however, that it became popular in the west.

It was so popular, that in the first decade of the 20th century lacrosse was the biggest sport in the west in terms of crowds and money. The centre of lacrosse and the top team in the province was New Westminster, with one of the most distinctive names in Canadian sport: the Salmonbellies.

New Westminster began its storied history and developed fierce rivalries, especially with Vancouver, in the early 1890s and 1900s. By 1908 the Salmonbellies were an awesome power, bringing the Canadian professional championship (Minto Cup) to the west for the first time, amid wild and jubilant celebration. With Queens Park as their home and crowds of up to 15,000, the 'Bellies would win this national title again in 1909, 1910, 1912 and 1913, led by names such as Gifford, Turnbull and Spring. The 'Bellies had some great nicknames for players in those days: "Doughy" Spring, "Dad" Turnbull, "Grumpy" Spring and "Biscuits" Peele.

With the introduction of the Mann Cup, emblematic of the Senior Amateur Championship of Canada, the Salmonbellies literally dominated the lacrosse world. Between 1915 and 1927 they won 10 Mann Cups. In 1928 the team added international honours to its record as it represented Canada at the Olympics in Amsterdam, where lacrosse was played as a demonstration sport.

The early 1930s saw lacrosse move from the field game to indoor arenas (box lacrosse). Competition for the Mann Cup, however, continued to rage between BC and Ontario through the '30s and into the '40s and '50s, with the Salmonbellies usually emerging as the representative from the west. During these three decades in which lacrosse essentially had everyone's undivided attention, the 'Bellies won the Canadian championship two more times, featuring players such as Alf Davey, Pete Meehan and Bill Wilkes Sr. along with later stars Jack Bionda, Jack Barclay and Cliff Sepka. Led by Fred Hume, the team's passionate owner, the 1937 victory, the first for the west in the box lacrosse era, was particularly sweet and inspiring.

Through the '60s, '70s and '80s the Salmonbellies (known for a brief time in the early '60s as the O'Keefes) continued to lead the west in the exciting, combative and competitive battle for the coveted Mann Cup against the always tough representatives from the east. During these three decades New Westminster remained strong, winning nine more Mann Cups. This was the era of Paul Parnell, Les Norman, Jack Bionda, Wayne Goss, Dave Durante, Al Lewthwaite, Ken Winzoski, Steve d'Easum and Geordie Dean.

At the end of the century, the Salmonbellies story encompassed 110 years of both lacrosse and community pride, combined with a liberal dose of tradition. Because of the memories, Queens Park Arena, where the 'Bellies played throughout, seems to have a certain mystique, a life all its own.

Since 1901 the Salmonbellies won far more Canadian championships (29) than any other lacrosse team in history. The Canadian Lacrosse Hall of Fame is strongly represented if not dominated by lacrosse greats connected with the "spiritual centre of Canadian lacrosse" — the city of New Westminster and the single greatest name in lacrosse history: the Salmonbellies. ❦

New Westminster Salmonbellies Senior Championships

Year
MINTO CUPS, PRE-JUNIOR
1908
1909
1910
1912
1913
MANN CUPS
1915
1916
1917
1920
1921
1922
1923
1924
1925
1927
1937
1943
1958
1959
1962
1965
1970
1972
1974
1976
1981
1986
1989
1991

WORLDS CHAMPIONS — WINNERS OF MINTO CUP. WESTMINSTER LACROSSE TEAM 1908.

HACKING PHOTO.

BCSHOF

General Highlights

1914

The Amateur Skating Association of Canada was formed in 1887 and by 1914 a separate organization for figure skating had been established, known as the Figure Skating Department of the Amateur Skating Association of Canada. The first official national figure skating championships were organized the same year. Louis Rubenstein was the first department president, a position he held until 1930. The department became known as the Canadian Figure Skating Association (CFSA) in 1939 and in 1947 the CFSA joined the International Skating Union, dropping its association with the Amateur Skating Association of Canada.

1914

In golf, Canada's first public golf course opened in Edmonton. The Duchess of Connaught presented a trophy for the Canadian Ladies Championships, and the RCGA issued Canada's first Rules of Golf.

1914

Baseball legend Babe Ruth had Canadian ties. As a boy in Baltimore he was befriended and introduced to baseball by Father Matthias (Martin Boutlier), a Jesuit priest originally from Nova Scotia. And, in his short stint in the Minor Leagues in 1914, Ruth hit his first of many professional home runs in Toronto playing against the baseball Maple Leafs.

1914-1918

The Amateur Athletic Union of Canada ceased operations during World War I.

1918

The Federal Minister of Health banned all amateur sport in Canada due to the outbreak of the flu epidemic, from October to late November.

1900-2000

At the turn of the 20th century there were about 50 golf clubs in Canada, a number that gradually rose to 115 by 1920. The first golf course boom occurred in the early 1920s as the number of courses went to over 300 in less than three years and to over 500 (and 200 golf professionals) by 1927. By 1950 the number exceeded 600. Numbers continued to rise throughout the century and by 1990 there were over 1700 courses. Coinciding nicely with the millennium, the RCGA (Royal Canadian Golf Association) noted that there were 2000 golf facilities in Canada by the end of the century.

1920

Vic Fleming drove *Louie Graham* to the first two-minute trotting mile recorded by a Canadian driver and Canadian-bred horse, albeit not on Canadian soil.

1923

Thomas Murphy drove *Peter Manning* to the first two-minute trotting mile on Canadian soil, in Windsor.

1923

For the first time, spectators had to pay to see the Canadian Open Golf Tournament — $1.00, per patron, per week.

1924

A proposal for a Canada Games was presented to the Amateur Athletic Union of Canada (AAU of C) at a meeting in Winnipeg, which endorsed the idea but lacked the funds to stage the games independently. Spearheaded by the federal government, the Canada Games finally became a reality in 1967.

1924

The first all-women's golf club was formed by Ada Mackenzie in Toronto.

1924

Cecil Eustace Smith was a product of the successful Toronto Skating Club. Smith competed during the 1920s and 1930s, starting at the age of 15, and in 1924 she became the first Canadian female ever to participate at the Olympic Games. Perhaps her greatest moment occurred in 1930 when, placing second only to the incomparable Sonja Henie, she claimed Canada's first ever medal at the World Figure Skating Championships.

1925

Leila Brooks of Toronto broke six world speed skating records.

1925

Vancouver's Percy Williams tied the 100m world record mark of 10.6 seconds.

1922-1927

Jimmy Hawboldt ran 55 marathon races between 1922 and 1927 (he won 38 and finished in the top three in all the others). Fellow Nova Scotian and two-time Boston Marathon champion Johnny Miles rated him the toughest competitor he ever faced. Hawboldt died in February, 2000, at the age of 94 in his hometown of Westville, N.S. He raced Miles six times and beat him three times. He was unbeatable in middle distance races and beat Miles every time over five miles. Hawboldt was a coal miner and the last living survivor of the MacGregor coal mine explosion.

1927

The Dominion Championship for the MacDonald Brier Tankard — named after the trophy presented to the champions — was held for the first time. The Brier became as revered in curling circles as the Stanley Cup became in hockey. The first Brier Champion was the rink from the Toronto Granite Club.

1927

Lord Willingdon, the Governor General of Canada, donated a Cup in his name for the first interprovincial amateur golf competitions. Spirited challenges for the Willingdon Cup would take place all century long.

1928

Canada sent its first figure skating team to the World Championships.

1929-2000

The Rugby Union of Canada was first formed in 1929, disbanded 10 years later at the beginning of World War II and in 1965 reincarnated as the Canadian Rugby Union. By 2000 it was known as Rugby Canada.

1913

Claire Demont was Canada's fastest human in 1913. He supposedly ran the 100-yard dash in a hand-held timed 9.6 seconds on an old cinder track. Demont tried not dream of representing Canada as a sprinter in the Olympic Games because he was employed as a compositor with a Glace Bay, Nova Scotia, newspaper and feared that spending two weeks travelling and competing would cost him his job. Demont's fears were groundless. The 1916 Berlin Olympics were cancelled because of World War I.

Highlights

General Highlights

1930

Canada's first night football game was played at Vancouver's Athletic Park. The game featured the UBC Thunderbirds and the Hamilton Tigers.

1931

World famous professional cyclist "Torchy" Peden of Victoria set a new world record for the mile.

1932

Canada hosted its first World Figure Skating Championships, in Montreal. The Worlds came to Canada five more times during the century: 1960 in Vancouver; 1972 in Calgary; 1978 in Ottawa; 1984 in Ottawa; and 1996 in Edmonton.

1932

Though rugby football was first played in Canada as early as the mid-1860s, the first international matches (i.e. national team matches) did not take place until 1932.

1932

Japan was chosen as the destination for Canada's first official rugby tour. At the evening dinner in Tokyo's Imperial Hotel, the Hon. Herbert Marler, Canada's ambassador to Japan, said that the visit of the Canadians was far more important than the visit of any trade or individual organization. That may very well have been the case, since those attending the match included a number of members of Japan's royal family as well as the ambassadors of Great Britain, the United States, France, Germany and the USSR.

1933

The Penguin Ski Club outside Montreal was the first women's ski club in Canada.

1933

The world's first ski tow was put into operation in Shawbridge, Quebec. It consisted of a rope stretched between a pulley at one end and the rear-wheel mount of a four-cylinder car at the other.

April 3, 1933

Ken Doraty claimed instant immortality by scoring in the sixth overtime period in the longest-ever Stanley Cup final game, helping the Toronto Maple Leafs defeat Boston 1-0.

1937

Lee Hanover was the first Canadian born and bred two-minute trotter.

Dr. Jack A. Wright was Canada's top-ranked male tennis player from 1926 to 1929 and in 1931. He won the international men's singles tennis title in Canada in 1927, 1929 and 1931 and added four Canadian doubles crowns in 1923, 1925, 1929 and 1931. He was a member of Canada's Davis Cup team from 1923-1933

1932

The Shield of Athletes, by R. Tait McKenzie

National Archives/CSFAC

It is not often remembered that when the modern Olympic Games were launched that they included competitions in the arts as well as sport. Among those who earned top honours was Canada's R. Tait McKenzie. Hailing from Almonte, Ontario, McKenzie was an outstanding athlete with Montreal's McGill University early in the century. He later became an internationally acclaimed medical doctor, physical educator and sculptor.

His most famous creation was the bronze medallion "Shield of Athletes." He entered the five-foot diameter piece in the art and culture competitions as part of the 1932 Olympic Games in Los Angeles, winning the top prize. By 1964 the sculpture, depicting each athletic event in the Olympics, became so popular around the world that it was adopted as the "Olympic Shield" at the Olympic Games in Tokyo.

1920-30s

The New Westminster Royals Soccer Club boasted some of the best club teams in Canada during the century. Part of the success of the teams, no doubt, came from the toe of Canada's top player in the 1920s and '30s, Dave Turner. Turner was born in Edinburgh, Scotland. When his family immigrated to Canada early in the century they first settled in Edmonton. Along with childhood friend George Graham (originally from Belfast, Ireland), Turner's teams easily won every club, city and provincial championship available. Looking for new competition, the young pair went to Vancouver in 1923 looking for a tryout with better teams. Their first tryout, with the Vancouver St. Andrews Club, was doomed from the start. Turner years later told sportswriter Jim Kearney: "The tryout was a disaster. It was down at the old Athletic Park. I had the ball on the wing and crossed it to my chum in front of the goal. He blasted his shot over the crossbar, over the fence and about 200 feet down the hill into False Creek. The ball was brand new and was never seen again. We were given the heave-ho. St. Andrews, as you probably know, was a Scottish team and didn't appreciate our carelessness." Turner and Graham ended up signing with Cumberland on Vancouver Island that year. The pair later returned to Vancouver and played for that same St. Andrews club for two years. Then it was off to Boston for a year to play professionally, followed by a season playing in Toronto. In 1927 the duo joined a Canadian All-Star squad, which toured New Zealand and Australia for four months. On returning to Vancouver, Dave Turner was approached by future Vancouver Mayor Fred Hume, who was then the enthusiastic owner of the New Westminster Royals Soccer Club. He signed Turner to a contract that included his tuition fees for UBC. Joined by his friend Graham, Turner was the key to the Royals' four Canadian championships: 1928, 1930, 1931, and 1936. He was renowned for creative play and possessing a scoring touch with either foot. In 1950, Turner was voted Canada's Soccer player of the half century by a wide margin.

Hockey

Patricks' Progress

**by Frederick Edwards
February 1, 1936**

The Patricks have always been rebels. To them, that anything in hockey had been done in a certain fashion was never a sound reason for continuing to do it in that fashion. It is because of this that, while there have been more spectacular brother acts in hockey, no fraternal pair has ever exercised so important an influence on the game. They are iconoclasts, innovators, defiers of tradition, creators of new devices.

In his school days and at McGill University, Lester Patrick was a forward. He played rover under the old seven-man system. When, entirely by chance and greatly to his surprise, he found himself, thirty-three years ago, wearing the uniform of the Brandon team in the Manitoba Hockey League, he was pressed into service as a defence man. The tactics of point and cover point were strange to him. He was a fast-skating stickhandler, and the first time the puck came to him in that Brandon game he began a weaving rush down the ice that ended in front of the opposing team's nets, giving the

goaltender, to whom such a thing had never happened before, a nasty turn.

Charlie McWhirter, who managed a Brandon department store and handled the hockey club for the fun of it, was annoyed with young Mr. Patrick. Such radicalism he felt, was fraught with peril to his defence. Anyway, it had never been done.

Of course, as every 1936 hockey fan knows, the Patrick plan worked. It not only worked but it developed into a defence rush play, one of the most spectacular features of the modern game.

Experts have figured that the Patricks have been responsible, directly or indirectly, for more than a score of changes in hockey customs and hockey rules. Some of these were important, others turned out of minor consequence; but every one of the Patrick innovations has remained in the game to become accepted practice.

"Frank and I," says Lester, "played our first hockey on the sidewalks of Point St. Charles. We cut sticks from the woods on Nun's Island, and used a tin can, a lump of ice, a stone, anything that came handy, for a puck."

After he left McGill, Lester Patrick turned out with the Montreal Juniors, helped them to win a Canadian championship, teamed up such future greats as Dr. George Cameron, Billy Meldrum and Grover Sargent. Next season he was out with Westmount Intermediates. Brother Frank was with him and so was a hefty curly-headed youth who later was to rival the Patricks' reputation as a big-time hockey manager. His name was Arthur Ross.

All through these years Lester Patrick was working in his father's office, playing hockey for the fun of it, never thinking that the game might turn into a career.

Lester knew what he wanted, or thought he knew. He wanted to be a cowboy, to rope steers and tame broncos. The Western fever had him; but not for long.

Seeking an occupation more suited to his training and ability, Lester Patrick contrived to catch on with a survey party then engaged in laying out Alberta's irrigation system in the territory north and west of Calgary.

Came winter, and Lester Patrick, feeling pretty well pleased with himself, money in his pocket and a sense of having conquered the West in his heart, started for home and the family. Three or four Montreal boys with whom he had played hockey back East were toiling on behalf of

Patrick innovations

- Defence rush
- Three zone system with blue lines
- Allowing goaltenders to fall to the ice to save a puck
- Forward pass
- Kicking the puck
- Awarding assists on goals scored
- Numbers on sweaters
- Substitution of a complete forward line
- The first artificial ice rinks in Canada
- Post-season playoff rounds for league championships
- Eliminating body checks near the boards to prevent injuries
- Separate dressing rooms for officials
- Delayed penalty calls until penalized team gains possession
- Penalty shots

the Brandon team. Lester stopped off to say "Hello" and listen to some home-town gossip. His friends met him at the station and said, "You're going to play for us."

In his first game, playing on the defence he staged the puck-carrying performance that made hockey history. It must have worked because Brandon that year won the Manitoba title and played off for the Stanley Cup, losing to Ottawa's famous "Silver Seven." In those days, to be beaten by Ottawa was an honour to be proud of.

During the winter of 1904-05 he played with the Westmount team in the Eastern Canada Hockey League. Next season he joined the famous old Wanderers of Montreal and helped them win the Stanley Cup.

Meanwhile, what of Frank Patrick, the younger brother?

He was always a good hockey player, but did not have Lester's dash. On the other hand he was a painstaking and thorough-minded referee, and he handled senior games in workmanlike fashion when he was only seventeen years old.

Father Patrick had extended his business connections to the Pacific Coast. Nelson was to be headquarters for his future activities, and so, quite casually, he closed out his Montreal affairs, and moved the entire family to West Kootenay.

Lester did not join the original exodus. He was captain of Wanderers, proud holders of the Stanley Cup.

Playing beside Lester on Wanderers' defence was Hod Stuart, one of the finest characters as well as one of the greatest players in the history of the game. Between the two there had developed almost a father and son relationship.

During that summer of 1907, Hod Stuart, on vacation with friends at Brockville, Ontario, dived from a boathouse dock into shallow water, struck bottom, broke his neck and died instantly.

After that, Lester Patrick says, he lost all personal interest in the future doings of Wanderers. He refused to listen to arguments and joined the rest of the Patricks at Nelson, just as soon as he could break away from Montreal.

In Nelson, neither of the Patrick brothers had any serious thought of hockey as a career. They were content to do their bit for the home town team for fun.

Frank Patrick, PCHL, one of the famed Patrick brothers.

Then, in December, 1908, the Edmonton team, Western champions, hurled a pre-season Stanley Cup challenge at Montreal Wanderers, and invited Lester to come along as a guest artist.

Edmonton lost the series, but that journey led to one of the strangest happenings recorded in connection with hockey, anywhere, any time.

As Lester tells it:

"When I got back to Nelson, father tackled me. He asked me if I had been paid. He kept after me, wanting to know if I had accepted anything more than my actual out-of-pocket expenses, and I had to own up that I had."

"All right, son. Now you write them a cheque for that extra money, and send it back to Edmonton, first mail."

So the Patrick brothers went through the season of 1908-09, playing for Nelson, with their amateur standing still as unsullied as the pure white snow capping the peaks of the adjacent Rockies. But way back East, things were happening that were destined to scramble their entire careers.

The staid, established old-line clubs were being raided into a state of frantic hysteria. Two leagues were operating, and no club manager knew for sure who was playing for what team from game to game.

Strange tales of fabulous salaries paid hockey players in the East came to the brothers Patrick, who remained calm. They had their lumber business to run, and they were all washed up as hockey players, and anyway probably none of it was true. That was their attitude until the day when Lester received three telegrams in one hour, each of them begging him to fix his own figure for playing hockey.

"Here's the way I figured it," says Lester Patrick. "I'd rather play in Montreal than anywhere else, so I wired them I'd come for a thousand dollars. Quebec didn't attract me, so I quoted them two thousand. I was quite sure I didn't want to play in Renfrew, and I asked them three thousand.

"And darned if the first acceptance I get isn't from Renfrew. I still didn't believe it, but I was doing some fast thinking. I wired back that I'd come if I could bring Frank along for two thousand."

They were back again in the spring of 1910, and they brought with them the germ of a Big Idea. At last with a complete plan they placed the whole matter before Father Patrick. All they wanted was to sell out the Patrick lumber interests and introduce major-league professional hockey to the West Coast.

Between them they beat down family opposition, talked to bankers, surveyed rink sites, toured the United States studying artificial ice machinery. The three-club league with a sixteen-game schedule opened its first season on January 3, 1912, and lasted for fifteen seasons without a break.

Pacific Coast champions won the Stanley Cup three times against the best the East could offer; and developed a host of young players, many of whom are actively playing the game today in the N.H.L. and in minor leagues.

The organization did a great deal for the development of the game in a general way; but its most important contribution to the advancement of hockey was its spirit of enterprise, its eagerness to try out new ideas, its genius for innovation.

The Pacific Coast League began to find the going pretty sticky in 1924, although the 1924-25 season was one of Lester Patrick's big years. His Victoria team won the championship, and then trimmed Montreal Maroons in the Stanley Cup series.

Tighter organization throughout the professional game, and the extension of the National Hockey League into the United States, first to Boston and then to Madison Square Garden, convinced the Patrick brothers that the pendulum had swung back to the East. This time they followed the swing.

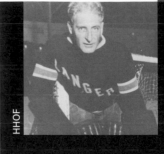

1927-1928

During the Montreal Canadiens — New York Rangers Stanley Cup final, New York goalie Lorne Chabot was injured in Game 2. Unable to find a suitable replacement for the rest of the game, Team Manager Lester Patrick, who was 44 at the time, went between the pipes – and won 2-1 in overtime.

Lester was appointed manager of the New York Rangers in 1925, the Rangers' first season. Under his leadership Rangers have made the play-offs for nine consecutive seasons, and have won the Stanley Cup twice.

Frank, after a few more years on the Coast managing the Patrick interests in British Columbia, turned the whole shebang over to brother Guy Patrick, and returned east, first as vice-president of the N.H.L. where his special chore was to direct referees — and a mean job that is — then, this year, as a manager of the Boston Bruins. 🍁

Lester Patrick and the New York Rangers, 1930s.

"As a rule, if there are any rules in this business, you don't want them to be too bright at anything but hockey. If they have little outside interest, and their minds aren't occupied elsewhere, they're more likely to concentrate on the game. A man may be almost illiterate, he may be unable to hold a responsible job, but by some queer quirk that I can't understand he may have the best hockey brains in the game. But what makes hockey brains, where they come from or how they work, no one knows."

- Lester Patrick, as quoted in Maclean's Magazine, March 15, 1950.

"There is only one way a boy can be sure to learn to play hockey — on the pond, on the creek, on a flooded lot. The foundation of hockey isn't really hockey at all. It's shinny, a wild melee of kids batting a puck around, with no rules, no organization, nothing but individual effort to grab and hold the puck."

- Lester Patrick, as quoted in Maclean's Magazine, March 15, 1950.

Vancouver Millionaires of the PCHA, 1911.

November 26, 1917

During a meeting in Montreal's Windsor Hotel, the National Hockey League (NHL) was formed, with Frank Calder voted in as its first President. Four teams played the first year in a 22-game schedule: the Montreal Canadiens, the Ottawa Senators, the Montreal Wanderers and the Toronto Arenas. A fifth team, the Quebec Bulldogs were accepted, but did not play the first year.

December 19, 1917

The first NHL game was played, with the Montreal Wanderer's Harry Hyland scoring five goals in a victory over the Toronto Arenas.

January 2, 1918

Westmount Arena, home to both the Montreal NHL teams, the Wanderers and the Canadiens, burned to the ground. Both teams moved into the smaller Jubilee Arena.

January 9, 1918

A new rule change allowed goaltenders to drop to their knees to stop shots. Ottawa's Clint Benedict is credited with encouraging the rule, since he apparently ignored it all the time anyway.

1918-1919

"Newsy" Lalonde again led his hockey league in scoring, this time with 30 points for the NHL's Montreal Canadiens. In his career, Lalonde played for teams in Cornwall, Sault Ste. Marie, Toronto, Montreal, Renfrew, Vancouver, Saskatoon and New York. During his summers, Lalonde swapped his hockey stick for a lacrosse stick, playing well enough to be voted Canada's Top Lacrosse Player of the first 50 years of the century.

March 1, 1919

"Newsy" Lalonde of Montreal scored a Stanley Cup playoff record five goals in a 6-3 win over Ottawa.

April, 1919

The influenza epidemic spread through North America and cancelled many events, including the final games of the 1919 Stanley Cup playoffs between the Seattle Metropolitans and the Montreal Canadiens. Five Montreal players were hospitalized and one, Joe Hall, died from the flu on April 19. "This has been the most peculiar series in the history of sport," said PCHA President Frank Patrick about the 1919 final. The games between the teams were tied at two, so no winner of the Cup was declared.

November 26, 1919

The Toronto Arenas franchise folded, cancelling its NHL season. The franchise was later sold to become the Tecumsehs, then the St. Patricks. Conn Smythe eventually bought the team and on February 14, 1927 renamed it the Maple Leafs.

1919-1920

The Quebec Bulldogs, accepted in 1917, entered the NHL. (The team was officially named the Athletics, but no one seemed to call them that.)

January 10, 1920

"Newsy" Lalonde of the Canadiens scored 10 goals in a 16-3 romp over the Toronto St. Patricks.

January 31, 1920

Joe Malone of the Quebec Bulldogs scored an unequalled seven goals in a game against the same Toronto St. Patricks — with an eighth disallowed on an offside.

1920-1921

The Hamilton Tigers joined the NHL and became the only new team in the century to record a shutout its first game — a 5-0 win over the Montreal Canadiens.

1921-1922

Harry "Punch" Broadbent of the Ottawa Senators scored in 16 consecutive games — a feat unmatched in the century.

March 31, 1923

Ottawa's King Clancy played every position at least once during a 1-0 Stanley Cup win over an Edmonton team. His stint playing goal came when regular Clint Benedict left the game briefly to get stitches for a cut.

March 14, 1923

Pete Parker called hockey's first radio broadcast for a Regina-Edmonton Western Canada League game. Foster Hewitt would call his first game, and the NHL's first, eight days later in Toronto.

September 18, 1922

Montreal Canadiens traded star player "Newsy" Lalonde to Saskatoon for then-unknown Aurèle Joliat — who went on to become a prolific goal scorer in his own right, including 13 goals and 22 assists in the 1922-23 season.

1924

The NHL introduced its first individual award — the Hart Trophy for the Most Valuable Player in the league during the regular season. Frank Nighbor of the Ottawa Senators was the first winner in 1924. A year later, Nighbor was also the first winner of the Lady Byng Trophy, awarded to the most gentlemanly player "who is also good."

1922

Somehow Toronto overlooked a rising hockey star from their own territory in Stratford, enabling the Montreal Canadiens to sign a young Howie Morenz — who went on to NHL fame as the "Stratford Streak."

March 9, 1924

The Hamilton Tigers of the NHL were suspended during the Stanley Cup finals against the Canadiens. The players had gone on strike over "back dues" which Tigers owner Percy Thompson denied. Hamilton lost its franchise for the remainder of the century and the entire team roster was sold for $75,000 to become the New York Americans.

November 29, 1924

The fabled Montreal Forum opened with a 7-1 Montreal Canadiens victory over the Toronto St. Patricks. Billy Boucher scored the first hat trick in the Forum the same evening.

November 28, 1925

Montreal Canadien's netminder Georges Vezina, who played every Canadiens game for 15 years, was replaced by Al Lacroix when Vezina came down with tuberculosis. On March 26, 1926, Vezina died from the dreaded disease. The NHL immediately named its "Best Goalie Award" the Vezina Trophy in his honour.

May 4, 1926

The PCHA President, Frank Patrick, sold the contracts of all League players to the NHL for $258,000, enabling three new franchises to begin play in the US — Chicago, Detroit and the New York Rangers.

1925-1926

Rookie Nels Stewart won the scoring race with 34 goals — a rookie scoring record not broken until 1970 by Gilbert Perreault.

February 14, 1927

Conn Smythe led a Toronto business group in purchasing the NHL St. Patricks, immediately renaming the team the Maple Leafs and changing the colours to blue and white from green and white.

1928-1929

The Montreal Canadiens eventually replaced Georges Vezina with George Hainsworth, who would win the Vezina Trophy in each of his first three years. In the 1928-29 season he recorded 22 shutouts and a goals-against average of 0.92 for the season — both NHL records that lasted the century.

1929-1930

The NHL allowed forward passing in all three zones, also adapting the offside rule.

The "Little Giant" in the Black Cap

Aurèle Joliat

"The little giant" was one of two nicknames proudly worn by Aurèle Joliat during his 16-season career with the Montreal Canadiens during the 1920s and 30s. Some also called him the "Mighty Atom." Not an imposing physical presence, he weighed in at less than 160 lbs (73 kg) upon his arrival in Montreal, maintaining just 140 lbs (64 kg) for most of his career.

But his limited size was never a problem for the nimble French-Canadian left winger. Coming from the same Ottawa roots as King Clancy and Frank Boucher, he learned to play hockey on the Rideau Canal. Boucher said of Joliat that he was as crafty as Howie Morenz was fast.

Born in Ottawa in 1901, he initially played rugby with the Ottawa Rough Riders and the Regina Wascana Boat Club. After fracturing his ankle during a rugby match, he decided to make a career out of hockey instead and joined the Saskatoon Sheiks. Not long after, Frank Boucher's brother Billy convinced Canadiens' owner Leo Dandurand to acquire the services of the nimble little player. In 1922, one of the first "big trades" saw Joliat move to Montreal in exchange for veteran star Newsy Lalonde. Despite being criticized for trading an established star, Dandurand and the Canadiens were not disappointed with the trade, watching Joliat overcome his small size by using a vast repertoire of spins and fancy footwork, not to mention his strong stick handling.

In his first season with Montreal, Joliat spent most of his time warming the bench. But in 1923 he was put on a line with Howie Morenz and Billy Boucher. The trio complemented one another perfectly on the ice.

During the following season, in 1924-25, Joliat scored 29 goals in just 24 games, without a doubt the best season of his career. Linemates Morenz and Boucher netted 27 and 18 goals respectively. The little giant and the "Stratford Streak" (Morenz) made hockey headlines, as the Canadiens finished the 1927-28 season in first place. Their star status helped popularize hockey in American cities like New York, Chicago, Detroit and Boston.

Busher Jackson

Joliat's small size clearly did not stop him from scoring goals. Like Morenz, he scored 270 in his career, despite suffering numerous serious injuries: six shoulder separations and three rib fractures, not to mention other common injuries of the era, such as five nose fractures. He was selected to the NHL's first all-star team in 1931, and the second team in 1932, 1934 and 1935. As his team's most valuable player, he won the Hart Trophy in 1934. His talents also graced three Stanley Cup winning squads (1924, 1930 and 1931).

Two of Joliat's adversaries were Toronto's Busher Jackson, left, and Ottawa's/New York's Nels Stewart, above.

Joliat always amused his teammates and opposing players with his little idiosyncrasies. Among them was the fact that the little giant invariably wore a black baseball cap during his games. It was even rumoured that he would refuse to chase the puck if the cap were knocked off his head.

Even long after his retirement, Joliat overflowed with energy and was often invited to special hockey events. He made one of his memorable appearances in 1968 at the old Madison Square Garden in New York for a ceremony marking the final hockey game to be played in that venerable arena. The Rangers had invited all living members of the Hockey Hall of Fame, including childhood friends Joliat and Frank Boucher.

One by one, the stars of the past jumped on the ice clad in their original team sweaters: Maurice Richard, Eddie Shore, Babe Pratt, Bill Cook, and Ching Johnson were just some of the names saluted by the crowd. But, as reporter Tim Moriarty of the Long Island Newsday wrote, "Aurèle stole the spotlight. He still wore the same black baseball cap that identified him during his career. He skated up and down the rink a few times and then spurred on by the crowd, went into a series of spins and tipped his hat to the spectators. It was an unforgettable display." Joliat was 67 at the time.

Joliat left behind the memory of an incredible little man who was a master stick handler and superb passer. Inducted into the Hockey Hall of Fame in 1945, he will always be remembered as "the little giant" in the black cap. ♣

1928

Track and Field

Canada at the Olympics

by Alexandrine Gibb (Manager of the Canadian Women's Olympic Track Team)
October 1, 1928

Myrtle Cook, 1928 Olympic gold medallist.

This year at Amsterdam, Holland, for the first time in athletic history, women athletes were given an official and definite place on an Olympic program. Women's athletics and women athletes were on trial before a world tribunal. That they made good beyond all shadow of a doubt is admitted wherever there are broad minded sportsmen.

This year, for the first time in her athletic history, Canada sent a team of women athletes to an Olympiad. Canada's women athletes were tried as they never had been tried before. And — they won the world's track and field championship.

It is no exaggeration at all to say that it was an amazing achievement. Look at what it meant and how it was done:

Six girls from Canada, drawn from a population of less than ten million, were pitted against the cream of the women athletes of twenty-one countries; against a total of one hundred and twenty-one competitors, drawn from a population of something like three hundred million.

Never before in the history of women's international athletics has the competition been so keen.

Team for team, the Canadian contingent of six was overwhelmingly outnumbered. The United States team totalled twenty; the German, nineteen; the Belgian, fourteen; the French, thirteen — to mention only the strongest, numerically.

And, when the last race was run, the unofficial score stood: Canada, 26; United States, 20; Germany, 18, with the rest trailing nowhere near the leaders.

If that's not an amazing achievement, then I don't know the meaning of the word amazing.

There may be a few old fogies who will express an opinion that athletics for women did not make good at Holland. But in the opinion of all the feminine authorities upon women's sports who witnessed and studied the effects of the competitions at Amsterdam, women's sports more than justified their place on the program. Some will argue that certain events, particularly the 800 metre one, were beyond the power and strength of women. They will try to prove their assertion by citing certain incidents which occurred at the conclusion of the 800 metre final race at the games.

Out of nine competitors in this final, four of them, the opponents of women's competitive sport claim, were run to utter exhaustion and were overtaxed in their strength.

1928 Olympic gold medallists in the 4 x 100m relay, from left to right, Florence Bell, Myrtle Cook, Ethel Smith and Fanny "Bobbie" Rosenfeld.

What are the facts? Four of the girls on crossing the finishing line turned to the infield and threw themselves upon the grass and two of the four were Canadians, Jean Thompson of Penetang, and Bobbie Rosenfeld of Toronto. The woman who won it, Mrs. Radke of Germany, finished her race out, slowed down gradually and showed less signs of distress than fifty percent of the men did at the same distance. The entry from Japan, Miss Hitomi, exasperated at not winning, threw herself on the grass and wept bitterly. The third finisher, Miss Gentzel, of Sweden, was unconcerned and finished off by running back to the tunnel entrance. The fourth and fifth finishers, our own two plucky Canadians, Jean Thompson and Bobbie Rosenfeld dropped on the grass. Little seventeen-year-old Jeannie, who had never previously been in a race where she was jostled or headed was broken-hearted. Bobbie Rosenfeld, who on the stretch down the track came from ninth position to close behind Jean when she saw the latter falter, and who coaxed the youngster to come on in, dropped down beside Jean to comfort her. Jean was

running her second 800 metre race in two days after being in bed suffering from an old tendon trouble.

Bobbie Rosenfeld's sportsmanship in this event was one of the high spots of the games. When she came up from behind, she refused to go ahead of the youngster, but stayed at Jean's shoulder to the finish and then let Jean finish fourth, taking a fifth for herself. In the annals of women's athletics, there is no finer deed than this. Remember, too, that Miss Rosenfeld was not trained for this distance, being a sprinter. She was put in the 800 metres only to encourage Jean and she carried out her allotted task magnificently.

So far as the Canadian team was concerned, the only real tragedy came in the 100 metres, when Myrtle Cook, of Toronto, was disqualified, after winning her way through the preliminary heats and the semi-finals, from actually running in the final with Ethel Smith and Bobbie Rosenfeld.

I think Bobbie Rosenfeld won. The finish was so close that there was room for doubt. I do not think the judges were unfair, I believe they all called it as they saw it. But they themselves were not agreed on the winner. The five judges at the finish were each picking one position. And both the judge who picked first and the judge who picked second chose Betty Robinson of the United States. Ethel Smith was undoubtedly third. Then where was Bobby Rosenfeld? In my opinion and that of a number of others at the finish, she either won or it was a dead heat.

Now for a word about the 400 metre relay. On the Saturday of the Olympics, the Canadian team, Bobbie Rosenfeld, Ethel Smith, Jane Bell, and Myrtle Cook, all of Toronto, won their preliminary heat with ease in forty-nine and two-fifth seconds, breaking the old Olympic record. The final on Sunday, with only six countries left in the contest, was a thriller from the gun to the finish. A terrific pace was set, and from the time Bobbie Rosenfeld, the lead-off girl, started we had a lead. True, it wasn't sufficient to be comfortable about, but still we were a yard ahead when she gave a pretty pass to Ethel Smith, Ethel ran like one possessed down that back stretch of the track. The wind was blowing her hair, and pressing her body back, too, all the way down to the turn, where she handed the baton to Jane Bell with a slight increase over the lead she had received from Miss Rosenfeld. Jane Bell ran the race of her life. Her portion of the run was around two curves in the track. It appeared to Jane that she was behind because the girls on the outside tracks were, apparently, in front of her on the turns. But when she straightened out for the final hand-over to Myrtle Cook she had a nice three-yard lead. The pass between Myrtle and Jane was nearly a flop. It was only when Miss Cook had nearly reached the line at which she must have the baton in her possession that Jane Bell reached her — Myrtle Cook was running at top speed — and Jane slapped it into her hand. A perfect pass- a fraction of a second later it would have been a catastrophe — Miss Cook was then running against the speedy winner of the 100 metres, the American, Miss Robinson. We think she gained slightly on her down the stretch. At any rate, we won with a comfortable margin — there could be no argument about that win at any rate! And we won in another new record time of forty-eight and two-fifth seconds, which I believe will stand on the books for some time to come.

How did we feel when it was all over! I doubt if any of us can tell. All I remember is that there were smiles, tears, and gasps of relief, up in the competitors' stand where the Canadian group was watching the contest. Out in the field the four runners ran together from the four corners of the track and hugged each other with delight. At last we had won a first in the girls' section — a first which meant that the Canadian flag was going to the masthead. And after all, that was what we were there for and we had met with success after a week of hard luck and some disappointments. It was the last day of the Olympics for us and we had to win then if ever. And when Ethel Catherwood, of Saskatoon, later in the day won another first in the high jump, our joy knew no bounds. Canada then, we all realized, was on the top of the heap in the girls' track and field events, even though we had lost first place in the 100 and 800 metres events and did not have a large enough team to send an entry into the other women's event, the discus. With our two firsts on one day, we had won the women's championship for Canada!

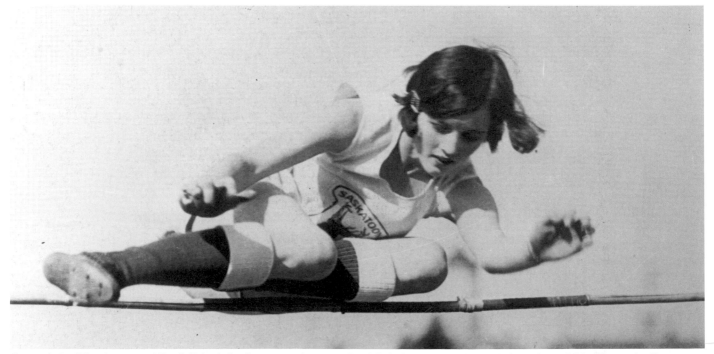

Canada's "Saskatoon Lily," Ethel Catherwood, won the high jump gold medal at the 1928 Olympic Games.

World's champion high jumper

Ethel Catherwood had to face a field of twenty-three jumpers. The United States had three and Miss Wiley, of that team, finished with a third, while our beauty won with a jump approximately five feet three inches. The Holland entry, Miss Gisolf, who holds the accepted world's record, could only secure a second when she ran up against the fair Canadian.

The high jump was held on the last day. Cold weather did not help the contestants in their endeavour to make new records. Miss Catherwood, tall with beautiful eyes, pretty hair and what the French call a photo-filmic face, previous to the commencement of competition, had been unofficially crowned Beauty Queen of the Olympiad without a dissenting voice. In actual competition she was given the unanimous verdict of the judges as the most graceful and perfect jumper any of them had ever seen in action. They should know. They were chosen from all nations to judge because of their knowledge of jumping. Miss Catherwood, for the first time in her career was up against real competition, but it did not phase her. Not for a moment. She took her turn at jumping, ran back to the big red Hudson Bay blanket, and remained there comfortably wrapped until her turn came. She did not remove her sweat suit until the bar was above five feet. Then she missed once and we held our breath in agony. Off came the sweat suit and she soared lightly over the bar with hardly a glance at the height. The huge amphitheatre was packed with spectators and there was a sharp indrawing of breath every time she jumped. Sufficient to say, of the Saskatoon Lily's popularity, when she defeated the home town favourite, Miss Gisolf, of Holland, for first place, the Hollanders, disappointed as they were at not getting a first, came across with real applause for our pretty Canadian.

There was a striking incident in the high jump which may have helped us win this event. To understand it, one has to go back to the heats of the 800 metres and the relay. Our dressing room we shared with several countries, including Belgians. The Belgian girls had no one to look after them, so the Canadian chaperone and I volunteered our services to massage them. The offer was gratefully accepted. Little did we think we would be more than repaid. But we were. When Miss Catherwood was jumping we were not permitted to have anyone out on the field with her. Practically every other country had two jumpers entered. We had only one. The Belgian jumpers entered noticed this. They sat down beside the Canadian entry, wrapped her up carefully in the big red blanket and took her spikes off after each jump and cleaned them of all mud and sand. They were delighted when she won. And they helped us in our success, with their kindly thoughtfulness.

1928

The Globe, Toronto, Wednesday, August 8, 1928, p. 6 (Sports Section)

Retain Six Events on Women's Olympiad

Amsterdam, Aug. 7 — The International Amateur Athletic Federation after a spirited debate today voted 16 to 6 to retain women's track and field events in the Olympic program. By a vote of 14 to 8 it rejected a full list of ten events asked by the Women's International Athletic Federation.

Those opposing the retention of the women's events in the Olympics were headed by a country whose women athletes won the present Olympic women's track and field meet — Canada. The Canadian delegates were supported by Great Britain, Ireland, Finland, Hungary and Italy.

The 800 metres event, which was the most hotly contested of all the program, was rejected by a 12-to-9 vote, with one abstention, while the broad jump, shot put and 200m flat also failed to command a majority. The six events which found favour with the Federation's delegates were the 100m flat, the 400m relay, the high jump, discus throw, the javelin, and the 80m hurdle.

Replying to the argument that women were not in the Ancient Greek Olympics, Lady Heath retorted that neither were the hop-step- jump, fencing and pistol shooting.

A woman speaks her mind

These are the events and Canada came home champions of the first women's Olympiad. I feel the results bear me out when I say they prove conclusively that competition in track and field sports has its place in the sphere of women's sport.

It is true Dr. A. S. Lamb, of Montreal, president of the Amateur Athletic Union of Canada, does not agree with me. He evidently thinks so little of what our sextet did against world wide competition that he voted against Canada or any other nation being permitted to have women participate at future Olympic games. This action on his part was received with consternation among our own team and women officials abroad, who could not understand why he should object to women at the Olympics when Canada had carried off the premier honours — surely a worth-while honour for any country.

The voting on the subject so important to athletic women all over the world resulted in women being included in the next Olympics by a vote of sixteen to six. Lucky for Canada and her girl athletes that Dr. Lamb's vote was not a deciding one.

Undoubtedly a number of things combined made Canada successful at the first women's Olympics. The main thing was that we had the best athletes in the world. Together they made an unbeatable team. Six of them and every one a point winner! Being handed a band of girls like this, every one of them in tip top condition, all that was necessary from the managing end was to keep them as they were. This was an easy matter with these girls. They went abroad on business for Canada — and that business came before all other things. ♣

The opportunities available to girls and women to participate in sport expanded greatly over the course of the 20th century. Even though various groups continue to work to increase access, by the end of the century there were no longer serious questions about either the rights or the appropriateness of women engaging in physical activities of their choice. Earlier in the century, however, there were people who felt that strenuous competitive sports were not only inappropriate for women, but were actually detrimental to their health. Two articles that appeared in Maclean's Magazine in 1938 illustrate the nature of the debate.

I DON'T LIKE AMAZON WOMEN

BY ELMER W. FERGUSON
AUGUST 1, 1938

Elmer Ferguson

Girls have a place in sport. I knew that when I saw a graceful figure standing atop a high diving board, a girl whose physical perfection was enhanced by a clinging one-piece bathing suit of the sort some old fogies with nasty minds would bar as indecent, when such garb in reality removed all possibility of suggestiveness. The girl leaned forward, arms arched, and floated off the high board, coming down to the water like a great sea bird, a thing of infinite grace, to strike smoothly, without a splash, and go streaking into the depths, leaving hardly a ripple behind.

Girls have a place in sport. I knew it seeing Kay Stammers and the late Suzanne Lenglen gliding over tennis courts, slashing back drives. I knew it seeing Joyce Wethered or some other graceful girl golfer swing with precise rhythm and a certain power on a teed-up ball, though I've seen some ponderous females tramping the links who added nothing whatever to the scenic effects with their Clydesdale strides, dripping perspiration, stertorous breathing and blowsily flushed faces.

That, indeed, is where I reach the dead-line. Sorry, but in girls' sport I can't go for those violent, face-straining, face-dirtying, body-bouncing, sweaty, graceless, stumbling, struggling, wrenching, racking, jarring and floundering events that some girls see fit to indulge in. Sorry again, but I like grace, sweetness, rhythm, freedom from sweat and freedom from grime

among the girls. Of course, it's a matter of taste. Some of the boys may like to see the girl-friend lumbering along from first to second in a softball game, hitting the dirt on her ear, and coming up with a lot of mud or sand ground into her visage. They may like to see the girls at hockey, a spectacle which I consider reaches the lower levels of competitive athletic entertainment after you've watched the grace and speed and certainty and skill with which males perform. They may like to see some nice girl body-check another and knock her down, half-stunned and breathless, though, in all truth, the girls in hockey skate in such rickety fashion, bobble along so uncertainly, that a good strong breeze will pretty nearly blow them off their stumbling feet, and body-checks are just so much wasted effort.

It's for health too. Amateur sport in Canada to my mind knows no more sincere and diligent advocate than Dr. A. S. Lamb, of the Department of Physical Education at McGill University. The good doctor is another of the little heckled band (I mean the girl sports writers continually give us the bird) opposing participation by girls in

Canada's 1932 Women's Olympic Track team.

violent sports in which he coincides with the opinions of Dr. H. M. Abrahams of London, Olympic 100-meter sprint winner of 1924. This is Dr. Lamb's sensible theory:

"There is almost universal agreement that well-directed play and recreative activities are most beneficial, particularly to our youth. Play is, however, a two-edged sword, and misdirected activities and emphasis may be quite harmful. In well-directed play, activities should be utilized which appeal to the natural interests, which harmonize with age and development

continued on page 52

"A friend of mine … believes that girls are possibly better sports than men. In his judgment, the girls fight just as hard during the game and, when they win, the congratulations of friends do not result in uncontrollable pride. When they lose they don't worry so much over defeat or think up so many alibis as do the men."

H.H. Roxborough, writing in Maclean's Magazine, February 15, 1929

ELMER, YOU'RE GOOFY

BY ROXY ATKINS
SEPTEMBER 15, 1938

So Elmer W. Ferguson doesn't like Amazon athletes. With his right to express a personal opinion, I can have no quarrel. But when he uses headlines in a national magazine to refer disparagingly to girls who participate in sports he doesn't like, then Mr. Ferguson ceases to be a protected individual.

By the way, who made Elmer a countrywide authority on women's sports? In the last ten years there have been Empire Games in Canada, England and Australia; there have been several world's championship competitions in Europe, and girls competed in every one of them. But I'll wager a mauve hair ribbon to a couple of new cigar bands, that this self-constituted authority never got nearer than St. Lawrence Main Street to any one of them.

While Elmer hasn't been a close observer of the things he decries, he does trot out the same old sketches so generally displayed by Paul Gallico, Andy Lytle, and other male sports writers who like to scare the girls back to their needlework.

For instance, Elmer says girls have a place in sports, providing it's figure skating, golf or diving. No one would question the desirability of those forms of recreation; every girl would pat "Fergie" on the back and say, enthusiastically, "Boy, you're right."

But what are most girls to use for the money it costs to figure skate or golf? Even if the working girl could spare the money required to figure skate and golf, or find transportation to the links, she still would be an outsider competitively, for the experts and near champions in both those sports practice and play in the daytime when their sisters are in the office or factory.

Diving and swimming do not present the same financial handicaps, and many girls who play the "hard games" can also get about in the water. But Mr. Ferguson should know his geography well enough to recognize that Canada has hundreds of rural communities where the girl who wanted to "lean forward, arch her arms and float like a great sea bird," would have to land in a bird bath or an open sewer. Yet in these lesser towns a softball diamond, a running track or even enough ice for a hockey game, is frequently available.

But what does Elmer hate in girls' sports? "Face straining, face-dirtying, body-bounding, sweaty, graceless, stumbling, struggling, wrenching, racking, jarring and floundering" are among his peeves.

Would Elmer have us run races with a powder puff in one hand and a mirror in the other? Of course athletic girls sometimes have dirty faces, but not often or for very long. Besides, it would be generally agreed that the outdoor, sports-loving girl has a naturally healthier colour than the nonplaying type who depends on artifice for her colour.

Fanny "Bobbie" Rosenfeld

Elmer, don't get it into your "noggin" that only the homely win the races, or smack the home runs, or toss the baskets. True, there are some champions who are not handsome, and that goes for figure skaters, golfers and tennis players too. Don't forget that.

I have never known a girl naturally beautiful, to lose any of her good looks and charm because she became sports-minded. But — and I say this with real experience — I have known many young girls, who were thin, scrawny, unattractive, prone to mixing with boy gangs and pointed for trouble ahead until they joined a ball team or a track club. Then, disciplined by training, physically developed through exercise and fresh air, socially developed by contacts with older girls and chaperones and broadened by travel, they have become young ladies whom it was a pleasure to meet and know. That's a fact, Mr. Ferguson. I'm not trying to paint a picture or get lost in a maze of words; I'm telling you that the team games you deplore have given a lift that no other means could provide to hundreds of girls right here in Canada.

Elmer also says, "The truth is that the legs of most girls' don't rate high on exposure." But how inconsistent this man is, for he also glories in "a girl whose physical

continued on page 53

and which have inherent values in the contribution they might make to better citizenship.

"The nature and characteristics of boys and girls differ very widely, and therefore care should be taken to foster activities from which the greatest benefits might be derived.

"Play, recreation, competition, are just as essential for our girls as for our boys, but this must in no way be interpreted to mean that intensive competition with its excessive emotional and physical stress is the type which should be participated in by girls and women."

That's the story, girls. The violent sports are no good for your looks, dignity, or health. Occasionally some writer comes out stressing the improvements of times and distances being made in women's sports, and hints that the day is coming when they'll equal the performances of males, which is a very stupid suggestion indeed, because they never will. ✤

"AMAZON WOMEN"

perfection was enhanced by a clinging one-piece bathing suit." But after all, Mr. Ferguson, if you don't like exposed legs at athletic meets, why not concentrate on the competition? Some men do.

Elmer, I thought at first that you didn't understand us girls. Now I know you don't even know your men. Would you be surprised to know that girls who play those sports you deplore are looked upon as gilt-edged securities in the marriage market? I can now recall, just at random, without any attempt to dig deep. Rosa Grosse, Myrtle Cook, Hilda Strike, Florence Bell, Peggy Matheson and "Dot" Brookshaw. Every one of the six was a sprinter, every one had a national reputation, each held some Canadian championship, every one at some time had a dirty face, every one had a strained face as she tore down cinder tracks and flung herself at the white woollen thread, every one qualified to be the kind of 'gal' Mr. Ferguson says men don't like. I really don't like to

confound the critics but — every one of the six married.

Don't let anyone tell you that women's efforts in sport are ridiculous. More than 2,500 paying spectators, mostly men, have crowded into Sunnyside Stadium in Toronto to see girls play the "violent" sport of softball, and cagey "sport-wise" Madison Square Garden recently paid $750 to a Toronto girls' team who were invited to play in a New York baseball tournament. Explain that $750 if you think girls' sports are ridiculous.

But after all, Mr. Ferguson, and I say this with all the femininity and grace I can command, "Girls are human beings. They want an equal chance with men to go places, to see the world, to parade before crowds, to win medals and cups, to hear the cheers of the spectators. They want a chance to play, to develop physically, to cultivate the spirit of sportsmanship, to meet nice people, to have an interest beyond the home and the office." ❦

"ELMER, YOU'RE GOOFY"

Basketball

Noel MacDonald

The best of the Edmonton Grads

NOEL MACDONALD
centre
PHOTO BY BLYTH STUDIOS

The Edmonton Grads compiled an unsurpassed record during their storied 25-year history, and there is no doubt that much of their success was due to their coach, J. Percy Page, who consistently pulled his teams together into a powerful unit. The focus was on teamwork, not on individual stars.

That said, there are many players whose individual performances rose above even the stellar standards set by the team, none more so than centre Noel MacDonald. After the team disbanded in 1940, both the fans and the coach concurred that the Grads' all-time leading scorer (averaging 13.5, 13.8 or 14.3 points per game, depending on the source, over seven seasons from 1933 to 1939) was the team's most outstanding player. On average, the Grads outscored their opponents by about 48-20.

Born in Mortlach, Saskatchewan in 1915 (the same year the Grads were formed), MacDonald's family moved to Edmonton during the 1920s after drought forced them off the family farm. She played basketball in public school and high school, eventually earning a spot on the McDougall High team that served as a feeder team for the Grads. She moved up to the big team in 1933, and never looked back.

The rules for women's teams were in a state of flux at the time, with some teams playing "girls" rules, and others playing "boys" rules. There was a centre-jump after every basket, and the Grads developed a whole series of plays off of MacDonald's ability to control the tip. At 6' 10 ", she was not only one of the tallest women on the court, but also fast, with extraordinary reflexes and good agility.

Even though she was the Grads' top scorer, she was no slouch on defence. In one notable match-up in her rookie year, she had the unenviable task of guarding Alberta Williams, a US all-star playing for the Tulsa Stenos. Williams stood one inch taller than MacDonald, and was known as a prolific scorer who could use either hand to drop a deadly hook shot. To add to the pressure, the teams were playing for possession of the Underwood Trophy, symbol of women's basketball supremacy in North America. MacDonald was simply expected to do her best to slow the American player down. She did much more though — she showed her future brilliance that night, outscoring her opponent 20-4 and leading her team to victory.

The Underwood Trophy was on the line again in 1936, this time with the formidable Eldorado Lion-Oilers making the challenge. They handed Edmonton a rare defeat in the first game of the best of five series, and were ahead by two near the end of the second game. MacDonald had played the whole game, and had 18 points to her credit, but was in a state of near exhaustion. Reaching into her reserves, she won a jump, tipped the ball to a teammate and scored on the return pass to tie the game. With time almost out, she took the next jump as well, and after a series of rapid-fire passes that typified the Grads' offence, got the ball back and shot from 25 feet out. The ball trickled in as time ran out, and the Grads went on to sweep the series. By the time they disbanded, the Grads had never lost the Underwood Trophy and it was given to them permanently.

It's a fairly safe bet that in addition to their other laurels, MacDonald and her teammates would have had Olympic gold medals to their credit if they had played in another era. The Grads played exhibition series at four Olympic Games from 1924 to 1936, never losing a game. Unfortunately for them, women's basketball wasn't an official Olympic event until 1976.

1939

The largest crowd up to that date to witness a basketball game in Canada gathered at the Edmonton Gardens as the Grads drew 6,792 fans.

Long-time Edmonton Grads captain Noel MacDonald retired after playing 135 games.

1940

The Edmonton Grads disbanded at beginning of World War II with the Underwood Trophy in their permanent possession. The team never started up again.

In typical fashion, MacDonald deflected praise aimed in her direction by emphasizing her teammates' accomplishments. When she was inducted into Canada's Sports Hall of Fame in 1971, she said, "I could go on through the team — each girl having her own outstanding characteristic and each of them able to shoot from anywhere on the floor with deadly accuracy in her own style. This is why I am not altogether comfortable at being chosen as the Grad for special recognition. On the floor we were not individuals, we were a team."

When Percy Page and the team's fans were asked to name its top players of all time, the list included stars like Etta Dann, Margaret MacBurney, Gladys Fry, Connie Smith and Babe Belanger. Despite her reluctance to claim the spotlight, though, Page and the public were unanimous that Noel MacDonald was the best of all time. ❦

Coach Percy Page and the 1932 Edmonton Grads.

The West Finally Wins — the 1935 Grey Cup

Winnipeg Blue Bomber Fritzie Hanson.

A Western football team didn't officially play for the Grey Cup until 1921 when Edmonton ventured into Toronto where they were skunked by the Argonauts 23-0. Still, given the steady improvement of Western teams relative to their more established Eastern counterparts, most assumed it would only be a matter of time before the Cup crossed the Red River on its way to a Prairie home.

By the end of the 1932 season such hopes were fading. The Regina Roughriders set the standard for futility by succumbing in their fifth straight Grey Cup appearance. There were few handicappers who would have taken action on a Western victory in the near future.

The East just seemed to have a better pool of recruits. Drastic action was required.

All that was to change in 1935. Ted Reeve, a budding journalist and a Canadian football star with Queen's University and Balmy Beach, poetically described the Winnipeg contenders:

> *"They have giants who hail from Minnesota,*
> *Their tackles would make a tree sag,*
> *And a tightly wound Swede from Dakota*
> *Who catches coyotes at tag."*

The 'Pegs had recruited college stars from Minnesota, Wisconsin, and North Dakota with the promise of a job and even under-the-table payments in an era when athletes were expected to play for the love of the game.

"They had a wiry, wonderfully fast little running backfielder in Fritz Hanson of North Dakota, who must be a direct descendant from the ten thousand Swedes who ran through the weeds, judging by the amazing amount of foot he displayed as he flashed across the mud to glory this season," said Reeve.

For the Cup final on December 7 Hamilton Tigers had the advantage of home field but almost from the start they were on the defensive as Bud Marquardt and Greg Kabat grabbed touchdown passes while Hamilton could only respond with a field goal. Nevertheless Hamilton managed to stay close, trailing 12-10 in the third quarter.

Then Hanson made a dazzling run. Taking a punt at his own 32-yard line he moved to the left before reversing field and then sprinting up the middle. The Hamiltonians seemed stunned by the suddenness of the move and could only watch him dash to their end zone.

Reeve rhapsodized:

> *"They sang 'On Wisconsin' and started*
> *To jump on the Tigers with zest,*
> *And they took the Grey Cup and departed*
> *To their little Grey home in the West."*

Over 6,000 saw the game but the depression era receipts were minimal and the 'Pegs didn't even have enough to cover their hotel and transportation costs. Not that they had to worry about defending the Cup. Eastern football authorities saw to that by imposing such harsh residency restrictions on imported players that the West didn't even challenge in 1936.

Canadian football however was to change forever as professionalism and the American influence grew over the next 15 years.

As Reeve himself observed:

> *"So remember the Red River Valley,*
> *And the ball team that cost them so dear,*
> *And get out the oughday, old pally,*
> *When you're gathering a club for next year."* ✤

June I, 1953

The Edmonton Eskimos hired a new head coach — Darrell Royal. At training camp he introduced the 1952 Heisman Trophy winner, Billy Vessels, who would go on to win the CFL MVP Schenley Award in 1953. In 1954 Royal would leave the CFL for Mississippi State University, but would talk one of his young athletes into playing professionally up north in Edmonton: Jackie Parker. Interestingly, the runner-up to Vessels for the 1952 Heisman was an outstanding young quarterback from the University of Maryland, Bernie Faloney, who also would end up in Edmonton in 1954. Faloney played in the CFL until 1966 and settled in Canada for life.

Football Highlights

February 13, 1944

The Tea Bowl
Four months before the D-Day invasion in Normandy, France in 1944, Canadian and American troops were stationed in England and played a football game. While on a joint training mission a few weeks beforehand, two generals from the respective armies met up and decided that "to help enliven the spirits of the men," a football game between the two bases would take place. The game, held at White City Stadium outside London, featured the "US Army Central Base Pirates" against the "Canadian Army Mustangs." The teams were enthusiastic, if a bit under-prepared, and the stands were packed. The first half was played under US rules and ended in a 0-0 tie. The second half, under Canadian rules, saw the Mustangs triumph 16-6 to win the game. The Canadians featured such stars as Huck Welch, Paul Rowe, Jeff Nicklin, Hec Creighton and Denis Whitaker (the star of the game).

Hector Naismith "Hec" Creighton

Elected to the Football Hall of Fame as a Builder, Hec Creighton was elected to the Canadian Rugby Union Rules Committee in 1947, where he re-wrote the rule book extensively over the next five years. He also revised the Intercollegiate Football Rule Book and then helped develop the national College Bowl. In his honour, the Hec Creighton Award was presented annually to the Most Outstanding Canadian Intercollegiate football player.

1946

The Regina Roughriders went provincial and became the Saskatchewan Roughriders.

1947

The Grey Cup was housed in the offices of the 1946 Champion, the Toronto Argonauts, when a fire broke out. All records and trophies were burned and melted, except one — the Grey Cup. On falling from a shelf it got hooked on a nail and was saved.

1949

The wearing of helmets in the CFL became mandatory.

1949

The Hamilton Tigers and Hamilton Wildcats combined forces and became the Hamilton Tiger Cats. The fans' rallying cry, OsskeeWeeWee, became known throughout the country.

Grey Cup, November 27, 1948

Calgary fans brought a week-long celebration to Toronto, beginning Canada's *Grand National Drunk* tradition of Grey Cups.

Fritzie Hanson, 1935.

1937

Hockey

He Shoots! He Scores!

You've heard Foster Hewitt's nerve-tingling hockey broadcasts – here's the man himself, telling you how he does it

by Foster Hewitt, as told to H. H. Roxborough
December 15, 1937

There was a time when Saturday evening seemed destined to be forever known as bath night. But ever since scientists started grabbing sounds out of the ether, a world of tap-turners has slowly evolved into a universe peopled with dial-twisters.

In a humble way I have contributed to this habit busting, for it has been my weekly chore during many years to participate in a sports program that has been estimated to reach three in every four radio-equipped Canadian homes.

This hockey broadcast, which has cut so deep into the clean sport of tubbing, goes on the air each Saturday night during the season at 9 p.m. Eastern Standard time. But my personal ritual has an earlier beginning.

Around 8:15 it is my custom to leave the ice level and begin my ascent to the radio gondola; and it is quite a climb. When I clamber up to the control room, I have attained the same altitude as the most remote spectator, and yet from even this elevation I must still climb up a narrow ladder to the catwalk situated thirty feet higher.

This lofty bridge is only two feet wide, and while it is protected by a railing on each side, the initial venture is about as comforting as walking along the roof-edge of an eight-story building.

Even when I have traversed the length of this walk I am still "up in the air," for I am compelled to descend an almost perpendicular stairway into a long narrow gondola, suspended from the rafters, which leaves me sixty feet above the ice.

I like to get up to the radio gondola while the teams are practicing because it gives me an opportunity to recognize the newcomers. You see, players can't be identified by position, for they roam all over the ice; neither can you spot entirely by appearance, for a team like Boston, wearing helmets, all look alike from up yonder. Neither are numbers and faces readily discernible. So I separate the players by another method.

My system is a combination of observation and memory. You may think I am "stretching it" a bit when I say that after seeing a player once in action I could forevermore name him, no matter what uniform he wore or where he played. It may be the way he stickhandles, the manner in which he extends his arms, how he skates, or perhaps the shape of his head. Somehow, every player has a peculiarity registered in my mental index file that, to me, is as sure as fingerprints are to a police specialist.

For the half-hour after I reach the gondola I am a silent observer, and not infrequently during this interval my imagination rides high and wide to the haunts of waiting hockey fans. It is reasonable for me to assume, from letters I have received, that in a lighthouse on the Bay of Fundy, a trawler on the North Atlantic fishing banks, a dormitory in a Maritime ladies' college, a Hudson's Bay trading post far north of Churchill, a theatre in a French-Canadian community in Northern Alberta, a construction camp many miles from rail in Ontario, a barber shop in a small Saskatchewan village, or in a British Columbia home where mail comes only once a month, there are sports lovers anxiously awaiting zero hour.

But this zero hour is subject to apparently wide variations, for at the moment when Pacific Coast listeners are hurrying through an early dinner, Newfoundlanders have cheated the sandman.

However, sharp at 6 p.m. in British Columbia, 9 p.m. in Toronto and 11 p.m. in the Empire's oldest colony, an associate tightens his grip on my shoulder, and the salutation, "Hello, Canada, and hockey fans in Newfoundland and the United States," reaches out, perhaps to New Zealand, England or South America, certainly to sun-kissed California and blizzard-blown polar posts.

The process by which the description of the game is transmitted to such remote distances is a story in itself. But some conception of the miracle may be gleaned from the unadorned statement that a single broadcast requires the employment of more than 200 radio technicians, an expenditure exceeding $4,000, and sufficient copper wire to encircle the globe.

The "Hot Stove Lounge" was heard between periods for years on Hockey Night in Canada.

All this planning and equipment is much more involved than the apparatus with which I "toyed" on what I believe was the world's first broadcast of a sport event.

Fifteen years ago, in Toronto's Mutual Street Arena, on a cold wintry night, I hunched for more than two hours on a stool with sawed-off legs, in a glass box, four feet high and three feet square, without even the slightest inflow of fresh air. This ventilation problem was aggravated by a vapor that soon clouded the glass and created the optical illusion that the players were skating in a dense fog. Then, just to make my radio baptism a really tough ordeal, Kitchener and Parkdale teams were tied at the end of the regular sixty minutes and prolonged my distress through an additional half-hour of overtime.

That initial broadcast was a painful introduction into the world of radio hockey, but there have been times in more recent years when the going has been tough.

You remember that historic game between Boston Bruins and Toronto Maple Leafs? It was the last in the play-off series, and the loser would be denied the chance to play Rangers for the Stanley Cup. The game began at 8:30 p.m. one early April night, and it ended when milkmen were delivering pints and quarts nearly five hours later.

During all the regular game and through 105 minutes of overtime I had to continue my comment, and toward the close there were times when I actually talked in my sleep. But I did have sufficient energy to hang on to the

Danny Gallivan's great moment in sport happened in 1950 when the Montreal Canadiens' regular play-by-play broadcaster, Doug Smith, fell ill. Gallivan's earlier broadcast of a Memorial Cup playoff game between Halifax St. Mary's and Montreal Royals had caught the ear of the producer of Montreal's NHL broadcasts and he was impressed with Gallivan's fresh and unique approach to the game. He was asked to fill in until Doug Smith returned. In 1952, Smith decided to switch over to CFL football with the Montreal Alouettes and Danny Gallivan embarked on what was to be a 32-year partnership with the Canadiens. He did play-by-play radio and TV commentary for more than 1,800 Canadiens' games and, along the way, the Sydney, Nova Scotia native re-wrote the style book with his unique vocabulary — "a cannonading slap-shot," "a patented Savardian spinerama," "an egregious giveaway" and other colourful phrases. He retired in 1984 and became a goodwill ambassador for Hockey Night in Canada. In 1991 the Canadian Association of Broadcasters inducted him in its Hall of Fame. He is a member of the Nova Scotia Sports Hall of Fame, the Hockey Hall of Fame and Canada's Sports Hall of Fame.

end and tell a tired world that Blair had barged through the Boston defence, passed the puck to the unguarded Doraty, and that the game little opportunist had bagged the only and deciding goal.

Broadcasting on the National Hockey League circuit offers a variety of perches for the broadcaster. In Chicago, the equipment is housed in the organ loft at one end of the rink. The location at Montreal is in the open, up in the crowd, surrounded by the fans, with English and French announcers working side by side. The Detroit booth is situated right on the boards, and has the advantage of a close-up view but also the disadvantage that there are angles where play is invisible, and somehow to be right on top of the game interferes with perspective.

Above all others, I prefer the bird's-eye view of Maple Leaf Gardens.

When the Gardens was being erected and the framework was going up, I began walking around to accustom myself to the height. After the gondola had been spotted and the ladder put down, I used to admire and even envy a steelworker who would shinny down the huge rivet-spotted girders with greatest of ease. One day, while aloft, I said to him, "Jim, have you had a look from the broadcasting gondola?"

"Nothing doing," he confided, "you're not going to get me walking down that ladder." And he wrapped his arms and legs around the steel and slid to safety.

Still, from this lofty gondola, be it as uncomfortable as the edge of a cliff or as inviting as a fireside chair, I am privileged to talk to millions.

Fortunately, my throat has given me little trouble. I have had an uninterrupted run exceeding 1,400 broadcasts. Yet when a night does come when I cough or a hoarseness is apparent, the days following that broadcast will be spent reading old-time recipes and modern remedies for coughs, sent to me by sympathetic listeners.

Invariably, it is my custom to broadcast with my head bare. Why, I don't know, but it is now a habit.

A few seasons ago Rangers were playing Leafs, and the New Yorkers were leading 4 to 0. Suddenly I realized I was wearing my derby. At once I told the listeners of my mistake, took off the hat, and believe it or not, Leafs turned around and won the game by 6 to 4. The next day a very ornate hat hanger was delivered to me by the postman.

But there must be a lot of good in the world. No reader of my mail could lose faith in human nature. I have received hand-painted birthday cards, gold razors, walking canes, and many other tangible expressions of goodwill. But it is not these I have in mind when I recall the countless letters that have come from shut-ins in hospitals, sanitoria and nursing homes; from deaf and dumb institutes where those who can hear spell the names and sketch the plays to the deaf; from unemployed in relief hostels; from kids whose dominant desire is to be professional hockey players, and elderly ladies who never saw a game in their three score and ten.

Apart altogether from monetary rewards, these appreciative listeners make broadcasting a real pleasure, and sustain me when some candid listener irreverently suggests that I'm so one-sided I can face both ways without turning around. ♣

Danny Gallivan, the legendary Montreal Canadiens voice for Hockey Night in Canda.

Highlights

Hockey Highlights

October 11, 1930

Conn Smythe used the money he won in a horse race ($20,000) to pay $35,000 (plus trading defenceman Art Smith) to the Ottawa Senators for star player King Clancy.

January 3, 1931

Montreal Maroons' Nels Stewart scored the NHL's fastest two goals of the century, four seconds apart in a 5-3 win over Boston.

February 14, 1931

For the first time in NHL play, three assists were awarded on one goal when Charlie Conacher scored with assists from King Clancy, Joe Primeau, and Busher Jackson.

November 12, 1931

Conn Smythe opened Maple Leaf Gardens in Toronto. Smythe built the Gardens in less than six months at a cost of $1.5 million during the Great Depression – paying union workers 20% of their wages in Gardens stock.

1937-1938

The icing rule was introduced to help keep offensive play moving.

1932-33

Edmonton native Eddie Shore of the Boston Bruins scored 35 points and became the first defenceman to win the Hart trophy as the NHL's Most Valuable Player.

March 17, 1934

Toronto's King Clancy celebrated St. Patrick's Day by wearing the old Toronto St. Patricks green and white sweater during the first period of a game against the Rangers. The referees made him change for the second period.

1934-1935

The season highlights included the Montreal Canadiens trading Howie Morenz to Chicago. He would return to the Habs later. The Ottawa Senators left their heritage and Canada to become the St. Louis Eagles, which folded after one season. The penalty shot was added to the rule book "for when players are fouled on a breakaway in good scoring position." The Toronto Maple Leafs' "Kid Line" of Charlie Conacher, Joe Primeau and Harvey "Busher" Jackson scored often, with Conacher defending his scoring title from the previous season with 57 points.

March 24-25, 1936

The Detroit Red Wings and the Montreal Maroons played the NHL's longest game of the century in the Stanley Cup finals – "Mud" Bruneteau scored on Montreal's Lorne Chabot after 176 minutes and 30 seconds of playing time to win the game 1-0. There were nearly nine periods of scoreless hockey.

HHOF — Turofsky Collection

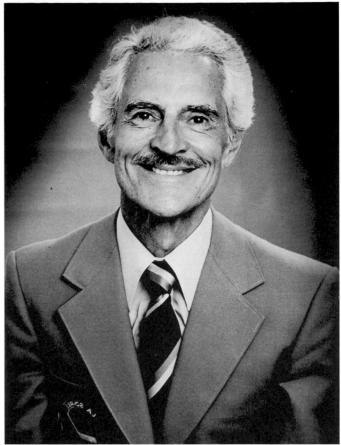

René Lecavalier of Montreal was an internationally acclaimed broadcaster with Radio Canada for more than 40 years. The French-speaking voice of the Montreal Canadiens, Lacavalier created a lexicon for francophone play-by-play announcers that became commonplace around the world.
Lecavalier, who also covered Olympic and other international sporting events, was to French-speaking Canadians what Foster Hewitt or Danny Gallivan were to English Canada. Some say, on a per capita basis, that the beloved voice of the Habitants and "La Soirée du Hockey with René Lecavalier" was even more popular.

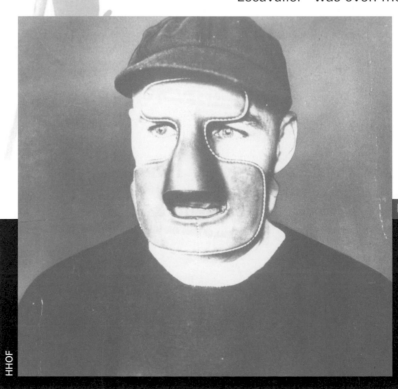

HHOF

February 20, 1930

Montreal Maroon's goalie Clint Benedict suffered a broken nose in a game on January 8 stopping a Howie Morenz shot. Benedict returned to the game, only to break his nose twice more. Finally, fed up, he returned to the ice wearing a leather mask. He soon discarded it, though, because "it's too hot and the nosepiece blurs my vision."

Ottawa – Hockey Capital

Modern hockey annals list the NHL Ottawa Senators as an expansion club. This tells only part of the story, though. In fact, Ottawa has been a hotbed of hockey since 1900 and Ottawa-based teams, including the one that gave the modern Senators their name, have won 10 Stanley Cups, four Allan Cups and two Memorial Cups.

Ottawa Senators' Frank Nighbor won the NHL's first Hart Trophy as the league's Most Valuable Player, 1924.

The legendary Ottawa Silver Seven, playing in the early 1900s, could in fact be considered organized hockey's first dynasty. During those years the Stanley Cup was a challenge trophy, and Ottawa won it and successfully defended it eight times from 1903 to 1906. Among the players was Frank McGee, who despite having the use of only one eye scored 14 goals in a 23-2 win over Dawson City in one Stanley Cup playoff game. (He was later killed in World War I action on September 16, 1916.) The Silver Seven also had the Smith brothers — Harry and Tommy, prolific scorers in their own right.

The first incarnation of the Ottawa Senators picked up where the Silver Seven left off and won the Stanley Cup for three straight years beginning with the 1908-09 season. They won again in 1920, 1921, 1923 and 1927. One of the players who shared the credit for these later Stanley Cup victories was the legendary King Clancy. He played nine seasons with the Ottawa Senators until 1930 when he was traded to the Toronto Maple Leafs for two players and $35,000 — a princely sum considering that around the same time the Boston Red Sox sold Babe Ruth to the New York Yankees for straight cash — $125,000.

The Stanley Cup itself was born in Ottawa. It was donated by the then Governor General, Lord Stanley of Preston, in 1892. Lord Stanley commissioned a silversmith to fashion the trophy and its finished cost was just under $50. By the end of the century it was insured for $75,000.

The Allan Cup, emblematic of Senior Amateur Hockey supremacy, was for many years as important to Canadians as the Stanley Cup. In 1908 the Ottawa Cliffsides brought home the Allan Cup for the first time. The RCAF won it in 1942, the Ottawa Commandos in 1943 and T.P. Gorman's Senators won it in 1949.

The Memorial Cup, symbol of supremacy in Junior hockey, has spent its share of time in Ottawa too. The Ottawa 67s, coached by Brian Kilrea, won the Memorial Cup in 1984 and again in 1999. ❧

James Naismith, 1861-1939

Dr. James A. Naismith is best remembered by history as the inventor of basketball, but he himself may have pointed to other achievements as the most significant ones in his life. In fact, but for an incident on the McGill University football field in Montreal one day, the Almonte, Ontario, native likely would have pursued a career as a minister instead of going into physical education. During a practice, one of his teammates responded to a problem by swearing loudly, which started Naismith thinking about the power of personal influence in people's lives. He soon decided that he would do the world the most good by helping people act on the motto "A sound mind in a sound body." For more than 40 years of teaching young people, this motto guided his steps. During his eulogy in 1939, Theodore Aszman said, "He did not conceive of his work as that of the ambulance driver picking up wrecks at the bottom of the cliff, but to build the fence at the top of the cliff to keep human lives from being wrecked."

The fact that Naismith was more concerned about the positive influence of sport on people's lives than on which sport they played likely made a difference to his original vision of basketball. When he invented the game he had actually only been given the task of developing an activity to catch the interest of an unruly group of students to fill in the time between the football and baseball seasons. With 13 basic rules, a couple of peach baskets and a soccer ball, Naismith introduced a sport that soon achieved worldwide popularity.

A natural highlight for him surely was in 1936 as basketball was introduced at the Olympic Games in Berlin. As a guest of the International Olympic Committee, he witnessed the gold medal game between the country of his birth (Canada) and the country where he invented the sport (USA). He also saw the exhibition games played by the women, and noticed the clear superiority of the Edmonton Grads team led by friend Percy Page.

Naismith was a lifelong friend of famed sculptor and educator R. Tait McKenzie (also from Almonte). He spent most of his working career at the University of Kansas, where he was originally hired in 1898 as a chapel director and physical education instructor. Throughout his life, he continued to emphasize building character as the most important benefit of sport. ♣

CBHOF

Cycling

King of the Crazy Marathons

by Trent Frayne

December 15, 1952

The scars of the depression cast a unique reflection on the entertainment tastes of North America through the hungry Thirties. The key word was endurance. Heroes of the era were tireless automatons like George Young, who splashed and sputtered twenty-one miles between Catalina Island and the California mainland; Ernst Vierkoetter, the Black Shark, who survived twenty-five miles in icy Lake Ontario to win the Wrigley Swim; the late Shipwreck Kelly, who so staunchly refused to come down from a perch on a flagpole that his name became a household word; any number of anonymous marathon dancers who shuffled, slept, collapsed and even married during their weeks of vertical agony; and Torchy Peden, who rode a bicycle in circles week after week in the six-day bike races.

Of all these sapping pursuits, none involved as much money or kept as many people out of bed as Peden's weird business of riding a bicycle a couple of thousand miles a week and never going anywhere. Until customer ennui forced them to the rug toward the late Thirties the six-day derbies packed arenas in Montreal and Toronto, in New York, Chicago, Cleveland, Los Angeles, San Francisco and scores of smaller cities. New York's Madison Square Garden frequently bettered a hundred and twenty-five thousand dollars for a single marathon, and Peden, a broth of a boy from Victoria, standing six-feet-three and weighing two hundred and twenty pounds, the largest and most indestructible of all riders, made close to twenty thousand dollars a year for his frenzied rides to nowhere.

Torchy, in his first four years as a professional, won twenty-four out of forty-eight races and before he hung up his spokes he had survived more races than any other rider, one hundred and forty-eight — which meant he'd been going around in circles for eight hundred and eight-eight days, or about two and a half years. If some of these trips weren't necessary they at least served to show Peden half the world — and vice versa — for he rode in England, Scotland, France, Germany, Poland and Denmark.

BC's Torchy Peden with a few of his awards.

Peden's endurance in this era of exertion-for-distance was no more remarkable than the grinds in which he furiously revolved his size thirteens. Citizens with nowhere else to go could wander in and out of the arenas at their leisure and a lot of them found the heated building an excellent place to dispose of a magnum of wassail on a cold winter's night. The races lasted six days, plus three hours, starting in most cities at nine o'clock on a Sunday night and concluding at midnight the following Saturday.

Riders were divided into two-man teams, usually by the race promoter, and one of them had to be on the track at all times, even if he were dozing, reading his mail or trying to pick the winner of the fifth at Hialeah. Tracks, made of pine and costing upward of five thousand dollars, were laid on the rink floor and were banked — as much as forty-five degrees at the turns — to provide traction for bikes that sometimes zipped along at forty-five and fifty miles an hour.

Each team had a pit beside the track which contained a bunk, a table, extra bikes and parts, and a trainer. Food was provided by the promoter and some of the world's most accomplished free-style grazers were bike riders, Peden among them. Before a race he would buy a chunk of round steaks, cut off the fat and grind it up with a dozen egg yolks. He'd salt it well and eat it on slices of whole-wheat bread while out on the track, between regular meals. For lunch and dinner Torchy would eat two or three pounds of sirloin steak that barely had been introduced to the frying pan. For breakfast he'd have fruit juice, cereal with milk, six slices of bacon and three eggs and a couple of cups of coffee. Most mornings he'd have two breakfasts.

According to BC sport historian Jim Kearney, the best all-around BC athlete of the century was Doug Peden. Peden excelled in swimming, track, basketball, rugby, tennis, baseball and cycling. He won a silver medal in basketball at the 1936 Olympic Games and later turned to professional cycling along with his more famous brother, Torchy.

When the riders were working — that is, riding — they wore brightly colored short-sleeved jerseys, short pants and they had their feet strapped to the pedals. Each partner caught about two and a half hours sleep during a quiet period from four a.m. to ten a.m. when the arenas were closed down, ostensibly so the cleaners could sweep out wayward husbands, peanut shells and other debris. But through the other eighteen hours of the day the arena owned an atmosphere all its own, particularly during jams and sprints. The riders would be going along at a good steady clip when one of them, usually Peden if there were a big crowd in the arena, would suddenly dart out from the pack and pick up half a lap before the others were aware of it.

Instantly, the arena became a bedlam. Down in the middle of the oval — in the flat, or infield — the relief riders would tumble out of their bunks and onto the bikes. The men on the track would be going at whirlwind speed and the relief teams would start on the flat, picking up speed until they were going top flight. They'd relieve their partners then, picking them up on the fly and touching them off. All the while Peden and his partner, often blond little Jules Audy, of Montreal, and in the latter days, his big black haired brother, Doug, would be striving desperately to lap the field. The jam might end with the lap being won, or it might be followed by another theft attempt by a rider endeavoring to utilize the letdown from the jam.

This was one of Peden's favourite tricks and it made him unpopular with the rest of the riders. While they were gasping for breath at the end of a sprint he'd drive his monstrous legs (at twenty-five inches, his thighs were a good four inches thicker than a model's waist, though not as pretty) down on the pedals to try to capitalize on the weariness of the others.

Spectators frequently added zest to the whirls by offering anywhere from twenty-five dollars to a hundred dollars for lap prizes, meaning for the team that could steal a lap on the field.

Torchy was singularly fortunate in avoiding serious injury. "A few broken ribs, a broken collarbone, a few small bones in my hands and feet and that's about all," he observed seriously. "Oh yeah, I lost a lot of teeth."

"Rivalries developed the same way they do in hockey," Torchy remarked recently. "A man would cut in on you, or block you, or interfere as you tried to pass and you were ready to slug him. You often did."

Peden and Piet Van Kempen, an outstanding Dutch rider, were such rivals and delighted in beating each other. Until Peden's thirty-eight victories set an all-time record the top score had been Van Kempen's thirty five.

In Montreal one time Van Kempen riled Peden by blocking him. As Torchy went high to pass, Van Kempen went high in front of him. Peden came down to go by and the Dutchman prevented it by moving low on the track, too.

Once more Torchy tried to pass and Van Kempen again blocked him.

"So I bluffed him high and went low and when I pulled past him I belted him with a terrific wallop in the stomach with my elbow," Peden recalls with some relish.

"From then on," Peden remembered, "we just raced."

The six-day fad had faded by 1938 when the Peden brothers won the second-last big race in New York, only brothers ever to click in that strange profession. The business was given a last chance during the World's Fair in 1939 but it folded faster than a dancer's fan.

But Peden had kept an eye on his future. In the good days he'd sent money to his father regularly and it was invested in dividend-bearing bonds. He enlisted in the RCAF in 1942, and served as a physical training instructor at Trenton and Edmonton.

In 1949 he tried to revive the six-day whirls in New England, but costs were too great and public interest too small. He promoted stock-car races for two summers, then a year ago he accepted an offer from the Canada Cycle and Motor Company to become a salesman in the Midwestern U. S.

There's a long sidewalk in front of a tree lined frame house in Clear Lake, Iowa, where Torchy lives today. More often than not you can see a six-year old boy spinning across the concrete on a junior-size two-wheeler. His name is William John Peden II.

"Pretty good rider, too," Torchy grinned not long ago, his blue eyes twinkling under hair still red and spiky. Then he added reflectively, "The other night, I was looking at television and you should have heard the people screaming. They were watching another sport that has been buried a long time. Wrestling. You never know, do you? You just never know." ❧

Torchy Peden riding with brother Doug, perhaps BC's best all-around athlete according to longtime BC sport historian Jim Kearney.

Highlights

General Highlights

1920s & '30s

Constance Wilson-Samuel was a dominant force on the Canadian figure skating scene during the 1920s and '30s. Her record included nine Canadian and three North American singles titles, the British Ladies title, wins in six Canadian and three North American pairs categories, and a Canadian fours title. She was a three-time member of the Canadian Olympic team and represented Canada at three World Championships, winning a bronze medal in 1932.

1920s & '30s

Montgomery "Bud" Wilson was Canada's premier male figure skater of the 1920s and '30s. The Toronto skater amassed an unprecedented 18 Canadian and 10 North American titles competing in the men's, pairs and fours events. His silver-medal victory in the men's category at the 1932 World Figure Skating Championships was the first by a Canadian. A three-time Olympian, Wilson's bronze medal performance at the 1932 Olympic Winter Games in Lake Placid marked the first Olympic figure skating medal won by a Canadian, and the first by a North American male.

1940-1946

The Amateur Athletic Union of Canada (AAU of C) ceased formal operations during World War II.

1942

Syl Apps was a member of the 1936 Olympic Track team, placing sixth in the pole vault in Berlin. On his return he joined the Toronto Maple Leafs, helping the team win the Stanley Cup in 1942. He left to serve in World War II in 1942, then returned to lead the Leafs to another series of Cups late in the '40s.

1943

Johnny Longden, on *Count Fleet*, became the first Canadian jockey to win the horse racing American Triple Crown (Kentucky Derby, Preakness, Belmont Stakes). Along with George Woolf, Ron Turcotte and Sandy Hawley, Johnny Longden was one of Canada's most successful jockeys of the century. He was the first North American rider ever to win 6000 races, ending up with 6,032 over a 40-year career. His highlight, of course, was riding Count Fleet to the Triple Crown. When he retired, Longden became a trainer.

1943

The *National Physical Fitness Act* was passed "to promote physical fitness for Canadians through various programs linked to sports and athletics."

September, 1945

Pitcher Dick Fowler threw a no-hitter for the Philadelphia Phillies.

1948

Suzanne Morrow and Wallace Distelmeyer performed the first-ever death spiral at the World Figure Skating Championships in Davos, Switzerland. This skating team also made Canadian history in 1948 by becoming the first pairs team to win Olympic and World medals (bronzes).

1949

The first game of the first year of the National Basketball Association was played in Canada, between the Toronto Huskies (who were there for one year only) and the New York Knickerbockers (Knicks).

1950

Ontario started a trend that went across the country in passing its own *Lord's Day Act*, which, in contrast to the 1906 federal law, permitted commercial sport events on Sundays.

1950

Dr. Jack Wright was voted Canada's outstanding tennis player of the first half century.

1950

Sandy Somerville and Ada Mackenzie were voted Canada's Male and Female Golfers of the first 50 years of the 20th Century.

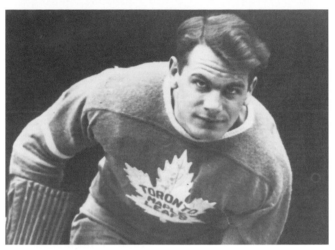

Future 1930s and '40s Toronto Maple Leaf star, Syl Apps, was on Canada's 1936 Olympic track team as a pole vaulter.

In 1950, Norm Baker was voted Canada's basketball player of the first half-century and the Edmonton Grads were voted the basketball team of the half-century. Norm Baker was a member of five national senior title basketball teams during the 1940s. He played with the Vancouver Hornets, establishing a record 1862 points for a 70 game schedule. Baker later toured Europe and North Africa with the "Stars of the World" in 1950. He played one professional season with the Boston Celtics.

The Maple Leafs Forever

King Clancy

Just about any young hockey fan growing up west of the Ontario-Quebec border during the century's last 75 years likely dreamed of someday wearing the blue and white of the Toronto Maple Leafs. While skating on a frozen pond or on a small-town ice rink in the 1930s, who wouldn't dream of playing alongside the likes of King Clancy, or Charlie Conacher and his "Kid line" teammates of Busher Jackson and Joe Primeau? A little later, the same dream would feature Syl Apps, Teeder Kennedy, and Turk Broda. During the 1960s, it might have been Frank Mahovlich, Davey Keon, Carl Brewer, Johnny Bower, or Tim Horton. Even after the NHL expanded in 1967 and the team's glory seemed to diminish a bit, countless young players would still try to emulate Darryl Sittler, Doug Gilmour, Wendel Clark or Curtis Joseph.

The reasons aren't hard to figure out: a central geographical location, lots of media coverage (including Foster Hewitt's legendary Hockey Night in Canada broadcasts that defined Saturday night in many a Canadian household), a patriotic name, a famous arena, star players and a succession of great teams. Besides, until the 1970s, fans who wanted to follow professional hockey had only two Canadian teams to choose from. Since the team's creation in 1927 and for nearly 50 years of the century, the Maple Leafs were a storied franchise, a team you wanted to belong to, to cheer, and to follow.

First known as the Arenas and then the St. Patricks, the Maple Leafs came to be after Conn Smythe headed a group of local businessmen in buying the ailing Toronto franchise on February 14, 1927. Along the way he renamed the team, changed its colours, built the most famous building in Canada and shaped the most popular franchise in Canadian sports history.

In the beginning

When Smythe purchased the team in 1926-27 its name was the St. Patricks (shortened to the St. Pats, of course), the players wore green and white and played out of the Mutual Street Arena (known as the Arena Gardens). Smythe had graduated from and coached hockey at the University of Toronto, scouted many young players playing with the East Toronto Maple Leaves, and, in 1926 he was only a few years removed from serving his country and wearing the Maple Leaf on his chest in World War I.

Somewhere in this eclectic mix Smythe came up with the name "Maple Leafs" (either from patriotism or a junior team), and new blue and white team colours (either U of T colours or as the Leafs long-serving Public Relations

Continued on page 70

Syl Apps

Les Canadiens sont là!

Hockey

"To you from failing hands we throw the torch; be yours to hold it high."

As any hockey fan knows, these immortal words are inscribed in bold, inspiring letters on the dressing room wall of the greatest hockey franchise of all time. Even though poet John McCrae clearly wrote *In Flanders Fields* for soldiers, it's possible that he actually saw the Canadiens play while practising medicine in Montreal in 1909, the year the team was founded. And, in a way, as Robert Miller mentioned in a Maclean's article in 1976, "…the Montreal Canadiens are soldiers, engaged in an unending crusade." McCrae's words were first published in 1915 (the first year the Canadiens won the Stanley Cup), and have been read by every single Montreal Canadien since.

George Hainsworth

The continuity of greatness of the Montreal Canadiens franchise, which saw the team win 24 Stanley Cups from 1911-2000, is Montreal's and all of Quebec's pride. The torch has been passed from generation to generation, from hero to hero, from failing hands to the hands of youth. To name just a few, the torch passed from the likes of "Newsy" Lalonde to Howie Morenz to the "Rocket" to "Big Jean" Béliveau to Guy Lafleur to Patrick Roy.

The Montreal Canadiens, also known as the Flying Frenchmen, les Habitants, or the Habs, were founding members of both the old National Hockey Association in 1909 and the upstart NHL in 1917. Throughout the century they captured the hearts and imagination of a culture, a province, a country … and gave rise to the victory refrain so often echoed by loyalists in the old Montreal Forum: *"Les Canadiens sont là!"*

In the beginning

Howie Morenz

J. Ambrose O'Brien, the owner of the Renfrew Millionaires, founded the Montreal Canadiens during a meeting of the National Hockey Association at the Windsor Hotel in Montreal, on December 4, 1909. In that first year, the Canadiens were managed by Jack Laviolette, played out of the old Westmount Arena, won their first "team" game against Cobalt 7-6 in the Jubilee Arena (only to have the result nullified when the CHA folded mid-season and its three remaining teams joined the NHA), lost their first "official" game 9-4 to Renfrew (in a revised schedule), and prior to the start of their second season were "granted" from the O'Briens to George Kennedy. It was Kennedy who is credited with first naming the team "Le Club Athlétique Canadien."

Continued on page 71

Bernie "Boom Boom" Geoffrion

Charlie Conacher

Continued from page 68

Director Stan Obodiac insisted, "Smythe chose blue for the Canadian skies and white for the colour of snow"). He also decided he needed a new arena. By 1931, he would arrange the financing and the construction of a new state-of-the-art home for his new team — Maple Leaf Gardens.

Maple Leaf Gardens – "The most famous building in Canada"

In 1931, in the middle of the Depression, Conn Smythe somehow managed to get his dream arena built. Raising money in this era was deemed a very risky business and more than a few thought Smythe had lost his senses. It would be just too difficult a project to succeed.

But Smythe was a seasoned leader, a Canadian Army Major who would serve in two world wars, and seldom listened to the opinions of others once he had his mind made up. He also had a valuable supporter in his friend and colleague Frank Selke. It took five and a half months, but together this dynamic duo built the most famous building in Canada.

Selke is best remembered as a hockey coach, but he was also a former union boss — a combination which would be pivotal to the creation of the Gardens and the team. Even when times were tough, when families did not know where the next paycheque was going to come from, Selke managed to convince the labourers to take stock shares in lieu of full wages during the Gardens' construction.

"In those hard times, construction work was hard to find, and it wasn't difficult to convince the trade unions that 80 per cent of a salary was

Frank Mahovlich

Continued on page 72

Canada

Continued from page 69

With the creation of the NHL in 1917, Kennedy and friends changed the club's official name to "Club de Hockey Canadien" and introduced the celebrated CH logo. When the Westmount Arena burned down on January 2, 1918, the club fled back to the Jubilee Arena and, when it too burned down in the summer of 1920, into its own home, the Mont-Royal Arena. After George Kennedy succumbed to the 1919 flu epidemic, his widow sold le Club to a group headed up by Leo Dandurand on November 3, 1921.

The Montreal Forum – hockey's temple

The building of the shrine of hockey, the Montreal Forum, began as an idea by Senator Donat Raymond and Sir Edward Beatty in 1924. Envisioning a new home for the Montreal Maroons that would seat 10,000 customers and include artificial ice, the Forum was constructed in a mere 159 days at an estimated cost of $1.2 million. Ironically, it was not the Maroons who opened the Forum, but the Canadiens who, because of ice problems at their own arena in Mont Royal, christened the new rink with a 7-1 drubbing of the Toronto St. Pats on November 29, 1924. By 1926 the Habs would make the Forum their permanent home.

Through the remaining years of the century the Forum hosted many a hockey moment — including Stanley Cup finals, international events, and scoring highlights. In 1937 it would even play host to the funeral of the "Stratford Streak," Howie Morenz, the star player who "died of a broken heart because he could no longer play as he wanted for the team he so loved." It is said that it is the ghost of Morenz and his fellow departed Habs that helped guide the Canadiens to victory in game after game after game at the Forum. From 1924 through 1996, when the team moved to the new Molson Centre, the Canadiens won nearly three games for every one they lost at home. Always, it seemed, Montreal would win when it counted. (The ghosts seemed to have trouble making their way to the new arena, though, where the team ran up a less than stellar home record between their move and the end of the century.)

Continued on page 73

Henri "Pocket Rocket" Richard

Hector "Toe" Blake

Continued from page 70

better than no salary," Selke had said. Smythe had concurred, "When the unions took our offers, the bankers got in on the act, loosening up a little money for us to go ahead. The contractors took some shares too, instead of cash or we never would have made it."

On November 12, 1931, the new Maple Leaf Gardens played host to its first NHL hockey game. Two and a half minutes into the first period of the first game, Mush March scored the first goal en route to a 2-1 victory by the visiting Chicago Blackhawks.

Nearly 70 years later, on February 13, 1999, the Maple Leafs bid farewell to the venerable Gardens, and moved to the more spacious, but less historic Air Canada Centre. Over the decades, Maple Leaf Gardens had become a shrine — synonymous with hockey in Canada. As a testimony to the respect due to the old arena, Toronto players wore a special crest on their sweaters during that season that read "Maple Leaf Gardens — Memories and Dreams."

The Toronto Maple Leafs – a team through the ages

1920s-30s:

King Clancy was a star player with the Ottawa Senators, an experienced Cup-winner. Smythe realized his team, now playing in its new facility, would require a star player with experience. For a then unheard-of sum of $35,000, Smythe purchased Clancy's contract, who would stay with the Leafs in various capacities for the next 60 years.

Within four years of purchasing the team, Smythe had assembled a squad that would not miss the playoffs for 15 years and would go to the finals nine times in that span. Toronto won its first Stanley Cup as the Maple Leafs in the very first year in their new home, 1932. Providing the explosive offence necessary to win the Cup was the famed "Kid Line" of Charlie Conacher, Busher Jackson and Joe Primeau. King Clancy and Hap Day provided the leadership on the blueline.

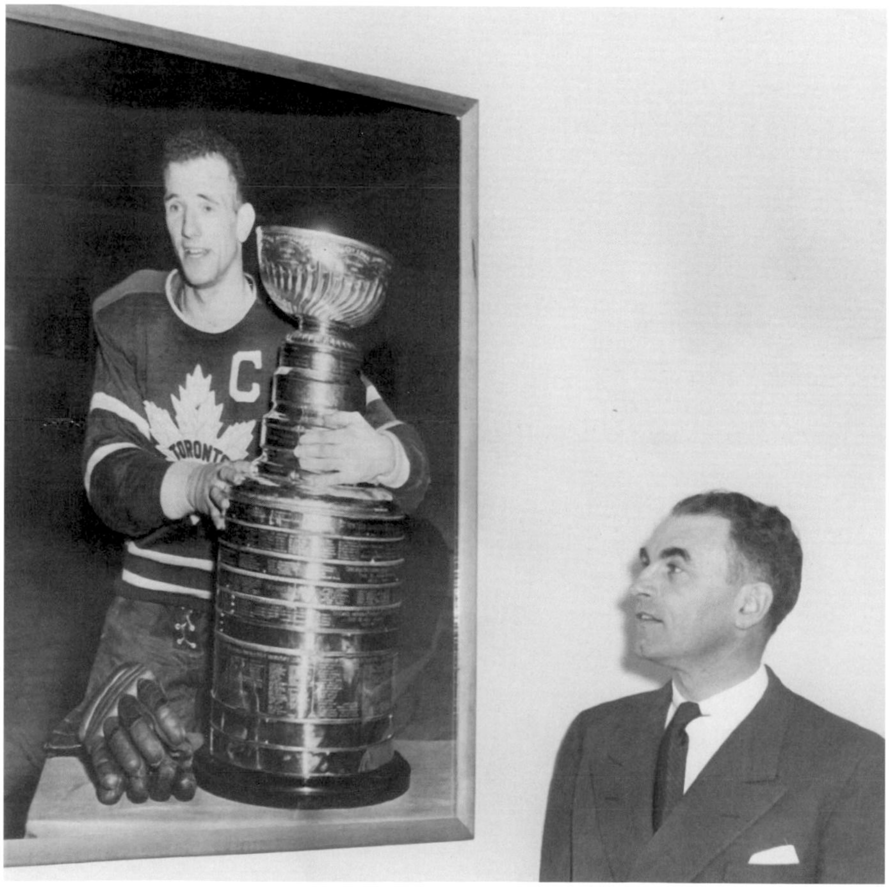

1940s

At the beginning of the decade, Smythe replenished his stars of the '30s with new players like Syl Apps, Turk Broda and fast-skating Gordie Drillon. In 1942 Hap Day took over from coach Dick Irvin (who departed for Montreal) and won the Cup in dramatic fashion — coming from three games down in the final to beat Detroit 4-3. This feat was unmatched in a Stanley Cup final for the rest of the century.

World War II depleted the Leafs roster, as it did with so many teams. As a result though, several new players were given a chance to

Continued on page 74

Joe Primeau remembering the Leafs' 1940's days of glory.

Canada

Continued from page 71

Bob Gainey hoisting the Stanley Cup, 1986

The players, the media, the hockey world and, most importantly, the fans would see the Forum as truly something special, unique, almost spiritual. On March 11, 1996, the final game was played at the Forum — and it was no surprise when the Canadiens won 4-1 over the Dallas Stars. The 24 Stanley Cup banners may have moved down the street to the new Molson Centre on March 16 of 1996, but the memories of 20th century hockey at its best still reside with the Forum as a backdrop.

In his passionate hockey book "The Game," former Canadiens star Ken Dryden captured the spirit of playing in the Forum:

"The Forum is hockey's shrine, a glorious melting pot of team, city and sporting tradition not elegant, not dramatic, not exciting or controversial. It is expansive, yet intimate, exuberant yet un-selfconscious. It supports and complements a game, never competing for your attention. And when a game ends, fading away, it gives you nothing to detail the impression it leaves — just a memory of the game and the unshakeable feeling that you've watched it in its proper place."

Le Bleu-Blanc-et-Rouge – too many accomplishments

There are many, many accomplishments of hockey's greatest franchise of the century, certainly too many to list at a single sitting. Suffice it to say that at the mid-century mark there were three or four clubs which could claim to be the top franchise in professional hockey, but only one of them would be standing at the end of the century, only one would have a record 24 Stanley Cups to show for its continued greatness. For a number of years, that was more championships than any North American team in any professional sport had won, until the New York Yankees won their 25th World Series in 2000.

Club highlights include:

- The only club to win five straight Cups (1956-60)

- The only club to win four straight Cups – twice (1956-60; 1976-79)

- The only club to win as many as six Cups in one decade, and they did it twice (1950s and 1970s)

- The only club to have its members play on 11 (Henri Richard), 10 (Jean Béliveau, Yvan Cornoyer) or 9 (Claude Provost) Stanley Cups

- The only club to have its goalie win as many as six Cups, and again they did it twice (Jacques Plante, Ken Dryden)

- The only club to have its goalie win the Vezina Trophy five times (Jacques Plante)

- The only club in the post-war era to lose less than 10 games in one season (1976-77, 8 losses)

Continued on page 75

Continued from page 72

play who may not have otherwise. One was future star and long-serving captain Ted "Teeder" Kennedy in 1943. Frank "Ulcers" McCool replaced the off-to-war Broda and recorded three consecutive shutouts en route to the Stanley Cup in 1945.

The end of the war saw many players return to the Leafs, and the composite team went on to be the first club to win the Cup three years running (1947-49). Clearly a major factor in the team's success was a former scoring star with the Chicago Blackhawks, Max Bentley, whom Smythe traded for during the 1947 season. Also in '47, rookie Howie Meeker scored five times in one game on his way to winning the league's rookie-of-the-year honours (beating out someone named Gordie Howe).

1950s:

The 1950s saw some early success and the arrival of new faces like George Armstrong and Tim Horton. The Leafs won only one Cup this decade, in 1951, on the ever-remembered overtime goal by Bill Barilko (who tragically died in a plane crash the following summer). Broda, Kennedy, Bentley, and Meeker all retired and were hard to replace. A steady stream of coaches did not help, until one named George "Punch" Imlach joined the club in 1958.

1960s:

Imlach went out and secured quality veterans like Johnny Bower and Red Kelly from other clubs to bolster the young legs of Davey Keon and Frank Mahovlich. With a solid core of players, including Bob Baun, Allan Stanley, Tim Horton and Carl Brewer on defence and forwards Bob Pulford, Billy Harris, Ron Ellis and captain George Armstrong up front, the Leafs would win three straight Cups (1962-63-64). They would cap the decade in 1967 in a thrilling six-game series against Montreal in Canada's Centennial year, winning the club's final Stanley Cup of the century.

1970s-80s-90s

The Leafs continued to be good, just not quite good enough. Star players like Norm Ullman, Paul Henderson, Darryl Sittler, Lanny McDonald and Brian Glenney would lead the team in the '70s, along with the league's first great European player, Borje Salming. The 1980s Leafs became a moribund franchise under the eccentric ownership of Harold Ballard, and had a revolving door of coaches, none of whom had great success. Led by Doug Gilmour and Wendell Clark, a couple of the teams in the 1990s came close to getting the Leafs back to the finals, but it never happened.

At the end of the century, the most famous building in Canada housed a lacrosse team only and the Leafs, in a sparkling new building but with still only a hint of success, had gone 33 years without winning the Stanley Cup, as the Toronto franchise had done 13 times earlier in the century. ❧

Toronto Maple Leafs
13* Stanley Cup victories

Year	Games	Opponent
1918*	3-2	Vancouver Millionaires (Toronto Arenas)
1922*	3-2	Vancouver Millionaires (Toronto St. Pats)
1932	3-0	NY Rangers
1942	4-3	Detroit Red Wings
1945	4-3	Detroit Red Wings
1947	4-2	Montreal Canadiens
1948	4-0	Detroit Red Wings
1949	4-0	Detroit Red Wings
1951	4-1	Montreal Canadiens
1962	4-2	Chicago Blackhawks
1963	4-1	Detroit Red Wings
1964	4-3	Detroit Red Wings
1967	4-2	Montreal Canadiens

HHOF

Continued from page 73

Era highlights include:

Dick Irvin, ex-Leaf coach behind the Hab bench.

- 1910s — Led by "Newsy" Lalonde, Didier Pitre, Georges Vezina and Joe Malone, the Habs won their first Cup in 1916. Malone set the first NHL scoring record in 1917 by netting 44 goals in only 20 games.

- 1920s-30s — Howie Morenz and Aurèle Joliat became the stars of the team in the '20s and '30s — winning scoring titles, Stanley Cups and many individual honours. The Club won one Cup in the '20s and two in the '30s, and were really just getting warmed up.

- 1940s — The famous rallying cry began in earnest this decade. With the demise of both the Maroons and Wanderers, it was left to the Canadiens to carry the pride of Montreal, and carry it they did. Toe Blake, Elmer Lach and a newcomer named Maurice Richard began to dominate the score sheets in the NHL. Richard would become the club's icon of the century, playing hockey with a fury not before seen, and become the first NHL player to score 50 goals in 50 games. The Habs would win two Cups in the '40s, but the real powerhouse was yet to come.

- 1950s — The "Flying Frenchmen" really took off in the '50s, winning five Cups during the decade, including the first four of five in a row that stretched into the '60s (1956-60). Toe Blake successfully retired as a player to coach the team and the club, after much luring, welcomed new icon Jean Béliveau and the Rocket's little brother Henri "the Pocket Rocket" Richard.

- 1960s — Springing to life in the modern media age, the Canadiens seemed to win the Cup every other year, and if they didn't win they came awfully close. The club won the Cup another five times in the '60s.

- 1970s — A new group of "Flying Frenchmen" led by Guy Lafleur took the torch in the '70s and flew — right into another six Cups in the decade, including four in a row from 1976 through 1979. Coached by Scotty Bowman, the club lost but eight games in the 1976-77 season (only once in the Forum). They would lose a mere 29 games in 240 tries in the three-year span from 1976-78. In what many called the "greatest, fastest, hockey game ever played," the club's international highlight was the 1976 New Year's Eve 3-3 tie with the Soviet Red Army team.

- 1980s-1990s — Dynasties were becoming rare in the NHL after the Oilers and Islanders of the '80s, and the Habs made a few less-popular player deals, but somehow Montreal would still manage to win the Cup a couple of times: in 1986 led by Patrick Roy in net and in 1993 when "St. Patrick" led the club to a record 10 overtime victories in the playoffs. ♣

Montreal Canadiens 24 Stanley Cup Victories

Year	Games	Opponent
1916	3-2	Portland Rosebuds
1924	2-0	Calgary Tigers
1930	2-0	Boston Bruins
1931	3-2	Chicago Blackhawks
1944	4-0	Chicago Blackhawks
1946	4-1	Boston Bruins
1953	4-1	Boston Bruins
1956	4-1	Detroit Red Wings
1957	4-1	Boston Bruins
1958	4-2	Boston Bruins
1959	4-1	Toronto Maple Leafs
1960	4-3	Toronto Maple Leafs
1965	4-3	Chicago Blackhawks
1966	4-2	Detroit Red Wings
1968	4-0	St. Louis Blues
1969	4-0	St. Louis Blues
1971	4-3	Chicago Blackhawks
1973	4-2	Chicago Blackhawks
1976	4-0	Philadelphia Flyers
1977	4-0	Boston Bruins
1978	4-2	Boston Bruins
1979	4-1	NY Rangers
1986	4-1	Calgary Flames
1993	4-1	Los Angeles Kings

Winning One for Johnny Canuck

There's never been an era in Toronto sports like that following World War II. While the hockey Maple Leafs were winning five Stanley Cups in seven years beginning in 1945, the football Argonauts were only slightly less efficient, taking five Grey Cups in the eight years ending in 1952.

No wonder the rest of the country came to resent Toronto and referred to the city derisively as Hogtown. Toronto's success was almost entirely a Canadian affair.

Royal Copeland and Joe Krol, "The Gold Dust Twins."

Teddy Morris, who coached the first three of those football champions and built the foundation on which the remaining two were won by Frank Clair, believed in the Canadian player and the Canadian game. His lineup of homebrews based their attack on end runs, daring laterals, and option plays in which Joe Krol and Royal Copeland employed both the run and pass. Players went both ways on offence and defence.

It was a game that made use of the whole field and ran counter to the American style of straight-ahead runs, drop back passing and the platoon system. Following the Argos devastating 35-0 victory over Winnipeg on December 1, 1945 an ashen-faced Winnipeg coach Bert Warwick concluded, "...as far as I'm concerned from now on we'll have to play this wide-open game they like in the East."

It was a game that should have changed the entire course of Canadian football, particularly as it was followed by two more Grey Cup triumphs, but within a decade the American way was victorious and Morris had lost his job.

Perhaps it would have worked had the successful team been anyone but Toronto. Even the Argonauts doubted themselves as Rod Smylie later noted, "The fan in 1952 would have found the game more interesting than in 1947. The greater use of passing and the American imports improved the game. We needed them particularly at the quarterback position."

1948 proved to be the turning point. Calgary coach Les Lear brought a professional American approach to the Stampeders and reinforced this with imports like Keith Spaith and Woody Strode. Few noticed the significance of his changes because in coming east to challenge for the Cup, the Stamps' fans brought something else, a spirit of adventure in which breakfast was served from chuck wagons on Yonge Street, while cowboys rode their horses into the lobby of the Royal York Hotel.

Off the field the Grey Cup was being reinvented as a uniquely Canadian festival, just as the game on the field was abandoning its distinctive identity.

"Canadian rugby, a good game to play and a wonderful game to watch is being ruined by Americanization," said Joe Krol a year later. No one was listening. ♣

Football Highlights

November 29, 1947

Grey Cup
Toronto's Joel Krol gave an outstanding performance in the Grey Cup game, and on his way to leading the Argonauts to victory was involved in every point scored, both passing and kicking.

1945-1952

The Toronto Argonauts won five of eight Grey Cups during these years with stars like Royal Copeland and Joe Krol, and coached by the legendary Frank Clair. For three of these years the Argonauts did not dress any import players, nor apparently did they need to.

1953-1983

Toronto-based teams often won championships in the first half of the century, but experienced a 30-year dry spell in the second half of the century.

November 27, 1954

Grey Cup
With his team trailing 25-20 in the Grey Cup, and with the Alouettes poised to take a commanding lead in the last minutes of the game, Edmonton's Jackie Parker picked up a fumble and returned it 92 yards for the tying touchdown. The convert won the game.

September 29, 1956

Montreal's magnificent receiver "Prince Hal" Patterson set a CFL record of 338-yards receiving against the Hamilton Tiger Cats. By the end of the century, Patterson still held the record for most pass receptions (29) as well as most pass receiving yards (580) in Grey Cup Games.

Hal Patterson

"Prince Hal" possessed a lot of charisma and provided 14 unbelievable seasons for CFL fans, scoring 75 career touchdowns. After playing with Montreal from 1953 to 1960, he was traded to Hamilton for the 1961 season, helping the Tiger Cats to the Grey Cup Game from 1960 to 1965.

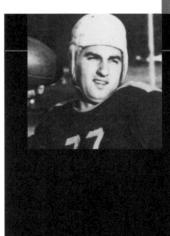

ROYAL COPELAND & JOE KROL

Royal Copeland and Joe Krol were known as the "Gold Dust Twins" during their days with the Argos from 1944 to 1956. Copeland was an Eastern All-Star running back in 1945, '46, '47 and '49 and was the only player in the century to score a touchdown in three consecutive Grey Cup games. One of the CFL's top players in a career that lasted from 1932 to 1953. Joe "King" Krol joined the Argos in 1945 and played on five Grey Cup winners, to go along with one he won as part of the 1943 Hamilton Tigers.

F o o t b a l l

1948 Grey Cup Parade

1948 Grey Cup

Grey Cup week is born

In 1948, for the first time in Grey Cup history, the antics of enthusiastic fans generated as much attention as the plays on the field. Don Mackay, Calgary's flamboyant Mayor and a former radio sports announcer, set the tone when he checked into Toronto's Royal York Hotel on horseback waving a white ten-gallon Stetson hat. Outside the hotel, well-behaved Calgary Stampeder football supporters showed a city and a nation how to party.

Grey Cup Week was born.

For the record, the 1948 Calgary Stampeders flew home with the Grey Cup. On the field, Calgary defeated Ottawa 12-7, capping a perfect 12-0 season – becoming the only Canadian Football League team ever to have gone undefeated in an entire season. Along the way, they established a league record by winning 22 consecutive games.

Meanwhile, hundreds of Calgary fans had made the three-day train ride to Toronto to watch their team play Ottawa in Varsity Stadium.

Staid Toronto had never quite seen anything like the exuberance and enthusiasm Calgary fans displayed. The moment the Stetson-topped supporters stepped down from the train at Union Station they began an impromptu square dance on the platform.

They brought a genuine Calgary Stampede chuckwagon and horses along with them and for the next few days turned Toronto on its ear. They hosted complimentary sidewalk pancake breakfasts. Toronto had seen buskers before but never Wild West rodeo and roping exhibitions on city sidewalks.

The Calgary cowboys rode their horses into the Royal York Hotel and through the lobby. Hotel staff said later they had never before witnessed noisier but more considerate fans. There was no damage to the hotel carpets or furniture.

There were 20,000 spectators in the stands at Varsity Stadium, but when the Stampeders arrived back in Calgary with the Grey Cup and the goal posts from Varsity Stadium, 30,000 Calgarians came out to salute them along the parade route through downtown Calgary. The victory celebration lasted a week.

The Stampeders organization was only three years old when Calgary descended on Toronto and changed the complexion of Grey Cup games forever. Football in Calgary dates back to 1909, though, when the Calgary Tigers were formed. The Tigers gave way to the Canucks in 1915 and then to the "Fiftieth Battalion" in 1923.

The Tigers surfaced again in 1928, making football history with the first forward pass in Canadian football. The team became the Altomahs in 1931 and the Bronks in 1935. The Stampeders first saw the light of day September 25, 1945. They played their first game against Regina a month later and won 12-0 before 4,000 fans.

When Albert Henry George Grey, Earl Grey, Governor General of Canada, donated a $48 cup for the Rugby Football Championship of Canada in 1909, little did he know it would become a national icon and a strong unifying symbol that brought West and East closer together.

Earl Grey was also a patron of the arts and donated trophies and prizes for music and drama. He was a horse fancier and horseracing enthusiast and probably would have been tickled pink watching the irreverent and good-natured hijinks in downtown Toronto in 1948. That week in Toronto, the Grey Cup became the property of the fans just as much as the players. ♣

1948 Grey Cup celebrations

1950 Mud Bowl

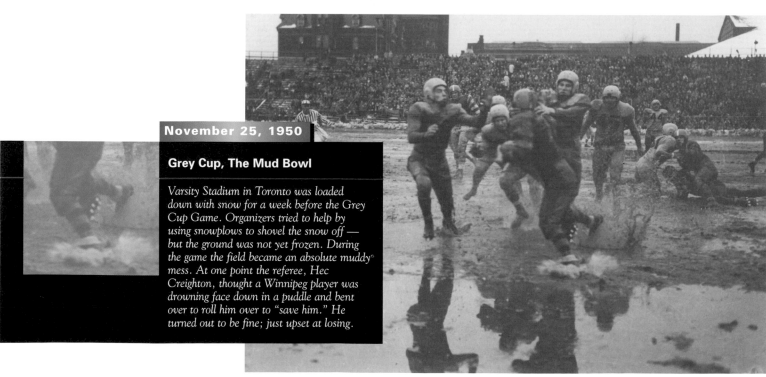

November 25, 1950

Grey Cup, The Mud Bowl

Varsity Stadium in Toronto was loaded down with snow for a week before the Grey Cup Game. Organizers tried to help by using snowplows to shovel the snow off — but the ground was not yet frozen. During the game the field became an absolute muddy° mess. At one point the referee, Hec Creighton, thought a Winnipeg player was drowning face down in a puddle and bent over to roll him over to "save him." He turned out to be fine; just upset at losing.

Highlights

Football Highlights

1958

The Canadian Rugby Union, which had recently changed its name to the Canadian Football Conference, became the Canadian Football League (CFL) for the remainder of the century.

September 14, 1958

Hamilton's all-star kicker Cam Fraser set a record of 785 yards punting in one game against Ottawa.

November 9, 1960

Ted Workman of the Montreal Alouettes orchestrated the biggest and possibly the most foolish trade of the century. Since neither he nor his new coach Perry Moss were able to work with star quarterback Sam Etcheverry and legendary receiver Hal Patterson, Workman traded them to Hamilton for Bernie Faloney and Don Paquette. Feeling his contract had been breached, Etcheverry went to the NFL Cardinals instead, which meant that Faloney ended up staying in Hamilton. Patterson, however, joined Faloney in Hamilton and would go to the Grey Cup in '61, '62, '63, '64. '65 and '67.

October 15, 1962

Hamilton Tiger Cat Joe Zuger led the Cats to a 67-21 drubbing of the Saskatchewan Roughriders — throwing a CFL record eight touchdowns passes in the game. A great punter, Zuger also set the CFL record of 45.5 yards per punt over 10 seasons.

November 20, 1965

Winnipeg's Ken Neilson took a Kenny Ploen pass 109 yards for a touchdown, establishing the record for the longest-possible pass reception in CFL playoff history.

1965

All-purpose back Dick Shatto retired in 1965 after 12 years with the Toronto Argonauts. He retired with more touchdowns and more offensive yards than any Argo before him, yet as an Argo during the 30-year drought, he retired with no Grey Cup victories.

November 30, 1957

Grey Cup – "Phantom Tackle"

Hamilton was winning the Grey Cup Game when Tiger Cat Ray "Bibbles" Bawel picked up a fumble and started running cleanly to the Winnipeg goal line. As he ran down the sideline a "mysterious" foot came out from the crowded sidelines, tripping up Bawel and robbing him of Grey Cup glory. Bawel shortly thereafter received a gold watch engraved "From the Tripper." Years later, a Toronto judge, David Humphrey, confessed to being the unnamed culprit.

October 10, 1960

Ottawa Rough Rider running back Ron Stewart rushed for 287 yards in a game against the Montreal Alouettes, a league record for the century. His efforts eclipsed the former record of 213 yards held by Hamilton's Gerry McDougall. Stewart's record-setting day is even more remarkable since he carried the ball only 15 times.

1955

Normie Kwong, the "China Clipper," won the CFL rushing title.

The "China Clipper" played 13 seasons with Calgary and Edmonton in the CFL. In 11 years of recorded statistics, he gained 9,022 yards with a 5.2-yard average. Combined with another great, Johnny Bright, Kwong gave the Eskimos a dynamic backfield that helped win three consecutive Grey Cups (1954-56).

June 10, 1958
On graduation from McMaster University, quarterback Russ Jackson negotiated his own first professional contract with the Ottawa Rough Riders for a reported $4500 a season. The unique contract included a $500 signing bonus and an open plane ticket back and forth to Toronto for Jackson to attend teacher's college in Toronto.

1955

Hockey

Maurice "Rocket" Richard

Hero of the Montreal Forum

Sport has the power to make an impact far beyond the boundaries of the arena or playing field where an event takes place, and nowhere was that more apparent in Canadian sport history than during the infamous "Richard Riot" in Montreal on March 17, 1955. The suspension imposed on Maurice "Rocket" Richard by NHL President Clarence Campbell, following an incident during which Richard struck a linesman, sparked intense protests by fans and eventually resulted in a full-fledged riot that demolished parts of downtown Montreal.

The facts of the incident are simple enough: during a late season game in Boston, Bruins' defenceman Hal Laycoe slashed Richard, causing a deep gash on his forehead. Richard retaliated with his stick, and in the ensuing struggle, punched the linesman who had stepped in to intervene. Several days later, all those involved in the incident were summoned to NHL President Clarence Campbell's office in Montreal to give their side of the story. Campbell then delivered his decision: for punching the linesman Richard would be suspended for the remaining three games of the regular season and the playoffs.

Had Richard been a player of lesser stature, the incident would have been quickly forgotten. But the Rocket was the NHL's leading scorer, a fiery competitor who was idolized in his native Quebec. He was a symbol of French Canadian pride. Infuriated fans flooded the NHL office with angry calls, some even going so far as to threaten Campbell's life for his decision.

The next day, the Detroit Red Wings came to Montreal for a game that would help decide if the Canadiens could hang on to first place in the standings. Campbell, not one to back down from a confrontation, was in attendance. As the game progressed, fans showered Campbell with an escalating array of insults, rotten fruit, eggs, bottles and more. At one point an unidentified person set off a tear gas bomb, sending a choking crowd rushing for the exits and cancelling the game. Some five hours of mayhem ensued outside the Forum, spreading 15 blocks down Ste. Catherine St., one of Montreal's main shopping streets. By the time it was over, nearly 40 people were injured and thousands of dollars in damage was done.

Richard himself took a dim view of the suspension as well, although after the riot he appealed to fans to support the team and accept Campbell's decision. Even years later, his thoughts still went back to that night when asked what he remembered most about his stellar 18-year career. "*I deserved a suspension of several games for shoving the linesman during my fight with Hal Laycoe of the Bruins,*" he said. "*I would have accepted that punishment if they had given it to me to serve, let's say at the beginning of the following season. But not for the rest of the season and the playoffs. That suspension removed all my chances of winning the scoring championship, the most coveted title for a hockey player. For me, that was the most memorable moment of my career.*"

The scale of public reaction to the Rocket's suspension is testimony to the importance of hockey, his stature as a national hero, and even the cultural tensions of the times. Some accused Campbell of racism, suggesting that an English player would have received a lighter sentence. Others simply felt the punishment was too severe, depriving their hero of a justly earned scoring title and crippling the home team on the eve of the playoffs. Richard had been provoked, they said, badgered into losing his temper by an opponent who simply wanted to get him off the ice. After all, opposing teams were always trying to find ways to contain him, and their methods were not always within the bounds of the rules or of sportsmanship.

Campbell was as widely praised in other circles for his decision as he was vilified in Montreal. Those who defended the suspension emphasized that no player, no matter how big a star, should be beyond the rules of the game. They also pointed out that the Montreal star had been involved in similar incidents before, yet previous punishments had seemed to have no effect. His passionate nature, resulting in outbursts like this, was no excuse.

Whether justice was done or not back in the late winter of 1955, Richard's place in the history books and people's hearts is assured. His playing statistics show that he won eight Stanley Cups, scored 544 regular-season goals and 82 playoff goals, and set various records that stood for 20 years or more after his retirement in 1960 (his record of six playoff

Hockey Highlights

January 28, 1937
Howie Morenz, again playing with the Montreal Canadiens, crashed heavily into the boards, breaking his leg in four places. On March 8, Morenz would succumb to a heart attack while in hospital — leading many Hab faithful to lament that, because of failing abilities to play the game he so loved, Morenz died of a broken heart.

March 17, 1938
Nels Stewart became the first NHLer to score 300 career goals, on his way to a record 324. His record was not surpassed until Rocket Richard laced up for the Canadiens en route to scoring 544 goals.

1938-1939
The Montreal Maroons took a sabbatical from the NHL, and never returned.

1940-41
During World War II at least 80 NHL players enlisted in the Armed Forces to join the war efforts. Among the thousands of Canadian dead were three up-and-coming NHLers: Red Tilson, Red Garrett and Joe Turner.

1940-1941
Boston Bruin centre Bill Cowley became the first player to win the scoring title with more assists than anyone else had points — he ended up with 45 assists and 17 goals for 62 points.

January 1, 1943
Max, Doug and Reggie Bentley formed the first all-brothers line in the NHL, and teamed up to score the winning goal in a 6-5 Chicago victory over the New York Rangers.

1943-1944
The red line was introduced in hockey, as was the rule prohibiting the two-line pass.

June, 1945
The NHL helped create the Hockey Hall of Fame to honour past heroes of the game.

overtime goals still remained unbroken when he died in 2000). As a tribute to his influence, the NHL introduced the Maurice Richard Trophy in 1999 to be given to the player scoring the most goals each season. It was the first time a post-season award was named after a player.

His presence on the ice went beyond statistics, though. Arguably the most valuable player of his day, his fiery personality and his passionate desire to win at all costs were what drew people's attention. Then there were his eyes. To call them smouldering and intense only begins to describe the gaze that could strike fear into the hearts of opponents.

When Richard died in 2000 after fighting cancer for three years, it was this immense presence on and off the ice that brought tributes from past and present Prime Ministers, other sporting heroes, and countless thousands of ordinary people. Richard's hope was that passion for the game would continue to motivate new players. "I can't imagine hockey in Canada being just another business," he said. "It has to stay our national sport for a long time and become the passion of other young people." ♦

Maurice Richard

Highlights

Rocket Richard Highlights

August 4, 1921
Maurice Richard was born in Montreal.

October 31, 1942
The Rocket played his first game with the Montreal Canadiens, wearing number 15, and picked up his first assist just 36 seconds into the game. The Habs won 3-2 over the Bruins at the Forum.

November 8, 1942
The Rocket scored his first goal in a 10-4 Montreal win over the New York Rangers at the Forum.

December 27, 1942
The Rocket's promising rookie season ended when he broke his ankle in a game. He ended the season with five goals and six assists in 16 games.

March 23, 1944
The Rocket scored all five goals in a 5-1 playoff win over Toronto, a modern-day NHL record.

April 6, 1944
The Rocket scored his first of three Stanley Cup final hat-tricks during a 3-1 win over Chicago.

December 28, 1944
The Rocket became the first post-war NHL player to score eight points in a game, getting five goals and three assists while drubbing Detroit 9-1.

February 25, 1945
Maurice "Rocket" Richard scored his 45th goal of the season, breaking Joe Malone's record of 44, which had stood for 27 years. Malone, though, had scored his 44 in only 20 games. The "Rocket" went on to score 50 goals in 50 games when he scored on the last day of the season, March 18. It was not until 1980-81 that anyone matched the 50-in-50 feat (Mike Bossy) and 1981 that someone would break it (Wayne Gretzky scored 50 goals in 39 games).

March 18, 1945
In his final game of the season, the Rocket became the first player to score 50 goals in 50 games.

January 15, 1949
The Rocket reached the 200 goal level with a goal against the Blackhawks in Montreal.

November 8, 1952
The Rocket scored his 325th goal, surpassing Nels Stewart on the all-time career goal list. It was the 10th anniversary of his first NHL goal.

October 10, 1953
The Rocket became the first player to register 350 career goals.

December 18, 1954
The Rocket became the first player to score 400 career NHL goals, surpassing Nels Stewart's record of 324.

March 17, 1955
The "Richard Riots" took place in Montreal after NHL President Clarence Campbell suspended the Rocket for his part in a stick-swinging duel with Boston's Hal Laycoe. Richard would miss the remainder of the season, including the playoffs, to miss his best chance at a scoring title by one point. Teammate Bernie "Boom Boom" Geoffrion won the title in the last game of the season.

October 15, 1955
The Rocket welcomed his baby brother Henri, who was 14 years younger, to the NHL and the Canadiens. The "Pocket Rocket" scored a goal in his first game. It was the first time the Rocket was as happy "as if I scored myself."

April 10, 1956
Montreal won its first of five straight Stanley Cups, an NHL record that remained standing at the end of the century.

October 19, 1957
The Rocket became the first player to score 500 career goals, scoring against Glenn Hall of Chicago, in his 863rd game with the Habs.

April 12, 1960
Montreal beat Toronto 5-2 at Maple Leaf Gardens in the third game of the Stanley Cup final, with the Rocket scoring his final NHL goal in the game, against Johnny Bower. Montreal went on to win its fifth straight Cup two games later.

September 15, 1960
During a morning pre-season scrimmage with the Canadiens, the Rocket scored four goals. In the afternoon, he and the Canadiens held a press conference to announce his retirement. Almost immediately, the Rocket was elected to the Hockey Hall of Fame.

October 6, 1960
The Montreal Canadiens retired the Rocket's famed Number 9 sweater.

June 25, 1999
The NHL created a new trophy for the league, the Maurice Richard Trophy, to be awarded each year to the league's leading goal scorer.

SUMMARY:
- 18 NHL seasons, all with the Montreal Canadiens
- 978 regular season games
- 965 points: 544 goals, 421 assists
- 82 playoff goals in 133 playoff games
- 8 Stanley Cups
- 26 career hat tricks
- 7 playoff hat tricks, including one game with 5 goals and two with 4

1946-1947

This was Gordie Howe's rookie year. Not surprisingly, he scored in his first game (against Turk Broda of the Toronto Maple Leafs).Yet, it was Howie Meeker who won the Calder Trophy that year as the NHL's Top Rookie.

1947-1948

One of the first "Biggest trades of the century" occurred when the Toronto Maple Leafs traded five players (Bob Goldham, Gaye Stewart, Bud Poile, Gus Bodnar and Ernie Dickens) to the Chicago Blackhawks for Cy Thomas and scoring sensation Max Bentley. It worked for the Leafs, as Toronto would keep the Stanley Cup for another year.

March 9, 1948

NHL President Clarence Campbell suspended two players — Don Gallinger and Billy Taylor — for "associating" with a known gambler, but no accusation of any direct wrongdoing was levelled at either player.

1948-1949

The Toronto Maple Leafs became the first NHL team to win the Stanley Cup three times in a row.

1949-1950

During a Stanley Cup semi-final loss in Toronto, the Red Wings' Gordie Howe was trying to check Teeder Kennedy of the Maple Leafs. Howe missed the check and crashed head first into the boards, and nearly died. He was rushed to hospital and his family was called in "just in case." Doctors drilled in a hole in his skull to relieve the pressure, and Howe recovered to play again, and again, and again…

During the next game, Detroit tried to avenge its star player: "*The Lord and 12 apostles couldn't have kept the Red Wings under control tonight,*" assessed Toronto GM and owner Conn Smythe.

1950-1951

Gordie Howe returned with a vengeance. After nearly dying on the ice the previous year, Howe returned to lead the league in goals, assists and points — a triple crown — a feat not accomplished since 1927-28 by Howie Morenz.

March 23, 1952

In the final regular-season game of the year, Bill Mosienko of the Chicago Blackhawks scored the century's fastest hat trick — in just 21 seconds! The Ranger goalie facing Mosienko was Lorne Anderson, and there is no record of Anderson ever playing again. Jean Béliveau recorded the second fastest hat trick, 44 seconds, in 1955. The fastest three goals for a team barely beats Mosienko's time — 20 seconds by Boston Bruins in 1970.

1951-1952

Terry Sawchuk of the Detroit Red Wings allowed a meagre average of 0.63 goals per game in the playoffs as the Red Wings won the Stanley Cup with eight straight wins over Toronto and Montreal. Sawchuk allowed no goals on home ice throughout the playoffs.

October 9 and November 1, 1952

Hockey Night in Canada went on television for the first time — first in French with René Lecavalier, and a few weeks later with Foster Hewitt in English.

Final Regular Season Game, 1953

Gordie Howe was trying to tie the "Rocket's" record of 50 goals in a season and had 49 goals entering his last regular season game. Fittingly, he was playing against the Canadiens who were desperately trying to preserve the "Rocket's" record. The Canadiens prevailed, but Howe still won the scoring title with a record 95 points and the Hart and Art Ross Trophies.

1953-1954

After lengthy negotiations and a serious threat to remain where he was, Jean Béliveau signed with the Montreal Canadiens, ending a stellar career with the Quebec Aces.

1941-42

The Toronto Maple Leafs fell behind the Detroit Red Wings 3-0 in games for the 1942 Stanley Cup, then shook up their line-up (replacing stalwarts Gordie Drillon and Bucko McDonald with the youthful Don Metz and Ernie Dickens) and won four straight. The seventh game was played at Maple Leaf Gardens before a then-record 16,128 partisans.

1939-1940

Boston's "Kraut Line" of three Canadians — Bobby Bauer, Milt Schmidt and Woody Dumart scored big and finished 1-2-3 in NHL scoring, with Schmidt winning the title with 52 points (Bauer and Dumart each got 43). It was the first of four times in the century that linemates would take the top three places in the scoring race.

March 18, 1952

The "Kraut Line Returns" — Bobby Bauer was enticed back from a four-year retirement to play in a game honouring the fabled line of Bauer, Milt Schmidt and Woody Dumart. Dramatically, they each got points, including Schmidt's 200th goal, en route to a 4-0 victory over Chicago.

Breaking a Barrier

Mary Baker joins the managing ranks

Moviegoers who enjoyed the 1992 film *A League of Their Own* could be excused for thinking that all the players in the All-American Girls Professional Baseball League that operated in the 1940s and 1950s were from the United States. A significant number came from Canada, in fact, and one of them, Mary "Bonnie" Baker, helped provide the inspiration for the composite lead character played by Geena Davis in the film.

Born in Regina in 1919, Baker had been discouraged many times from playing ball. "My father just hated the game, hated it" she said for emphasis, "I got whipped more than once because I stayed in school to play ball."

She would eventually join the Moose Jaw Royals softball team that toured the United States for six weeks in the late 1930s, where she impressed American softball scouts.

Baker later turned down an offer to play semi-professional softball in Montreal when her husband objected. A few years later, Hub Bishop, who also worked as a hockey scout for the Chicago Blackhawks, asked Baker if she'd like to try out for the new women's league in the United States. Her husband was now stationed in Europe. "So when I got this offer from the All-American Girls' league," Mary recalls, "He didn't know I was gone till I wrote from South Bend."

The league was the brainchild of Phil Wrigley, the chewing gum magnate and owner of the Chicago Cubs of baseball's National League. It started in 1943 to counter the public's declining interest in baseball as the war sapped the established major leagues of their star players. It outgrew its original purpose of providing a substitute for men's major league baseball, however, and lasted through the 1954 season.

While the league was largely made up of American women, there was a sprinkling of other nationalities. About 10% of the league's total roster over those years was Canadian. Of those, almost half were from Saskatchewan.

Baker was everything Wrigley could have wanted in a league player. She modelled on the side, represented the league on the popular television show, "What's My Line," and was a rugged catcher who once almost came to blows with another Canadian, Gladys "Terrie" Davis, over a strike call in the league's inaugural season.

Even though it broke new ground by providing opportunities for women to play professional baseball, the league was staunchly conservative when it came to other things. All of its field managers were male, and the post was often offered to former big leaguers like Jimmy Foxx in hopes that they would attract a fickle public to buy tickets.

Baker's leadership qualities helped change that, albeit for only part of a season. For the second half of the 1950 season, she was named the field manager of the Kalamazoo Lassies, following the team's relocation from Muskegon. Her leadership behind the plate and her promotion of the league's All-American identity, despite her Canadian citizenship, spurred the great experiment of 1950 as the League broke ranks with its own history. She managed to move the team from last-place to fourth, but at season end the league resolved that the experiment of having a female manager would not be repeated.

"They didn't want me beating former big-league stars," Baker said.

She remained with the league until 1953 before returning home to Regina where she starred for local softball teams and became Canada's first female radio sports director. ❦

Highlights

General Highlights

1950s-'60s

BC is renowned for producing top quality rugby players and perhaps its best ever was 1950s and '60s star Ted Hunt. A consummate all around athlete, Hunt also boxed (UBC light heavyweight champ), ski jumped (on the 1952 Canadian Olympic Team), returned punts and kicked field goals for the BC Lions ('56-'58) and helped Vancouver win two Mann Cups in lacrosse (1961 and 1964). Sport was also a family affair for Hunt: his wife was Pan Am Games swimming star Helen Stewart, sister of Olympian Mary Stewart.

1959

Whenever Jack Bionda was healthy enough to play a full season of lacrosse, he was the west coast league's scoring champion. To boot, every time he moved to a new team he led them to a BC Championship. 1959 was perhaps his best year, when he led the New Westminster Salmonbellies to the Mann Cup, was named the Mann Cup MVP, and won the Mike Kelly Medal as the outstanding player in the series. Having played across the country, Bionda is a member of five Halls of Fame.

1950s

In the 1950s, Frances Dafoe and Norris Bowden were the seven-time Canadian figure skating champions in dance, waltz and ten-step. They were also two-time North American pairs champions and the Canadian Senior Pairs champions from 1952-55. They were the world silver medallists in 1953 and gold medallists at the 1954 and 1955 World Championships, earning them the distinction of being the first Canadian pair ever to win a world crown. In 1956 they were the world and Olympic silver medallists.

1956-60

Barbara Wagner and Robert Paul, from the Toronto Cricket, Skating and Curling Club, dominated world pairs skating for four years from 1956-60. Winning the Canadian senior pairs title in 1956, they went undefeated as Canadian champions from 1956-60. They also claimed two North American titles and were World Champions from 1957-60. Their electrifying performance at the 1960 Olympic Games in Squaw Valley resulted in first place marks from all judges and earned them the distinction of becoming the first Canadian, and North American, pair ever to win an Olympic gold medal.

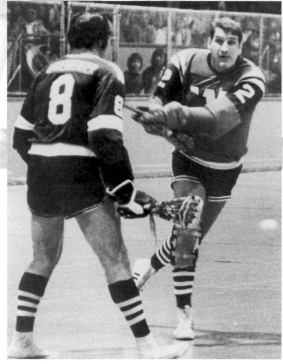

Jack Bionda

Frances Dafoe and Norrie Bowden.

Ada Mackenzie, First Lady of Canadian Golf

Ada Mackenzie, the first lady of Canadian golf, won so many titles even she lost track. At 13 years old, she won her first match with her father, and continued playing and winning almost every year until her death in 1973 at the age of 81.

One win, however, does stand out from the rest: the 1925 Canadian Ladies Open. When Ada won that, she brought the title home to Canada for the first time. At the time, it was a very important win for Canadian women golfers. It signaled that foreign golf stars were not invincible, and that a homegrown Canadian could play with the best of them.

The Canadian Ladies Open had been re-introduced in 1920 after World War I. Year after year, either an American or a British golfer won the match-play event.

Leading up to the 1925 tournament, Ada was considered a contender, but most of the attention was paid to the two American heavyweights: Dorothy Campbell Hurd and Alexa Fraser (nee Stirling). Dorothy was the US Champion, and heavily favoured to win. While Alexa Fraser had become a Canadian through marriage, it was as Alexa Stirling that she made her name as America's leading female golfer. The pundits predicted Dorothy and Alexa would end up fighting it out for the title.

Ten Americans and 22 Canadians qualified for the event. Alexa led the qualifying round with an 83, and Ada's 85 beat out Dorothy's by a stroke.

The course was playing quite slow, after two days of heavy rain, but it was in generally good condition.

By the third round, Dorothy was knocked out by Toronto's Sydney Pepler Mulqueen, in a match many called the best of Sydney's career. It was starting to look like a Fraser-Mackenzie final.

Ada was paired with Sydney in the semi-finals, and took the round with nary an opening for Sydney to break through. When Alexa won her round, the lines were drawn for the final battle.

Both Ada and Alexa could have been excused for not playing their best. A year earlier, Alexa had undergone major surgery, and had rarely played competitive golf since. For her part, Ada had also been somewhat absent from the competitive golf course, having focused her energies on opening her Ladies' Golf and Tennis Club.

Despite this, the pair put on an excellent exhibition of golf that day, the different strengths of each golfer making for a close, and exciting match.

The 36-hole final was scheduled to be played in two rounds of 18, one in the morning and one in the afternoon. The morning round was close, with many holes tied. Fraser had strong drives, and Ada seemed to be the one in trouble. Yet while her driving presented Fraser with three good chances to take the lead, she failed to capitalize. By the end of the first round, they were tied.

The first hole of the afternoon round sealed the fate of the game. Fraser again had an opportunity to take the lead, but she missed. Ada, whose approach and putting were superior, won the hole in one stroke. And she never looked back. Ada continued to dominate the approach and putts, even as Fraser's impressive long game seemed to put Ada at a disadvantage before every hole. By the 32nd hole, the homegrown Canadian had built up an insurmountable lead and won the match.

Ada had spent considerable time working on her approach and putting, and clearly, her practice paid off. She three-putted only once, and single-putted 14 of the 32-holes. She played the better golf that day, and for her efforts, brought home the Canadian Ladies Open title, and the Duchess of Connaught Gold Cup.

Ada went on to win the Canadian Ladies Open three more times, in 1926, 1933 and 1935. She was the Ladies' Closed Champion six times; the Ladies' Senior GA Champion seven times, and so on, and so on, and so on. She was also a great supporter of Canada's next great female golf star, Marlene Stewart-Streit.

One last notable moment: in 1950, at the ripe age of 59, this indefatigable athlete won the Ontario ladies golf championship against a much younger rival. It was the ninth time she'd won the title. ♣

Highlights

Golf Highlights

1905
M. Thompson of New Brunswick won her first of four straight Canadian Ladies' Golf Championships.

1919
Ada Mackenzie won her first of 10 National Amateur Championships. She also won some 27 other tournaments through 1950.

Ada Mackenzie was Canada's first star female golfer, winning often throughout her long and storied career.

G o l f

Marlene Stewart-Streit

From caddie to Canadian champion

It could be said Marlene Stewart-Streit got into golf for the money, but stayed for love.

When she was 12, she learned that caddies could make a dollar a round toting bags at the local golf course. Even though she was young and small, she was also tough and determined — two attributes that would carry her far in life. So Stewart (her maiden name) became a caddy, fell in love with the sport, and became one of Canada's greatest female golfers of the century.

Her family was living in Fonthill, Ontario, at the time, and the local golf course was the Lookout Point Golf Club. There, Stewart caddied for older players, but she soon began following the footsteps of the club professional, Gordon McInnes — quite literally. McInnes was heard to joke, "I can rarely go into the pro shop without tripping over Marlene's shoes."

When Gordon would go out to hit a few balls, Stewart would chase his stray balls. In return, the pro would let Stewart drive a few herself, and so it began.

From the start, Stewart had a natural, easy swing. But she also thrived on practice. The caddies were allowed to play one round a week on their own, and by the time she was 14, Stewart was as good as any of the boys.

By 15, she had saved up for her very own clubs. And, equipped with her own matched set, she entered her very first competition, the junior girls' Ontario championship. Playing against much older competitors, Stewart placed third.

But true to form, Stewart felt she could have done better and needed to work on a few things — namely, her ability to concentrate. In that competition, she let herself get too complacent on easy shots, but soon realized there was no such thing as an easy shot in golf. Whether it was a 200-yard drive or six-inch putt, it demanded full concentration.

So Stewart began to focus on every shot. Soon, the five-foot, 108-pound diminutive golfer became a steel-nerved competitor unfazed by pressure. In 1951 at the age of 17, she played a famous round against Ada Mackenzie, the pioneer of Canadian women's golf. First Stewart was ahead, but Mackenzie, the experienced competitor, held on and seemed to be close to breaking through. As Mackenzie put it, "Then we came to the hole that really counted. If Marlene was to weaken in a pinch, then this would be the test. But she didn't! She won the hole and I never caught her again. Let me tell you, that young girl doesn't panic."

Mackenzie added, "You'll be hearing from her for a long time."

Those were prophetic words. That same year, Stewart won the National Women's Open tournament, the first time a Canadian had won it in 13 years. In 1953, she won the British Women's Open golf championship—the first such title for a Canadian golfer.

Then came 1956. Many athletes lead solid careers topped by one golden, defining moment. For Stewart, that moment was more like a golden, defining year.

That year, Stewart was unstoppable. She won the North and South, the US Intercollegiate, the Ontario Amateur, the Canadian Closed, the Canadian Open and the Jasper Park Totem Pole.

When she teed off at the US Women's National Golf championship in September that year, she was attempting her seventh victory in a row.

The field at the Meridian Hills Country club in Indianapolis was lower in entries than in 1956, with 105 competitors, compared to as many as 200 in previous years. But what it lacked in quantity it made up for in quality. Competitors included the British Open title holder, the defending US champion, and a host of past US champions and runners-up. Also playing that year was the first-ever black female competitor in the history of the tournament, Ann Gregory.

Not only was Stewart facing formidable competition, but she had tried for the US title three times before. The best she'd mustered was fifth in 1954. In the end, however, it was Stewart's steely nerves that won her the championship.

In the final 36-hole match-play round, Stewart was lagging behind JoAnne Gunderson, a 17-year-old whiz kid who hailed from Washington State (and later who became more popular as JoAnne Carner). She trailed by one hole after the first 18 holes. Then, Stewart's short game began to falter, and Gunderson surged ahead. With 12 holes to go, Stewart racked up a four-hole deficit. She was facing certain defeat.

But ever composed and unfazed by the pressure, Stewart came back, and how. At the 25th, the two bogied. Then, Stewart won the next two holes. On the 28th, they tied. But the pressure was now getting to Gunderson, who lost the 29th, and when she three-putted from 15 feet on the 30th, Gunderson let Stewart even things out.

From that point on, Stewart was in control. They tied the 31st, Gunderson bogied the 32nd, and Stewart kept ahead for the next two.

Finally, the duelling competitors were at the 35th hole. Stewart sank the ball in an 11 1/2 foot putt. Her short game was back on. Gunderson came three feet short on a 10 1/2 foot putt.

Fighting back with a tremendous rally, Stewart had won the US Women's National Golf title.

If that was not sweet enough, the icing on the cake came in December that year. Stewart was chosen outstanding woman amateur golfer for 1956 by the Los Angeles Times National Sports Award board. ♣

Marlene Stewart-Streit

One of the most revered and recognized female golfers in Canada and around the world, Marlene Stewart-Streit personified the dedication and determination of Canadian golfers. Streit was the only player from anywhere to have won the Canadian, US, British and Australian Amateur Championships in her career and was one of the inspirations behind many of Canada's top young female professional and amateur golfers. Among her many accomplishments were 11 Canadian Ladies Open Amateur Championships, nine Canadian Ladies Closed Amateur Championships, three Canadian Ladies Senior Championships and two USGA Senior Women's Championships.

Career Highlights:

- 1953 British Ladies' Amateur Champion
- 1956 United States Women's Amateur Champion
- 1956 North & South Ladies' Champion
- 1956 United States Inter-Collegiate Champion
- 1956 Totem Pole Champion
- 1961 Low Amateur in United States Open
- 1963 Australian Ladies' Champion
- 1985 United States Senior Women's Champion
- 1994 United States Senior Women's Champion
- 1953 Co-Champion of the US Mixed Foursomes
- 1958 Co-Champion of the US Mixed Foursomes
- 1959 Co-Champion of the US Mixed Foursomes
- 1959 Helen Lee Doherty Tournament Champion
- 1960 Helen Lee Doherty Tournament Champion
- 1961 Helen Lee Doherty Tournament Champion
- 1965 Helen Lee Doherty Tournament Champion
- 1951, 1954, 1955, 1956, 1958, 1959, 1963, 1968, 1969, 1972, 1973 Canadian Ladies' Open Amateur Champion
- 1950, 1951, 1952, 1953, 1954, 1955, 1956, 1957, 1963, 1969 Canadian Ladies' Closed Amateur Champion
- 1987, 1988, 1990, 1993 Canadian Ladies' Senior Champion
- 1950, 1956, 1957, 1958, 1968, 1969, 1970, 1972, 1974, 1976, 1977 Ontario Ladies' Champion
- Voted one of 10 top international women golfers in January 1999 by Golf World Magazine.

Moe (Murray Irwin) Norman

There was never a more colourful character in golf than Moe Norman. His legendary accuracy and prolific tournament record were renowned and revered throughout the world by fellow golfers. Among his many victories were two Canadian Amateurs, two CPGA Championships and five CPGA Senior Championships along with multiple victories in the Ontario, Manitoba and Saskatchewan Opens.

Career Highlights:

- 1955, 1956 Canadian Amateur Champion
- 1966 Canadian Professional Golfers Champion
- 1974 Professional Golfers Champion
- 1980-1985 Canadian Professional Golfers Association Seniors Champion
- 1958 Ontario Open Champion
- 1963 Saskatchewan Open Champion
- 1963 Ontario Open Champion
- 1965 Manitoba Open Champion
- 1966 Alberta Open Champion
- 1966 Manitoba Open Champion
- 1967 Manitoba Open Champion
- 1968 Saskatchewan Open Champion
- 1971 Alberta Open Champion
- 1976 Alberta Open Champion

Stan Leonard

Vancouver's Stan Leonard won his first of eight CPGA Championships in 1940. After years of being a club pro, Leonard finally joined the new PGA Tour in 1957, promptly winning the Greensboro Open in North Carolina, at the time a very major golf tournament in the US The next year Leonard would win the very prestigious Tournament of Champions in Las Vegas and be voted the World Golfer of the Year for 1958.

Career Highlights:

- 1957 Greater Greensboro Open Champion
- 1958 Tournament of Champions
- 1960 Western Open Champion
- 1952 Northwest Open Champion
- 1960 Canadian Match Play Open Champion
- 1940, 1941, 1950, 1951, 1954, 1957, 1959, 1961, Canadian Professional Golfers Champion
- 1945, 1950, 1951, 1952, 1955, 1958, 1959, 1960, Low Canadian professional, Canadian Open
- Winner of a total of 44 tournaments during his career

Highlights

1900s

Cal Bricker was an excellent university athlete, winning two all round track and field championships in 1905 and 1906. His specialties were the running broad jump (long jump) and the hop, step and jump (triple jump). At the 1908 Olympic trials he set a long jump record of 24'1½", which he held for 27 years. At the 1908 Games he took the bronze medal in the long jump and placed fourth in the hop, step and jump. In 1912, while a dentistry student, Bricker made the Olympic team bound for Stockholm where he placed second in the long jump to win the Olympic silver medal.

1920s

At the Canadian track and field championships, Cyril Coaffee tied Charlie Paddock's world record for the 100 yard dash. This sprint of 9.6 seconds stood as a national record for more than 25 years. He was also the national 200 yard champion for many years. Throughout the 1920s he faced many of the world's best sprinters in international meets and came away with his share of victories. In 1926 and again in 1927 Coaffee competed against the great Percy Williams and won.

1920s

"Cap" Fear joined the Toronto Argonauts in 1920 as an outside wing and remained for three league titles and a Grey Cup. From 1928-1932 Cap played for the Hamilton Tigers winning two league titles and two Grey Cups. Fear was selected to six eastern Canada All-star teams. Like many athletes of his time Fear was more than talented at many sports including rowing, hockey and boxing. With the Argonaut rowing club he stroked the lightweight eights and fours to Canadian Henley victories on the same day.

1920s

Football great Pep Leadley joined the Hamilton Tigers Intermediate team in 1915 at 17 and helped them win a Canadian championship. After two seasons with the Tigers Interprovincial team, he entered Queen's University, where, as a drop kicking backfielder, he helped Queen's win the college title from 1921 to 1925 and three Grey Cups from 1922 to 1924. Leadley rejoined the Hamilton Tigers in 1926 and added two more Grey Cup triumphs before he retired in 1930.

1955

Canada's Sports Hall of Fame was established at the CNE grounds in Toronto "To preserve the record of Canadian sports achievements and to promote a greater awareness of our nation's heritage of sport."

Hockey

Is Jean Béliveau the Best Ever?

by Trent Frayne
March 3, 1956

Jean Béliveau, a bland and bashful centre for the Montreal Canadiens, is a unique figure in the history of hockey. He has glided serenely through a career in which cities, hockey magnates and even politicians have engaged in push-and-pull struggles for his services and he has been virtually a one-man industry paying off the mortgage on a multi-million-dollar rink. Now only twenty-four years old and one of the highest paid hockey players in history, Béliveau has emerged from this seething cauldron to a cool pedestal completely devoid of controversy: modern hockey authorities, who agree on almost nothing, believe he is the most gifted player of all time, and potentially the greatest.

A few savants, such as Lynn Patrick, the general manager of the Boston Bruins, are convinced already. "No question about it," Patrick says flatly, "he's the finest player I've ever seen."

Older and possibly more meditative heads await the test of time and toss in occasional riders based on the fact that Béliveau has not yet completed three seasons in the National Hockey League and therefore cannot possibly be compared with, say, Eddie Shore, Howie Morenz or Béliveau's team mate Maurice Richard. Art Ross, who built hockey in Boston starting in 1924 and who retired last year as vice-president of the Bruins, calls Béliveau the greatest *young* player he ever saw, and it was Ross who took young Eddie Shore to Boston. Conn Smythe, the president of the Toronto Maple Leafs, says that if Béliveau goes along at his present clip for another seven or eight years he'll be the greatest ever.

In fact Smythe, a Toronto loyalist who rarely tosses garlands of love beyond his native city's borders, employs Montreal's Béliveau as his end-all illustration in a running war he's conducted in recent years with people who feel modern hockey has deteriorated.

"Béliveau is the greatest thing that could have happened to the modern game," cries Smythe, in the manner of a man who has just found his missing laundry ticket. "They say there's no room left for stick-handling and brains and technique. When has there ever been a better stick-handler? Who has ever shown more savvy? Who ever got a shot away faster?"

Hot battles swirled around him before he reached the NHL; in fact, two prominent hockey executives fought so strenuously to gain his services as a junior that they have few kind words for one another to this day. They are Frank Selke, the managing director of the Canadiens, and Frank Byrne, who was the owner of the Quebec Citadels of the now-defunct Quebec Junior Hockey League.

To keep him in Quebec City when he graduated from junior ranks, men close to Premier Duplessis became involved, and it was widely believed in Quebec that the license to operate a tavern in the Montreal Forum—a big money maker for the Canadian Arena Co., which operates the Forum and the NHL Canadiens—would be revoked if Béliveau were enticed to Montreal by the Canadiens. He stayed in Quebec City for two seasons where record crowds flocked to worship him and spend money that helped pay for the lavish new Coliseum, a bowl devoid of posts that seats 10,338 people and frequently bettered that total with standees during Béliveau's stay.

Béliveau has always delivered on the ice. He has led the scorers in every league in which he's ever played except the NHL, and it seems likely that he'll do that this year. Last season he was two points behind the leader, team mate Bernie (Boom Boom) Geoffrion, and this season he was the league's leading scorer every week through mid-season. One night against Boston, he scored four goals and Terry Sawchuk, the Boston goaler, reluctantly admitted he was beaten cleanly on all of them, a rare confession by any goalkeeper.

Hap Day, the general manager of the Toronto Maple Leafs, was asked recently if there were any known way of stopping Béliveau. He said crisply, "Of course there is. But it isn't legal."

Curiously, the average spectator has to watch Béliveau play several games before he begins to appreciate what makes him so good. "That's because Jean makes the game look easy," explains Dick Irvin, the coach of the Chicago Blackhawks, who served in the same capacity with the Canadiens during Béliveau's first two seasons in the NHL. "You've got to look closely to appreciate his finesse."

Toronto's star right-winger of the Thirties, Charlie Conacher, is generally conceded to have owned the hardest shot in hockey, but Conacher himself figures Béliveau's is its equal. "*Le Gros Bill*," says Conacher, grinning at his French, "gets his shot away a little faster, too." The nickname, *Le Gros Bill*, was hung on Béliveau six years ago by Quebec newspaperman Roland Sabourin. It's the title of an old French-Canadian folk song, *Le voila Le Gros Bill* (Here Comes Big Bill).

Even Béliveau's teammates worship at the shrine, and Doug Harvey and Dollard St. Laurent, a Canadiens defence pair, occasionally stand at the blueline during a game and shout unbelievingly to one another when they see some new facet of Béliveau's technique. "There ought to be two leagues," St. Laurent told Vince Lunny, sports editor of the Montreal Herald, one night after a game, "one of the pros and one for Béliveau."

And he steadily has been becoming a better hockey player. "It's something new every game," says linemate Bert Olmstead. "He has such remarkable reflexes, can so quickly take a pass in front of the net and fire the puck hard and accurately. He has the same sense of direction as the Rocket, and is big and strong in front of that net, hard for the defencemen to knock down."

Kenny Reardon, assistant managing director of the Canadiens, was asked recently if there were anything about Béliveau that bothered him.

"Just one thing," he replied, "How'd you like to have the job of signing him when his five-year contract runs out?" ❦

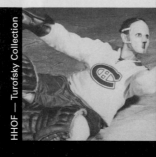

HHOF — Turofsky Collection

November 1, 1959

Goaltender Jacques Plante wore a face mask for the first time. After taking a shot in the face from Andy Bathgate, Plante left the ice to get stitched up, only to return wearing a mask. He was the first to wear a protective mask on a regular basis. Coach Toe Blake did not initially approve of the idea, but yielded when Plante said, "If they let me wear it all the time, I can play until I'm 45." He did.

"Le gros Bill," in 1971, Jean Béliveau retired from the National Hockey League. He played on 10 Stanley Cup winning Montreal Canadiens teams between 1956 and 1971.

Hockey

The Best Defence

Doug Harvey helped change the game of hockey

by Barbara Wickens
January 8, 1990

Doug Harvey, who was named an all-star 11 times during the 21 seasons that he spent in the National Hockey League (NHL), never seemed to care what other people said about him. During the 1950s when Harvey was a brilliant playmaker for the Montreal Canadiens, fellow hockey players called him one of the best defencemen of his time — perhaps of all time. For his part, Harvey once told a reporter that he could not rate his own playing because "I have never seen myself play."

In later years, the hard drinking Harvey appeared equally unconcerned when he was confronted by rumours that he was, as one reporter put it, "living in a bottle."

Born in the sporting-conscious west-end Montreal district of Notre-Dame-de-Grace, Harvey was a natural athlete who played semi-professional football and baseball as well as hockey. He broke into professional hockey with the Canadiens in 1947. During his 14 seasons with the Canadiens, in a period when the club also boasted such stars as Maurice (Rocket) Richard and Jean Béliveau, the Canadiens won 5 consecutive Stanley Cups between 1956 and 1960, a feat unmatched in league history.

Harvey won the Norris Trophy as the NHL's top defencemen seven times. In 1961, after he became active in the recently formed players' association, Harvey was traded to the New York Rangers, where he played for three seasons and coached for a year. Then he played with minor-league teams in St. Paul, Minn., Quebec City, Baltimore and Pittsburgh. With the NHL expansion to 12 teams from six in 1967, Harvey played for the St. Louis Blues. He finally retired from playing in 1969 at the age of 44 with a lifetime total of 88 goals and 452 assists. He was elected to the Hockey Hall of Fame in 1973.

Tom Johnson, vice-president of the Boston Bruins and a fellow defenceman with Harvey on the cup-winning Canadiens, once said that Harvey was unrivalled as a defenceman in his era and could control the tempo of a game at will. A pinpoint passer, Harvey perfected the long pass out of his own end zone. With Harvey, the Canadiens became so successful on the power play that the NHL changed its regulations so that a penalized team returned to full strength immediately after opponents scored a goal. Harvey's legacy to the game was written, in the record book — and the book of rules. ♦

1961-1962

Canadien Doug Harvey was traded to New York from Montreal to become a player-coach. He promptly won his seventh Norris Trophy as the league's best defenceman.

Hockey Highlights

February 5, 1960

Red Kelly was a star defenceman with the Detroit Red Wings during the 1950s. As with many of his teammates before him, he was traded from the Red Wings. At first he was traded to New York, but he resisted and said he'd retire instead, nullifying the deal. Detroit surprisingly accepted his plea then shipped him to Toronto, a move Kelly accepted. He would be an integral member of Toronto's Stanley Cup winning teams of the 1960s, but as a forward.

1959-1960

Bobby Hull scored twice in the last game of the regular season to overtake Boston's Bronco Horvath and win his first Art Ross scoring title.

September 15, 1961

After scoring four goals in a training camp game, Maurice "Rocket" Richard retired from hockey. His 18-year career left him with 17 NHL scoring records, including most goals (544), most game winning goals (82), playoff overtime goals (6) and a legion of fans, French and English.

March 16, 1961

Following in the footsteps of his long-time teammate Rocket Richard, Montreal's Bernie "Boom Boom" Geoffrion became the second NHLer to score 50 goals in a season (scoring 22 goals in his last 21 games). The 50th came against the Leafs' Cesare Maniago. Toronto's Frank Mahovlich scored 48 goals that season.

1961-1962

For the first time in NHL history there was a scoring championship tie – between Bobby Hull of the Chicago Blackhawks and Andy Bathgate of the New York Rangers. Hull was awarded the Art Ross Trophy for the scoring title because he netted more goals (50-28), becoming the third player to score 50 goals in one season.

June 6, 1962

Some of the wreckage from former Leaf Bill Barilko's plane crash in 1951 was found in northern Ontario. Surely by coincidence, the Leafs won the Stanley Cup the same year, their first since the crash year.

1962

Red Kelly became the fourth NHL player to enter the House of Commons as a Member of Parliament. Interestingly, he defeated a young Alan Eagleson in the election, who was just starting his inroads in the hockey world.

1962-1963

Gordie Howe won his sixth and final Art Ross Trophy as the NHL scoring leader — a record he would hold until Wayne Gretzky came along.

November 6, 1962

Glenn Hall's goaltending streak of 502 consecutive regular season and playoff game appearances came to an end when he pinched a nerve in his back. Denis DeJordy replaced him.

June 4, 1963

Montreal traded Jacques Plante and two other players to the New York Rangers for Gump Worsley and three players in an unexpected blockbuster NHL trade.

February 22, 1964

Andy Bathgate was traded to the Toronto Maple Leafs by the New York Rangers.

HHOF — Turofsky Collection

The "Rocket"

HHOF — Graphic Artists

Toronto's Red Kelly, a star at Maple Leaf Gardens and on Parliament Hill.

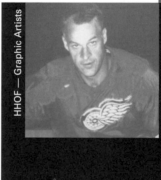

HHOF — Graphic Artists

November 10, 1963

Two historic events occurred in the same game, as Gordie Howe scored his 545th career goal against the Montreal Canadien's Charlie Hodge to overtake Rocket Richard, while Terry Sawchuk recorded his 94th career shutout tying George Hainsworth's long-standing record. On January 18, Sawchuk broke the record with a 2-0 win over Montreal.

1964

Stanley Cup

Bobby Baun and the Toronto Maple Leafs were down 3-2 in games to the Detroit Red Wings. Baun put his foot out to stop a Gordie Howe shot and was carried off the ice on a stretcher in serious pain. The game went into overtime, with Baun returning to score the winner. The Leafs won the Cup with a 4-0 victory the next night. Baun finally went to have an x-ray on his ankle, and found that it was broken (well, cracked at least, but the myth that grew up around the goal made it seem like it was broken).

1957

Hockey

Nobody's Too Big for Ted Lindsay

by Trent Frayne
October 26, 1957

Hockey's scrappy little all-star leftwinger has battled the largest and roughest men on the ice. Now, as president of the new players' union, he may be taking on his toughest opponent of all — the NHL owners.

Straight ahead is the only direction Ted Lindsay has ever travelled in thirteen years in the National Hockey League. As a snarling, mocking, richly talented performer for the Detroit Red Wings from 1944 until he was traded to the Chicago Blackhawks last summer, he recognized no detours in becoming the highest-scoring leftwinger of all time, and one of the stormiest. For thirteen years Ted Lindsay has never backed down from anyone and now, this fall, in addition to moving to a new challenge with the lowly Hawks, he is taking on the largest order of them all — the men who run the league.

He'll do this as president of the National Hockey League Players' Association, a union formed by the ice-bound serfs in awesome secrecy during a three-month period last winter, with Lindsay as one of the principal instigators and organizers. When its existence was announced by Lindsay at a press conference in New York last February, the club owners and league executives expressed an astonishment matched only by that of most hockey fans. The sudden materialization of a players' union was unexpected in itself; still more remarkable was the materialization as the players' spokesman and president, their archenemy during working hours, the little hellion, Lindsay.

Lindsay's announcement on the formation of the players' united front was made with studied understatement. "We have organized to promote and protect the best interests of the players," he said: "We don't intend to start a revolution. We aren't displeased or discontented about a single thing."

Opposition from the game's executives is not likely to faze Lindsay in the committee rooms because he's been overcoming opposition, some of it unbelievably violent, ever since he broke into the league.

He feels that one incident illustrating the need for a union is the case of Jim Thomson, who was shipped off to the minors by his outspoken employer, Conn Smythe, and was on the minor-league roster all summer until his sale in August to Chicago. "It doesn't seem fair that after twelve years in the big league a player can be shipped off like that," he says. "There ought to be greater recognition of a man who has proven himself. He ought to become a free agent and allowed to make a deal for himself."

The players also feel the owners could contribute more to the players' pension fund than the administrative costs they now bear.

It isn't the snarling stick-flicking Lindsay who talks of these things, a scarred thirty-two-year-old veteran of a hundred hockey wars. It's the other Lindsay, a calm young business executive, neatly dressed, and controlled.

It would appear, then, that this Lindsay — the one with the velvet glove — will prove quite as formidable as the other—the one who climbed to the top carrying a big stick and never backed down from anyone. ❦

INKERMAN ROCKETS

Inkerman is a farming community of 100 souls south of Ottawa, but for a brief, shining moment in the late 1940s and early '50s it was a powerhouse in Junior hockey. Local farmers dug down and each contributed five dollars to buy a set of second-hand red and white sweaters with the letter "R" already sewn on. It was decided to name the team "Rockets." The Inkerman Rockets won five straight Ottawa and District titles. In 1951 the team reached the Memorial Cup quarter finals before losing out to Jean Béliveau and the Quebec Citadelles. Quebec then fell to the powerful Barrie Flyers who won the Memorial Cup that year. Inkerman Rocket centre Brian McFarlane, later a nationally known hockey broadcaster and author, had the almost impossible chore of keeping Béliveau off the score sheet. One of Inkerman's marquee players was 16-year old Prescott, Ontario, defenceman Leo Boivin who went on to play 22 seasons in the NHL with Toronto, Boston, Detroit, Pittsburgh and Minnesota.

HHOF — Turofsky Collection

HHOF — Turofsky Collection

Early days of basketball.

Highlights

Basketball Milestones of the 1900s

1936 Olympics

Basketball's first appearance as a medal sport took place at the Berlin Olympics in 1936. James Naismith witnessed the finals, as his adopted country (the United States) defeated the country of his birth (Canada) 19-8 on a rainy day in Berlin, with the game played on a muddy outdoor clay court. In an ironic human interest twist, the Canadian team was mostly comprised of the Dominion Champions from the Windsor Young Men's Hebrew Association (YMHA), who were limited in their off-time due to the Nazi organizers' restrictions on the movement of Jewish people throughout Germany at the time.

1930s

Edmonton's Margaret Vasheresse was the longest serving member of the Grads (1926-36). She held the record for most career points (2,079) and set a world record in 1931 by sinking 61 consecutive free throws during a half time exhibition.

November 1, 1946

The first Basketball Association of America (BAA) game was played at Maple Leaf Gardens between the Toronto Huskies and the New York Knickerbockers. Hank Biasatti and Gino Sovran, both Canadians, played for the Huskies in that first game and through their inaugural season. Just before the 1950 season, the BAA incorporated the key National Basketball League (NBL) franchises and formed a new league now known as the NBA (National Basketball Association).

1950

Noel Robertson MacDonald, the centre for the Edmonton Grads, was voted as the outstanding female basketball player of the first half-century.

1950

Norm Baker was voted as the outstanding male basketball player of the first half century.

1952

Vancouver native Bob Houbregs, known as "hook shot Houbregs," was the NCAA player of the year in 1952 as well as a two-time all-American. He led the Washington Huskies to three Pacific Coast Conference titles, also winning the scoring titles in 1951, '52 and '53. He went on to a solid five-year NBA career followed by a stint as the general manager of the Seattle Supersonics.

1952-60

Tillsonburg Livingstons — This small southwestern Ontario team twice captured CABA titles, earning the right to represent Canada in the Summer Olympics. In 1952 and in 1960 the Livies were also the Dominion Champions.

1964, 1968, 1972, 1976

Al Rae was the only person to referee in four Olympic Games.

1950-2000

Fred Thomas, Pascal Fleury and Ferguson Jenkins are the only Canadians to have suited up for the Harlem Globetrotters in their 75 years of entertaining crowds around the world.

1972-1988

Jack Donohue, a native New Yorker who first coached at Power Memorial High School with a young Lew Alcindor (Kareem Abdul Jabbar), then at Holy Cross University, embarked on a 16-year term at the helm of the Canadian National team, elevating the development of basketball in Canada throughout his tenure.

1976

Phil Tollestrup was the third leading scorer at the 1976 Olympic Games in Montreal where he captained Canada to a fourth-place finish. At the Games he was also named to the All-Olympic Team.

1976

The 1976 Montreal Olympics saw women's basketball added to the list of fully recognized Olympic sports. It was fitting for this to happen in Canada, the nation of basketball inventor James Naismith's birth as well as home of the most dominant basketball team in history, the Edmonton Grads.

1979

Sylvia Sweeney was named the MVP of the Women's World Championships in 1979 after leading Canada to its best finish ever, a bronze medal.

1977-80

Chris Critelli won two CIAU Championships with Laurentian University in Sudbury in 1977 and 1978 and followed this up with two NCAA Titles with Old Dominion University in Norfolk, Virginia in 1979 and 1980. Winning a league championship is always special, winning it two times in a row is powerful, and winning it twice consecutively in two different elite leagues (four times in a row) is almost unheard of.

1980s

Canadian Misty Thomas was the only women's basketball player to have her number retired from the University of Nevada-Las Vegas (UNLV). Thomas was the daughter of Paul Thomas, and together they were the only father and daughter team inducted in the Canadian Basketball Hall of Fame.

1980s

Bev Smith was a two-time all-American with the University of Oregon in the early 1980s then a leader on many of Canada's National Women's teams.

1983

At the FISU Games (University Games) in Edmonton, Canada upset the mighty USA team and captured its most significant gold medal in basketball of the century.

1976-88

Romel Raffin was the only Canadian of the century named to four Olympic basketball teams. Beginning with the fourth-place 1976 team coached by the legendary Jack Donohue, Raffin was also named to the 1980, 1984 and 1988 teams. Unfortunately, the 1980 Games coincided with the Moscow boycott, so he did not actually play in those Games.

1980-2000

The University of Windsor (formerly Windsor Assumption) has placed three former coaches into the Canadian Basketball Hall of Fame. Paul Thomas was inducted in 1980, Red Nantais in 1981 along with the 1936 Olympic team, and Hank Biasatti in 2000.

1986

Leo Rautins, the first high schooler to make the national men's team (at 16), was the most heavily recruited Canadian high school player of his time. He was the first-ever Canadian drafted in the first round of the NBA draft (17th overall).

1987

Mike Smrek, a back-up centre to Kareem Abdul Jabbar of the Los Angeles Lakers, became the first Canadian to capture an NBA crown in 1986-87, repeating the feat in 1987-88. Bill Wennington followed with two championship years with the Chicago Bulls in the mid 1990s and Rick Fox enjoyed two championship runs with the LA Lakers in 1999-2000 and 2000-2001.

1992-94

The Winnipeg Wesman Women's team achieved an unmatched women's record of 88 straight wins and three straight championships from 1992 to 1994. This streak matched the collegiate men's record of 88 set by the UCLA Bruins of 1972-74.

1994

Will Njoku, a player for St. Mary's University of the Atlantic Universities Athletic Association, was drafted 41st overall by the Indiana Pacers in the 1994 NBA Draft, the first Canadian university player ever drafted into the NBA.

1990s

Ron Foxcroft, an internationally and NCAA renowned referee, invested personal funds to develop the Fox 40 whistle, the pea-less whistle which became the whistle of choice around the globe.

October 31, 1997

Violet Palmer became the first female to referee an NBA game on Hallowe'en Night, 1997, in Vancouver as the Grizzlies hosted the Dallas Mavericks.

1998

Stacy Dales, of Brockville, Ontario, was selected as a first-team all-American after her junior year at Oklahoma University. She later became a dominant force for the Canadian team at the 2000 Olympic Games in Sydney.

Bob Abate

Hockey

NHL Goalies

Goalie mask, 1980s

Terry Sawchuk

It has often been said that hockey goaltenders are a breed apart, particularly those that are good enough to reach the NHL They simply have to be "different" in order to stand the pressure of getting hard rubber pucks shot at them from all directions, at speeds that can exceed 160 km/hr. Not only that, but goaltenders have to live with the pressure of knowing they are the team's last line of defence — a mistake in goal costs more than a mistake anywhere else.

Terry Sawchuk, considered by many to be hockey's greatest goalie ever, was no exception. Particularly later in his career, his personality, combined with some difficult circumstances thrown at him by life, often made him appear a moody, unapproachable loner. His sudden and tragic death at the age of 40 only served to further the myth that grew up around the man who more than 30 years later continued to reign as the undisputed shutout king of the NHL His record of 115 shutouts (including 12 in the playoffs) may never be equaled.

Shut out king Terry Sawchuk.

Born in 1929 and raised in the Winnipeg suburb of East Kildonan, Sawchuk grew up listening to Foster Hewitt's radio broadcasts of Hockey Night in Canada and idolizing Toronto Maple Leafs' goalie George Hainsworth (whose NHL shutout record Sawchuk broke in 1964). When it came time for him to learn to play hockey, he naturally gravitated towards playing goal. Not only did his NHL hero play that position, but his older brother Mike, who had tragically died of a heart attack at age 17, was also a goalie.

As his skills grew, Sawchuk attracted the attention of NHL scouts, in his case representing the Detroit Red Wings. He eventually signed with Detroit, which at the time had one of the best player development systems in the league, headed up by the legendary Jack Adams.

While many players, goalies in particular, take some time to mature, Sawchuk showed that he was NHL caliber almost from the start. Playing at Detroit affiliates in the United States Hockey League and the next year in the American Hockey League, he won Rookie of the Year honours both times. When he was called up to the parent team for the 1950-51 season, he did it again, winning the Calder Trophy for the NHL's best rookie, and narrowly missing the Vezina Trophy as the league's best goaltender.

One of the things that set Sawchuk apart from his colleagues was his characteristic crouch in front of the net. A style eventually widely adopted, it enabled him to see the action better through a sea of legs, to block low shots without going down, and to manoeuvre faster. His lightning reflexes ensured that when he did go down, he was up again faster than anyone.

George Hainsworth

His unpredictable temperament also set him aside from his fellow players — literally. Starting off happy-go-lucky, he became less and less sociable as his career progressed, whether it was with his teammates, the media or his fans. Some traced the change in his personality back to a crash diet he was put on when he showed up 15 kg overweight to training camp in his second NHL year. Certainly the pressures of the job didn't help, especially when combined with his tendency to blame himself when the team performed poorly. Nor did his many injuries, which at various points in his career meant that he played countless nights in severe pain. He thought that short-term consolation might be found in drinking, but in the end alcohol also contributed to his problems. The net result was that even those who knew him well realized that he was better off left alone when a sour mood overtook him.

In all, Sawchuk played for five teams, but is best remembered for his exploits with Detroit and Toronto. With the Red Wings he was part of an indomitable team that won three Stanley Cups during his first five-year stint with the team — in 1952, 1954 and 1955. Sawchuk allowed fewer than two goals per game on average during that period, winning the Vezina Trophy three times.

Chicago Blackhawk, Glenn Hall.

Bill Durnan

Johnny Bower

It looked like the Red Wings, still a young team, could continue winning Cups for a few years to come. During the 1955 off-season, though, "Trader Jack" Adams inexplicably made deals for half of his winning combination. His reasons were open to question (as many did at the time), but it was undisputable that Sawchuk, who had considered himself a Red Wing for life, was unhappily sent to Boston.

The struggling Bruins hoped Sawchuk would help turn around the team, while adding to their box office appeal. Even though his heart was elsewhere, he obliged. His first season there was unremarkable, but in his second season, he had the best goals against average and the Bruins were leading the league almost midway through the year. Then Sawchuk contracted mononucleosis. After only two weeks recovery for a disease that normally requires at least six, he was back between the pipes. Whether it was due to management's pressure or Sawchuk's desire not to let his teammates down, he went back too early, as quickly became apparent. Rather than simply taking more rest, he blamed himself, and his self-esteem, fragile at the best of times, took a severe beating. Feeling he was washed up (a refrain that he repeated regularly in later years), he sank into despondency, and announced his decision to leave the team and hockey.

No one could persuade him to give Boston another chance, and after a while the team stopped trying. Happily for him, Adams wanted him back in Detroit, and made a deal with Boston. Back in his beloved Red Wings uniform, he played well, but lacked the powerful supporting cast that had powered his club to the Stanley Cup earlier in the decade. After a few years of rebuilding, though, they made it to the final several times in a losing cause — once against Chicago (1961) and twice against Toronto (1963 and 1964). In 1964, while Gordie Howe was breaking Maurice "Rocket" Richard's goal scoring record, Sawchuk quietly broke Hainsworth's shutout record.

Charlie Gardner

Despite his success, Detroit again let him go, this time by allowing Toronto to pick him up in the waiver draft. The Maple Leafs wanted to team Sawchuk up with Johnny Bower, feeling this would give them the strongest goaltending in the league. Both goalies were getting a little long in the tooth by this point, particularly since the lack of facemasks in those days made facial injuries more common. Sometimes it seemed like the Leafs needed both goalies just to have enough spare parts on hand to keep one of them healthy.

The Leafs failed to make the finals the next two years, although Bower and Sawchuk did win the Vezina Trophy together in 1965. The aging Leafs team had one last chance in the 1966-67 season. With the exception of a mid-season stretch Sawchuk and Bower seemed to coordinate their injuries so at least one of them was available to play. This continued in the playoffs, with Sawchuk playing most of the semi-final series because Bower was hurt. He shone for the entire series, including stopping 22 Chicago shots in the third period of Game Five alone. In the final against Montreal, the two split the duties, with Sawchuk stopping 40 shots in Game Six to bring the Stanley Cup back to Toronto for what would be the last time in the century.

Had Sawchuk retired at this point, his story might have had a happier ending. But the league was expanding, and the Los Angeles Kings offered him $41,000 to keep playing (he had been used to toiling for $18,000).

Tony Esposito recorded 15 shutouts in his rookie season — and won both the Calder and Vezina trophies.

Patrick Roy

With riches like these available, he picked up stakes and moved to California. Although he showed flashes of his old brilliance, his body just couldn't keep up to the pace any more.

From Los Angeles he had another quick stint in Detroit, and then went to the New York Rangers. In both his last two assignments he was clearly seen as a backup goalie and mentor to the team's first-string goalie.

It was only a matter of time before Sawchuk would be forced to retire, but fate took a hand in the matter. Barely two weeks after the Rangers were knocked unceremoniously out of the playoffs, he got into a violent argument with Ron Stewart, a former Leafs teammate now also with the Rangers. Both were drinkers, and both had bad tempers when under the influence. While at a Long Island bar, Stewart confronted his teammate about expenses and work that needed to be done in the house the two shared. The quarrel escalated into a fight that continued after they left the bar and went home. During the tussle, the two fell, and Sawchuk's stomach hit either Stewart's knee or a nearby barbecue grill heavily. He was taken to hospital in agony, but several surgeries couldn't repair damage to his gall bladder and liver. Just over a month later, on May 31, 1970, the great, but troubled goalie died. ❧

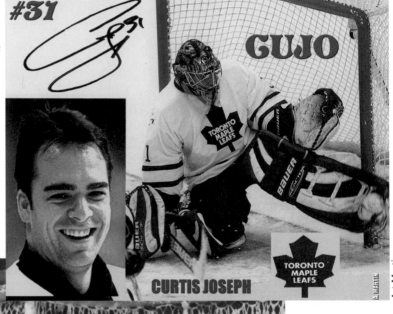

CURTIS JOSEPH

Jacques Plante

F o o t b a l l

The Lansdowne Park "Duck"

The late Geoff Crain has the distinction of being the very first Canadian quarterback drafted in Canadian professional football. Both Winnipeg Blue Bombers and Toronto Argonauts claimed him in the early '50s. The McGill College starting quarterback elected to play for Winnipeg and was understudy to "Indian Jack" Jacobs.

Playing with the Blue Bombers, he completed 20 of 43 passes for four touchdowns before being traded to his hometown Ottawa. It was not the era of Canadian born quarterbacks and the Rough Riders used him for punt returns. Playing at quarterback, he completed 10 of 22 passes for two TDs — both by Hall of Famer and Schenley Award winning end, Bobbie Simpson.

Geoff Crain's best known pass happened on October 24, 1959, during a game at Ottawa's Lansdowne Park between Ottawa and Toronto. His clandestine throw was carried out with military precision and willing accomplices.

Dave Wright, founder and owner of The Snow Goose crafts shop on Sparks Street provided a dead Mallard he bagged hunting at Montebello. Gerry O'Flanagan, former Argo, then an Ottawa TV sportscaster, and the late great sportswriter Eddie McCabe outfitted Geoff with an empty typewriter case and a Press Box pass.

Pat MacAdam

Geoff was at the game with his parents, Ed (The Colonel) and Louise, and he excused himself, made his way to the Press Box, then outside in pouring rain and up a ladder onto the roof of the covered stands.

The only other person on the roof was a motion picture cameraman who was filming official game footage. When he first saw Geoff Crain he thought he had a "jumper" on the roof with him. When he saw Geoff produce the dead duck he knew for sure he was in the presence of madness.

The late Lee Snelling was the Official Timer. Ottawa's great Hall of Famer and All-Star, lineman Kaye Vaughan, was in on the caper. Kaye Vaughan later married Olympic skier Lucile Wheeler and he wrote from their home in the Eastern Townships: "Big Lee was up on his chair with his blank pistol raised and then came the shot. The duck came plummeting down from the roof and landed with a thud on the pavement beside Lee Snelling."

Bobbie Simpson, who now lives in retirement in Ottawa, recalls "it was the last play of the quarter on our own 45-yard line. I was in the three-point stance but I was watching the roof. So was Kaye. I didn't see the duck land because by that time I got knocked flat on my ass by an Argonaut. I looked over after I picked myself up off the ground and saw the duck about 10 feet in from the sidelines. I got up and went down again in the mud and rolled over laughing."

General Highlights

1954

Bill 475, "An Act to Repeal the *National Physical Fitness Act*," passed through Parliament, removing Government responsibility for issues "of a sporting nature."

1955

Marilyn Bell became the youngest person, at 17, to swim the English Channel. The same year, her coach, Gus Ryder (who also coached world marathon champion Cliff Lumsdon), was named Canada's "Man of the Year."

1959

Keith Waples became the first Canadian to drive a Canadian-bred trotter to a two-minute mile on Canadian soil.

1959

Harry Jerome of Vancouver tied the world 100m record of 10.0 seconds, a record that stood until 1968.

1947-1958

Trev Deely competed in numerous motorcycle races, winning many and setting track records in the process. He was a three-time competitor in the 200 mile road race in Daytona Beach, Florida, riding a Harley-Davidson. In 1972 he was given the rights to distribute Harley-Davidson products in Canada, and was the first Canadian appointed to the Board of Directors for Harley-Davidson. He was inducted into the Canadian Motor Sports Hall of Fame in 1995.

1959

Vancouver's Stan Leonard was named the World Golfer of the Year.

1961

Bill 475, which had eliminated the federal government's role in sport in 1954 was rescinded, as the "*Fitness and Amateur Sport Act*" was passed by Parliament. The new Act outlined federal involvement in the development and promotion of fitness and amateur sport in Canada. The first Fitness and Amateur Sport Directorate was formed shortly thereafter.

1962

No official international matches were played during Canada's 1962 rugby tour to Great Britain, and the win-loss record was less than flattering. A 3-3 draw with the mighty Barbarians, however, remained as one of the highlights of Canada's rugby history. Captained by D.L. "Buzz" Moore, who played in all 16 of the tour matches, the Canadians braved the mud and the rain at Gosforth. One reporter said it was the worst conditions in the area since World War I. Moore, who was invited to become an honourary Barbarian at the evening dinner, became the first player born and raised in Canada to join this world-renowned club. (Grahame Budge, who was born in Manitoba, had been named a Barbarian in 1950, but he grew up and learned to play rugby in Scotland, also playing on that country's national team.)

1962, Donald Jackson performed the first-ever triple Lutz in competition at the World Figure Skating Championships in Prague, Czechoslovakia, en route to becoming the first Canadian male to win the world championship.

Two weeks after Canada's tie with the Barbarians, though, the Wales Under-23 squad shut Canada out 23-0. Buzz Moore was again feted by his competitors and was carried off the Cardiff Arms pitch on the shoulders of his opponents as the band played and the crowd sang "Alouette."

1962

The outstanding brother and sister pair, Maria and Otto Jelinek, immigrated to Canada in 1951 and joined the Oakville Skating Club. Overcoming some severe injuries, they became the 1961 and 1962 Canadian pairs champions, and claimed the 1961 North American pairs title. A dedication to excellence and drive for perfection led them to the world stage, where they became bronze medallists at the 1957 and 1958 World Figure Skating Championships and silver medallists in 1960. In 1962 they won the World Figure Skating Pairs title, coincidentally in their native Prague.

1963

17-year old Nancy McCredie broke the Canadian women's shot put record by an incredible 10 feet.

Hervé Filion from Anger, Quebec, was one of North America's all-time great harness drivers. His highlights are numerous, and include:

- 1968 – being the top North American harness driver with 407 wins
- 1970 – winning his first world harness racing championship
- 1971 – being the top North American driver
- 1972 – setting a money-winning world record in Harness Racing with 605 wins in the year as the top North American driver
- 1974 – being the top North American driver for the fourth time
- 1970-76 – six times as the North American leading money winner in harness racing — '70, '71, '72, 73, '74, '76

Kaye Vaughan recalls that the crowd reaction was quite interesting: "Spectators in the Old Stands were particularly quiet at this point. Then, as word spread from those who actually saw the duck fall and could appreciate the situation the quiet turned to a buzzing. After about 20 seconds had elapsed the entire stands erupted in laughter and guffaws. By this time, all of the 14,696 fans were collapsing with laughter — with the possible exception of Lee Snelling. The laughter rolled across the field like a wave."

When Geoff returned to his seat the first thing his mother said to him was: "Geoff, do you know that some silly bastard just threw a dead duck off the roof?"

"The Colonel" just looked at Geoff and managed a knowing smile. ❧

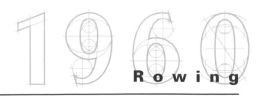

1960

R o w i n g

Can Frank Read's Oarsmen Outrace the World – Again?

by Ray Gardner
July 2, 1960

Driving his crews like galley slaves, UBC's rowing coach has twice turned gangs of green kids into international champions, almost overnight. This summer, at Rome, he may do the impossible for the third time.

During the past ten years, while most other Canadian athletes have hardly made the grade as even second-rate contenders in international competition, rowing crews from the University of British Columbia have won a secure place among the world's best oarsmen.

The young rowers from UBC have swept to victories in the Olympic and British Empire Games and once came close to winning their sport's supreme prize, the Grand Challenge Cup of England's Royal Regatta at Henley-on-Thames.

Their record is all the more remarkable because part of it has been achieved in competition against United States crews from colleges that spend lavish sums to provide the finest coaches and equipment and boathouses where the oarsmen may live while in training.

In contrast, rowing, until recently, had always been a neglected sport at UBC. Six years ago the university spent only a few hundred dollars on rowing and even now spends only six thousand, less than a tenth of what is spent by some US colleges.

UBC doesn't even have its own boathouse. The crews must travel from the campus right across Vancouver to use the facilities of the Vancouver Rowing Club. When they were training for the 1956 Olympics, UBC oarsmen lived for a time in a condemned house and worked as laborers to pay the rent.

The university has no paid rowing coach but depends upon the voluntary efforts of Frank Read, a prosperous, forty-nine-year-old Vancouver hotel owner.

In the ten years since he took on the job, Read has proven that money couldn't buy a better coach. It took him four years to learn how to coach and to produce his first champions, an eight-oared crew that won a gold medal at the 1954 British Empire Games. Since then, seven other UBC crews have finished either first or second in top-flight international competition.

Bob Osborne, the University of British Columbia's physical-education director, describes the record compiled by Read's rowers as "almost unrivaled in the annals of amateur sport in Canada."

BCSHOF

Robert Bédard was Canada's top-ranked male tennis player between 1956 and 1965 and he was only a few times ranked lower than third between 1952 and 1970. Bédard won the Canadian international singles tennis title in 1955, 1956 and 1958 and the doubles crown in 1955, 1957 and 1959. He represented Canada in Davis Cup play between 1953-1961, playing 31 singles and doubles matches.

"It has been accomplished," he says, "by hard work and the sheer force of Frank's personality."

Read's great achievement came when he took two crews to the 1956 Olympics in Melbourne and brought back a gold and a silver medal. Canada won only two gold medals during the entire games.

The UBC four-without-coxswain swept to three victories in three races. In every race its margin of victory was so great none of the rival crews appears in any picture taken near the finish line. In the final, they beat the United States by five lengths. (In this event one of the four rowers, in place of a cox, steers the boat.)

Read's eight-oared crew lost to the United States in its final race by only half a length.

The victory of the coxless four caused a sensation. Three of the crew were raw beginners who had never rowed a shell until nine months before the Olympics. The fourth man had only three month's more experience, none of it gained in first-class competition.

When Read told a French newspaperman at Melbourne that the four had been trained in only a few months, the Frenchman said, bluntly, "*C'est impossible.*"

"Of course it was impossible," says Read. "I think it was the most phenomenal effort ever made in international athletic competition. At least I don't know of any parallel."

David Helliwell, a young Vancouver accountant who rowed in Read's Olympic eight, says, "He is a strict disciplinarian. He allows no talking, no gum-chewing in his boat. He'll tolerate no dramatics at the end of a race, no collapsing over the oars. Everyone must sit up straight, as though the race were only beginning."

The boys who have rowed under him, and even older men who have worked with him, idolize Read. They all picture him as the hard-bitten coach with a heart of gold. On the water, they say, he is strict and tough but never unfair or tyrannical. Away from the water, they insist, he is a kind and sympathetic friend.

After the Olympics, Read retired from rowing to attend to his hotel business and was succeeded by John Warren, one of the boys he'd taught to row. Warren took three crews to the 1958 Empire Games in Wales and won a gold medal and two silver medals. Last year, David Helliwell coached a UBC eight that placed second in the Pan-American Games at Chicago.

Now Read has come back for a second crack at the Olympics. But, he insists, it is not for Olympic medals alone that he drives his boys to such extremes.

His philosophy is that through rowing a boy may, as he expresses it, "discover himself."

"All of us," he explains, "have more courage and more capacity for understanding and developing than we ever call upon. By demanding the supreme effort from these boys, I believe they will discover these latent forces and thus be able to drive themselves to the supreme effort in everything they undertake in life. ❦

Highlights

General Highlights

1964

Joe Kapp was the only man in the modern era to play quarterback in a Rose Bowl game, Grey Cup Championship and a Super Bowl. Kapp quarterbacked the Grey Cup Champion 1964 BC Lions, and also played for the Minnesota Vikings, setting a record as the last NFL quarterback in the century to throw seven touchdowns in a single game.

1966

Harry Jerome tied the world 100-yard mark of 9.1 seconds.

1966

Barrie Burnham, playing for his club Meralomas, established a world rugby record when he scored in every possible way during one match (for which he has mention in the Guinness Book of World Records).

1967

The long-discussed *Canada Games* finally became a reality when the first *Canada Winter Games* were held in Quebec City. The first *Summer Canada Games* were held in Halifax in 1969.

1968

The Air Canada Silver Broom replaced the Scotch Cup, emblematic of the World Curling Championship. Canada won the first five Air Canada Silver Brooms.

Doug Sturrock

Johnny Bright

The powerful fullback gained 10,909 yards in 13 CFL seasons with Calgary and Edmonton. He was top rusher in the West four times, a Western All-Star seven times and the Most Outstanding Player in the CFL once. Along with Jackie Parker and Normie Kwong, he led the Eskimo charge to three straight Grey Cup wins in the mid-1950s.

John Barrow

In 14 years with the Tiger Cats, John Barrow earned All-Star status 16 times. For four consecutive years, from 1957 to 1960, he was an All-Star Tackle on offence and defence. He helped Hamilton to nine Grey Cup Games and in 1962 he was selected as the CFL's top lineman.

Jackie Parker

"Ole Spaghetti Legs" starred for the Edmonton Eskimos from 1954 to 1962, the Argos from 1963 to 1965 and BC Lions from 1966 to 1968. He played on three Grey Cup winners with Edmonton, won the Schenley as the CFL's top player three times, and was an All-Star for eight straight years. He scored 750 points in his career, including a dramatic 84-yard touchdown run in the 1954 Grey Cup game.

Norm Fieldgate

Norm Fieldgate played for the BC Lions from their birth in 1954 to 1967, and was the lone original Lion to celebrate the club's first Grey Cup victory in 1964. An All-Canadian once and All-Western All-Star three times, he played more than 200 games as offensive and defensive end.

Ken Ploen

Kenny Ploen played 11 seasons with the Winnipeg Blue Bombers, making six Grey Cup finals, and winning four. He was a Western All-Star quarterback in 1957 and 1965 and an All-Canadian in 1965.

Earl Lunsford

The "Earthquake" played six seasons for the Calgary Stampeders and became the first player in the history of pro football to rush for a mile in one season (1,794 yards in 1961).

"Ole Spaghetti Legs," Jackie Parker above and lower left.

1954-1955-1956

Grey Cups
The Montreal Alouettes and the Edmonton Eskimos played three straight Grey Cups, with Sam "The Rifle" Etcheverry and Jackie Parker quarterbacking their respective clubs. The Eskimos won each encounter.

Ed McQuarters, 1960s-70s

Ed McQuarters played with Saskatchewan from 1966 to 1974, making the CFL and Western All-Star teams in 1967, '68 and '69, and winning the Schenley Award Winner as Most Outstanding Lineman in 1967. In a home workshop accident in the winter of 1971 he lost his left eye, but courageously returned to action in August later that year to play four more seasons.

Bronco Nagurski, 1950s-60s
Perhaps the best football name of the century, and the player was good too.

Bill Symons

Bill Symons played from 1966 to 1973, mostly with the Toronto Argonauts. In 1968, he became the first Argo to rush for over 1,000 yards (1,107 yards on 164 carries for nine touchdowns).

Wayne Harris

For 11 consecutive seasons, from 1961 to 1972, the Calgary middle linebacker was a Western Conference All-Star in the CFL. He was an All-Canadian eight times. After losses in two Grey Cup appearances, Harris was named the game's MVP in 1971 — the year Calgary won.

Bill Baker

The "Undertaker" was known for his ferocious pass rush. He was named to the CFL All-Star team four times, All-Western team five times, played in the Grey Cup in 1969 and 1972 and was named the Outstanding Defensive Player in 1976. Baker played with the Saskatchewan Roughriders in 1968-73, with the BC Lions from 1974-76, and again with the Roughies in 1977-78.

Jim Corrigall

Jim Corrigall played his entire career (1970-1981) with the Toronto Argonauts. Corrigall was an Eastern All-Star as a defensive end eight times and was also honoured four times as a CFL All-Star. His best season was in 1975, when he was chosen the Most Outstanding Defensive Player in the league and was the Argonauts' nominee for Most Outstanding Player and Canadian.

Dave Fennell

"Doctor Death" was a leading force with the Edmonton Eskimos' defensive line from 1974 to 1983. He was one of the leaders on the team that won five consecutive Grey Cups from 1978 to 1982 as well as one in 1975. He was the Defensive Star of the 1978 Grey Cup, and the Defensive and Canadian Star of the 1982 Championship. He was a CFL and Western All-Star at defensive tackle from 1977 to 1981 and the Most Outstanding Defensive Player in 1978. Fennell won the Most Outstanding Canadian Award in 1979.

Peter Dalla Riva

Peter Dalla Riva played 14 seasons with the Montreal Alouettes from 1968 to 1981 at tight end. He led the team in receiving during five of those seasons and became the franchise's all-time leader in touchdown catches. He was an All-Star in 1972, 1975 and 1976, and played in six Grey Cup games, winning three. In 1981, the Montreal franchise retired his number 74.

Al Wilson

Al Wilson played 15 years with the BC Lions from 1972 to 1986 as a guard and centre. He was an All-Western All-Star and All-Canadian All-Star for seven consecutive years from 1975 to 1981. He was voted the Most Outstanding Offensive Lineman in 1977. Wilson participated in Grey Cup games in 1983 and 1985, winning the championship in his second try.

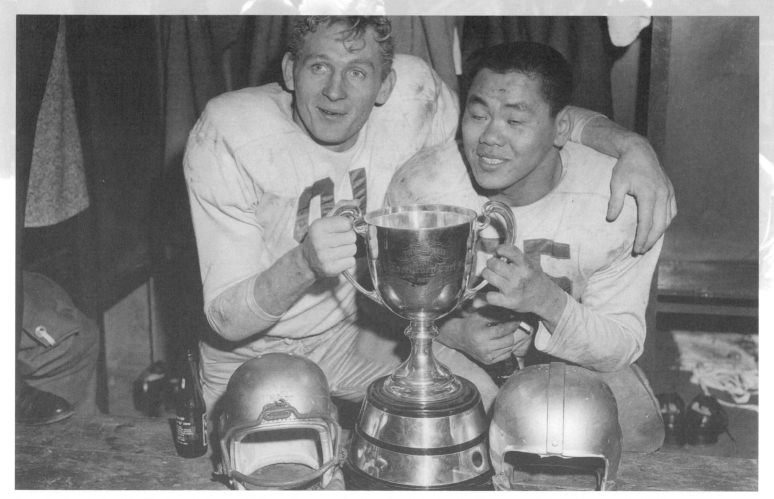

Quarterback Jackie Parker, left, and his stalwart running back Normie Kwong of the Edmonton Eskimos share a drink from the Grey Cup, 1955. They would team up to share three consecutive Grey Cup drinks, in 1954, 1955 and 1956.

1962

F o o t b a l l

December 1 & 2, 1962

Exhibition Stadium, Toronto
The Grey Cup game that lasted two days

The 1962 Fog Bowl

It was almost the Grey Cup that wasn't. What a world war couldn't stop in the 1940s, a pea soup fog almost did in 1962, as Canadian Football League Commissioner Sydney Halter wrestled with his options. On the field the Winnipeg Blue Bombers and Hamilton Tiger Cats played one of the better games in the Cup's history, though few could see it.

Faced with the likelihood of stopping the December 1 game and resuming it the next day, Halter finally declared, "If play is started Sunday it will be finished regardless of the weather. But if it is impossible to start, I intend to recommend to the league executive that the game remain unfinished and declared no contest."

While climatic conditions could be blamed for much of that Saturday's fog, at least some was owed to Tiger Cat coach Jim Trimble who, when asked what his pre-game strategy was, replied, "You want me to keep telling people we'll beat them, but I won't. We intend to waffle'em." No one was ever quite sure what he meant, but whatever it was it obviously didn't work.

Before over 32,000 fans at Toronto's Exhibition Stadium as well as a continent-wide television audience watching across Canada and the United States, the game had plenty of thrills. Garney Henley ran 74 yards for an early Hamilton lead but ominously Don Sutherin missed the extra point. Early in the second quarter Leo Lewis capped an 83-yard Blue Bomber drive and Gerry James's point after gave Winnipeg a 7-6 lead.

Regina-born James was one of that era's outstanding two-sport stars having spent several previous seasons with hockey's Toronto Maple Leafs beginning in 1954. He was still active in Saskatchewan's senior hockey league in 1972.

Lewis and Henley, who starred on both offence and defence, led the two teams. They exchanged touchdowns as the fog continued to swirl in the stadium. Down 28-26 in the fourth quarter, the Tiger Cats moved into field goal position but again Sutherin kicked wide for a single point. Shortly after the missed field goal, the fog took over completely, obscuring the scoreboard from view. There really was no choice but to stop the game.

Halter's earlier indecision on the game's fate was blamed on the presence of American broadcasters but such criticism was tempered by his recognition that many westerners who'd come east by train could not stay for Sunday's resumption.

The game resumed under clear skies and before only 15,000 fans able to return on Sunday for the final nine minutes and 29 seconds. Hamilton, led by backup quarterback Frank Cosentino, moved the ball into good field position several times. Penalties and bad decisions prevented them from getting at least the one point that would have necessitated a repeat of the previous season's overtime.

Winnipeg won 28-27, capturing its fourth Grey Cup in five years. ❧

November 30, 1963

Grey Cup

Angelo Mosca of the Hamilton Tiger Cats hit BC's star running back, Willie Fleming, "apparently" out of bounds, but no call was made. Fleming, however, had to leave the game and the Cats went on to win the Cup.

CFHOF

Canada

Our
Century
in Sport

Football

Russ Jackson

**Quarterback — Ottawa Rough Riders
1958-1969**

In a league that relies heavily on imported American players in certain positions, Russ Jackson was most likely the best, and sadly the last good, Canadian-born quarterback to play in the Canadian Football League. Jackson had an outstanding 12-year career with the Ottawa Rough Riders, culminating in three Grey Cup victories.

Following a stellar collegiate career with his hometown McMaster Marauders in Hamilton, Jackson agreed to sign with Ottawa's Rough Riders after negotiating his own contract, itself a rare occurrence at the time let alone what he negotiated: a $4500 base salary, a $500 signing bonus and an open plane ticket back and forth from Ottawa to Toronto in order to complete his teaching certificate at the Ontario College of Education.

Fears that a Canadian-bred quarterback would not be capable of leading a modern football team were quickly put to rest. Jackson, under the leadership of experienced CFL coach Frank Clair, proved himself to be one of the best quarterbacks in the CFL … for the century.

Perhaps Jackson's most outstanding moment was also his last — winning the 1969 Grey Cup and being selected the game's MVP. Jackson had announced his retirement prior to the game and was determined to go out with a memorable performance. He did just that, leading the Riders to a 29-11 win over the Roughriders from Saskatchewan. Jackson routinely mixed runs and passes to keep the hard-charging western Roughies off balance for most of the day. His running and scrambling ability seemed to wear out the Saskatchewan defenders, and on one memorable manouevre, he side-stepped and ducked Ed McQuarters, turning a sure loss into a large touchdown gain by dumping a short pass to an open Ron Stewart. Jackson would end the day with 13 completions for 254 yards, four touchdowns and very importantly, no interceptions. He also scrambled for 31 yards on five rushes.

In 1960, Jackson had beaten out Ron Lancaster for the Ottawa starting QB position, and it was the same Lancaster whom Jackson met on the field for his last game in 1969. Said Lancaster in defeat: "He just went out in an unbelievable way. For most of us the end comes when they throw you out, boo you out or your body gives out. He goes out with everything — there's nothing left for him to win."

In an era when CFL stars routinely worked at other jobs in the off-season, Russ Jackson had pursued a teaching career while playing. When he retired from football he continued teaching, eventually becoming a high school principal. ❧

Russ Jackson, Career Highlights

1960, '68, '69
Grey Cup Champion

1966
Grey Cup Finalist

1963, '66, '69
Schenley Award
for Most Outstanding Player

1959, '63, '66, '69
Schenley Award
for Most Outstanding Canadian

1973
Inducted into
the Canadian Football Hall of Fame

1969
Canada's Athlete of the Year
(Lou Marsh Trophy)

Member of the Order of Canada

1966, '68, '69
Quarterbacked the CFL All-Star Team

1962, '63, '66, '67, '68, '69
Six time Eastern Division All-Star

1963, '64, '65, '66, '67
Five-time Passing Yards Leader (season)

1963, '66, '67, '69
Four-time Pass Attempt Leader (season)

First All-time Leader Most Passing
Touchdowns, Grey Cup Game: **4**

Tied for First All-time Leader Most
Passing Touchdowns, Grey Cup: **8**

Highlights

Canada's Sports Hall of Fame

1930s to 1980s

Herman Smith "Jackrabbit" Johannsen was born in Norway but settled in Canada after World War I. He eventually moved to Piedmont, Quebec, located in the Laurentian mountains. In 1932 he began spreading ski trails across the Laurentians. It was members of the Cree and Ojibway tribes that gave him the nickname "Jackrabbit." In 1979, at the age of 104 he became involved with the Jackrabbit Ski League, a nationwide ski program started in his honour. He has been the subject of several documentaries as well as a book titled Jackrabbit-his first one hundred years.

Father David Bauer

"Jackrabbit" Johannsen

1960s

Father David Bauer — Born into a Kitchener, Ontario, hockey family, the speedy left winger was a member of the Oshawa team that won the 1943 Memorial Cup. Bauer gave up his big league aspirations and joined the priesthood, also turning his talents to coaching. Holding fast to the belief that hockey players should not have to give up their pursuit of education in order to play high calibre hockey, Bauer conceived the idea of a national team composed of university players based at one school. He coached this team from 1964 to 1969.

1979

Soccer has always been highly popular in BC In 1979 the Vancouver Whitecaps of the NASL won the league championship, and over 100,000 fans turned out for the team victory party in Robson Square.

1960s

Doug Rogers was one of Canada's most successful judo competitors. In 1964 he won a national title and captured a silver medal at the Olympics. The following year he won a bronze medal at the World Championships. His success continued at the 1967 Pan-Am Games, where he earned both gold and silver medals. Rogers than turned to coaching others in his beloved sport. He guided the UBC Judo team to Western Canada university titles in 1975, 1976 and 1977. Perhaps Rogers' most unique achievement was in Japan where he became the first-ever Caucasian to captain an all Japanese team.

Jocelyn Lovell

1970s

Colourful and sometimes controversial, Jocelyn Lovell was primarily responsible for bringing Canadian cycling back into the international limelight. In a career that spanned 20 years he won more than 40 Canadian titles at varying distances. He turned the 1974 Canadian championships into a one man show by sweeping nearly every event from the sprints to the 102 mile road race. His greatest success came at the 1978 Commonwealth Games in Edmonton, where he won three gold medals all in Games record times. Later the same year he won a silver medal at the World Cycling Championships.

1980s

Michelle Cameron began her synchronized swimming career in 1976 with her hometown Calgary Aquabelles. From 1981 to 1988 the Calgary team won six of eight national championships. In 1983 Cameron was a member of the Canadian team that swam before an IOC committee in Los Angeles and at the Pan Pacific games in Australia to gain full acceptance for synchronized swimming as an Olympic sport. The highlight of Cameron's career was her gold medal performance with Carolyn Waldo in the duet event at the 1988 Olympics.

Vancouver's Doug Rogers, Judo 1964 Olympic Silver medallist.

Gordie Howe

Eulogies for Each Other

by Bobby Orr
November, 1971

I find it tough to talk about Gordie. What can you say? He was just a fantastic hockey player. He did everything exceptionally well. You hear a lot about him, you could watch him on TV, but you had to watch this man *play* the game to really appreciate him. The things he did, a lot of people wouldn't even notice them.

Like wandering around the net. Whenever he was around the net he'd start taking guys out all by himself. He knew one of his men might have the puck so he'd just take you out of the play. Suddenly you'd look up and see one of his guys coming in on the net and you couldn't do anything about it because Gordie'd moved you out of the way. A lot of guys do that but when you're talking about Gordie, well, Gordie did it well.

Floral Saskatchewan native and Detroit hockey legend, Gordie Howe.

Gordie was fast. You watch a rookie, a young player: he does a lot of skating he doesn't have to do. Gordie only skated when he had to. Other than that he just paced himself. When he had to he skated fast. A rookie skates fast all the time. Gordie knew when to go and when not to go. That's just being smart. You get tired out too fast. I'm sure he'd slowed down a little from his prime — I wish I could have played with him, just to have seen him 13 years ago — but I remember an afternoon game in Boston. I was piddling around our end and as I crossed the blue line Gordie came from nowhere, he must have come from behind me, and poke-checked the puck off me and one of his teammates picked it up and went for a goal. He's an amazing guy.

Some hockey players mature late. The play-making, the big fakes, the things that make the game exciting to watch — they do it later. But Gordie, Gordie played that way for 25 years and still had it coming. An old fox doesn't forget, and Gordie never forgot. You'd watch him in a game when the other team had just scored a go-ahead goal in their favour. They were hot. The pace was picking up. And Gordie would say to himself, "The pace has got to slow down," and he'd take the puck and mess around, and the other team would cool off. And he'd done what he wanted to do. He'd put out the fire. He did that pretty well, too.

In my first year in the National Hockey League we were playing Detroit and I had a habit — I still have it but then it was really bad — of making a pass and then watching it. "Look at the pretty pass." Anyway, I was going in behind the Detroit net, this game, and I threw the puck out on one side and I was watching it as I came around the other side and Gordie came across and gave me — this was my first lesson — a good shot. Someone told me later, I don't know whether it was true, that he had read that Gordie said he just wanted to let me know he was still around.

He was a tough son of a moose, but he had to be. Guys are always trying to make reputations for themselves, they've got to run the big guys, so Gordie was the man they tried. I'm sure he threw the odd elbow but he wasn't a dirty player the way people say. There's a story about how Gordie and Carl Brewer were lying on the ice, holding each other during a fight. It was Brewer's first year in the league, and Howe is supposed to have said to him, "Look, in this league when two players are holding each other like this they both let go." So Brewer let go and Howe is supposed to have punched him. That's the story but I don't believe it. There are bound to be stories about a player like Gordie. Besides, he didn't have to do that kind of thing. He could let you go and still give it to you.

A player will be remembered for being a great stickhandler or maybe he added something to the game, like when a defenceman falls to block shots. There's no way Gordie will be remembered for just one thing. Gordie will be remembered as the greatest hockey player. He did everything. You just didn't know what the man was going to do. It's just incredible. One time he'd be coming in on you and he'd make a certain move, so you'd watch for it the next time. But the next time he'd do something else. He had a whole bag of tricks. The thing with Gordie is that he was a perfect athlete.

A lot of people don't understand hockey players. They think we're different. People write me about how much money I make. They'll say, "Who do you think you are, asking for x number of dollars a year? I thought you played for the love of the game." If I didn't like the game, I wouldn't play it. But hockey is my trade. It's how I make my living. During the season that's all we do, that's all we eat, that's all we drink is hockey. A great hockey player like Gordie, a real professional, he's just a car mechanic. You take a car in, 1,400 car mechanics can't figure out what's wrong with it, except this one guy, who's a good mechanic, who's good at his job, who really studies his job.

But Gordie is a professional off the ice, too. I don't know, he was so great maybe this didn't happen to him, but there are days when you're so tired and everything that you just want to walk away from people. They expect so much of you — "He shouldn't smoke, he shouldn't drink, he shouldn't stay out after ten o'clock at night . . ." It's unfair, and there's the odd day when they just don't know when to leave you alone, so maybe you ignore them and they don't like it. But Gordie was so good to people, especially kids. And his family — I think I met Mrs. Howe in my second year in the league and I met the kids in my third year and they're just the greatest family. His kids are so polite. I had only met Mrs. Howe once and a few years ago I was walking with my bags through the airport in Montreal for an all-star game or something and a lady yelled at

me, "Hey Bob, how are you?" At first I didn't recognize her but it was Mrs. Howe. It's just a fantastic family.

The finest athlete of them all — that's what Gordie is. And when I say athlete I'm talking about *any* sport. Take everything into consideration: his age, his record, his condition. There are some pretty good athletes around, great boxers, great football players, everything, but Gordie is in a league by himself. I'd be proud to be half the man on or off the ice that Gordie is. Here's a guy, he played professional hockey for 25 years, he was 43 years old, and he still ran the game. I mean you can't say anything. The guy has got to be the greatest. He's *still* the greatest. The only thing is his wrist, it's bothering him. That's why he retired. Otherwise, he could have played till he was 50. He could. He's in that great shape! The son of a moose, he could have played till he was 50. And that would have been fine with me — as long as he sat out every game against Boston. ❧

Howe facing Toronto's Johnny Bower in the 1960s.

Gordie Howe Highlights

March 31, 1928

Gordie was born in Floral, Saskatchewan.

November 1, 1945

Gordie played his first professional hockey game at age 17, with the Omaha Knights of the United States Hockey League.

October 16, 1946

Gordie joined the NHL's Detroit Red Wings. He played against Toronto in his first of 1,767 games in the NHL. Wearing number 17, he got in two fights, and scored his first goal in a 3-3 tie. He started to wear his famous number 9 on October 29.

November 3, 1948

Gordie played in his first of an NHL-record 23 All-Star games.

March 28, 1950

In a playoff game against the Maple Leafs in Toronto, Gordie accidentally crashed into the boards head-first after missing a check on the Leafs' Teeder Kennedy, fracturing his skull. An emergency 90-minute operation to relieve pressure on his brain saved his life. His team went on to win the Stanley Cup on April 23. The next season Gordie showed those who recommended that he should leave the game that he was still the same player, winning the Art Ross Trophy as the league's leading scorer.

December 25, 1956

In his most prolific night of scoring, Gordie scored a hat-trick in both goals and assists, leading the Red Wings to an 8-1 victory over the New York Rangers.

November 28, 1957

Gordie got his 409th career assist, surpassing Montreal's Elmer Lach and making him the NHL's all-time assist leader.

January 16, 1960

In scoring a goal and an assist against the Blackhawks in his 888th career game, Gordie became the NHL's all-time scoring leader with 947 points, surpassing the great Maurice Richard.

November 27, 1960

Gordie became the first NHLer to score 1000 career points, playing in his 938th game. A year later on November 26, 1961, he became the first player to ever play 1000 NHL games.

November 10, 1963

Gordie became the NHL's all-time goal leader, again surpassing Maurice Richard, by scoring his 545th career goal against Montreal in a 3-0 Detroit win.

October 29, 1970

Gordie picked up two assists in a 5-3 Detroit win over the Bruins, becoming the NHL's first 1000-assist man.

February 18, 1971

Gordie scored his 20th goal of the season, a mark he reached an NHL record 22 consecutive years.

June 7, 1972

Gordie was elected to the Hockey Hall of Fame, but by June 5, 1973, he was persuaded to come out of retirement and play alongside sons Mark and Marty for the new WHA's Houston Areos.

April 21, 1978

Gordie's proudest moment may have occurred during a WHA game in Toronto. He scored a goal on the first shift after hearing he had become a grandfather for the first time, showing himself that he "...was not just old, but a good old."

April 6, 1980

After the WHA folded, four teams joined the NHL, with Gordie playing for Hartford. He scored his 801st, and last, NHL goal in a game appropriately played against the Detroit Red Wings.

April 11, 1980

After more than 30 years, Gordie played in his final NHL game ... at least for the century.

October 3, 1997

Just to prove how ageless he really was, Gordie suited up for one final professional hockey game, at least for the century, playing one shift with the Detroit Vipers of the International Hockey League. This made Howe the only player ever (and likely the only athlete ever) to play professionally in six decades — 1940s, 1950s, 1960s, 1970s, 1980s and 1990s.

SUMMARY:

- **NHL:**
  - 26 seasons
  - 1,767 games
  - 801 NHL goals
  - 1,049 assists
  - 1,850 points
  - 21 All-Star selections (12 on the first team)
  - 6 Art Ross Trophies (leading scorer)
  - 6 Hart Trophies (MVP)
- 33 professional hockey playing seasons (1 USHL, 26 NHL, 6 WHA)
- 160 points in 157 regular season and playoff WHA games
- 1967 Lester Patrick Award for outstanding service to hockey in the US
- Order of Canada

HHOF — Graphic Artists

January 4, 1954

The Montreal Canadiens' Bert Olmstead became only the second NHL player to score eight points in a single game. He registered four goals and four assists in a 12-1 victory over Chicago. The "Rocket" had been the first player to do so, 10 years earlier.

1954

The Soviet Union gave Canada the first of many shock treatments as the Soviet team trounced the Canadian senior team (Toronto East York Lyndhursts) 7-2 to win the World Championships.

March 10, 1955

The Zamboni made its NHL debut at Maple Leaf Gardens.

June 3, 1955

Terry Sawchuk, arguably the NHL's best goalie at the time, was traded from the Detroit Red Wings to the Boston Bruins. That spring, Detroit Manager "Trader" Jack Adams inexplicably traded all but nine of his players and Detroit's two-year run of Cups was over.

March, 1955

After winning the NHL's Hart Trophy and scoring or assisting on four of the six Leaf goals in a losing semi-final series against Detroit, Toronto's long-time captain Ted "Teeder" Kennedy retired. The Leafs also retired Kennedy's number 9 jersey.

1956

The Soviet Union beat Canada 2-0 in the medal round en route to its first Olympic gold medal. Canada, represented by the Kitchener-Waterloo Dutchmen, ended up with the bronze medal.

1956-1957

The Montreal Canadiens' power play was so potent that the league made a rule change to enable a penalized player to return to the ice if his team was scored upon while he was serving his penalty. The new rule remained through the century.

November 5, 1955

Jean Béliveau scored three times in 44 seconds for the second fastest hat trick in the century.

January 16, 1957

Terry Sawchuk walked out on the Boston Bruins midway through his only season there, citing mononucleosis. Sawchuk sat out the remainder of the season, to re-surface again the next season back with Detroit.

February 11, 1957

"Terrible Ted" Lindsay was elected the first president of the NHL players' association. Lindsay promptly got traded to the lowly Chicago Blackhawks. Facing intense pressure from owners, the fledgling players' association folded quickly.

October 19, 1957

The "Rocket" became the first NHL player to score 500 goals, scoring against Glenn Hall of the Chicago Blackhawks. Richard had also scored his 100th, 200th and 400th goals against Chicago netminders.

January 28, 1958

The country monitored the critical condition of Montreal's Bernie "Boom Boom" Geoffrion for 48 hours following his collapse at the Montreal Forum for a ruptured bowel. The star player recovered fully, though, scoring six goals in 10 playoff games later that season.

March 22, 1959

Montreal's Dickie Moore set an NHL scoring record with 96 points for the year, breaking Gordie Howe's 95-point record set in 1952-53.

1959-1960

Montreal won its fifth straight Stanley Cup, the only team to do so in the century.

HHOF — Turofsky Collection

1951

During his brief NHL career, rushing defenceman and Timmins, Ontario, native Bill Barilko won four Stanley Cups and played in three All-Star Games with the Toronto Maple Leafs. Yet it is his final goal that will always be remembered. In the first overtime period during the fifth game of the Stanley Cup finals against the Montreal Canadiens, with the Maple Leafs up three games to one (and three overtime victories to one!), Barilko rushed to the Montreal net.

Falling as he shot, he scored at the 2:53 mark of the first overtime, clinching Toronto's seventh Stanley Cup. As nice a goal as it was, what made it memorable, and tragic, was that it was Barilko's last. On August 26 of that year, a fishing plane carrying Barilko and a friend went missing in northern Ontario. No traces of the accident were found until 1962 — the next year Toronto won the Cup.

1930s

Renowned announcer Foster Hewitt cried out the names of the Toronto Maple Leafs "Kid Line" for years to hockey fans across the continent, making Charlie Conacher, Joe Primeau and Harvey "Busher" Jackson household names. The three jelled like few lines before them had, with Primeau leading the play with his slick stickhandling, often passing off to either Conacher to launch one of his wicked shots, or to the ever-flashy Jackson to slide the puck softly into the net.

HHOF — Turofsky Collection

Hockey

Dr. Jekyll and Mr. Hull

by Jack Batten
March, 1973

Bobby Hull felt lousy. He was sitting slack and tired against the rich grey upholstery in the back seat of Ben Hatskin's black Lincoln Continental. Hatskin, president of the Winnipeg Jets and Hull's boss, was behind the steering wheel, guiding the car with one nonchalant hand through the brilliant cold winter noon in downtown Winnipeg.

Hatskin wheeled the Continental into the driveway of the Fort Garry Hotel. Handshakers ringed around Hull in the hotel lobby, businessmen who showed him big grins and admiring deference. There was another emotion at work, too, something like gratitude. "Thanks for coming to Winnipeg, Bobby," one man said.

Bobby Hull, the Golden Jet.

HHOF/O-PEE-CHEE

The businessmen belonged to the Kiwanis Club, and Hull was a head-table guest at their luncheon meeting.

The luncheon's advertised speakers took their turns at the microphone, three Kiwanians, including the Lieutenant-Governor, who reminisced for 15 minutes each about their trip to Moscow during the Canada-Russia hockey series. "The Russians," one of them said, "seem to enjoy their regimentation." The three finished and the president asked Hull for a few words. He hadn't expected to speak, and for a moment, as he stood up, he looked touchingly vulnerable.

The moment of vulnerability passed in a hurry. Hull talked for 15 minutes. He was relaxed, funny and frank, neither a dumb jock nor a smart-ass jock. He told the audience that Harry Sinden had phoned him in August to say he was on Team Canada but that the NHL owners later overruled Sinden. He sank a shaft into Al Eagleson, whom Hull clearly doesn't like, referring to him as a Judas character. He said Team Canada might not have won the series "if they hadn't crippled Kharmalov who always controlled the play when he was out there." And he ended, dramatically timed, on a ringing climax: "You people have been overdue for pro hockey for too damn long, and I'm proud to be a part of the Jets." The Kiwanians rose and cheered.

The two men who organized the WHA, Gary Davidson, a lawyer from Santa Ana, California, and Dennis Murphy, a marketing executive from Fullerton, California, warmed up for the job by starting the American Basketball Association.

"Except nobody took us seriously," says Winnipeg's Ben Hatskin. "Not until we signed Bobby."

Hatskin worked out the deal with Hull: one million dollars out front, another million in Hull's bank account by December 1, 1972, a third million over the next 10 years for services as left winger, coach, and, not the least, public relations man. "So," Hatskin explains, "at the next owners' meeting I told them the whole league was gonna benefit — right? — and everyone should throw in for the front million dollars." Which is why the huge blow-up of the Hull payment hanging in the Jets offices shows the crucial cheque to be drawn on the account of WHA Properties Limited.

But will the WHA last?

Back on the farm near Belleville, Ontario.

Bobby Hull

Before making his dramatic jump to the WHA in 1972, "Golden Jet" Bobby Hull won the NHL scoring title playing for the Chicago Blackhawks three times, the Hart trophy as the league's most valuable player twice, and the Lady Byng trophy for sportsmanship once. In 16 NHL seasons the left-winger scored 610 regular-season goals, 62 playoff goals and totalled almost 1300 points.

"Last?" says Ben Hatskin. "Why else spend millions on Bobby Hull?"

Five thousand, one hundred and five people showed up for the Jets game against Los Angeles on the night, a Tuesday, of the Kiwanis luncheon.

The game was a laugher, 8-0 Jets. The level of play was often closer to senior amateur than to NHL professional. And most of the evening's entertainment value came in those moments when Hull powered his slap shots, when Hull wheeled at his own blue line and headed up ice waiting for the pass that he and everyone else in the building knew was coming his way, when Hull swept in on the Los Angeles goal in that characteristic move of his, guiding the puck in the curve of his stick with one hand, holding off the checkers with the other.

Larry Hornung, a defenceman, scored Winnipeg's seventh goal. The announcement over the Arena's public-address system gave the goal to Bordeleau. Hull shouted something at the officials' bench near the Jets' own bench. One of the officials picked up the phone connecting him to a booth high over the ice. A few seconds later, a man rushed from the booth into the press box.

"Bobby says Hornung scored," the man said, flustered.

"That's right," a reporter answered him, and the man hurried back to the booth.

Someone asked, who was that?

"The official scorer."

The public-address system announced a change in the last goal, Hornung not Bordeleau, and the reporter said, "They take Bobby's word for most things around here."

"Well," Hull said later, "you gotta remember the officials haven't had 25 years experience running big league hockey like they have in the NHL. We're all brand new."

"I'd say Bobby has meant at least 1,500 more tickets for every game he's played," Hatskin says. "He's also brought

in a different class of people. At first, when the courts wouldn't let him on the ice, we had mostly kids coming to the games. Now we got all classes. You have to remember that, in comparison to the big NHL cities, Winnipeg isn't the richest place in the world. A hockey ticket's a big investment for a working guy out here even if he has been dying to get pro hockey in his own city for a long, long time."

After the last tape recorder had left, Hull splashed some water on his face, loosened his tie and contemplated his role in the WHA: "The guys you deal with, the WHA owners I mean, have a different attitude than in the NHL. But I could have stayed with the Blackhawks and not worried about money or about missing part of the season like I've just done. Life would have been much simpler for me. But, hell, the WHA is something that's been needed. It's made room for more guys to play and make a living, and it brought entertainment to people who used to be able to only get big league hockey on TV."

"Know what this is all about?" Hull said after the game. "Know what we're in? What the league is?"

"What?"

"Show business."

Then Hull packed up his gear, getting ready for the trip to, let's see, Philadelphia next, two games with the Blazers. Taking the show on the road. 🍁

Hockey

How Roger Doucet Wrote the Soviet National Anthem

The Hymn of the Soviet Union (A. V. Aleksandrov) is one of the most stirring national anthems ever composed. The late Roger Doucet, who sang *O Canada* for many years at the Montreal Canadiens' hockey games, was one of the most stirring singers in Canada. The two were made for each other. There was just one problem — in 1976, the year of the first Canada Cup of Hockey, the Hymn had no words. They had been quietly dropped after 1956, because they contained too many references to the late Soviet dictator Josef Stalin.

CP Wire Photo

In the summer of 1976 Doucet asked the Department of External Affairs if they could find him the official lyrics to the anthems of all four European participants in the Canada Cup. He was told there was no problem with the Czechs, Finns or Swedes, but he'd just have to hum the Soviet anthem very loudly. No more was heard of the matter until the first Soviet match against Czechoslovakia in Montreal in September 1976, when Doucet strode onto the ice and with his legendary élan proceeded to sing *both* teams' anthems. The External Affairs representative at the game almost had a diplomatic heart attack. After the game (and a couple of stiff drinks) he asked interpreter Aggie Kukulowicz where Doucet had come up with the lyrics.

Doucet had unearthed a copy of the old Stalinist lyrics. He himself couldn't speak or read Russian, but he took them to the Russian Department at Université de Montréal and asked them to "fix them up."

Before the game, he showed the result to the Soviet team officials and asked if they minded him singing the new lyrics. As the story goes, they looked at each other and shrugged — and that September evening the *Hymn of the Soviet Union* was first heard sung in all its glory on Soviet State Television by a generation of Soviet citizens who had never heard it before. In 1977, the Soviet Parliament adopted the new lyrics — without, of course, crediting Roger Doucet. ♦

March 12, 1966

Bobby Hull of the Chicago Blackhawks became the first NHL player to score more than 50 goals in a season when he scored against Cesare Maniago for his 51st. He received a 10-minute standing ovation from the hometown fans and, in typical Hull fashion, told the crowded media gathering afterwards "It felt wonderful and was certainly a load off my back. It was a thrill getting the goal, but the biggest thrill was that roar from the crowd." Hull went on to score a record 54 for the year, and won both the Art Ross and Hart Trophies, setting an NHL scoring record with 97 points.

February 9, 1966

The NHL announced it would expand to 12 teams for the 1967-68 season with six new teams in the US

1966-1967

Stan Mikita won the Lady Byng, Art Ross and Hart Trophies as the NHL's most gentlemanly player, highest scorer and most valuable player. It was the first time these three awards were won in the same year by the same person.

1966-1967

Rookie Bobby Orr joined the Boston Bruins to a well-deserved fanfare.

1966-1967

With three players in their 40s, and nine more in their 30s, the Toronto Maple Leafs became the oldest Stanley Cup Champions in history, averaging over 31 years of age as a team.

1967-1968

In a blockbuster trade that wold prove disadvantageous to Chicago, Boston received Phil Esposito, Ken Hodge and Fred Stanfield from Chicago for Pit Martin, Gilles Marcotte and Jack Norris. Meanwhile, Toronto dealt local favourite Frank Mahovlich, as well as Garry Unger, Pete Stemkowski and a retired Carl Brewer to Detroit for Norm Ullman, Paul Henderson and Floyd Smith.

December 4, 1968

Gordie Howe became the first player to score 700 career goals, scoring against Pittsburgh.

June 7, 1968

The National Hockey League Players Association finally became a reality when the players chose Bob Pulford as the NHLPA's first official President and Alan Eagleson as its Executive Director.

November 7, 1968

Red Berenson of the St. Louis Blues scored a modern-era record six goals in one game against the Philadelphia Flyers and Doug Favell.

March 2, 1969

Boston's Phil Esposito scored twice against Pittsburgh to become the first NHL player to reach the 100 point plateau in a season.

March 30, 1969

On the eve of his 41st birthday, Gordie Howe reached the 100-point plateau for the only time in his career, getting four points in his final game of the season.

1968-1969

The NHL had three 100-point scorers for the first time. Phil Esposito won the scoring title with 126 points, Bobby Hull got 107 — including a then-record 58 goals — and the ageless Gordie Howe at 41 scored a career high 103 points.

1969-1970

Bobby Orr became the first defenceman to win the NHL scoring title, amassing 33 goals and 87 assists for 120 points in winning the Art Ross Trophy. Orr also won the Norris, Hart and Conn Smythe Award, the first player to win four major awards in one year. For good measure he also scored the overtime winning goal for the Stanley Cup.

Despite being one of the century's top defencemen, Brad Park never won the Norris Trophy, finishing second in voting to Bobby Orr four times and twice to Denis Potvin.

March 11, 1971

Phil Esposito scored a double — on the same night he netted his 59th goal and 127th point against the LA Kings, surpassing previous records in both categories. "Espo" ended the season with 76 goals and 152 points, shattering both previous records.

1970-1971

Just a few years after Phil Esposito became the first 100-point man, Bobby Orr became the first NHL player to get 100 assists, finishing with 102 for the year.

1971

The mighty Boston Bruins, fresh from setting some 37 NHL records, prepared to play an overmatched Montreal Canadiens squad in the first round of the playoffs. Canadiens coach Al MacNeil wanted to try something different (since they hadn't beaten the Bruins all year) so he inserted eight-game rookie Ken Dryden in net. The ploy paid off, incredibly. Dryden went on to stonewall the Bruins' heavy scorers in seven games, then stymied the Blackhawks in the Stanley Cup final, again in seven games. Dryden and the Canadiens won the Cup, and Dryden earned a very deserved Conn Smythe Trophy. Interestingly, because Dryden played only eight regular-season games in 1970-71, the next season he was still eligible for the Calder (rookie) Trophy — which he won.

1971

Both Jean Béliveau and Gordie Howe, longtime NHL stalwarts and traditional "superstars" and heroes, retired before the 1971-72 season. The only difference was that Béliveau stayed retired! Howe came out of retirement to play in the WHA and later returned to the NHL.

August 26, 1971

Bobby Orr signed the NHL's first million dollar contract, then proved he was worth it by winning the Hart Trophy again, the last time in the century a defenceman would win the Hart.

1971-1972

A 10-year-old named Wayne Gretzky scored 378 goals in one novice season — and was interviewed on Hockey Night in Canada.

1971-1972

Bobby Orr and the Bruins won the Stanley Cup over the New York Rangers and the famous GAG (goal-a-game) Line of Jean Ratelle, Rod Gilbert and Vic Hadfield. Said Ratelle afterwards: "We played them pretty even, but they had Bobby Orr and we didn't."

1971-1972

In what turned out to be his final NHL season for seven years, the Blackhawks' Bobby Hull again scored 50 goals in a season. Hull would soon leave the Hawks for the Winnipeg Jets of the WHA, returning briefly to the NHL in 1979-80 after the WHA folded.

June 27, 1972

The WHA started up as a minor hockey "joke," then signed star Bobby Hull to a $250,000-a-year 10-year contract with a $1 million signing bonus to stop the NHL's laughter.

1973-1974

Borje Salming of Sweden became the first star player from Europe in the NHL, paving the way for many, many, others.

February 13, 1973

Frank Mahovlich, now with Montreal, scored his 1000th career point. Later that season, on March 21, he scored his 500th goal.

1974

The Philadelphia Flyers, starring Bobby Clarke from Flin Flon, Manitoba, were the first NHL "expansion" club to win the Cup, doing so in six games over the Boston Bruins and an ailing Bobby Orr.

1973-1974

During its second year, the WHA's Houston Aeros lured Gordie Howe out of retirement by signing him to play with two of his sons, Mark and Marty. That season, Houston won the league championship and the Avco Cup, with Howe acknowledged as the league's MVP after scoring 100 points.

1974

The Soviets played and beat a WHA All-Star team in the second Canada-Russia series. The Canadians managed three ties and one victory in the eight-game series.

1974-1975

Bobby Orr scored a record 46 goals for a defenceman, earning his second Art Ross trophy for winning the scoring championship. He remained the only defenceman to win any scoring titles, let alone two. Orr never played a full season again due to a series of serious knee operations.

1974-1975

Bobby Hull, the former Blackhawk but this year a star with the WHA's Winnipeg Jets, scored a league record 77 goals. During his seven-year WHA stay, Hull scored a league career record 303 goals in 411 games. Yet, in 1975 it was Gordie Howe's Houston Aeros who won the AVCO Cup, with the 40-something Howe scoring 34 goals.

"Crazy Canucks," left to right, Ken Read, Jim Hunter, Dave Irwin and Dave Murray

Ken Read and the Crazy Canucks

"The Canucks, they ski like crazy."

So remarked the European press as they watched the Canadian men's downhill ski team burst onto the World Cup scene in the mid 1970s. The Crazy Canucks attacked the legendary race-courses of the Alps, their devil-may-care, flat-out style driving them from unknowns to international fame and World Cup wins.

For Canada and men's alpine skiing, these were heady, exciting times. The Crazy Canucks were heroes, loved by all Canadians for their wild style and prowess.

Oddly, up until that point, the men's ski team had been almost a non-entity. Canadian women, like Lucy Wheeler and Nancy Greene, were the ones who had established themselves as forces to be reckoned with in the downhill. But Canadian men were noticeably absent from the world scene, that is, until the Crazy Canucks began careening down the slopes.

It started when a young man from Calgary served notice to the alpine world that the Canadian men were ready to take up their rightful mantle. That young man was Ken Read, unofficial leader of the Crazy Canucks. On December 7, 1975, Read scored a breakthrough, history-making World Cup win at Val d'Isère. It was the first-ever World Cup win for a North American male.

The Europeans were shocked — as was only appropriate. Not only did Read win, but the rest of the scoreboard was littered with Canadian flags too: teammate Dave Irwin took fourth, Jim Hunter ninth, Steve Podborski 10th, and Dave Murray 13th. It was an incredible day. Dark muttering began about how the Canadians wouldn't survive, given the way they were skiing.

Yet the victories kept coming. A few days after Read's win, Irwin won at Schladming's Planai course later in December, 1975. On February 13, 1978, Read and Murray were first and second respectively at Chamonix, while Irwin was seventh. Nipping at everyone's heels, Podborski took ninth.

"Crazy Canuck" Ken Read, in action

Canada

"Crazy Canuck" teammates celebrating Steve Podborski's 1982 World Cup championship season.

Clearly, the Crazy Canucks were more than a fluke, although the Europeans remained skeptical. The "crazy" label was dismissive, really. It meant the Canadians might win a couple, but sooner or later they'd pay for all the risks they took. Although the Chamonix wins were heralded by the European press at the time, in the 120-page fact book published by the World Cup, the Canadian domination was written off in one line: the Crazy Canucks had won because the European skiers were too relaxed after the World Championships.

Far from being demoralized, the Canadians were only egged on by this attitude. In January, 1980, Read delivered a final blow to the European ego, winning back-to-back races in Kitzbuhel and Wengen.

In the skiing world, a win at Kitzbuhel is arguably more prestigious than an Olympic gold. The latter is worth more to the rest of the world, but the former has acquired an unique status within ski circles. Conquering the famed Hahnenkamm mountain is the Holy Grail of downhill racing, and probably as difficult to attain. It packs every element of downhill into a hellish two-minute unforgiving free-for-all. The racer must be "on" the whole way down: every inch of the course demands commitment, faith and instinct. There is no room for recovery from even the minutest of mistakes.

The Lauberhorn at Wengen, unlike the Hahnenkamm, is more forgiving, but at four and a half kilometers, it is the longest race on the circuit. The extra 30 seconds it takes to do the course delivers a special kind of hell on the racer, as heart, lung and muscles scream for rest.

With these two victories by Read, the last doubting Thomas on the World Cup circuit was silenced. The European press went crazy over Read, who, already loved at home, became an international hero in a select category reserved for the greats: Jean-Claude Killy, Karl Schranz, Roland Collumbin and Franz Klammer.

After displaying such prowess, Read was the odds-on favourite for the 1980 Olympic Winter Games. But it was not to be. Shortly after launching down the Lake Placid course, Read's binding came loose, a scant eight seconds into the race. He was out of the running.

But there was another Crazy Canuck on the hill that fateful day, who would take up the torch. Steve Podborski had come into his own and he had the honour of bringing home the Olympic bronze, another Canadian first for this illustrious group.

While the critics had long been silenced, one quest still lay before the Canucks: the men's overall world cup downhill title. Read had come the closest, missing it by 0.02 seconds in 1980. It was up to the new leader, Podborski, to secure the title in 1982. The highest honour for men's alpine was finally brought home to Canada, land of ice and snow. ♣

1980

In 1980, Ken Read would be Canada's flagbearer of the Lake Placid Olympics. In 1988, Read would join Cathy Priestner in bringing the Olympic flame into his hometown stadium for the Calgary Games. And in 1992, Read would lead Canada's summer team as Chef de mission in Barcelona.

High Jumper Arnie Boldt: 1.96 Metres on One Leg

Despite the solo achievements of Terry Fox and Rick Hansen, sport for athletes with a physical disability didn't become well-recognized in Canada until the late 1990s, and perhaps didn't become *really* well-recognized until the Sydney 2000 Paralympics, when for the first time Canadian athletes competed before record crowds of sports-mad Australians, and were featured in stories in the national media. But before wheelchair racer Chantal Petitclerc, before Terry Fox, and before Rick Hansen, there was Arnie Boldt.

Arnie was born in 1958 in Osler, Saskatchewan. A childhood amputee growing up in a rural area where physical injury was fairly common and not much noticed, he took an early interest in track and field. Since nobody bothered to tell him a guy with one leg couldn't do it, he went right ahead and did it. By 1976 he had been introduced to formal competition for amputees, and in that year he began a 20-year career as a high-performance athlete at the Torontolympiad for the Physically Disabled, the predecessor of today's Paralympics.

His glory days were the late 1970s and early 1980s competing in the high jump against able-bodied athletes for the University of Saskatchewan and University of Manitoba. In CIAU meets he regularly averaged over 2 metres. In the days before Paralympic sport became well known, his approach to the bar was unforgettable to anyone who saw it, especially at an able-bodied event. A run-up was impossible of course. Arnie *hopped* up — one, two, three and takeoff in a tight curl (called the "Fosbury Flop") over the bar. His best jump ever in a disabled/amputee event (unfortunately not sanctioned by the IAAF) was in 1980 in Italy with a jump of 2.04 metres and his best indoor performance, at the Tribune Games in Winnipeg in 1981, was 2.08 metres. His world and Paralympic high jump record, which still stood 20 years later, was 1.96 metres at the 1980 Games for the Physically Disabled in Arnhem, the Netherlands.

Arnie's athletic achievements also took him to Hollywood, at least via Tunisia, Malta, and the Seychelles. In 1984 he was stunt stand-in for Walter Matthau in an action epic called Pirates, in which he ended up getting about as much screen time as Matthau himself did. Earlier, in 1977, he had made a TV movie for CBC called *Crossbar*, loosely based on his own achievements.

Arnie retired from active competition just a little too soon to take advantage of the extension of Federal financial support (the "carding" system) to top-level athletes with a disability. He continued to devote himself to the development of young amputee and disabled athletes. ♦

Sandra Post

Canada's first golfer on the LPGA Tour, Sandra Post left a fine amateur career for the professional ranks and never missed a beat. Following victories in three successive Canadian Junior Girl's Championships, Post focused on turning professional for the 1968 season. Her victory in the LPGA Championship, and a fifth in the World Series of Golf, garnered her LPGA Rookie of the Year honours and started a glorious career that included back-to-back wins at the 1978 and 1979 Dinah Shore and another six LPGA victories. Career Highlights:

- 1999 Captain of the inaugural Nation's Cup between Canada and the United States
- 1981 McDonald's Kids Classic Champion
- 1980 West Virginia Classic Champion
- 1979 ERA Real Estate Classic Champion
- 1979 Lady Michelob Champion
- 1979 Colgate Dinah Shore Winners Circle Champion
- 1978 Colgate Dinah Shore Winners Circle Champion
- 1978 Lady Stroh's Open Champion
- 1968 LPGA Champion
- 1964, 1965, 1966 Canadian Junior Girls Champion

1962-78

Jockey Ron Turcotte began his horse racing career as a hot walker for E.P. Taylor's Windfield Farms in 1959 but he was soon wearing jockey silks and winning races. In 1962 and 1963 the New Brunswick native was named Canada's top jockey. In 1972, he rode Riva Ridge to victory in the 1972 Kentucky Derby and Belmont Stakes. His repeat Derby win in 1973 aboard the great Secretariat made him the first jockey with back-to-back Kentucky Derby wins. He went on to complete the Triple Crown by riding Secretariat to victory in both the Belmont and the Preakness. Turcotte and Secretariat were the first American Triple Crown winners since 1948. The pair won the Kentucky Derby in record time, the Preakness in mud and the Belmont by a record 31 lengths. In a tribute to his Canadian partners (Lucien Laurin from Quebec was the trainer), Secretariat ran his last race at Toronto's Woodbine race track, winning the Canadian International Stakes race easily. With a career total of 3033 wins to his credit, Turcotte was forced to retire in 1978 following a fall from his horse at Belmont, which left him in a wheelchair.

1969

Sandy Hawley, from Oshawa, Ontario, shared the record for Queen's Plate victories at four (together with Robin Platts and Avelino Gomez). He enjoyed incredible success in the United States and Canada and was twice winner of the Lou Marsh Trophy as Canada's athlete of the year.

Highlights

General Highlights

1960s

Wayne MacDonnell (Badminton) — At the pinnacle of international badminton competition, the Thomas Cup is contested every three years and is considered to be the Davis Cup of badminton. In his first year on the National Team in 1961, Wayne MacDonnell won six straight matches, surprising everyone and was the only player to go undefeated. He set a Canadian record by being named to the six-man Thomas Cup team a total of six times out of a possible six opportunities over a 15 year period (1961-1976). He won the Canadian singles championship a record six times between 1962-1967. During his elite badminton career, he played an average of 10-12 tournaments per year without losing a single match to another Canadian.

1968

Bill Symons was the first Toronto Argonaut to rush for over 1,000 yards in a season.

1970

Jerome Drayton of Toronto set the world record for the 10-mile run at 46:37.8.

1970

The first *Arctic Winter Games* were held in Yellowknife, NWT.

1970

The Amateur Athletic Union of Canada (AAU of C) ceased operations permanently.

1971

Debbie Brill of Vancouver became the first North American woman to clear six feet (approx. 1.83m) in the high jump.

1972

Jocelyne Bourassa was an outstanding amateur golfer throughout the 1960s and took the LPGA pro tour by storm in the early 1970s. She won the 1973 La Canadienne in her second season. In addition to being named the LPGA's rookie of the year, she was named the 1971 and 1972 French Canadian Athlete of the Year and 1972 Canadian Female Athlete of the Year.

1972

Runner Penny Werthner of Ottawa set the world record in the 1000m at 2:45.9.

Hockey

A Flower for all Seasons

by Roy MacGregor
October 16, 1978

I retired in 1971, the same year Guy arrived and he came to me and asked me what I thought about him taking my sweater number: "If you want it, take it," I told him, "But don't you think you already have enough on you? Why don't you pick another number and make it famous yourself?" **– Jean Béliveau**

The man an entire province prayed for when Jean Béliveau moved on has arrived at his full bloom. It is hardly possible to believe today that those same hands that ruffle children as if their imaginations were crops he himself had planted, once struggled to put down his desperate feelings in poetry. It is harder still to realize these same friendly eyes could have spilled tears over the red, white and blue of the *les Canadiens* — colored chesterfield in Jean Béliveau's office as Lafleur sat crying over whatever it was that had gone so wrong with his promised life.

But eyes can also weep for joy. And Antoine Viau, who has waited much of his life for this moment, is dampening slightly as he stands watching his beloved Canadiens skate and shoot and actually breathe. The Montreal Forum is empty of fans, but Guy Lafleur — who an hour earlier has said "What good is money when you play and lose?" — is skating with Stanley Cup intentions during a $25-per-man pre-season scrimmage. His wispy hair matted with the cream cake his team-mates have used to celebrate his 27th birthday, Lafleur commands his magic to turn a 4-2 deficit into victory. In the dying minutes he scores, sets up the tying goal, then single-handedly wins the game in overtime with a phantom shot from the point. For Antoine Viau, who sweeps floors nights at the American-owned IBM plant, the state of *les Canadiens* is, in many ways, the state of his own well-being. "Ah, Lafleur," Viau says, courteously speaking English to the reporter who helped him sneak in, "Lafleur...Lafleur...I love it!"

The gender is accidental but telling, for Guy Lafleur is more symbol than human to a great many Québecois. "There is," says Jerry Petrie, Lafleur's agent, "probably more pressure on him to perform from the people in this province than there is on René Lévesque." For them, Lafleur occupies the highest office in the land.

"Guy is the true throwback," says Ken Dryden, the Canadiens goaltender. "I look out sometimes and see the St. Lawrence skater, not the player, and it is a beautiful thing to behold."

"The Flower is a very strange person," says Lafleur's line mate and good friend Steve Shutt. It is not for any obvious idiosyncrasy such as his superstitious tap of the goal netting to start each game and period; what is truly odd, in Shutt's evaluation, is that

Guy Lafleur accepting the Lou Marsh Trophy as Canada's Athlete of the Year, 1976.

Lafleur is "the farthest thing from an athlete you'd ever want to see off the ice." A loyal consumer of Molson's ale (the brewery owns the team) and a chain smoker who two weeks ago switched to a pipe — Lafleur does little more than work out with suntan oil in the off season. "He shows up at camp, puts on his skates and it's the first time he's been on them since the playoff," says Larry Robinson of the Canadiens. "And the frightening thing is he just flies by everyone immediately."

"It's because he's so hyper," says Shutt. "He winds himself up like a coil." The bad nerves are a mixed blessing: what Lafleur gains in reflex and metabolism he gives up in what it does to his mental fitness. Before particularly important games he has been discovered in the dressing room at three o'clock in the afternoon — his equipment on, his skates tightened — fully five hours before game time. By the time the puck is dropped he is strained, which partially explains his periodic slumps in critical games.

His priorities always place the team and the game first, and either his fans or family second. Only once, when the team was in a rare slump, has Lafleur deliberately tried to inspire by anything but his own standard of play. He moved from his locker to the play blackboard near the showers, picked up the chalk, thought a moment, and then scribbled, "A winner never quits and a quitter never wins." He then moved back to his locker where he sat staring up at the approving, legendary faces of *les Canadiens* of past years, and he read again the lines of the poet John McRae that are stenciled just below the ceiling. "To you from failing hands we throw the torch; be yours to hold it high."

As Béliveau had before him, Lafleur left the small town for Quebec City and their resulting glory was comparable. As an "amateur" junior, Lafleur made close to $20,000 a year, drove a free Buick and dressed in the finest "gift" clothes. He wore the No. 4, Béliveau's signature in Montreal, and Lafleur made sure he kept a poster of his idol taped to the wall beside his locker.

In Lafleur's final year — when he scored an astonishing 130 goals — it was arranged that the sensation would come to Montreal. By rights, as the best amateur in the country, he should have gone to the last-place California Golden Seals, but a celebrated sleight of hand by Montreal's general manager Sam Pollock saw the Canadiens come up with Lafleur.

So much was Guy Lafleur on people's minds — despite never having played a single professional game — that a manufacturer was rushing production to get a Lafleur-endorsed table-hockey game out in time for Christmas.

"Le démon blond," Guy Lafleur in full flight.

By the third winter, however, the Lafleur game was off the market. Not only had the rookie award gone to his team-mate Ken Dryden, but the word around the league was that Lafleur was "yellow." The junior promise had become a professional deceit.

The unhappy sessions in Jean Béliveau's office weren't providing a solution either. It took a gamble by Béliveau in the spring of 1974 to provide the remedy. Béliveau let it be known that he was less than pleased with the performance of his heir, and he castigated Lafleur for not working hard enough. The effect, at first devastating, became "a wake up" for Lafleur and he emerged from his sulk by announcing, "I'll show the bastards." When training camp opened, he discarded his yellow stigma with his helmet and the new Guy Lafleur suddenly and aggressively emerged as Béliveau reincarnate. A broken finger probably cost him the scoring championship that year, but he has held the title for the three years since.

There have, however, been darker sides that are not pasted in any album but linger anyway. And this has led him to wonder rather than gloat. In April of 1976, the Montreal police were investigating the holdup of a Brinks truck when they stumbled on a plot to kidnap Lafleur before the playoffs began and hold him for a rumored $250,000 ransom.

For a full two months, Lafleur lived in sight of two detectives. His wife Lise, and their eight-month-old son Martin stayed for a while in a hotel and then with her parents in Quebec City.

Lafleur's play disintegrated and when the fans and press squeezed him for answers he had to fight to keep it from pouring out.

The very next year he made up for that small lapse by winning the Conn Smythe Trophy as the most valuable player during the playoffs. But there was a new threat to deal with. One of the Boston Bruin players, John Wensink, whose hockey talent is to Lafleur's what punk rock is to Beethoven, proudly announced: "If I get on the ice, Lafleur will not come out alive." Lafleur survived, of course. Wensink, who has trouble catching his own wind, had to make do with Lafleur's as the Canadiens star flew by and led his team to its record 20th Stanley Cup. But the incident had its effect on Lafleur. "It's supposed to be a sport," he says of his beloved game, "not butchery." ❦

HHOF/London Life

1976

Darryl Sittler's Year

Stanley Cup quarter-finals

In Game Six between Toronto and Philadelphia, Darryl Sittler's scoring went into high gear again — equaling an NHL record of five goals in one playoff game.

September

The first Canada Cup featured a six-team invitational tournament with the best professionals from Canada, Russia, Czechoslovakia, Sweden, Finland and the USA Canada won this first unofficial professional world championship with a two-straight-wins performance in a best of three final against the Czechs. Darryl Sittler scored the Series winner with a dramatic chase to the puck and deke around the goalie. Bobby Orr played his only international tournament and, naturally, received the MVP for the Canada Cup.

1976 Canada Cup

Darryl Sittler scored the overtime winner in the 1976 Canada Cup, taking the advice of Don Cherry who told him "Fake a shot. Dzurlla will come out. Shift to your left and you'll have plenty of open net." Sittler did just that.

February 7
Toronto's Darryl Sittler scored six times and added four assists for an NHL record 10 points in an 11-4 rout over the Boston Bruins. His six goals came against Dave Reece. No other NHLer scored 10 points in a game during the century.

November 7, 1975

In a surprise move, the Boston Bruins traded centre Phil Esposito and defenceman Carol Vadnais to the New York Rangers for Jean Ratelle, Brad Park and Joe Zanussi.

November 1975

In a game between the Toronto Maple Leafs and the Philadelphia Flyers a brawl broke out, which was very common for Flyers' games in those days. This time, though, four of the "Broad Street Bullies" were charged with assault through the Attorney General's Office of Roy McMurtry in Ontario, who was attempting to crack down on hockey violence. Later the same season, Brian Glennie of the Leafs was charged after a game against Detroit. Two of the Flyers were found guilty of bodily assault, while the others were cleared.

June 9, 1976

Bobby Orr did the unthinkable and signed a contract with the Chicago Blackhawks as a free agent. His Chicago stint was cut short by yet another knee operation part way through his first season. Orr would play but 20 games for Chicago, scoring four goals and 23 points on wobbly knees.

1976-1977

The Montreal Canadiens lost but eight times in an 80-game schedule, recording NHL records of 60 victories and 132 points. Steve Shutt scored 60 goals and Guy Lafleur won the Art Ross Trophy as the league's leading scorer. The Habs won the Stanley Cup easily for the second straight season.

1977-1978

Laval junior graduate Mike Bossy scored a record 53 goals in his rookie season with the NHL New York Islanders. Bossy went on to win the Calder (Rookie) Trophy by the widest margin in the century.

1977-1978

Guy Lafleur won his third straight scoring title and second consecutive MVP award for the season, as the Habs again won the Stanley Cup for the third year in a row.

March, 1978

The NHL voted to include the four remaining WHA clubs — Edmonton, Winnipeg, Hartford and Quebec (although it was called an expansion). The WHA folded.

November 8, 1978

Finally succumbing to knee operations, his only real foe, Bobby Orr retired at age 30.

January, 1979

The 1979 Challenge Cup between the Soviets and the NHL was played over three games in New York. The NHLers won the first game 4-2, with the Soviets triumphing in Game 2. The deciding game became a no-contest, with the Soviets easily taking the Cup and the game 6-0.

April, 1979

In the seventh game of a Stanley Cup semi-final match in Montreal, the Boston Bruins, coached by Don Cherry, led with less than two minutes to play. Ever anxious, the Bruins got called for too many men on the ice. On the ensuing power-play Guy Lafleur tied the game. The Habs' Yvon Lambert scored in overtime to win the series. The Canadiens went on to win their fourth consecutive Cup.

1979-1980

In Wayne Gretzky's first NHL season after a year with the WHA, he won the Hart (MVP) and Lady Byng (Sportsmanship) Awards and tied Marcel Dionne for the scoring lead — but Dionne received the Art Ross because he scored more goals (53 to Gretzky's 50). Gretzky was the youngest player to score 50 goals, but was ruled ineligible for the Calder (Rookie) Trophy because of his year in the WHA.

1979-1980

At age 51, Gordie Howe returned to the NHL after retiring nine years earlier. In his final hockey season, Howe scored 15 goals and 41 points in 80 games for the Hartford Whalers.

January 7, 1981

Marcel Dionne became the 13th, and at the time fastest, player to reach the 1,000-point plateau in the NHL, playing in his 740th game (Phil Esposito held the previous record at 823 games).

January 24, 1981

Mike Bossy of the New York Islanders scored two goals in the last five minutes of a game against the Quebec Nordiques, tying the 50-goals-in-50-games record set by Rocket Richard in 1945.

March 19, 1981

After trailing the Maple Leafs 1-0 following the first period of an NHL game in Toronto, the Buffalo Sabres, led by Gilbert Perreault, set an NHL record for goals in a period by scoring nine in the second period. The Leafs scored three times in the period as well, leading to another NHL record for most goals in a period by both teams — 12.

March, 1981

The Gretzky assault on the record book really took off when he broke Phil Esposito's 10-year old scoring mark with 164 points. His total included 109 assists, which broke the assist record held by Bobby Orr.

December 30, 1981

Wayne Gretzky shattered the 50-goals-in-50-games standard set by Rocket Richard and only tied the year before by Mike Bossy. The "Great One" scored his first 50 goals in just 39 games in decisive fashion — scoring five times in the 39th game.

1981-1982

"The record book became his," said Gordie Howe. Wayne Gretzky scored 92 goals and 120 assists for 212 points, each record far surpassing what anyone else had done before.

1981

Quite frankly, Canada was embarrassed by the Soviets in the final of the second Canada Cup, losing 8-1 in the decisive game. Alan Eagleson refused to allow the Soviets to take the Canada Cup trophy home, though, even after finding the Soviets packing it up.

1982-1983

Wayne Gretzky's new record of 125 assists was more than anyone else got points (the first time since Bill Cowley had achieved this distinction in 1940-41). Gretzky was partially driven to this achievement because in the 1980-81 season he had tied Marcel Dionne in scoring, but lost the scoring race because Dionne had more goals. This year it didn't matter.

1983-1984

Wayne Gretzky and the Oilers took control of the NHL. The team scored a record 446 goals during the regular season , and then won its first Stanley Cup in four straight games over the Islanders. Paul Coffey scored 126 points, breaking the great Bobby Orr's mark for the most points by a defenceman. Jari Kurri and Glen Anderson joined Gretzky in scoring more than 50 goals in the season. Gretzky set another new scoring mark of 205 points. His average of 2.77 points per game was the highest ever, including the score-happy early century days of hockey. Along the way, Gretzky recorded a 51-consecutive game-scoring streak.

1984-1985

Quebec junior scoring sensation Mario Lemieux was drafted by the lowly Pittsburgh Penguins. Finally agreeing to a contract, the emerging star scored on his first shift in the NHL, going on to win the Calder Trophy for the best rookie of the year.

1984

After narrowly beating the Soviets in overtime (which included Paul Coffey's sensational defensive play on a two-on-one break), Canada defeated Sweden in the final to win the Canada Cup and reclaim professional hockey supremacy.

1985-1986

Two seemingly unbreakable records were broken. First, Paul Coffey of the Oilers broke Bobby Orr's goal record for a defenceman by scoring 48 for the season, and then Gretzky topped his own scoring mark by accumulating 215 points in winning both the Art Ross and Hart Trophies. Gretzky was the only player to score over 200 points in a season throughout the century — which he did four times in five years.

1986

Tied 2-2 with under a minute to play in Game 7 of the Western Final in the Stanley Cup playoffs against the Calgary Flames, Edmonton Oilers defenceman Steve Smith accidentally cleared the puck into his own net and the mighty Oilers were defeated.

March 14, 1986

Paul Coffey set the record for points in a game by a defenceman, registering eight points against the Detroit Red Wings.

December, 1986

On the final day at the World Junior Championships, the Canadians needed to beat the Soviets by five goals to win the gold medal. With the score 4-2 at the time, a bench-clearing brawl broke out and both teams were disqualified from the tourney, handing Finland its first Junior Championship.

February 11 & 13, 1987

Rendez-Vous '87 in Quebec City saw the NHL All-Star game replaced by the NHL Stars playing a two-game series against the Soviets. In spectacular play, the teams split the two games.

Niatross, the Once in a Lifetime Horse

All too often in sports, behind the story of glory in competition lurks a tale of infighting, greed, egos and court battles. Such was the story of Niatross, hailed as the greatest standard bred racehorse of all time.

On the track, the story is like a dream. As a three-year old pacer, a two-legged gait that is faster than the traditional trot, Niatross was unbeatable. In the words of trainer/driver Clint Galbraith, "Niatross was a once in a lifetime horse."

Born and raised in Tara, Ontario, Galbraith left for greener pastures in the US when he was 18. There, he met horse owner Elsie Berger, another ex-patriate born in Stayner, Ontario, who now made her living in the US.

Berger bred and raised Niatross, while Galbraith trained and drove the young colt. Recognizing his potential, Galbraith offered to buy into the horse, but Berger would not hear of it. She simply gave him half.

When he began racing Niatross as a two-year-old, Galbraith was very careful not to push the horse too far. Often, young horses are pushed too early, and their as-yet-undeveloped bones cannot handle the pressure. Galbraith didn't take Niatross to the track until early June, 1979, when he put the young colt in a qualifying, or no-purse, race. Niatross won easily, in 2:01.2, and Galbraith begin to realize what he had on his hands.

After a few more easy races, Galbraith entered Niatross in the Woodrow Wilson, the most valuable race in harness or thoroughbred racing history. He won it in 1:55.4.

Throughout the first half of 1980, Galbraith kept bringing Niatross along, and the great colt kept responding, continuing to trim seconds off his time. Galbraith began to see that history was in the making.

The big moment for Niatross was not winning a record number of races to win, or winning the Little Brown Jug, harness racing's most prestigious title, or even winning harness racing's Triple Crown. It was breaking the 1:50 time mark for a mile.

In 1970, pacer Steady Star had set the record for the fastest mile in standard bred racing history at 1:52.

In October 1980, Niatross blew that record away in a time trial held in Lexington, Kentucky. During a time trial, a harness horse races alone, aided by galloping thoroughbred prompters. Galbraith guided Niatross to the quarter-mile in 27 3/5 seconds. The half went in 54 3/5 and the crowd of almost 5,000 fans, grooms, trainers, owners and horsemen began to go wild. When the horse and driver reached the three-quarter mile mark in 1:21 4/5, it was clear to everyone that history was going to be made. With the crowd screaming and cheering, Galbraith brought Niatross home with a final quarter of 27 2/5. He tapped the big colt but once with the whip.

1968

Hervé Filion

In 1968, Hervé Filion put Canada into the harness racing limelight when he set the world record for winning drives. One of eight sons of a trucker, Filion was Canada's highest-paid professional athlete for a number of years. He was elected to Canada's Sports Hall of Fame in 1969 and named Canada's Athlete of the Year in 1971.

How did the boy from Angers, Québec, get there? Well, he was hard working and hard driving—no pun intended. In 1968, when Filion decided to make his mark, he literally drove himself to harness racing superstardom. He worked non-stop from February to Christmas, often racing at two different tracks in the same day. One day, he finished a race at 4 p.m. in Carlisle, Pennsylvania, and showed up for work at 8 p.m. in Boston — 300 miles away. By November, he was the North American champion, and a month later, the new world champion with 407 wins, toppling the previous record of 384.

When the time flashed up on the teletimer, the crowd roared. Niatross had paced the mile in 1:49 1/5, wiping nearly three seconds off of Steady Star's record.

Overcome with emotion, many in the crowd broke down and cried. Joe O'Brien, who had driven Steady Star to the 1971 record, rushed onto the track to congratulate Galbraith.

By the time Niatross retired, he had won 37 races out of 39 starts and earned over $2 million, the most by a harness horse at the time, and remarkable even in thoroughbred circles.

Off the track, however, the story was a nightmare. Even as the great pacer was shattering every track record in harness racing history, his Canadian-born owners were involved in an ugly dispute with a New Jersey-based syndicate of investors.

The dispute went as follows: Berger and Galbraith had sold half of Niatross in the summer of 1979 to the 27-member syndicate, led by New Jersey stockbroker Louis Guida. Guida wanted to retire Niatross to stud as early as possible, to avoid the risk of injury, and — clearly — begin to collect on the investment through stud fees.

Berger and Galbraith claimed the syndicate was breaching the original contract by treating the great horse like a "commodity." As true horse people, Berger and Galbraith wanted to continue racing Niatross and continue making harness racing history.

Throughout 1980, Niatross's year of fame and glory, his owners were locked in a protracted and ugly court battle. When Galbraith had a bad start in a race with Niatross, Guida publicly accused him of taking the colt on a "suicide drive." For a trainer, this is an unthinkable insult.

Unfortunately for Berger and Galbraith, in the end a judge ruled that they had signed away their rights. Niatross was retired on January 1, 1981, and sent to a stud farm in Lexington, Kentucky. His career on the track was over. But it would live on in history. ♦

General Highlights

1974

Cindy Nicholas of Scarborough was 16 when she swam across Lake Ontario in record time: 15 hours and 18 minutes. In 1975, she set the record for crossing the English Channel in 9 hours, 46 minutes. In the summer of 1976 Nicholas again swam across the English Channel, becoming the first Canadian to swim the Channel three times. For good measure, in 1977 she swam across the English Channel and back again, setting the round-trip record of 19 hours and 55 minutes.

1975

Saskatoon native Diane Jones set the world pentathlon record of 4540 points.

1976

Women's basketball became an official medal sport for the first time at the Montreal Olympic Games, with Canada finishing eighth. The men's team, led by coach Jack Donohue, had its best finish since the silver medal in 1936, ending up in fourth.

1976

A modern pioneer of artistic skating, Toller Cranston had a staggering influence on men's figure skating (the European press routinely refer to him as the "skater of the century"). Cranston eschewed traditional figures for the artistry, flamboyancy and the sheer joy of free skating. He was six-time Canadian men's champion, from 1971 to 1976, also winning the newly created Skate Canada competition. At the 1974 World Figure Skating Championships in Munich he earned a bronze medal. His highest honour came at Innsbruck, during the Olympic Winter Games in 1976, where the 26-year-old Cranston won an Olympic bronze medal.

1977

Leo Rautins joined the Canadian National Basketball team at the age of 17.

1978

Vern Taylor performed the first-ever triple Axel in competition at the World Figure Skating Championships in Ottawa.

1978-94

Badminton player Claire Backhouse-Sharpe holds the record for the most appearances by a female athlete representing Canada at the Commonwealth Games (1978-1994). At the Commonwealths, she won silver and gold in 1982, silver in 1986 and silver in 1990. She won a total of 15 Canadian national titles during her 17-year career (2 Junior, 3 Intermediate and 10 Senior).

1973-1986

Bob Lenarduzzi played for the Vancouver Whitecaps during the team's entire 10-year existence in the North American Soccer league (NASL) from 1974 to 1984. He was the only player in the NASL to play 288 games and to play all 11 positions on the field, earning spots on the NASL all-star team in 1979,1981 and 1984. Lenarduzzi was selected as the 1978 Player-of-the-Year in the NASL. He was also a key member of Canada's National Team from 1973 to 1986 playing a total of 28 World Cup qualifying games — more than any other player.

Doug Sturrock

1979, Progress in Canadian rugby was apparent when a Canadian side defeated the France B squad 14-4 in 1979 at Lille.

1978

Rudy Plichie is in a category all by himself in the Canadian Boxing Hall of Fame. In 1978, he became the only "Cut Man" ever elected to the Hall. "Cut men" are the ring corner paramedics who have a minute between rounds to staunch the blood flow from cuts — usually over boxers' eyes. Rudy Plichie was the best in the business. In 2000 he was 66 years old and retired from his dangerous job as an underground mine rescue specialist. He was so highly respected that the legendary Angelo Dundee tried to persuade him to join the Dundee Camp and move to Florida permanently. Rudy elected to stay in Canada. Tyrone Gardiner, former Canadian lightweight champion, told about the time he suffered a deep cut in the third round and "the doctor was about to stop the fight, but with Rudy's work he let the bout continue." Gardiner TKO'd his opponent "in the fifth round in a fight I just as easily could have lost." Rudy Plichie is the only Canadian ever to serve on Ring Magazine's Ratings USA panel. He was in the corners for Maritime, Canadian, British Empire, Commonwealth, North American and world title bouts. He was co-manager and trainer for five Canadian and one North American champion.

Federal Ministers of Amateur Sport in Canada

1961	The Fitness and Amateur Sport Act was passed
1972	Marc Lalonde
1976	Iona Campagnolo
1979	Steve Paproski
1980	Gerald Reagan
1982	Ray Perrault
1983	Céline Hervieux-Payette
1984	Jacques Olivier, Jean Lapierre, Otto Jelinek
1988	Jean Charest
1990	Perrin Beatty, Marcel Danis
1991	Pierre Cadieux
1993	Michel Dupuy
1996	Sheila Copps
1999	Denis Coderre

CSA

1973-1986

Bruce Wilson was the first Canadian-born player selected to the North American Soccer League (NASL) All-Star Team. In his 11 year, 275 game NASL career, he played a record breaking 161 consecutive games, was selected an All-Star seven times, and in 1978 was "Player of the Year" (Defender). Wilson was the captain of the Canadian National Team for 10 years and led the team to the quarterfinals in the 1984 Olympics and the FIFA World Cup finals in Mexico in 1986.

1972-1983

Marjorie Blackwood was the top-ranked tennis player in the country from 1977 to 1979 and a three-time Canadian National Champion. She reached a high of 48th on the world rankings in 1983 and captured 14 titles in singles and doubles play in her career. She represented Canada on the Federation Cup team from 1972-1980.

1970s

Bev Boys, from Pickering, Ontario, was Canada's leading diver of the 1970s, winning Commonwealth gold medals in both the three and 10 metre events.

1970s

Multisport performer Sandy Robertson played championship basketball, squash and pro baseball. In 1971 he was given a well-deserved spot in BC's Sports Hall of Fame. By 1978 he was joined by his son Bruce, who won a silver medal at the 1972 Olympic Games in the 100m butterfly. Bruce broke the previous world record in the final, but not by as much as the immortal Mark Spitz did. He went on to win gold in the same event at the 1973 World Championships.

1936-1980

Balance. Precision. Co-ordination. The Athans family from Kelowna BC had all three in spades. The father, George Sr., was on the 1936 and 1948 Olympic teams for tower and springboard diving. He won two bronze medals at the 1938 British Empire (Commonwealth) Games and improved that to gold for the 1950 Games. The mother, Irene (Hartzell) Athans, was a national synchronized swimming champion for five years. The oldest son, George Jr., was Canada's national water-ski champion for 10 straight years and the overall world champion in back-to-back competitions in 1971 and 1973. Middle son Greg was five times the national junior champion and three times national senior men's champion in water skiing. He then turned to the snow and became the world freestyle-ski champion in 1980. Youngest son Gary, at 17, made the national teams for both alpine and water-skiing.

1975-2000

Canadian girls and women took up rugby with a passion in the last 25 years of the century. Canada's women's national team stepped onto the international scene in 1987 by facing the USA. Highlights include a 16-7 win over Holland in the opening match of the 1998 Women's Rugby World Cup and the first two victories over arch rival USA in 1999 and 2000. After coming close several times in their previous 12 meetings, Canada scored a try in the final minutes to win 16-11 in the 1999 match. One year later at Saranac Lake they duplicated this result by outscoring the United States 17-10.

Gary Cowan

There are very few accomplishments in amateur golf that eluded Gary Cowan. His record included winning one Canadian Amateur Championship and two US Amateur Championships; being low amateur at both the Canadian Open and the Masters Tournament; and being medallist at the World Amateur Team Championship. In International play, he was a fierce competitor, representing Canada 19 times in tournaments.

Career Highlights:

- 1999 — Named the Canadian Male Amateur Golfer of the Century
- 1981 Simon Bolivar Trophy Tournament (winner with Doug Roxburgh)
- 1971 United States Amateur Champion
- 1971 North and South Amateur Champion
- 1971 New Zealand Centennial Trophy Tournament Canadian Team Member (Winning Team)
- 1966 United States Amateur Champion
- 1965 America's Cup Canadian Team Member (Winning Team)
- 1964 Low Amateur in Masters
- 1962 World Amateur Golf Team Championships Individual Title
- 1961 Canadian Amateur Champion
- 1956 Canadian Junior Champion

Canada Introduces Short Track Speed Skating to the World

"Go fast, turn left," read one fan's sign at the short track speed skating venue at the 1998 Olympics in Nagano. That brief phrase describes the essence of the sport that Canada introduced to the Olympic world ten years earlier at the Calgary Olympics — the first one to the line wins, and between the start and the finish it sometimes seems like anything goes.

A latecomer on the scene, short track had some difficulty establishing its credentials on the world scene. It had been referred to as "roller derby on ice," an impression created partly out of ignorance of the sport but based on the reality that crashes are common on the tight 111-m oval and that the extremely close quarters on the ice can make it look like a contact sport. Still, no one denies that it provides a higher level of excitement for spectators than does its older, more sedate cousin, long track speed skating.

To a large extent, short track is a Canadian creation, brought about by the necessity for speed skaters to practice in standard arenas during times of the year when full-size, natural-ice outdoor ovals are not available. For the first few years after the first world championships were held in 1978, Canadians were the dominant team. Other countries, notably East Asians, quickly developed strong athletes too, pushing world standards higher and higher.

CSI/COA

The success of the short track demonstration events at the Calgary Olympics in 1988 helped make it an official part of the program in Albertville in 1992. Hopes were high for a Canadian sweep of the four gold medals up for grabs, but the team had to settle for one gold and two silvers.

Two years later, in Lillehammer, Canadians won two silvers and a bronze in six events. Bad luck and bad judging cost the Canadian team better results, and even led some to consider short track's Olympic status in jeopardy. "That's short track," became an oft-repeated phrase, sometimes spoken philosophically to explain the unpredictable nature of a sport that was still unfamiliar to media and the public, but other times laden with irony and sarcasm when apparent rule infractions went unpunished.

Nevertheless, short track was back, better and more competitive than ever in Nagano. The Canadians rebounded from Lillehammer to win two gold and two bronze. At the Olympics and world championships, Canadian skaters proved that even though the stakes kept escalating, they were up for the challenge.

At the 1992, 1994 and 1998 Olympics, short track accounted for 11 of the 35 medals won by Canadians. Not bad for a newcomer on the block. ❧

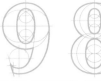
Éric Bédard

The present and future of short track speed skating

"The glory, the receptions and the honours have taken nothing away from the Nagano double medallist's refreshing amiability." That's how a reporter from Montreal's *La Presse* described the young man from the small Quebec village of Ste-Thècle who had just ascended to the pinnacle of his sport with a gold medal as part of the short track relay team, after winning an individual bronze medal in the 1000m.

His international career started to take form after the 1995 Canada Games, where he set four Canadian records on his way to four gold medals. Needless to say, he finished first in the overall standings.

In a sport where the competition is notoriously fierce, Bédard earned a berth on the Canadian team as an individual skater, battling against skaters who would later be his teammates in the relay.

Claude Parent

"It was certainly a powerful feeling to receive my bronze medal at the Nagano Olympics in 1998," he said. "It was my first Olympic medal, but a few days later, the gold medal I won with my teammates in the relay gave me an even bigger feeling of satisfaction. That medal proved that we were the best team in the world. It was an indescribable feeling. Being part of a team, contributing to success with your teammates, and working together to reach a goal teaches you really important life lessons."

That same year, Bédard and his teammates captured the World Team Championships in Italy. Along the way, they again proved to be the best relay team. It came as no surprise that they were named the "Team of the Year" in 1998.

Bédard wasn't ready to quit yet. At the end of the century he had already embarked on his drive towards the 2002 Olympics in Salt Lake City. After an injury-plagued year in 1999, he won gold in the 500m at the World Championships and silver in the 1500m. His performances earned him second place in the overall standings behind Korean Min Ryoung. With his teammates he then won the World Team Championships.

At the end of the century, Bédard was well-positioned to move towards his goal of a gold medal in Salt Lake City. ❧

The Quebec Air Force –

The Laroche family and friends pioneer a new sport

It must be that pioneering spirit. Whatever the reason, Canadians have been leaders in the development of many sports, including freestyle skiing. Of the three main events in freestyle — aerials, moguls and ballet — Canadians have gained the most fame and acclaim in the former two.

Born in the late 1960s as a sort of counter-culture alternative to established downhill racing, freestyle was originally the domain of acrobatic young skiers who were often derisively called hotdoggers. Leading the pack was a loose grouping of acrobatic aerialists from La Belle Province who became known as the Quebec Air Force.

CSI/COA

Philippe Laroche

Canada

CSI/COA

Lloyd Langlois

One of those pioneers was former world champion John Eaves, who was there for the sport's heyday in the early 1970s. Promoters would offer large prizes to daredevils such as Eaves to perform dizzying aerial stunts, with little regard for safety. It's little wonder that Eaves went on to become a professional stuntman for James Bond films.

As the sport gained safety and respectability, a number of Quebec skiers followed in Eaves' footsteps, including aerials legends such as Lloyd Langlois of Magog, and several brothers from the famous Laroche family of Lac Beauport: Alain, Yves, and Philippe. (Sister Lucie Laroche opted for the more staid sport of downhill racing.) Another rising star was, of course, moguls champion Jean-Luc Brassard.

Both Langlois and the various members of the Laroche family garnered world titles and international acclaim for their gravity-defying aerial prowess. Along the way, the sport matured out of its daredevil beginnings and became a more serious athletic competition.

But the characteristics of the sport that excited both athletes and spectators remained. In the aerials, competitors launch themselves off steep ramps of hard-packed snow and soar into the air to execute complex combinations of somersaults and/or twists, before flying back down to earth and landing neatly. In the moguls event, competitors race down a mogul-packed run. Along the way, each skier must complete two "airs," or jumps, which go by colourful names such as the Daffy, the Chopper, or Brassard's specialty, the Iron-Cross Cossack. In contrast with the more serious atmosphere at most sporting events, both events are held with rock or rap music blasting the air.

Canada initially introduced the Olympic world to freestyle by making it a demonstration event at the 1988 Olympics in Calgary. By the 1992 Albertville Olympic Games, the hotdoggers were there in full force to shake up the staid Olympic program. Aerials were a demonstration sport, while the mogul event was an official one. Canada took the aerials in a 1-2 finish, with Philippe Laroche winning the gold and Nicolas Fontaine the silver.

Canada's skiers were shut out of the moguls medals in 1992, but their pioneering efforts paid off at the 1994 Winter Olympic Games in Lillehammer, when Jean-Luc Brassard captured the gold medal, and the hearts and imagination of Canadians, in the demanding moguls event. Veterans Philippe Laroche and Lloyd Langlois, meanwhile, captured silver and bronze in the aerials event, the first time since 1932 and only the second time ever that two Canadians had stood on the podium in an individual Winter Olympic event. ♣

Philippe Laroche won the demonstration aerials at the Albertville Olympics, 1992

1987

Man in Motion

The End of an Odyssey

by Malcolm Gray
June 1, 1987

Rick Hansen raised his gloved hands in celebration after rolling his wheelchair across the parking lot of Vancouver's Oakridge mall. There, before 7,000 cheering spectators, Hansen triumphantly concluded an incredible odyssey during which he, accompanied by a six-member crew, wheeled through 34 countries in 26 months. Only 300 invited guests and onlookers braved the wind and rain in that same lot on March 21, 1985, when Hansen set out on his 40,073 km journey — the equivalent of the circumference of the globe. But thousands of well-wishers applauded his passage on the final stretch of the Man in Motion World Tour through the flat, fertile farmland of the Fraser Valley and into Vancouver last week. They did so in recognition of the fact that Hansen's remarkable feat has fostered awareness of the plight — and potential — of the handicapped and at the same time raised more than $14 million for spinal-cord research, rehabilitation and wheelchair sports.

Hansen proved that he could surmount such challenges as the 40°C heat of the Australian desert and the windswept passes of the Swiss Alps and Canadian Rockies. And in response, government officials and ordinary citizens around the world opened their hearts — and wallets — to the handsome wheelchair athlete. But tour officials acknowledged that Canadians had contributed all but $28,000 of the $14 million that the marathon raised for research and rehabilitation projects. And at journey's end, as Hansen, his road crew members and support staff at the marathon's downtown Vancouver headquarters contemplated adjusting to life after the tour, the British Columbia government provided the largest donation — a $3 million pledge to match the private contributions of BC residents.

Hansen's achievement recalled similar successes by two other BC marathoners. In 1985 Steve Fonyo, a one legged runner from Vernon, raised $13 million for cancer research on a cross-Canada run. And a similar fund-raising effort in 1980 by Terry Fox generated $24 million. But Fox was forced to end his run near the halfway point by a recurrence of the cancer that had taken his right leg — and eventually killed him in 1981. Last week, on the final day of his journey, Hansen passed through Fox's home town, the Vancouver-area town of Port Coquitlam. There, before a welcoming crowd of several hundred people, many waving yellow ribbons and balloons in greeting, he paid tribute to his predecessor. Said Hansen: "He stands as a man who was not afraid to reach for his dreams, a man who knew that failing was not reaching, not trying to be the best that you can with what you have."

Certainly, Hansen acknowledges that he had to struggle to regain his sense of self-worth after being tossed from the back of a pickup truck in June, 1973. That accident severed his spinal cord and left him permanently paralyzed below the waist. But he persevered and met a series of goals that he set for himself. He began by getting out of hospital and returning to school, eventually becoming the first disabled person to receive a degree in physical education from the University of British Columbia. And in 1980, he said Fox's run inspired him to consider another challenge: wheeling his way around the world.

Still, he needed all his resolve and dedication. The marathon began with Hansen and his crew estimating that they only had enough money for one week. But they persevered, gaining corporate sponsors and overcoming setbacks that included 100 flat tires and two occasions when Hansen collapsed from fatigue in Greece. The grueling roadwork over, Hansen still must attend to unfinished business. For one thing, he must choose six experts in spinal-cord research and rehabilitation of the handicapped to join him and two other members on a special committee. Their task: to allocate grants from about $1-million worth of yearly interest from the trust fund.

Hansen also found romance on his epic journey. On Oct. 10 the 29-year-old athlete will marry his fiancée Amanda Reid. She is a 27-year-old physiotherapist who joined the tour two weeks after it began — and signed on for the duration in order to attend to Hansen's nagging wrist and shoulder injuries. Both Hansen and the auburn-haired Reid say that their love evolved slowly during their two years together in the road — and that meeting the demands of the tour always came first. Now they can plan their life together — and both say that they would like to have children. But they have not decided on the number. Reid wants two children while Hansen would like to have four.

Ahead of them lie such simple pleasures as going to the movies — and even walking in the park — Hansen is able to walk for several kilometers with the aid of leg braces and crutches. And even though an event that he described as "the greatest challenge of my life" is over, Hansen is unlikely to fade from public view. For one thing, the Vancouver publishers Douglas & McIntyre expect that his biography, *Rick Hansen, Man in Motion*, will be an instant bestseller. To that end the publishers are printing 50,000 copies of the book — written by veteran Vancouver sports columnist Jim Taylor — for a scheduled launch in September. Still, after rolling his chair through the yellow tape that marked the end of his journey — in a ceremony broadcast live across the country by CBC TV — Hansen said that he has yet to make plans for his future. Declared Hansen: "I am looking forward to a good rest." The applause that marked his homecoming indicated that he had earned it. ♦

Canada's Rick Hansen, the "Man in Motion."

Montreal Expos

1969-2000

Baseball Highlights

National Archives

Former Canadian Prime Minister and lifelong baseball fan Lester Pearson throws out the first pitch at the first Major League Baseball game played in Canada, April 14, 1969, at Montreal's Jarry Park.

May 27, 1968

Major League Baseball's National League (NL) awarded two expansion franchises for the 1969 season: Montreal and San Diego. Charles Bronfman, head of the Seagram's distilling empire, was the Montreal Expos first owner.

April 8, 1969

The Expos played the first game in team history against the New York Mets at Shea Stadium, winning 11-10.

April 14, 1969

The Montreal Expos played their first home game at Jarry Park in front of 29,184 fans, beating the St. Louis Cardinals 8-7.

April 17, 1969

Pitcher Bill Stoneman shut out the Philadelphia Phillies 7-0, en route to registering the two-week old Montreal Expos' first no-hitter.

June 25, 1969

Bob Bailey and Bobby Wine executed the first triple play in Expos' history at Jarry Park.

October 2, 1972

Bill Stoneman pitched his and the Expos' second career no-hitter in a 7-0 victory over the New York Mets at Jarry Park in Montreal.

April 15, 1977

The Expos played their first game at Olympic Stadium in Montreal in front of 57,592 fans, but lost 7-2 to the Philadelphia Phillies.

April 20, 1977

Catcher Gary Carter became the first Expos' hitter to hit three home runs in the same game, doing so against the Pittsburgh Pirates' Jim Rooker during the Expos' inaugural homestand at Olympic Stadium.

October 1, 1978

Ross Grimsley became the only Montreal Expo in the century to register a 20-win season.

October 1979

The Expos finished second in the NL East to the Pittsburgh Pirates, remaining in the pennant race until the final series of the season.

September 10, 1980

Rookie pitcher Bill Gullickson struck out 18 Chicago Cubs in one game, a team record that lasted the century.

October 1980

The Expos again maintained their playoff hopes until the final day of the season, but ended up finishing second in the NL East, one game behind the Philadelphia Phillies.

May 10, 1981

Pitcher Charlie Lea threw the third no-hitter in Expos' history in a 4-0 win against the San Francisco Giants at Olympic Stadium.

October 3, 1981

Due to a player-management dispute, this baseball season saw two half seasons played. In the final game of a strike-interrupted season, the Expos beat the New York Mets to clinch the 1981 second-half NL East title.

October 10, 1981

The Expos won their first National League East division title, defeating the first-half title-holding Philadelphia Phillies in the best-of-five division series 3 games to 2.

October 19, 1981

On a day Montrealers remember simply as "Blue Monday," Los Angeles Dodgers outfielder Rick Monday ended the Expos' hopes of a trip to the World Series with a game-winning, ninth-inning home run off Steve Rogers in the fifth and deciding game of the NL Championship Series at Olympic Stadium. The Dodgers went on to beat the New York Yankees in the Fall Classic, the third consecutive season that the Expos were eliminated by the eventual World Series Champions.

July 13, 1982

Montreal hosted the first Major League Baseball All-Star game held outside the United States.

October 3, 1982

Al Oliver became the first Expos' hitter to win a batting title, with a .331 batting average. Teammate Tim Raines would win the team's second four years later, hitting .336 in 1986.

July 28, 1991

El Presidente! El Perfecto! Montreal Expos' Dennis Martinez pitched the 15th perfect game in Major League Baseball history, beating the Dodgers 2-0 in Los Angeles. Just two days earlier, Mark Gardner of the Expos had pitched nine innings of no-hit baseball against the Dodgers, only to lose the game in the 10th inning.

August 12, 1994

Ruining what would likely have been the finest season in Montreal's history, Major League Baseball players went on strike and ended the season prematurely. The Expos finished six games ahead of the Atlanta Braves in first place in the NL East, finishing with the best record that year in baseball with a 74-40 record. The Expos finished 34 games over .500, their highest mark at the end of any season through the century.

June 3, 1995

Expos' starter Pedro Martinez pitched a perfect game for nine innings at San Diego, but with the score tied 0-0 the game went into extra innings. He gave up a lead-off double in the 10th, thus losing his bid for a perfect game. He was replaced by closer Mel Rojas, as Montreal went on to win the game 1-0.

December 1997

Pedro Martinez became the first Expos' pitcher and first Dominican to win baseball's coveted Cy Young Award, awarded to the top Major League pitcher. Martinez won 17 games to go along with a 1.90 ERA and 305 strikeouts in 206 2/3 innings pitched.

Toronto Blue Jays

1977-2000

Baseball Highlights

1977

Major League Baseball came to Toronto on April 7, 1977. The hometown Blue Jays defeated the Chicago White Sox 9-5, with rookie Doug Ault hitting two home runs in the Jays' first game. Otto Velez hit .442 for the month of April. Bob Bailor hit .310 over the season, the highest mark ever for a player on a first-year expansion club.

1980

John Mayberry became the first Blue Jay to hit 30 homers in a season.

1983

The Blue Jays were contenders in 1983 for the first time. The club's designated hitters, Cliff Johnson and Jorge Orta, combined to hit 34 home runs and 113 RBIs, while the Jays' .277 team hitting average led the entire American League. Lloyd Moseby became the first Jay to score more than 100 runs, as he hit .315 with 18 home runs, 81 RBIs and 27 stolen bases. Willie Upshaw became the first Jay to record 100 RBIs, hitting 27 homers as well.

1984

The Blue Jays won 19 one-run victories in the first half of the season, then dropped 25 of 40 one-run games over the second half of the season. They finished with 89 wins, in second place behind the World Series winning Detroit Tigers.

1985

The Blue Jays won the American League East on October 5, 1985 when Doyle Alexander beat the Yankees 5-1. The Jays finished with 99 wins and went on to play the Kansas City Royals in the AL Championship Series, losing a tight seven-game series.

1986

The Blue Jays Jesse Barfield and George Bell both drove in a club record 108 runs, with Barfield also setting a club record with 40 homers.

1987-1991

Jimmy Key and Dave Stieb combined to win 291 games for Toronto during the '80s and early '90s.

1987

In September, Toronto and Detroit staged one of Major League Baseball's most dramatic pennant races. Toronto had held a solid lead most of the year before the two teams played seven games against each other over the last 10 days of the season. The games were all decided by one run, with Toronto finishing two games back of Detroit with 96 wins, the second-highest in the majors to Detroit's 98. The Blue Jays hit a major-league record 10 home runs in one game on September 14. George Bell (47 HRs and 134 RBI) earned American League MVP honours.

1988

The Blue Jays had a slow start in 1988 and trailed the Division leaders by 11.5 games in mid July. After the All-Star break, though, the Jays enjoyed the best second-half record with 45 wins, ending up two games out of first. The club led the league in home runs (158), triples (47), total bases (2330) and slugging percentage (.419). Fred McGriff's 34 homers led the AL, and the pitchers combined for a league-high 17 shutouts.

1989

The Blue Jays won their second American League East crown in 1989, playing most of the season in the new SkyDome. With a team record 20 wins in August, the Jays pulled into a first place tie with Baltimore on the last day of the month. Back-to back wins over the Orioles on the last weekend of the season clinched the East Division title. In the American League Championship Series, the Jays lost to the Oakland A's in five games.

September 2, 1990

Dave Stieb pitched the first no-hitter in franchise history against the Cleveland Indians. Stieb also pitched the 100th complete game of his career on May 28, shutting out Oakland 1-0.

1991

The Blue Jays won the American League East title again, but lost another chance to go to the World Series, losing to the Minnesota Twins in the AL Championship Series. The Jays became the first team in baseball history to draw 4,000,000 fans over the course of the season.

Toronto Star — J. Goode

Joe Carter celebrating his 1993 home run that gave the Toronto Blue Jays their second consecutive World Series title.

1992

Toronto Blue Jays, 1992 World Series Champions.
The 1992 Blue Jays were a well-balanced team, with Dave Winfield, Jack Morris, Alfredo Griffin and David Cone joining the club for the season. After clinching their second consecutive American League East title, the Jays defeated the Oakland A's in six games to reach the World Series for the first time. After an opening game loss to the Atlanta Braves, the Jays then won three straight, two as a result of dramatic ninth-inning comebacks. Atlanta won game five, but then Jays made baseball history, becoming the first team based outside the USA to win the World Series, with a 4-3 game six victory in 11 innings.

1993

Toronto Blue Jays, 1993 World Series Champions.
The Blue Jays did not rest after their 1992 championship and entered the 1993 season with 11 new faces. John Olerud, Robbie Alomar and Paul Molitor finished 1-2-3 in the AL batting race as the Jays won their third straight American League East title. Pitcher Dave Stewart registered two wins as the Jays defeated the Chicago White Sox in six games to win the American League pennant. They faced the Philadelphia Phillies in the World Series, splitting the first two games in Toronto before the Jays captured two of the next three in Philadelphia, including a record-setting 15-14 game four. Back in Toronto's SkyDome for game six, the Jays saw a 5-1 lead become a 6-5 deficit heading into the bottom of the ninth. Rickey Henderson and Paul Molitor reached base, setting the scene for Joe Carter to hit his historic home run off Mitch Williams to give the Jays their second straight championship. Carter's home run was only the second Series-ending home run in baseball history.

1996

In Toronto's 20th season, Blue Jay pitcher Pat Hengten became the first club Cy Young Award winner, posting a 20-10 record and leading the American League with 10 complete games and 265.2 innings pitched.

1997

The Blue Jays acquired free agent pitcher Roger Clemens from Boston. His 21 victories tied a club record and his 292 strikeouts set a new one, earning Clemens the Club's second and his fourth Cy Young Award.

1998

Pitcher Roger Clemens earned his fifth, and the team's third, Cy Young Award with a 20-6 record.

Hockey

HHOF

Sipping from Stanley

by Malcolm Gray
June 6, 1988

At 27, Wayne Gretzky is no longer a fresh-faced kid — and the hairstyle that he now favours reflects the blunt, no-nonsense approach taken by the Edmonton Oilers in this year's National Hockey League playoffs. Gretzky's hairstyle — army-recruit sidewalls and punk-like on top — gives him a lean, hungry look that matches Edmonton's drive to be one of the greatest sports dynasties of modern times. The Oilers took a giant step toward that goal last week by winning their fourth Stanley Cup with a convincing four-game sweep of the Boston Bruins. And for a team whose past triumphs relied heavily on dazzling displays of individual talent, coaches and players alike stressed that winning through disciplined team play was one of the sweeter aspects of victory. Declared Edmonton associate coach John Muckler: "They were all good, but this is the best Oiler *team* to win the cup."

Certainly, the Oilers were almost invincible in the playoffs, losing only two of 18 games after a relatively mediocre season that saw them finish third in the regular-season play. Indeed, Las Vegas bookmakers picked another Alberta team — the Calgary Flames — as the odds-on favourites to win the Stanley Cup this year. But the Flames, like the Bruins, fell in four games in postseason play that featured several unusual events. The strangest was a power blackout at the steamy Boston Garden last week caused by transformer malfunction outside the building. That power loss forced the cancellation of the fourth game in the Oilers-Bruins

series — a contest that was also notable for frequent delays caused by fog rising from the ice surface in the sweltering 30°C temperature of the 60-year-old building. Despite such distractions, the Oilers brushed aside their playoff opponents, and the players quietly measured themselves against such great teams of the past as the Montreal Canadiens, the winners of five straight Stanley Cups between 1956 and 1960. Declared Gretzky: "The scary thing is we're going to be better next year."

It will be unsettling news for opposing checkers if Gretzky gets better. Within a year the game's most outstanding player has captained three championship teams. He did so by sandwiching a Canada Cup win over the Soviet national team last September between Edmonton's Stanley Cup victory over the Philadelphia Flyers in 1987 and their successful defence of the cup last

HHOF — Paul Bereswill

HHOF — Paul Bereswill

week. And for the second time in his career, Gretzky won the Conn Smythe Trophy as the most valuable player in NHL postseason play, amassing 43 points with 12 goals and a record-breaking 31 assists.

One play alone in Edmonton's 6-3 win in the final game over the Bruins had his coach Glenn Sather grasping for superlatives. As the second period drew to a close Gretzky gained control over the puck and then moved up ice, eluding a check near the Boston blue line. He hesitated briefly, then flicked the puck softly toward a corner of the net where winger Craig Simpson stood. Time remaining on the clock as Simpson redirected the puck past Bruin goaltender — and former Oiler — Andy Moog: two seconds. Said Sather: "I've been watching Wayne play since he was 17. He's a great example for every kid in this country."

Sather himself said that he does not like to refer to the Oilers as a dynasty. Declared Sather: "It makes you sound like you're bragging. When I think of a dynasty, I think of the Ming dynasty." Still, he has been careful to avoid a pattern that is familiar to such great teams as the New York Islanders. In 1984 the Oilers dethroned that team, a collection of veteran superstars that had remained largely intact since the Islanders won the first of four straight Stanley Cups in 1980. But only nine members of Edmonton's first championship team in 1984 have survived to celebrate the Oilers' fourth win last week. Kevin Lowe, a steady defenceman, is a member of that Old Guard and he said that he finds the final act of

each session — taking the team's picture — a bittersweet occasion. Said Lowe: "Every year Slats (Sather) makes changes, and you know that three or four guys who are in that picture are not going to be with the team next season."

Lowe, who stoically suited up for most of the playoffs with a broken wrist and three cracked ribs, is 29. But other key members of the team, including forwards Mark Messier, Glenn Anderson and goaltender Grant Fuhr, are 27 years of age or younger. As a result, Lowe echoes Gretzky's prediction that the Oilers will be a championship-calibre team for years to come. Said Lowe: "We want to win as many Stanley Cups as possible. I think we're one cup away from being recognized as the greatest hockey team of all time." ❧

HHOF — Paul Bereswill

HHOF

The Edmonton Oilers – the Last Canadian Dynasty?

The Edmonton Oilers' five Stanley Cup wins over seven seasons from 1984 to 1990 mark the last time during the 20th century that a Canadian team dominated the NHL. The team's nucleus formed during its years as a World Hockey Association franchise, when the team was coached by hockey mastermind Glen Sather and featured local boy Mark Messier as one of its stars. Wayne Gretzky joined the team in 1978, the year before the Oilers and three other WHA teams merged with the NHL. From that point on, the team only got better.

In 1983, they surprised everyone by beating the Montreal Canadiens on their way to the Stanley Cup finals, where they lost in four straight games to the New York Islanders. In 1984, they got their revenge, bringing the Islanders' dynasty to an end and bringing the Cup to Edmonton for the first time. A young team, the Oilers looked strong enough, on paper and on the ice, to repeat their performance for a number of years to come.

The next year they did it again, this time over the Philadelphia Flyers. The convincing victory came courtesy of the maturing talents of Gretzky and Mark Messier with an excellent supporting cast.

They were favoured to make it three in a row in 1986, but what seemed like the only Oiler weakness of the era surfaced with a vengeance. The team was accused of lacking maturity and focus, which meant that despite having the best regular season record they were unable to adjust quickly to a setback in the playoffs. Cross-province rivals the Calgary Flames shocked them with a seven-game victory in the second round of the playoffs. The loss was all that much harder to take because the winning goal was actually scored by Oiler Steve Smith into his own net.

With a full year to correct the problems, they finished first in the league again in 1987. This time, they did a better job of overcoming the roadblocks en route to beating the Philadelphia Flyers again for their third Cup.

With its deep pool of talent, it looked like Edmonton could carry on indefinitely. But trouble arose when star defenceman Paul Coffey revealed he was unhappy with owner Peter Pocklington and coach Glen Sather. With his departure for Pittsburgh, the club was weakened, but still strong enough to beat Boston in the 1988 Cup final in just five games.

Then came The Trade — Gretzky's move to the Los Angeles Kings. Following a year after Coffey's departure, his was a loss the club could not adjust to. They went out in the first round of the 1989 playoffs, ironically the victims of Gretzky's Kings.

It seemed like the dynasty was ended and that Edmonton would never win without Gretzky. The club finished second in the Smythe division the next year, and did not look impressive in eking out a seven-game opening round playoff win over Winnipeg. But with Bill Ranford replacing an ailing Grant Fuhr in goal, they caught fire, overpowering first Los Angeles and then Chicago. By the time they defeated Boston in five games to win the 1990 Stanley Cup, Ranford had earned the Conn Smythe Trophy as the most valuable player in the playoffs. ❧

HHOF

1988-1989

Mario Lemieux took advantage of the downfall of the Oilers to win his second straight scoring title, registering a career high of 199 points for the season (the highest non-Gretzky total in the century).

October 15, 1989

Wayne Gretzky passed Gordie Howe as the NHL all-time scoring leader with a three-point game — an early assist (tying Howe at 1850), a tying goal with 53 seconds left (breaking the record with 1851), and the overtime winner (en route to many, many more).

March, 1990

The first Women's World Hockey Championships saw Canada win its first of six straight gold medals in the 1990s.

1990-1991

Canadian-born Brett Hull scored 86 goals, joining his father Bobby as a Hart Trophy winner — the only father-son duo to achieve such heights.

January 2, 1992

In the largest player trade in the century, the Toronto Maple Leafs and Calgary Flames swap 10 players, including Doug Gilmour coming to Toronto.

April 1-10, 1992

The NHL players strike when the iron is hot — at playoff time. Sane heads, and a good deal for the players, saved Canada's springtime ritual of the Stanley Cup playoffs, this time won by Mario Lemieux and the Pittsburgh Penguins.

June 30, 1992

Eric Lindros refused to play for the Quebec Nordiques, the team which had selected him as the first player in the 1991 Junior Draft. Quebec took its time, and eventually sold Lindros' rights, but two clubs claimed to have made a deal — the New York Rangers and the Philadelphia Flyers. The Flyers won out in arbitration, but it cost them six players, two draft picks and $15 million. The Flyers never won the Cup with Lindros during the century; Quebec was sold and moved to Colorado in 1996, where they won the Cup in their first year.

September 23, 1992

Manon Rhéaume became the first female to play a game involving NHL teams. She played net for Tampa Bay in an exhibition against the St. Louis Blues.

December 10, 1992

The Ottawa Senators live again. An Ottawa group received an expansion franchise and returned NHL hockey to the nation's capital after a mere 60-year hiatus.

1992-1993

The Montreal Canadiens won 10 overtime games en route to the team's 24th Stanley Cup of the century — by far the most in the NHL. The Toronto Maple Leafs franchise is second with 13 (11 by the Leafs and one each by the St. Pats and the Arenas).

January 11, 1993

Mario Lemieux announced that he had been diagnosed with cancer (Hodgkin's Disease). After missing two months of play, he returned to action March 2 and scored a goal and an assist. Remarkably, Lemieux scored 56 more points to close out the season and win the Art Ross Trophy as the league's top scorer. He also won the Hart (MVP) and Masterton (Perseverance) Trophies.

March 23, 1994

Wayne Gretzky surpassed Gordie Howe on the all-time goal scoring list, marking his 802nd career goal against Vancouver's Kirk McLean.

February, 1994

At the Lillehammer Olympics, Canada and Sweden end the gold medal game in a tie. Canada took an early lead in the five-goal shootout, but Sweden's Peter Forsberg scored on a remarkable one-handed backhand deke on Canada's Corey Hirsch to win the gold medal. It was Canada's second consecutive Olympic silver.

1995-1996

Coaching the Detroit Red Wings, Scotty Bowman won his 1,607th game behind the bench, becoming the NHL's winningest coach (passing Al Arbour). Bowman also led Detroit to 62 wins for the season, surpassing the 60-win season (with two fewer games on the schedule) of the 1976-1977 Montreal Canadiens, which had also been coached by Bowman.

December 2, 1995

Patrick Roy always played goal with his heart. The sacred Montreal netminder, however, was embarrassed in an 11-1 loss to Detroit on this night. Upset with not being pulled from the game, Roy told the Canadiens' President, sitting behind the bench during the game, that he had played his last game in Montreal. Four days later, Roy was traded to Colorado. Later that same season, Roy led the Avalanche to their first Stanley Cup.

February 27, 1996

Wayne Gretzky was traded again, this time by choice to the St. Louis Blues, where he played just part of one season.

December, 1996

Canada's juniors won their fifth consecutive World Junior Championship.

April 16, 1999

Wayne Gretzky played his last hockey game in Canada, in Ottawa against the Senators.

September 1, 1999

The NHL Board of Governors confirmed Mario Lemieux as the new owner and Chairman of the Pittsburgh Penguins.

December 27, 2000

Mario Lemieux returned to the NHL from a three-year retirement to score a goal and two assists against Toronto in his first game back.

HHOF — Dave Sandford

April 18, 1999, Wayne Gretzky retired after playing as a New York Ranger in his last game against the Pittsburgh Penguins, a 2-1 overtime loss.

Frank Nighbor

Mario Lemieux

Wayne Gretzky

Hart Trophy winners (NHL MVP)

Year	Player	Team	Year	Player	Team
1924	Frank Nighbor	Ottawa Senators	1962	Jacques Plante	Montreal Canadiens
1925	Billy Burch	Hamilton Tigers	1963	Gordie Howe	Detroit Red Wings
1926	Nels Stewart	Montreal Maroons	1964	Jean Béliveau	Montreal Canadiens
1927	Herb Gardiner	Montreal Canadiens	1965	Bobby Hull	Chicago Blackhawks
1928	Howie Morenz	Montreal Canadiens	1966	Bobby Hull	Chicago Blackhawks
1929	Roy Worters	New York Americans	1967	Stan Mikita	Chicago Blackhawks
1930	Nels Stewart	Montreal Maroons	1968	Stan Mikita	Chicago Blackhawks
1931	Howie Morenz	Montreal Canadiens	1969	Phil Esposito	Boston Bruins
1932	Howie Morenz	Montreal Canadiens	1970	Bobby Orr	Boston Bruins
1933	Eddie Shore	Boston Bruins	1971	Bobby Orr	Boston Bruins
1934	Aurèle Joliat	Montreal Canadiens	1972	Bobby Orr	Boston Bruins
1935	Eddie Shore	Boston Bruins	1973	Bobby Clarke	Philadelphia Flyers
1936	Eddie Shore	Boston Bruins	1974	Phil Esposito	Boston Bruins
1937	Babe Siebert	Montreal Canadiens	1975	Bobby Clarke	Philadelphia Flyers
1938	Eddie Shore	Boston Bruins	1976	Bobby Clarke	Philadelphia Flyers
1939	Toe Blake	Montreal Canadiens	1977	Guy Lafleur	Montreal Canadiens
1940	Eddie Goodfellow	Detroit Red Wings	1978	Guy Lafleur	Montreal Canadiens
1941	Bill Cowley	Boston Bruins	1979	Bryan Trottier	New York Islanders
1942	Tom Anderson	Brooklyn Americans	1980	Wayne Gretzky	Edmonton Oilers
1943	Bill Cowley	Boston Bruins	1981	Wayne Gretzky	Edmonton Oilers
1944	Babe Pratt	Toronto Maple Leafs	1982	Wayne Gretzky	Edmonton Oilers
1945	Elmer Lach	Montreal Canadiens	1983	Wayne Gretzky	Edmonton Oilers
1946	Max Bentley	Chicago Blackhawks	1984	Wayne Gretzky	Edmonton Oilers
1947	Maurice Richard	Montreal Canadiens	1985	Wayne Gretzky	Edmonton Oilers
1948	Buddy O'Connor	New York Rangers	1986	Wayne Gretzky	Edmonton Oilers
1949	Sid Abel	Detroit Red Wings	1987	Wayne Gretzky	Edmonton Oilers
1950	Charlie Rayner	New York Rangers	1988	Mario Lemieux	Pittsburgh Penguins
1951	Milt Schmidt	Boston Bruins	1989	Wayne Gretzky	Los Angeles Kings
1952	Gordie Howe	Detroit Red Wings	1990	Mark Messier	Edmonton Oilers
1953	Gordie Howe	Detroit Red Wings	1991	Brett Hull	St. Louis Blues
1954	Al Rollins	Chicago Blackhawks	1992	Mark Messier	New York Rangers
1955	Ted Kennedy	Toronto Maple Leafs	1993	Mario Lemieux	Pittsburgh Penguins
1956	Jean Béliveau	Montreal Canadiens	1994	Sergei Fedorov	Detroit Red Wings
1957	Gordie Howe	Detroit Red Wings	1995	Eric Lindros	Philadelphia Flyers
1958	Gordie Howe	Detroit Red Wings	1996	Mario Lemieux	Pittsburgh Penguins
1959	Andy Bathgate	New York Rangers	1997	Dominik Hasek	Buffalo Sabres
1960	Gordie Howe	Detroit Red Wings	1998	Dominik Hasek	Buffalo Sabres
1961	Bernie Geoffrion	Montreal Canadiens	1999	Jaromir Jagr	Pittsburgh Penguins
			2000	Chris Pronger	St. Louis Blues

Phil Esposito

Re-Writing History with a Stick

Wayne Gretzky's Records and Accomplishments

MINOR HOCKEY in Brantford:

Season	Level	Goals Scored
1967-68	Novice	1
1968-69		27
1969-70		104
1970-71		196
1971-72		378
1972-73	Pee Wee	105
1973-74		196
1974-75	Bantam	90
8 SEASONS		1,097

OHL Jr. A Sault Ste. Marie Greyhounds, 1977-78:

64 games, 70 goals, 112 assists, 182 points

WHA Indianapolis Racers / Edmonton Oilers, 1978-79:

Racers:	8 games	2 goals	4 assists	6 points
Oilers:	68 games	43 goals	61 assists	104 points
Totals:	76 games	44 goals	65 assists	110 points

NHL Quick Summary:

Most Career Points	2,857
Most Career Assists	1,963
Most Career Goals	894
Most Points One Season	215
Most Points One Season Including Playoffs	255
Most Assists One Season	163
Most Goals One Season	92
Most Goals from Start of Season	61
Longest Point Scoring Streak	51
Most 3-or-more Goal Games, Career	50
Most Game Winning Goals in Playoffs	24
All-Star Games	15
Most 100-or-more Point Seasons	15
Most Consecutive 100-or-more points	13
Most 50-or-more Goal Seasons	9
Most 60-or-more Goal Seasons	5
Most 3-goal Games, One Season	10
Art Ross Trophy (Scoring)	10
Hart Trophies (MVP)	9
Stanley Cups	4
Conn Smythe Trophy (Playoffs MVP)	2

HHOF

HHOF — Dave Sandford

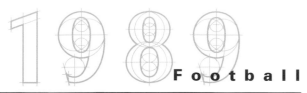

November 26, 1989

SkyDome, Toronto

Possibly the Greatest Grey Cup Game Ever Played

(They might disagree in Hamilton)

The 1989 Saskatchewan Roughriders, Grey Cup Champions.

Afterwards Dave Ridgway said he warned his teammate Glen Suitor: "I told him he could talk to me about anything other than football. So we discussed camping which I've never done. He promised to take me out and let the bears eat me."

That may have been just the small humorous edge Ridgway needed to freeze out whatever nerve-wracking demons he had prior to kicking the game-winning field goal in perhaps the most memorable Grey Cup match ever played.

The 1989 final had a promising cast. The Saskatchewan Roughriders, bridesmaids on so many occasions, were hoping to win only their second championship ever. The Hamilton Tiger Cats, who could commute by GO Train to Toronto's SkyDome, had won 13.

It didn't start off well for Saskatchewan. Two field goals and a Mike Kerrigan to Tony Champion touchdown pass gave the almost hometown Tiger Cats a 13-1 lead early in the first quarter. The Roughies jitters disappeared in the second quarter, however, as Kent Austin threw touchdowns to Ray Elgaard, Jeff Fairholm, and Don Narcisse while Hamilton replied twice with TDs of their own. The Ti-Cats entered the half ahead by 27-22.

Surely the teams couldn't maintain this scoring pace for the rest of the game!

In the third quarter Saskatchewan began to assert themselves as they forced Hamilton punter Paul Osbaldiston to concede a two-point safety touch. Two plays later Don Narcisse picked up 52 yards for the Roughriders. Saskatchewan completed the drive a few plays later and took the lead as Tim McCray crossed the goal line.

Toronto Star — J. Mahler

Canada

CFHOF

Exchanging field goals the western contenders had a 40-33 lead with two minutes remaining in regulation time. Undaunted, Hamilton's Kerrigan led his team downfield. With less than a minute remaining, he threw a desperate and final third down pass to the end zone. Tony Champion, who had already caught seven passes, dove backwards in mid-air to make a spectacular touchdown grab and then crashed onto the artificial turf. There were 43 seconds left.

Overtime was imminent but Saskatchewan quarterback Kent Austin had other ideas. He completed four straight quick passes to take his team to the Hamilton 26-yard line with three seconds remaining on the clock.

That's when Ridgway and Suitor had their little talk.

"If I missed the field goal I wanted it to go far enough to get us the single point or force them to kick it back out," Ridgway later said.

He didn't have to worry as the ball went straight through the uprights to win Saskatchewan the Grey Cup, outscoring Hamilton 43-40. ♣

Toronto Star — J. Mahler

Hamilton Tiger Cat Tony Champion making a spinning, diving, catch on third-and-goal to score what Hamilton fans thought was the tying touchdown in the final minute of the 1989 Grey Cup game. Saskatchewan came back, though, to kick the winning field goal with three seconds left.

CFL Most Outstanding Player Award

Year	Player	Team
1953	Billy Vessels	Edmonton
1954	Sam Etcheverry	Montreal
1955	Pat Abbruzzi	Montreal
1956	Hal Patterson	Montreal
1957	Jackie Parker	Edmonton
1958	Jackie Parker	Edmonton
1959	Johnny Bright	Edmonton
1960	Jackie Parker	Edmonton
1961	Bernie Faloney	Hamilton
1962	George Dixon	Montreal
1963	Russ Jackson	Ottawa
1964	Lovell Coleman	Calgary
1965	George Reed	Saskatchewan
1966	Russ Jackson	Ottawa
1967	Peter Liske	Calgary
1968	Bill Symons	Toronto
1969	Russ Jackson	Ottawa
1970	Ron Lancaster	Saskatchewan
1971	Don Jonas	Winnipeg
1972	Garney Henley	Hamilton
1973	George McGowan	Edmonton
1974	Tom Wilkinson	Edmonton
1975	Willie Burden	Calgary
1976	Ron Lancaster	Saskatchewan
1977	Jimmy Edwards	Hamilton
1978	Tony Gabriel	Ottawa
1979	David Green	Montreal
1980	Dieter Brock	Winnipeg
1981	Dieter Brock	Winnipeg
1982	Condredge Holloway	Toronto
1983	Warren Moon	Edmonton
1984	Willard Reaves	Winnipeg
1985	Merv Fernandez	BC
1986	James Murphy	Winnipeg
1987	Tom Clements	Winnipeg
1988	David Williams	BC
1989	Tracy Ham	Edmonton
1990	Mike Clemons	Toronto
1991	Doug Flutie	BC
1992	Doug Flutie	Calgary
1993	Doug Flutie	Calgary
1994	Doug Flutie	Calgary
1995	Mike Pringle	Baltimore
1996	Doug Flutie	Toronto
1997	Doug Flutie	Toronto
1998	Mike Pringle	Montreal
1999	Danny McManus	Hamilton
2000	Dave Dickenson	Calgary

Prime Minister Pierre Trudeau was always a strong supporter of the CFL, and of the Grey Cup game. In 1968 he practised his placekicking for weeks, and showed up for the ceremonial kickoff wearing a kicking shoe. He set the ceremonial kickoff distance record. Here he is shown presenting the 1969 Grey Cup to the Ottawa Rough Riders' Russ Jackson.

November 26, 1978

Quarterback Ron Lancaster, "the Little General," led the Saskatchewan Roughriders for most of the 1960s and '70s. When he retired, he held the CFL century records for most passing yards in a career with 50,535-yards, and most passing touchdowns in a career with 333. He was selected as the league's Most Outstanding Player twice in his 19 seasons.

Four times an All-Canadian All-Star and seven times an All-Western All-Star, Lancaster also played three seasons for Ottawa in a career that went from 1960 to 1978. He won the Schenley Award as the league's Most Outstanding Player in 1970 and 1976 and retired holding most CFL career passing records.

1963-1975

Saskatchewan Roughrider George Reed rushed for more yards than any pro running back in any league, carrying the ball 16,116 yards in his 13-year career.

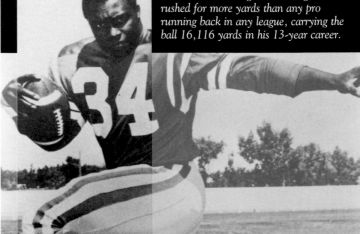

November 25, 1971

CFL legend Jackie Parker was elected to the Canadian Football Hall of Fame. He starred with the Edmonton Eskimos from 1954-62, and later with the Argos and the BC Lions. He played on three Grey Cup winners with Edmonton and won the Schenley as the CFL's top player three times. He starred as quarterback, halfback and defensive back. Parker, who also kicked, ended up with 750 career points scored (including 88 touchdowns); passed for another 88 touchdowns; kicked 40 field goals, 103 converts and 19 singles; and, was a Canadian All-Star eight straight years.

May 6, 1974

Bernie Faloney was inducted into the Canadian Football Hall of Fame. He played with Edmonton and Montreal as well, but his most productive years were as a quarterback with the Tiger Cats from 1957-63. He was voted the Most Outstanding Player in the CFL in 1961. He took Hamilton to the Grey Cup in '57, '58 '59, '61, '62 and '63. He is most remembered for returning a punt 111 yards in a playoff game against the Argonauts and, even though that play was called back on a penalty, the return is said to have broken the back of the Argonauts, who lost the game in overtime.

1969

Leo Cahill was the somewhat overconfident coach of the Toronto Argonauts who predicted that "only an act of God can beat us now" in the playoffs. The Argos lost to the Ottawa Rough Riders in the Eastern Final.

1967

The CIAU organized a Championship Football Game for University teams, the College Bowl for the Vanier Cup.

1974

Marc Lalonde, the federal minister for Health and Welfare, drafted legislation to prevent the fledgling World Football League from entering Canada, thus scaring off the proposed Toronto Northmen, who went south to become the Memphis Southmen. The legislation never reached the House of Commons.

1974

The Montreal Alouettes signed US college star Johnny Rodgers, who did quite well for himself on the field, even though according to him: "I'm just an ordinary superstar."

November 27, 1977

The most people ever to witness a Grey Cup in the century — 63,318 — assembled at Montreal's Olympic Stadium as the hometown Alouettes defeated Edmonton 41-6. Olympic Stadium also holds the record for the second highest Grey Cup game attendance of 62,113 set November 25, 1979 when the Als were on the short end of a 17-9 score against the Eskimos.

November 27, 1977

Punter Hank Ilesic made his first appearance in a Grey Cup game. In his career, he would earn seven Grey Cup rings — more than any other player in the century — in nine Grey Cup appearances with the Edmonton Eskimos ('77, '78, '79, '80, '81, '82) and with the Toronto Argonauts ('83, '87, '91).

July 29, 1984

Saskatchewan's Dave Ridgway kicked eight field goals against the Ottawa Rough Riders, a CFL record.

July 23, 1988

Saskatchewan's Dave Ridgway again kicked eight field goals, this time against the Edmonton Eskimos, tying his own CFL record.

September 22, 1996

Tiger Cat Paul Osbaldiston kicked eight field goals in a victory over Ottawa, tying a CFL record held by Mark McLoughlin of Calgary and Saskatchewan's Dave Ridgway (who did it twice: against Ottawa on July 29, 1984 and Edmonton July 23, 1988).

November 30, 1986

Henry "Gizmo" Williams played in his first Grey Cup as an Edmonton Eskimo. In his 13 seasons the Gizmo would set the record for most career punt return yards (10,598) and 26 touchdowns. He also set records for career kickoff return yards (7,231), and most punt returns for touchdowns in a career (26), in a season (5) and in a game (2).

September 9, 1990

Winnipeg Blue Bomber cornerback Rod Hill picked off five passes against the Hamilton Tiger Cats, setting a CFL single game interception record.

July 14, 1994

Winnipeg quarterback Matt Dunnigan set a CFL record for most yards passing in one game with 713 yards in a victory over the Edmonton Eskimos.

October 14, 1995

The largest regular season one game attendance at Regina's Taylor Field was 55,438 (with the addition of temporary seating) when Saskatchewan beat Calgary 25-23. Given that the regular capacity of Taylor Field was 27,732, this was a tight game in more ways than one.

Jim Young was inducted into the Canadian Football Hall of Fame. The Hamilton Westdale High School product played for the Queen's University Golden Gaels, then went directly to the NFL Minnesota Vikings for two years. In a unique trade between the leagues, Young joined the BC Lions in exchange for the rights to Willie Fleming. (Other sources have his Canadian rights held by the Toronto Argonauts who traded him to BC in return for Dick Fouts and Bill Symons.) From 1967-79, Young played in 197 games with the Lions where he became known as Dirty 30 for his aggressive style of playing receiver. Young would be the Lions' nominee for the Schlenley's Most Outstanding Player Award in '67, '69, and '72. He was also their nominee for Most Outstanding Canadian in '67, '69, '70, '71, '72, an award he won twice. From 1989 to 1992, he would join the Lion's front office.

September 4, 2000

Labour Day

The Hamilton Tiger Cats and the Toronto Argonauts renewed their Labour Day rivalry as they had so many times in the past. The rivalry is older than any other in North America, dating back to 1873. The first game in 1873 saw the Hamilton Football Club lose to the Toronto Argonauts on The University of Toronto grounds, but the Tiger Cats established a decided edge in victories over the next century or so. Since the modern-era of professional football began in 1950, the Ti-Cats held a 24-6 record in Labour Day games against the Argonauts in Hamilton through the century, outscoring the Argos Toronto 743-542 in those games.

Calgary and Edmonton developed a Labour Day tradition of their own, playing 36 times in the "Battle of Alberta" classic. The Eskimos held the edge in that series as of the end of the century, 20-15-1.

CFHOF

The Edmonton Eskimos dominated the Grey Cup game in the 1970s, winning five straight times and losing in a sixth. Here, Tom Wilkinson (left), Larry Highbaugh (13) and Dan Kepley (43) raise the 1979 cup just presented to them by Prime Minister Joe Clark.

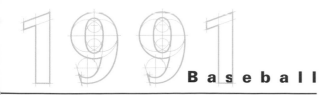

The First Canadian in Baseball's Hall of Fame

It only happened once during the century. On July 21, 1991 a Canadian ballplayer entered the Baseball Hall of Fame in Cooperstown, New York as one of its honoured members. At the ceremony, Ferguson Jenkins paid special tribute to his parents and the people of Chatham, Ontario where his improbable road to baseball immortality began.

Baseball has a long and distinguished history in Canada with roots as old as those in the United States, but rarely has it produced as talented a player as "Fergie" and no other Canadian reached the sport's highest pinnacle of achievement in the 20th century.

The only Canadian inducted into Baseball's Hall of Fame in the century, Chatham's Ferguson Jenkins.

Jenkins, always a talented pitcher, built his reputation on the strength of pin-point accuracy and a slider he estimated he could get in the strike zone 80% of the time. The righthander's 284 major league wins, 594 pitching starts, career strikeout to walk ratio of better than 3:1, (3192 strikeouts and 997 bases on balls) and seven seasons with 20 or more wins, are the stuff of record books and memories.

He was the winner of Canada's leading sports award, the Lou Marsh Trophy, in 1974; Canadian male athlete of the year on four occasions; subject of a wonderful National Film Board documentary, "King of the Hill" produced in the early 1970s; and a recipient of the Order of Canada.

"Fergie" grew up in Chatham, Ontario, a community of 40,000 just 50 miles northeast of the US border. Prior to the American Civil War it was a centre of anti-slavery activity and one of the northern terminuses for the Underground Railway which brought fugitive slaves to Canada. One of those was the Jackson family from which Fergie is descended on his mother's side. It was from that side as well that he claimed two other traits.

"My father says I got my size (6 foot, 5 inches) from her and my precision pitching because she was so exacting," Jenkins claimed in his autobiography. From his father he inherited a love for baseball and, apparently, fishing, which had been the family's occupation in Barbados. Ferguson senior was an outfielder for several Chatham teams and it was at these games that Fergie's parents met.

By the time Jenkins left Chatham in 1962 to begin his professional baseball career he was already something of a local legend, having played hockey for a Junior B affiliate of the Montreal Canadiens, and starred in high school basketball (he later barnstormed with the Harlem Globetrotters). In baseball the limited Ontario schedule had restricted his starts to seven or eight in each of three seasons of amateur ball. Despite this small number of games it remained an old joke in Chatham that he had 5,000 coaches because that's how many took credit for his later success.

Fergie debuted for the Philadelphia Phillies in 1965 and his first pitch put Dick Groat on his back (presumably deliberately). Pat Corrales, his catcher that day, recalled, "The next three deliveries were on the black [just catching the side of the plate]." Jenkins later criticized such tactics. "I figure if a pitcher wants to go headhunting," he told a Sport Illustrated reporter, "he should play hockey instead of baseball."

He is best remembered for six glorious seasons with the Chicago Cubs between 1967 and 1972, during each of which he won 20 or more games. This part of his career culminated with winning the Cy Young Award in 1971 as the National League's premier pitcher. His greatest disappointment was never reaching the World Series, as the Cubs finished second three times and third three times during his best years.

After a mediocre 1973 season he was traded by the Cubs to the Texas Rangers and rebounded with a 25-win season in 1974. While Fergie slipped somewhat from the quality of his first decade in the majors he remained a reliable starter who usually worked late into games until his eventual retirement after the 1983 season.

After his major league career ended Jenkins played a season in Ontario's amateur Inter-County League in 1984 and in 1989 pitched in the Florida based Senior Professional Baseball Association. He later coached with the Chicago Cubs but found his greatest pleasure in farming, an occupation he grew up with. His induction into the Baseball Hall of Fame remained one of the proudest moments of his storied career. ❧

The 1971 Cy Young Award winner was Chicago Cub Fergie Jenkins.

1940s — Canadian-born AAGPBL players

The All-American Girls Professional Baseball League (AAGBPL) was very popular in the 1940s and many Canadian women joined the league. Made famous by the movie "A League of Their Own," the league began in 1943 and ended in 1954. The games were played exclusively in the United States, but at least 64 Canadian women participated in the league, many of them considered league all-stars. These women were named honourary inductees of the Canadian Baseball Hall of Fame in a ceremony on June 4, 1998. Seventeen women who played in the league attended the ceremony. Some of the women who played in the AAGBPL were:

Ontario
Barbara Barbaze
Dorothy Cook
Gladys Davis
Helen Nelson
June Schofield
Thelma Walmsley

Manitoba
Doris Barr
Dorothy Hunter
Eleanor Callow
Autrey Haines Daniels
Dorothy Ferguson Key
Olive Bend Little
Ruth (Middleton) Gentry
Doris Shero Witiuk
Mary Kustra Shastal
Yolande Teillet Schick
Evelyn Wawryshyn Litwin Moroz

Alberta
Olga Grant
Kay Helm McDaniel
Marjorie Hanna
Helen Nicol Fox
Penny O'Brien
Vickie Panos
Martha Rommelaire
Anne Jane Thompson

Saskatchewan
Velma Abbott
Elizabeth Berthiaume
Catherine Bennett
Virginia Carrigy Piersol
Terry Donahue
Janet Anderson Perkins
Julianna Dusanko
June Emerson
Gene George
Thelma Grambo Handeby
Marg Jones Davis
Mary Baker
Daisy Junor
Ruby Knezovich
Elsie Wingrove Earl
Lucella MacLean Ross
Lena Surkowski (Lee) Delmonico
Mildred Warwick McAuley
Agnes Zurowski Holmes
Arleene Johnson Noga
Chris Jewett
Betty Petryna
Muriel Coben

British Columbia
Marge Callaghan Maxwell
Helen Callaghan Candale
Colleen Smith McMulloch

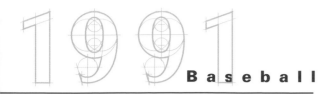
Larry Walker

Baseball Superstar

By the 12th of August of the 1994 major league baseball season, Larry Walker of the Montreal Expos was batting .322 with 19 home runs, 86 RBI, 15 steals, and had a spectacular 44 doubles. He was closing in on the National League's all-time record of 64 two-base hits in a season. The Expos' record of 74-40 was the best in the major leagues.

Unfortunately, the season ended at that point because of a player strike. The strike not only delayed Walker's pursuit of several all-time bests for a Canadian-born baseball player, but also sank the Expos' excellent prospects for post-season play.

The next regular season game Walker played was in 1995 with the Colorado Rockies and the Expos had by then also jettisoned Marquis Grissom, and pitchers Ken Hill and John Wetteland.

Associated Press AP

Born in Maple Ridge, British Columbia in 1966, Walker was signed as a non-drafted free agent by the Expos in 1984 after foregoing a promising hockey career. He was a diamond in the rough who had "a real fire in him," said his first professional coach Gene Glynn.

Though he had to learn to hit the curveball, Walker was a quick study and had reached the big leagues by 1989. It was soon obvious that he had the makings of a superstar. He used his strong arm to throw out complacent runners who jogged to first on apparently "sure" base hits to right field. He hit for power and average and was everything a Canadian major league team could want.

"I'm from Canada and I like to think I represent my country well," he said. Such sentiments, however, couldn't keep him in Montreal, where management bemoaned its economic inability to compete with big market teams, and yet by letting players like Walker go, condemned the Expos to second class status among major league teams.

In the expansion city of Denver, Walker found the climate perfectly aligned with his prodigious blasts, much to the chagrin of opposing pitching staffs. In 1995 he hit 36 home runs. Injury cut short his 1996 season but the next year he reached heights never reached by another Canadian and only by a few major leaguers in baseball history.

He flirted with the elusive .400 batting average for much of that season before finishing with a .366 average, 49 home runs, 130 runs batted in, and 33 stolen bases. He was an easy choice for the National League's Most Valuable Player. No Canadian had ever before earned this honour.

Highlights

1900s

Jimmy Archer

Jimmy Archer was called one of the greatest catchers ever by Chicago Cubs' legend Johnny Evers. Archer was the catcher for two pennant winning teams — the 1907 Detroit Tigers and the 1910 Chicago Cubs (where he was part of the Tinker-to-Evers-Chance era). He once threw out three base runners in an inning, and was recorded as the first catcher to throw out a runner from the squatting position. He was born in Dublin, Ireland, raised in Montreal and later moved to Toronto with his family.

1902

Justin Clarke

Justin Jay Clarke was one of the first Canadian players to have an extended major league career, playing nine seasons with Cleveland, Detroit, St. Louis, and Pittsburgh. Clarke's finest moment in baseball, though, was June 15, 1902 when he slugged eight home runs in a game playing for Corsicana of the Texas League.

1910s

Russell Ford

Russell Ford started playing Major League Baseball in 1909 with the New York Highlanders (now known as the Yankees). He threw a shutout in his first major league start in 1910 and went on to win 26 games that year (the first Canadian to ever win 20 games in a season).

1910s

Jack Graney

Jack Graney played in 1,402 games between 1908 and 1922, but he is best remembered as the first major league batter to face the legendary Babe Ruth. Other career highlights included leading the American League in walks twice (1917, 1919), being the first Canadian to pinch hit in a World Series game (1920), and being the first player to bat wearing a number on his uniform (1916).

1920s

Frank O'Rourke — "Blackie" O'Rourke enjoyed a 14-year major league career, appearing in 1,131 games, and was the only Canadian playing in the majors during the four-year span from 1926 to 1929.

1930s

George Selkirk

Huntsville, Ontario's George Selkirk is forever remembered as the man who replaced Babe Ruth in the New York Yankees outfield. During his career with the Yankees (1934 to 1942), Selkirk earned the nickname "Twinkletoes" for his fast feet in the outfield. He enjoyed a solid nine-year major league career, finishing with 108 home runs and a .290 batting average, two all-star game appearances, five seasons in which he hit .300 or better and two seasons in which he registered more than 100 RBIs (1936, 1939). "Twinkletoes" belted a home run in his first World Series at bat in 1936, and was part of five World Series Championship teams with the Yankees.

George "Moonie" Gibson enjoyed a 14-year major league career with the Pittsburgh Pirates and New York Giants, playing in 1,213 games. He was the Pirates' catcher in the 1909 World Series against Detroit, registering his best season in 1914 with a .285 batting average. After his playing career was over, Gibson became a well-respected manager — managing the Pirates (1920-1924, 1932-1934) and the Cubs (1935). He was the last Canadian-born manager in the major leagues in the century, and in 1950 he was selected as Canada's baseball most outstanding baseball player at the first half century.

Colorado manager Don Baylor said, "He has learned an unbelievable amount about the game. Being Canadian has nothing to do with it. He's just a tremendously gifted player."

His only disappointment that season was not winning the Lou Marsh Trophy as Canada's athlete of the year, although he did win that award in 1998. The 1995 honours went to Jacques Villeneuve, winner of the world's Formula One drivers' championship.

Walker's career totals continued to grow in the following years with back-to-back batting titles in 1998 and '99, a first for a Canadian in the modern era. Despite injuries taking their toll, by the end of the century he appeared on his way to career statistics that would eventually earn him a spot in baseball's Hall of Fame.

"I don't make the game any harder than it is," he said in a philosophical moment, "A guy hits the ball, you catch it and throw it back in. It's a simple game if you just stick to the fundamentals and don't try to do too much." ❧

Highlights

Baseball Highlights

Phil Marchildon, 1940s

1940s

Richard Fowler
Dick Fowler enjoyed a 10-year major league career with the Philadelphia Athletics. The 6'5", 215-pound, pitcher's highlights include pitching all 16 innings in a 1-0 loss to the St. Louis Browns in 1942 and tossing a no-hitter in September 1945 (first Canadian to ever throw a no-hitter) in his first start after serving three years in the Canadian military.

1940s

John Heath
John Heath was the first American League player to register 20 doubles, 20 triples, and 20 home runs in one season (George Brett in 1979 was the only other person who accomplished this feat in the century). Dubbed the "muscular monster" by former roommate and pitching great Bob Feller, Heath enjoyed a productive 14-year major league career, from 1936 to 1949. The outfielder from Fort William, Ontario, compiled a .293 career batting average with 194 home runs and 887 runs batted in.

1940s

Phil Marchildon
"Fidgety Phil" Marchildon was one of the American League's most durable pitchers in the 1940s, completing 82 of his 162 career starts. Going straight from the Northern Ontario minor leagues to Connie Mack's Philadelphia Athletics, his career highlights include a 17-win season in 1942 and a 19-win season in 1947 – a season many consider to be one of the best ever by a Canadian-born pitcher. Marchildon lost three seasons during the prime of his career (1943 to 1945) to military service.

1945

Goodwin Rosen
Toronto-born outfielder Goody Rosen was the first Canadian-born major leaguer to be named to an all-star team (1945). His .325 batting average (third in the National League), 197 hits, and 19 outfield assists that season earned him a 10th place finish in the MVP voting.

1969

For many years, Montrealers supported the old Montreal Royals as a farm team of the Brooklyn, and later Los Angeles, Dodgers. In 1969, a number of years after the Royals had moved away, the Montreal Expos joined the National League, becoming the first team outside the USA in Majors League Baseball.

April 14, 1969

Major league baseball came to Canada to stay in 1969, when the Montreal Expos made quaint Jarry Park their first home. Dedicated baseball fan and former Canadian Prime Minister Lester "Mike" Pearson threw out the first pitch. The Expos did not disappoint the full capacity crowd, beating the St. Louis Cardinals 8-7 in their home, and country, opener.

1960s

Ronald Piche
"Monsieur Baseball" was a hard-throwing right-handed pitcher who toiled in the majors for six seasons (1960-1963, 1965-1966) with the Milwaukee Braves, California Angels, and St. Louis Cardinals. He joined the Montreal Expos' front office in 1970, serving in several different capacities and earning the nickname "Monsieur Baseball."

1960s

Ron Taylor
Relief pitcher Ron Taylor registered 72 saves in a major league career that spanned 11 seasons (1962 to 1972) with four major league teams: St. Louis,

Ron Taylor, 1960s

Houston, New York Mets and San Diego. He was the only Canadian pitcher to ever win a League Championship Series game in the century, and was also the only Canadian to win two World Series championships with two different teams (St. Louis 1964, New York 1969). After retiring from baseball in 1972, he returned to Toronto, where he earned a degree in medicine from the University of Toronto and became the only former player to return to major league baseball as a team doctor.

John Hiller, Detroit Tigers, 1973

1960s & '70s

John Hiller
Relief pitcher John Hiller's career lasted from 1965 to 1980. He pitched in 545 games, recording 87 career victories, 125 saves, and a career ERA of 2.84, striking out 1,035 batters in his career (second to Fergie Jenkins in career strikeouts by a Canadian). In early 1971, Hiller suffered a massive heart attack that caused him to miss all of the 1971 season and a large portion of 1972. Hiller returned to enjoy his best season in 1973, when he recorded 38 saves (a major league record at the time) and was named American League Fireman of the Year for relief pitchers.

1969

Claude Raymond
Claude Raymond pitched for the Montreal Expos in their 1969 inaugural season, becoming the first Canadian-born player to play for a Canadian major league team.

Canada

T

Our Century in Sport

156   The Games of Our Lives

Bobby Porter

1970s

Reggie Cleveland

Reggie Cleveland was only 17 when he signed his first major league contract with the St. Louis Cardinals, on his way to 105 career victories in Major League Baseball (second only to Fergie Jenkins for career wins during the century by a Canadian). His finest major league season was in 1973 with a 14-10 win-loss record and a 3.01 ERA, but his personal highlight was starting game six (the first Canadian-born pitcher to ever start a World Series game) of the infamous 1975 World Series. In 13 years in the major leagues, he played for Boston, Texas and Milwaukee.

1976

Toronto came close to obtaining the financially-troubled San Francisco Giants baseball team, but the deal fell through with a last-minute court injunction. Shortly thereafter, though, the Toronto Blue Jays joined the American League as an expansion team.

April 7, 1977

The Blue Jays celebrated their first-ever home opener in Toronto with a victory over the Chicago White Sox. Doug Ault hit two home runs in the game to instantly become the first Blue Jay hero. The game, appropriately, was played on a snow-covered field.

Vancouver native Dave McKay was the only Canadian on the field for that first game. Despite snow falling at Exhibition Stadium, the Blue Jays' starting second baseman had a pair of hits and drove in the winning run in the 9-5 victory over the White Sox. He was also the first and only Canadian of the century to hit a home run in his first at bat in the major leagues.

1970s

Terry Puhl

Melville, Saskatchewan's Terry Puhl played 15 years in Major League Baseball. His 1,534 career games are the most by a Canadian-born player in the century. Puhl posted the best fielding percentage (.993) by an outfielder who has played in 1000 games or more in the century. He was also a good hitter, averaging over .300 in three different seasons and finishing with a career batting average of .280. He was selected to the 1978 all-star game and hit .526 in the 1980 National League Championship Series.

1991

Canada's national youth baseball team defeated Cuba, the United States, and Chinese Taipei en route to winning the 1991 World Youth AAA Championship at Brandon, Manitoba. Daniel Brabant of Longueil, Quebec, was selected the top pitcher in the tournament, while shortstop Todd Betts of Scarborough, Ontario and second baseman Jason Lee of Edmonton were tournament all-stars.

Bobby Porter

Canada's 1999 Pan Am Games baseball team excited the country en route to winning a bronze medal.

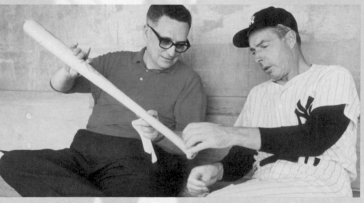

Andy O'Brian with the legendary Joe DiMaggio.

Hockey

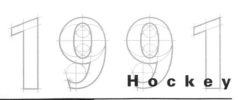

HHOF

Lucky Lindros

by Bruce Wallace
September 9, 1991

The overhead lights in Toronto's Maple Leaf Gardens have been turned off and the dim lighting that remains obscures the dinginess of one of hockey's most famous shrines. The players on Team Canada, their practice over, have all left the building on a steamy August afternoon. But 18-year-old Eric Lindros, widely considered to be the best player of his generation and the still-unscarred face of Canada's hockey future, sits in the empty stands. Hooking the legs of his six-foot five-inch, 224-lb body over the seat in front of him, Lindros throws his head back and bellows at the rafters and the ghosts of the Gardens. "This is my barn," he shouts to the deserted arena. "I love you." Then, Lindros speaks wistfully of his future in hockey. "I don't know if I ever want to get away from Toronto," says Lindros. "Can you imagine this place if the Leafs won another Stanley Cup after all these years?" His voice softens and he stares toward the ice. "Imagine," he says. "The Leafs. Alive again."

HHOF — Paul Bereswill

Even at 18, Eric Lindros is accustomed to making dreams come true. Without ever having played a game in the National Hockey League (NHL), he proved during Team Canada tryouts for the Canada Cup showdown that he could excel alongside the Canadian hockey elite by winning a place on the team. But while he prepared to play this month for his country against the best in the world in the Canada Cup series, Lindros found his ambitions stalled by an off-ice obstacle that not even his extraordinary size, speed or shot could overcome. His right to play in the NHL is controlled by the Quebec Nordiques, who used their first choice in the league's draft last June to pick him. But the strong-willed Lindros, who describes himself as a "rebel," says that he has no intention of playing hockey in Quebec City. "Sometimes, you have to look at the political aspect of the thing," he told Maclean's in the Gardens. "If things are not going well politically in a certain climate, then you have to think twice about whether or not you want to be there."

In a wide-ranging interview, Lindros told Maclean's why he was unwilling to go to Quebec City. "The people that come out of high school with the best grades go to the best universities. The people with the lower grades have fewer choices," he said. "Why should a player who comes out of junior hockey with top marks go to a city that is not his choice?"

Lindros has signalled that he possesses grand hockey ambitions, and intends to achieve them his way. On the ice, he is a menacing presence to opponents: a marauding, extremely physical player with spectacular scoring skills and a locomotive drive to win at all costs.

But just as NHL owners salivate at the prospect of adding Lindros to the league's marquee, the confident teen-ager who has yet to play a professional game is sending shivers through the hockey establishment by refusing to play in Quebec. "Everyone has the right to work where they want to work," said Lindros. "The old way has got to change." Still, critics have expressed concern that an unrestricted campaign by players to defy the draft system and play with the team of their choice would undermine franchises in small markets, especially those in Canadian cities that include Quebec City and Winnipeg.

Lindros has not endeared himself to the residents of Quebec City. There, fans comforted themselves during their team's losing 1990-91 season with the knowledge that their last-place finish would give them the right to pick the most heralded junior hockey player since Mario Lemieux and, before that, Wayne Gretzky. But as far back as last May, Lindros told Nordiques president Marcel Aubut that he would not play in Quebec City. Lindros and his parents, Carl and Bonnie Lindros, insist that playing in the small, predominantly francophone market would lessen his value for off-ice endorsements.

Since then, relations between the two sides have deteriorated further. "It's an ego thing," said Eric Lindros of Aubut's refusal, so far, to trade him to another club. Despite reports in the Quebec press saying that Lindros was seeking a three-year contract that would pay him $3 million a year, Carl Lindros told *Maclean's* that "we have never made a financial demand of Quebec." Still, many Quebecers now refer sarcastically to Lindros as "the son of Bay Street." Said Albert Ladouceur, a hockey writer for the daily *Journal de Quebec*: "The fans here are hurt by his attitude." And by citing political reasons for his refusal to join the Nordiques, Lindros may provoke a backlash that extends beyond the hockey world.

The Quebec furor is only the latest in a short career that has been almost as noteworthy for its turmoil as for its brilliance. Lindros has challenged hockey's ways of doing business in the past. In 1989, when the Sault Ste. Marie Greyhounds of the Ontario Hockey League (OHL) drafted him from the Toronto-based St. Michael's College Junior B team, he refused to obey the rules and move, arguing that he wanted to play hockey for a team based closer to his family's Toronto home. The league finally gave in and changed its rules to allow Lindros to be traded to the Oshawa Generals.

Still, some critics say that Lindros's self-driven approach to the game turned into obstinacy when the Greyhounds drafted him. And when the OHL initially balked at changing its bylaw that prevented any team from trading its first-round draft pick for a year, Lindros simply went to play for a commercially sponsored junior team in Detroit. Seven months later, the league relented, allowing a trade to Oshawa for three players, three future draft picks and $80,000. With Lindros in the line-up, Oshawa sold out every game in its 4,200-seat arena and won the 1990 Memorial Cup, Canada's junior hockey championship. Lindros also played on Canada's last two world junior championship teams. And Lindros led the OHL in scoring last year, with 71 goals and 78 assists in 57 games.

Fans in Sault Ste. Marie never forgave Lindros. Said Greyhounds director Sherwood Bassin: "People in the Soo were offended. They felt that their families and their community had been affronted, the same as Quebec now feels." The anger spilled out in May when Lindros returned to Sault Ste. Marie during the league's playoffs. The fans taunted him by waving pacifiers and hanging signs with messages that included: "Lindros wants his mommy."

Clearly, Lindros presents a challenge to the foundations of the NHL's established business practices. But the pressure has also taken a toll on an 18-year-old who, despite his talent and self-assuredness, is uneasy about his future. "All my friends are taking off for

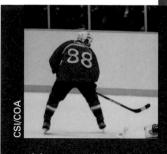

After helping Team Canada win its fourth Canada Cup, Lindros split the 1991-92 season between the Ontario Hockey League Oshawa Generals, the Canadian national team and the Canadian Olympic Team. The Olympic Team won a silver medal at the 1992 Olympics in Albertville, France. At the end of the season, the Nordiques agreed to trade him, with both the New York Rangers and the Philadelphia Flyers believing they had acquired his rights. An arbitrator eventually ruled in favour of Philadelphia, which gave up six players and $15-million (US) for Lindros's rights. Although beset by injuries, including a number of concussions, by the end of the 1999-2000 season Lindros had scored 659 points in eight seasons. He won the Hart Trophy as the league's most valuable player in 1995.

universities," said Lindros, who has registered for an economics course at Toronto's York University in the fall. "It makes me really nervous to not know what I'll be doing." And in refusing to report to Quebec while making it known that he would be willing to play in Toronto, he runs the risk of becoming a symbol of the growing tensions between Quebec and the rest of Canada. "I'd take a pay cut to play in Canada," he said. "But why would someone take a cut to play in a place where they are not happy?" ✦

Friends – of a Kind

Coolheaded Quebecers duel for gold on the short track

by Barry Came
February 3, 1992

Sylvie Daigle and Nathalie Lambert have spent much of the past decade chasing each other at breakneck pace around tight ovals of ice. The two Quebec women are Canada's queens of the wild and woolly sport known as short-track speed skating, where as many as eight contestants repeatedly hurtle in close proximity around a surface smaller than a hockey rink, often reaching speeds in excess of 25 m.p.h. Lambert, a 28-year-old Montrealer, is the reigning world champion. Daigle, 29 and a native of Sherbrooke, has won the world crown five times in the past 12 years and last November set a new world record for the 500-m distance. Both rank among Canada's best hopes for Olympic gold next month in Albertville, where short-track speed skating, a demonstration contest at the 1988 Olympics in Calgary, finally opens as a full-fledged medal event.

The spirited rivalry between the two young women has been a feature of Canada's speed skating effort since 1981, when Lambert won a place on the national team that Daigle had joined the previous year. But while it has been a fierce rivalry, it has also been a friendly one. Indeed, both skaters are quick to credit the other with providing the inspirational spark needed to excel in world-class competition. "We have always challenged each other to do better," said Daigle as she carefully taped two battered, nine-year-old skates at Montreal's Michel Normandin arena, the home of the country's national team. "We have pushed each other for so long now that I think if one of us quit, maybe the other wouldn't be as good," declared Lambert the following day as she prepared for a training session at the same rink, on the northern edge of the city. Yves Nadeau, head coach of the short-track team, added, "They have a lot of respect for each other's abilities, and that has helped to lift them both to a very high level."

Of the two, Daigle's record is the more impressive. The slim, dark-eyed athlete, the youngest in a family of five daughters and one son, has excelled almost from the moment she first laced on a pair of speed skates. She was only 9 when she competed in her first major competition, the Quebec Games. By the time she was 16, she had won a short-track world championship and a place on the national team. She represented Canada in the 500-m event in the traditional long-track speed skating at the 1980 Olympics in Lake Placid, NY, when she was 17.

At 18, she was ranked ninth in the world in long-track, the event that propelled fellow Quebecer and national teammate Gaétan Boucher, winner of two gold medals and a bronze in the 1984 Games, onto the world scene. But chronic weakness in the muscles in the front of her legs forced Daigle to abandon long-track racing, in which competitors skate against the clock around a 400-m oval.

But it did not keep her out of the shorter version of the sport, a rough-and-tumble race against individuals around a 110-m circuit that some have called an icebound Roller Derby. She won another short-track world crown

Two Canadian short-track speed skating greats, Sylvie Daigle (far right) and Nathalie Lambert (2nd on left) teamed up with Annie Perreault (far left) and Angela Cutrone to win the 1992 Olympic gold medal in the relay.

CSI/COA

in 1983 and two more as the decade drew to a close. In the 1988 Olympic Games at Calgary, when short-track was a demonstration event, Daigle won a gold and a silver medal.

Although Daigle narrowly lost the 1991 world championship last March to archrival Lambert, she quickly demonstrated that she remains a major force in the sport. In November, she trounced all the competition during a pre-Olympic event at the Albertville Ice Hall, sprinting past the world's current top-ranked skater, Yahei Zang of China,

Sylvie Daigle

and establishing in the process a world record for the Olympic distance. She covered the 500m on the small oval in 46.72 seconds, the first woman to beat the 47-second mark. "Sure it felt good," Daigle recalled, quickly adding: "But it was just a first step. I haven't won an Olympic medal yet."

The remark reflects Daigle's levelheaded approach to the sport that she has come to dominate. "Sylvie's an intelligent girl," said teammate Lambert. "It's one of the main reasons why she's so hard to beat." Throughout the past 10 years, Lambert has been spending a lot of time and effort attempting to accomplish that goal. But it was not until last March that the Montreal native finally managed to edge past her good friend and longtime rival for the world championship in short-track speed skating. Lambert had come close several times previously, winning bronze medals in the 1984 and 1985 world championships and silver medals in 1986 and 1987. And in both 1989 and 1990, Lambert defeated Daigle for the Canadian short-track championships only to fall short of victory during the worlds. In 1990, she skated all year without a loss, including a world-record performance over 1000m — a feat that was later disallowed because it had not been timed electronically.

But that same year, during the world championships in Amsterdam, she could only manage to place a disappointing fourth overall in the standings. "I was really strong and had the edge on everyone in 1990," Lambert recalled. "I even won the first race at the worlds," she went on, before pausing to add with a sheepish grin: "Then I screwed up."

Events took a different turn in March, when the world competition was held in Sydney, Australia. Daigle beat Lambert for the 1991 Canadian championship, which seemed to set the stage for yet another Daigle win at the worlds. But Lambert, taking part in her ninth world championship, dominated the three-day event. She won the opening 1,500m; Daigle finished second. Then, Daigle won the 1,000m. Going into the final 27-lap, 3,000m event, she and Daigle were tied in overall standings. But Lambert swept into the lead from the start

and never relinquished it, holding off a last-minute rush from Daigle to win the crown. Daigle took the silver medal. In view of all the years she had skated in Daigle's shadow, it was a satisfying win for Lambert. As she remarked at the time, "I feel really happy to have finally beaten Sylvie because every year it is between me and her."

Despite Lambert's win at the worlds last year, however, most of the experts give Daigle the edge in the race for the Olympic gold in the individual short-track event. And that includes national team head coach Nadeau. "Sylvie is going to have the advantage at Albertville because the Olympic race is a 500m sprint," he told *Maclean's*. "Sylvie is smaller than Nathalie and she has better acceleration. She's a natural sprinter with phenomenal early speed. Nathalie has more endurance and she can probably match Sylvie's top speed, but it takes her longer to get up a head of steam. Over 500m, unless she gets a break at the start, she simply may not have the time." Much the same applies in the other women's short-track event — the 3,000m relay — where quick acceleration is the major asset as each of the four teammates sprint 750m. But whatever the eventual outcome, both Daigle and Lambert have the potential to raise Canadian speed skating to levels of international prestige that have not been achieved since the heady days of Boucher's double-gold performance. ❧

Nathalie Lambert

CSI/COA

Highlights

General Highlights

1980-1992

Carrie Serwetnyk was the first female to enter the Canadian Soccer Hall of Fame. She blazed the early trail for women in soccer, represented Canada 19 times in international matches and played professionally in Japan.

1983

Vancouver's Italian community flocked to a rugby match at Swangard Stadium in 1983 to see their former countrymen finish at the wrong end of a 19-13 score to the red-shirted Canadians. Only one try was scored by each team, with Jim Donaldson tallying for Canada, and future World Cup captain Mark Wyatt kicking four penalty goals. Though Canada lost to Italy one week later in Toronto the stage was set for Canada's biggest step forward in its history when it earned a spot in the inaugural Rugby World Cup in 1987.

Doug Sturrock

1984

A KILREA DYNASTY — The winningest Junior A hockey coach, Ottawa 67s' coach Brian Kilrea can say with pride that the name Kilrea is engraved on every major sports trophy in Canada. Brian coached two Ottawa 67s' teams to Memorial Cups in 1984 and 1999. "Uncle Hec" won a Stanley Cup with Detroit Red Wings in 1936. "Uncle Kennie" won an Allan Cup with the Ottawa Commandos in the 1942-43 season and "Young Hec" played in the Canadian Football League and won a Grey Cup.

1984

Barbara Underhill and Paul Martini got used to winning ways. They were the 1978 Junior Canadian pairs champions, and from 1979 to 1983 they were five-time Canadian pairs champions. In 1983 they became World bronze medallists and winners of numerous international competitions. Their crowning achievement came in 1984 when they became the World pairs champions.

1987

Toronto Blue Jay George Bell hit 47 home runs in 1987 and was voted the American League MVP, becoming the first player from a Canadian-based major league team to be named the League's Most Valuable Player.

1987

Participation in the 16-team Rugby World Cup tournament in New Zealand was a true test of Canada's standing in the world and gave them a measuring stick for future preparation. The Canadians opened with a fantastic win against Tonga, but then lost to both Ireland and Wales.

Doug Sturrock

1987

Brian Orser

A dominant force in Canadian and World figure skating, known widely for his ease and flair in making triple jumps, Brian Orser was the only man in Canadian singles skating to have won all three major Canadian titles: Novice (1977), Junior (1979) and Senior (from 1981-1988). He also captured the Skate Canada International titles in 1983, 1984 and 1987. He won back-to-back Olympic silver medals (1984 in

Sarajevo, 1988 in Calgary), four World silver medals (1984, 1985, 1986 and 1988) and one bronze (1983). In 1987, Orser became the third Canadian male to capture the World Figure Skating Championship.

1987

At the 1987 World Track Championships in Rome, Canadian Ben Johnson came first in the 100m with a then-record time of 9.83 seconds. The record stood until after Johnson tested positive for steroids at the 1988 Olympic Games in Seoul. He later admitted to enhancing his performances over the years with the use of steroids, and as a result, his 1987 Championship and record were erased from the books.

1982-88

Toronto's Carling Bassett was the only Canadian to have broken into the top-10 in singles on the professional tennis tour during the century, reaching a career-high Number 8 world ranking in 1985. She ranked Number 1 in Canada from 1982 to 1986. Bassett represented Canada as a Federation Cup team member from 1982-1987. In 1983, she was named as the "Newcomer of the Year" by the Women's Tennis Association. At the 1986 Wimbledon Championships, Bassett reached the fourth round, the highest of the century for Canadian women, and was dubbed "Darling Carling" by the Fleet Street tabloids.

1988

Following an impressive eighth place showing at his first of three Olympics in 1988, Kurt Browning performed the first-ever quadruple toe loop in competition at the World Figure Skating Championships in Budapest, Hungary. Browning was the Canadian and World Senior Men's Champion in 1989, 1990 and 1991, and became the first Canadian man to win three consecutive World titles. Performing his memorable "Casablanca" routine, he added his fourth Canadian and World crowns in 1993, the most World titles won by a Canadian singles skater.

January 20, 1989

Mario Lemieux joined Wayne Gretzky as the second NHL player to score 50 goals in less than 50 games to start the season. Lemieux scored his 50th in his 44th game, against the Winnipeg Jets. (Gretzky scored 50 in 39 games.)

1990

Kris Draper scored in the NHL and the AHL before he had even tried on a Major Junior A hockey sweater. A native of Toronto, he was drafted by the Winnipeg Jets at 18. The young forward scored his first NHL goal in his very first NHL game with the Winnipeg Jets in their 1990-91 season's opening 7-2 win over Toronto Maple Leafs. Draper played a total of three games and was injured. He was sent down to the Moncton Hawks of the American Hockey League and scored twice in 10 games. He was cut by the Hawks and then and only then did he play his very first ever game of Major Junior "A" hockey. He was returned to Junior ranks and finished the season with Ottawa 67s where he amassed 61 points on 19 goals and 42 assists. He played 17 more games with Winnipeg over the next two years but spent most of the two seasons in Moncton. He was then traded to Detroit where he became a regular for five seasons.

July 28, 1991

Montreal Expos' Denis Martinez pitched a no-hit perfect game against the Dodgers in LA.

September 2, 1990

After being close a few times, including one game with two out in the bottom of the ninth inning, Toronto Blue Jay pitcher Dave Stieb pitched the club's first no-hitter against the Oakland A's.

1991

Elvis Stojko performed the first-ever quadruple combination jump (quad-toe/double toe) in competition at the World Figure Skating Championships in Munich, Germany.

Doug Sturrock

Doug Sturrock

1991

Canada rebounded in style from the 1987 Rugby World Cup experience, peaking at the right time in the leadup to the 1991 Cup. The Canadian side defeated six of their seven opponents, including for the first time, Argentina (in both Vancouver and Buenos Aires), Japan and Scotland.

1991

Canadian rugby followers long remember the day that Canada first beat an established founding country of the International Rugby Football Board. Hosting Scotland in an international match in Saint John, New Brunswick, fans saw the Canadian forwards monopolize possession and Mark Wyatt achieve a world record by kicking eight penalty goals. The Canadian Rugby Union's annual report noted: "The Scottish Manager's remarks at the after-dinner banquet that 'Scotland had come to Canada and had learned' was a significant turnaround from the countless years of such speeches in which the opposite sentiment had been expressed."

1991

In their 1991 Rugby World Cup pool games, Canada dismissed Fiji and Romania before losing to France 19-13. The two wins earned them the right to a quarter-final match against New Zealand, which had won the first World Cup and was one of the year's favourites. Even though New Zealand won 29-13, Canada's forwards were superb and at times had New Zealand scrambling. Memorable tries were scored by Chris Tynan and Al Charron.

1991

Canadian rugby players continued to gain international respect during the 1990s. Canada's National Team halfback combination of Chris Tynan and Gareth Rees played against each other in the traditional pre-Christmas Oxford and Cambridge University match: Tynan for Cambridge and Rees for Oxford.

1964, '68, '72, '76, '80, '84, '92

Christilot Hanson Boylen was named to seven Olympic equestrian (dressage) teams, the highest number for a female athlete.

1980-92

Glenn Michibata was a top-10 player in the Tennis Canada singles rankings for 12 years, holding the number 1 spot from 1981-1983. He was named the Tennis Canada Player of the Year in 1983 and 1985, and won the national closed singles crowns in 1981 and 1982 and doubles in 1985 and 1989. In the ATP Tour world singles rankings, Michibata reached a career high of 48th in 1986. He reached the Australian Open doubles final in 1990 and was semifinalist at the French Open and Wimbledon in 1991 with Grant Connell.

1993

Grant Connell was the number 1-ranked doubles player on the ATP world tennis tour in 1993, becoming the only Canadian male to reach a number 1 world ranking in tennis. He was the first Canadian to win a world championship on the professional tour (playing doubles with Patrick Galbraith in 1995) and won 22 doubles titles (he was also a 26-time doubles finalist — including four Grand Slams). In singles competition, he reached as high as the number 67 ranking on the ATP Tour in 1991. Connell represented Canada as a Davis Cup team member from 1987-1997.

June 5, 1994

The perennially strong Brazilian soccer team would win the World Cup one month later, but on June 5, 1994, in Edmonton, all they could do was manage a 1-1 draw against the feisty Canadians.

1995

Despite losses to England, Scotland and New Zealand in the build-up for the 1995 Rugby World Cup in South Africa, Canada got off to a good start in their "pool of death" with a superb 34-3 dismissal of Romania. Against Australia, following a disastrous opening ten minutes in which they conceded two tries, the tough-tackling Canada squad gave the Wallabies all they could handle before losing 27-11. The eventual winner South Africa scored 20 unanswered points against Canada in a very physical and confrontational contest, easily securing the victory.

1996

Local boy (Scarborough, Ontario) Paul Tracy won the Toronto Molson Indy car race.

1997

The new era of professional rugby altered the players' situations, with several of Canada's best players grabbing the opportunity to play for money overseas in England, Wales or France. The best known of the Canadians playing abroad was British Columbia's Gareth Rees, who won the English Courage League Division 1 scoring title while playing for league champion London Wasps. Rees also captained the Wasps against a World XV squad the same year and in 1998 led all United Kingdom players in points scored. Not many years earlier it would have been unheard of for a Canadian to play in Britain, let alone win scoring titles.

1999

Early in the year, Canada's rugby team won the newly-formed Pacific Rim Tournament against national teams from Japan, the USA, Hong Kong, Fiji, Tonga and Samoa and qualified for the 1999 World Cup in France. They were placed in a pool with France, Fiji and Namibia. The matches against France and Fiji could have gone either way, but Canada simply failed to do enough things right, and lost. On the other hand, against Namibia they could do no wrong and registered their biggest win ever, routing the Africans 72-11. Canada did not advance after pool play, though. Team captain Gareth Rees participated in a record-setting fourth World Cup. He appeared in every one of Canada's games, and made every kick at goal—11 conversions and nine penalties — in the three games, as well as scoring on a drop goal against Fiji.

Post-1965

Other countries have honoured Canadian rugby players by inviting them to play in special or commemorative games. Buzz Moore was the first to be asked by the Barbarians (a form of all-star team for rugby players) and he was followed by Mike Luke, Angus Stewart, Mark Wyatt, Norm Hadley, Dave Lougheed, Al Charron, Gareth Rees, Glenn Ennis , Mike Schmid, Rod Snow and Kevin Whitley. Honours have also been accorded over the years to Barrie Leigh (Irish RFU President's XV), Hans de Goede, Mike Luke, Graham Taylor (Overseas XV), Ro Hindson (South Pacific Barbarians), Al Charron, Rod Snow and Gordon MacKinnon (World XV) and Al Charron and Mike James (French Barbarians).

1990s

The men's national rugby team played more international matches in the 1990s than in the previous 60 years combined.

1997

Elvis Stojko performed the first-ever quadruple toe/triple toe loop combination in the free program of the ISU Champions Figure Skating Series Final.

1990s

In a 13-year career before his tragic death in 2000, Greg Moore progressed through the North American Championships, earning various titles and honours, and quickly catapulted to the heights of professional car racing. He was the youngest driver ever to win a sanctioned CART event and broke the record for most career Indy Lights victories in 1995 with 13 wins. At 22 years of age he became the youngest winner in CART history, holding off Mario Andretti to take the checkered flag at the Milwaukee Mile.

1994

British Columbia native Dave Barr entrenched his already established role in Canadian golf history as the leader of the Canadian victory at the Dunhill Cup Championship in 1994. With the 1985 World Cup Team Championship under his belt, three PGA Tour victories and 12 Canadian Tour titles, Dave's record includes a second-place finish in the 1985 US Open. He was also the first Canadian to surpass the $2 million mark in earnings on the PGA Tour. Canada's winning Dunhill Cup team featured two other British Columbians: Ray Stewart (Abbotsford) and Rick Gibson (Victoria). Victory at the Dunhill Cup in St. Andrews, Scotland, marked the first time a Canadian golf team had even advanced past the round robin qualifying. The trio beat players who ranked among the top 50 in the world and achieved a stunning upset over a very strong American team in the final.

1993

Hockey

More than Magnificent

Mario Lemieux caps a remarkable year

by D'arcy Jenish
April 26, 1993

Rick Aston sits in his cab in front of a downtown Pittsburgh hotel. Waiting for a fare, he has a perfect view of a 10-storey-high mural, painted on the side of an office tower, that depicts Pittsburgh's most renowned sports stars. From baseball, there are former Pirates Roberto Clemente and Bill Mazeroski; from football, ex-Steelers "Mean" Joe Greene and Jack Lambert. The fifth is from hockey: the Penguins' Mario Lemieux. "He's the greatest hockey player ever," Aston tells a visitor, "and maybe the greatest athlete ever."

Overhearing Aston, fellow driver Randy Barrett jumps out of a nearby cab. "No way Lemieux's the greatest athlete ever," Barrett snaps. "A great athlete is a versatile player, like a Bo Jackson or a Deion Sanders, who can play more than one sport. Lemieux wouldn't last 15 minutes on a football field." But Aston has the last word: "So, those guys wouldn't last 15 minutes on the ice. And whoever led any league after missing a quarter of the season with cancer? That's like someone hitting 50 home runs in 90 games. Anyway, the Penguins are winners, and we like winners in Pittsburgh."

In a sport known for blinding speed and frequent violence, Mario Lemieux is all flamboyance and mystery. Game after game, the towering centreman makes dazzling plays that leave fans, teammates and opponents asking the same question: How did he do that? Off the ice, Lemieux is a different person: quiet, private, unassuming. And he remained that way even as he led the Penguins to the National Hockey League's best regular-season record this year — and seized the scoring crown despite missing 23 games for

treatment of Hodgkins' disease, a cancer of the lymphatic system. In early April, after Pittsburgh tied the NHL record for consecutive wins — 15 — with a victory over the vaunted Montreal Canadiens, the Penguin players were in a celebratory mood. But Lemieux spent nearly an hour in the trainer's room having his standard post-game back massage. When he emerged, many of his teammates had departed. With typical reserve, Lemieux assessed the Penguins' latest achievement: "It's nice to tie a record by beating a team with so much history behind it."

This spring, the once-woeful Penguins have an opportunity to earn their own distinguished place in hockey history. If they can win a third straight Stanley Cup, the Penguins would enter the pantheon of modern hockey dynasties, joining several Montreal Canadiens and Toronto Maple Leaf teams; and the Edmonton Oilers and New York Islanders of the 1980s. Even without another Cup, Lemieux is in the midst of a remarkable year. After the discovery of a malignant node in his neck in early January, he returned to the Penguins lineup on March 2 — less than 12 hours after completing his final radiation treatment — and went on a scoring rampage that propelled him past Pat Lafontaine of the Buffalo Sabres in the scoring race. Off the ice, Lemieux and his long-time, live-in companion, Nathalie Asselin, are expecting their first child at the end of this month. And in June, Lemieux and Asselin will be married at a church in their hometown of Montreal.

Lemieux's path to Pittsburgh began in Montreal where he grew up in the working-class district of Ville-Emard.

The youngest of three sons of now-retired construction worker Jean-Guy Lemieux and his wife, Pierrette, young Mario was selected first overall in the June, 1984, draft of overage junior hockey players. But he was reluctant to join the Penguins and refused to put on a team sweater for the traditional post-draft photos. Eventually signing, he had problems adjusting to life away from his familiar French-Canadian surroundings. "He was very quiet and very shy," recalled Nancy Mathews, Lemieux's landlady during his first season with Pittsburgh: "The language problem was very difficult for him."

On the ice, however, Lemieux quickly emerged as one of the NHL's most potent offensive forces. It was as a member of Team Canada in 1987, he says, that he reached a turning point in his personal development. Practising and playing with the world's best during the Canada Cup tournament, he says, was an inspiring experience. He went on to win two straight NHL scoring championships and, along the way, formed an attachment to Pittsburgh. "It's a great city, not too big, not too small," he said. "I enjoy the whole package."

For many veteran observers of the NHL, Lemieux has fulfilled his potential as both an athlete and a franchise player. Dick Irvin, a Canadiens play-by-play broadcaster, has visited Pittsburgh annually since the early 1970s and remembers the state of hockey before Lemieux arrived. "We used to leave here for the last time every season," he said, "and we'd wonder whether we were going to be back the following winter. The rink was only half full. There was no publicity. The media coverage was sparse. We used to ask ourselves, 'How can this team last?' The whole atmosphere is different now, and it's all due to Mario."

Although Lemieux rarely reveals much of his character publicly, he has earned widespread admiration for his courage under adversity. Two years ago, he sat out the first 54 games of the regular season recuperating from back surgery and a related infection — only to return and lead the Penguins to their first Stanley Cup. This year, he was on track to break Gretzky's single-season scoring record of 215 points when, in January, doctors discovered that he had Hodgkin's disease. The early diagnosis, and prompt treatment, left Lemieux with an excellent chance for total cure.

Since then, the Penguin star has received get-well messages from people all over the world. Mathews, who now sorts his mail and helps prepare responses, said that on four occasions since January she has loaded the trunk and backseat of her car with bags of mail for Lemieux. "He's handled himself exceptionally well for all he's gone through," she said. "It's hard to find the words to tell you how I feel about Mario Lemieux." ❧

Mario Lemieux highlights

From 1984 until he announced his first retirement in 1997, Lemieux won the NHL scoring title six times. Over 12 NHL seasons, he scored 613 regular season goals, the only player to achieve similar per-season statistics to those posted by Wayne Gretzky. "Super Mario" also led his Pittsburgh Penguins to two Stanley Cups, won the Hart Trophy as the league's most valuable player three times and the Conn Smythe Trophy as the MVP in the Stanley Cup playoffs twice. In 1999, he became the first player in the modern era of sports to buy the team he once played for, when he and a group of investors acquired the Penguins.

The final chapter of Lemieux's story remained unwritten, however. On December 8, 2000, at the age of 35, he announced that he was making a comeback as a player. He played his first two games back on December 27 and 30, serving notice that he remained a force to be reckoned with by scoring an assist on his very first shift. By the end of the second game, he had notched two goals and five assists, passing the 1500-point plateau in career scoring.

CSI/COA

Winning all but Nagano

by Hayley Wickenheiser

The top moments of my sport career are playing in the first Olympic women's hockey tournament in 1998 and right along with that are the World Championships in 1997 when we beat the United States in overtime.

The 1997 World Championships were really exciting because it was the first time I had competed at the Worlds in Canada, with the championships being in Kitchener, Ontario. The crowd was electric, the people were excited and everybody was going crazy. It was the second time the World Championships had been held in Canada, but our profile had been raised, and that really helped with the momentum. Then there was the rivalry with the US, of course, being so close to them. We had beaten them so handily in previous years, so taking the game into overtime that year was a real white knuckler. It was very intense and very exciting.

We always knew that they had the talent, but it was just the way they competed. For the first time they played three full periods of intense hockey and really wanted to beat us. That was the first time we had experienced that from them. What had separated us before was the commitment level, the way we approached the game as a team, and the seriousness of the players. We take the game very seriously and it's only in the last five or six years that other countries have started to as well. 1997 was the turning point, not only for the United States, but Finland too. We just barely beat Finland in the semi-final. It was a very close tournament the whole way through, so that's why it was so exciting to win it.

When I was growing up, my heroes were Gretzky and Messier. I watched the NHL and the Oilers of the 1980s. That's really how I learned how to play hockey, in a way, because I tried to emulate what those guys did on the ice.

CSI/COA

Watching the first Women's World Championships on TV in 1990 was the first time I'd ever seen women's hockey. From that moment on, I knew that's what I wanted to do. Growing up I'd always played with the boys, so to see women playing at that level was very inspiring.

I joined the national team in 1994 when I was only 15. It was pretty exciting, but I was also pretty intimidated because I was playing with some women who were old enough to be my mother. They really helped me along and took me under their wing. France St. Louis, who was our captain at the time, was really instrumental in making me feel a part of the team, along with Stacy Wilson.

When we went to the 1998 Olympics in Nagano, it was nice to have the men's team there too. They understood what we were going through and I think we understood the expectations placed on them. We had a closed door meeting with Bob Clarke, Patrick Roy and Eric Lindros just before the beginning of the competition. They talked about what it's like to play in a pressure situation, what to expect and what it would be like. I think it helped our team a lot.

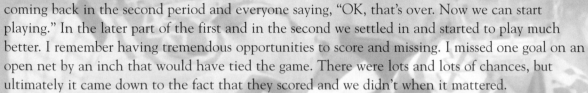

There was much more tension in the final game in Nagano than in the World Championships. The game was the same, the teams were the same, but for some reason that Olympic spotlight magnified everything. The buildup to it was lengthy and intense, and that made it seem like there was a lot more at stake.

I hardly remember anything about going out on the ice for the warmup. There were a lot of people, a lot of noise. I think our team was uptight to start with in the first period. I remember coming back in the second period and everyone saying, "OK, that's over. Now we can start playing." In the later part of the first and in the second we settled in and started to play much better. I remember having tremendous opportunities to score and missing. I missed one goal on an open net by an inch that would have tied the game. There were lots and lots of chances, but ultimately it came down to the fact that they scored and we didn't when it mattered.

At the end of the third period, as the last minute ticked down, I remember thinking, "Oh, no. We're not going to win." I was almost shocked — I didn't know what to think.

Standing on the blue line during the medal ceremony, I was emotionless. I stared straight ahead and didn't hear or see what was going on around us. It was just way too difficult. In the dressing room our captain, Stacy Wilson, pulled out a little music box that played "O Canada". It was going to be for when we won the gold medal, but she played it anyway. We all stood up in our uniforms and we sang the national anthem in our dressing room privately. It was a pretty emotional moment. And then that was it. I sat in my equipment for about an hour, until we had to go to the press conference.

It was emotional too for the press that had followed us through that year and the people that were constantly around us. They had tears in their eyes, just like we did. The men's team saw us after we had lost, and a lot of the guys didn't know what to say. Of course after they lost to the Czech Republic we knew exactly what they were going through. It was a tough time for everybody and there wasn't a lot said. Everybody knew it was the gold medal or nothing. I think the players on both teams felt that way. At least we brought home a silver medal, but to us at the time it was like winning no medal.

As time went by we started to realize that a silver medal is quite an achievement as well. You realize that perspective is important. It came down to one game. On that day we didn't play well, and they did. At the same time, it's something that always sticks in the back of your mind, and going into Salt Lake City in 2002 we have a bit of unfinished business.

After the Olympics Bob Clarke asked me if I wanted to come to the Philadelphia Flyers' training camp in 1998 as a way of improving my skills. It was very challenging to have to keep up with them for ten intense days and I learned a lot. Physically it was very demanding and it made me a better player when I came back to the women's team.

I hope that a women's professional league is on the horizon. Everyone's waiting to see what happens in Salt Lake City — that's going to be the big measuring stick. From there, we need to look at the North American market to get it going. I can foresee a six-team league in the Eastern part of Canada and the US to start with. We need more players and better players, and we also need some good financial backing and maybe the support of the NHL as well. ❧

Doug Flutie

An American made for the Canadian game

Quarterback — BC, Calgary & Toronto
1990-1997

Quite simply, Doug Flutie was one of the best players to play in the CFL this century. His statistics are naturally impressive, but even more so given that they accumulated over only an eight-year career.

Toronto STar — J. Goode

Following a Heisman-trophy winning US college career, Flutie played in the USFL and the NFL before being recruited north of the border by the BC Lions in 1990. He played well in his first season for the Lions, but it was during his second season that he began re-writing the CFL record book: 730 pass attempts, 466 completions and 6,619 yards. He also earned the first of his six Most Outstanding Player Awards for the 1991 season.

Flutie signed with the Calgary Stampeders as a free agent for the 1992 season, and would go on to lead the Stampeders to their third Grey Cup Championship. He was named the MVP of the '92 Grey Cup game in a 24-10 victory over the Winnipeg Blue Bombers, completing 33 of 49 pass attempts for 480 yards and two touchdowns. He received his second straight Most Outstanding Player award after the season.

During the 1993 and 1994 seasons, Doug continued to show how his passing, scrambling and running talents were suited to the CFL and received the Most Outstanding Player award after each season. In 1993, he tied for the CFL lead in rushing touchdowns with 11 and went over the 6,000-yard passing mark for the second time in his career. In 1994, Doug passed for a CFL record 48 touchdowns, and would run the ball for a career high 760 yards on only 96 attempts for a staggering 7.9 yards per carry average.

Following financial hardships for the Calgary organization, and a subsequent contract dispute with the Stampeders, Doug joined the Toronto Argonauts for the 1996 season. He excelled there too, leading the Argonauts to a 15-3 season, and earning his fifth CFL's Most Outstanding Player Award as well as his second Grey Cup ring.

The 1997 CFL campaign was Doug Flutie's last. His 47 touchdown passes that season left him one off his record-setting season mark set in 1994. He was named the Most Outstanding Player for a record sixth time, and won the Grey Cup for the third time in his career and second in as many years with the Toronto Argonauts. In accepting his Grey Cup MVP Award, Doug graciously gave the car he had won for his performance to the top Canadian in the game, teammate Paul Massotti. ❧

CFL Awards

1992, '96, '97
Grey Cup Champion

1992, '96, '97
Grey Cup MVP

1991, '92, '93, '94, '96, '97
CFL Most Outstanding Player Award

1991, '92, '93, '94
Western All-Star

1996, '97
Eastern All-Star:
CFL Records

1991, 1993-4, 1996-7
Led the CFL in Passing Attempts

1991, 1993-4, 1996-7
Led the CFL in Passing Completions

1991, 1993-4, 1996-7
Led the CFL in Passing Yardage

1991, 1993-4, 1996-7
Led the CFL in Touchdown Passes

1992
Set the CFL Record for Most Passing Yards, Attempts and Completions in one season

Most Pass Attempts All-Time, Grey Cup: **171**

Most Pass Completions All-Time, Grey Cup: **108**

Most Passing Yards All-Time, Grey Cup: **1,421**

2000

Hockey

The Modest Man from Motown

by James Deacon
February 7, 2000

There are stories for every scar on Steve Yzerman's otherwise handsome mug, and they are not for the faint of heart. They tell of a man who, though comparatively slight by modern National Hockey League standards (five-11, 185 lb.), isn't afraid of the rough going. Take, for example, the reddish crescent-moon dent where the bridge of his nose meets the centre of his forehead. That came from stopping a Paul Coffey slapshot just before last year's All-Star Game in Tampa. The force of the blast broke his nose and some other small bones, but as he was being wheeled to an ambulance headed for hospital, he called over to the Red Wings' equipment manager and said: "I think I'll need a visor on my helmet if I'm going to play in Tampa."

He did not go to Florida — doctors made sure of that. And although the story, like the scars, testifies to his remarkable focus and competitive spirit, it masks another truth about the man known as Stevie Y. He's not that tough. If you want to watch him squirm, offer him a compliment. Tell him his career achievements put him among the greatest players ever to lace up skates. Or insist that his sticking with the Detroit Red Wings for his entire career, through bad times and good, sets a shining example of loyalty in an era of money-driven transience. Then watch: he'll turtle. He'll tell you he's just been lucky to play so long for stable owners and with good linemates.

Hockey fans aren't fooled. In league-wide voting, they elected the 34-year-old Yzerman as the starting centre on the North American squad that will play a similarly elected team of European NHLers in Toronto. Along with being among the top 10 scorers going into last weekend's games, Yzerman recently overtook Bobby Hull and Mario Lemieux in career goals and now sits seventh all-time. Over lunch in the players'

HHOF — Dave Sandford

lounge at Joe Louis Arena last week, Yzerman deflected the accolades. "I can relate to Mario, because I played with him," he says, sitting at a table beside a huge black-and-white of former Wings Gordie Howe and Alex Delvecchio. "But Bobby Hull? Guys like him are kind of like gods. Their 600 goals are different from the 600 goals I have. They played fewer games, and it was more defensive then."

The distinction is well made, but it does not detract from what he has achieved. When he was named Detroit's first pick in the 1983 draft of junior players, Yzerman was saddled with the pressure of leading a then-dreadful team back to glory. He was initially a scoring sensation — he had 65 goals and 90 assists in 1988-1989. But in the mid-1990s, after general manager Jim Devellano and later Ken Holland began to improve Detroit's supporting cast, and when Scotty Bowman joined as coach, Yzerman, the team's captain since he was 21, transformed himself into a player known as much for defence as for scoring. The combination worked: the Wings won back-to-back Stanley Cups in 1997 and 1998, and they appear ready to contend again this year. "I get more attention for being a 20-goal scorer than when I scored 50," he says, chuckling at the irony.

He claims he has mellowed with age, a family of his own and, particularly, the car accident that crippled teammate Vladimir Konstantinov only days after the 1997 Cup victory. "I don't take the game as seriously as I used to," he says. "I know that winning, one way or another, isn't going to change my life."

The greatest compliment comes from crusty Detroit legend Ted Lindsay, now 74, who stopped by the Wings' locker room last week. "If you wanted to program the ideal child, hockey player, citizen, he's the guy you'd copy," says Lindsay. ♣

During the course of the 20th century,
multi-sport competitions grew
to a phenomenal popularity,
expanding opportunities
for interaction between virtually
every country in the world.
Canadians participated in most
of these events from the start, adding
greatly to our sporting tradition as well
as making our mark internationally.
Canada at the Games
relates our rich tradition of participating
in and hosting the Olympics,
Paralympics, Pan American Games,
Commonwealth Games, Canada Games
and Special Olympics.

Canada

Our Century in Sport

1900-2000

Chapter II

Canada at the Games

Flag Bearers

Flag Bearers

by James Deacon
September 18, 2000

CSI/COA

Brian Orser,
Calgary, 1988

On their jerseys and in their hearts, these Olympians carry the hopes of Canadians

James Worrall has been at the centre of Olympic life for more than 60 years, but the north Toronto apartment he shares with his wife, Birgitte, doesn't show it. The living room is bright, comfortable and noticeably bereft of Games memorabilia. So Worrall, 86, has to dig into his files when a visitor asks to see a photograph of him at the opening ceremonies at the 1936 Olympics. From a tired manila envelope, he slides a faded black-and-white photograph showing a procession of Canadian coaches and athletes marching into Berlin's Olympic Stadium. Out in front is Worrall himself, carrying the flag. He was 22 then, a 400-m hurdler from Montreal. He was surprised that he was chosen to carry the flag since Phil Edwards had been appointed team captain. But Worrall was a good athlete, a silver medallist at the 1934 British Empire Games, and he was tall, six-foot-four, which meant that Canada's emblem would be held high as the team passed by German Chancellor Adolf Hitler.

In hindsight, it was an occasion of heavy political import. It just didn't seem so at the time. As was then customary, the Canadians passing Hitler's box offered the Olympic salute — the same raised-right-arm salute that was adopted by the Nazis. Many athletes, Worrall says, didn't even know the German leader's name, let alone his policies.

More than politics, Worrall remembers the pageantry. "It was an awesome moment," he says, "coming out of the tunnel and into the sunlight, into the stadium in front of 100,000 people."

That was just the beginning of Worrall's Olympic career. In Toronto, where he moved to study law and set up a practice, he worked as a volunteer to establish provincial and national amateur sport federations, including what now is the Canadian Olympic Association. He served as Canada's chef de mission at the 1956 and 1960 Summer Games. In 1967, Worrall was appointed to the International Olympic Committee, and in 1980, he was a candidate for IOC president, losing to Juan Antonio Samaranch. In all, Worrall attended 14 games, and he has been honoured for various contributions to Canadian sport. But the greatest, he says, was the one given to him in Berlin. "That is something you cannot really describe," he says of his feelings in 1936. "But yes, I was very proud to be out in front, carrying the Canadian flag." 🍁

Courtesy of Jim Worrall

James Worrall, Canada's flag bearer at the 1936 Olympic Games Opening Ceremonies, Berlin.

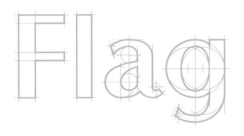

Canadian Olympic Flag Bearers, Opening Ceremonies, 1900-2000

Year	City	Flag Bearer	Sport
1900	Paris	None	
1904	St. Louis	None	
1906	Athens	None	
1908	London	Unknown/multiple	
1912	Stockholm	Duncan Gillis	Track & Field
1916	Cancelled	–	–
1920	Antwerp	Archie McDiarmid	Track & Field
1924	Paris	Hector Phillips	Track & Field
1928	Amsterdam	Joseph Wright, Jr.	Rowing
1932	Los Angeles	George Maughan	Boxing
1936	Berlin	James Worrall	Track & Field
1940	Cancelled	–	–
1944	Cancelled	–	–
1948	London	Robert McFarlane	Track & Field
1952	Helsinki	William Parnell	Track & Field
1956	Melbourne	Robert Steckle	Wrestling
1960	Rome	Carl Schwende	Fencing
1964	Tokyo	Gilmour Boa	Shooting
1968	Mexico City	Roger Jackson	Rowing
1972	Munich	Doug Rogers	Judo
1976	Montreal	Abby Hoffman	Track & Field
1980	Moscow	Sue Holloway *	Canoeing
1984	Los Angeles	Alex Baumann	Swimming
1988	Seoul	Carolyn Waldo	Synchro Swimming
1992	Barcelona	Michael Smith	Track & Field
1996	Atlanta	Charmaine Crooks	Track & Field
2000	Sydney	Caroline Brunet	Canoeing

* Canada named a team but officially did not participate in these boycotted Games.

Canadian Olympic Winter Flag Bearers, Opening Ceremonies, 1924-2000

Year	City	Flag Bearer	Sport
1924	Chamonix	Ernie Collett	Hockey
1928	St. Moritz	John Porter	Hockey
1932	Lake Placid	Unknown / Multiple	
1936	Garmisch	Unknown / Multiple	
1940	Cancelled	–	–
1944	Cancelled	–	–
1948	St. Moritz	Hubert Brooks	Hockey
1952	Oslo	Gordon Audley	Speed Skating
1956	Cortina	Norris Bowden	Figure Skating
1960	Squaw Valley	Robert Paul	Figure Skating
1964	Innsbruck	Ralph Olin	Speed Skating
1968	Grenoble	Nancy Greene	Alpine Ski
1972	Sapporo	Karen Magnussen	Figure Skating
1976	Innsbruck	Dave Irwin	Alpine Ski
1980	Lake Placid	Ken Read	Alpine Ski
1984	Sarajevo	Gaétan Boucher	Speed Skating
1988	Calgary	Brian Orser	Figure Skating
1992	Albertville	Sylvie Daigle	Speed Skating
1994	Lillehammer	Kurt Browning	Figure Skating
1998	Nagano	Jean-Luc Brassard	Freestyle Ski

Caroline Brunet, Sydney, 2000

Canadian Press/COA

Kurt Browning, Lillehammer, 1994

CSI/COA

Canada Hosts the
Commonwealth

The First British Empire Games

Percy Williams winning British Empire gold in the 100m.

The idea for a multi-sport competition between countries of the then British Empire was first proposed as early as 1891, but it would be nearly 40 years before the British Empire Games became a reality. An "Inter-Empire Sports Meeting" held in conjunction with the Festival of Empire to celebrate the coronation of George V in 1911 helped keep the idea alive, as did the support of various sport officials from around the far-flung Empire.

Canadians were on the forefront of efforts to make the Games a reality. In 1924, Norton Crowe, Secretary of the Amateur Athletic Union of Canada for 19 years, encouraged the Union to take a more active role. M.M. "Bobby" Robinson, a sports reporter for the Hamilton Spectator and Manager of the Canadian track and field team for the 1928 Amsterdam Olympics, joined the cause and spent part of his time at the Olympics persuading other countries to agree to hold the first Games in Hamilton in 1930. During a time of economic difficulty it was no easy task to cajole commitments to participate from countries scattered all over the globe, united only by their loyalty to the British Crown. In the end, helped in part by travel subsidies offered to some countries, 400 athletes from 11 countries made their way to the Steel City.

The Games were patterned after the now well-established Olympics, but with a few key differences. Organizers wanted them to be "free from both the excessive stimulus and the babel of the international stadium. They should be merrier and less stern, and will substitute the stimulus of novel adventure for the pressure of international rivalry." The exclusion of team sports and restricting the program to nine sports ensured the Games would remain a manageable size for both organizers and participants. There was also no point system for medal winners that would enable one country to be declared the overall winner of the Games.

Canada Hosts the World

Hosting the Commonwealth

1930	Hamilton	The British Empire Games
1954	Vancouver	The British Empire and Commonwealth Games
1978	Edmonton	The Commonwealth Games
1994	Victoria	The Commonwealth Games

Hosting the Americas

1967	Winnipeg	The 5th Pan American Games
1999	Winnipeg	The 13th Pan American Games

Hosting the Olympic World

1976	Montreal	The XXI Olympic Games
1988	Calgary	The XV Olympic Winter Games

First Place Canadians at the Festival of Empire Games – 1911

London, England

Sport	Event	Athlete
Track & Field	100 yd	F.J. Halbhaus
	200 yd	F.J. Halbhaus
	1 mile	J. L. Tait
Swimming	1 mile	George Hodgson

Commonwealth

The City of Hamilton agreed to house and feed the athletes, as well as underwrite any financial losses. The seating in the stadium was increased, a new swimming pool built, a marsh dredged for a rowing course, and the city was ready. The program included six sports: athletics, lawn bowling, boxing, rowing, swimming/diving, and wrestling.

Opening day was a civic holiday, and some 20,000 spectators took advantage of their day off to attend the opening ceremonies. Prime Minister R.B. Bennett welcomed the athletes, also conveying the best wishes of King George V and the Prince of Wales. Governor General Lord Willingdon officially opened the Games.

Canadian sprint hero Percy Williams, winner of two gold medals at the 1928 Olympics, took the oath of allegiance on behalf of his fellow competitors, promising to compete "in the spirit of true sportsmanship, recognizing the rules which govern them, desirous of participating in them for the honour of our Empire and the glory of sport." When competition started, he lived up to his billing as the world's fastest human, but on his way to the gold medal in the 100m he pulled a muscle as he neared the finish line. It was an injury that would effectively end his competitive career.

Fittingly, Canada won the first gold medal of the Games, when Gordon Smallcombe took top honours in the hop, step and jump. Alf Phillips provided another Canadian highlight, winning both the highboard and springboard diving events. Canadians also won all seven wrestling events.

On August 22, midway through the Games, representatives from all the participating countries unanimously pronounced the Games a success and agreed that they should be held every four years. The British Empire Games Federation was formed to oversee the development of a new tradition that would eventually include more than 60 countries. ❧

1930 British Empire Games poster.

Opening Ceremonies of the First British Empire Games at Hamilton's Scott Park, 1930.

July 30 - August 7, 1954, Vancouver, BC

Fifth British Empire and Commonwealth Games

By 1954, the changing political reality of the former British Empire had led to adding "Commonwealth" to the name of the Games. With more than two decades of tradition behind them, their scale had increased substantially. But even with 24 countries and 662 athletes participating, their character remained as always as Canada played host for the second time. The airplane was by now the preferred mode of transportation, which meant that grateful athletes could measure their travel time in days or hours, rather than weeks.

The nine sports on the program this time around were athletics, cycling, fencing, lawn bowling, rowing, swimming/diving, weightlifting and wrestling. For the first time, photo finishes and electronic devices were used to help judges decide the winners of various events. Track athletes also had the benefit of racing on a state-of-the-art cinder track inside the brand-new Empire Stadium.

Spectators who flocked to Empire Stadium on August 7 witnessed two of the more dramatic moments of the Games. Many were there to witness the much-anticipated matchup of the world's two fastest mile runners: Roger Bannister of England and John Landy of Australia. These first men ever to run a sub-four-minute mile, had never before met in competition, and the event almost

Opening Ceremonies at Vancouver's Empire Stadium, 1954.

Canada

eclipsed the Games themselves. Bannister won the hard-fought race by .8 seconds, but it marked the first time two runners in one race had ever gone below four minutes. The race went down in the history books as the "Miracle Mile." Less well-remembered is the fact that a Canadian, Richie Ferguson, won the bronze medal in a time that would have easily won a gold medal in 1950.

Equally riveting, although for different reasons, was the finish of the marathon. England's Jim Peters had about a 15-minute lead when he entered the stadium with one lap of the track to go. In a state of complete exhaustion, he staggered onto the track, falling repeatedly. Spectators and officials watched in agony, unable to help lest Peters be disqualified. After 20 minutes of struggle and 11 falls, he had staggered and crawled only halfway around the track before he collapsed in the arms of an English team official. He thought he had crossed the finish line, but it was still 200 yards away.

English athletes dominated many of the track events, while Canadians earned their share of medals in lawn bowling and rowing. Canada was also the top country in weightlifting, winning three gold and two silver medals.

Earl Alexander of Tunis, who had officially opened the Games, wrote later that he was most impressed by "the spirit of true sportsmanship which was present throughout and shown not only by the competing athletes from all parts of the Commonwealth but by the large crowd of spectators. It was a real gathering of sportsmen." ❦

The 1950 Canadian Commonwealth team setting off for New Zealand.

Canada

Our
Century
in Sport

The Miracle Mile

Copyright — Charlie Warner

The fateful glance by Australian John Landy as he misses England's Roger Bannister passing him by.

The only constant thing about sports records is that someday they will be broken. Some benchmarks take on an almost mythical aspect, though, particularly if they steadfastly resist athletes' efforts to attain them. So it was during the 1940s and the early part of the 1950s with the standard for the one mile run. For a decade, runners came excruciatingly close to breaking through the magic four-minute mark, but came up just short.

That state of affairs persisted until May, 1954, when British medical student Roger Bannister made history with the first sub-four-minute mile: 3:59.4. As so often happens, once the barrier had been breached, it seemed to become easier for others to rise to the same level, and just six weeks later Australian agronomy student John Landy sped to a 3:58 mile in Finland.

Both these efforts were under controlled conditions, though, with half-mile runners pacing both men to a high enough pace for part of the distance in order to reach their goals. Could they repeat the performance in competition?

All eyes turned to Canada, where Landy and Bannister would meet at the 1954 British Empire and Commonwealth Games in Vancouver in August. The games were a huge sporting event, and left a sports legacy in the Vancouver area that lasted for many years. The magnitude of the event was almost eclipsed, though, by the hype surrounding the mile event.

On August 7, 1954, eight men from five nations lined up for the race on the state-of-the-art cinder track, but it was clear early on that six of them were racing for third place. Landy started fast, his strategy being to open up a wide lead in the knowledge that his finish was not as strong as Bannister's. For much of the race his tactic appeared to be working, as he built up a lead that at times was more than 10 metres. The crowd of more than 32,000 in the brand-new Empire Stadium roared its approval as the duel unfolded. Everyone, from veteran sports writers to the public, knew they were witnessing history in the making.

The event that captured the world's attention produced one of the most dramatic sports photos of all time, taken by Vancouver Sun photographer Charlie Warner. He stood on the sidelines that memorable day hoping for a good angle as Bannister and Landy raced around the track. At the crucial moment when Landy looked back, Charlie snapped that immortal photo that would win him international acclaim for "best sports action picture" of 1954.

Bannister never lost sight of Landy, though, and midway through the third of four laps started to whittle away at the lead. At the end of three laps there were only two metres separating the two. The split time of 2:58 proved they were on schedule to go under four minutes, and the crowd anxiously awaited Bannister's famed finishing kick. Landy knew it was coming too, and vainly tried to pick up the pace after checking over his shoulder where his opponent was.

Bannister stuck close, though, and about 80 metres from the finish made the move that would be remembered as the defining moment of the race. At the same moment Landy chose to peek over his left shoulder to check his rival's whereabouts again, Bannister surged past him on the right. A spent Landy couldn't answer the challenge, and Bannister moved four metres ahead. He crossed the line in 3:59.6 to Bannister's 3:58.8, but his place in the history books was assured as both men breached the four-minute barrier.

The Miracle Mile, as it came to be known, had attracted media attention from around the world. *Sports Illustrated*, just being launched, made the event the feature of its inaugural issue. For the first time, film footage of the race was flown by a Royal Air Force jet to London so that British and European audiences could see the race just hours after it happened. Vancouver was put on the international map in a way it had never known.

Almost forgotten in the hype of the day and even in the retelling of the story, is the fact that Canadian Richie Ferguson won the bronze medal. To give an indication of how fast the race was relative to the standards of the day, his time of 4:04.6 was more than six seconds faster than the previous British Empire and Commonwealth Games record. The 1950 record of 4:11 had in fact been set by another Canadian — William Parnell. Bannister's mark was, of course, in turn also equaled and bettered in subsequent years, but never in as dramatic a fashion. ❧

The Miracle Mile finish, with Bannister (left) and Landy both breaking the four-minute barrier.

Queen Elizabeth II

August 3-12, 1978, Edmonton, Alberta

11th Commonwealth Games

When the members of Edmonton's bid committee arrived at the Olympics in Munich in 1972, where the host of the 1978 Commonwealth Games was being chosen, they had an interesting challenge ahead of them. They were not just up against a rival bid from Leeds, England, but had to overcome widespread ignorance about the very existence of Edmonton, let alone its qualifications to host a major sports event. A number of intense days of lobbying convinced voters from other Commonwealth countries that Edmonton was not a suburb of Toronto, did have running water and indoor plumbing, and that snow would in fact not be a factor during the month of August. Nor would the city of 600,000 have to fly in food daily for the expected influx of 3000 athletes and officials.

The geography lesson complete, Edmonton's bid was approved. Meanwhile, political and economic associations between the countries of the former British Empire continued to change, and the Games were re-christened for the fourth time in 1974, becoming simply the Commonwealth Games rather than the British Commonwealth Games. While the number of sports on the program remained at nine, the scale of the Games continued to grow. In Edmonton 1474 athletes from 46 countries competed.

Diane Jones Konihowski delivering the 1978 Commonwealth Baton to Queen Elizabeth II.

Diane Jones Konihowski, Canada's star pentathlete, ran the final relay leg into the stadium during the Opening Ceremonies with the specially carved Games baton carrying a message from Queen Elizabeth II. For the first time ever, the Queen opened the Games personally, praising the human qualities brought out in the sporting rivalries and friendships that had developed at the Games in the 50 years since the original decision had been made to hold them. Diver Bev Boys took the Oath of the Games on behalf of all the athletes.

Some of the most memorable of Canada's 45 gold medals at the Games came from stars Jones Konihowski and hometown swimmer Graham Smith. Both had been considered medal contenders two years earlier in the Montreal Olympics, but Jones Konihowski had come away empty-handed while Smith was shut out in the individual events, winning a silver medal in the 4 x 100m medley relay. Given a second chance for glory in front of loyal fans, neither one disappointed.

Jones Konihowski won the pentathlon in decisive fashion, her score of 4768 shattering the previous Commonwealth Games record by more than 300 points. Several of her individual performances in the five parts of the pentathlon would have put her in medal contention in the open versions of those events. In the end she won the gold by more than 500 points over her nearest competitor and pundits were suggesting that she would contend for the gold medal at the 1980 Olympics in Moscow. Unfortunately, those Games were to be boycotted by Canada.

Smith was also favoured to win in Edmonton, but carried far more than the usual weight of expectation on a local athlete predicted to do well. Less than two years earlier, his father had died of cancer, living just long enough to see Smith and his sister Becky compete in Montreal (Becky earned bronze medals in the 400m individual medley and the 4 x 100m freestyle relay). In Edmonton, the pool was subsequently named the Dr. Donald F. Smith Memorial Pool in memory of a man who had pioneered competitive swimming in Edmonton. Smith was either undaunted or inspired by the pressure of competing in a pool named for his father, and swam the races of his life on the way to four individual gold medals and two more in relays. His total of six gold medals was unmatched in Commonwealth Games history.

Outside of competition, even the "Friendly Games" were affected by the political controversies of the day that spilled over into the sports arena. In an echo of the African boycott of the 1976 Montreal Olympics, Nigeria withdrew from the Edmonton Games in continued protest over sporting ties between New Zealand and the apartheid regime in South Africa. This cloud had an ironic silver lining, though: Precious Patrick McKenzie, a diminutive 4'11" weightlifter who left his native South Africa in 1964 because his race prevented him from being named to the national team, won a gold medal competing for ... New Zealand. It was his fourth consecutive win, going back to 1966, when he competed for England. ♣

Commonwealth champion
Graham Smith, 1978

National Archives

Jones Konihowski in competition

Commonwealth

All That Glitters

Victoria lowers a curtain
on the Commonwealth Games

by Chris Wood
September 5, 1994

Victoria's 1994 Commonwealth Games Opening Ceremonies.

For the hundreds of winners showered in gold, silver and bronze over 10 days of Commonwealth Games that ended on Aug. 28, winning meant different things to different people. England's Linford Christie appeared almost offhanded as he sprinted to the gold medal in the 100m in a Commonwealth record time of 9.91 seconds. There was nothing even remotely casual, though, about the elated runner who followed Christie across the line and then literally rolled on the ground with excitement: Horace Dove-Edwin's silver was the first-ever, from any major games, for his tiny, impoverished west African country of Sierra Leone and its 4.3 million people. Declared the 27-year-old sprinter: "This medal is for them."

Among Canadians, runner Angela Chalmers delivered the goods before an ecstatic home-town crowd, winning the 3,000m race in 8:32.17, shaving six seconds off her own Commonwealth Games record. Toronto decathlete Michael Smith won his second gold in as many Commonwealth Games, shaking off two years of injury-plagued doldrums. "I came in here ranked No. 1 in the Commonwealth," he said. "I wanted to go out of here No. 1." Overall, Canada emerged from the Games as No. 2 in the medal tally, trailing Australia, whose athletes virtually ruled the Commonwealth pool, winning 25 swimming golds.

Such comparisons, however, seemed at odds with the relaxed atmosphere that prevailed last week in Victoria. Certainly, the crowds of up to 70,000 people who thronged into the closed-off, downtown streets for free nightly concerts and fireworks were anything but chauvinist, cheering for all the medallists who were introduced from a stage on the BC legislature lawn. An appearance by Chalmers and fellow-Victorian Robyn Meagher, who took the 3,000m silver, prompted a heartfelt, unscheduled rendition of O Canada. But, in a gesture in keeping with the Games' oft-cited friendly spirit, the nightly throng saved its warmest ovation for the unassuming Dove-Edwin.

The Games themselves did have their critics. Controversy struck the boxing ring in the second week, when several African coaches accused white judges of racism in their decisions. Some people carped about the steep price of tickets to the most popular events (up to $125 for seats at the opening and closing ceremonies) or the slow delivery of competition results on the Games' IBM-designed computer system. BC taxpayers, meanwhile, will have to wait until the end of the year to receive a full accounting of the $160 million — including federal, provincial and corporate contributions — spent to mount the Games.

Whether such massive undertakings are worth the public expense at any time is a subject bound to provoke debate. One answer to the question, however, could be glimpsed in the number of representatives from other cities who came to Victoria to take notes for their own plans to host similar games.

As athletes from around the globe headed home after closing ceremonies, they could take with them memories of achievement and fellowship that promised to endure long after the last anthem was played and the last firework had sputtered out over Victoria Harbour. ♦

Hometown hero Angela Chalmers raises her arms in victory after being presented the gold medal for her Commonwealth Games record-breaking 3,000m race in Victoria.

Canadian Press CP

1930

HAMILTON
21 gold, 14 silver, 19 bronze

After years of batting the idea around, a plan to organize the first British Empire Games was presented at the 1928 Olympic Games by Bobby Robinson, a sports reporter for the *Hamilton Spectator*. Two years later Hamilton hosted the first Games. Triple jumper Gordon "Spike" Smallacombe won the first gold medal in the history of the Commonwealth Games in Hamilton. Olympic legend Percy Williams won the 100m sprint gold medal, sustaining a career-ending injury in the process. Diver Alf Phillips won gold medals in both the tower and springboard events, with Pearl Stoneham winning the women's tower event.

Percy Williams, Hamilton, 1930

1950

Auckland, New Zealand
8 gold, 8 silver, 13 bronze

Diver George Athans, who had won two bronze medals in 1938, returned after a 12-year absence and won the gold medal on the 3-metre springboard and a silver on the tower event. William Parnell won the mile race on the track, taking more than six seconds off the Games record.

Harold Webster, Marathon gold medallist, 1934, London

1934

London, England
17 gold, 25 silver, 9 bronze

Swimmer Phyllis Dewar became the first athlete to win four gold medals at a single Commonwealth Games. Toronto pole vaulter Syl Apps, later an NHL star with the Maple Leafs, won the gold medal in his event.

1938

Sydney, Australia
13 gold, 16 silver, 14 bronze

Swimmer Robert Pirie was the first to win five medals at a single Games, winning two gold and three silver medals. On the track, John Loaring won two gold medals, in the 440 yard hurdles and the 4 x 110 yard relay.

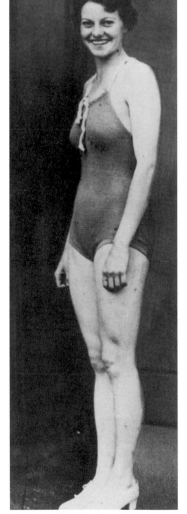

Phyllis Dewar, 1934

Canada's Rich Ferguson came third in the Miracle Mile.

1954

VANCOUVER
9 gold, 20 silver, 14 bronze
Often overlooked and forgotten, but running the race of his life, Richard Ferguson of Canada won the bronze medal behind Roger Bannister of England and John Landy of Australia in "The Miracle Mile." It marked the first time two runners broke the four-minute mile in the same race. Hometown weightlifter Doug Hepburn won the heavyweight gold medal.

1958

Cardiff, Wales
1 gold, 10 silver, 16 bronze
Canada's only gold came from the men's eights crew from UBC, who repeated their 1954 victory in less than ideal conditions. Irene MacDonald won silver in springboard diving.

1962

Perth, Australia
4 gold, 12 silver, 15 bronze
On the track, middle distance runner Bruce Kidd won the gold medal in the six-mile event. In the pool, Mary Stewart won the 110 yard butterfly, and future International Olympic Committee executive member Dick Pound won the gold medal in the 110 yard freestyle.

Irene MacDonald

Richard Pound

Vancouver's Doug Hepburn

Mary Stewart

Bruce Kidd

1966

Kingston, Jamaica
14 gold, 19 silver, 23 bronze
In the Games that would make her world-famous, Canada's "Mighty Mouse" Elaine Tanner won four gold medals and three silver medals in the pool, setting two world records in the process. Swimmer Marion Lay also won gold in the pool, winning the 110 yard freestyle. Sprinter Harry Jerome claimed the gold medal in the 100m on the track, while Abby Hoffman earned perhaps her greatest victory in the 800m.

Elaine "Mighty Mouse" Tanner

1974

Christchurch, New Zealand
25 gold, 19 silver, 18 bronze
Swimmer Bruce Robertson was the most decorated Canadian at the Games, earning two gold, two silver and two bronze medals. Also in the pool, Wendy Cook won both the 100m and 200m backstroke events, Patti Stenhouse was first in 100m butterfly, and Leslie Cliff took the 200m and 400m individual medleys. Diver Bev Boys again won the gold medal on the tower, while Cindy Shatto, daughter of famed Toronto Argonaut Dick Shatto, was victorious on the springboard. Cyclist Jocelyn Lovell won a medal of each colour, including a repeat gold medal performance in the 10-mile scratch race. Weightlifter Russ Prior repeated as the heavyweight gold medallist. Canadian shooters won four out of six gold medals.

Jocelyn Lovell

Debbie Brill receives her 1970 Commonwealth Games high jump gold medal from HRH, Queen Elizabeth II

1970

Edinburgh, Scotland
18 gold, 24 silver, 22 bronze
High jumper Debbie Brill began her long and illustrious international career by capturing her first Commonwealth Games title. Cyclist Jocelyn Lovell set a Games record en route to victory in the 10-mile scratch race, and also added silver and bronze medals. Diver Bev Boys won on both the tower and the springboard. Weightlifter Russ Prior won his first heavyweight title.

Bev Boys

Leslie Cliff

1978

EDMONTON
44 gold, 29 silver, 34 bronze

Canada's Edmonton gold rush started in the water. Competing before a hometown audience in Edmonton in the swimming pool named for his late father, Graham Smith won six gold medals. Butterfly specialist Dan Thompson won the 100m; George Nagy was victorious in 200m butterfly; first to touch in 100m freestyle was Carol Klimpel as was Cheryl Gibson in 200m backstroke, Robin Corsiglia in the 100m breaststroke, Lisa Borsholt in the 200m breaststroke, and Wendy Quirk in the 100m butterfly. Wendy Cook repeated her champion ways in the 100m backstroke. Diver Linda Cuthbert triumphed on the tower, as did Janet Nutter on the springboard. Out of the pool, gymnast Philip Delesalle won double gold, and Elfi Schlegel won the women's individual all-round title. High jumper Claude Ferragne took gold, with Phil Olsen winning the javelin event, and Bruce Simpson topped the pole vaulting field. The winning discus thrower was Borys Chambul for the men and Carmen Ionesco in the women's event. Diane Jones Konihowski broke the Games' pentathlon record en route to her gold medal. Another hometown athlete, Wendy Clarkson, won silver and bronze in badminton, with Jane Youngberg and Claire Backhouse being the silver medallists in doubles. Trapshooter John Primose successfully defended his 1974 gold title and cyclists Jocelyn Lovell and Gord Singleton triumphed in the tandem sprint. Lovell added two more golds: in the 10-mile race and individual 1000m time trial. Hamiltonian Russ Prior won his third straight heavyweight weightlifting title. Egon Beiler repeated as the featherweight wrestling champion, while Wyatt Wishart won the heavyweight title, Kelly Perlette the light-middleweight, S. Daniar the light-heavyweight, R. Gibbons the super-heavyweight, Richard Deschatelets the middleweight, and R. Fortin the light-heavyweight title.

The Friendly Games — Sprinters Angella Taylor of Canada and Jamaican Merlene Ottey.

Graham Smith

1982

Brisbane, Australia
22 gold, 23 silver, 32 bronze

Success for Canada in the pool again as swimmer Alex Baumann won gold medals in the 200m and 400m individual medleys, setting a new world mark in the 200m event. Breaststroke specialist Victor Davis won one gold, and frustrated at having just missed a second gold, kicked over some chairs in the un-amused presence of Queen Elizabeth II. Anne Ottenbrite won a gold and two silvers; Mike West topped the field in the 100m backstroke and Cam Henning was first in the 200m backstroke. Dan Thompson repeated as the 100m butterfly champion and Kathy Bald was tops in the 100m breaststroke. On the mats, five Canadian wrestlers — Richard Deschatelets, Bob Robinson, Chris Rinke, Clark Davis, and Wyatt Wishart — won gold medals.

John Primrose

Alex Baumann

1986

Edinburgh, Scotland
50 gold, 34 silver, 31 bronze
An African nation boycott of the Games left only 26 countries competing in the Edinburgh Games. Alex Baumann won three gold medals in the pool. On the track, Mark McKoy triumphed in the 110m hurdles for the second straight Games. Ben Johnson defended his 1982 100m title and Dave Steen repeated as the Commonwealth decathlon silver medallist. Sprinter Angella (Taylor) Issajenko won gold and silver medals and Jillian Richardson was second in the 400m. Debbie Bowker won two silvers, in the 1500m and 3000m. Lynn Williams won the 3000m and was third in the 1500m. Toronto's Milt Ottey repeated as the Games' high jump champion. In the pool, Mark Tewksbury headed the field in the 100m backstroke; Sandy Goss was the 200m backstroke champion; breaststroker Victor Davis duplicated his 1982 gold medal performance; Jane Kerr won the 100m freestyle race; Allison Higson was first in 100m and 200m breaststroke; and Donna McGinnis won the 200m butterfly.

Dave Steen

Mark McKoy

1990

Auckland, New Zealand
35 gold, 41 silver, 37 bronze
Curtis Hibbert and Lori Strong swept the gymnastics medals. Mary Fuzesi won the individual all-round title and the hoop and ribbon gold medals in rhythmic gymnastics. Angela Chalmers won gold in both the 1500m and 3000m. Michael Smith captured Canada's first Commonwealth decathlon gold medal. Gold medallist in the 30-km walk was the 1986 silver medallist Guillaume Leblanc. And, Mark Tewksbury repeated as Commonwealth champion in the 100m backstroke.

Mark Tewksbury

1994

VICTORIA
41 gold, 42 silver, 46 bronze
Gymnast Stella Umeh won two gold and two silver medals. Angela Chalmers and Michael Smith added to their Commonwealth Games gold medal collection, in the 3000m and decathlon respectively. Jeff Adams won the gold medal in the demonstration 800m wheelchair race. Carole Rouillard won the women's marathon. Cyclist Tanya Dubnicoff was a gold medallist on the track. Paige Gordon, Anne Montminy, and Myriam Boileau swept the tower diving events, while Annie Pelletier was victorious on the one-metre and three-metre springboards.

CPC

Jeff Adams

1998

Kuala Lumpur, Malaysia
30 gold, 31 silver, 38 bronze
Diver Alexandre Despatie scored a major upset with his victory on the tower, while Eryn Bulmer topped the three-metre springboard. Gold medal performances by Lyne Bessette, Eric Wohlberg, and Tanya Dubnicoff told the story in cycling. Erika-Leigh Stirton won all five individual events in rhythmic gymnastics. Individual medley specialist Joanne Malar won golds, two silvers and a bronze medals. And, swimmer Marianne Limpert topped the field in 200m IM.

CSI/COA

Tanya Dubnicoff

CSI/COA

Joanne Malar

Canada's Gold Medals at the Commonwealth Games, 1930-2000

Games	Medallist	Sport	Event
1930:	Alf Phillips	Diving	Highboard
Hamilton, Canada	Alf Phillips	Diving	Springboard
20 Gold Medals	Pearl Stoneham	Diving	Highboard
	E. Boles, B. Richards	Rowing	Double Sculls
	F. Munro Bourne	Swimming	100yd Freestyle
	Men's Team	Swimming	4x200yd Freestyle Relay
	Jack Aubin	Swimming	200yd Breaststroke
	Percy Williams	Track & Field	100yd
	Alexander Wilson	Track & Field	440yd
	Men's Team	Track & Field	4x110yd Relay
	Leonard Hutton	Track & Field	Long Jump
	Gordon Smallacombe	Track & Field	Triple Jump
	Victor Pickard	Track & Field	Pole Vault
	Jim Trifunov	Wrestling	Bantamweight
	Clifford Chilcott	Wrestling	Featherweight
	Howard Thomas	Wrestling	Lightweight
	Reg Priestley	Wrestling	Welterweight
	Mike Chepwick	Wrestling	Middleweight
	L. McIntyre	Wrestling	Light Heavyweight
	Earl McCready	Wrestling	Heavyweight
1934:	Robert McLeod	Cycling	10 Miles Scratch
London, England	Judith Moss	Diving	Springboard
17 Gold Medals	George Burleigh	Swimming	100yd Freestyle
	Men's Team	Swimming	4x200yd Freestyle Relay
	Men's Team	Swimming	3x100yd Medley Relay
	Phyllis Dewar	Swimming	100yd Freestyle
	Phyllis Dewar	Swimming	400yd Freestyle
	Women's Team	Swimming	4x100yd Freestyle Relay
	Women's Team	Swimming	3x100yd Medley Relay
	Harold Webster	Track & Field	Marathon
	Samuel Richardson	Track & Field	Long Jump
	Syl Apps	Track & Field	Pole Vault
	Robert Dixon	Track & Field	Javelin
	Women's Team	Track & Field	660yd Relay
	Robert McNab	Wrestling	Featherweight
	Joseph Schleimer	Wrestling	Welterweight
	Terry Evans	Wrestling	Middleweight
1938:	Thomas Osborne	Boxing	Heavyweight
Sydney, Australia	Robert Pirie	Swimming	100yd Freestyle
13 Gold Medals	Robert Pirie	Swimming	440yd Freestyle
	Women's Team	Swimming	4x110yd Freestyle Relay
	Men's Team	Track & Field	4x110yd Relay
	Men's Team	Track & Field	4x440yd Relay
	John Loaring	Track & Field	440yd hurdles
	Harold Brown	Track & Field	Long Jump
	Eric Coy	Track & Field	Discus
	James Courtwright	Track & Field	Javelin
	George Sutherland	Track & Field	Hammer
	Robina Higgins	Track & Field	Javelin
	Terry Evans	Wrestling	Middleweight

Games	Medallist	Sport	Event
1950:	George Athans	Diving	Springboard Diving
Auckland, New Zealand	Peter Salmon	Swimming	110yd Freestyle
8 Gold Medals	William Parnell	Track & Field	1 mile
	Leo Roininen	Track & Field	Javelin
	Gerard Gratton	Weightlifting	Middleweight
	James Varaleau	Weightlifting	Light Heavyweight
	Henry Hudson	Wrestling	Welterweight
	Maurice Vachon	Wrestling	Middleweight
1954:	Mickey Bergin	Boxing	Light Welterweight
Vancouver, Canada	Wilfred Greaves	Boxing	Light Middleweight
9 Gold Medals	William Patrick	Diving	Highboard
	Men's Team	Fencing	Men's Sabre Team
	Men's Team	Rowing	Eights
	Men's Team	Track & Field	4x110yd Relay
	Gerald Gratton	Weightlifting	Light Heavyweight
	Keevil Daly	Weightlifting	Middle Heavyweight
	Doug Hepburn	Weightlifting	Heavyweight
1958:	Men's Team	Rowing	Eights
Cardiff, Wales			
1 Gold Medal			
1962:	Harold Mann	Boxing	Light Middleweight
Perth, Australia	Richard Pound	Swimming	110yd Freestyle
4 Gold Medals	Mary Stewart	Swimming	110yd Butterfly
	Bruce Kidd	Track & Field	Six Miles
1966:	Gilmour Boa	Shooting	Small Bore – 22 Rifle
Kingston, Jamaica	James Lee	Shooting	Centre Fire Pistol
14 Gold Medals	Ronald Jacks	Swimming	110yd Butterfly
	Men's Team	Swimming	4x110yd Medley Relay
	Marion Lay	Swimming	110yd Freestyle
	Women's Team	Swimming	4x110yd Freestyle Relay
	Elaine Tanner	Swimming	110yd Butterfly
	Elaine Tanner	Swimming	220yd Butterfly
	Elaine Tanner	Swimming	440yd Individual Medley
	Harry Jerome	Track & Field	100yd
	David Steen	Track & Field	Shot Put
	Abby Hoffman	Track & Field	880yd
	Pierre St. Jean	Weightlifting	Middleweight
	Robert Chamberot	Wrestling	Light Heavyweight
1970:	Jamie Paulson	Badminton	Men's Singles
Edinburgh, Scotland	Jocelyn Lovell	Cycling	10 Miles Scratch
18 Gold Medals	Bev Boys	Diving	Highboard
	Bev Boys	Diving	Springboard
	William Kennedy	Swimming	100m Backstroke
	William Mahony	Swimming	100m Breaststroke
	William Mahony	Swimming	200m Breaststroke
	A. Byron MacDonald	Swimming	100m Butterfly
	Toomas (Tom) Arusoo	Swimming	200m Butterfly

Games	Medallist	Sport	Event
	George Smith	Swimming	200m Individual Medley
	George Smith	Swimming	400m Individual Medley
	Men's Team	Swimming	4x100m Medley Relay
	Angela Coughlan	Swimming	100m Freestyle
	David Steen	Track & Field	Shot Put
	George Puce	Track & Field	Discus
	Debbie Brill	Track & Field	High Jump
	Russ Prior	Weightlifting	Heavyweight
	Edward Millard	Wrestling	Heavyweight
1974: Christchurch, New Zealand 25 Gold Medals	Bev Boys	Diving	Highboard
	Cindy Shatto	Diving	Springboard
	John Primrose	Shooting	Shotgun - Clay Pigeon
	Harry Willsie	Shooting	Shotgun Skeet
	Jules Sobrian	Shooting	Free Pistol - .22 Single Shot
	William Hare	Shooting	Rapid Fire Pistol - .22 Semi Automatic
	Men's Team	Swimming	4x100m Freestyle Relay
	Men's Team	Swimming	4x100m Medley Relay
	Women's Team	Swimming	4x100m Freestyle Relay
	Wendy Cook	Swimming	100m Backstroke
	Wendy Cook	Swimming	200m Backstroke
	Patti Stenhouse	Swimming	100m Butterfly
	Leslie Cliff	Swimming	200m Individual Medley
	Leslie Cliff	Swimming	400m Individual Medley
	Women's Team	Swimming	4x100m Medley Relay
	Yvonne Saunders	Track & Field	400m
	Glenda Reiser	Track & Field	1500m
	Jane Haist	Track & Field	Shot Put
	Jane Haist	Track & Field	Discus
	Russ Prior	Weightlifting	Heavyweight
	Mitchell Kawasaki	Wrestling	Light Flyweight
	Egon Beiler	Wrestling	Featherweight
	Terry Paice	Wrestling	Light Heavyweight
	Claude Pilon	Wrestling	Heavyweight
	William Benko	Wrestling	Heavyweight Plus
1978: Edmonton, Canada 45 Gold Medals	Kelly Perlette	Boxing	71kg
	Roger Fortin	Boxing	81kg
	Jocelyn Lovell	Cycling	1000m Time Trial
	Men's Team	Cycling	Tandem Sprint
	Jocelyn Lovell	Cycling	10 mile
	Janet Nutter	Diving	Springboard
	Linda Cuthbert	Diving	Tower
	Elfi Schlegel	Gymnastics	Individual
	Women's Team	Gymnastics	Team Event
	Philip Delesalle	Gymnastics	Individual
	Men's Team	Gymnastics	Team Event
	Yvon Trempe	Shooting	Free Pistol

Games	Medallist	Sport	Event
	Jules Sobrian	Shooting	Rapid Fire Pistol
	Desmond Vamplew	Shooting	Full Bore Rifle
	John Primrose	Shooting	Trap
	Graham Smith	Swimming	100m Breaststroke
	Graham Smith	Swimming	200m Breaststroke
	Graham Smith	Swimming	200m Individual Medley
	Graham Smith	Swimming	400m Individual Medley
	Dan Thompson	Swimming	100m Butterfly
	George Nagy	Swimming	200m Butterfly
	Men's Team	Swimming	4x100m Freestyle Relay
	Men's Team	Swimming	4x100m Medley Relay
	Carol Klimpel	Swimming	100m Freestyle
	Cheryl Gibson	Swimming	200m Backstroke
	Robin Corsiglia	Swimming	100m Breaststroke
	Lisa Borsholt	Swimming	200m Breaststroke
	Wendy Quirk	Swimming	100m Butterfly
	Women's Team	Swimming	4x100m Freestyle Relay
	Women's Team	Swimming	4x100m Medley Relay
	Claude Ferrone	Track & Field	High Jump
	Bruce Simpson	Track & Field	Pole Vault
	Phil Olsen	Track & Field	Javelin
	Borys Chambul	Track & Field	Discus
	Carmen Ionesco	Track & Field	Discus
	Diane Jones Konihowski	Track & Field	Pentathlon
	Michel Mercier	Weightlifting	60kg Class
	Russ Prior	Weightlifting	110kg Class
	M. Cardinal	Weightlifting	110kg+ Class
	Ray Takahashi	Wrestling	Flyweight
	Egon Beiler	Wrestling	Featherweight
	Richard Deschatelets	Wrestling	Middleweight
	Stephen Daniar	Wrestling	Light Heavyweight
	Wyatt Wishart	Wrestling	Heavyweight
	Robert Gibbons	Wrestling	Heavyweight Plus
1982: Brisbane, Australia 26 Gold Medals	Women's Team	Badminton	Women's Doubles
	Shawn O'Sullivan	Boxing	Light Middleweight
	Willie de Wit	Boxing	Heavyweight
	Tom Guinn	Shooting	Free Pistol
	Jean-François Senecal	Shooting	Air Rifle
	Men's Team	Shooting	Skeet - Team
	Mike West	Swimming	100m Backstroke
	Cameron Henning	Swimming	200m Backstroke
	Victor Davis	Swimming	200m Breaststroke
	Dan Thompson	Swimming	100m Butterfly
	Alex Baumann	Swimming	200m Individual Medley
	Alex Baumann	Swimming	400m Individual Medley
	Kathy Bald	Swimming	100m Breaststroke
	Anne Ottenbrite	Swimming	200m Breaststroke
	Women's Team	Swimming	4x100m Medley Relay

Games	Medallist	Sport	Event
	Mark McKoy	Track & Field	110m Hurdles
	Angella Taylor	Track & Field	100m
	Women's Team	Track & Field	4x400m Relay
	Bruno Pauletto	Track & Field	Shot Put
	Debbie Brill	Track & Field	High Jump
	Milt Ottey	Track & Field	High Jump
	Bob Robinson	Wrestling	62kg
	Chris Rinke	Wrestling	82kg
	Clark Davis	Wrestling	90kg
	Richard Deschatelets	Wrestling	100kg
	Wyatt Wishart	Wrestling	+100kg
1986:	Scott Olson	Boxing	Light Flyweight
Edinburgh, Scotland	Bill Downey	Boxing	Featherweight
51 Gold Medals	Asif Dar	Boxing	60kg
	Howard Grant	Boxing	Light Welterweight
	Dan Sherry	Boxing	Light Middleweight
	Lennox Lewis	Boxing	Super Heavyweight
	Debbie Fuller	Diving	Highboard
	Debbie Fuller	Diving	Springboard
	Men's Team	Rowing	Coxless Fours
	Men's Team	Rowing	Double Sculls
	Women's Team	Rowing	Coxless Pairs
	Women's Team	Rowing	Coxed Fours
	Canadian Team	Shooting	Full Bore Rifle - Pairs
	Canadian Team	Shooting	Small Bore Rifle, Prone - Team
	Canadian Team	Shooting	Air Rifle - Team
	Guy Lorion	Shooting	Air Rifle - Individual
	Canadian Team	Shooting	Free Pistol - Team
	Mark Tewksbury	Shooting	100m Backstroke
	Sandy Goss	Swimming	200m Backstroke
	Victor Davis	Swimming	100m Breaststroke
	Alex Baumann	Swimming	200m Individual Medley
	Alex Baumann	Swimming	400m Individual Medley
	Men's Team	Swimming	4x100m Medley Relay
	Jane Kerr	Swimming	100m Freestyle
	Women's Team	Swimming	4x100m Freestyle Relay
	Allison Higson	Swimming	100m Breaststroke
	Allison Higson	Swimming	200m Breaststroke
	Donna McGinnis	Swimming	200m Butterfly
	Sylvie Fréchette	Synchronized Swimming	Solo
	Women's Team	Synchronized Swimming	Duet
	Ben Johnson	Track & Field	100m
	Atlee Mahorn	Track & Field	200m
	Graeme Fell	Track & Field	3000m Steeplechase
	Mark McKoy	Track & Field	110m Hurdles
	Ray Lazdins	Track & Field	Discus
	Milt Ottey	Track & Field	High Jump
	Men's Team	Track & Field	4x100m Relay
	Angella (Taylor) Issajenko	Track & Field	200m

Games	Medallist	Sport	Event
	Lynn Williams	Track & Field	3000m
	Women's Team	Track & Field	4x400m Relay
	Denis Garon	Weightlifting	100kg
	Kevin Roy	Weightlifting	110kg
	Ron Moncur	Wrestling	Under 48kg
	Chris Woodcroft	Wrestling	Under 52kg
	Mitch Ostberg	Wrestling	Under 57kg
	Paul Hughes	Wrestling	Under 62kg
	Dave McKay	Wrestling	Under 68kg
	Gary Holmes	Wrestling	Under 74kg
	Chris Rinke	Wrestling	Under 82kg
	Clark Davis	Wrestling	Under 100kg
	Wayne Brightwell	Wrestling	100kg +
1990:	Chris Johnson	Boxing	Middleweight - 75kg
Auckland,	Mary Depiero	Diving	1m Springboard
New Zealand	Anna Dacyshyn	Diving	Platform
35 Gold Medals	Men's Team	Gymnastics	Team Artistic
	Curtis Hibbert	Gymnastics	Individual All Round
	Curtis Hibbert	Gymnastics	Parallel Bars
	Curtis Hibbert	Gymnastics	Rings
	Curtis Hibbert; Alan Nolet	Gymnastics - TIE	Horizontal Bar
	Women's Team	Gymnastics	Team Artistic
	Lori Strong	Gymnastics	Individual All Round
	Lori Strong	Gymnastics	Balance Beam
	Lori Strong	Gymnastics	Floor Exercise
	Mary Fuzesi	Rhythmic Gymnastics	All Round
	Madonna Gimotea	Rhythmic Gymnastics	Ball
	Mary Fuzesi	Rhythmic Gymnastics	Hoop
	Mary Fuzesi	Rhythmic Gymnastics	Ribbon
	Guy Lorion	Shooting	10m Air Rifle
	Guy Lorion; Mart Klepp	Shooting	10m Air Rifle - Team
	Mart Klepp	Shooting	50m Free Rifle, 3 Position
	Mart Klepp; J-F Senecal	Shooting	50m Free Rifle, 3 Position - Team
	Mark Tewksbury	Swimming	100m Backstroke
	Gary Anderson	Swimming	200m Backstroke
	Jon Cleveland	Swimming	200m Breaststroke
	Gary Anderson	Swimming	200m Individual Medley
	Men's Team	Swimming	4x100m Medley Relay
	Keltie Duggan	Swimming	100m Breaststroke
	Nathalie Giguere	Swimming	200m Breaststroke
	Nancy Sweetnam	Swimming	200m Individual Medley
	Sylvie Fréchette	Synchronized Swimming	Figures
	Kathy Glen; Christine Larsen	Synchronized Swimming	Duet
	Sylvie Fréchette	Synchronized Swimming	Solo

Games	Medallist	Sport	Event
	Guillaume Leblanc	Track & Field	30km Walk
	Michael Smith	Track & Field	Decathlon
	Angela Chalmers	Track & Field	1500m
	Angela Chalmers	Track & Field	3000m
1994: Victoria, Canada 41 Gold Medals	Casey Patton	Boxing	Featherweight - 57kg
	Mike Strange	Boxing	Lightweight - 60kg
	Rowan Donaldson	Boxing	Middleweight - 75kg
	Dale Brown	Boxing	Light Heavyweight - 81kg
	Tanya Dubnicoff	Cycling	1000m Sprint
	Jason Napper	Diving	1m Springboard
	Annie Pelletier	Diving	1m Springboard
	Annie Pelletier	Diving	3m Springboard
	Anne Montminy	Diving	10m Platform
	Men's Team	Gymnastics	Men's Team Artistic
	Alan Nolet	Gymnastics	Horizontal Bar
	Stella Umeh	Gymnastics	Individual All Round
	Stella Umeh	Gymnastics	Vault
	Women's Team	Rhythmic Gymnastics	Team
	Mark & Matt Bedlington	Shooting	Pairs Running Target -Men
	Jean Pierre Huot	Shooting	Individual Air Pistol - Men
	Michel Dion	Shooting	Individual SB Rifle, 3 Position - Men
	Wayne Sorensen; Michel Dion	Shooting	Pairs SB Rifle, 3 Position - Men
	J. Senecal & W. Sorensen	Shooting	Pairs Air Rifle - Men
	Helen Smith	Shooting	Individual Air Pistol - Women
	Sharon Bowes	Shooting	Individual SB Rifle - Women
	S. Bowes; C. Ashcroft	Shooting	Pairs SB Rifle, 3 Position -Women
	Stephen Clarke	Swimming	100m Freestyle
	Andrew Haley	Swimming	100m Freestyle - S9
	Lisa Alexander	Synchronized Swimming	Solo
	Lisa Alexander; Erin Woodley	Synchronized Swimming	Duet
	Jeff Adams	Track & Field	800m Wheelchair
	Jeff Adams	Track & Field	1500m Wheelchair
	Men's Team	Track & Field	4x100m Relay
	Michael Smith	Track & Field	Decathlon
	Angela Chalmers	Track & Field	3000m
	Carole Rouillard	Track & Field	Marathon
	Selwyn Tam	Wrestling	52kg Class
	Robert Dawson	Wrestling	57kg Class
	Marty Calder	Wrestling	62kg Class
	Christopher Wilson	Wrestling	68kg Class
	David Hohl	Wrestling	74kg Class
	Justin Abdou	Wrestling	82kg Class
	Scott Bianco	Wrestling	90kg Class
	Greg Edgelow	Wrestling	100kg Class
	Andrew Borodow	Wrestling	130kg Class

Games	Medallist	Sport	Event
1998: Kuala Lumpur, Malaysia 30 Gold Medals	Michael Strange	Boxing	Light Welterweight
	Jeremy Molitor	Boxing	Welterweight
	Mark Simmons	Boxing	Heavyweight
	Lyne Bessette	Cycling	Individual Road Race
	Eric Wohlberg	Cycling	Individual Road Time Trial
	Tanya Dubnicoff	Cycling	Sprint
	Alexandre Despatie	Diving	Platform
	Eryn Bulmer	Diving	3m Springboard
	Alexander Jeltkov	Gymnastics	Horizontal Bar
	Kris Burley	Gymnastics	Horizontal Bar
	Erika-Leigh Stirton	Rhythmic Gymnastics	Individual All Around
	Erika-Leigh Stirton	Rhythmic Gymnastics	Clubs
	Erika-Leigh Stirton	Rhythmic Gymnastics	Ribbon
	Erika-Leigh Stirton	Rhythmic Gymnastics	Hoop
	Erika-Leigh Stirton	Rhythmic Gymnastics	Rope
	James Paton	Shooting	Individual Full Bore Open
	Igorov Metodi	Shooting	Individual Rapid Fire Pistol
	Christina Ashcroft; Sharon Bowes	Shooting	Pairs Air Rifle
	Michel Dion; Wayne Sorensen	Shooting	Pairs Small Bore Free Rifle - 3 positions
	Christina Ashcroft; Sharon Bowes	Shooting	Pairs Small Bore Free Rifle - 3 positions
	Joanne Malar	Swimming	400m IM
	Mark Versfeld	Swimming	200m Backstroke
	Marianne Limpert	Swimming	200m IM
	Mark Versfeld	Swimming	100m Backstroke
	Valerie Hould-Marchand	Synchronized Swimming	Solo
	Jacinthe Taillon; Kasia Kulesza	Synchronized Swimming	Duet
	Sebastien Groulx	Weightlifting	69kg Snatch
	Sebastien Groulx	Weightlifting	69kg Total
	Akos Sandor	Weightlifting	105kg Snatch
	Akos Sandor	Weightlifting	105kg Clean & Jerk
	Akos Sandor	Weightlifting	105kg Total

Canada Hosts the Pan Am Games

1967 How Winnipeg Rose to the Pan-Am Test

by Hal Tennant
September 1967

It was the morning after the fifth Pan-American Games ended in Winnipeg. And Jack Matheson, the *Tribune*'s sports editor, was talking like an unbeliever just back from witnessing a divine miracle. "I don't know what happened to the people of this town in the last couple of weeks," he told a local radio audience, "but whatever it is, I like it."

Matheson had as much cause to be dazed as Games organizers had to be delighted. Four years ago, he declared publicly that Winnipeg was "a two-bit town" that would never shell out any worthwhile amount of money to see amateur cyclists, fencers and high jumpers — even if they were the hemisphere's best. From then on, out of civic loyalty rather than hard-headed conviction, Matheson consistently boosted the Games in his daily sports column. But privately he remained part of an army of skeptics — until Winnipeggers went on that 15-day sports-watching binge which ended early in August. In their fervor to see 2,700 athletes from 28 countries compete in 23 types of individual and team events, the fans, mostly from around Winnipeg, shelled out something like one million dollars — twice what Games organizers themselves had dared hope for.

What's more, even blasé US reporters who have covered Pan-Am and Olympic Games all over the world were impressed with the way Winnipeg's seven-million-dollar show was run. They marvelled that the Games could go so smoothly with so many tasks allotted to 9,000 inexperienced citizen-volunteers. Among these were lawyers and doctors who simply put their practices aside for the duration; retired executives who slipped happily back into harness; housewife-interpreters who brushed up on their college Spanish; and boy scouts who handed out oranges to athletes.

Mind you, there were foul-ups and incidents. One afternoon of gymnastics was going into the books as a sellout when somebody noticed, belatedly, that one quarter of the 10,000 tickets were still sitting, unsold, in a box-office drawer. The Olympic flag which had been blessed by the Pope and flown at three previous Pan-Am Games was swiped by two teenagers, who returned it sheepishly, in response to a front-page editorial in the *Tribune*. When Cuba lost a basketball game to Mexico, 71 to 66, Havana's semi-official newspaper, *El Mundo*, decided it was all a plot on the part of the US referee. And a US walker named Ron Laird took a wrong turn near the end of the 20,000-meter event and found himself facing a high-wire fence instead of the finish line. (He got the gold medal anyhow.)

But all that was just comic relief. The important thing was that Canadian athletes were winning 92 medals, Canadian stars like Elaine Tanner were providing some of the meet's biggest thrills (she got two gold medals for swimming) and Winnipeg was putting on a show every bit as good, in its way, as Montreal's Expo 67.

By the time the Games were over, old Pan-Am boosters like Mayor Stephen Juba and Pan-Am executive-director Jim Daly were insisting that the big winner was not really the US (with 227 medals) but the city of Winnipeg, with $4.5 million worth of new sports facilities, including an Olympic-calibre pool said to be second only to Japan's. ✦

A wet Prince Philip opens the 1967 Pan Am Games

All that Glitters

by Brian Bergman
August 16, 1999

From the outset, hosting the 1999 Pan-American Games was seen by many Winnipeggers as a chance to put their city squarely in the international spotlight. And as the 17-day sporting extravaganza drew to a close last weekend, it was clear the Games had done just that — though not always in the manner civic boosters might have envisioned. Drug scandals (three) and political defections (five) by visiting athletes or hangers-on generated lavish media coverage. The Pan-Am Games, so often dismissed as a sedate stepsister of the Olympics, had suddenly become a hot ticket.

The intrigue began even before the Games were under way, when Cuban pistol shooter Juncosa Reyes sought political asylum in Canada. He was soon joined by at least three other reported refugees from one of the world's last Communist outposts, including a reporter, a softball coach and a track-and-field star. The cheeky *Winnipeg Sun* published a step-by-step guide for would-be defectors and ran a contest urging readers to predict the number of Cubans who would flee the island state before the Games were over. Back in Havana, Cuban President Fidel Castro raged that the Canadian media were "exhorting people to defect" and for a time it looked as if Canada-Cuban relations were heading for the Dumpster.

Controversy erupted again on Aug. 1, when Pan-Am officials stripped the Canadian in-line hockey team of its gold medal after discovering that goal-tender Steve Vézina had taken three banned substances, including huge amounts of anabolic steroids.

By midweek, however, Vézina's transgression had been overshadowed by an even more startling revelation. Cuban high jumper Javier Sotomayor lost his gold medal after testing positive for cocaine. Sotomayor is the Wayne Gretzky of the high-jumping world and an iconic figure in his homeland. The first person to clear eight feet in the high jump, he holds 17 of the 25 top records in the sport. Cuban sporting officials rallied around Sotomayor, professing his innocence and hinting darkly that he'd been framed.

The rapid-fire controversies threatened to obscure the fact that, for Canadian athletes at least, the 1999 Pan-Am Games marked a watershed. With just a few events remaining, by Saturday Canada had accumulated 54 gold, 43 silver and 69 bronze medals — the country's best showing ever in Pan-Am competitions. Last week alone, Canadian supremacy was evident in several fields, but nowhere more than in the swimming pool. Among the gold-medal performances: Calgary's Curtis Myden, 25, in the 400m individual medley; Vancouver's Jessica Deglau, 19, in the women's 200m freestyle and Winnipeg's Kelly Stefanyshyn, 17, who wowed the home-town crowd with her victory in the 100m backstroke.

As for Winnipeg itself, the Games proved, at times, to be a mixed blessing. Despite sluggish advance sales, organizers said that by last Friday they had sold 464,000 tickets — homing in on their target of 500,000. As well, Sunday's closing ceremonies at the 23,000-seat Winnipeg Stadium were looking like a sellout — thanks in part to the Guess Who, the legendary Winnipeg rock group whose members performed together for the first time since 1983. And while the scent of scandal guaranteed plenty of international ink, a survey compiled by the *Winnipeg Free Press* showed that not all the attention was flattering. True, *The Washington Post* praised Winnipeg's multicultural character and vibrant arts scene. However, the *Los Angeles Times* declared that Winnipeg's Games were "this summer's place not to be," while *The Dallas Morning News* deemed Winnipeg "this northern version of the Bermuda Triangle, this outpost city within an outpost nation."

The spotlight is sometimes harsh. ✦

The Pan Am Games returned to Winnipeg July 23, 1999.

Associated Press AP

277 Canadian Gold Medallists at the Pan Am Games, 1955 – 2000

Year	Gold Medallists	Sport	Event	Location	
1955	Beth Whittall	Swimming	400m Freestyle	Mexico City	Mexico
1955	Beth Whittall	Swimming	100m Butterfly	Mexico City	Mexico
1955	Helen Stewart	Swimming	100m Freestyle	Mexico City	Mexico
1955	Leonore Fisher	Swimming	100m Backstroke	Mexico City	Mexico
1959	Team	Equestrian	Team Three-Day Event	Chicago	USA
1959	Ernestine Russell	Gymnastics	Individual All-Around	Chicago	USA
1959	Ernestine Russell	Gymnastics	Vault	Chicago	USA
1959	Ernestine Russell	Gymnastics	Uneven Parallel Bars	Chicago	USA
1959	Ernestine Russell	Gymnastics	Balance Beam	Chicago	USA
1959	G. Ouellette	Shooting	Small Bore Rifle-Prone	Chicago	USA
1959	G. Ouellette, C. White, E. Gering, E. Tiilen	Shooting	Small Bore Rifle-Team Prone	Chicago	USA
1959	G. Ouellette	Shooting	Small Bore Rifle-Three Positions	Chicago	USA
1959	Team	Swimming	400m Medley Relay	Chicago	USA
1963	Thomas Dinsley	Diving	Springboard	Sao Paulo	Brazil
1963	Fredrick Weiler	Gymnastics	Individual All-Around	Sao Paulo	Brazil
1963	Fredrick Weiler	Gymnastics	Floor Exercises	Sao Paulo	Brazil
1963	Fredrick Weiler	Gymnastics	Vault	Sao Paulo	Brazil
1963	Men's Team	Rowing	Eights	Sao Paulo	Brazil
1963	Abby Hoffman	Track & Field	800m	Sao Paulo	Brazil
1963	Alex Oakley	Track & Field	20km Walk	Sao Paulo	Brazil
1963	Don Bertoia	Track & Field	800m	Sao Paulo	Brazil
1963	Nancy McCredie	Track & Field	Shot Put	Sao Paulo	Brazil
1963	Nancy McCredie	Track & Field	Discus	Sao Paulo	Brazil
1963	Team	Yachting	Dragon Class	Sao Paulo	Brazil
1967	A. Simonyik	Canoe/Kayak	K-1 500m	Winnipeg	Canada
1967	B. Cordner	Canoe/Kayak	C-1 1000m	Winnipeg	Canada
1967	A. Simonyik	Canoe/Kayak	K-1 1000m	Winnipeg	Canada
1967	B. Norris & D. Bossy	Canoe/Kayak	C-2 10,000m	Winnipeg	Canada
1967	Marcel Roy	Cycling	Individual Road Race	Winnipeg	Canada
1967	Jocelyn Lovell	Cycling	Kilometre Time Trial	Winnipeg	Canada
1967	James Day	Equestrian	Individual Show Jumping	Winnipeg	Canada
1967	Susan McDonnell	Gymnastics	Uneven Parallel Bars	Winnipeg	Canada
1967	Doug Rogers	Judo	Open Category	Winnipeg	Canada
1967	Michael Johnson	Judo	Light Heavyweight	Winnipeg	Canada
1967	Alphonse Mayer	Shooting	English Match Rifle-Individual	Winnipeg	Canada
1967	Elaine Tanner	Swimming	100m Backstroke	Winnipeg	Canada
1967	Elaine Tanner	Swimming	200m Backstroke	Winnipeg	Canada
1967	Ralph Hutton	Swimming	200m Breaststroke	Winnipeg	Canada
1967	Andrew Boychuk	Track & Field	Marathon	Winnipeg	Canada
1967	Harry Jerome	Track & Field	100m	Winnipeg	Canada
1967	Nancy McCredie	Track & Field	Shot Put	Winnipeg	Canada
1971	Elizabeth Carruthers	Diving	Springboard	Cali	Colombia
1971	Nancy Robertson	Diving	Platform	Cali	Colombia
1971	Christilot Hanson	Equestrian	Individual Dressage	Cali	Colombia
1971	Team	Equestrian	Team Dressage	Cali	Colombia
1971	Team	Equestrian	Team Show Jumping	Cali	Colombia
1971	Team	Equestrian	Team Three-Day Event	Cali	Colombia
1971	Donna-Marie Gurr	Swimming	100m Backstroke	Cali	Colombia
1971	Donna-Marie Gurr	Swimming	200m Backstroke	Cali	Colombia
1971	Leslie Cliff	Swimming	200m Individual Medley	Cali	Colombia
1971	Leslie Cliff	Swimming	400m Individual Medley	Cali	Colombia
1971	Sylvia Dockerill	Swimming	100m Breaststroke	Cali	Colombia
1971	Jamie Wright	Swimming	200m Breaststroke	Cali	Colombia
1971	Women's Team	Swimming	4x100m Medley Relay	Cali	Colombia
1971	Abby Hoffman	Track & Field	800m	Cali	Colombia
1971	Brenda Eisler	Track & Field	Long Jump	Cali	Colombia
1971	Debbie Brill	Track & Field	High Jump	Cali	Colombia
1971	Debbie Van Kiekebelt	Track & Field	Pentathlon	Cali	Colombia
1971	Stephanie Berto	Track & Field	200m	Cali	Colombia
1971	Chun Hon Chan	Weightlifting	Flyweight Snatch	Cali	Colombia
1975	Chris Clarke	Boxing	Lightweight	Mexico City	Mexico
1975	Jocelyn Lovell	Cycling	Kilometre Time Trial	Mexico City	Mexico
1975	Janet Nutter	Diving	Platform	Mexico City	Mexico
1975	Christilot Boylen	Equestrian	Individual Dressage	Mexico City	Mexico
1975	Brad Farrow	Judo	Featherweight	Mexico City	Mexico
1975	Rainer Fischer	Judo	Middleweight	Mexico City	Mexico

1975	Wayne Erman	Judo	Lightweight	Mexico City	Mexico
1975	Men's Team	Rowing	Fours with Cox	Mexico City	Mexico
1975	Lynn Chenard	Swimming	100m Backstroke	Mexico City	Mexico
1975	Bruce Pirnie	Track & Field	Shot Put	Mexico City	Mexico
1975	Diane Jones	Track & Field	Pentathlon	Mexico City	Mexico
1975	Joyce Yakubowich	Track & Field	400m	Mexico City	Mexico
1975	Women's Team	Track & Field	4x400m relay	Mexico City	Mexico
1975	Egon Beiler	Wrestling	up to 62kg Freestyle	Mexico City	Mexico
1975	Howard Stupp	Wrestling	up to 62kg Greco-Roman	Mexico City	Mexico
1979	Claude Langlois	Cycling	4000m Individual Pursuit	San Juan	Puerto Rico
1979	Gordon Singleton	Cycling	Match Sprint	San Juan	Puerto Rico
1979	Gordon Singleton	Cycling	Kilometre Time Trial	San Juan	Puerto Rico
1979	Monica Goermann	Gymnastics	Individual All-Around	San Juan	Puerto Rico
1979	Monica Goermann	Gymnastics	Uneven Parallel Bars	San Juan	Puerto Rico
1979	Sherry Hawco	Gymnastics	Balance Beam	San Juan	Puerto Rico
1979	Women's Team	Gymnastics	Team Event	San Juan	Puerto Rico
1979	Brad Farrow	Judo	Light Lightweight	San Juan	Puerto Rico
1979	Louis Jana	Judo	Middleweight	San Juan	Puerto Rico
1979	Men's Team	Rowing	Double Sculls	San Juan	Puerto Rico
1979	Men's Team	Rowing	Pairs without Cox	San Juan	Puerto Rico
1979	Guy Lorion Jr.	Shooting	Individual Air Rifle	San Juan	Puerto Rico
1979	Men's Team	Shooting	Team Free Pistol	San Juan	Puerto Rico
1979	Men's Team	Softball		San Juan	Puerto Rico
1979	Anne Gagnon	Swimming	200m Breaststroke	San Juan	Puerto Rico
1979	Helen Vanderburg	Synchronized Swimming	Solo	San Juan	Puerto Rico
1979	Kelly Kryczka & Helen Vanderburg	Synchronized Swimming	Duet	San Juan	Puerto Rico
1979	Bruce Simpson	Track & Field	Pole Vault	San Juan	Puerto Rico
1979	Diane Jones	Track & Field	Pentathlon	San Juan	Puerto Rico
1979	Scott Neilson	Track & Field	Hammer Throw	San Juan	Puerto Rico
1979	Douglas Yeats	Wrestling	up to 62kg Greco-Roman	San Juan	Puerto Rico
1979	Howard Stupp	Wrestling	up to 68kg Greco-Roman	San Juan	Puerto Rico
1979	Terry Neilson	Yachting	Laser Class	San Juan	Puerto Rico
1983	Men's Team	Field Hockey		Caracas	Venezuela
1983	Louis Jani	Judo	Middleweight 86kg	Caracas	Venezuela
1983	Mark Berger	Judo	Heavyweight +95kg	Caracas	Venezuela
1983	Men's Team	Rowing	Double Sculls	Caracas	Venezuela
1983	Men's Team	Rowing	Quadruple Sculls	Caracas	Venezuela
1983	Men's Team	Softball		Caracas	Venezuela
1983	Women's Team	Softball		Caracas	Venezuela
1983	Anne Ottenbrite	Swimming	100m Breaststroke	Caracas	Venezuela
1983	Kathy Bald	Swimming	200m Breaststroke	Caracas	Venezuela
1983	Women's Team	Synchronized Swimming	Team	Caracas	Venezuela
1983	Charmaine Crooks	Track & Field	400m	Caracas	Venezuela
1983	Dave Steen	Track & Field	Decathlon	Caracas	Venezuela
1983	Laslo Babits	Track & Field	Javelin	Caracas	Venezuela
1983	Ranza Clark	Track & Field	1500m	Caracas	Venezuela
1983	G. Kallos	Wrestling	90kg Greco-Roman	Caracas	Venezuela
1983	Jeff Stuebing	Wrestling	up to 74kg Greco-Roman	Caracas	Venezuela
1983	Ray Takahashi	Wrestling	up to 52kg Freestyle	Caracas	Venezuela
1987	Jack Chubaty & Max Tracy	Canoe/Kayak	C-2 1000m	Indianapolis	USA
1987	Curt Harnett	Cycling	1km Time Trial	Indianapolis	USA
1987	Christilot Boylen	Equestrian	Individual Dressage	Indianapolis	USA
1987	Ian Millar	Equestrian	Individual Show Jumping	Indianapolis	USA
1987	Team	Equestrian	Team Dressage	Indianapolis	USA
1987	Team	Equestrian	Team Show Jumping	Indianapolis	USA
1987	Jean-Paul Banos	Fencing	Individual Sabre	Indianapolis	USA
1987	Men's Team	Field Hockey		Indianapolis	USA
1987	Sandra Greaves	Judo	Middleweight 66kg	Indianapolis	USA
1987	Men's Team	Rowing	Lightweight Double Sculls	Indianapolis	USA
1987	Michele Murphy	Rowing	Lightweight Single Sculls	Indianapolis	USA
1987	Silken Laumann	Rowing	Single Sculls	Indianapolis	USA
1987	Women's Team	Rowing	Pairs without Cox	Indianapolis	USA
1987	Guy Lorion Jr.	Shooting	Individual Air Rifle	Indianapolis	USA
1987	Men's Team	Shooting	Team Air Rifle	Indianapolis	USA
1987	Men's Team	Shooting	Team Free Rifle	Indianapolis	USA
1987	Patrick Vamplew	Shooting	Free Rifle, Prone	Indianapolis	USA
1987	Sharon Bowes	Shooting	Individual Air Rifle	Indianapolis	USA
1987	Men's Team	Softball		Indianapolis	USA
1987	Keltie Duggan	Swimming	100m Breaststroke	Indianapolis	USA
1987	Gideon Ng	Table Tennis	Singles	Indianapolis	USA
1987	Gideon Ng & Horatio Pintea	Table Tennis	Doubles	Indianapolis	USA

1987	David Bolduc	Weightlifting	110kg Snatch	Indianapolis	USA
1987	David Bolduc	Weightlifting	110kg Clean and Jerk	Indianapolis	USA
1987	David Bolduc	Weightlifting	110kg Total	Indianapolis	USA
1987	D. Garon	Weightlifting	100kg	Indianapolis	USA
1987	D. Garon	Weightlifting	100kg Snatch	Indianapolis	USA
1987	D. Garon	Weightlifting	100kg Clean and Jerk	Indianapolis	USA
1987	Doug Cox	Wrestling	up to 90kg Freestyle	Indianapolis	USA
1987	Donald MacDonald & David MacDonald	Yachting	Star Class	Indianapolis	USA
1991	Corrina Kennedy	Canoe/Kayak	K-1 500m	Havana	Cuba
1991	Tessa Desouza & Corrina Kennedy	Canoe/Kayak	K-2 500m	Havana	Cuba
1991	Richard Young	Cycling	Match Sprint	Havana	Cuba
1991	Tanya Dubnicoff	Cycling	Match Sprint	Havana	Cuba
1991	Danny Foster	Equestrian	Individual Show Jumping	Havana	Cuba
1991	Lorraine Stubbs	Equestrian	Individual Dressage	Havana	Cuba
1991	Team	Equestrian	Team Dressage	Havana	Cuba
1991	Women's Team	Rhythmic Gymnastics	Team All-Around	Havana	Cuba
1991	Mary Fuzesi	Rhythmic Gymnastics	Hoop	Havana	Cuba
1991	Alison Keagan	Roller Skating	Figures	Havana	Cuba
1991	Women's Team	Rowing	Lightweight Pairs without Cox	Havana	Cuba
1991	Women's Team	Rowing	Fours without Cox	Havana	Cuba
1991	Men's Team	Shooting	Team Air Rifle	Havana	Cuba
1991	Men's Team	Shooting	Team Free Pistol	Havana	Cuba
1991	Team	Shooting	Team Trap Shooting	Havana	Cuba
1991	Sharon Cozzarin	Shooting	Individual Air Pistol	Havana	Cuba
1991	Men's Team	Softball		Havana	Cuba
1991	Kristen Topham	Swimming	50m Freestyle	Havana	Cuba
1991	Kristen Topham	Swimming	100m Butterfly	Havana	Cuba
1991	Jae Hoon Lee	Tae Kwon Do	Welterweight 76kg	Havana	Cuba
1991	Jeff Eckard & Nigel Cochrane	Yachting	470 Class	Havana	Cuba
1991	Shona Moss	Yachting	Laser Class	Havana	Cuba
1991	Lawrence Lemieux	Yachting	Finn Class	Havana	Cuba
1995	Rob Rusnov	Archery	70m	Mar Del Plata	Argentina
1995	Rob Rusnov	Archery	90m	Mar Del Plata	Argentina
1995	Denyse Julien	Badminton	Singles	Mar Del Plata	Argentina
1995	Denyse Julien & Darryl Yung	Badminton	Mixed Doubles	Mar Del Plata	Argentina
1995	Iain Sydie & Anil Kaul	Badminton	Doubles	Mar Del Plata	Argentina
1995	Jaimie Dawson	Badminton	Singles	Mar Del Plata	Argentina
1995	Sian Deng & Denyse Julien	Badminton	Doubles	Mar Del Plata	Argentina
1995	Catharine Willis	Bowling	Individual	Mar Del Plata	Argentina
1995	William Rowe	Bowling	Individual	Mar Del Plata	Argentina
1995	Women's Team	Bowling	Team	Mar Del Plata	Argentina
1995	Mike Oryschak & Danny Howe	Canoe/Kayak	C-2 500m	Mar Del Plata	Argentina
1995	Women's Team	Canoe/Kayak	K-4 500m	Mar Del Plata	Argentina
1995	Alison Sydor	Cycling	Mountain Bike - Cross Country	Mar Del Plata	Argentina
1995	Brian Walton	Cycling	Points Race	Mar Del Plata	Argentina
1995	Brian Walton	Cycling	Individual Road Race	Mar Del Plata	Argentina
1995	Tanya Dubnicoff	Cycling	Match Sprint	Mar Del Plata	Argentina
1995	Anne Montminy	Diving	Platform	Mar Del Plata	Argentina
1995	Annie Pelletier	Diving	3m Springboard	Mar Del Plata	Argentina
1995	Ewan Beaton	Judo	Bantamweight 60kg	Mar Del Plata	Argentina
1995	Keith Morgan	Judo	Light Heavyweight 95kg	Mar Del Plata	Argentina
1995	Nicolas Gill	Judo	Middleweight 86kg	Mar Del Plata	Argentina
1995	Nicole Poirier	Karate	+52kg Kumite	Mar Del Plata	Argentina
1995	Silken Laumann	Rowing	Single Sculls	Mar Del Plata	Argentina
1995	Women's Team	Rowing	Double Sculls	Mar Del Plata	Argentina
1995	Alex Gyori	Shooting	Individual Double Trap, 150 targets	Mar Del Plata	Argentina
1995	Men's Team	Shooting	Team Double Trap, 150 targets	Mar Del Plata	Argentina
1995	Men's Team	Softball		Mar Del Plata	Argentina
1995	Gary Waite	Squash	Singles	Mar Del Plata	Argentina
1995	Heather Wallace	Squash	Singles	Mar Del Plata	Argentina
1995	Men's Team	Squash	Team	Mar Del Plata	Argentina
1995	Team	Squash	Grand Champion	Mar Del Plata	Argentina
1995	Women's Team	Squash	Team	Mar Del Plata	Argentina
1995	Curtis Myden	Swimming	200m Individual Medley	Mar Del Plata	Argentina
1995	Curtis Myden	Swimming	400m Individual Medley	Mar Del Plata	Argentina
1995	Joanne Malar	Swimming	200m Individual Medley	Mar Del Plata	Argentina
1995	Joanne Malar	Swimming	400m Individual Medley	Mar Del Plata	Argentina
1995	Lisa Flood	Swimming	100m Breaststroke	Mar Del Plata	Argentina
1995	Lisa Flood	Swimming	200m Breaststroke	Mar Del Plata	Argentina
1995	Horatio Pintea & Lijuan Geng	Table Tennis	Mixed Doubles	Mar Del Plata	Argentina
1995	Lijuan Geng	Table Tennis	Singles	Mar Del Plata	Argentina

1995	Lijuan Geng & Barbara Chiu	Table Tennis	Doubles	Mar Del Plata	Argentina
1995	Women's Team	Table Tennis	Team	Mar Del Plata	Argentina
1995	Glenroy Gilbert	Track & Field	100m	Mar Del Plata	Argentina
1995	Women's Team	Triathlon	Team	Mar Del Plata	Argentina
1995	Jaret Llewellyn	Water Skiing	Tricks	Mar Del Plata	Argentina
1995	Jaret Llewellyn	Water Skiing	Jumping	Mar Del Plata	Argentina
1995	Team	Water Skiing	Team	Mar Del Plata	Argentina
1995	Penny Davis & Leigh Pearson	Women's 470		Mar Del Plata	Argentina
1995	Caroll-Ann Alie	Yachting	Mistral Class	Mar Del Plata	Argentina
1999	Brent Olynyk & Iain Sydie	Badminton	Doubles	Winnipeg	Canada
1999	Iain Sydie & Denyse Julien	Badminton	Mixed Doubles	Winnipeg	Canada
1999	Robbyn Hermitage & Milaine Coutier	Badminton	Doubles	Winnipeg	Canada
1999	Karen Furneaux	Canoe/Kayak	K-1 500m	Winnipeg	Canada
1999	Marie-Josée Gibeau-Ouimet & Carrie Lightbound	Canoe/Kayak	K-2 500m	Winnipeg	Canada
1999	Stephen Giles	Canoe/Kayak	C-1 1000m	Winnipeg	Canada
1999	Women's Team	Canoe/Kayak	K-4 500m	Winnipeg	Canada
1999	Eric Wohlberg	Cycling	Individual Time Trial	Winnipeg	Canada
1999	Tanya Dubnicoff	Cycling	500m Time Trial	Winnipeg	Canada
1999	Emilie Heymans	Diving	Platform	Winnipeg	Canada
1999	Eryn Bulmer	Diving	3m Springboard	Winnipeg	Canada
1999	Ian Millar	Equestrian	Individual Stadium Jump	Winnipeg	Canada
1999	Men's Team	Fencing	Team Sabre	Winnipeg	Canada
1999	Men's Team	Field Hockey		Winnipeg	Canada
1999	Alexander Jeltkov	Gymnastics	Horizontal Bar	Winnipeg	Canada
1999	Lise Léveillé	Gymnastics	Balance Beam	Winnipeg	Canada
1999	Women's Team	Gymnastics	Team	Winnipeg	Canada
1999	Yvonne Tousek	Gymnastics	Floor Exercises	Winnipeg	Canada
1999	Yvonne Tousek	Gymnastics	Uneven Bars	Winnipeg	Canada
1999	Nicolas Gill	Judo	100kg	Winnipeg	Canada
1999	Emilie Livingston	Rhythmic Gymnastics	Individual All-Around	Winnipeg	Canada
1999	Men's Team	Roller Skating	Roller Hockey	Winnipeg	Canada
1999	Marnie McBean	Rowing	Single Sculls	Winnipeg	Canada
1999	Theresa Luke & Emma Robinson	Rowing	Coxless Pairs	Winnipeg	Canada
1999	Kim Eagles	Shooting	Air Pistol	Winnipeg	Canada
1999	Men's Team	Softball		Winnipeg	Canada
1999	Graham Ryding	Squash	Singles	Winnipeg	Canada
1999	Melanie Jans	Squash	Singles	Winnipeg	Canada
1999	Men's Team	Squash	Team	Winnipeg	Canada
1999	Women's Team	Squash	Team	Winnipeg	Canada
1999	Curtis Myden	Swimming	400m Individual Medley	Winnipeg	Canada
1999	Curtis Myden	Swimming	200m Individual Medley	Winnipeg	Canada
1999	Jessica Deglau	Swimming	200m Freestyle	Winnipeg	Canada
1999	Jessica Deglau	Swimming	200m Butterfly	Winnipeg	Canada
1999	Joanne Malar	Swimming	400m Individual Medley	Winnipeg	Canada
1999	Joanne Malar	Swimming	200m Individual Medley	Winnipeg	Canada
1999	Kelly Stefanyshyn	Swimming	100m Backstroke	Winnipeg	Canada
1999	Laura Nicholls	Swimming	100m Freestyle	Winnipeg	Canada
1999	Lauren van Oosten	Swimming	200m Breaststroke	Winnipeg	Canada
1999	Morgan Knabe	Swimming	200m Breaststroke	Winnipeg	Canada
1999	Shamek Pietucha	Swimming	200m Butterfly	Winnipeg	Canada
1999	Women's Team	Swimming	4x200m Freestyle Relay	Winnipeg	Canada
1999	Women's Team	Swimming	4x100m Freestyle Relay	Winnipeg	Canada
1999	Claire Carver-Dias & Fanny Letourneau	Synchronized Swimming	Duet Free	Winnipeg	Canada
1999	Women's Team	Synchronized Swimming	Team Free	Winnipeg	Canada
1999	Roxanne Forget	Tae Kwon Do	49kg	Winnipeg	Canada
1999	Graham Hood	Track & Field	1500m	Winnipeg	Canada
1999	Joel Bourgeois	Track & Field	3000m steeplechase	Winnipeg	Canada
1999	Mark Boswell	Track & Field	High Jump	Winnipeg	Canada
1999	Sharon Donnelly	Triathlon		Winnipeg	Canada
1999	Jody Holden & Conrad Leinemann	Volleyball	Beach Volleyball	Winnipeg	Canada
1999	Women's Team	Water Polo		Winnipeg	Canada
1999	Andrew Ross	Water Skiing	Slalom	Winnipeg	Canada
1999	Jaret Llewellyn	Water Skiing	Tricks	Winnipeg	Canada
1999	Marysse Turcotte	Weightlifting	58kg Combined Clean & Jerk and Snatch	Winnipeg	Canada
1999	Miel McGerrigle	Weightlifting	63kg Combined Clean & Jerk and Snatch	Winnipeg	Canada
1999	Guivi Sissaouri	Wrestling	up to 58kg Freestyle	Winnipeg	Canada
1999	Kelly Hand	Yachting	Laser Radial Class	Winnipeg	Canada
1999	Oskar Johansson	Yachting	Sunfish Open Class	Winnipeg	Canada
1999	Richard Clarke	Yachting	Finn Class	Winnipeg	Canada

Canada

Our
Century
in
Sport

Gérard Côté lights the torch on Mount Royal

Montréal 1976

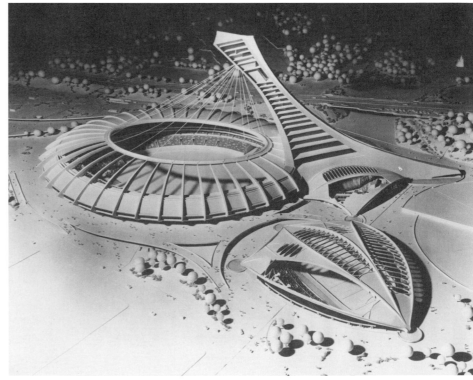

the World, 1976

Abby Hoffman leads in Canada

Decathlon star Bruce Jenner

The perfection of gymnast Nadia Comaneci

Finnish running sensation Lasse Viren

Montréal 1976

Mayor Jean Drapeau

International Politics at the 1976 Olympics

How many Chinas?

Starting in 1949 with the Communist Revolution, two governments claimed to rule China: the People's Republic of China (Mainland/Communist) Government in Beijing and the Republic of China (Nationalist) Government in Taiwan. Both claimed that China was indivisible; the only question was who ruled it.

Until 1976, Mainland China had never participated in an Olympics. When the Nationalists fled to Taiwan in 1949, their Olympic Committee fled with them. By the late 1950s when Beijing became interested in participating, they got the brush-off from the International Olympic Committee. Taiwan competed through the '50s and '60s as the uncontested "Republic of China."

In 1972, Canada had recognized the Beijing (Mainland) government as the legitimate government of China, and de-recognized the government in Taiwan. Beijing, which was beginning to take an interest in the outside world, began lobbying Canada to help them get into the 1976 Olympics, which of course to them meant getting Taiwan *out*.

Canada knew from the start that it was in trouble. The government had given the usual assurances to the IOC that all accredited Olympic Family members would be admitted for Montreal "subject to the normal regulations" as the official letter put it. The government knew that it had to try to negotiate something with the IOC. The only other option was to choose between breaking its word to China or to the Olympic Movement. To the government, the former was unthinkable. If a promise had to be broken, they knew which one it would be.

Discussions with the IOC proved fruitless. The Government conveyed to the IOC in at least two meetings that there would be "difficulties" with Taiwan's status at Montreal. The hope was that the IOC would recognize the problem and do something to help out. The IOC, wrapped in its ideology that sport is outside of politics and unused to the nuance of international negotiation, either failed to understand the signals or simply assumed that it was unthinkable for the Canadian government to go back on its promise of admission to all.

It turned out that it was quite thinkable. After all of the teams had arrived in Montreal, Canada informed the IOC that "pursuant to the normal regulations" the Taiwanese entry visas were being revoked.

Canada had seriously underestimated the outrage that would result from outright defiance of Olympic tradition. US President Ford considered calling the US team home in protest. Prime Minister Trudeau appeared on ABC-TV to justify the Government's position and was given one of the roughest rides of his career.

In the end, Canada backed down, sort of. Trudeau told the IOC that he did not care what flag was flown or what anthem was played as long as the Taiwanese did not call themselves the "Republic of China." The Beijing Government was upset at this apparent betrayal, but the Taiwanese unintentionally saved the day by pulling out. No Chinese team at all competed in Montreal.

Ironically, the Montreal impasse led the IOC, Taiwan, and Mainland China to settle their differences. In 1979, the three parties adopted a formula which permitted both Olympic Committees to participate, and which endures to this day. Canada's IOC Member Jim Worrall, who had suffered through the abortive discussions with the Canadian Government in 1975-76, played a leading role in helping to negotiate the settlement.

Equally ironically, the Taiwan affair completely masked another, just as contentious, international issue that came to the boil only a day or so later, this time, out of Africa.

African Boycott – overlooked

South Africa had been expelled from the Commonwealth in 1961 for its apartheid policies. After a threatened African boycott of the 1968 Mexico Olympics, the IOC expelled South Africa in 1970. However, South African teams, especially in rugby, continued to tour Commonwealth countries such as England and New Zealand, and the African opposition to apartheid turned to secondary boycotts (of other countries) to cut off this angle of attack.

In 1976 New Zealand's government was not greatly sympathetic to the African position. (They were also very pro-rugby; the call for Team Canada to boycott the touring Russian hockey team in 1980 will stir at least some sympathy among Canadians for the difficulty encountered by New Zealand in deciding about maintaining sporting ties with South Africa.) In the end, they permitted the New Zealand All-Blacks (so named for their jersey colour) to tour South Africa.

This was the last straw for the Supreme Council for Sport in Africa, the political leaders of the anti-apartheid movement in sport. They announced at their Mauritius meeting in early 1976 that if New Zealand was not expelled from the Montreal Olympics, a boycott of those Games would ensue.

Unfortunately for the African cause, *nobody noticed in time*. The IOC took the position that this was a political matter outside their jurisdiction, and that in any case rugby was not an Olympic sport. The Canadian Government took the view that this was a matter to be sorted out between the IOC, the Africans and New Zealand, and no concern of theirs. By the time African teams began arriving in Montreal in early July, the issue had not been resolved and the Africans fully expected on-the-spot pressure immediately before the Games to have an effect, as it had had against Rhodesia in Munich four years earlier.

As the opening of the Games approached, though, the Taiwan crisis burst upon the world and by the weekend before the Games, African teams were already leaving Montreal in dribs and drabs without anyone paying particular attention. By opening day, 22 nations, practically all of Africa, had withdrawn. The IOC and the Canadian Department of External Affairs had been caught flat-footed by their complete absorption in the Taiwan crisis. It took some days to understand what had happened and what it might mean for the future.

Immediately after Montreal, the international track and field, soccer, and swim federations expelled South Africa. Canada was to host the 1978 Commonwealth Games in Edmonton. The Supreme Council again threatened a boycott, and this time External Affairs paid full attention. Following an intensive two-year diplomatic campaign, almost every Commonwealth African nation did come to Edmonton.

Earlier in 1978, the Commonwealth Heads of Government had pledged to fight apartheid in sport by every legal means available to them. But the issue was to plague Commonwealth relations until the apartheid regime in South Africa came to an end in 1991, and an integrated South African team participated in the 1992 Barcelona Olympics. ❦

Montreal Games

Heroes of the XXI Olympiad

by Michael Posner
August 9, 1976

CODA

The Americans landed on Mars and the earthquake flattened Tangshan. There were riots in South Africa, murders in Northern Ireland, carnage in Lebanon. Pitcher Randy Jones won his eighteenth game and Jerry Pate captured the Canadian Open. Sony Inc. reported that second quarter profits were up 100%. The franc dropped against the dollar and the price of gold dipped to a three-year low. Lady Banting and Mickey Cohen died. It rained, at last, in Europe.

All of this the world briefly noted and then ignored. For 16 days last month, the attention of millions was riveted elsewhere, on the city of Montreal and the Games of the XXI Olympiad. Nothing rivaled it. For several hours every day North Americans sat enthralled before their television sets, suddenly learned in the finer points of Greco-Roman wrestling. Even *Sesame Street* was preempted. The world's leading newspaper ran Olympic stories on page one. No fewer than seven magazines displayed the pubescent form of the gymnast Nadia Comaneci — the first woman to score a perfect mark in the Olympics — on their covers. In Montreal, scalpers exchanged $30 seats for $200 in hard cash. Spectators lined up for hours to secure standing room tickets or a brief glimpse of the Olympic Village. Telly Savalas, Mick Jagger and Queen Elizabeth came to call. In the streets of a city in which even the women who hawk Jehovah's Witnesses literature are chic, there was singing until 3 a.m.

It was an occasion. Conceived in fantasy and reared amid controversy, the Montreal games — to the surprise of everyone — were executed with near-flawless precision. Predictably, there were complaints about security, but the indefatigable presence of Canadian army officers clearly had its intended effect. The closest approximation to an incident was the crashing of the closing ceremonies by a lone streaker. In the end, even Roger Taillibert's Stade Olympique, an edifice of classic proportions, was ready (if not finished). And though the debt for this fortnight's festival was estimated at $1.5 billion and still climbing, Montrealers seemed to accept it with Gallic indifference. Spent or misspent, the money had already changed hands; one might as well enjoy it.

Every Olympiad engenders its own set of heroes, new demigods of sport. To the scrolls that bear the now legendary names of Kuts and Zatopek and Nurmi, the Montreal games will add Lasse Viren, the inscrutable Finnish game warden, and the first man to win both the 5,000- and 10,000- metre races in consecutive Olympics; Nadia Comaneci, the sullen 14-year-old princess of the balance beam, a child in everything but grace; Vasili Alexeyev, the strongest man in the world; Alberto Juantorena, a six-foot two-inch Cuban revolutionary with the speed of Secretariat and the strength of Man O' War — it is not for nothing that his teammates call him El Caballo; Irene Szewinska, a 30-year-old Polish housewife and mother, competing in her fourth Olympics and winning the 400 metres (her seventh medal) in world record time; Bruce Jenner, the essence of the American way and quite simply the finest all-round athlete in the world; and Kornelia Ender, owner of four gold medals, the fastest swimmer of her generation.

There was once a time when North Americans knew little and cared less about the sport of gymnastics. That was before Olga Korbut. In league with ABC, the network of the Olympics, Korbut's acrobatic flourishes in Munich created an instant audience of millions.

Four years ago, the Russians — Korbut, Ludmila Tourischeva, Nellie Kim — were the best in the world. But in Montreal they were all eclipsed by a four-foot six-inch, sad-eyed elf named Nadia Comaneci, who in the opinion of the judges and the crowd, could do no wrong. Seemingly oblivious to the frantic whirr of movie cameras and motor drives, the crackle of flash bulbs or the fierce stress of Olympic competition, Comaneci moved through her daring routines with unflappable cool — never missing so much as a toe point. On the balance beam — a four-inch width of padded spruce, four feet above the floor, she flipped effortlessly into somersaults, handstands and splits. On the uneven bars, she whipped her elastic body through breathtaking manoeuvers: handstands and full twists at high speed. Seven times during the competition, perhaps swayed by the crowds in the Montreal Forum, the judges accorded Comaneci the sport's highest honour — a mark of 10.

Individuals aside, the single most impressive achievement of the Montreal games was the performance of the German Democratic Republic. In all, GDR won 90 medals, including 40 golds — more than the United States or Japan or Great Britain. But the tally does not begin to suggest the East Germans' depth. In most competitions, GDR athletes scored as many fourth, fifth and sixth place finishes as they did firsts, seconds or thirds. By 1980, presumably, the second rank will have developed into champions, and a new breed of champions, and a new breed of juniors will have taken their place. They will be graduates of the most awesomely efficient sports system in the world, launched a mere 15 years ago.

The GDR juggernaut was best witnessed in the Olympic swimming pool, a handsome, 10-lane affair conducive — it had been forecast — to fast times. And so it was: East German women set eight world records en route to winning 11 of 13 events. For most finals, the only issue in doubt was who would win second and third. First place almost invariably went to a strapping East German fraulein, usually named Kornelia (Konny) Ender, a 17-year-old swimming machine blessed with size 36 shoulders and a pair of biceps most men would be proud to claim.

And what of Canada — the first host nation in Olympic history that failed to win a single gold medal? On paper, the country's 11-medal total (eight alone in the swimming pool) is not exactly imposing. But the Canadian effort was actually a vast improvement over the team's performance in Munich. In the silver medals of high-jumper Greg Joy, canoeist John Wood and equestrian Michel Vaillancourt; in the performance of the sprint relay teams, in the stubborn determination of Jack Donahue's basketball squad (which finished fourth), there are grounds for optimism.

Every Olympiad carries its own asterisk. In 1968 at Mexico City, the army opened fire on protesting students, killing eight. In 1972 at Munich, the violence moved indoors: 11 Israelis dead from the guns of Arab terrorists. In 1976, a 29-nation walkout, the largest boycott in Olympic history. Politics has never been too far removed from international sport, but seldom have their diverging interests been so ensnarled. First, to the dismay of an American press corps grimly determined to misunderstand the issue, Ottawa told the International Olympic Committee that Taiwan, otherwise known as the Republic of China, could not pretend to represent the interests of mainland China to 22 million Canadians who knew better.

Far more serious was the black African walkout (28 nations in all), ostensibly in protest of a tour of South Africa by a New Zealand rugby team. "Sports ties with the racist regime of South Africa constitute implicit support for apartheid," declared one African official. "This must not go unnoticed. If New Zealand stays, we leave."

The long-term effects of the African power play are difficult to read. In any event, it is just one of myriad problems the IOC must soon grapple with. If politics does not savage the games, the costs of staging them may, and the IOC must soon decide whether lofty Olympic ideals are worth a billion dollars and the threat of terrorism, whether all 21 Olympic sports are worth keeping; whether a permanent site in Greece (or elsewhere) ought not be established. In the months to come, in the cozy salons of Geneva and Lausanne, the IOC will do its work. The heroes of the XXI Olympiad have done theirs and taken their rightful place in history. ♣

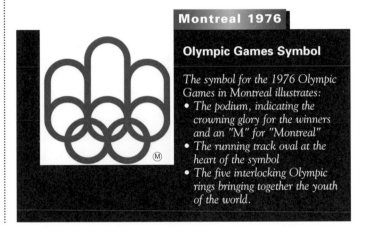

Montreal 1976

Olympic Games Symbol

The symbol for the 1976 Olympic Games in Montreal illustrates:
- *The podium, indicating the crowning glory for the winners and an "M" for "Montreal"*
- *The running track oval at the heart of the symbol*
- *The five interlocking Olympic rings bringing together the youth of the world.*

The "Big Owe" — Montreal's Olympic-sized debt

While the organizers of the Montreal Olympics drew rave reviews for the organization of the games, things were less rosy on the financial front. Mayor Jean Drapeau's infamous quote, "The Montreal Olympics can no more have a deficit than a man can have a baby," would come back to haunt him with a vengeance.

The initial estimates for the cost of the Games started as low as $125 million, but by the time the dust settled the price tag was a whopping $1.5 billion. Much of the cost overrun was related to the construction of facilities and infrastructure, most of which would continue to be used by the people of Montreal long after the Games were over. In fact, if the cost of facilities were removed from the equation, the operation of the Games themselves actually made a profit of $150 million.

Much of the criticism was focused on the oval-shaped Olympic Stadium with its revolutionary retractable roof. Construction delays meant it was unfinished, although usable, when the Games started. Throughout its history, it has been plagued by controversy and structural problems, and the "Big Owe" became a widely-recognized symbol of the flaws in Drapeau's original Olympic dream.

Ultimately, the Malouf Report found that the cost overruns came from various sources, including planning errors, labour problems and suspected widespread corruption. Regardless of the cause, part of the legacy of the Games was debts owed by the City of Montreal and the Province of Quebec that would take more than 20 years to pay off.

Montreal Welcomes Olympic Royalty

Princess Anne

One of the best-recognized athletes at the Montreal Olympics in 1976 was actually better known outside of sport circles. She was Anne Elizabeth Alice Louise Windsor, the Princess Royal and member of the British equestrian team. Princess Anne lists her biggest achievement as "Olympic sportswoman." Despite her royal status, Princess Anne and her then husband and fellow British equestrian competitor, Captain Mark Phillips, stayed in Olympic equestrian village in the same quarters as their fellow competitors.

Canadian Press CP

HRH Princess Anne on "Goodwill."

Despite the presence of royalty on the team, the honour of carrying the flag into the Olympic Stadium at the head of the British team fell to Rodney Patterson, a member of Great Britain's sailing contingent. Meanwhile, Princess Anne's mother, Queen Elizabeth II, prepared to declare the Games opened.

Riding "Goodwill" in the three-day equestrian event, Princess Anne finished a disappointing 24th overall in the dressage portion. The next day during the endurance and cross-country trials, her mother stood near the second fence. All went well until the 19th fence, when Goodwill hit a soft patch, his hind legs crossed and he hit the rails over a ditch. Princess Anne was thrown and mildly dazed and concussed. She got back up on her horse but remembers nothing of the remaining 17 fences, which Goodwill took with ease.

Competing in Montreal was only part of Princess Anne's involvement with international sport. For five years, she was President of the British Olympic Association before being named to the International Olympic Committee in 1988. In 1986 she succeeded her father, Prince Philip, Duke of Edinburgh, as President of the International Equestrian Federation. ♣

July 27, 1976

Michel Vaillancourt

Michel Vaillancourt almost didn't make it onto the Olympic equestrian team for the 1976 Olympics. Neither the 22-year-old rider nor his seven-year-old horse Branch County had a significant amount of experience by Grand Prix jumping standards, but the pair finished second at the Canadian trials to be named to the team. At the Games, his older and more experienced teammates were expected to do better, but finished well back. Meanwhile, Vaillancourt surprised everyone (including himself) by finishing in a tie with two other riders for second after the regular round of competition. The three riders would have to negotiate the tight, 470m course again in order to decide the silver and bronze medals. Adding to the challenge was a thunderstorm with driving rain that delayed the competition. When Vaillancourt and Branch County finally took to the soggy course, they incurred only a single knockdown for four faults, while their opponents incurred eight and 15 faults respectively. The silver medal, Canada's only medal in equestrian events in 1976, was his. "My goal was to be in the top 10," said Vaillancourt later. "I was happy just to have made it as far as the jumpoff. Winning the medal was a bonus." If it hadn't been for the boycott of the 1980 Olympics in Moscow, Vaillancourt may have added to his medal count. As it was, he joined Jim Elder, Ian Millar and Mark Laskin in winning the gold medal in team jumping at the 1980 Rotterdam Show Jumping Festival, an alternative competition to the Moscow Games that featured the top competitors in the world.

CSI/COA

Canada
Our
Century
in Sport

The Olympic Boycotts of 1980 and 1984

Should Canada have gone to Moscow? Were the medals from boycotted Games "tarnished"?

Even after 20 years to reflect, these are hard questions to answer. Perhaps they aren't even the right questions to ask, because they really mean: "Are the Olympics a suitable vehicle to convey a political point?" And perhaps the only answer to that is: whether or not they are a *suitable* vehicle, in the international climate of the day they were an *inevitable* vehicle.

Politics had been present in one way or another at many Olympic Games, and had been particularly overt since 1968. By 1976, international sport was essentially a "virtual battlefield" in the geopolitical tensions of the day. After Montreal, it was almost unconsciously accepted that *something* would happen at Moscow; the question really was what, and where would it come from?

In 1980 the Cold War was at its coldest, with elevated levels of paranoia in both the West and in the USSR. The United States was struggling with its international fortunes. Vietnam was only seven years past, and US foreign policy had not had great success post-Vietnam. Then on November 4, 1979, the Iranian Hostage Crisis began, which was a fatal thorn in the side of the Carter Administration throughout 1980. In April 1980, while the Olympic boycott debate was at its height, the US Armed Forces humiliated themselves in an abortive rescue attempt.

Consideration of American actions on the world stage at this period must take into account the feelings of impotence and humiliation evoked by the Iranian crisis.

By contrast, the USSR had a string of foreign policy successes in 1979 and looked far stronger than it really was, big navy and nuclear weapons notwithstanding. Nobody anywhere could imagine that 12 years later there would be *no* Soviet Union, or that it would fall apart from within. The Communist regime could still take a major decision. And on Boxing Day, 1979 it decided to invade Afghanistan.

The West had to respond to the invasion. Just *how* it would respond was up for debate. Seven years after Vietnam, the United States was in no mood for direct military action, but a direct military confrontation with the USSR in Afghanistan was out of the question anyway. Both sides understood that if Soviet and American troops ever met in anger, the result could be World War Three. An alternative response had to be sought. Economic sanctions of various sorts were applied by the NATO powers, with varying enthusiasm. But one target virtually stood out against the skyline — the Moscow Olympic Games.

World record holder swimmer Graham Smith, left, missed Moscow, and his chance at Olympic glory, as did Debbie Brill, right, and a host of other Canadian athletes.

By (again almost inevitable) coincidence the Communist Party of the Soviet Union had given the United States the perfect excuse for a boycott. Whether President Carter was actually aware of it or not when he began to talk of a boycott, the Party Activists' Handbook for 1980 (which gave the party line on absolutely everything) claimed that the award of the 1980 Olympics to Moscow was proof of international validation of the foreign policy and Communist ideology of the Soviet Union. Even though this was clearly normal Soviet-style propaganda (when challenged on the point by IOC President Lord Killanin, Brezhnev was reported as saying, "That is a good line, da."), this was a gauntlet the West felt it had to pick up.

Almost from the beginning, the Afghan War was a military and political disaster for the Soviet Union; "the Soviet Vietnam." But it is not conceivable that any Western action including a boycott of the Olympics could have led to the evacuation of Afghanistan in 1980. Both sides had too much on the line to be able to blink. The boycott, along with the various other sanctions, was a symbolic expression of international disapproval.

Several NATO governments stood aside from the boycott issue, allowing their Olympic teams to go or stay as they saw fit. The British team defied its government and went anyway. The Canadian Olympic Association took an early position that it would not respect demands for a boycott. In theory, the COA could have sent a team to Moscow, since the Canadian Government (itself as divided on the issue as the nation was) threatened only to cut off games mission funding if the COA decided to go. A reduced team might still have gone, but the Olympic Trust of Canada, the COA's fundraising arm composed of senior businessmen, also threatened a funding cutoff. The pressure, added to strident pressure in some sections of the Canadian media, was too much. Canada did not go to Moscow.

Diane Jones Konikowski, just one of the many Canadian athletes missing their Olympic dreams in 1980.

From that moment on, the Los Angeles counter-boycott was inevitable, however much anyone might have hoped otherwise. IOC President Samaranch, an experienced diplomat who turned the Olympic Movement into a serious political force after Moscow, acknowledged that the Olympics had become an international diplomatic football.

The boycott had done what Carter wanted it to — it had humiliated the Soviet Union publicly. What he did not count on, or perhaps especially care about, was that it would spark a gut-felt need to retaliate.

Were the medals at both Games "tarnished" by the boycotts? At the time, much was made of the "asterisk" medals and records by commentators who thought that they were. But at both Moscow and Los Angeles it was clear that, to the general public at least, those who did come, came, and those who stayed away were quietly forgotten until the next major event at which they appeared. We can only speculate on what Canada might have won at Moscow. In 1984 at Los Angeles, to paraphrase Lenin, many athletes found gold lying in the streets and picked it up. Today the medals won at Los Angeles are no less bright than those from any other Games. The losers in both Games were the athletes who missed their only chance at an Olympic Games, casualties of a war in which no shot was fired. ❧

Canada Hosts the Winter World

From Olympia to the Calgary Games

by Ralph Surette
November 30, 1987

The windblown snow in St. John's, Nfld., created a fitting backdrop for the start of the odyssey. Originating at Olympia, Greece, where it was ignited on Nov. 14 at the Temple of Hera, goddess of the Olympics, the Olympic flame last week began its epic 88-day journey across Canada — to Calgary and the 1988 Olympic Games. Atop St. John's historic Signal Hill, Prime Minister Brian Mulroney passed the flame — flown to Canada from Greece in two coal miners' lamps — to a cauldron and ignited the Olympic torch. Then, the first torchbearers — figure skating legend Barbara Ann Scott-King, 59, gold medal winner at the St. Moritz Winter Olympics of 1948, and Ferd Hayward, 76, Newfoundland's first-ever Canadian Olympic athlete, who competed as a race walker at Helsinki in 1952 — carried the flame for the first kilometre of its 18,000 km journey. Said Scott-King: "To an athlete, the Olympic torch is almost sacred. I saw it from afar at St. Moritz. I never thought I'd get to touch it, to carry it. I am thrilled."

By Feb. 13, when it arrives at Calgary's McMahon Stadium for the Games' opening ceremonies, 7,000 Canadians will have carried the 1.7-kg torch. Wearing red and white jogging suits, the torchbearers — the majority of whom were selected by lottery — will each carry the torch one kilometre. The marathon relay will cover 8,250 km by road, 2,750 km by snowmobile from Northern Ontario to Saskatchewan — and more than 6,000 km by aircraft on a tour through the Northwest Territories. On a route

that will take it to every territorial and provincial capital, the flame will also travel by sea and dogsled. Explained Sandy Hunter, media director for the torch relay: "The route was designed so that the flame will be no more than a two-hour drive away for 90 per cent of the Canadian population."

The appeal of the Olympic symbol was clear last week as citizens of St. John's crowded along the flame's route and broke spontaneously into choruses of O Canada. Flag- and balloon-waving children raced out of every school along the way to touch the maple handle of the torch, shaped like the Calgary Tower. Carrying the flame out of St. John's, Brett Thornhill, a 20-year-old Memorial University student, was asked by relay organizers to slow down. "I can't slow down," he said. "I'm on too big a

CODA — Tibor Bognor

high. I've thought about it day and night for weeks." Equally enthusiastic, thousands of people cheered at later ceremonies when the flame arrived in the Newfoundland communities of Mount Pearl, South Conception Bay and Holyrood.

Like Thornhill, 6,520 torchbearers were chosen by lottery. The others — including former Olympians, native Canadians who will carry the flame in and near reserves, and handicapped people — were chosen by their own special organizing groups in coordination with the flame relay sponsor and organizer, Petro Canada. The company mailed 10 million invitations to Canadians to participate and received 6.5 million responses. David Pagnucco, for one, a 30-year-old miner from

Barbara Ann Scott and Ferd Hayward run the first leg of the Olympic Torch Relay from Signal Hill in St. John's Newfoundland.

12-year old Robyn Perry lighting Calgary's 1988 Olympic Flame.

Cranbrook, BC, who carried the torch on the first day, said that he sent in "thousands, thousands. I didn't count them." The youngest runner will be four-year-old Bruno Levesque from Jacquet River, NB, scheduled to run near Edmundston. The oldest torchbearer is Joe Chase of Wetaskawin, Alta., who will be 101 years old when he carries the torch in his town.

The torchbearers are accompanied by a 40-vehicle caravan — including four motor homes, TV transmission trucks and vans carrying the 70-member relay staff. In addition to relay coordinators and medical personnel, escort runners are on hand. They jog along with the torchbearers, carrying a first-aid kit and a fire extinguisher. Preparation for the relay is so detailed that organizers have produced a 10-cm-thick instruction manual for each week of the torch's 13-week journey. The document records every hill, shopping plaza, bridge and stop sign along the way.

And to ensure that the flame is not lost en route, 11 miner's lanterns were ignited with the flame at Olympia. Four travel with the relay; the others were flown to Calgary. Each night the torch — housing a cannister containing one of three fuel mixtures especially developed for the relay — is extinguished, then reignited from one of the miner's lamps for the first runner the next morning. But despite the careful planning, the torch was accidentally extinguished three times on the relay's first day.

At week's end, the Olympic flame reached Sheet Harbour, NS, and runners in Dartmouth, the first stop next week, waited for their turn to carry the torch — and a chance to play their part in the longest Olympic flame relay ever held. ♦

The Canmore Olympic Nordic Centre.

1988

Calgary Games

'For the Glory of Sport'

February 22, 1988
by Bob Levin with Hal Quinn,
June O'Hara and Bruce Wallace

In the end, Calgary's mercurial weather could hardly have been more co-operative. The temperature dropped to an appropriately wintry -4°C. The wind whipped the flags around McMahon Stadium, and the sun, as if on cue, broke through a heavy cloud cover just in time to spotlight the start of the opening ceremonies of the XV Olympic Winter Games. In the stands, 60,000 excited spectators wore colour-coded ponchos that awaited them at their seats. From an overview, the spectators formed the Olympic rings, the Calgary Games snowflake and the Canadian flag. Down on the field, which was covered in snow-simulating sand, the extravaganza — featuring 6,500 performers aged 9 to 84 — was an eclectic affair laced with a rousing western theme. Indians from five native Albertan bands charged onto the field on horseback. Two giant inflated dinosaurs swayed in the breeze, and Calgary Stampede chuck wagons came rolling on — discreetly followed by pooper-scooper crews. Up went the flags of the 57 participating nations, the largest number even in a Winter Games, and the Lord Strathcona mounted troop escorted Gov. Gen. Jeanne Sauvé riding in an open carriage onto the field.

Snappy: Then came the athletes, smiling and waving. They were representing some 1,700 in all, headed by Greece, where the ancient Games began. The crowd cheered approvingly, saving its most resounding roar for last, when the 129 Canadian athletes marched on. Led by flag bearer and world figure skating champion Brian Orser, considered the country's best hope for a gold medal, the Canadians were decked out in long red coats with white

leather fringe. The noise level continued to rise as costumed dancers did a snappy two-step, accompanied by performers Ian Tyson and Gordon Lightfoot singing *Four Strong Winds* and *Alberta Bound*. In the stands, the athletes and spectators stomped and clapped and started the ubiquitous "wave," which went twice around the stadium, paving the way for the dignitaries. Organizing-committee chairman Frank King, in a brown fur hat, declared that "the dream has become a reality." International Olympic Committee president Juan Antonio Samaranch thanked Canadians for building such "splendid facilities," and then Sauvé read the customary salutation: "I declare open the Games of Calgary."

Electrifying: Eventually, 10 present and former Canadian Olympians carried in the Olympic flag. Some 1,000 pigeons fluttered out of the stadium, and the Games' best-kept secret was finally revealed: to the rhythmic sound of Indian drums, former Canadian downhiller Ken Read and speed skater Cathy Priestner, two Calgary residents, dashed into the stadium carrying the Olympic torch, completing the 88-day cross-country relay. They stopped at the north end of the stadium to greet wheelchair athlete Rick Hansen, then handed the torch to 12-year-old Robyn Perry, a Calgary student representing future Olympians. The freckle-faced seventh grader then climbed the final flight of 65 steps and lit the Olympic cauldron. With an electrifying whoosh it shot into the air. As the Canadian Forces Snowbirds flew overhead, leaving a smoke trail of nine colours, they carried the soaring hopes of a city, country — and a host of grinning athletes. ♦

CSI/COA

1988 Flagbearer Brian Orser.

Prime Minister Brian Mulroney and Sport Minister Otto Jelinek (1962 World Champion figure skater) check out the Torch Relay passing through Ottawa.

CSI/COA

1988
Calgary Games

Double-bronze medallist, Karen Percy

Laurie Graham

CSI/COA

CSI/COA

Calgary's Opening Ceremonies, 1988 Olympic Winter Games

1988

Calgary Games

Making the Magic Last

**by Bob Levin
March 7, 1988**

Suddenly, the party was almost over. The days were dwindling away, and the other Olympics — the ones in the Calgary streets in which Games-goers vied to have the most enjoyable time imaginable — were in their final, frenzied phase. On the Stephen Avenue mall, under a sparkling blue sky, strollers gobbled fat hotdogs, watched jugglers and listened to reggae and rock. They traded pins feverishly, their chests laden with enough metal to make a general proud. They snapped pictures and jammed souvenir stores, trying to hang on to the memory — to their piece of personal and sports history. "The Stampede's nothing compared to this," marvelled Rose Deak, busily selling Olympic sweatshirts at the Tropicana shop. Outside, as a choir at Olympic Plaza sang *Over the Rainbow*, 28-year-old Brian Arnelien of Clifford, Ont., summed up the prevailing mood. "Nobody wants the Games to end," he gushed. "If they lasted a month, I'd stay the whole time — that's how much fun I'm having."

It was a moment that defied mere logic, that could be described, but not entirely dissected. It went beyond sport to something very much like magic, and not even the area's troublesome winds could blow it away. During the last week of the Games, as calm, northerly air broke down the tumultuous Pacific flow that had forced 22 postponements, Canadians embraced a host of new heroes. There was Karen Percy, the blond Banff skier who schussed to her second bronze medal, and Italy's Alberto Tomba, who garnered two golds. Canadian ice dancers Tracy Wilson and Robert McCall skated off with a bronze, while supreme ski jumper Matti Nikanen — the Flying Finn — soared to his second and third

golds. In speed skating, Yvonne Van Gennip of the Netherlands and Bonnie Blair of the United States successfully assaulted the East German stronghold. But perhaps the best came nearly last: in a dramatic Saturday-night showdown, Katarina Witt, the dazzling East German figure skater, grabbed the gold, and Canada's Elizabeth Manley — with a stunning performance — overcame American Debi Thomas to take the silver. "I've had dreams about this night," said an exuberant Manley. "I'm so happy!"

Medals: As closing ceremonies neared, the Soviets held a sizable lead in the medals race, followed impressively by the East Germans. The Canadians' count at the weekend stood at five medals — two silver and three bronze — and critics questioned whether or not that was sufficient payoff for the federal government's $25-million BestEver program. Sport Minister Otto Jelinek told Maclean's that the money was designed to encourage participation at the local level, not just winning Olympic medals. And in any case, he noted, the Canadians had more top-eight finalists in Calgary than in any previous Games. "I'm not disappointed in the performance of the team," he said. "I'm disappointed for the individual athletes who wanted to do better."

The bottom line at the beginning of the week was that the Games seemed to be grinding to a halt. At Mount Allan and Canada Olympic Park, event after event succumbed to nine days of above-normal winds, which averaged 38 km/h on one gusty day. Spectators grumbled. Organizers said that the Games might have to be extended beyond the ceremonies. Torjorn

Two-time Olympic silver medallist Brian Orser

CSI/COA

CSI/COA

Lloyd Langlois

began to roll up the score. Team Canada had only two real scoring chances in the entire game — shooting wide both times — and the final tally was 5-0. The Soviets swept on to blast Sweden to capture the gold. The Canadians, meanwhile, mounted a stirring recovery, besting West Germany and Czechoslovakia — and leaving the home team with hope of a medal if West Germany could beat Sweden on Sunday.

Complaints: The soviets also continued to lead the way in cross-country skiing, taking 13 of the 24 total medals. But the traditionally strong Swedes saved face by winning the team competition, and their star, Gunde Svan, topped the 50-km field. In the biathlon, the East Germans skied and shot their way to dominance. But in the two-man bobsleigh, highly favoured East German pilot Wolfgang Hoppe — who complained that dirt blown onto the track made going down it "like driving on sandpaper" — was upset by Soviet Ianis Kipours. The Canadians did manage to score in the demonstration sport of short-track skating, winning one gold, six silver and two bronze medals.

And so the competition wound down. The world had come to Calgary on a cold February afternoon and, 16 eventful days later, it was preparing to go. The ubiquitous television cameras, which had transformed the area into a vast set and local residents into extras, would soon be carted away. The athletes and visitors would travel home to all parts of the globe. Ahead lay Calgary's collective hangover — and perhaps an Olympian letdown — and after that the endless assessments of costs and benefits. But in the waning days last week, Calgarians seemed intent on making the magic last, on savoring the moment. "If I stayed here 100 years," said Mike Batson, doorman at the VIP-packed Palliser Hotel, "I'd never see anything like this again. Never." ❦

Yggeseth, an official of the Fédération internationale de ski, warned that the constant delays inflicted "mental cruelty" on the ski jumpers — and that winds could prevent Canada Olympic Park from being used for World Cup competition.

But Tuesday dawned clear and still, and a festive crowd of 80,000 thronged to see the twice-delayed 90-m ski jump. "you can't ask for a better day than today," beamed spectator David Powers, 32, of Calgary. Nykanen took advantage of the conditions to complete a first-ever sweep of both the 70-m and 90-m jumps, with Canada's Horst Bulau leaping to a best-ever seventh. The next day Nykanen crowned his conquest by leading the Finns to first in the team competition — and, for the moment, the jury remained out on the future of Canada Olympic Park. "I've never seen it so windy here for so many days," said Bulau. "It's really too bad it had to happen during the Olympics."

Miracle: At the weekend, there was also no verdict on the Canadian hockey team's quest for a medal. The dream of a home-ice miracle was buoyed two months earlier in Moscow when Team Canada topped the Soviets to win the Izvestia tournament. After a disappointing performance the first week, the offence-weak Canadians needed a win over Sweden on Feb. 22 to move to the medal round with two points and a shot at the gold. But all they could manage was a 2-2 tie, advancing with a single point. Meanwhile, the superb Swedes, although in disarray after a series of defeats in other international tournaments, cruised undefeated through the preliminary round to advance with four points.

That set up the inevitable confrontation between the Soviets and their Canadian hosts. With the US squad eliminated in the first round, ABC TV pressed for a schedule change to position the Soviet-Canada game in prime time, leading Canadian head coach Dave King to comment, "It's great to be America's team — North America's, South America's, whatever." The show lasted until the second period, when the dominant Soviets

CSI/COA

Elizabeth Manley

The Canada Games

1967-2000

It was Norton Crowe, on his retirement in 1924 from 19 years of service to the Amateur Athletic Union of Canada in various capacities, who is first recorded as musing about the possibility of organizing a "Canadian Olympic Games." With government support, he felt it would provide a good venue to help develop Canadian athletes for international competition.

Even though it was well-received by Crowe's colleagues at the time, the Depression, followed by World War II, helped push the concept of an all-Canadian multi-sport competition to the back shelf. There were also those who felt that "politics and sport don't mix," and that the federal government should not get involved in the first place. Others saw sport in broader terms as a cultural asset; a means not just to promote fitness and health, but also to cultivate national pride and understanding between regions.

A group of the latter got together just after World War II and formed the National Sports Advisory Council, and for the next 10 years tried to persuade Members of Parliament and cabinet ministers to support sport. In 1959, they finally managed a small coup, getting then Prime Minister John Diefenbaker to visit Canadian athletes competing at the Pan American Games in Chicago. The same year, their efforts also got an unexpected boost from none other than Prince Philip, when he made reference in a speech to the Canadian Medical Association to Canadians not being as healthy or physically fit as they might be. His comments made headlines, and gave royal encouragement to programs that would foster participation in sport and recreation.

Finally, in 1961, Prime Minister Diefenbaker announced the first-ever federal grant for amateur sport in Canada. In addition to providing money for national teams, the Fitness and Amateur Sport Act gave the green light to moving ahead with plans for a national competition. A plan developed to hold the Canada Games every two years, alternating between winter and summer.

Quebec City volunteered as the host of the inaugural Canada Winter Games, and in 1963 an organizing committee was up and running. Under the presidency of Georges Labrecque, the committee had two more hurdles to jump before getting down to business.

First, the federal government insisted on agreements being in place from all provincial governments before it would agree to provide its own funding. Labrecque embarked on a cross-country mission, and succeeded in getting all the premiers to buy into the concept.

The second hurdle was that the conditions of the federal funding did not allow for using any of the money for capital projects, such as building a new arena or playing field. This flew in the face of the evolving philosophy of the Canada Games, which included the idea that they

Canada Games Council

should be staged in smaller centres in order to leave behind legacies of facilities and trained people for the purpose of developing sport in those regions.

It was too late to change things for the Quebec City Games, but by the time the 1969 Canada Summer Games were held in Halifax, the federal government had agreed to share the capital costs as well as paying for the full net operational costs. Provincial and municipal governments paid the rest. The funding formulas have varied over the years, and have been augmented by sponsorship money, but the principal of three levels of government sharing the cost has remained.

Over the years, the Games have left behind a legacy worth well over $120-million in the host communities, not to mention the expertise gained by the staff and volunteers who run the events.

Canada Games Council

The organizers of the Canada Games also wanted a good balance between elite competition and widespread participation. They wanted to avoid discouraging smaller provinces or territories with less developed sport systems and therefore fewer chances of winning medals from participating. A point system was developed that meant that even a 12th place finisher would add to a provincial or territorial team's total. At the end of each Games, honours went not just to the top team (the Games flag), but also to the most improved team (the Centennial Cup) and the team that best combined performance and sportsmanship (the Jack Pelech Award).

Since 1967, the Games have been held in St. John's, Newfoundland, Burnaby, BC, and more than a dozen communities in between. They have fulfilled their mandate as a competitive opportunity that all young athletes can aspire to, while also acting as a springboard for international stars. Greg Joy, a gold medallist in the high jump at the 1973 Canada Games (and a silver medallist at the 1976 Montreal Olympics), summed it up well when he said, "It really opened my eyes to the other sports and the other athletes. It brings you up to that certain level that just competing in your own sport really doesn't do." ♣

Canada Games Council

Canada Games Council

The Canada Games
Winter

1967 – Quebec City, Quebec

Frigid -30° C temperatures, a last-minute, makeshift Games torch and a savage blizzard couldn't dampen the spirits of organizers, fans and athletes determined to make sure the first Canada Games were a success. A 76-cm snowfall on Day Four could have sunk the games, but instead became their finest hour as everyone pitched in to keep the program on track.

1971 – Saskatoon, Saskatchewan

Saskatoon's contribution to Canada Games history included building a mountain on the prairie in order to host skiing events. More than two decades later, Blackstrap Mountain was still in use as a public skiing facility. Equally imaginative, an unused department store was turned into the athletes' dormitories.

1975 – Lethbridge, Alberta

Instead of one community, these Games were hosted by a dozen in the Lethbridge area. The potential logistical nightmare was overcome by more than 4000 volunteers, while a fleet of school buses and cars solved the transportation problems.

1979 – Brandon, Manitoba

Even without mountains to build or islands to move, the challenge of organizing events and accommodating 2000 athletes and officials was daunting. One of every nine people in the city of 38,000 helped out in some way. Fundraising efforts yielded more than $1-million in cash and services to help stage the Games.

1983 – Saguenay-Lac-St-Jean, Quebec

With no major logistical problems, and a half-million dollar surplus, these Games were among the smoothest yet organized. Despite a lack of snow leading up to the Games, a fresh blanket fell as if on cue just before they started.

1987 – Cape Breton, Nova Scotia

It was inevitable that Games held in Cape Breton would have a vibrant cultural element. Each province and territory sent entertainers who performed all around the region. The new arena built for the Games helped bring an American Hockey League franchise to Sydney.

1991 – Charlottetown, PEI

These were the first Games to be hosted by an entire province. Competition was close, as it was at many Canada Games, with the Ontario team edging out the Quebec team by a single point. In the spirit of the Games' "Unity through sport" motto, the Quebec athletes were the first on their feet to applaud the victors.

1995 – Grande Prairie, Alberta

The smallest city ever to host the Games, Grande Prairie got unprecedented commitment from volunteers to produce a world-class celebration of sport and culture. Quebec gymnast Alexandre Jeltkov set a new record by winning eight medals.

1999 – Corner Brook, Newfoundland

Corner Brook was smaller even than Grande Prairie, but volunteer commitment again ensured success. Led by Lee Churchill, a local cross-country skier who won three gold medals, Newfoundland won more medals than ever before. The host province also won the Jack Pelech Award for sportsmanship.

The Canada Games

1969 – Halifax-Dartmouth, Nova Scotia

The challenges facing the organizers included having to literally move a small island (featureless and free of vegetation) to create the rowing and canoeing venue. Corporate sponsors were invited to help out for the first time, and the official Canada Games symbol, song and flag were developed.

1973 – New Westminster-Burnaby, BC

Before creating what *Sports Illustrated* called "the finest rowing course in the western hemisphere," engineers had to devise a way to remove countless water lilies from Burnaby Lake. The Games legacy included a new pool complex, two renovated stadiums, and upgraded softball, baseball, lawn bowling and field hockey facilities.

1977 – St. John's, Newfoundland

St. John's submitted a late, but enthusiastic bid to host the Games. A flurry of construction gave the city $8-million worth of new or renovated facilities. Newfoundland won its first individual medals ever in Canada Games competition.

1981 – Thunder Bay, Ontario

Employing a volunteer army totaling more than 7000 people, the Games united the City of Thunder Bay as nothing before had. The competition was characterized by record setting, including nine on the second day of track and field competition and nine on the first day in the pool.

1985 – Saint John, New Brunswick

After an unsuccessful bid in 1977, the time was ripe for Saint John to host the Games. The city was transformed from a conservative, uneventful community to what newspapers called "an enchanted city." A labour dispute that had threatened to cancel the Games was resolved at the last minute.

1989 – Saskatoon, Saskatchewan

This was the first time a city had hosted the Games twice (the Winter Games were held in Saskatoon in 1971). A record 8500 volunteers helped out, and Saskatchewan's athletes did their part by winning the Centennial Cup for the most improved team.

1993 – Kamloops, BC

Held in the city's centennial year, the Games set more than 50 competitive records, not to mention attendance records. For the first time, events were held for athletes with disabilities.

1997 – Brandon, Manitoba

For only the second time, a city played host to the Summer Games after having hosted the Winter Games (1979). The growth of the Games in the intervening years meant that the challenge was still not an easy one, though. With 7000 volunteers, Brandon continued the tradition of improving the Games each time out.

Logos courtesy of Canada Games Council

Special Olympics

The Birth of the Special Olympics in Canada

In the early 1960s, testing of children with mental disabilities revealed that they were only half as physically fit as their non-disabled peers. It was initially thought that their low fitness levels were a direct result of their disability, but a Toronto researcher and professor, Dr. Frank Hayden, questioned this assumption. Working with a group of children on an intense fitness program, he demonstrated that, given the opportunity, mentally disabled people could become physically fit and acquire the physical skills necessary to participate in sport. His research proved that low levels of fitness and lack of motor skills development in people with mental handicaps were a result of nothing more than a sedentary life style. In other words, their mental disabilities had resulted in an unfair exclusion from the kinds of physical activity and sports experience readily available to other children.

CSO

Inspired by his discoveries, Dr. Hayden began searching for ways to develop a national sports program for mentally disabled people. It was a goal he eventually achieved, albeit not in Canada. His work came to the attention of Eunice Kennedy Shriver and the Kennedy Foundation in Washington, D.C., and led to the creation of the Special Olympics. The first sports competitions organized under the Special Olympics banner were held at Soldiers' Field in Chicago in 1968. To ensure that Canada was represented, Dr. Hayden called on an old friend, Harry "Red" Foster.

The late Harry "Red" Foster was an outstanding sportsman, a famous broadcaster, a successful businessman and a humanitarian whose tireless work on behalf of people with a mental disability had already brought him international acclaim. Inspired by his mother's devotion to his younger brother, who was both blind and mentally disabled, Foster began early in his career to devote much of his time, energy and wealth to addressing the problems faced by individuals with a mental disability and their families.

Accompanying a floor hockey team from Toronto to those first Games in Chicago, Foster was quick to see the Special Olympics as a further opportunity to enhance the lives of mentally disabled Canadians. Upon returning to Canada he set about laying the foundation for the Special Olympics movement. The following summer, 1969, the first Canadian Special Olympics event was held in Toronto. From that modest beginning, the Special Olympics movement quickly spread across the country and grew into the national sports organization it is today. ❧

Highlights

Canadian Special Olympics

1968

Canada was represented by a floor hockey team from Toronto at the first International Special Olympics Games held at Soldiers' Field in Chicago. Canada became the first nation outside of the United States to participate in Special Olympics.

1969

The first Canadian Special Olympics (CSO) Games and National Hockey League (NHL) Floor Hockey Tournament were held in Toronto.

1974

Canadian Special Olympics was incorporated as a national, charitable volunteer organization.

The third Canadian Special Olympics and NHL Floor Hockey Tournament were held in Winnipeg, with 1,000 athletes participating.

1981

Canadian Special Olympics Summer Games were held in Ottawa. Five hundred athletes and 136 coaches participated. Prior to the Games, the first NHL Floor Hockey Training Camp was held in Toronto.

1984

Canadian Special Olympics hosted the International NHL Floor Hockey Tournament as part of Toronto's Sesquicentennial celebrations. Over 400 mentally disabled athletes participated. All NHL teams were represented.

Canadian Special Olympics Honourary Head Coach Lanny McDonald was awarded the International Special Olympics Award for Distinguished Service to mentally disabled people.

1986

Canadian Special Olympics Summer Games were held in Calgary, Alberta. Eight hundred athletes and 200 coaches participated.

1988

The first Canadian Special Olympics Winter Games were held in Edmundston, New Brunswick in March of 1988. Approximately 300 athletes and coaches attended.

1993

Canadian Special Olympics was represented by a team of 150 athletes and coaches at the World Winter Games held in Schladming and Salzburg, Austria. These Games were the first World Games held outside of the United States.

1994

25th Anniversary of Canadian Special Olympics.

CSO

CSO

CSO

CSO

Canada Goes to the Paralympic Games

The Paralympic Movement

The Paralympic Games are the ultimate competition for premier athletes with a disability and by the end of the century were linked to the respective Olympic summer and winter celebrations. The Paralympics involve athletes who are blind or partially sighted, paraplegics and quadriplegics, athletes with cerebral palsy, amputees, and since 1996, events with full medal status for athletes with a mental disability.

The fundamental philosophy guiding the Paralympic movement is that athletes with a disability should have opportunities to pursue their highest goals in sport, equivalent to those of non-disabled athletes. ♣

Paralympics

CANADIAN PARALYMPIC COMMITTEE

COMITÉ PARALYMPIQUE DU CANADA

The Canadian Federation of Sport Organizations for the Disabled (CFSOD) foundations were laid in 1976, when Toronto hosted the 1976 Olympiad for the Disabled (later to become known as the Paralympic Games). It was the first Canadian city to become host of a major, international sporting event for athletes with a disability and was funded by the federal government. In 1981 CFSOD was incorporated with the mandate to "coordinate those activities common to member sport organizations for the physically disabled on matters pertaining to promotion, rule integration, coaching integration and participation in national and international competitions and administration involving more than one disability group." Since 1987, CFSOD was involved in coordinating National Games for Paralympic athletes.

Brantford became the first host of the Canadian Games for the Physically Disabled with a long-term sponsorship agreement with the Canadian Foresters. From 1989 through 1993 the games were known as the Canadian Foresters Games. Successful National Games were subsequently held in Richmond, BC in 1989, Brantford, Ontario in 1991 and the last Foresters Games of the century were held in 1993 in Abbotsford, BC

Over the years, Canada has become known as a world leader in sport for athletes with a disability. In 1989 Dr. Robert Steadward from Edmonton, Alberta, then president of CFSOD, became the first President of the International Paralympic Committee (IPC), an organization which has authority over all world multi-disability games.

In April 1993 the CFSOD name changed to the Canadian Paralympic Committee (CPC). At the end of the century, it was a nonprofit, charitable, private corporation recognized by the International Paralympic Committee as the National Paralympic Committee of Canada, with a mandate "to promote the Paralympic movement to the fullest by providing the professional management of Canada's Paralympic Teams."

The Canadian Paralympic Committee (CPC) logo features a maple leaf with three coloured drops that symbolize people with a disability around the world striving for international friendship and strength through unity. The configuration represents the three disability groups (locomotor, sensory and intellectually disabled). The horizontal bars in the maple leaf represent equality and humanity. The IPC logo and all that it represents is incorporated into the maple leaf to be distinctly Canadian.

Chantal Benoit

CPC

Sledge hockey

CPC

Canada at the Summer Paralympic Games – Medal Totals

Year	Location	Team Size	Gold	Silver	Bronze	Total
1960	Rome, Italy	No Team	–	–	–	–
1964	Tokyo, Japan	No Team	–	–	–	–
1968	Tel Aviv, Israel	Unknown	6	6	7	19
1972	Heidelberg, Germany	Unknown	5	6	9	20
1976	TORONTO	Unknown	28	18	32	78
1980	Arnhem, Holland	100	71	37	27	135
1984	New York, USA & Stoke-on-Trent, UK	146	80	65	55	200
1988	Seoul, Korea	140	53	44	52	149
1992	Barcelona, Spain	137	27	20	32	79
1996	Atlanta, USA	132	24	23	24	71
2000	Sydney, Australia	162	38	33	25	96

Canada at the Winter Paralympic Games – Medal Totals

Year	Location	Team Size	Gold	Silver	Bronze	Total
1980	Geilo, Norway	20	2	2	1	5
1984	Innsbruck, Austria	22	1	5	4	10
1988	Innsbruck, Austria	21	5	3	4	12
1992	Tignes, France	22	2	4	6	12
1994	Lillehammer, Norway	37	1	2	5	8
1998	Nagano, Japan	32	1	9	5	15

Canada Hosts the Paralympic Games

Toronto '76

"Every four years the games grow bigger and better. We tried to make them the best ever and they will remain so, at least in our memories, until supplanted by the 1980 games."

That's how Organizing Committee Chair Dr. Robert Jackson described the Toronto area's goals in hosting the 1976 Olympiad for the Physically Disabled. The TorontOlympiad, as it was known, was the second largest sports event in Canada that year (after the Montreal Olympics), with 1560 athletes from 40 countries competing. More than 250 existing games and world records were broken, not counting those set in the blind and amputee categories, which were being held for the first time. One of the big stories of the games was Canadian high jump sensation Arnie Boldt, who could clear heights on one leg that many jumpers with two legs couldn't dream of. An appreciative crowd watched Boldt clear 1.86m for a new world record. A well-rounded athlete, he also set a world record in the long jump and played on the Canadian volleyball team. Although run on a tight budget, the games were a huge competitive success, and scored points with the public too. Dr. Jackson commented afterwards that, *"People who came initially out of curiosity, came again out of respect for the courage and ability of the participants, and developed an increasing appreciation of the Games as a unique sports spectacular in their own right."* ♣

1968-2000

Canadians have participated at the Summer Paralympic Games since the Tel Aviv Summer Games in 1968, and at every Winter Paralympic Games since the first games in 1976. The Paralympic Games name was used for the first time in Seoul, Korea, in 1988.

1968

Tel Aviv, Israel
Canada attended its first Paralympic Games, then known as the Games for the Physically Disabled, in 1968. This first team brought home 17 medals, including six gold.

1976

Toronto, Canada
Called the TorontOlympiad, the Toronto Games gave official recognition to blind and partially sighted athletes and included for the first time amputees. 1600 athletes from 42 countries competed in events which also included wheelchair athletes. The games resulted in significant growth of the Paralympic movement in Canada.

1968-72

Joyce Murland and E. Reimer were two of Canada's first multi-medal and multi-games Paralympians. Murland would get two field medals each in 1968 and 1972, while Reimer would earn nine field medals between 1968 and 1976, including five gold and four silver.

Arnie Boldt

1976-92

Arnie Boldt became the only Paralympic athlete inducted into Canada's Sports Hall of Fame in the century. Boldt jumped amazing heights and distances, on one leg. The gold medal in high jumping seemed his alone as he won in 1976, 1980, 1984, 1988 and 1992. Not surprisingly, he set the world record time after time. He also won gold medals in the long jump in 1976 and 1980, adding a silver medal in 1988. At the 1976 games in Toronto, he also competed on the men's volleyball team.

1980-84

Future "Man in Motion" Rick Hansen competed in the 1980 and 1984 Paralympic Games. He won the 800m wheelchair gold medal in 1980 and added a silver medal in the 1500m. In 1984 he upped his collection, winning gold medals in both the 1500m and the marathon.

1980-84

Blind swimmer Timothy McIsaac won five medals in 1980, including four golds in world record time. He returned in 1984 to win seven more medals, five of which were world record, gold medal, times.

1980-92

Not to be outdone by her male counterpart, Yvette Michel also won multiple medals in blind swimming, but over four games. In 1980 she won four gold and a silver with three world records. In 1984 she netted six medals overall, with four more golds and two world records. In Seoul, 1988, she won seven swim medals, with one being gold. And, in her final games in 1992 she would add three more medals in Barcelona.

1984-88-92

In track and field competition, Joanne Bouw won 10 field event Paralympic medals in three Games between 1984 and 1992, including eight gold medals.

1992

Barcelona, Spain
Joanne Mucz won five gold medals and set five world records in the pool at the 1992 Paralympic Games in Barcelona: 100m freestyle; 400m freestyle; 100m breaststroke; 100m butterfly; and, 200m individual medley.

Joanne Mucz

1992

Barcelona, Spain
Collette Bourgonje of Saskatoon won Paralympic medals in both the winter and summer games, in wheelchair racing and nordic sit-skiing.

1992-1996-2000

Women's wheelchair basketball was introduced to the Paralympic Games in 1992. For these and the remaining games in the century, Canada would be the only winners of the gold medal, winning in Barcelona, Atlanta and Sydney.

1996

Atlanta, USA
Atlanta produced many multiple medal winners from Canada. Quebec's Dean Bergeron won five men's wheelchair medals, while Chantal Petitclerc also won five in women's wheelchair events, including setting a world record in the 100m sprint. In the pool, Marie Claire Rose won six medals, including two gold, both in world record time, in the 100m breaststroke and the 200m individual medley. In blind swimming, Walter Wu brought home six medals, including five gold and two world records. In 2000, Wu added five more medals to his collection, two of which were gold.

2000

Sydney
In the pool, Stephanie Dixon won four gold medals in world record time, and added two individual silver medals and two more golds in relay events. Danielle Campo would also bring home multiple medals, winning six in the pool, including three individual and two relay gold medals. Jeff Adams continued his success in wheelchair events, netting two gold medals, two silver and one bronze. Chantal Petitclerc added four medals to her wheelchair resume, two gold and two silver. The women won their third straight basketball title while the men's wheelchair basketball team won their first.

Rick Hansen

Jeff Adams

CPC

Chantal Petitclerc

When an injury left Chantal Petitclerc a paraplegic at the age of 13, a career in international sport was the furthest thing from her mind. After her accident, she initially took up swimming as a way of staying in shape, and then discovered a taste for physical challenges. Several years later, she met long-time coach Pierre Pomerleau, who encouraged her to try wheelchair racing. Petitclerc never looked back, reaching the top step of many Canadian podiums over the next few years. A coaching change and renewed aggressiveness helped her make the jump to international competition in the early 1990s. A versatile athlete, her competitive victories ranged from 100m sprints to marathon races. The Canadian record book records her name beside every distance in the T4 class, and she also set a 100m world record in 1996, only to break it in 1999. With a trophy room that includes numerous world championship and Paralympic medals, Petitclerc closed the century out in style by winning four medals (including gold in the 200m and the 800m) at the 2000 Paralympics in Sydney. At the end of the century, one of her goals remained unrealized, though: that of having wheelchair racing recognized as an official event at the Olympic Games. ♣

CPC

Jeff Adams

From his first participation in the Paralympics in 1988, wheelchair racer Jeff Adams worked his way into being one of Canada's most recognized athletes. In a career that continued after the end of the century, he set Canadian and world records; won medals at the Paralympics, Olympic demonstration events and world championships; and took his sport to new heights. When he took to the track to race, beating his competitors was just one of the things on his mind. Adams also worked tirelessly to build and promote his sport's appeal to the mainstream spectator. He recalls the 800m race at the 1994 Commonwealth Games in Victoria as one of the highlights of his career, not just because of his gold medal in the event, but also because of the crowd's reaction. "It wasn't a token round of applause that we got; it was people standing up and stomping and screaming and slapping each other on the back." Along with the high points have come some disappointments, including the 1500m demonstration event at the 1992 Olympics in Barcelona. The world record holder going into the race, Adams was poised to win, when one of his push rings came off and he was relegated to seventh place. "I think of what I do as a performance," he said. "If you cross the line first, you celebrate, and you make the crowd part of your celebration lap." ♣

Chantal Benoit

The Canadian women's wheelchair basketball team owned the 1990s, winning three straight Paralympic titles (1992-2000) and two world championships (1994 and 1998). A big part of their success came thanks to the efforts of Chantal Benoit, who first joined the team in 1984. She has been called the Michael Jordan of wheelchair basketball as a testimony to her ability to dominate a game. Opposing teams have even paid her the ultimate compliment by trying to develop a defensive strategy based on shutting down her potent offensive skills. Their success was limited, though. At the 1992 Paralympics in Barcelona, for example, Benoit scored 18 points in a 35-26 Canadian victory over the favoured American team. Her play also earned her the Most Valuable Player award at the 1998 world championships. Benoit emphasizes that Canada's success has been very much a team effort. Following the win at the 1996 Paralympics in Atlanta, she said, "*We were really centred on our game. For each move of the opposite team, we adjusted our game, defence or offence, so it was very hard for the other teams to read what we were doing. In amateur basketball everyone has a position and a role to play, and with that team we were not the starting five; we were the starting 12.*" ❦

Andre Viger

In 1986, Andre Viger won his second of three Boston Marathon wheelchair titles in a world best time of 1:43:25. Viger's three victories in the most famous of marathons in North America seemed appropriate, since he was one of the pioneers of marathon racing for wheelchair athletes. ❦

Boston Marathon Champion
1984 (2:05:20)
1986 (1:43:25)
1987 (1:55:42)

1984 Paralympics

Gold	Marathon, category 3
Bronze	Marathon, category 4

1988 Paralympics

Bronze	800m, category 3
Bronze	5,000m, category 3
Silver	10,000m, category 3
Gold	Marathon, category 3

1992 Paralympics

Gold	10,000m, category TW3-TW4
Gold	4x100m Relay, category TW3-TW4
Silver	4x400m Relay, category TW3-TW4

Canada Goes to the

1900: Paris, France

Team: Unofficial (at least 2)
1 Gold, 0 Silver, 1 Bronze = 2 Medals
Flagbearer: None

Medal	Medallists	Sport	Event
Gold	George Orton	Track & Field	3,000m Steeplechase
Bronze	George Orton	Track & Field	400m Hurdles

1904: St. Louis, USA

Team: Unofficial 43
4 Gold, 1 Silver, 1 Bronze = 6 Medals
Flagbearer: None

Medal	Medallists	Sport	Event
Gold	Etienne Desmarteau	Track & Field	56-pound Weight Toss
Gold	Galt Football Club: George Ducker; John Fraser; John Gourley; Alex Hall; Albert Johnson; Robert Lane; Ernest Linton; Gordon McDonald; Fred Steep; Tom Taylor; William Twaits	Soccer	Soccer
Gold	George Lyon	Golf	Golf
Gold	Winnipeg Shamrocks: Eli Blanchard; V. Brennaugh; George Bretz; William Burns; George Cattanach; George Cloutier; Sandy Cowan; Jack Flett; Benjamin Jamieson; Hilliard Laidlaw; H. Lyle; William Orris; L.H. Pentland	Lacrosse	Lacrosse
Silver	A. Bailey; Phil Boyd; Thomas Loudon; Donald McKenzie; George Reiffenstein; W. Rice; George Strange; William Wadsworth	Rowing	Eights
Bronze	Mohawk Indians: Almighty Voice; Black Eagle; Black Hawk; Flat Iron; Half Moon; Lightfoot; Man Afraid Soap; Night Hawk; Rain in Face; Red Jacket; Snake Eater; Spotted Tail	Lacrosse	Lacrosse

1906: Athens, Greece

Team: Unofficial 4
1 Gold, 1 Silver, 0 Bronze = 2 Medals
Flagbearer: None

Medal	Medallists	Sport	Event
Gold	William Sherring	Track & Field	Marathon
Silver	Don Linden	Track & Field	1,500m Walk

1908: London, UK

Team: 91
3 Gold, 3 Silver, 9 Bronze = 15 Medals
Flagbearer: Unknown/multiple

Medal	Medallists	Sport	Event
Gold	The All Canadas: Patrick Brennan; John Broderick; George Campbell; Angus Dillon; Frank Dixon; Richard Duckett; C. Fyon; Tommy Gorman; Ernest Hamilton; Henry Hoobin; A. Mara; Clarence McKerrow; D. McLeod; George Rennie; Alex Turnbull	Lacrosse	Lacrosse
Gold	Walter Ewing	Shooting	Clay Pigeon
Gold	Robert Kerr	Track & Field	200m
Silver	George Beattie	Shooting	Clay Pigeon
Silver	George Beattie; Walter Ewing; Mylie Fletcher; D. McMackon; George Vivian; A.W. Westover	Shooting	Team Clay Pigeon
Silver	J. Garfield MacDonald	Track & Field	Triple Jump
Bronze	William Anderson; Walter Andrews; Frederick McCarthy; W. Morton	Cycling	4,000m Team Pursuit
Bronze	N.B. Jackes; F.P. Toms	Rowing	Coxless Pairs
Bronze	Gordon Balfour; Becher Gale; Douglas Kertland; Walter Lewis; Charles Liddy; Irvine Robertson; Geoffrey Taylor; Julius Thomson; George Wright	Rowing	Eights
Bronze	Charles Crowe; William Eastcott; H. Kerr; D. McInnis; William Smith; B.M. Willi	Shooting	Military Rifle Team
Bronze	Calvin Bricker	Track & Field	Long Jump
Bronze	Con Walsh	Track & Field	Hammer Throw
Bronze	Robert Kerr	Track & Field	100m
Bronze	Edward Archibald	Track & Field	Pole Vault
Bronze	Aubert Côté	Wrestling	54kg

Olympic Summer Games

1 9 0 0 - 2 0 0 0

1912: Stockholm, Sweden

Team: 36
3 Gold, 2 Silver, 2 Bronze = 7 Medals
Flagbearer: Duncan Gillis, Track & Field

Medal	Medallists	Sport	Event
Gold	George Hodgson	Swimming	400m Freestyle
Gold	George Hodgson	Swimming	1,500m Freestyle
Gold	George Goulding	Track & Field	10,000m Walk
Silver	Duncan Gillis	Track & Field	Hammer Throw
Silver	Calvin Bricker	Track & Field	Long Jump
Bronze	Everard Butler	Rowing	Single Sculls
Bronze	William Happeny	Track & Field	Pole Vault

1916: Berlin, Germany

Games not held due to World War I

1920: Antwerp, Belgium

Team: 47
3 Gold, 3 Silver, 3 Bronze = 9 Medals
Flagbearer: Archie McDiarmid, Track & Field

Medal	Medallists	Sport	Event
Gold	Bert Schneider	Boxing	66.68kg (Welter)
Gold*	Winnipeg Falcons: Robert Benson; Wally Byron; Frank Frederikson; Chris Fridfinnson; Mike Goodman; Haldor (Slim) Halderson; Konrad Johannesson; Allan (Huck) Woodman	Hockey	Hockey
Gold	Earl Thompson	Track & Field	110m Hurdles
Silver	Chris Graham	Boxing	53.53kg (Bantam)
Silver	Georges Prud'homme	Boxing	72.57kg (Middle)
Silver	George Vernot	Swimming	1500m Freestyle
Bronze	Moe Herscovitch	Boxing	72.57kg (Middle)
Bronze	Chris Newton	Boxing	61.24kg (Light)
Bronze	George Vernot	Swimming	400m Freestyle

*Retroactively awarded

1924: Paris, France

Team: 73
0 Gold, 3 Silver, 1 Bronze = 4 Medals
Flagbearer: Hector Phillips, Track & Field

Medal	Medallists	Sport	Event
Silver	Arthur Bell; Ivor Campbell; Robert Hunter; William Langford; Harold Little; John Smith; Warren Snyder; Norm Taylor; William Wallace	Rowing	Eights
Silver	Archie Black; Colin Finlayson; George MacKay; William Wood	Rowing	Coxless Fours
Silver	William Barnes; George Beattie; John Black; James Montgomery; Sam Newton; Sam Vance	Shooting	Team Clay Pigeon
Bronze	Doug Lewis	Boxing	66.68kg (Welter)

1928: Amsterdam, The Netherlands

Team: 71
4 Gold, 4 Silver, 7 Bronze = 15 Medals
Flagbearer: Joseph Wright Jr., Rowing

Medal	Medallists	Sport	Event
Gold	Percy Williams	Track & Field	100m
Gold	Percy Williams	Track & Field	200m
Gold	Florence Bell; Myrtle Cook; Fanny Rosenfeld; Ethel Smith	Track & Field	4x100m Relay
Gold	Ethel Catherwood	Track & Field	High Jump
Silver	Jack Guest; Joseph Wright Jr.	Rowing	Double Sculls
Silver	Fanny Rosenfeld	Track & Field	100m
Silver	Jim Ball	Track & Field	400m
Silver	Donald Stockton	Wrestling	79kg Freestyle
Bronze	Ray Smillie	Boxing	66.68kg (Welter)
Bronze	John Donnelly; Frank Fiddes; John Hand; Frederick Hedges; Athol Meech; Jack Murdoch; Edgar Norris; Herbert Richardson; William Ross	Rowing	Eights
Bronze	Garnet Ault; Munroe Bourne; Walter Spence; Jim Thompson	Swimming	4x200m Freestyle
Bronze	Ethel Smith	Track & Field	100m
Bronze	Jim Ball; Phil Edwards; Stanley Glover; Alex Wilson	Track & Field	4x400m Relay
Bronze	Maurice Letchford	Wrestling	72kg Freestyle
Bronze	Jim Trifunov	Wrestling	56kg Freestyle

1932: Los Angeles, USA

Team:102
2 Gold, 5 Silver, 8 Bronze = 15 Medals
Flagbearer: George Maughan, Boxing

Medal	Medallists	Sport	Event
Gold	Horace Gwynne	Boxing	53.52kg (Bantam)
Gold	Duncan McNaughton	Track & Field	High Jump
Silver	Hilda Strike	Track & Field	100m
Silver	Mary Frizzell; Mildred Frizzell; Lillian Palmer; Hilda Strike	Track & Field	4x100m Relay
Silver	Alex Wilson	Track & Field	800m
Silver	Dan McDonald	Wrestling	72kg Freestyle
Silver	Earnest Cribb; Peter Gordon; George Gyles; Harry Jones; Ronald Maitland; Hubert Wallace	Yachting	Team 8m
Bronze	Noel DeMille; Charles Pratt	Rowing	Double Sculls
Bronze	Doan Boal; Earle Eastwood; Harry Fry; Joseph Harris; Cedric Liddell; George MacDonald; Stanley Stanyar; Albert Taylor; William Thoburn	Rowing	Eights
Bronze	Alex Wilson	Track & Field	400m
Bronze	Jim Ball; Phil Edwards; Ray Lewis; Alex Wilson	Track & Field	4x400m Relay
Bronze	Phil Edwards	Track & Field	800m
Bronze	Phil Edwards	Track & Field	1,500m
Bronze	Eva Dawes	Track & Field	High Jump
Bronze	Philip T. Rogers; Gerald Wilson; Gardner Boltbee; Kenneth Glass	Yachting	Team 6m

1936: Berlin, Germany

Team: 109
1 Gold, 3 Silver, 5 Bronze = 9 Medals
Flagbearer: James Worrall, Track & Field

Medal	Medallists	Sport	Event
Gold	Francis Amyot	Canoeing	C-1 1000m
Silver	Gord Aitchison; Ian Allison; Art Chapman; Charles Chapman; Edward Dawson; Irving Meretsky; Robert Osborne; Doug Peden; James Stewart; Malcolm Wiseman	Basketball	Men's
Silver	Harvey Charters; Frank Saker	Canoeing	C-2 10,000m
Silver	John Loaring	Track & Field	400m Hurdles
Bronze	Harvey Charters; Frank Saker	Canoeing	C-2 1000m
Bronze	Dorothy Brookshaw; Hilda Cameron; Jeanette Dolson; Aileen Meagher	Track & Field	4x100m Relay
Bronze	Phil Edwards	Track & Field	800m
Bronze	Betty Taylor	Track & Field	80m Hurdles
Bronze	Joseph Schleimer	Wrestling	72kg Freestyle

1940: Games Not Held — WW II

Games not held due to World War II

1944: Games Not Held — WW II

Games not held due to World War II

1948: London, UK

Team: 106
0 Gold, 1 Silver, 2 Bronze = 3 Medals
Flagbearer: Robert McFarlane, Track & Field

Medal	Medallists	Sport	Event
Silver	Douglas Bennett	Canoeing	C-1 1000m
Bronze	Norman Lane	Canoeing	C-1 10,000m
Bronze	Dianne Foster; Patricia Jones; Nancy MacKay; Viola Myers	Track & Field	4x100m Relay

1952: Helsinki, Finland

Team: 113
1 Gold, 2 Silver, 0 Bronze = 3 Medals
Flagbearer: William Parnell, Track & Field

Medal	Medallists	Sport	Event
Gold	George Genereux	Shooting	Clay Pigeon
Silver	Don Hawgood; Ken Lane	Canoeing	C-2 10,000m
Silver	Gerald Gratton	Weightlifting	75kg

1956: Melbourne, Australia / Stockholm, Sweden*

Team: 99
2 Gold, 1 Silver, 3 Bronze = 6 Medals
Flagbearer: Robert Steckle, Wrestling

Medal	Medallists	Sport	Event
Gold	Walter d'Hondt; Donald Arnold; Lorne Loomer; Archie MacKinnon	Rowing	Coxless Fours
Gold	Gerald Ouellette	Shooting	Prone Rifle
Silver	David Helliwell; Phillip Kueber; Richard McClure; Douglas McDonald; William McKerlich; Carleton Ogawa; Donald Pretty; Lawrence West; Robert Wilson	Rowing	Eights
Bronze	Jim Elder; Brian Herbinson; John Rumble	Equestrian	3-day Event
Bronze	Irene MacDonald	Diving	3-metre
Bronze	Gilmour Boa	Shooting	Prone Rifle

* Due to stringent Australian quarantine rules, Stockholm hosted the equestrian events six months prior to Melbourne.

Canada

1960: Rome, Italy

Team: 97
0 Gold, 1 Silver, 0 Bronze = 1 Medal
Flagbearer: Carl Schwende, Fencing

Medal	Medallists	Sport	Event
Silver	Donald Arnold; Walter d'Hondt; Nelson Kuhn; John Lecky; David Anderson; William McKerlich; Archie MacKinnon; Glen Mervyn; Sohen Biln	Rowing	Eights

1964: Tokyo, Japan

Team: 118
1 Gold, 2 Silver, 1 Bronze = 4 Medals
Flagbearer: Gilmour Boa, Shooting

Medal	Medallists	Sport	Event
Gold	George Hungerford; Roger Jackson	Rowing	Coxless Pairs
Silver	Doug Rogers	Judo	+80kg
Silver	Bill Crothers	Track & Field	800m
Bronze	Harry Jerome	Track & Field	100m

1968: Mexico City, Mexico

Team: 143
1 Gold, 3 Silver, 1 Bronze = 5 Medals
Flagbearer: Roger Jackson, Rowing

Medal	Medallists	Sport	Event
Gold	Jim Day; Jim Elder; Tom Gayford	Equestrian	Grand Prix Jumping, Team
Silver	Ralph Hutton	Swimming	400m Freestyle
Silver	Elaine Tanner	Swimming	100m Backstroke
Silver	Elaine Tanner	Swimming	200m Backstroke
Bronze	Angela Coughlan; Marilyn Corson; Marion Lay; Elaine Tanner	Swimming	4x100m Freestyle

1972: Munich, Federal Republic of Germany

Team: 220
0 Gold, 2 Silver, 3 Bronze = 5 Medals
Flagbearer: Doug Rogers, Judo

Medal	Medallists	Sport	Event
Silver	Leslie Cliff	Swimming	400m Individual Medley
Silver	Bruce Robertson	Swimming	100m Butterfly
Bronze	Eric Fish; Robert Kasting; William Mahoney; Bruce Robertson	Swimming	4x100m Medley
Bronze	Donna-Marie Gurr	Swimming	200m Backstroke
Bronze	Paul Côté; John Ekels; David Miller	Yachting	Soling

1976: Montreal, Canada

Team: 414
0 Gold, 5 Silver, 6 Bronze = 11 Medals
Flagbearer: Abby Hoffman, Track & Field

Medal	Medallists	Sport	Event
Silver	John Wood	Canoeing	C-1 500m
Silver	Michel Vaillancourt	Equestrian	Grand Prix Jumping
Silver	Cheryl Gibson	Swimming	400m Individual Medley
Silver	Clay Evans; Gary MacDonald; Stephen Pickell; Graham Smith	Swimming	4x100m Medley
Silver	Greg Joy	Track & Field	High Jump
Bronze	Nancy Garapick	Swimming	100m Backstroke
Bronze	Nancy Garapick	Swimming	200m Backstroke
Bronze	Gail Amundrud; Barbara Clark; Anne Jardin; Becky Smith	Swimming	4x100m Freestyle
Bronze	Robin Corsiglia; Wendy Hogg; Anne Jardin; Susan Sloan	Swimming	4x100m Medley
Bronze	Becky Smith	Swimming	400m IM
Bronze	Shannon Smith	Swimming	400m Freestyle

1980: Moscow, USSR

Canada did not compete: 0 Medals
Unofficial Team: 221
Unofficial Flagbearer: Sue Holloway, Canoeing

1984: Los Angeles, USA

Team: 436
10 Gold, 18 Silver, 16 Bronze – 44 Medals
Flagbearer: Alex Baumann, Swimming

Medal	Medallists	Sport	Event
Gold	Larry Cain	Canoeing	C-1 500m
Gold	Alwyn Morris; Hugh Fisher	Canoeing	K-2 1000m
Gold	Sylvie Bernier	Diving	3-metre
Gold	Lori Fung	Rhythmic Gymnastics	All Around
Gold	Dean Crawford; Mark Evans; Mike Evans; Blair Horn; Grant Main; Brian McMahon; Kevin Neufiled; Paul Steele; Pat Turner	Rowing	Eights
Gold	Linda Thom	Shooting	Sport Pistol
Gold	Alex Baumann	Swimming	200m IM
Gold	Alex Baumann	Swimming	400m IM
Gold	Anne Ottenbrite	Swimming	200m Breaststroke
Gold	Victor Davis	Swimming	200m Breaststroke
Silver	Willie de Wit	Boxing	91kg (Heavy)
Silver	Shawn O'Sullivan	Boxing	71kg (Light Middle)
Silver	Alexandra Barré; Sue Holloway	Canoeing	K-2 500m
Silver	Larry Cain	Canoeing	C-1 1000m
Silver	Steve Bauer	Cycling	Road Race
Silver	Curt Harnett	Cycling	1,000m
Silver	Barbara Armbrust; Marilyn Brain; Angela Schneider; Lesley Thompson; Jane Tregunno	Rowing	Four with Cox
Silver	Betty Craig; Tricia Smith	Rowing	Coxless Pairs
Silver	Victor Davis	Swimming	100m Breaststroke
Silver	Victor Davis; Sandy Goss; Tom Ponting; Mike West	Swimming	4x100m Medley
Silver	Anne Ottenbrite	Swimming	100m Breaststroke
Silver	Carolyn Waldo	Synchronized Swimming	Solo
Silver	Sharon Hambrook; Kelly Kryczka	Synchronized Swimming	Duet
Silver	Angela Bailey; France Gareau; Marita Payne; Angella Taylor	Track & Field	4x100m Relay
Silver	Charmaine Crooks; Molly Killingbeck; Marita Payne; Jillian Richardson	Track & Field	4x400m Relay
Silver	Jacques Demers	Weightlifting	75kg
Silver	Bob Molle	Wrestling	+100kg Freestyle
Silver	Evert Bastet; Terry McLaughlin	Yachting	Flying Dutchman
Bronze	Dale Walters	Boxing	54kg (Bantam)
Bronze	Hugh Fisher; Alwyn Morris	Canoeing	K-2 500m
Bronze	Alexandra Barré; Lucie Guay; Sue Holloway; Barb Olmsted	Canoeing	K-4 500m
Bronze	Mark Berger	Judo	+95kg
Bronze	Robert Mills	Rowing	Single Sculls
Bronze	Danielle Laumann; Silken Laumann	Rowing	Double Sculls
Bronze	Bruce Ford; Doug Hamilton; Mike Hughes; Phil Monckton	Rowing	Quadruple Sculls
Bronze	Mike West	Swimming	100m Breaststroke
Bronze	Cameron Hemming	Swimming	200m Backstroke
Bronze	Reema Abdo; Michelle MacPherson; Anne Ottenbrite; Pam Rai	Swimming	4x100m Medley
Bronze	Ben Johnson	Track & Field	100m
Bronze	Sterling Hinds; Ben Johnson; Tony Sharpe; Desai Williams	Track & Field	4x100m Relay
Bronze	Lynn Williams	Track & Field	3,000m
Bronze	Chris Rinke	Wrestling	82kg Freestyle
Bronze	Terry Neilson	Yachting	Finn
Bronze	Steve Calder; Hans Fogh; John Kerr	Yachting	Soling

1988: Seoul, South Korea

Team: 354
3 Gold, 2 Silver, 5 Bronze = 10 Medals
Flagbearer: Carloyn Waldo, Synchronized Swimming

Medal	Medallists	Sport	Event
Gold	Lennox Lewis	Boxing	+91kg (Superheavy)
Gold	Carolyn Waldo	Synchro Swimming	Solo
Gold	Michelle Cameron; Carolyn Waldo	Synchro Swimming	Duet
Silver	Egerton Marcus	Boxing	75kg (Middle)
Silver	Mark Tewksbury; Victor Davis; Tom Ponting; Sandy Goss	Swimming	4x100m Medley
Bronze	Ray Downey	Boxing	71kg (Light Middle)
Bronze	Cynthia Ishoy; Eva-Marie Pracht; Gina Smith; Ashley Nicoll	Equestrian	Team Dressage
Bronze	Lori Melien; Allison Higson; Jane Kerr; Andrea Nugent	Swimming	4x100m Medley
Bronze	Dave Steen	Track & Field	Decathlon
Bronze	Frank McLaughlin; John Millen	Yachting	Flying Dutchman

1992: Barcelona, Spain

Team: 314
7 Gold, 4 Silver, 7 Bronze = 18 Medals
Flagbearer: Michael Smith, Track & Field

Medal	Medallists	Sport	Event
Gold	Kathleen Heddle; Marnie McBean	Rowing	Coxless Pairs
Gold	Kirsten Barnes; Jessica Monroe; Brenda Taylor; Kay Worthington	Rowing	Coxless Fours
Gold	Lesley Thompson; Kathleen Heddle; Marnie McBean; Kirsten Barnes; Megan Delehanty; Jessica Monroe; Brenda Taylor; Kay Worthington; Shannon Crawford	Rowing	Eights
Gold	Derek Porter; Michael Rascher; Bruce Robertson; Andy Crosby; Mike Forgeron; Robert Marland; Darren Barber; Terry Paul; John Wallace	Rowing	Eights
Gold	Mark Tewksbury	Swimming	100m Backstroke
Gold	Sylvie Fréchette	Synchro Swimming	Solo
Gold	Mark McKoy	Track & Field	110m Hurdles
Silver	Mark Leduc	Boxing	63.5kg (Light Welter)
Silver	Penny Vilagos; Vicky Vilagos	Synchronized Swimming	Duet
Silver	Guillaume Leblanc	Track & Field	20km Walk
Silver	Jeff Thue	Wrestling	130kg Freestyle
Bronze	Chris Johnson	Boxing	75kg (Middle)
Bronze	Curt Harnett	Cycling	Sprint
Bronze	Nicolas Gill	Judo	86kg
Bronze	Silken Laumann	Rowing	Single Sculls
Bronze	Stephen Clarke; Jon Cleveland; Marcel Gery; Mark Tewksbury	Swimming	4x100m Medley
Bronze	Angela Chalmers	Track & Field	3,000m
Bronze	Eric Jesperson; Ross Macdonald	Yachting	Star

1996: Atlanta, USA

Team: 307
3 Gold, 11 Silver, 8 Bronze = 22 Medals
Flagbearer: Charmaine Crooks, Track & Field

Medal	Medallists	Sport	Event
Gold	Kathleen Heddle; Marnie McBean	Rowing	Double Scull
Gold	Donovan Bailey	Track & Field	100m
Gold	Donovan Bailey; Carlton Chambers; Robert Esmie; Glenroy Gilbert; Bruny Surin	Track & Field	4 x100m Relay
Silver	David Defiagbon	Boxing	91kg (Heavy)
Silver	Caroline Brunet	Canoeing	K-1 500m
Silver	Brian Walton	Cycling	Ind. Points Race
Silver	Alison Sydor	Cycling	Cross Country
Silver	David Boyes; Gavin Hassett; Jeffrey Lay; Brian Peaker	Rowing	Ltwt. Coxless Fours
Silver	Alison Korn; Theresa Luke; Maria Maunder; Heather McDermid; Jessica Monroe; Emma Robinson; Lesley Thompson; Tosha Tsang; Anna Van der Kamp	Rowing	Eights
Silver	Silken Laumann	Rowing	Single Sculls
Silver	Derek Porter	Rowing	Single Sculls
Silver	Marianne Limpert	Swimming	200m IM
Silver	Lisa Alexander; Janice Bremner; Karen Clark; Karen Fonteyne; Sylvie Fréchette; Valerie Hould-Marchand; Christine Larsen; Cari Read; Erin Woodley	Synchronized Swimming	Team
Silver	Gia Sissauori	Wrestling	57 kg Freestyle
Bronze	Curt Harnett	Cycling	Sprint
Bronze	Clara Hughes	Cycling	Ind. Road Race
Bronze	Clara Hughes	Cycling	Ind. Road Time Trial
Bronze	Annie Pelletier	Diving	3m Springboard
Bronze	Laryssa Biesenthal; Kathleen Heddle; Marnie McBean; Diane O'Grady	Rowing	Quad Sculls
Bronze	Curtis Myden	Swimming	200m IM
Bronze	Curtis Myden	Swimming	400m IM
Bronze	John Child; Mark Heese	Volleyball	Beach

2000: Sydney, Australia

Team: 311
3 Gold, 3 Silver, 8 Bronze = 14 Medals
Flagbearer: Caroline Brunet, Canoeing

Medal	Medallists	Sport	Event
Gold	Daniel Nestor; Sebastien Lareau	Tennis	Doubles
Gold	Simon Whitfield	Triathlon	Triathlon
Gold	Daniel Igali	Wrestling	Freestyle 69kg
Silver	Caroline Brunet	Canoeing	K-1 500m
Silver	Anne Montminy; Emilie Heymans	Diving	Synchronized 10m Platform
Silver	Nicolas Gill	Judo	100kg
Bronze	Steve Giles	Canoeing	C-1 1000m
Bronze	Anne Montminy	Diving	10m Platform
Bronze	Karen Cockburn	Gymnastics	Trampoline
Bronze	Mathieu Turgeon	Gymnastics	Trampoline
Bronze	Buffy Alexander; Laryssa Biesenthal; Heather Davis; Alison Korn; Theresa Luke; Heather McDermid; Emma Robinson; Lesley Thompson; Dorota Urbaniak	Rowing	Eights
Bronze	Curtis Myden	Swimming	400m IM
Bronze	Lyne Beaumont; Claire Carver-Dias; Erin Chan; Jessica Chase; Catherine Garceau; Fanny Letourneau; Kirstin Normand; Jacinthe Taillon; Reidun Tatham	Synchronized Swimming	Team
Bronze	Dominique Bosshart	Tae Kwon Do	+67kg

1900

- **Paris, France** — At least two Canadians competed in the second Olympic Games, held in Paris, but they traveled and competed with the American team. Both George Orton and Ronald MacDonald were studying in the US and were asked to go with the teams from the University of Pennsylvania and Boston College respectively. Orton is well remembered for winning the 3000m steeplechase and getting a bronze in the 400m hurdles. At the time though, MacDonald may have been the more popular of the two. He had won the 1898 Boston Marathon and was considered a strong favourite in the 1900 Olympic marathon. On the day, though, he officially finished seventh of the seven who finished the race. He argued that the first three finishers did not run the entire course and, years later, claimed that he and the sixth placed American were the only two who actually completed the course.

The first Olympic champion from Canada, George Orton, 1900.

1904

- **St. Louis, USA** — Etienne Desmarteau was a Montreal policeman who also threw the 56-pound weight. He asked his employers for time off to attend the Olympic competitions in 1904, and was not only turned down, but fired. He received assistance from the MAAA (Montreal Amateur Athletic Association), beat all the competitors to win the gold medal and returned a conquering hero. He also returned home as a reinstated policeman. Sadly, Desmarteau died of typhoid a year later. At the time, he was credited as Canada's first Olympic gold medallist.

- The Galt Football Club sponsored its own way to the Olympic Games by winning several soccer events in 1903. In St. Louis, they scored 11 goals to the competitors none and walked away with the first Olympic gold medal in a team sport for Canada.

- Lacrosse was one of Canada's most popular sports in 1904, and the Shamrock Lacrosse Club from Winnipeg did the country proud by winning the Olympic gold medal in St. Louis.

- Canada's fifth-ever gold medal was won by one of the more interesting characters in Canadian sport history. George Lyon from the Rosedale Golf Club in Toronto was the only foreign competitor in the only Olympic golf event in the century. Lyon was a star athlete in many sports late in the 19th century and had not taken up golf until he was 37. In 1904 he was 46 and thought of as a long shot in the event, having really only played in Canada up until then and being "a bit old." In the final match-play pairing, though, Lyon defeated his 23-year old American counterpart. On receiving his gold medal, Lyon walked on his hands the entire length of the clubhouse.

1906

Athens, Greece, *The Intercalated Games*

To celebrate the 10th anniversary of the modern Olympic Games, organizers decided to stage a Games back in Athens, host of the first modern Games in 1896. These were known as the Intercalated Games. The 1906 Games were actually the first Olympics to which Canada sent a team, as opposed to the individual athletes from Canada who participated on their own in 1900 and 1904. Although at the time they were treated as full-fledged Olympic Games, over time they were eliminated from some records as unofficial. In 1906, though, it did not dampen the enthusiasm of Canadian participants. The Canadian team included marathon champion Billy Sherring, race walker Don Linden, pole vaulter Ed Archibald and middle distance runner Elwood Hughes.

1906

- **Athens, Greece** — Don Linden of Toronto won the silver medal in the 1500m walk, but easily could have (and many thought should have) won the gold. During the race, two of the four judges disqualified the American first-place finisher for improper footwork (i.e. running). Linden and the officials agreed to a walk-off the next day between the two. The American did not show up and the officials, somehow, let the result from the previous day stand.

- Fifty years after the event, Linden discussed the incident with sport historian and columnist Henry Roxborough:

  "Bonhag, an American runner, had been defeated in his 5-mile race, so he looked around for another event that might restore his prestige. He had never competed in a walking race in his life; but he approached me and said he was thinking of entering …. And asked for some advice. ….So half-jocularly and half-seriously, I told him what shoes to wear, how to stride, what the rules were; and I really encouraged him to enter. As I now recall, there were nine competitors, and the eager Bonhag went out in front, right from the starter's gun. I trailed him a couple of yards where I could watch him closely and we were soon well ahead of the others. However, it didn't take me long to learn that Bonhag was so determined to stay ahead that he began skipping, which is a form of running. I also noticed that the judges, most of whom were as green as Bonhag, were pointing to the American's head and shaking their heads. Bonhag continued walking so illegally that no honest walker could ever have caught him; and he finished ahead of me by a couple of yards.

  That race was walked on Monday, and later I was told that the judges had conferred and had agreed that Bonhag had broken the rules; so, they had ordered a re-walk to be held between Bonhag and myself at 9:30 Wednesday morning. At that hour, I was on the track and ready; and so was the Crown Prince of Greece, who was one of the judges. But Bonhag never appeared and neither did he ever give an explanation; no re-walk was held, and the original result went into the records.

  If, on a certain day in April, 1906, I had only kept my mouth shut, I would have been an easy world's champion. But I surely talked myself out of it."

- Hamilton's Billy Sherring had built a strong marathon-running reputation by 1906. With a mixture of hard work, friends and the money from a winning horseracing bet, Sherring made his way to Athens. He confidently wrote home: *"If the early pace is too fast, I'll drop back. I don't want to fall on my head like I did in Boston. Anyway, you can bet I will be right in the fight the last few miles, and the fellow who beats me will have to be a dandy."* Canadian teammate Elwood Hughes, having run his races already, decided to help out. Hughes rode his bike ahead of the pack to gauge the leaders. He then rode back along the course to inform Sherring what was up ahead. Having held back almost half a mile when the eager runners took off on an early quick pace, Sherring, with more surveillance assistance from Hughes, caught the last two runners at the 20-mile mark and strode into the Stadium well in front. Escorted by the Crown Prince of Greece, Sherring won the Olympic Marathon in Athens. So impressed were the Greeks, they offered him an olive twig from the sacred Altis, a marble statue, four silver cups, honourary Greek citizenship and a goat. He left the goat with his landlady in Greece.

- Pole vaulter Ed Archibald ran into misfortune in 1906. In training he had been regularly jumping over 12 feet. En route to the Athens Games from Toronto, Archibald traveled via Rome. On the train ride through Italy, he placed his pole (12 feet in length, with a sharp point on one end) in the hands of the conductor, who would store it safely up with the engine. He never saw the pole again. He never had confidence in the poles provided to him in Greece (a vaulter gets very attached to a specific pole), and one almost impaled him. The winning height was under 12 feet.

1908

- **London, England** — These were the first Olympic Games that Canada officially sent a team to (the 1906 Games being deemed "Intercalated" and not given an Olympic number). Canada did quite well for a new entrant and came away with three gold, three silver and nine bronze medals.

- J.G. MacDonald won silver in the "hop, step and jump," with Cal Bricker winning the bronze. In the hammer throw, Con Walsh came second. Ed Archibald kept his pole this time and won a bronze in the pole vault. A. Cote came third in bantam wrestling, as did the Canadian cyclists in the team pursuit. Walter Ewing and George Beattie led Canada to a 1-2 finish in clay-pigeon shooting. A disappointment for Canada at the Games was the failure of Canada's top sculler, and 1904 winner of the Henley Diamond Skulls, Lou Scholes to win any medal at all.

- The gold medal won by the All-Canada field-lacrosse team, to be fair, needs a little explanation. Canada did indeed win the gold medal game against the British, 14-10. The British, however, were the only other team in the competition! The game featured a great example of sportsmanship: when Canadian Frank Dixon broke his stick with the score tied 9-9, R.G. W. Martin of Great Britain offered to sit out the game until a new stick could be found.

- Bobby Kerr of Hamilton became the star of the Games, and not just with Canadians. He had joined the "fast firefighters" of the International Harvester Fire Brigade as a teenager. First representing Canada in 1904, he had hoped to go to the Olympics in Athens in 1906, but money was scarce and he couldn't afford to go. Still, he was gaining a reputation as a fast runner, perhaps the fastest around. En route to London for the 1908 Olympic Games, he won both the 100m and 200m at the British AAU Games two weeks before.

In London, Kerr ran in both the 100m and 200m races (the only participant to run both) and was the favourite to win the 100 over the American challenger. After a series of preliminaries, Bobby Kerr slipped out of the starting blocks in the final. A South African came from nowhere to win, with three of the four judges giving Kerr the nod for the silver. Alas, the head referee sided with the lone judge and Kerr was awarded the bronze. Not satisfied, he rebounded two days later to win the 200m Olympic gold by less than a foot, edging out two Americans.

- The world's leading marathon runner in 1908 was Tom Longboat. He was heavily favoured to win the race, especially by the London bookmakers. However, July 24, 1908 was not Tom's day — it turned unusually hot and humid. Running with a solid lead at the 20-mile mark, Longboat became exhausted, overheated and collapsed. He did not finish the race, and all of Canada was disappointed. Of course, he would go on to a famous professional marathon-running career. While Tom Longboat was forced to quit after leading the marathon, three other Canadians — Wood, Simpson and Lawson — finished fifth, sixth and seventh respectively in a field of 58.

Highlights

1912

- **Stockholm, Sweden** — These were Canada's second official games as a team. In addition to the triumphs of George Goulding and George Hodgson, Canada had some other noteworthy results in Stockholm. Cal Bricker got another Olympic medal in the running broad jump; Duncan Gillis of Vancouver earned BC's first Olympic medal with a silver in the 16-pound hammer throw; William Happeny won a bronze in the pole vault, as did Frank Lukeman in the pentathlon and Ed Butler in the single sculls.

- George Hodgson had won the one-mile swimming race at the 1911 Coronation Games in London and was deemed a favourite in both the 400m and 1500m swims. And, in one glorious week in July, 1912, George Hodgson won two Olympic titles and broke four world records. He broke three of them on July 10; on the way to the 1500m record he also broke the 1000m and mile records. He had lowered the 1500m record by an astonishing 2 minutes and 33 seconds. In the process of winning the 400m swim, Hodgson set another world record.

- Canada's other gold medal in 1912 went to George Goulding in the 10,000m walk. George Goulding was born in England and grew up in Toronto. In 1908 he had gone to the Olympics as both a runner and a walker, finishing fourth in the 3,500m walk and 22nd in the marathon. By 1912 he was the heavy favourite for gold in the "long-walk." He kept up such a pace that three of the 10 finalists had to drop out and another three were called for lifting (running) and disqualified. Having just heard of the safe arrival of his newborn son back in Canada, Goulding continued his blistering pace. He entered the Stadium some 30 metres ahead of his nearest competitor, and actually won by some 80 metres. Here is Goulding's own account of that race:

"In the final. I took the lead right from the start. When I was about 40 yards ahead of Webb (England), I thought the judges were after me. One of them said something in Swedish which I didn't understand; but when I turned toward him I saw a broad grin on his face and concluded he must have said something nice. Still, it was a ticklish moment, for the judges had the right to pull anyone off the track without previous warning.
With other judges I could have improved my time; but during the last mile, when I had a lead of about 75 yards, I slowed considerably and took no chance of being disqualified. Besides, in the first heat, I had rubbed the skin off my toes, while wearing almost new shoes; and in the final my feet were really torturing. However, in winning, I soon forgot the pain and remembered only the pleasure."

Ever thrifty, the laconic Goulding sent a telegram to his wife and newborn back in Canada after the race *"Won – George."*

"Won – George"

1920

- **Antwerp, Belgium** — These Games marked the presentation of the first Olympic Flag, with its now famous five interlocking rings. The Canadian team found themselves without a Canadian flag for the Opening Ceremonies, and so carried in a bare pole.

- Transplanted Canadian Earl Thompson won the gold in the 110m hurdles. Montreal's Bert Schneider became the first Olympic bantamweight boxing champion, and the boxing team ended up with Schneider's gold, two silver and two bronze medals to win the boxing competitions. George Vernot, also from Montreal, earned two Olympic swimming medals: a silver in the 1500m freestyle and a bronze in the 400m swims. The trapshooting team won the bronze, for a total of two gold, three silver and three bronze medals at the Games.

- Earl Thompson was born near Prince Albert, Saskatchewan in 1895. When he was eight his family moved to California, meanwhile retaining their Canadian citizenships. Thompson became a superb all-round athlete, who went on to receive an athletic scholarship to Dartmouth College where he captained the track team. During WW I, Thompson took time off from his studies to fight with the RCAF. In 1920, he was one of the world's best hurdlers, and it was expected he would represent the US. However, being a Canadian citizen, having recently fought with the Canadians in WW I, and having competed in and won the Canadian Olympic Trials, he had to represent the land of his birth — much to the chagrin of the Americans. Thus, Thompson won his 110m hurdle Olympic gold medal wearing Canadian colours. His 14.8 seconds in the 110m hurdles was both an Olympic and world record (the more standard race at this time was the 120 yard hurdle, in which Thompson also held the world record at 14.4 seconds).

- Interestingly, gold medal boxing champion Bert Schneider also represented Canada, even though he was born in Cleveland and had retained his American citizenship. As an infant, Schneider had moved to Montreal and became part of the Montreal boxing community early on. He won the Canadian trials, and after defeating an American in the semi-finals, won his gold in a final match that went into an extra round.

George Hodgson, 1912

Hockey Gold

In 1920, Canada was invited to send what it believed was an Olympic hockey team. It was an Olympic year, the request came from the IOC, and the competition was to be played in the Olympic city of Antwerp. Figure skaters were also invited to compete. At the time, the Winnipeg Falcons had just won the Allan Cup for the Senior Amateur Hockey Championship in Canada, so they were asked to go. During the tournament the Falcons demonstrated their clear superiority by soundly defeating all opponents. They beat the USA, Sweden and Czechoslovakia by a combined score of 28-1! When the players received their medals, they also received a scroll stating these were "the first Winter Olympic Games." Yet, somehow no official word came that these were in fact the first winter games. Then, a full five years later in 1925, IOC officials retroactively made the 1924 Chamonix "International Sport Week" the first Olympic Winter Games. It took years, but eventually the Falcons were recognized as official Olympic Champions, but for the 1920 summer Games.

1924

- **Paris, France** — For the first time in the century, Canada did not win an Olympic gold medal, and earned no track and field medals at all. Canadians did get three silver and one bronze medals in other events and received a number of fourth and fifth place finishes.

- *"The Olympic Games are attended by the world's best athletes and judged by the world's worst officials,"* commented Judge J.A. Jackson of Lethbridge, Alberta, after witnessing an apparent injustice to Regina's Jim Trifunov in wrestling. Trifunov was considered a strong contender for a medal, perhaps even the gold. In a preliminary match, though, he apparently out-classed his opponent only to hear that he had been disqualified retroactively by the referee for a "rolling fall." The rules of the day specifically stated that "a rolling fall shall NOT count." There was no appealing a referee's decision and Trifunov was eliminated.

Earl Thompson, 1920

Wrestler Jim Trifunov, 1924

Ethel Catherwood, 1928

1928

- **Amsterdam, The Netherlands** — "The Matchless Six." Once in a while it happens. The six Canadian women who made the trip to Holland performed so well that the small team out-pointed much larger teams to win the unofficial Track Championship at the Games. Ethel Catherwood of Saskatoon won the high jump, and but for a judging error likely could have set a world record. Myrtle Cook was expected to challenge for the 100m gold, but two false starts in the final had her eliminated. Her two teammates, Fanny "Bobbie" Rosenfeld and Ethel Smith, though won silver and bronze in the 100m. Many believed that Rosenfeld actually crossed the line first, but a protest went nowhere. These three, plus sprinter Florence Bell, joined forces to win the 4x100m relay. The team of only six, then, ended up earning two first, two seconds, and one each of third, fourth and fifth places to lead the world.

Myrtle Cook, 1928

- The men's team also enjoyed success. The 100m and 200m finals each had two Canadians running and the 400m final included three. Jimmy Ball of Winnipeg earned a silver in the 400m, narrowly missing the gold.

- The star of the games was no doubt the 100m and 200m champion, Percy Williams from Vancouver. The Manager of the Canadian track team later reported:

  "The finalists in order of stations at the starting mark were: Wycoff, United States; Macallister, United States; London, Great Britain; Williams, Canada; Legg, South Africa. On the first attempt, Legg, with a reputation for flying starts, broke ahead of the gun. On the second attempt, Wycoff was the offender. The third time, the field was away in perfect alignment, with Williams the first to show in front. His effort from the 50m mark, was so determined that he was able to win decisively by almost 3 feet in 10.8 seconds. [The time was so fast, that by 1936 Games it was not beaten, but only equalled by the great and more famed Jesse Owens from the USA] Williams has rare courage and perfect control over his emotions. He is gifted with determination that is marked at all times, possessing a driving finish which was the most powerful of any sprinter competing in Amsterdam."

  A short while after his Olympic victory, Williams and a friend noticed a large gathering outside his hotel. Williams recalled: *"We joined the mob. Looking over their shoulders I asked a person in front of me why they were there and he said 'We're waiting for the Canadian runner Williams to come out of the hotel.' I didn't tell him who I was. I stood around waiting too, and talking to the people — it was much more fun."*

- Canada also sent some non-track athletes to Amsterdam: Don Stockton from Montreal won a silver in middleweight wrestling; Flagbearer Joe Wright Jr. and Jack Guest teamed up to win a silver in the double sculls; and the crew from the Argonaut Rowing Club in Toronto won a silver in the Men's eights. Bronze medals went to the 1600m swim relay team, Jim Trifunov and Maurice Letchford in wrestling, and welterweight boxer Ray Smilie from Toronto.

- In 1928 Bob Pearce was still representing Australia in the Olympics, but he would later immigrate to Canada to shine for his new country in rowing. In Amsterdam he had an interesting twist of events en route to a gold medal in the single sculls:

  "I had beaten a German and a Dane in earlier heats and I was racing a Frenchman, when I heard wild roars from the crowd along the bank of the canal. As I glanced, I could see some spectators vigorously pointing to something behind me. I peeked over one shoulder and what I saw I didn't like, for a family of ducks, in a single file, were paddling slowly from shore to shore. It's funny now, but it wasn't at the time, for I had to lean on my oars and wait for a clear course; and all the while my opponent was pulling ahead into a five-lengths lead."

  Pearce went on to win not only that race, but the Olympic final as well.

1928 4 x 100m sprint relay Olympic Champions — Canada.

Single sculls champion, Australian Bob Pearce, 1928.

Although women's basketball did not gain official Olympic status until 1976 in Montreal, the Edmonton Grads went undefeated in Exhibitions at the Olympic Games in Paris, Amsterdam, Los Angeles and Berlin.

1932

- **Los Angeles, USA** — This was the first year for an Olympic Village that housed all the athletes at the Games. Hollywood met the sports world, and seemed quite interested in the Canadians. During the Games, movie star Mary Pickford and her husband Douglas Fairbanks hosted the Canadians at their estate. Later, 400m relay bronze medallists Ray Lewis and Phil Edwards noted an interesting twist: "During the competition there was a lull in the action, and we went down to a box where the movie stars were sitting and asked for their autographs. When they heard we were from Canada they asked for ours. So I signed for Gary Cooper!"

- Duncan McNaughton was born in Cornwall, Ontario and early on moved with his family to Vancouver. He eventually accepted an athletic scholarship at the University of Southern California in LA This would prove fortuitous, for if he had lived elsewhere he may never have gone to the Olympics. He had not participated in the Canadian trials and was at first not allowed on the team. After pestering the Canadian Olympic officials, both in letters and finally in person when the team arrived in LA, McNaughton was finally allowed to compete. He stated:

  "I'd been disqualified for diving over the bar in the 1930 British Empire Games in Hamilton and a lot of Canadian officials weren't too happy with me. Anyway, they told me I'd have to meet the Canadian standard of six feet two inches to qualify for the Olympic team. I thought this was a little ridiculous as I'd been clearing that height all year in competition and so I told them to stuff it … In any case, I didn't know until the day before the Olympic event whether I'd be in the high jump or not."

Edmonton Grads, 1932

It was a good thing too. After a jump-off, McNaughton won Canada's only men's gold medal in high jumping of the century. (Ethel Catherwood won Canada's only women's gold in 1928.)

- Toronto's Horace "Lefty" Gwynne was "a jockey in real life" who had taken up boxing with his six-year old brother when he was but four. In LA Gwynne did not study the other boxers and did not even look to see who he was fighting until arriving at the arena for the bout. Lefty won the gold medal in the bantamweight handily, and returned to Toronto an Olympic hero. After a civic celebration in which the Mayor gave him a watch, Gwynne came right out and said: "thanks…but can I have a job." The Mayor apparently laughed. Gwynne fought professionally until 1939, but never worked for the City of Toronto.

- Hilda Strike officially came in second in the women's 100m final in LA. Years later it was confirmed that the winner of the race, Poland's Stella Walsh, was in fact anatomically a man.

- Famous sculptor and physical education professor, R. Tait McKenzie won a gold medal in the "Medals and Reliefs" section of the Olympic Art Competition for his distinguished work "Shield of the Athletes."

- Phil Edwards won more Olympic medals than any Canadian during the century. In 1932, he won his second, third and fourth of five career bronze medals. In LA Edwards won bronzes in the 800m, 1500m and the 4 x 400m relay.

Horace "Lefty" Gwynne, 1932

Duncan McNaughton, 1932

1936

- **Berlin, Germany** — This was the first year of the Olympic Torch Relay, which went from the site of the ceremonial lighting of the torch in Olympia, Greece to the start of the Opening Ceremonies. These Games were also held under the ever-darkening shadow of Nazi rule in Germany. Up until this time the athletes of the world would march around the stadium, dipping their country's flag (except the USA) to the head of state while offering the Olympic salute. The salute would cause much consternation to many athletes, since it so closely resembled the Nazi salute. Many countries opted against the salute; Canada was one of the last countries to ever do the salute, as it was banned after these Games. Flagbearer Jim Worrall noted *"we talked about not doing it, but in the end we decided that it would be best to be polite, to do what is in the laws of the time, and to do the salute. We really did not think much about it afterwards."*

- Canada won only a single gold medal at the Games, earned by canoeist Francis Amyot in the 1000m. In the final, Amyot forced a fast pace, trying to burn out his Czech challenger. It worked for the first 500 metres, but then Amyot was caught and even slightly passed. It was not he who faltered, however, but the Czech. Amyot caught him and took the lead for good with 50 metres to go — to earn a decisive victory.

- Although Canada earned but one gold, we still managed some other memories to treasure: middle distance runner Phil Edwards earned his fifth Olympic bronze medal, a Canadian record that would last the century; John Loaring got a silver medal in the 400m hurdles in only his second try in the event; the women's 4x100m relay team received a bronze after the leading German team dropped their baton; Betty Taylor surged to a bronze medal in the women's 80m hurdles; and in welterweight wrestling, Joe Schleimer also earned a bronze. Coming sixth in the pole vault was future Toronto Maple Leaf Syl Apps.

- In front of both the Canadian inventor of basketball James Naismith, and Pierre de Coubertin, father of the modern Olympic Games, the Canadian men's basketball team won the silver medal in the inaugural basketball competitions. It would be the only medal for a Canadian basketball team in the century. The team was made up mostly of players from the University of Windsor, with support from a few BC players. All games were played outdoors, including the final against the USA on a court wet from a recent rain.

- The Edmonton Grads again won the women's basketball exhibition, also in front of both Naismith and de Coubertin, following an undefeated nine-game exhibition tour of Europe.

1948

- **London, England** — Two Olympics cancelled because of WW II did nothing but increase the desire of athletes to continue friendly competitions in the athletic arena. War ravaged London provided an exceptional backdrop to begin the Games anew. Crowds flocked to the events and Britons everywhere welcomed the world to their Games.

- The Olympic motto says "The important thing is not to win, but to take part." For the next few Games, Canada upheld this, always sending "large teams with beautiful uniforms," that didn't win nearly as many medals as previous teams had. In 1948, Canada earned but three medals: a silver by Doug Bennett in the C-1 1000m canoe, a bronze by Norm Lane in the C-1 10,000m canoe, and another bronze by the women's 4x100m relay team. To quote Henry Roxborough:

"This summary indicates that Canada's 1948 Summer Olympic team was one of Canada's poorest. There was no Williams, Edwards or Wilson to stir the native pride, and not once did the Canadian ensign wave from Wembley's central staff. And yet, to illustrate the power of statistics, no fewer than 27 Canadians returned from the London Games with diplomas signifying that in some event they had placed in the top six."

1936 Olympic Track Team

George Généreux, 1952

1952

- **Helsinki, Finland** — Canada's 1952 Chef de Mission noted in his final report: "The results achieved by Canada's athletes were disappointing, and it was obvious that many of them were not really good enough for the class of competition encountered." Nonetheless, Canada did send a team of 113 competitors.

- A 17-year old high school student from Saskatoon provided Canada with its only gold medal in Helsinki, and its first summer gold since 1936. George Généreux won the Olympic clay-pigeon shooting title during a two-day competition. Trailing after the first day, Genereux held firm the second day to record 97 "kills" and outscore the leaders over the two days. Prior to the Games, Genereux was asked what score he would need to win the event, and he remarked "192." His winning two-day total was just that.

- Gilmour Boa must have the record for coming the closest to winning an Olympic medal without actually receiving one. In Helsinki, Boa competed in the prone small-bore rifle event. Two shooters achieved a perfect score of 400. Boa and an American rival came close, each scoring 399. Rather than award a second bronze medal, the judges looked more closely at the inner rings of the shooter's targets, and Boa was declared fourth. Gerald Gratton received a-well-earned silver in the middleweight weightlifting competition, having equalled the previous Olympic record only to get silver behind a new Olympic and World record. Also, Don Hawgood and Ken Lane of Toronto joined up in their canoe to get another silver for Canada in 10,000m C-2 event.

1956

- **Melbourne, Australia** — Actually, the first events of the 1956 Olympics took place in Stockholm, rather than Melbourne, with Canada winning a bronze in the three-day equestrian event. (Equestrian events were held in advance in Europe because the long quarantine period required at the time for horses entering Australia made it logistically impossible to hold the events Down Under.) The course for the cross-country event was slippery, severe and dangerous, and many horses did not make it around; many others committed many jumping faults. Somehow, though, the Canadians came through with the

Gerald Ouellette and Gilmour Boa, 1956

least number of faults and on the last day vaulted from seventh to third to win the bronze.

- Canada received a gold in rowing, specifically in the coxless fours (Archie McKinnon, Lorne Loomer, Walter D'Hondt, Don Arnold). The crew from UBC had only rowed for a year, and in the final they were so nervous that they nearly missed the water on their first stroke. They recovered nicely, however, and caught the leaders by the halfway mark, pulling ahead to a five-length victory.

- The gold-medal fours were actually spares for the eights, also from UBC. The eights did what no Canadian crew had done before and came home with an Olympic medal, a silver, narrowly missing the gold behind the world champion German crew.

- After a poor performance in the three-position small-bore event, Windsor's Gerald Ouellette and his teammate Gilmour Boa decided they would both use Boa's rifle in the prone competition. This meant, though, that they would have to split the 2 1/2 hour time limit between them. Boa went first, and coached by Ouellette tied his world record of 598 for an early lead in the contest. Then, with only half the time remaining, Ouellette went, coached by Boa. Encouraged to take a couple of breaks to calm his nerves, Ouellette shot 60 straight bull's eyes for a perfect score of 600 to win the gold medal. (It was not deemed a world record, however, because afterwards the course was found to be about 1.5 metres short). Boa ended up with the bronze.

- On the same day the shooters were setting their sights on medals, so too was diver Irene MacDonald of Hamilton. Heading into the final dives, MacDonald was in second

place, but she had aggravated a previous elbow injury. She balked on her second of six final dives and it cost her several points. It did not look good. But then she went to the dressing room, hurriedly got her elbow "frozen," and returned to perform four solid dives. She won Canada's first diving Olympic medal ever — a bronze.

1960

- **Rome, Italy** — These were disappointing Games for Canada, recording its worst medal-count of the century, with a solitary silver in men's eights rowing. The UBC crew had only rowed together for four months, but the crew was made up of three of the 1956 gold medal fours and one member of the eights silver crew. Under the guiding hand of coach Frank Read, the team came together, worked hard, and battled Germany back-and-forth right to the finish.

- Richard Pound was then a young student in Montreal and made it to the finals of the 100m freestyle, where he finished sixth. Pound also earned points in the relay swim — but his top Olympic marks would come later as an IOC Executive Board member for the last 20 years of the century. Mary Stewart of Vancouver would also reach the final of her 100m swim event, but would not match her times recorded before the Games. Perhaps Canada's biggest disappointment was 100m sprinter Harry Jerome. In the Olympic trials Jerome had tied the world record of 10.0 seconds and was a clear favourite for a medal in Rome. In the semi-finals, though, Jerome was leading by a good margin when he sustained a serious thigh injury, and was eliminated.

A perfect 600 for Gerald Ouellette, 1956

George Hungerford, left, and Roger Jackson, 1964

1964

- **Tokyo, Japan** — Canada's lone gold medal in Tokyo came from an unexpected source. George Hungerford and Roger Jackson had never rowed together before they went to Tokyo, and neither was initially all that pleased to be put in the coxless pairs boat. Both were reserves for the more popular, featured, eights crew from the UBC. Hungerford was actually on the crew, but lost his seat when he contracted mononucleosis in the months leading up to the Games. Ironically, the eights never made it to the final, but the new coxless pairs team did. The pair won their heat and were fortunate to draw a lane in the final near the side of the course, close to a partial breakwater. From there, the pair jumped to an early lead and held on to win by about one-half of a second over a Dutch pair. So unexpected was the result that no Canadian media were there to cover the race.

- Harry Jerome rebounded from his 1960 injury to again be one of the world's fastest men in 1964. In Tokyo he was the only person to qualify for the finals in both the 100m and the 200m. Jerome came close to the world record in the 200m heats, but his form didn't quite hold up in the final, where he placed fourth. In the 100m final, though, Jerome's form was fine and fast and he won the bronze behind Bob Hayes of the US, who tied the world record of 10.0 seconds in the race — a record held by Jerome.

- Toronto's Bill Crothers was not really expected to challenge for a medal in Tokyo; his time in the 800m was about 4 seconds slower than the world record held by Peter Snell. But, in the final, Crothers attempted to stay with favourite Snell who broke from the pack on the backstretch on the final lap. Using a finishing kick even he wasn't sure he had, Crothers passed two runners in the final 100m to break the old Olympic record, claim a silver for Canada just a stride back of Snell, and make a lifelong memory for Canadians.

- Judo is an historic sport, with deep roots in Japan, so it was appropriate it made its Olympic debut in Tokyo. What was surprising to the Japanese, however, was that a Canadian would win the heavyweight silver medal. Doug Rogers defeated a Taiwanese in the first round, a Mexican in the second and a Soviet in round three. In the final he met an old foe, the great Onokuma of Japan. The contest went the full time limit and in a close decision, Rogers was given the silver.

1968

- **Mexico City, Mexico** — Amid the ceremony and the politics of the 1968 Mexico Games, the Canadians attracted comparatively little attention. Canada again walked away with a small scattering of medals, but counted a number of top finishes, including those by Gerald Ouellette in small-bore rifle, Abby Hoffman in the 800m, Harry Jerome in the 100m sprints, Andy Boychuk in the marathon, and Beverly Boys in diving.

- Harry Jerome again threatened for a 100m medal, making the finals for the second Games in a row. His bronze in 1964 was his lone Olympic medal, but ever since he first set a world record at 19, he was always in the finals of any field of top-runners. In Mexico, Jerome ran the final just .1 second slower than he had nine years earlier, recording a 10.1. That year though, 10.0 won the gold — and Jerome's one-tenth of a second dropped him back to seventh. Only two tenths of a second separated the world's top eight runners.

- Swimming seemed to be on the rise for Canada in the Mexico City Games. Ralph Hutton was the only swim competitor to qualify for the freestyle finals in each the 200, 400 and 1,500m races. He won the silver in the 400m.

Harry Jerome, 1964

1968

Canada's Mighty Mouse, Elaine Tanner, was expected to do well in the pool in Mexico, and she did — just not as well as she had planned. Tanner was a world record holder and had success in both the recent Pan American and Commonwealth Games. She was expecting at least one gold medal, more likely two or three. But, a poorly organized training camp that did not include her personal coach caused her to be a bit unprepared. She entered the waters the favourite in each race, and came away with silver medals in each of the 100m and 200m backstrokes and a bronze in the women's 400m relay. It should have been a time of rejoicing, but the country's expectations weighed heavily on a 17-year old girl, and Tanner came away disappointed she did not win gold. Tanner mused after the Games: "Usually, before a race you're concentrating on strategy, the other swimmers, the race. But at Mexico all I could think about was the 20 million people who were expecting me to win."

1972

- **Munich, West Germany** — Pomp and ceremony have long been associated with the Games, for they bring out a sense of tradition, of timeliness and an opportunity for the host nation to showcase itself. Munich had promised all this and more; until the unthinkable happened. The Games proceeded as expected in the arena, and then … a shooting, a murder, and 17 people dead in the Munich Massacre. Canada played no role in this darkest moment in Olympic history, except as a witness to the terrorist acts. The Games continued, but would never be the same again.

- According to Henry Roxborough, *"Our summer team in 1972 are best remembered for being among those present."* These were not our best Games in the medal count, but we did have some highlights: in Track and Field, Abby Hoffman again advanced to the 800m finals, the only track person to reach that stage this year; Bruce Simpson achieved a fifth place in the pole vault; in high jumping, both men (John Beers and John Hawkins) made the top 10, as did Debbie Brill (eighth) in the women's event. Statistically in track and field, though, our combined team placed 26th. Canada fared better in the water events, winning a bronze in the soling class yachting event and receiving two silver and two bronze in swimming. Canada fared reasonably in other disciplines as well, just not getting medals: Doug Rogers earned a fourth and seventh in two judo events; the equestrians received two sixth place finishes; Carroll Morgan placed fifth in the super heavyweight boxing competition; Don Jackson was sixth in archery and John Primrose was seventh in trap shooting. Overall, in the unofficial medal count, Canada placed 27th.

- **Swimming.** The Canadian men's and women's teams each received two medals in the pool. Bruce Robertson swam his 100m butterfly faster than anyone had in 1968, but in 1972 he was facing Mark Spitz who had an even faster time, leaving Robertson with a silver. The men's 4x100m, medley relay of Robertson, Bob Kasting, Erik Fish and Bill Mahoney took the bronze in a time 2.5 seconds faster than the winning time in Mexico. Leslie Cliff earned a silver in the 400m women's medley and came fifth in the 200m. Finally, Donna-Marie Gurr won a bronze medal in the 200m backstroke event.

Bruce Robertson, 1972

1976 Montreal

1976

MONTREAL, CANADA

As an athlete, Abby Hoffman represented Canada at many international sporting events, winning her share of 800m races and consistently ranking in the top 10 in the world for several years. She ended her long career in Montreal. An Olympic medal may have eluded her, but she experienced an unique Olympic moment, which all Canada shared July 17, 1976. In front of 70,000 spectators, and a television audience of about 1 billion, some 8,000 athletes marched into Olympic Stadium in Montreal for the first Olympic Games hosted in Canada. As Olympic tradition dictates, the host nation came last. Hoffman, taking the honour of carrying Canada's Maple Leaf Flag, came in first, followed closely by the 414 Canadian team members. Dressed in brilliant red and white, the team brought the whole Olympic Stadium to its feet in a collective cheer. Then the marchers stopped in front of the royal box and Queen Elizabeth II and the crowd grew hushed. Almost in unison, Hoffman dipped Canada's flag toward its head of state, the team turned their heads to the right, and waved like mad. The noise was deafening. Canada would play host to the Olympics.

1976

- Coincidently and happily, Canada earned its first medal on the first day of hosting its first Olympics. The women's 4 x 100m medley relay swim team of Wendy Hogg, Robin Corsiglia, Susan Sloan and Anne Jardin swam to a bronze medal.

- Canada became the first nation to host an Olympic Games and not win a gold medal; the only one to do so in the century. (For good measure, Canada did not win an Olympic Winter gold in hosting the 1988 Winter Games either). Canada ended up with five silver and six bronze medals. Eight of the 11 medals were won by the swim team, and one each in equestrian (Michel Vaillancourt — silver), track (Greg Joy — silver) and canoeing (John Wood — silver).

- Nancy Garapick was the lone Canadian to win two individual medals in Montreal — getting bronzes in both the 100m and 200m backstroke events. Becky Smith won a 4 x 100m freestyle swim relay bronze and a silver in the 400m individual medley, and Anne Jardin won two swimming relay bronzes.

- It is interesting to note that one of the stars at the Montreal Olympic Games, the men's decathlon champion and World record holder Bruce Jenner, seemingly the typical all-American, was actually born in Montreal while his father was completing medical school at McGill University.

- Lucille Lessard of Loretteville Quebec won two women's world archery championships in 1974. She went on to place fifth at the Montreal Olympics — Canada's highest ranking at the Games in the century.

- Women's basketball became an official medal sport for the first time at the Montreal Olympic Games.

- Sue Holloway of Ottawa became the first Canadian to compete in the summer and winter Games in the same year. Sue was on the 1976 cross-country ski relay team in Innsbruck; when the summer came she jumped in a canoe to paddle for Canada in the C-2 competition in Montreal.

Michel Vaillancourt, 1976

1976

What makes a moment so memorable that it becomes etched in a country's collective memory? No one can know for sure, but when Greg Joy won a silver medal in the high jump in Montreal we all knew this was one such moment. Joy was not one of the favourites, but he was not a long shot either. The clear favourite was American Dwight Stones, the world record holder. Stones, however, hated jumping in wet conditions as it did not suit his fast-approach style. When he arrived at the Games, he noted that the planned retractable roof on the Olympic Stadium was not installed. He called the Olympic organizers "rude" for not finishing what they had planned. In translation, the French newspapers in Montreal classified his remarks to meaning "all French Canadians were rude." During the preliminary rounds, each time Stones stepped up, he was soundly booed. On the next day, Stones returned wearing a shirt reading "I love French Canadians." But the damage had been done and the enemy-of-the-day was an American. Then it started to rain, and Stones slipped down to a third place finish. This was enjoyed by the crowd, but not nearly as much as the fact that he was also beaten by a Canadian — Greg Joy. Joy was in contention all day and when he cleared 2.23m (7'3/4") to pass Dwight Stones for good, the jump seemed to have been made for the whole country. His gold medal hopes were dashed at the next height, but that day's silver medal became a Canadian golden moment — we beat the brash American, and we all watched.

Greg Joy, 1976

1984

- **Los Angeles, USA** — Another Games, more politics and another boycott of nations. This time Canada did go the Games, while a host of Soviet-bloc countries did not. Because many top athletes did not attend, Canadians likely ended up with more than their usual share of medals. Like 1980, though, it was not the fault of the athletes. The Canadians who won medals in LA earned them fairly — they earned more medals in fact, than any Canadian team in the 20th century. Canada ended up with: 10 golds, 18 silvers and 16 bronzes for an unprecedented 44 Olympic medals in one Games.

- Canada's first of 10 golds came in a thrilling, tie-breaking shoot-out in sport pistol on the first day of the Games. Until then-unknown Linda Thom of Ottawa defeated her American challenger and became an instant celebrity — at least during these Games.

- It was appropriate that Canada's flagbearer at these Games, Alex Baumann, would lead the swim team on its record setting ways. Baumann won his first gold by lowering his own world record in the 400m medley. Five days later he won his second gold of the Games, this time in the 200m medley.

- Victor Davis came close to his dream of a gold medal when he beat his previous world record in the 100m breaststroke, only to finish second. Not stopping there, three days later Davis charged to the lead in the 200m breaststroke, and held on to realize his dream, a world record and an Olympic gold

medal. Davis added his third medal of the Games when he led the 4x100m relay team to a silver.

- Another then-unknown Canadian stepped up to deliver her best as an Olympic performance, this time in the pool. Eighteen-year old Anne Ottenbrite swam away with three medals of her own — one each of gold, silver and bronze. She became the first-ever Canadian female to win a gold in the pool, doing so in the 200m breaststroke. She then earned a silver in the 100m breaststroke and helped the 4x100m medley relay team to a bronze.

- Canada's most thrilling silver may have come in the 190 km cycling road race. Fenwick Ontario's Steve Bauer and his American challenger, Alexi Grewal, pulled away from the pack during the later stages of the race. Dueling head-to-head for the last kilometres, the duo exchanged leads and headed into a last-gasp sprint for the gold, with Bauer winning the silver less than a "wheel" away from the gold.

- Expected to reach the final against American Frank Tate, light middleweight boxer Shawn O'Sullivan from Toronto's Cabbagetown gave it all he could and just might have won. In the second of three rounds in the championship bout, Tate was twice given a standing eight-count and somehow managed to win the round on four of the five judges' cards. Tate's gold medal announcement was met with a chorus of boos, but not by O'Sullivan: "It was an unfortunate decision. I dearly wish things had gone differently, but

they didn't, and there's no gain in crying over spilled milk." Interestingly, it had gone the other way for O'Sullivan in his semi-final bout against Christophe Tiozzo of France. The judges ruled it a 3-2 victory for Tiozzo, but after an automatic referral to an appeals jury, O'Sullivan was given the nod 4-1.

- The women's springboard was expected to be an American vs. Chinese showdown, but 20-year old Ste. Foy native Sylvie Bernier took home the Olympic gold instead. Having a history of not performing her best under pressure situations, Bernier refused to follow the results of the first rounds of dives, preferring to sit by the side of the pool listening to "Flashdance" on her headphones. It wasn't until after her final dive that her coach told her how close she was to the gold. Only one challenger was left to dive and a score of 70.0 would deprive Bernier of the gold. The American, Kelly McCormick, came close, scoring a 67.2, but not close enough — Sylvie Bernier became the Olympic champion.

- Canada's rowing eights crew took off as fast as it could, opening up an overwhelming lead, and hung on to win the gold by 10 feet.

- Grand Prairie native Willie de Wit, Canada's heavyweight boxing hope, had defeated his challenger in two previous bouts, once by knockout. This time, though, de Wit was defeated 5-0 on points in the final bout by Henry Hillman, who had narrowly won a very controversial semi-final match.

- The sport of rhythmic gymnastics made its Olympic debut in 1984, and Vancouverite Lori Fung stylishly hung on to claim the first-ever Olympic gold in the sport.

- Kayakers Hugh Fisher and Alwyn Morris knew each other well before the Games, and became forever entwined during them. Fisher and Morris combined to win the K-2 1000m event, then settled for a bronze in the K-2 500m final as well. Morris, a Mohawk from the Kanawake Reserve carried with him to each medal ceremony a decorated eagle feather given to him by a native Californian band, symbolizing a sharing of his victory with the native people of North America.

- Larry Cain took off in a flurry and left others in his wake en route to winning Olympic gold in the 500m C-1 canoe race in Los Angeles, the first canoe gold for Canada since Francis Amyot in 1936. Cain returned a short while later to paddle off with a silver in the C-1 1000m as well.

- Unofficial 1980 flagbearer Sue Holloway partially made up for her disappointment in not attending the Games in Moscow by teaming with Alexandra Barre to earn a silver medal in the K-2 500m canoe race. The two then joined with Barb Olmstead and Lucie Guay to win a bronze in the K-4 500m event.

- Sisters can work wonders together, as Laumanns Danielle and Silken teamed up to win a bronze medal in the double sculls. Silken, of course, would return in 1988, 1992 and 1996.

1980

Moscow, Soviet Union

The Olympics have often been politicized, regardless of the idealistic notions that the Games should rise above such antics. The validity of the decision could be debated, and certainly was at the time, but in 1980, Canada did not go to the Olympic Games for political reasons. 1980 became Canada's sporting moment that could have been. The Canadian Olympic Association held a reception in Toronto honouring those athletes who would have gone to Moscow, and even named paddler Sue Holloway as its flagbearer. Many great sporting moments took place in Moscow, but none of them were Canadian.

1976 Winter and Summer Olympian, Sue Holloway was selected as Canada's flag bearer for the boycotted 1980 Moscow Games.

1988

- **Seoul, Korea** — In the first Olympics spared from a major boycott since 1972, the Seoul Olympics proved a positive experience for Canada ... with one major exception.

- There were big expectations for "The Bens" — the horse Big Ben and the sprinter Ben Johnson — in Seoul. Big Ben and rider Ian Millar were the favourites to win the equestrian show jumping event, and most of Canada got caught up in the expectation. Unfortunately, it was not to be — the long overseas trip over had exhausted the star horse and he finished out of the medals. Canada, though, did win an equestrian bronze in the team dressage event.

- The other Ben had won a 100m sprint bronze in the 1984 LA Olympics, and followed that up with World Championship victories indoors and outdoors, in rain and shine. He and rival Carl Lewis of the US seemed to put the rest of the world's sprinters on hold and run their own races. On September 24, 1988, Ben Johnson was crowned the Olympic 100m champion, defeating Lewis in a world record time of 9.79 seconds. All of Canada rejoiced as one, in a way we had not done since Paul Henderson's last minute goal

against the Russians in 1972. We were proud, and happy. Then, on September 27, 1988, the world was told that Ben's post-race urine sample had tested positive. He was caught with the steroid stanozolol in his body — a clear contravention of the rules. On September 28, 1988, Canadian Chef de Mission Carol Anne Letheren retrieved Ben's gold medal, gave it to the IOC, who in turn presented it to the person who came second in the race, but was the first clean runner across the line, Carl Lewis.

- Victor Davis was disappointed in his individual results in the pool. The 1984 Olympic champion in the breaststroke finished out of the medals by less than a second. He was determined to go home with a medal, though, and led a young swim medley team that also included Tom Ponting, Mark Tewksbury and Sandy Goss. The team that on paper would have been expected to finish about sixth picked up a silver medal.

- Despite the Ben Johnson scandal, there was some success on the track for Canada. Dave Steen from Vancouver won the country's only decathlon medal of the century, finishing in third spot for a bronze medal, just 160 points out of first (but as he pointed out, "also 160

CSI/COA

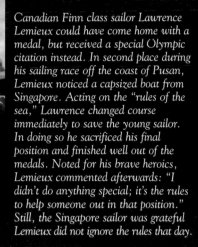

Canadian Finn class sailor Lawrence Lemieux could have come home with a medal, but received a special Olympic citation instead. In second place during his sailing race off the coast of Pusan, Lemieux noticed a capsized boat from Singapore. Acting on the "rules of the sea," Lawrence changed course immediately to save the young sailor. In doing so he sacrificed his final position and finished well out of the medals. Noted for his brave heroics, Lemieux commented afterwards: "I didn't do anything special; it's the rules to help someone out in that position." Still, the Singapore sailor was grateful Lemieux did not ignore the rules that day.

points out of sixth"). The two-day competition involved ten events in running, jumping and throwing. Dave was a top-six contender and, with solid efforts he could get a medal. He performed well under pressure, but he was still in eighth spot when the final event, the gruelling 1500m, took place. He was deemed such a long shot that Canadian television reporters at the Games were not at the event, and only a very small handful of other reporters may have been there. It didn't matter, as Steen beat out his friend and 1980 and 1984 champion

Daley Thomson of Britain with his best-ever 1500m, good enough for the Olympic bronze medal, and a run into the Canadian history books with Canada's first-ever Olympic decathlon medal.

- Carolyn Waldo became the first female Canadian to win two gold medals at an Olympic Games — she won the solo synchronized swimming event on September 30 (just three days after the world found out about Ben Johnson, which had caused morale and performances to plummet on the Canadian team), then teamed with partner Michelle Cameron to claim the duet gold on October 1.

- In Seoul, the future heavyweight boxing champion of the world was still competing as a Canadian, although he would win his world crown as a British citizen. Lennox Lewis was born in England, immigrated to Canada with his mother at 12, grew up and learned how to box in Kitchener, Ontario. He made the Olympic team easily in 1988, then defeated all comers in Seoul to claim the gold — Canada's first in boxing since 1932.

- Canada received a medal of each colour in boxing. To go with Lennox Lewis' gold in the heavyweight division, Toronto middleweight Egerton Marcus fought through a broken hand to win a silver, and light middleweight Ray Downey from Halifax earned a bronze.

CSI/COA

Dave Steen, 1988

1992

- **Barcelona, Spain** — Heading into the Barcelona Olympics, two clear favourites for gold came from Canada, both defending world champions: Sylvie Fréchette in synchronized swimming, and Silken Laumann in single sculls rowing. Neither came home from Spain with gold, but both came away with spirit, Canadian support, empathy, and Olympic honours. Ten weeks prior to the Games, Laumann was severely injured when a German boat slammed into her in a warm-up accident, crushing her right leg. Told she would not be able to compete, Silken found the resolve to train enough to make the team, then to make the finals, then to row to a bronze medal. The medal was bronze, but the effort golden. Meanwhile, Fréchette underwent two horrid experiences in the space of two weeks. First, on the eve of her departure for Spain, Fréchette's fiancé committed suicide. Personally distraught, Sylvie decided to go to Spain anyway and try to recover. Then, during the compulsory figures portion of the competition, a

Brazilian judge mis-inputted her score (entering 8.7 instead of 9.7), an error which cost Fréchette the gold medal. She went home with a silver. Sixteen months after returning home, thanks to the efforts of a number of officials, Sylvie Fréchette's gold-medal performance was finally recognized. Before a standing ovation in the Montreal Forum, IOC member Richard Pound retroactively awarded Fréchette a gold medal.

Saturday, October 2, 1993 *Sylvie strikes Gold! MONTREAL (CP) — Sylvie Fréchette will leave a golden legacy. The International Swimming Federation (FINA) decided yesterday to recommend that the International Olympic Committee give Fréchette a gold medal after a judging mistake cost her one at the 1992 Barcelona Olympics. "What this means most to me is that 25 or 50 years from now, it would have said, Sylvie Fréchette silver medal and now it will say gold," the 26-year-old synchronized swimmer said. The move will result in two solo synchronized swimming gold medallists from Barcelona. Kristen Babb-Sprague, wife of Blue Jays third baseman Ed Sprague, will keep the medal she won. Fréchette will get one of her own. FINA's decision came as a result of an appeal launched by the Canadian Olympic Association. Although the swimming federation can only make a recommendation to the IOC, Canadian officials called IOC approval "a virtual certainty." There was no immediate word on when the IOC would make its ruling. Dick Pound, a Canadian lawyer and the IOC member who led the COA's 14-month effort to review the situation, said that the*

Mark McKoy, 1992

decision "has done more than any single action I can imagine to show that FINA really has the best interest of athletes at heart. "It took wisdom and courage to review the matter again when it might have been easier to sweep it under the carpet."

1992

- Hurdler Mark McKoy was part of the tainted Olympics of Seoul, but that did not tarnish his efforts in Barcelona in 1992. After serving a two-year suspension because of steroid use in the 1980s, McKoy accepted an invitation from friend Colin Jackson of Wales to train in Britain. The two agreed not to compete against each other until Barcelona, by which time Jackson had become the clear favourite for gold. Jackson showed well in the preliminaries, but the final belonged to McKoy, who led from start to finish and lay to rest any lingering doubts from Seoul. McKoy was an Olympic champion. It was Canada's first track and field gold since Duncan McNaughton's high jump gold in 1932, and the first running gold since Percy Williams in 1928. *"Born in Guyana, McKoy lived in England, attended university in the United States, married a German, and, after the Olympics, became an Austrian citizen. But on the day he became an Olympic champion, Mark McKoy literally wrapped himself in the Canadian flag."* That flag, given to Mark at the end of his race, came from a 20-year old Canadian named Michael Cantelon, attending the Barcelona Olympic Youth Camp.

- The men's rowing eights had the closest rowing final of the century. Germany was the pre-race favourite, having won the three previous world championships, but did not perform their best in Barcelona and settled for a bronze. That left Canada and Romania fighting for the top spot. The Romanians took the early lead and

held it for the first half of the race. The Germans faded, but the Canadians seemed to get even stronger. Nearing the three quarter mark of the race, the Canadian crew surged into the lead only to lose it again to the Romanian eight. Back and forth the lead went until the final 100 metres, with Canada narrowly in the lead. At the finish line, it remained Canada in first, by less than a foot.

- The rowing competitions took place outside Barcelona in a town called Banyoles. There Canadian rowing achieved its greatest accomplishment of the century, netting four gold medals to go with Silken Laumann's bronze. Marnie McBean and Kathleen Heddle each earned two gold medals, one in the pairs event with each other, the other in the women's eights crew. Heddle and McBean would go on to more gold in 1996.

- Ben Johnson had sat out his two-year suspension from the 1988 Olympics and made the 100m team again, but this time could only find enough speed to make the semi-finals, where he received lots of media coverage, but still came last in his heat. Bruny Surin, though, became the next speeding star from Canada, making the finals of the 100m and ending up in fourth.

- Swimmer Mark Tewksbury overcame a typically slow start in the 100m backstroke final, to edge out his American rival in a new Olympic record time and claim a gold medal, to go with his silver in the 1988 relay and a bronze with the 1992 relay squad.

- Other Barcelona highlights included Nicolas Gill earning a silver in Judo, Guillaume Leblanc's silver in the 20km race walk, Angela Chalmers racing to a bronze in the women's 3000m, and Graham Hood becoming the first Canadian since 1936 to reach the final of the 1500m.

Sylvie Fréchette, 1992

Mark McKoy, 1992

1996

- **Atlanta, USA** — The partially boycotted Games of 1984 provided Canada with its greatest medal haul in terms of quantity, but the Olympic Centennial Games in 1996 provided the best combination of quantity and quality of the century. Canada ended the Games with its second best ever medal take — 22 medals, three gold, 11 silver, eight bronze — against a record number of competitors and participating countries.

- Donovan Bailey erased any memory of 1988 Ben Johnson in winning the 100m final, becoming not only the fastest man in the world but also the world record holder. In an event long cherished and owned by the Americans, Bailey led Canadian pride in capturing the "fastest man" title in the Americans' own backyard.

CSI/COA

Donovan Bailey, 1996

CSI/COA

Silken Laumann, 1992

- The only regret the men's 4x100m relay team had after winning the Olympic gold medal was in celebrating a bit early and not setting a world record. Robert Esmie started the race and followed the message he had shaved on his head, "Blast Off." Glenroy Gilbert took the baton second and raced a personal best down the backstretch, where he handed it to a waiting Bruny Surin. Surin had the reputation as being able to run the corners best, and when he handed the baton to anchor Donovan Bailey, Canada was in the lead to stay. In a state of exhilaration, Bailey raised his arms in celebration with about 15m still to run. They won the gold but missed the world record by .29 of a second.

- Kathleen Heddle and Marnie McBean earned their third career gold medal in Atlanta — the most Olympic golds by any Canadian in the century. (The pair had won gold in Barcelona in pairs and as part of the women's eight crew.) This time in double sculls (each pulling on two oars), Heddle and McBean took an early lead and held it throughout the race, after challenges by both the Chinese and Dutch teams. In the end it was a clear win, but as McBean observed "I felt like we were just hanging on out there."

- This time Silken Laumann came to the Games in top shape. She put in a valiant effort in the single sculls, dueling with eventual winner Ekaterina Khodotovich of Belarus throughout the race, but finally coming in second by two seconds. "No regrets" said Silken, who then retired from the sport that had caused her so much happiness and anguish over the years. For Derek Porter it was different. He fought a hard race against Xeno Mueller of Switzerland and was visibly shocked when his competitor survived the ordeal to win the gold. Porter's silver, as close as it was to gold, resulted in him staying in the sport for four more years and trying for gold again in Sydney. He did not get it.

Kathleen Heddle, left, and Marnie McBean, 1992-1996

- Marianne Limpert claimed a medal, in her case a silver, when another Canadian favourite faltered. Hamilton's Joanne Malar was expected to do well in the women's individual medley swimming events. But it was Limpert, from Fredericton, who posted her personal best time in the 200m final and received a silver behind Ireland's Michelle Smith. Meanwhile, Calgarian Curtis Myden was working on his own medley success. He set a Canadian 400m individual medley record in winning a bronze medal, then turned around to win another bronze and set a Canadian record in the 200m final as well.

- In the women's 100km cycling road race, Clara Hughes from Winnipeg sidestepped a crash that ended the day for one of the favourites, Ottawa's Linda Jackson, then fought off the expected heat and unexpected mid-race rain to claim a bronze medal. In rowing, Canada sent 10 boats to the Games, eight of which made the finals and none of which finished lower than seventh.

In addition to Laumann, Heddle & McBean, and Porter, the women's quads won bronze, the men's lightweight fours earned a silver and the women's eights crew won a surprise silver medal. In the individual kayak, Caroline Brunet showed she was a force to reckon with in powering her way to a silver medal in the K-1 500m race. Brian Walton from Vancouver displayed courage and motivation in coming from far behind in the cycling points race (160 laps of the velodrome) to earn a silver medal. Walton's performance inspired Thunder Bay native Curt Harnett to his third Olympic medal, this one a bronze in the individual sprint event. "Walton's performance was the most awesome thing I've ever seen," said Harnett afterwards. Canada earned medals in two new sports as well: Torontonians John Child and Mark Heese teamed up in beach volleyball to win a bronze and Alison Sydor from Vancouver won a silver in the mountain bike race.

CSI/COA

2000

- **Sydney, Australia** — Daniel Nestor and Sebastian Lareau were seeded fourth in the Olympic doubles tennis tournament. Playing together all year on the professional tennis tour prepared them to meet the world's number one ranked tandem, local favourites Mark Woodforde and Todd Woodbridge. The Canadians beat the most successful doubles team of all-time, on their own court in front of very partisan Australian fans, to win the Olympic gold medal, Canada's only tennis medal of the century.

- The new sport of triathlon made its first appearance in Sydney. A day after athletic disaster hit Canadian medal hopefuls Carol Montgomery and Sharon Donnelly in the women's triathlon, Simon Whitfield gave a tremendous sprint in the final 300 metres of the men's event to overtake the leader and win the gold medal. He was the country's first gold medallist in Sydney, and his teammates voted him to be the flagbearer for the closing ceremonies — the final Canadian Olympic flagbearer of the century.

- The gold medal somehow eluded Caroline Brunet, Canada's "queen of kayaking," again. After winning a silver medal in Atlanta in 1996, Brunet decided to train for four more years to reach the top of her profession. She did that, becoming the world champion in 1998 and 1999. Even though the wind-delayed race day conditions in Sydney were less than ideal, Brunet hung tough and earned her second Olympic silver.

- Nicolas Gill of Montreal was a medal favourite heading into Sydney, and most likely was the number 2 judoka in the world. He bettered his bronze medal in 1996, losing only to world number one Kosei Inoue of Japan in the Sydney final to earn an Olympic silver medal.

- Over the last 40 years of the century our rowing team earned a reputation for Olympic excellence. In Sydney, that excellence was tested, and just when it looked like we might be left out of the medals for the first time in a long while, the women's eights came through the waters to earn an Olympic bronze. In the crew were the 1999 coxless pairs world champions, Emma Robinson and Theresa Luke, who had finished a heart breaking fourth the day before.

Caroline Brunet

- Individual medley swimmer Marianne Limpert set a new Canadian record in the 200m individual medley, just missing the podium and finishing fourth in the finals. Limpert also set the 200m freestyle Canadian record, swimming leadoff for the 4x200m freestyle relay.

- Dominique Bosshart won a bronze medal in the over-67kg taekwondo category, winning her bronze medal bout 11-8. Perhaps her best bout, though, was her 9-8 victory over Adriana Carmona of Venezuela, whom she had never beaten before.

- Swimmer Curtis Myden of Calgary broke his own Canadian record in the 400m individual medley, and earned his third Olympic bronze. (He won two in Atlanta.)

- Swimming a routine depicting all of the Olympic sports, the synchronized swim team earned a bronze medal, behind Russia and Japan.

- Kevin Sullivan was the first North American since 1988 to finish as high as fifth in the Olympic 1500m final, and first Canadian since Phil Edward's bronze medal in 1932 to reach that level.

- Canada's men's basketball team teased us all in 2000. Lightly regarded before the Games, the team's 5-2 record did not do justice to its eventual seventh-place finish. Led by Steve Nash, the tournament assist leader averaging 6.9 a game, the Canadians defeated the host Australia team and the defending world champions from Yugoslavia in round robin play. In the quarterfinal, though, the Canadians came up empty against the French team and despite their good record were eliminated from the medals.

- Canoeist Steve Giles from Nova Scotia achieved his life long goal of making the Olympic podium, earning a bronze medal in the C-1 1000m event.

- Diver Anne Montminy was in her third Olympic Games. She desperately wanted to win a medal, and she did so twice. She earned her first medal, a bronze, in the women's 10m-platform event, and later won her second teaming up with Emilie Heymans to win a silver in the new 10m synchronized diving event. Montminy was Canada's only double medallist in Sydney.

Associated Press AP

Simon Whitfield

CSI/COA

2000

Sydney, Australia

Daniel Igali was born in Nigeria, but became a world champion wrestler after immigrating to Canada. Going to Sydney as the world champion must have added some pressures on the young man, but on the final day of Olympic competition, and after several close and tension filled matches, he overcame the pressures to win Canada's only wrestling gold medal of the century. So elated was Igali after his victory, he knelt and kissed the Canadian flag he had draped on the mat, providing Canadians with one of the most memorable moments of the Games.

Canada Goes to the

1924: Chamonix, France

Team: 12
1 Gold, 0 Silver, 0 Bronze = 1 Medal
Flagbearer: Ernie Collett, Hockey

Medal	Medallists	Sport	Event
Gold	Toronto Granites: Jack Cameron; Ernie Collett; Albert McCaffery; Harold McMunn; Duncan Munro; W. Beattie Ramsay; Cyril Slater; Reg Smith; Harry Watson	Hockey	Men's

1928: St. Moritz, Switzerland

Team: 25
1 Gold, 0 Silver, 0 Bronze = 1 Medal
Flagbearer: John Porter, Hockey

Medal	Medallists	Sport	Event
Gold	University of Toronto Grads: Charles Delahay; Frank Fisher; Grant Gordon; Louis Hudson; Norbert Mueller; Bert Plaxton; Hugh Plaxton; Roger Plaxton; John Porter; Frank Sullivan; Joseph Sullivan; Ross Taylor; Dave Trottier	Hockey	Men's

1932: Lake Placid, USA

Team: 53
1 Gold, 1 Silver, 5 Bronze = 7 Medals
Flagbearer: Unknown

Medal	Medallists	Sport	Event
Gold	Winnipeg Hockey Club: William Cockburn; Cliff Crowley; Albert Duncanson; George Garbutt; Roy Hinkel; Vic Lindquist; Norman Malloy; Walter Monson; Ken Moore; Romeo Rivers; Harold Simpson; Hugh Sutherland; Stan Wagner; Aliston Wise	Hockey	Men's
Silver	Alex Hurd	Speed Skating	1,500m
Bronze	Montgomery Wilson	Figure Skating	Singles
Bronze	Alex Hurd	Speed Skating	500m
Bronze	William Logan	Speed Skating	1,500m
Bronze	William Logan	Speed Skating	5,000m
Bronze	Frank Stack	Speed Skating	10,000m

1936: Garmisch-Partenkirchen, Germany

Team: 30
0 Gold, 1 Silver, 0 Bronze = 1 Medal
Flagbearer: Unknown

Medal	Medallists	Sport	Event
Silver	Port Arthur Bearcats: F. Maxwell Deacon; Ken Farmer; Hugh Farquharson; James Haggarty; Walter Kitchen; Ray Milton; Francis (Dinty)Moore; Herman Murray; W. Arthur Nash; Dave Neville; Ralph Saint-Germain; Alex Sinclair; William Thompson; N. Friday; G. Saxberg	Hockey	Men's

1940: No Games, WW II

Games not held due to World War II

1944: No Games, WW II

Games not held due to World War II

1948: St. Moritz, Switzerland

Team: 36
2 Gold, 0 Silver, 1 Bronze = 3 Medals
Flagbearer: Hubert Brooks, Hockey

Medal	Medallists	Sport	Event
Gold	Barbara Ann Scott	Figure Skating	Singles
Gold	RCAF Flyers: Hubert Brooks; Murray Dowey; Bernard Dunster; Roy Forbes; Andy Gilpin; Orval Gravelle; Pat Guzzo; Wally Halder; Ted Hibberd; Ross King; André Lapperierre; Louis Lecompte; Julius Leichnitz; George Mara; Ab Renaud; Reg Schroeter; Irving Taylor	Hockey	Men's
Bronze	Suzanne Morrow; Wallace Distelmeyer	Figure Skating	Pairs

Olympic Winter Games
1924-2000

1952: Oslo, Norway
Team: 39
1 Gold, 0 Silver, 1 Bronze = 2 Medals
Flagbearer: Gordon Audley, Speed Skating

Medal	Medallists	Sport	Event
Gold	Edmonton Mercurys: George Abel; Jack Davies; Billie Dawe; Bruce Dickson; Don Gauf; Bill Gibson; Ralph Hansch; Bob Meyers; Dave Miller; Eric Paterson; Tom Pollock; Al Purvis; Gordie Robertson; Louis Secco; Frank Sullivan; Bob Watt	Hockey	Men's
Bronze	Gordon Audley	Speed Skating	500m

1956: Cortina d'Ampezzo, Italy
Team: 37
0 Gold, 1 Silver, 2 Bronze = 3 Medals
Flagbearer: Norris Bowden, Figure Skating

Medal	Medallists	Sport	Event
Silver	Frances Dafoe; Norris Bowden	Figure Skating	Pairs
Bronze	Lucile Wheeler	Alpine Skiing	Downhill
Bronze	Kitchener-Waterloo Flying Dutchmen: Denis Brodeur; Charles Brooker; William Colvin; James Horne; Arthur Hurst; Byrle Klinck; Paul Knox; Ken Laufman; Howie Lee; James Logan; Floyd Martin; Jack MacKenzie; Don Rope; George Scholes; Gerry Theberge; Bob White; Keith Woodall	Hockey	Men's

1960: Squaw Valley, USA
Team: 44
2 Gold, 1 Silver, 1 Bronze = 4 Medals
Flagbearer: Robert Paul, Figure Skating

Medal	Medallists	Sport	Event
Gold	Anne Heggtveit	Alpine Skiing	Slalom
Gold	Barbara Wagner; Robert Paul	Figure Skating	Pairs
Silver	Kitchener-Waterloo Flying Dutchmen: Bobby Attersley; Maurice Benoit; James Connelly; Jack Douglas; Harold Hurley; Ken Laufman; Floyd Martin; Robert McKnight; Cliff Pennington; Don Rope; Bobby Rousseau; George Samolenki; Harry Sinden; Darryl Sly	Hockey	Men's
Bronze	Donald Jackson	Figure Skating	Singles

1964: Innsbruck, Austria
Team: 62
1 Gold, 0 Silver, 2 Bronze = 3 Medals
Flagbearer: Ralph Olin, Speed Skating

Medal	Medallists	Sport	Event
Gold	Douglas Anakin; John Emery; Vic Emery; Peter Kirby	Bobsleigh	4-Man
Bronze	Debbie Wilkes; Guy Revell	Figure Skating	Pairs
Bronze	Petra Burka	Figure Skating	Singles

1968: Grenoble, France
Team: 71
1 Gold, 1 Silver, 1 Bronze = 3 Medals
Flagbearer: Nancy Greene, Alpine Skiing

Medal	Medallists	Sport	Event
Gold	Nancy Greene	Alpine Skiing	Giant Slalom
Silver	Nancy Greene	Alpine Skiing	Slalom
Bronze	National Team: Roger Bourbonnais; Ken Broderick; Ray Cadieux; Paul Conlin; Gary Dineen; Brian Glennie; Ted Hargreaves; Fran Huck; Marshall Johnston; Barry MacKenzie; Billy McMillan; Steve Monteith; Morris Mott; Terry O'Malley; Danny O'Shea; Gerry Pinder; Herb Pinder; Wayne Stephenson	Hockey	Men's

1972: Sapporo, Japan
Team: 60
0 Gold, 1 Silver, 0 Bronze = 1 Medal
Flagbearer: Karen Magnussen, Figure Skating

Medal	Medallists	Sport	Event
Silver	Karen Magnussen	Figure Skating	Singles

1976: Innsbruck, Austria

Team: 60
1 Gold, 1 Silver, 1 Bronze = 3 Medals
Flagbearer: Dave Irwin, Alpine Skiing

Medal	Medallists	Sport	Event
Gold	Kathy Kreiner	Alpine Skiing	Giant Slalom
Silver	Cathy Priestner	Speed Skating	500m
Bronze	Toller Cranston	Figure Skating	Singles

1980: Lake Placid, USA

Team: 59
0 Gold, 1 Silver, 1 Bronze = 2 Medals
Flagbearer: Ken Read, Alpine Skiing

Medal	Medallists	Sport	Event
Silver	Gaétan Boucher	Speed Skating	1,000m
Bronze	Steve Podborski	Alpine Skiing	Downhill

1984: Sarajevo, Yugoslavia

Team: 69
2 Gold, 1 Silver, 1 Bronze = 4 Medals
Flagbearer: Gaétan Boucher, Speed Skating

Medal	Medallists	Sport	Event
Gold	Gaétan Boucher	Speed Skating	1,000m
Gold	Gaétan Boucher	Speed Skating	1,500m
Silver	Brian Orser	Figure Skating	Singles
Bronze	Gaétan Boucher	Speed Skating	500m

1988: CALGARY, Canada

Team: 117
0 Gold, 2 Silver, 3 Bronze = 5 Medals
Flagbearer: Brian Orser, Figure Skating

Medal	Medallists	Sport	Event
Silver	Brian Orser	Figure Skating	Singles
Silver	Elizabeth Manley	Figure Skating	Singles
Bronze	Karen Percy	Alpine Skiing	Downhill
Bronze	Karen Percy	Alpine Skiing	Super-G
Bronze	Tracy Wilson; Rob McCall	Figure Skating	Dance

1992: Albertville, France

Team: 117
2 Gold, 3 Silver, 2 Bronze = 7 Medals
Flagbearer: Sylvie Daigle, Speed Skating

Medal	Medallists	Sport	Event
Gold	Angela Cutrone; Sylvie Daigle; Nathalie Lambert; Annie Perreault	Speed Skating	Short Track 3,000m relay
Gold	Kerrin Lee-Gartner	Alpine Skiing	Downhill
Silver	National Team: Dave Archibald; Todd Brost; Sean Burke; Kevin Dahl; Curt Giles; Dave Hannan; Gord Hynes; Fabian Joseph; Joe Juneau; Trevor Kidd; Patrick Lebeau; Chris Lindberg; Eric Lindros; Kent Manderville; Adrien Plavsic; Dan Ratushny; Brad Schlegel; Wally Schreiber; Randy Smith; Sam St. Laurent; Dave Tippett; Brian Tutt; Jason Wooley	Hockey	Men's
Silver	Frédéric Blackburn	Speed Skating	Short Track 1,000m
Silver	Frédéric Blackburn; Michel Daignault; Mark Lackie; Sylvain Gagnon; Laurent Daignault	Speed Skating	Short Track 5,000m relay
Bronze	Myriam Bédard	Biathlon	15km
Bronze	Isabelle Brasseur; Lloyd Eisler	Figure Skating	Pairs

1994: Lillehammer, Norway

Team: 104
3 Gold, 6 Silver, 4 Bronze = 13 Medals
Flagbearer: Kurt Browning, Figure Skating

Medal	Medallists	Sport	Event
Gold	Myriam Bédard	Biathlon	7.5km
Gold	Myriam Bédard	Biathlon	15km
Gold	Jean-Luc Brassard	Freestyle Skiing	Moguls
Silver	Elvis Stojko	Figure Skating	Singles
Silver	Philipe Laroche	Freestyle Skiing	Aerials
Silver	National Team: Mark Astley; Adrian Aucoin; David Harlock; Corey Hirsch; Todd Hlushko; Greg Johnson; Fabian Joseph; Paul Kariya; Chris Kontos; Manny Legace; Ken Lovsin; Derek Mayer; Pter Nedved; Dwayne Norris; Greg Parks; Alain Roy; Jean-Yves Roy; Brian Savage; Brad Schlegel; Wally Schreiber; Chris Therien; Todd Warriner; Brad Werenka	Hockey	Men's

		Sport	Event
Silver	Susan Auch	Speed Skating	500m
Silver	Nathalie Lambert	Speed Skating	Short Track 1,000m
Silver	Christine Boudrias; Isabelle Charest; Sylvie Daigle; Nathalie Lambert	Speed Skating	Short Track 3,000m relay
Bronze	Edi Podivinsky	Alpine Skiing	Downhill
Bronze	Isabelle Brasseur; Lloyd Eisler	Figure Skating	Pairs
Bronze	Lloyd Langlois	Freestyle Skiing	Aerials
Bronze	Marc Gagnon	Speed Skating	Short Track 1,000m

1998: Nagano, Japan

Team:
4 Gold, 5 Silver, 4 Bronze = 13 Medals
Flagbearer: Jean-Luc Brassard, Freestyle Skiing

Medal	Medallists	Sport	Event
Gold	Dave MacEachern; Pierre Lueders	Bobsleigh	2 man
Gold	Sandra Schmirler; Marcia Gudereit; Joan McCusker; Jan Betker; Atina Ford	Curling	Women's
Gold	Ross Rebagliati	Snowboarding	Giant Slalom
Gold	Catriona Le May Doan	Speed Skating	500m
Gold	Annie Perreault	Speed Skating	Short Track 500m
Gold	Francois Drolet; Marc Gagnon; Jonathon Guilmette; Eric Bédard; Derrick Campbell	Speed Skating	Short Track 5000m Relay
Silver	Richard Hart; George Karry; Mike Harris; Collin Mitchell; Paul Savage	Curling	Men's
Silver	Elvis Stojko	Figure Skating	Singles
Silver	Team Canada: Jennifer Botterill, Thérèse Brisson, Cassie Campbell, Judy Diduck, Nancy Drolet, Lori Dupuis, Danielle Goyette, Geraldine Heaney, Jayna Hefford, Becky Kellar, Kathy McCormack, Karen Nystrom, Lesley Reddon, Manon Rhéaume, Laura Schuler, Fiona Smith, France St-Louis, Vicky Sunohara, Hayley Wickenheiser, Stacy Wilson	Hockey	Women's
Silver	Jeremy Wotherspoon	Speed Skating	500m
Silver	Susan Auch	Speed Skating	500m
Bronze	Eric Bédard	Speed Skating	Short Track 1,000m
Bronze	Christine Boudrias; Isabelle Charest; Annie Perreault; Chantale Sevigny; Tanya Vicent	Speed Skating	Short Track 3,000m relay
Bronze	Kevin Overland	Speed Skating	500m
Bronze	Catriona Le May Doan	Speed Skating	1,000m

CSI/COA

Jean Luc Brassard, 1994

Canadian Press/COA

Catriona Le May Doan, 1998

Canada

Our
Century
in Sport

Highlights

Canada's Olympic Winter Highlights

1924

- **Chamonix, France** — The first Olympic Winter Games were not officially recognized until almost two years after they ended. Regardless, Canada sent a team to the Chamonix Winter Sports Festival and received its share of medals, which became the first winter Olympic medals for Canada.

- The Canadian hockey team (from the Granite Club in Toronto) began its domination of Olympic hockey by shellacking opponents 30-0, 22-0, and 33-0 in round robin play. In the semi-finals, Canada defeated Britain 19-2. The final was a bit closer, with the Canadians winning the gold medal in a 6-1 victory over the USA. It is interesting to note that the games were played outdoors on a lake with boards a mere six inches high. A net was hung behind the end boards to stop shots from careening off the snow-banks at the base of Mont Blanc, thus alleviating local fears of potential avalanches.

Constance Wilson

1928

- **St. Moritz, Switzerland** — The University of Toronto Grads represented Canada at the Games, winning the gold again in decisive manner. The team had won the Allan Cup in Canada the year before, under regular coach Conn Smythe. Smythe was busy with the NHL by the time of the Games, though, and left the coaching to W.A. Hewitt. His assistant coach was a young Harold Ballard, the future Maple Leafs owner. The organizers were afraid of Canada running up huge scores again, so a unique structure was set up. Ten countries had sent teams, and nine of them were placed in three pools of three teams each. Canada would watch. The winning teams from each pool would then play Canada. Canada met the three challengers and triumphed easily, 11-0 over Sweden, 13-0 over Switzerland and 14-0 over Great Britain to claim the gold medal.

- Besides hockey players, Canada also sent four skiers, four figure skaters and three speed skaters to the 1928 Winter Games. Cecil Smith and Constance Wilson placed fifth and sixth respectively in women's figure skating while the others failed to place in their events.

1932

- **Lake Placid, USA** — Canada's proximity to Lake Placid meant more Canadian competitors and spectators could afford to go to the Games. Even some of the snow was Canadian, as organizers trucked in snow from Quebec to ensure that the cross-country ski trails had enough snow.

- Montgomery Wilson earned Canada's first Olympic figure skating medal, a bronze, while his sister Constance finished fourth in the women's division. The brother and sister then joined up for a fifth in the pairs competition.

- Canada did well in speed skating thanks in part to the fact that races were run in the North American mass-start format, rather than the European pairs against the clock format. In the 500m, Canadians finished third (Alex Hurd), fourth (Frank Stack) and fifth (William Logan). In the 1500m they same three finished second (Hurd), third (Logan) and fourth (Stack). Logan earned a bronze in the 5000m while Stack earned one in the 10,000m.

- Women's speed skating was a demonstration event in Lake Placid. Canada's Jean Wilson won both the 500m and 1500m contests in world record times. Rather than a gold medal, the demonstration winners won trips to Japan —

sadly never taken by Wilson. She contracted a rare muscular disease and died within a year after her victories.

- Canada's Frank Stack was a very durable speed skater — in addition to competing in 1932, he qualified for the 1936 Games but could not afford to attend. He then waited through the war years and the two cancelled Olympics, to return to Olympic competition in both 1948 and 1952.

- Dog-sled racing was a demonstration event as well in 1932 — and Canadians finished 1-2-3, with Emile St. Goddard of Le Pas, Manitoba taking the top honours.

- Only four nations made it to the hockey competitions, and Canada (represented by the "Winnipegs") anxiously awaited the results after each game. It came down to Canada and the USA in the final. In a thrilling and close match, the teams remained tied 2-2 after two overtime periods. Canada was awarded the gold because of its 2-1 victory over the Americans in round robin play.

1924 Olympic Hockey team

1936

- **Garmisch-Partenkirchen, Germany** — *"It is doubtful that anyone participating in the Olympic Games is a representative of the Government of this country…"* With this logic in place, Canada entered the 1936 Winter Games in Nazi Germany with the Canadian government's blessing. Canada sent a small team, and achieved less than stellar results. We sent no bobsleigh entry nor male skiers of any sort and only one speed skater. In figure skating we finished fourth in men's singles and sixth in the pairs event. And, in hockey we received the first blow to our ego this century, ending up with a silver medal.

- In 1936, 45 year old Canadian Edwina Chamier went to the Olympic Winter Games to compete in the alpine skiing combined event. Her participation made her the oldest woman Olympic Winter Games competitor in the century, 45 years, 318 days.

Jean Wilson

Frank Stack

1936

Hockey Silver

It was initially thought that the 1935 Allan Cup Champions would play in the 1936 Olympics. Many of the Halifax Wolves, however, had either turned professional or left Halifax by the time of the 1936 Olympics. Thus, the runner-up team from Port Arthur went to represent the country. At the same time, 14 amateurs from Western Canada left the country to play in England, without the consent of the Canadian Amateur Hockey Association (CAHA), and were suspended. However, in a gesture of goodwill, the CAHA agreed to allow two of the defecting members, Jimmy Foster and Alex Archer, to play for Great Britain in the Olympics. This decision would haunt Canada for many years. In a round robin game against Britain, goalie Jimmy Foster stymied Canada much of the game, turning aside shot after shot and leading to Canada's first-ever Olympic hockey defeat. Canada, though, easily won all its remaining games, and expected to play Britain again in the final. However, as H.H. Roxborough later wrote, "In the final series, Canada defeated both the United States and Czechoslovakia, and a victory over Britain would have assured the Olympic hockey championship. Should Canada have won? Well, it will never be known, for the Gods of Garmisch decided that because Britain had defeated Canada in the preliminary round, Britain was not obliged to play Canada again for the title. In simpler language, the match in round 2 would also stand for round 3. … Thus, in a subtle and irritating manner, Canada lost the Olympic title that had previously been won by the Falcons, Granites and Grads. Canada's only consolation was that many on the British team had been developed in Canada and that this was an instance of the pupils defeating the teachers."

1936 Olympic Hockey Team

Maria and Otto Jelinek

1948

- **St. Moritz, Switzerland** — The RCAF Flyers and Barbara Ann Scott were the toasts of the winter world in 1948.

- **Pairs Skating** — Canadians Suzanne Morrow and Wallace Diestelmeyer became the first pair to execute the death spiral in competition, en route to a bronze medal for Canada.

1952

- **Oslo, Norway** — Canada earned a surprise bronze medal in the men's 500m speed skating event. Winnipeg native Gordon Audley was "hoping for fifteenth or twentieth" but as luck would have it was drawn to race with world champion Finn Helegeson from Norway. Pushed on by his competitor, Audley came through in third place overall to capture the bronze medal.

- Canada's hockey hopes were carried by the Edmonton Mercurys this time. The days of Canada merely showing up to trounce an opponent were over, but our pride in hockey shone through. Winning a few close games put Canada near the gold medal, and the final game tie with the USA put them over the top to retain the Olympic hockey title. It would be our last Olympic title of the century.

Die Eröffnungsfeier / Opening of the Olympic Gam.

The Edmonton Mercurys, 1952

Dafoe and Bowden, 1956

1956

- **Cortina d'Ampezzo, Italy** — It had to happen sometime. Having lost only one Olympic Hockey match to date, the Canadian squad, represented by the '55 Allan Cup winning team Kitchener-Waterloo Dutchmen, lost twice in one Olympics. In the last Olympic tournament played on outdoor ice, the Dutchmen started off with victories over Germany, Italy, Austria and Czechoslovakia, then lost 4-1 to the Americans during a blinding snowstorm. Still, Canada entered the final round with a chance to win the gold medal, and if they could beat the upstarts from the Soviet Union by three goals, would win the gold. Alas, the Canadians were defeated 2-0 in the final game, relegating them to a tie in the standings with the Americans, who claimed the silver because of their earlier victory.

- At the 1952 Games, the Canadian pairs figure skating tandem of Frances Dafoe and Norris Bowden had placed a respectable fifth at their first Games. By 1954 the Canadian pair had climbed the world ladder to become World Champions, and again claimed the World crown in 1955. They were definite favourites heading into Cortina. It was not to be, however, as the final skate ended in controversy. Entering the final minute of their skate, the Canadian pair faltered very slightly on a lift, upsetting their timing. It was enough to make the nine judges take caution in marking the closest final in Olympic figure skating history. Both the Canadian and

Austrian pairs ended with four first place votes. The Canadians also registered four for second, and inexplicably one for third (the Hungarian judge had placed the Hungarian pair above both the top contenders). The winning Austrian couple ended with five second place votes — had they received one more second place vote, Dafoe and Bowden would have been Olympic Champions on points, but in the end settled for winning the silver.

- Laurels do not only go to the victor. Until Cortina, Canada had not won anything on the Olympic ski slopes, but a 21-year old from St. Jovite, Quebec would change that. This year's downhill for the women was similar in style to a giant slalom in that there were many gates at the top of the course. Canada's Lucile Wheeler liked the giant slalom, and came in sixth in the specialty on the first day of the Games. When it came to the downhill, she was ready. Wheeler finished the top portion of the course in first place. Going so fast she almost fell in the middle section, she maintained her speed enough to win Canada's first Olympic ski medal — a bronze in the women's downhill.

1960

- **Squaw Valley, USA** — The Kitchener-Waterloo Dutchmen returned to fight for Canada's Olympic hockey honour again, and improved on their 1956 bronze performance — but not enough for some observers. This time Canada defeated the strong Soviet team, 8-5, as well as teams from Sweden, Czechoslovakia, Japan and Germany. Then Canada's club representative was defeated 2-1 by an American All-Star squad to earn a silver medal. More than any previous hockey defeat, the loss in Squaw Valley to the Americans put Canada in a state of national mourning. It also led to the charge for Father David Bauer's dream of creating a National Team for Canada.

- Figure skating is big in Canada, bigger still when we produce world champions like Barbara Wagner and Bob Paul. After finishing sixth at the 1956 Winter Olympics, Wagner and Paul continued their rise in winning the Canadian, North

Wagner and Paul, 1960

American and ultimately the World Championships in pairs figure skating. They were so popular, that prior to the Games in Squaw Valley the Canadian duo went on at least seven European skating tours. They were the heavy favourites in 1960 and came through in shining colours — earning first place marks from each judge to win the Olympic gold medal. Two weeks after the Games, they won the world championships again. (The sister-brother tandem of Maria and Otto Jelinek also performed well, earning a fourth place in Squaw Valley where many thought they had earned at least the bronze. At the Worlds, they came through in second place — but their time was yet to come.)

- In 1960 at Squaw Valley, Anne Heggtveit became Canada's first Olympic champion in alpine skiing. As Lucile Wheeler's roommate in 1956, the Ottawa native learned from her earlier Olympic experiences. By 1960, Heggtveit was primed to perform well in all three skiing disciplines, but had disappointing runs in the downhill and giant slalom, finishing 12th in each event. But near the end of the Games she made up for it — big time. *"Beatings are tough to take … you've got to get hardened by them. Today makes up for all those losses."* She made up for the losses with a vengeance, racing down the slalom course in a time three seconds faster than her second place competitor, a margin of victory almost unheard of in ski racing. Heggtveit's 1960 roommate, by the way, was another future champion, then 16-year old Nancy Greene.

- Future World Figure Skating Champion Donald Jackson performed well enough in his first Games to earn the bronze medal, while 15-year old Donald McPherson, also a future World Champion, finished in 10th spot.

Lucile Wheeler, 1956

Highlights

1964

- **Innsbruck, Austria** — Canada had no bobsleigh track in 1964, and the event wasn't even held in 1960. Yet, after 1964, the sport became well known in Canada. Vic Emery spearheaded a Canadian campaign to race in the bobsleigh after he got hooked on the sport while watching it at the 1956 Games. Attracting his brother John and friends Peter Kirby and Doug Anakin, Emery led the team to one of Canada's greatest Olympic achievements — winning the Olympic gold medal in the four-man bob. Their winning time was more than a second faster than the runners up, a margin unheard of in a sport measuring times in the hundredths of seconds.

- Hockey was at the forefront of the Canadian consciousness in Innsbruck, as Canada sent a national team to the Olympics for the first time rather than a club team. Coach Father David Bauer had been the former Vice Principal at Toronto's famed St. Michael's College and the head of its hockey program. When the school decided against playing Junior A hockey, Bauer's attention turned to developing a national team for international competitions. His

planned worked, sort of. The Canadian squad, made up mostly of collegiate talents and some ex-professionals, played well against the European "shamateurs," but for the first time in Olympic history Canada finished out of the hockey medals, settling for a fourth place finish.

- Fifteen-year old Petra Burka from Toronto won the bronze medal in women's figure skating and, when the 1964 Olympic champion retired, Burka went on to win the World Championship in 1965. She turned professional prior to the 1968 Olympics in Grenoble and did not compete there, though it is tempting to wonder if she could have won Canada's second individual figure skating gold medal of the century.

- Canadian pairs figure skating was at its zenith in this era. Following the silver medal in 1956 by Dafoe and Bowden, the gold medal performance of Wagner and Paul in 1960, and the World Championship by the Jelineks in 1962, it was left to Debbi Wilkes and Guy Revell to uphold the medal streak. And they did, earning Canada a bronze medal. Following the Games, however, it was found that the silver-medal pair from Germany had signed professional skating

Bobsleigh gold, 1964

contracts prior to the Olympics and thus, given the rules of the day, were disqualified. The Canadian bronze turned to silver.

1968

- **Grenoble, France** — The strong efforts of the '64 Olympic hockey team kept the national program alive for four more years. This time, still playing with collegians and ex-professionals and against the "professionals from the communist states," Father David Bauer's Olympic team came away with a well-earned bronze medal. Still, it was a disappointment to Canadians to be prevented from sending better qualified representatives to the Olympics. It was such a strong feeling that Canada refused to send any hockey team at all to either the 1972 Games in Sapporo or the 1976 Games in Innsbruck.

Petra Burka

1968

Grenoble, France

In 1967 Nancy Greene of Rossland, British Columbia, won the inaugural World Cup despite missing three of nine meets. The following year she participated in her third Olympics. After finishing tenth in the downhill and second in the slalom, she realized that the giant slalom was her last chance to win a gold medal. The Canadian coaches brought her to the top of the slope 45 minutes early and suggested that they fill the time by eating a snack at a nearby restaurant. Over tea and rolls they became involved in a spirited discussion about ski politics. Suddenly, one of the coaches realized the race had already started. When they reached the start hut, the fifth skier was already in the gate. Greene was number nine. In fact, the coaches had planned the whole thing so that Greene would be distracted from her nervousness. When it came her turn to start in the gate, she told herself "Anne Heggtveit won a slalom gold when I was on the team in 1960, and she washes her clothes the same way I do." Greene skied a perfect race, but when she turned around to look at the electronic clock, the numbers were still moving. "My heart almost stopped," she recalled later. "I thought, I've just skied the race of my life and they missed my time." After two or three seconds the clock malfunction was corrected and her time appeared. "But that's all it took for my blood pressure to shoot out of sight. I had a headache for the next two days." (David Wallechinsky The Complete Book of the Winter Olympics 1998, pg 191)

Nancy Greene, 1968

Kathy Kreiner, 1976

1972

- **Sapporo, Japan** — Disagreeing with the international hockey federation over the eligibility of "communist professionals" and not North American professional hockey players, Canada refused to send a hockey team to Sapporo.

- Figure skater Karen Magnussen won an Olympic silver medal in 1972, Canada's only medal of the Games. Compulsory figures were still very much a part of the judging in 1972. Magnussen was superb in the free skate portion of the program, winning it convincingly. Because of her compulsory figure marks she had to settle for the silver, even though the eventual winner had finished seventh in the free skate. Undaunted, Magnussen returned to the world stage in 1973 to claim the World Championship.

- "Jungle" Jim Hunter did not finish in the top three of any Olympic events in 1972, but he did receive a bronze medal. How so? Hunter skied in all three alpine disciplines — the downhill, giant slalom and slalom — and finished in the top ten in each one. This was good enough to earn an alpine combined bronze by the International Ski Federation, even though alpine combined was not an Olympic medal event.

1976

- **Innsbruck, Austria** — Cathy Priestner had won six Canadian speed skating championships before heading to Innsbruck in 1976. There, she sped through the 500m race winning an Olympic silver medal.

- Canada's third medal of the Games came in men's figure skating. This time, it was the artistry of Toller Cranston, long a critic of figure skating judges, that earned him an Olympic bronze medal.

Sylvia Burka, 1972

1980

- **Lake Placid, USA** — Father David Bauer returned Canada to the Olympic hockey stage in Lake Placid for the first time since 1968, only to see his collection of collegians again be trampled by the powerful Soviet national team. Even so, Canada still had a chance to advance to the medal round, but lost to Finland 4-3.

- Gaétan Boucher was still an up-and-coming speed skater in 1980, known for quick starts and long, powerful strides. For his 1000m race, Boucher was selected to skate with the heavy favourite from the USA, Eric Heiden. (Heiden would win all five events that year.) This was both good and bad. Bad in the sense that Heiden had remarkable times and to even think of beating him was tough. It was good because if Boucher could stay with Heiden, he would be assured a very fast time. The latter proved correct, as Boucher sped to an Olympic silver medal in a personal best time.

CSI/COA

Steve Podborski, 1980

1984

- **Sarajevo, Yugoslovia** — In the hockey tournament, Canada defeated the Americans 4-2 (right before the match, the US successfully prevented Canada from using two players who had signed professional contracts with NHL clubs), Austria 8-1 and advanced to the medal round with a 4-2 win over Finland. Canada lost the first medal round game 4-0 to the Czechs then had to face the powerhouse Soviet team to stay alive. Goaltender Mario Gosselin was superb, kicking aside 26 point-blank shots and allowing four. The rest of the team, though, managed only 10 shots on the Soviets and ultimately lost 4-0. Disheartened, Canada then lost a nail-biter 2-0 to the Swedes to finish out of the medals.

- *"I went to Sarajevo expecting, not hoping, to win."* With these words speed skater Gaétan Boucher enjoyed the best Games of the century by a Canadian. On February 10 Boucher started his assault on the Canadian record book, earning a bronze medal in his weakest event, the 500m sprint. On February 14 he won the 1000m gold medal by almost a full second. Then, two days later on February 16, Boucher again won gold, this time in the 1500m. Including his silver medal in Lake Placid in 1980, Boucher won two golds, a silver and a bronze to become Canada's most decorated winter Olympian of the century.

- Brian Orser came tantalizingly close to that elusive gold medal in Sarajevo. Trailing American Scott Hamilton after the figures competition by a large margin, it was thought that gold was out of the reach. But the final free skate counted for 50% and Brian came through with a dazzling performance, winning the free skate comfortably. It was good, but not quite good enough — Orser got the silver, Canada's highest men's Olympic figure skating result in the century (for good measure, of course, Orser would win the silver again in 1988, and Elvis Stojko won back-to-back silvers in 1994 and 1998).

1980

In the most anticipated ski race for Canadians since Nancy Greene in 1968, the favourite in the men's downhill race was Canadian Ken Read. A winner of several World Cups, Read was at the time a leading figure in downhill racing. The course seemed to his liking, and he had skied very well all season. Read burst out of the starting gate and immediately began his attack of the course. Then it happened — his ski binding separated from his boot as he rounded only the third gate. Through mechanical failure, Read was out of the one race he had physically and mentally trained for all his life, in just 8 seconds! Just when Canada was disheartened, however, along came the youngest Crazy Canuck, Steve Podborski. It was "Pod" and not Read who would go on to become Canada's first male alpine medallist, skiing a smooth race to garner a bronze medal. Podborski's initial thoughts upon hearing about Read's misfortune were not what you'd call charitable: "There you jerks, that'll teach you!" directed at the Canadian media, for adding so much pressure to the race.

Olympic Champion, Gaéten Boucher, 1984

CSI/COA

Ken Read, 1980

CSI/COA

Brian Orser, 1984

1988

- **Calgary, Canada** — Canada's 1988 Olympic flagbearer was reigning world figure skating champion Brian Orser. Entering the stadium last, as by custom, Orser led a Canadian team numbering 117 athletes wearing splendid full-length red winter coats with matching white shoulder braids and stetsons.

- Capping off the longest Olympic torch relay to date, Ken Read and Cathy Priestner entered McMahon Stadium carrying the Olympic Torch right on schedule. They paused to pass it to the round-the-world-wheelchair athlete Rick Hansen, and then passed it to Robyn Perry, a Grade 7 student and local figure skater, representing the future of sport, who lit the torch to begin the Games.

- Canada did enjoy success in Calgary, just not golden success. Canada ended the Games with five medals: two silver and a bronze in figure skating and two bronze medals by Karen Percy in alpine skiing.

- A local star emerged in Calgary — Karen Percy. Percy had won the Canadian slalom championships a few weeks before the Olympics and felt confident, but in the downhill it was expected that veteran Laurie Graham would be Canada's main hope. It was Percy, though, buoyed by a groundswell of local support, who emerged as the first Canadian medal winner in Calgary — getting a bronze. Karen duplicated the feat a few days later in the super giant slalom event, becoming only Canada's second double Olympic

alpine medallist of the century (Nancy Greene won gold and silver in 1968).

- In the figure skating dance competition, Canadians Tracy Wilson and Rob McCall came through with a stunning final performance to capture the bronze medal in Calgary, behind two Soviet couples.

- Men's figure skater Brian Orser entered the Games as the previous silver medallist, the reigning world champion, Canada's flagbearer and, really, our greatest hope for a gold medal. The pressure must have seemed enormous on the Penetanguishene native, especially in light of the fact that he was front and centre of the biggest-hyped event at the Games — *"The Battle of the Brians."* As expected, the final came down to Orser, skating last, and Brian Boitano of the USA. Boitano's skate was near perfect, with just enough room for Orser to squeak through with a perfect performance of his own. He almost made it. Skating with his usual brilliance and flash, Orser electrified the crowd with his trademark triple jumps. Then suddenly, he two-footed a landing and turned a planned double jump into a single. When the night ended, Brian Orser had won his second straight Olympic silver medal.

- The surprise of the Games for Canadians came from Ottawa native Elizabeth Manley. Playing a decidedly second, if not third, fiddle to the expected contest between Katarina Witt of East Germany and American Debi Thomas, Manley was hoping for a top six placing, and wishing for a medal. She got

her wish, and more. Manley came through the middle and almost got the gold, winning the free skate with a flawless performance and placing a very close second to Witt. Liz Manley won an Olympic silver medal. (To show naysayers her performance was no fluke, Manley duplicated her silver medal feat at the world championships the next month.)

- In hockey the national team again came up empty-handed as the powerful Soviets won another gold medal. Canada came fourth. And, the world of speed skating waved goodbye to an all-time great in Gaétan Boucher. Boucher, Canada's most decorated winter Olympian wanted to retire on his own terms, in his own country, and *"go out in a blaze of glory."* It did not happen quite as scripted, as Boucher narrowly ended up out of the medals.

Karen Percy, 1988

Liz Manley, 1988

1988

CALGARY, CANADA

Canada played host to the Olympics for the second time in 1988, this time for the Winter Games in Calgary. The Games were a financial, organizational and entertaining success not matched up to that point by any other winter host. Unfortunately, in competition Canada became the first host nation to not win a single winter gold medal, reminiscent of 1976 when we became the first summer host not to win gold. Canada was the only country to host an Olympic or Olympic Winter Games without winning gold throughout the century.

1992

- **Albertville, France** — These were the last of the Winter Games to be held in the same calendar year as the Summer Games, as the schedule changed to alternate Summer and Winter Games every two years. The events in Albertville were scattered among 13 venues throughout the Savoie region, making travelling a challenge, but the backdrops scenic. In competition Canada did quite well for itself — garnishing two gold, three silver and two bronze medals — even though we had hoped for much more.

- A lot was expected of our figure skaters, but this was not their year. World Champion Kurt Browning was hampered by a bad back all year long and fell during his short program, ultimately ending up what was for him a disappointing sixth. He was shocked. His colleague Elvis Stojko made his first Olympic foray and skated brilliantly. In what appeared to be the most proficient short program the officials somehow put Stojko in fourth, and after many triple jumps in the long program he actually slipped to seventh overall. Judging is not always objective, even for future world champions. Isabelle

Brasseur and Lloyd Eisler had hoped to challenge for the gold medal in the pairs event, but in the end skated well enough to earn a bronze medal.

- *"About a year and a half ago, I woke up and I'd had a dream that somebody was saying 'Médaille d'Or, Kerrin Lee-Gartner — Canada,' and I don't even speak French!"* On one of the most difficult downhill courses for women in the world, and certainly in Olympic competition in the century, Rossland, BC native Kerrin Lee-Gartner won Canada's only Olympic downhill gold medal of the century.

- Sylvie Daigle started her career as a long-track speed skater, then specialized in short-track racing and became a five-time world champion. Entering the inaugural Olympic 500m event in Albertville she was the clear favourite for the gold medal. But fate intervened when American Cathy Turner (a skater with a rough and tumble reputation) cut inside Daigle early in the race, making contact with Daigle's skate. No call was made by the referee, and Canada's gold-medal hopeful was forced out of the race. Not yet done with her career, Sylvie then backboned the women's relay team to its gold

medal, leaving Turner in her wake in the process. The Olympic champion team also included Nathalie Lambert, Angela Cutrone and Annie Perreault. *"It was my last chance. It was the perfect end to our dream,"* said Daigle afterwards.

- The men's short-track team also left its mark in its Games debut, winning two silvers. Frédéric Blackburn

surprisingly scorched his way around the track for his silver in the 1000m event, then led the men's relay team to a silver of its own.

- In two years, Myriam Bédard would become a household name in Canada; in 1992 she was still on her way up and settled for Canada's first-ever medal in biathlon, earning a bronze in the 15km event.

Kerrin Lee-Gartner

After years of sending young teams against seasoned international veterans, Canada finally received long overdue Olympic recognition in hockey in 1992, after a very close call. Having placed first in its round-robin play, Canada faced the fourth-placed German team in its first sudden-death playoff in the medal round. What was thought to be an easy victory, turned into a memorable sporting moment. Canada held a slim 3-2 lead when the Germans scored to tie the game with about two minutes to play, and the subsequent 10-minute overtime solved nothing. This meant a five-man shootout to determine who would advance and who would end up sixth. The two teams tied at 2 goals each in the shootout, which now meant a sudden-death shootout. Eric Lindros (at the time a holdout with the Quebec Nordiques) scored on Canada's first chance; then goalie Sean Burke faced Petr Draisaitl of Germany. The German's shot got through Burke's legs, but only barely enough to reach the goal line and not across it. Canada won. The national team then defeated the Czechs in the semi-finals, 4-2, to set up the gold medal game against the Unified Team (countries from the former Soviet Union which was in the process of breaking up at the time). After two periods the score was 0-0 and it looked like Canada might have a chance to redeem lost Olympic pride. It was close, but in the end the ex-Soviets won the gold medal game 2-0. Canada had won its first Olympic medal, a silver, since winning bronze in 1968.

Sylvie Daigle

CSI/COA — Scott Grant

The powerful Soviet hockey team had been disbanded, most star European players had joined the NHL and so were not playing in the Olympics, and Canada itself was allowed to send a few professionals currently not in the NHL: Paul Kariya, Corey Hirsch and Petr Nedved to name a few. Our hopes were high that these would be the Games when we won back the gold medal in our sport, last won by Canada in 1952 by the Edmonton Mercuries. The national team came oh-so-close again, easily earning the right to play in the quarter-finals against the Czech Republic. It was a tight 2-2 game that went into overtime. Kariya scored at the five-minute mark to send Canada into the semis against Finland, which had played a very strong tournament so far. A large pro-Finland crowd cheered wildly as the Finns jumped into an early 2-0 lead. But it was short-lived: Canada scored 5 unanswered goals and ultimately won 5-3, winning the right to play in the gold medal game, this time against Sweden. In a classic contrast of playing styles the game featured the wide-open passing game popular in Europe versus the tight-checking, grinding, game used by the Canadians. Both styles seemed to work during regulation time. The Swedes outshot Canada 42-21, but a combination of solid goaltending by Corey Hirsch and timely goals by Canada sent the game into overtime tied 2-2. Overtime solved nothing, so it would be a penalty-shootout that would decide the gold medal. Talk about pressure. Canada had the early lead in the initial five-shot format, then had to settle for another tie to send the shoot-outs into sudden-death. The first team to score when the other didn't would be the Olympic champion. Sweden went first. Peter Forsberg against Hirsch. Forsberg went for a deke, an apparently obvious deke for Hirsch who followed the puck the whole way….until Forsberg deftly changed direction and barely pushed a backhand around the now-sprawled Hirsch. Kariya was next up. He had scored earlier in the game on a high wrist shot against Tomi Salo, but this time the Swede stopped it — and all of Sweden rejoiced while Canada sighed. The image of Forsberg's classic deke, a move he had only tried in practice a few times, became a popular postage stamp in Sweden.

1994

- **Lillehammer, Norway** — Kurt Browning carried the Canadian flag to lead a 104-athlete team to Lillehammer, Norway, for some of the most picturesque moments in sport history. The team's uniforms, red and black "Mountie-style" outfits were a big hit. Our athletes did well too, earning 13 medals: three gold, six silver and four bronze.

- In alpine skiing our hopes were high for the women. Kate Pace was the reigning downhill champion and the 1992 gold medallist, Kerrin Lee-Gartner was still in top form. It was not to be for the women, though, as both ended up in the top 10, but out of the medals. In a pleasant surprise for those watching back home, a Canadian did earn an alpine medal after all, but from the men's side. Edi Podivinsky had been on the men's national team for a few years, achieving his share of top World Cup downhill results, but no wins and only a few podium finishes. He put it all together when it counted, though, on a sunny morning in Norway. Canada's new "Pod" earned only Canada's second bronze medal in men's Olympic alpine skiing. (The first "Pod," Steve Podborski, won a bronze in 1980.)

- In figure skating, Canadians were dreaming of a best-ever haul of medals. That didn't happen, but we did have our moments: reigning

Elvis Stojko

CSI/COA

world champion Kurt Browning was favoured to win the elusive gold medal, and compatriot Elvis Stojko was to be there if he faltered. Unlike 1992, Browning was healthy and prepared — but a fall in the short program sent his Olympic hopes down the drain. A classic free-skate pulled Browning up to only seventh. Stojko, though, was always ready. Skating with intense athleticism, Elvis jumped his way to the silver medal — a position he had expected, except that he had expected to see Kurt Browning in first.

- As far as the women's figure skaters were concerned, it was very safe to say that Josée Chouinard was distracted. There was a media circus surrounding the women as a result of the Nancy Kerrigan — Tonya Harding affair (in which Harding was accused of having Kerrigan's knees hit with a crowbar before the Games!). Harding, though, affected the Canadian champion in a different way. As Harding was skating her long program, she suddenly stopped, went to the officials' bench in tears and pleaded to be given some time to replace a surprisingly broken skate lace. To the crowd's amazement, she was given a reprieve, but the next skater had to be rushed onto the ice ill-prepared. That happened to be Chouinard. Neither she nor her coaches complained, but the three falls she encountered in her program clearly were at least partly the result of the Harding incident. Both skaters finished out of the medals and away from their dreams.

- Isabelle Brasseur and Lloyd Eisler had won the world championships in pairs figure skating the previous year. They were mentally and physically ready to challenge for Olympic gold, even with the addition of professionals raising the calibre of the field. But in the days leading up to the competition the petite Brasseur fell hard in practice and cracked a rib. Skating bravely and with pain in every stride, the pair came through with a dazzling performance for a bronze medal. Happy despite missing out on the ultimate prize, Eisler ceremoniously carried Brasseur on his shoulders to the podium to receive their hard-earned medals.

- Winnipeg's Susan Auch carried the nation's long-track speed skating hopes by herself, successfully earning Canada's first women's medal since 1976, a silver medal in the 500m sprint.

- The short track skaters came through again with medal performances. The defending women's 3000m champions almost repeated, ending up with the silver medal after the Chinese team, which had placed second in the race, was disqualified for interference.

- Team veteran Nathalie Lambert attacked the final of the women's 1000m, trying to lead from the start and steer clear of any trouble (which had ended her high hopes in Albertville). Her game plan almost succeeded as she finished between two Korean skaters to earn the silver medal.

- It is safe to say that short-track speed skater Marc Gagnon's Olympic bronze medal in 1994 was as confusing as it was gratifying. In his 1000m semi-final heat, Gagnon slipped and fell, losing his chance to compete in the final. In short-track they have a B-Final though, just in case, and Gagnon won that. When two of the four skaters in the A-Final were disqualified, that left Marc Gagnon, winner of the B-Final, with a bronze medal.

- Myriam Bédard's performance in Lillehammer made her a household name in Canada and put her sport on the map. First, she went out and demolished the field in the 15km biathlon, winning by an unheard margin of 46 seconds, with only two of 20 missed targets in the shooting. Then, unknowingly using a mixed set of skis (one for sprinting and one for longer distances), Bédard made a final push down the stretch in the 7.5 km event to claim her second gold of the Games by one second. Myriam Bédard tied Gaétan Boucher's best-Canadian record for the century in claiming two golds at one Winter Games.

- In the freestyle ski moguls event, Jean-Luc Brassard of Grand-Ile Quebec skied a near-perfect run, fast and cunningly clever with his classic Iron Cross — Cossack jump combination to win the Olympic gold medal.

- Brassard's freestyle aerial teammates were defending world champion Lloyd Langlois and two-time world champion Philippe Laroche. Each thought they had a chance for Olympic gold. In the end, Swiss veteran Sonny Schoenbaechler narrowly defeated both Canadians, who still got two of the three medals awarded: the silver for Laroche and the bronze for Langlois.

1998

- **Nagano, Japan** — A star of the 1994 Games, freestyle skier Jean-Luc Brassard was asked to carry the Canadian flag at the Opening Ceremonies in Nagano. He fulfilled his role proudly at the Ceremonies, but found that when he needed to compete the next day he performed poorly. A favourite to be on the podium, he afterwards traced his poor results back to the fact that he had carried the flag the day before.

- Canada bettered its positive showing of 13 medals at Lillehammer four years earlier with 15 — six gold, five silver, and four bronze. Speed skaters, both short and long track, accounted for nine of those medals. Canada's strong showing came despite disappointing results in men's hockey and freestyle skiing (no medals) and surprising losses in gold medal games in men's curling and women's hockey.

- The Canadian men's curling team looked like it had a lock on the gold medal during the Games. The rink headed by skip Mike Harris ended the round robin 6-1 and easily

defeated USA in the semi-finals. Lead George Karrys was then caught bragging about how the 60th best club in Canada could defeat the top European clubs. The skip lowered this estimate somewhat, saying, "*It's more like the top 40,*" but the jinx was in. Canada lost the gold medal game to Switzerland 9-3 to end up with the silver.

- The Canadian speed skating team was strong, accounting for nine of the 15 medals won by Canada in Nagano. "*We came here knowing we had a strong team, and today we proved it,*" said gold and bronze medallist Catriona Le May Doan.

- Catriona Le May Doan won gold in the 500m, bronze in the 1000m in long track speed skating, and carried Canada's flag at the Closing Ceremonies. In the 500m, she beat out sentimental favourite and Winnipeg native Susan Auch, the first time Canadians had finished 1-2 in a winter Olympic event.

- Canadian men finished 2-3-4 and 5 in a remarkable showing in the 500m speed skating race. Jeremy Wotherspoon won the silver with Kevin Overland taking the bronze. Sylvain Bouchard was fourth and Patrick Bouchard was fifth. "*I don't know what impressed me more,*" said coach Derrick Auch, "*having four in the top five of an Olympic event or having five (long-track) speed skating medals from different athletes.*"

CSI/COA

- Elvis Stojko put on another show for the ages and walked, or rather limped, away with his second straight Olympic silver medal in figure skating. Stojko concealed a painful groin injury leading up to the Games. But when a pinched nerve and a case of the flu caught up to him as well, he could no longer hide his pain. Grimacing with agony during his final free skate — which included a remarkable eight triple jumps on basically one leg — and even during the medal ceremony, the world saw a courageous effort fall just short of a golden moment.

- The figure skaters were most disappointed with the fourth place finish of ice dancers Shae-Lynn Bourne and Victor Kraatz. The duo was inexplicably placed fifth after the compulsory dance. Their routine was done to the music from Riverdance that was the talk of the Games. The result basically took them out of the medal hunt. Most galling was the allegation that the final placings were decided BEFORE the event took place. Whether accurate or not, the report on judging at the Games left most with a rather bad taste.

CSI/COA

Jean-Luc Brassard leading in the Canadian Team at Nagano, 1998

Canadian Press/COA

Catriona Le May Doan, left, and Susan Auch testing out their gold and silver speed skating medals, 1998.

Finally, our top players, but not our top result.

- These were the final Winter Games for Brian Stemmle. The veteran downhill skier came oh-so-close to his best race ever. Disappointed in his three previous Olympic Games results (26th in the 1994 Olympic super-G, 23rd in the 1992 downhill and a fall in 1988 in the Calgary downhill), Stemmle was determined to ski his best at Nagano. He neatly manoeuvered past a tricky section of the course that had slowed or eliminated much of the competition, and posted the best time of the field for the first two-thirds of the race. Then disaster struck — the Aurora, Ontario, native caught a ski in loose snow, missed a gate, and was eliminated. Just like that, his career was over. "*I thought I was doing well in the turn and I just got on the high side a little bit and couldn't hold my balance and ended up missing the gate,*" Stemmle said. "*I just lost concentration for a second. It's hard, it's really hard,*" he continued, "*I've been in four Olympics and bombed out in all of them. It (Olympics) is a great experience and a great time, but to be successful is really tough.*"

- Snowboarder Ross Rebagliati had a wild Olympic experience in the first-ever snowboarding events at the Games. Rebagliati came down the hill in first place, received his gold medal to a stirring rendition of O Canada, then retired to the Athlete's Village to enjoy the rest of the Games. Two days after his event he had a test result come back — positive. It was found that he had traces of marijuana in his system, an illegal substance at the Games, and would therefore have to hand back his medal. The Canadian team protested, arguing that even if it was positive, the substance clearly would not have helped him. Rebagliati himself argued that he must have acquired traces through inhaling second-hand smoke back in Whistler, where using marijuana is, well, popular. The initial appeal failed, but had to go to a separate arbitration panel before his medal could be removed. There, at the final hearing possible before the medal was lost, the case was thrown out on a technical discrepancy between the ski federation and the Olympic organization. Ross Rebagliati was still an Olympic champion.

- Marc Gagnon, Derrick Campbell, Eric Bédard and François Drolet led for most of the race in the men's 5000m short-track speed skating final and narrowly upset the favoured South Korean team to win the Olympic gold medal. For

Gagnon it was a bittersweet moment. He was favoured in his earlier 500m and 1000m individual races, but fell in both. His dream, and even his expectations, were finally met with the relay performance. Gagnon fought back tears as he told a television audience how he felt: "*It means a lot. I had a tough beginning to these Games, falling in the 1000m and again falling today in the 500m. It was very disappointing. But I forgot about it right away, I went to the relay and was confident we could do it. I'm so proud. I'm so proud.*"

- Canada had great and not-so-great success on the bobsleigh run. Driver Pierre Leuders and his brakeman Dave MacEachern from PEI, won the gold medal in the two-man event. But the four-man was a logistical nightmare all the way through. Disgruntled veteran driver Chris Lori was asked by teammates to drive the four-man sled and let Leuders concentrate on the two-man. Lori thought it was a great opportunity to win that elusive Olympic medal. Canadian bobsleigh officials, and Leuders, disagreed and put Leuders in Canada I with the top team. They finished ninth compared to the 11th place finish for Canada II driven by Lori. "*The two-man gold, though, is really what we should remember,*" said the officials.

- The Canadian women's hockey team were the four-time world champions, in fact the only world champions in women's hockey, coming into Nagano. They expected the gold medal, but knew they would be in tough against a strong American team. In the end, perhaps as a result of being overly-tight throughout the tournament, the Canadians lost a 3-1 heartbreaker in the final game. The score actually flattered Canada, for if goaltender Manon Rhéaume had not played so splendidly in the second period, the score could have been much worse. After standing and listening to The Star Spangled Banner during the medal ceremony, the Canadians returned to their dressing room, to sing O Canada together privately.

"*They played better,*" said Judy Diduck, of Sherwood Park, Alberta. "*They played three periods. We played one. Hats off to them.*" "*We came to get gold. We didn't get it. But this is a silver medal at the Olympics,*" said Canadian captain Stacy Wilson.

"*It came down to one game,*" said Fiona Smith, also of Sherwood Park. "*We played our hearts out. We went into our dressing room

and sang our own national anthem. Canada should have been proud of us. I'm wearing an Olympic silver medal, and how many people have one of these? It's been a huge thrill to play in the first women's hockey tournament in Olympic history. The Olympic experience has been phenomenal.*"

- Since the Canadian men's team had been announced on November 29, 1997, Canadians had talked not of which teams would be in the Olympic final, but who Canada would be playing in the game. After years, decades in fact, of trying to get our best hockey players in the Olympics, the Games would at long last include the top NHL players. Yet, however close we came, however hard the players tried, they did not meet expectations on the ice. Canada suffered a heartbreaking loss in a shootout semi-final against the Czech Republic, the eventual gold medallists, then inexplicably lost 3-2 to Finland in the bronze medal game to come home with a fourth place finish.

- In a surprising move by Canadian hockey coach Marc Crawford, he elected to use Ray Bourque in the pivotal shoot-out against the Dominic Hasek-led team from the Czech Republic. Sitting on the bench during the losing cause

were the likes of all-time NHL scoring leader Wayne Gretzky, and sharpshooters Mark Recchi and Steve Yzerman.

- After losing in the tie-breaking shootout 1-0 (and therefore the game 2-1) against the Czech Republic, all-time NHL scoring leader Wayne Gretzky took a moment to sit by himself on the Canadian team bench, head down, dejected. The player who almost single-handedly made hockey popular even in spaces where it was never played, who had campaigned long and hard to allow professional hockey players to play in the Olympics, who had come so close to achieving his dream of being an Olympic champion, was alone with millions of eyes watching him. It was an image rarely seen of the gifted "Great One," and reflected the country's agony in watching others play "our" game better.

- The last Winter Games of the century saw Canada achieve a first — ending up with more medals than the Americans. When Canada won the men's 5000m short-track speed skating on the second last day of the Games, it gave Canada 15 medals to the Americans' 13. Yet, if Canada hadn't won that gold, the Americans would have won the gold medal count 6-5.

Canada

Our Century in Sport

Canada's Olympic Summary

Canada's Olympic Medal Summary, 1900-2000

Year	Games	Gold	Silver	Bronze	Total	Team Size
1900	Paris	1	0	1	2	2 (unofficial)
1904	St. Louis	4	1	1	6	43 (unofficial)
1906	Athens	1	1	0	2	4 (unofficial)
1908	London	3	3	9	15	91
1912	Stockholm	3	2	2	7	36
1916	Cancelled due to WW I	–	–	–	–	–
1920	Antwerp	3*	3	3	9	47
1924	Paris	0	3	1	4	73
1928	Amsterdam	4	4	7	15	71
1932	Los Angeles	2	5	8	15	102
1936	Berlin	1	3	5	9	109
1940	Cancelled due to WW II	–	–	–	–	–
1944	Cancelled due to WW II	–	–	–	–	–
1948	London	0	1	2	3	106
1952	Helsinki	1	2	0	3	113
1956	Melbourne	2	1	3	6	99
1960	Rome	0	1	0	1	97
1964	Tokyo	1	2	1	4	118
1968	Mexico City	1	3	1	5	143
1972	Munich	0	2	3	5	220
1976	MONTREAL	0	5	6	11	414
1980	Moscow (did not attend)	0	0	0	0	221 (unofficial)
1984	Los Angeles	10	18	16	44	436
1988	Seoul	3	2	5	10	354
1992	Barcelona	7	4	7	18	314
1996	Atlanta	3	11	8	22	307
2000	Sydney	3	3	8	14	311
TOTALS	**24 Olympic Games**	**53**	**80**	**97**	**230**	**3831**

*1920 Gold Awarded Retroactivley

CSI/COA

Canada's Olympic Summer Medal Summary, 1900-2000, By Sport

Sport	Gold	Silver	Bronze	TOTALS
Basketball	0	1	0	1
Boxing	3	7	7	17
Canoeing	3	8	5	16
Cycling	0	4	5	9
Diving	1	1	3	5
Equestrian	1	1	2	4
Golf	1	0	0	1
Gymnastics	0	0	2	2
Hockey	1	0	0	1
Judo	0	2	2	4
Lacrosse	2	0	1	3
Rhythmic Gymnastics	1	0	0	1
Rowing	8	12	12	32
Shooting	4	3	2	9
Soccer	1	0	0	1
Swimming	7	13	19	39
Synchronized Swimming	3	4	1	8
Taekwondo	0	0	1	1
Tennis	1	0	0	1
Track & Field	14	15	23	52
Triathlon	1	0	0	1
Volleyball	0	0	1	1
Weightlifting	0	2	0	2
Wrestling	1	5	5	11
Yachting	0	2	6	8
TOTALS	**53**	**80**	**97**	**230**

Canada's Olympic Winter Medal Summary, 1924-2000

Year	Games	Gold	Silver	Bronze	Total	Team Size
1924	Chamonix	1	0	0	1	12
1928	St. Moritz	1	0	0	1	25
1932	Lake Placid	1	1	5	7	53
1936	Garmisch-Partenkirchen	0	1	0	1	30
1940	Cancelled due to WW II	–	–	–	–	–
1944	Cancelled due to WW II	–	–	–	–	–
1948	St. Moritz	2	0	1	3	36
1952	Oslo	1	0	1	2	39
1956	Cortina d'Ampezzo	0	1	2	3	37
1960	Squaw Valley	2	1	1	4	44
1964	Innsbruck	1	0	2	3	62
1968	Grenoble	1	1	1	3	71
1972	Sapporo	0	1	0	1	60
1976	Innsbruck	1	1	1	3	60
1980	Lake Placid	0	1	1	2	59
1984	Sarajevo	2	1	1	4	69
1988	CALGARY	0	2	3	5	117
1992	Albertville	2	3	2	7	117
1994	Lillehammer	3	6	4	13	104
1998	Nagano	6	5	4	15	154
TOTALS	**18 Olympic Winter Games**	**24**	**25**	**29**	**78**	**1149**

Canada's Olympic Winter Medal Summary, 1924-2000, By Sport

Sport	Gold	Silver	Bronze	TOTALS
Alpine	4	1	5	10
Biathlon	2	0	1	3
Bobsleigh	2	0	0	2
Curling	1	1	0	2
Figure Skating	2	7	9	18
Freestyle Skiing	1	1	1	3
Hockey	6*	5	2	13
Snowboarding	1	0	0	1
Speed Skating	6	10	11	27
TOTALS	**25***	**25**	**29**	**79***

*Includes 1920 Hockey gold won at the Summer Olympic Games in Antwerp.

Myriam Bédard, 1992

In the excitement of celebrating
victory, it is sometimes easy
to forget the stories of those
who finished behind the leader.
Silver or bronze medals
can run the gamut from being
the unexpected pinnacle of
an athlete's career to being
a bitter disappointment
at not winning gold.
Sport is also no stranger
to disappointment, hardship,
and even tragedy.
These are the stories that are told in
Clouds and Silver Linings.

Canada

Our
Century
in Sport

1900-2000

Chapter III

Clouds
and
Silver
Linings

1980

'There's a hero'

Since the time of Terry Fox's death in 1981, annual Terry Fox Runs have been held across Canada and in dozens of other countries in memory of his Marathon of Hope. As of 2000, some $250 million had been raised for cancer research worldwide. This Maclean's article was written just after he was forced to quit his run.

The Agony and the Ecstasy of Terry Fox

**by Warren Gerard
September 15, 1980**

He wasn't suddenly smitten, but early last week Terry Fox knew something was terribly wrong. The hopping, running 22-year-old amputee was well over the halfway mark in his coast-to-coast odyssey to show Canada he could *do* it — and to raise funds for cancer research. From April 12, when he dipped his artificial limb into the Atlantic Ocean at St. John's and began to run, until last week and 5,342 km later, Terry Fox had become a national symbol of courage, and some close to him said even stubbornness. But it wasn't to end as Terry Fox thought, and as every Canadian hoped, reminded daily as they were by the catchy jingle on radio and television, *Run Terry, Run.* Rather, it ended on the Thunder Bay bypass headed for the Red River Road in Northern Ontario. For two days, maybe three, he hadn't felt right — but he wasn't about to quit. Then, at the 29 km point on Tuesday's run, he recalled, "There was hardness of breath. I was coughing. I started to choke. I didn't know what was going on." In severe pain, he still wouldn't quit. People were lining the road ahead and he wanted to run out of people before he quit. "There was no way I was going to stop running, not with all those people there." So he ran another mile and then there were no more people. And for Terry, no more road.

His parents, Rolly and Betty Fox, flew from their home in Port Coquitlam, BC, to be with Terry. The cancer that had caused him to have his leg amputated had returned, this time to his lungs. That afternoon, his silent father on one side of a stretcher bed, his mother, unable to hold back the

emotion, on the other, Terry held a press conference: "Do you want to ask questions or should I just say what I want?" He went ahead. "I didn't think this would happen, it was an unbelievable shock. I mean, I've been doing great, doing those 26 miles every day, up those hills, I had less than 2,000 to go. I thought I was lucky as I could get. Well, you know I had primary cancer in my knee 3 1/2 years ago, and now the cancer is in my lungs, and I really have to go home and have some more x-rays, and maybe an operation that will involve opening up my chest, or more drugs. I'll do everything I can. I'm gonna do my very best, I'll fight, I promise I won't give up."

During the run, Cancer Society officials found out just how stubborn and determined Terry was. Even though they made repeated requests that he have regular medical checkups, he refused: "There's no doctor in the world who has had an amputee who's doing anything on an artificial leg like I am. If I went to see a doctor, he'd have a pessimistic approach to me."

It was as if he were inspired, and nothing, no one, would change his heart. When he first thought of the idea three years ago even his mother, Betty, despite knowing intimately her son's stubborn gutsiness, told him he was "crazy." He went to see Blair MacKenzie, executive-director of the BC and Yukon division of the Cancer Society, who said that when he first saw the young, curly-headed youth limp into his office on a metal-and-plastic leg he was skeptical. "We get a lot of requests that are a little off-centre, so I said, fine, organize it yourself, and he did. I was really taken with him."

Terry organized a dance and approached Vancouver businessmen for support. "I'm not a dreamer," he said in his appeals for aid, "and I'm not saying that this will initiate any kind of definitive answer or cure to cancer, but I believe in miracles. I have to." At the same time, Terry, a B-average student at Simon Fraser University, had been training. At first he hobbled through the streets of Port Coquitlam, for almost a kilometer, then he increased the distance by the same amount each week — up to 42 km a day.

As Terry, in his odd hop-and-run style moved westward, the country became more aware of what he was doing. On May 18, he was in Sherbrooke, NS saying the trip so far was a "piece of cake." On June 4, he was in Fredericton, NB, losing weight and having problems with his artificial leg. But now the money was coming in — $100,000, and the $1-million mark looked good. On June 21 he was in Quebec: "At a press conference nobody knew what we were talking about."

On a couple of occasions he was nearly run off the road by transport trucks, and police barred him from the Trans-Canada Highway as a traffic hazard. He was pelted by hailstones as big as golfballs and the leg continued to fall off, and to hurt. On his way he met Governor-General Ed Schreyer and Prime Minister Pierre Trudeau, who said he didn't have time to run with Terry. He met his hockey heroes, Darryl Sittler and Bobby Orr. Sittler later said he would carry on the run if that's what Terry

wanted. In Toronto, the crowds were overwhelming — 10,000 at city hall — and cops were seen to cry.

At the point where he stopped in Northern Ontario, out of sight of the crowds, proud, still determined, Terry Fox had done something that no individual had ever done before — he had raised almost $2 million for cancer research.

At week's end he was still in hospital in good spirits. Meanwhile, the country is in a flurry of fund-raising for cancer research. Contributions are coming from everywhere. Governments, cities, small communities are making pledges. The CTV network said it would open up four hours of prime-time Sunday night television for a tribute to Terry Fox. Pledges will be taken. One radio station, CKFM, in Toronto has raised more than $236,000. The country is in a frenzy of giving — not so much, perhaps, for cancer research, but for Terry Fox.

Terry bravely promises to return, to finish the run he started, next year, the year after — maybe. But he accomplished what he set out to do. It was summed up by Sheila Fox (no kin to Terry) of Kitchener, Ont., a Cancer Society representative, who said "You know, they say the United States is built on a history of heroes while Canadians have none to look up to. But when I looked down the street today and saw Terry, I said 'There's a hero.'" ❧

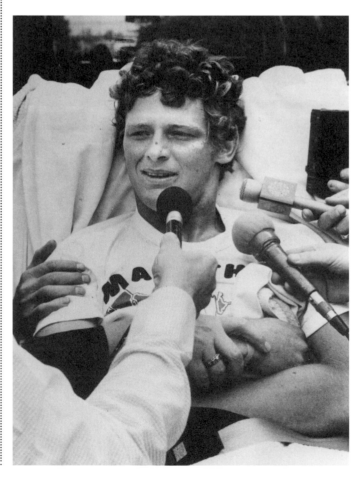

1906 – 1927

Track and Field

The Rise and Fall of Tom Longboat

by Fergus Cronin
February 4, 1956

A two foot wooden marker over an Indian grave near Brantford, Ont. is the only monument today to a man who once was the best known athlete in the world. His was a Horatio Alger story in reverse. For him there was no long struggle against odds, no interminable hours of training for a gradual and painful climb to the top. He started very near the top in 1906 and was not long in reaching it. Then, over the years, he worked his way to the bottom. Literally, his was a story of Public Hero to Garbage Collector.

He was a naive, long-limbed youth of nineteen, five-foot-ten and a half in height and weighing about one hundred and forty pounds, when he took time out from his farm work on the reserve to try his luck in the 1906 edition of a race sponsored by the Hamilton Herald and known as the Around-the-Bay Race.

Longboat stepped up to the starting line wearing a thirty-five-cent cotton bathing suit and a pair of seventy-five-cent rubber sneakers. It was during this race that Longboat's peculiar style of running was first noted. He had a long slow stride that was deceiving in its speed and seemed to carry him over the ground with the least possible exertion.

The Herald reported the next day: "Marsh was the pacemaker in the early part of the race, but right behind him was Longboat, who occasionally shot to the front just to test his speed."

Marathon runner Tom Longboat, 1908.

Longboat beat Marsh by a full three minutes, and his time of one hour, 49 minutes and 25 seconds was only 42 seconds behind the record — in spite of the fact that toward the end of the race he had taken a wrong turning and ran seventy five yards before someone turned him back.

Members of the West End YMCA of Toronto convinced Longboat he should join their ranks and represent them in the Boston Marathon, an annual event since 1897 and the only one of the old running classics still held today.

The Boston event was twenty-five miles in open country, much of it uphill. There were one hundred and twenty six entries, but Longboat was confident. As he climbed aboard the train he told a reporter with a grin that became his trademark, "No more Tom Longboat. I'm Cyclone Jack now." Before he was through, the public and the newspapers had many pet names for him, probably the favourite of which was "the Bronze Mercury."

April 19, 1907, was a miserable day in Boston. Runners had to buck snow, rain and slush. But Longboat won with ease. He finished in two hours, 24 minutes and 24 seconds, a record that stood for four years and was broken only after the course was made easier.

It was an era in which the individual champion rather than the team was idolized and, in the fashion of Sullivan and Corbett, the fighters, and Ned Hanlan, the oarsman, Longboat became Public Hero No. 1 to most Canadians and many Americans in a period that came to be known for "the marathon craze."

He was likeable but headstrong. He soon balked at the training rules of the West End Y, claiming with some truth, that he hadn't done much training before and saw no need for it now. He broke the Y's rules against smoking and drinking and was suspended.

But he was not long without a sponsor. Two robust Toronto Irishmen, Tom Flanagan and Tim O'Rourke, joint owners of the Grand Central Hotel, had just organized the Irish-Canadian Athletic Club, whose avowed purpose was to promote amateur sport. In reality, however, it was a semi-professional club with headquarters in the hotel, whose athletes were the objects of heavy betting. Longboat joined the club — sometimes he was called "the Irish Indian" — and his training was taken over by Flanagan.

In spite of Longboat's reluctance to train, the prospect of representing Canada in the 1908 Olympic Games in London appealed to him.

The Olympic Marathon was the longest race Longboat had yet run — 26 miles, 385 yards, the distance run in 490 BC from Marathon to Athens by a Greek soldier with news of victory. The sun was scorching as fifty-five marathoners from a dozen countries lined up four deep on the east lawn of Windsor Castle.

At 2:33 p.m. the pistol cracked. Longboat, in a white jersey adorned with a maple leaf and the number 72, leaped to the front like a deer and set a killing pace. He appeared to be in perfect condition and led for a few miles, but the hills and the heat and the pace began to tell on him.

At about the nineteen-mile mark he had slowed to a walk, then stopped altogether. He proceeded to the stadium in a car and was carried in on a stretcher for medical attention. Later Flanagan said, "It was the heat that beat him. We lost honestly." But Canadians and others could not believe he had failed them and rumours were widespread that Longboat had been doped. Only recently a fan (E.V.E. Harris, of Sacramento, Calif.) wrote in a sports magazine "I had followed (Longboat) on a bicycle twice while training over the full route and never saw him distressed. You can never convince

Tom Longboat winning the 1907 Boston Marathon.

Longboat Highlights

1907

Famed long-distance runner Tom Longboat was twice suspended and reinstated for professionalism, but it didn't keep him from winning the Boston Marathon in world record time and helping to stimulate international interest in marathon racing. It would not be until after the Olympic Games in 1908 that Longboat would sign an official professional racing contract.

During his career, Tom Longboat was often called "the greatest distance runner of them all." He won the 1907 Boston marathon by a wide margin, somehow faltered in the 1908 Olympic marathon after leading most of the race, turned professional, won many races both in North America and Europe, and set the record for the 15 miles.

1909

Tom Longboat and Alfie Shrubb of England faced each other in the marathon "race of the century" at Madison Square Garden in New York. Before over 12,000 spectators, Longboat would pass his rival for good during the 24th mile to win and be regarded as the world's best long distance runner.

me that he wasn't 'jobbed' or that possibly $100,000 was not won on his failure."

Back in New York a pair of promoters, Pat Powers and Harry Pollock, proceeded to capitalize on the intense public interest in marathons, sparked by the Olympics. The pair induced Dorando and Hayes [Olympic gold and silver medallists respectively] to turn professional and run against each other in the Garden over the full marathon distance. Then Powers set out to get Longboat too to turn pro and race Dorando, but another professional had been vainly trying to take on Longboat since well before the Olympics.

He was Alfred Shrubb, reputed to be a perfect running machine, a cocky little Englishman who held all world distance records from one and a half to eleven miles. And after the Olympics, in spite of a campaign of taunting and ridicule by Shrubb, Flanagan felt that Longboat had to redeem himself if he was to be successful as a professional.

COG-WA-GEE
LONGBOAT

The Indian proceeded to do just that, winning race after race. William Stark, president of the Canadian AAU, said "I think he has since his return (from the Olympics) proven himself the greatest long-distance runner of the century."

Sports writers and the sporting public began to demand a showdown between Longboat and Shrubb but Powers offered Flanagan a portion of the gate receipts if Longboat would take on Dorando. Flanagan agreed to a race in the Garden on Dec. 15, 1908. It was a sell-out.

Longboat was now a professional and, at twenty-one, recognized as the best long-distance runner in the world.

Longboat and Shrubb were finally signed to run a marathon in Madison Square Garden on Feb. 5, 1909. At last the two greatest runners of the world were to match skills in what was considered the world's greatest race.

At the pistol, Shrubb shot away amid frantic cheering and gained a complete lap (a ninth of a mile) in the first mile and a half. Longboat, loping along with a stride of six feet, six inches, made no effort to keep up.

Longboat's only chance lay in Shrubb's collapsing and there was no indication of this. During the twenty-first mile Shrubb stopped and changed his shoes while Longboat recovered a lap and a half. The crowd rose to its feet and screamed with excitement. At the end of twenty-two miles Shrubb was still seven laps ahead, but apparently weakening while Longboat looked as strong as ever.

The noise was terrific as Longboat reduced the lead to four laps in the twenty-third mile. Shrubb began to limp and his lead was reduced to two laps. As Longboat's steady pace ate up the remaining distance Shrubb began staggering from side to side. Longboat spurted past him.

Since turning professional, Longboat had been giving Flanagan trouble. "He was all right until he started to make money," Flanagan said later. "There were times when he did not feel like running, when he refused to train properly and just generally went prima donna on me."

So Flanagan, who had become manager for Jack Johnson, later to become world's heavyweight boxing champion, sold Longboat's contract to Powers for two thousand dollars.

Then Powers organized the daddy of all marathons, to be held in the open at the New York Polo Grounds which could hold twice as many spectators as the Garden. The race, held April 3, 1909, offered five thousand dollars to the best of six men representing five nations: Longboat, Shrubb, Dorando, Hayes, Matt Maloney (another American) and Henri St. Yves, a dark horse from France, imported by Powers and Pollock and whom no one in America had ever heard of.

Twenty-five thousand people saw Longboat give up in the twentieth mile. Shrubb fell into a walk in the twenty-second, St. Yves won and Dorando came

second. Longboat, at twenty-one, was on his way down.

When World War I broke out, Flanagan donned the uniform of a captain. With Col. Dick Greer he formed the 180th Sportsmen's Battalion and Longboat joined as a private. But army discipline did little to change the Indian's unpredictable nature.

The war ended, but Longboat's troubles had only begun.

He drifted from job to job, farming in Alberta — working in a steel mill in Buffalo, odd jobs anywhere — and in 1922, now thirty-five, he returned penniless to Toronto and a job in a rubber plant. His name flared again briefly when he challenged Paavo Nurmi, the remarkable Finn, but the AAU refused to reinstate Longboat as an amateur. By 1927 he had hit the low point of his career — a job as helper on a Toronto garbage wagon.

What became of the thousands Longboat won in his prime? In his first three years as a professional he earned about seventeen thousand dollars.

Longboat blew his money on liquor, fancy clothes and foolish investments in real estate. He had no idea how to handle it.

"He was a better man as an Indian than he was trained as a white man," Flanagan said recently. "I often thought if we could have kept him on the reservation and brought him out just to run, what he could have done would have been even more remarkable." ✦

1908

One of Canada's top athletes ever, and likely our greatest of the 19th century, was rowing champion Ned Hanlon. In 350 recorded races, the Toronto native won a remarkable 344. Dubbed The Boy in Blue, Hanlon died at age 53 in 1908. In 1920 the rowing fraternity erected a massive 20-foot statue on the CNE grounds in Toronto in his honour. A movie life story on Hanlon, The Boy in Blue, was made in 1990.

Sam Langford, the "Boston Tar Baby"

There are many great moments in sport but then there are also moments that aren't so great. Nova Scotia boxer's Sam Langford's great moment, a shot at the world title, eluded him because he was black.

Sam Langford's stone fists and his skillful boxing propelled him to the very top of his profession. Promoters and champions avoided him because they thought he was too good. But, the real reason was that racially-prejudiced promoters and the general public wanted to keep division titles as the private preserve of white fighters. As late as the 1950s, former heavyweight champion Jack Dempsey funded the Jack Dempsey White Hope Tournament in an attempt to win back the heavyweight crown for the white race.

Langford is rated by *Ring Magazine* as one of the top ten heavyweight boxers of all-time. He began his fight career when he weighed only 132 pounds and fought his way up through all the divisions. Despite his success in the ring, however, once his career was over he was found living blind and destitute in a Harlem, New York, tenement.

Nicknamed "The Boston Tar Baby," he never held a world title but he fought and defeated most of the world champions in non-title bouts. He stood only 5' 6" tall but he had a 73" reach. He was both a classic boxer and a devastating puncher with both hands.

In his 21-year ring career he fought nearly 300 recorded professional fights. He scored 129 knockouts in 181 wins, lost 22 and drew nine. Sixty-six other bouts were non-decision exhibitions. Most of his losses were after he was 35 years of age and going blind.

At the age of 12 he ran away from home in Weymouth Falls, Nova Scotia, and rode the rails to Boston. He fought his first fight in 1902 when he was 16 and scored a sixth round knockout. When he was only 18 he defeated world welterweight champion, the great Joe Gans, in a non-title bout. That same year he fought a 15-round draw with Joe Walcott, former world welterweight champion.

In 1906, barely 20 years old, he lost a 15-round decision to black heavyweight champion, Jack Johnson. Johnson weighed in at 186 pounds and Langford was 156 pounds. Johnson had Langford on the canvas twice. Two years later, Johnson was heavyweight champion of the world but he would never give Langford a rematch during the seven years he held the title between 1908 and 1915.

Few of Langford's opponents fared well against him: He knocked out Jack O'Brien, then the current light heavyweight champion, in five rounds. He fought the great "Michigan Assassin," Stanley Ketchel, middleweight champion, to a draw. He sent "Fireman"

1906-08

Tommy Burns won the world heavyweight boxing title, defeating Marvin Hart in Los Angeles. Burns successfully defended the title 15 times, in sanctioned and exhibition bouts. On his 16th defence on December 25, 1908, though, he lost the heavyweight title to boxing's first black champion, American Jack Johnson, while touring in Australia.

Jim Flynn to the canvas for the count in the first round. Fighting in Paris, he finished off his opponent only 17 seconds into Round One.

The victories continued. In 1923 he was heavyweight champion of Mexico and Spain. He won the Mexican title with a knockout and scored six consecutive KOs defending the title over a three month period. Ring historians rank Langford alongside ring greats Archie Moore, Bob Foster, Gene Tunney, Michael Spinks and Ezzard Charles.

He fought in Canada, all over the United States, in Australia, France, Spain and Mexico. But, he would never be allowed to enter a North American ring as a title challenger.

In the 1920s Sam Langford was slowly going blind. In 1926 he was knocked out in the first round by an unseeded "nobody" — Brad Simmons — in Oklahoma and was persuaded to retire. In 1944 a sportswriter found him living in a cheap tenement — alone, blind and penniless. The ensuing publicity resulted in a trust fund which allowed him to live his last years in comfort.

He died in Cambridge, Massachusetts, in 1956. Ring Magazine named him to its Hall of Fame — the first non-champion ever elected. ❦

1914-18

WW I took the lives of many Canadians, including hockey players. Many teams wound up joining en masse, leaving shortages at home in the leagues. A year after winning the Allan Cup for Senior Hockey supremacy in 1915, the Winnipeg Monarchs joined the Winnipeg 61st Battalion and headed for France. The Winnipeg Falcons teamed up with the 223rd Battalion and joined the war efforts in 1917, with Falcons Olie Turnbull, Buster Thorsteinson and George Cumbers making the supreme sacrifice for their country. The famed Ottawa Senator, Frank One-Eye McGee, must have talked his way through his army physical since he passed it with perfect eyesight. He paid the sacrifice in 1916 at the Somme. Future Toronto Maple Leaf owner Conn Smythe was the captain with the University of Toronto Blues in 1915 when he coaxed Gordon Southam of the newspaper family to pay for a Sportsman's Battery. The Battery took part in the great Vimy Ridge battles, with Southam not returning, and Smythe never forgetting.

1930s

Two Ottawa amateur boxers are forgotten footnotes to ring history. Harvey Lacelles scored a five round decision over Walker Smith in Smith's last amateur bout in Ogdensburg, New York. Smith turned professional, changed his name and became better known as Sugar Ray Robinson, eventual winner of several world titles. Harvey Lacelles never did turn pro. Johnny Page spoiled Carmen Basilio's last fight as an amateur by out-boxing him and winning a five round decision over the hard hitting American brawler in Utica, New York. Basilio went off to war with the US Marines and came home safely to win and lose six world titles. Johnny Page also went off to war with the RCAF as a Pilot Officer Air Gunner with 405 City of Vancouver Squadron, but he did not come home to resume his ring career. He was killed when his Halifax bomber was shot down over Holland during a raid on Bremen, Germany, on June 28, 1942. He was only 23.

1900

At the start of the century George Dixon was the world featherweight boxing champion (and had been for most of the previous 10 years). He didn't make it long into the new century though, losing the title on January 9, 1900.

1927
Swimming

George Young, Yesterday's Hero

by Robert Thomas Allen
September 1, 1949

On January 16, 1927, George Young, the 17-year-old son of a Toronto cleaning woman, defeated 102 of the world's best swimmers in the $25,000 Wrigley Marathon; he was the only contender to cross the 20 mile channel between Santa Catalina Island off the coast of California, and Point Vincente on the mainland.

Shortly before dawn, after 15 hours and 46 minutes in the water, he reached shore at Miramont Club beach, raised his arms to 5,000 spectators and touched off a story that, before it ended, involved the frustration of a city, the snubbing of a mayor, a bitter front-page feud, a legal tangle involving a battery of lawyers, banks and trust companies, and a red-hot controversy that, 22 years later, can still be fanned into fist fights.

The story of George Young illustrates a lot of things; but, most of all, it illustrates the cruel fickleness of the public, who one day can hoist a man to world fame as the greatest living model of sterling youth, filial love, clean living and courage, and the next, tag him with the sports fan's term of derision: "a bum."

Those who have swum with him and worked with him know that he isn't a quitter or a phoney. Professional swimmers, and others connected with the sport, unanimously regard George Young as one of the greatest swimmers that world has produced. Not a few consider him *the* greatest swimmer.

At his peak Young was once offered a $250,000 movie contract and a $5,000 a week personal appearance tour. Actually he made more than $60,000. But when I visited him in Philadelphia a few weeks ago, he was working as a machinist in the roundhouse of the Pennsylvania Railway for about $50 a week. He still looks back to the time, but less and less frequently, when he shot like a rocket across the front pages of the continent and soared to the giddy heights of fame.

When news of the big California swim being sponsored by chewing gum magnate Wm. Wrigley, Jr., reached Toronto, George and a pal, Bill Hastings, then Canadian high-diving champion, decided to go down there so that George could give it a try.

After a futile attempt to raise funds, they got enough from their mothers to get by, and started off on Bill's motorcycle; Bill driving, George bundled in the sidecar.

They reached Los Angeles early in December with a

couple of honeymooners who had picked them up somewhere in Arkansas after the motorcycle had collapsed, and went directly to the home of Henry ("Doc") O'Byrne, a Toronto man. It came out later that Mrs. Young had signed an agreement giving O'Byrne 40% of anything George earned.

Few people would have given a bent nickel for George's chances. He was in with the toughest competition in the world. Many rated the Catalina as a more difficult swim than the English Channel. The water was frigid and the channel swept by powerful tides.

There was no official record of anyone having swum it. It had taken a 15 man team, swimming in relays, more than 23 hours to do it. Yet Young was to swim it in 15 hours and 46 minutes. His performance was one of the greatest swimming feats ever recorded.

Young's feat was so sensational that, later, when he was dropped from the public pedestal, some people refused to believe that he actually swam the Catalina. But a Wrigley representative sat in Young's rowboat together with his oarsmen, 10 or more passenger-laden boats followed close by with their search lights on him, and a tugboat accompanied him for the entire swim.

He went into the lead in the first stage of the marathon, his long, powerful glide soon hopelessly outdistancing, at an average of 44 strokes to the minute, early sprinters doing 50 to 70.

Young was never headed after overtaking Chicago's Norman Ross, one of the top distance swimmers of the US, who later publicly declared George to be one of the greatest swimmers of all time.

Although the airline distance was about 20 miles, to take advantage of the currents Young swam closer to 30. He had to get through a 200-yard patch of heavy oil and two fields of kelp, a weed that at low tide lies on top of salt water like a cake of shredded wheat.

There was another hazard that has no official rating, but which was very real to George. It was a shark he saw swimming along with him early in the race. Californians had explained that the sharks in the channel did not attack humans, but George remained unconvinced and for every moment of his swim he was scared nearly out of his grease.

Norman Ross was taken out at 2:40 a.m. a beaten man. Pete Meyer, who came closest to Young's feat, succumbed to the cold a mile and a half from the mainland. Charles Toth and Henry Sullivan, both of whom had swum the English Channel, were forced to give up. Mrs. Martha Stager of Portland, Oregon, and Margaret Hauser of Long Beach, California, got within a few miles from shore but were defeated by the cold and tides. Clarabelle Barrett, a Pelham NY schoolteacher was taken out at 1:11 a.m.

Radio reports began to come through that a 17-year-old Canadian lad was still in there and looked as if he was going to finish. Crowds gathered at Miramont Club Beach and lit beacons. A mile from shore, in view of the beacons, George began to fight the outflowing tide. He fought it until the flow eased, just holding his position for more than an hour, while the crowd tried to make him hear their shouts of "Come on, George!" He made shore at 3:41 a.m.

George Young became the big news and the big attraction of North America, and he stood to make a pile of money on top of his $25,000.

Yet at the peak of his fame, things were happening which were fated to turn his brilliant success into a personal tragedy.

Although George was making appearances at Grauman's Egyptian theatre and the Paramount, the sports writers warned O'Byrne that he was losing thousands of dollars every day by not lining up some really fat contract for George while he was hot.

O'Byrne turned down one offer of a $250,000 movie contract from Carl Laemmle Jr. because he wanted $300,000. C. C. Pyle, noted for the big cheques he'd obtained for footballer "Red" Grange and tennis star Suzanne Lenglen, said that the Young party had already missed the boat.

Wm. Wrigley Jr., acting on his own initiative, clapped George's $25,000 into trust for him until he was 29, set a lawyer to the task of trying to straighten things out, then washed his hands of the affair.

By the time the Catalina prize money came through there were assignments against it. When the trust was terminated in 1939, Young's mother and his wife, Margaret, to whom he'd assigned his interests, collected about $14,000, out of which they spent $3,000 to fix up the gift house where they were all living. (It was later sold.)

Today, at 39, George is a hefty, rather awkward-moving man 5 feet, 8 3/4 inches tall, weighing 218 pounds, with a paunch and enough grey hair to show. He doesn't smoke or drink, and in spite of a bit of extra beef which could soon be worked off, he's in good shape.

And the man who was once offered a $250,000 movie contract hasn't got a dime.

Sober George didn't hit it off with Margaret, his fun-loving first wife, and they were divorced. Margaret has custody of their 11 year-old son whom George supports.

Did he enjoy being a hero? It was a pretty wonderful feeling, he says, all that money and excitement, especially for a 17 year-old kid in his circumstances.

"I found out, when the returns were in, that the financial side of it wasn't as glorious as I thought," he adds now "but all that acclaim made me feel like a million dollars anyway."

"Sometimes now, when I'm going down the street, strangers stop me and say: 'Aren't you George Young?' It's good to be remembered. That's something money can't buy.

"The trouble is" — George has a habit at times like this of resting his head on the back of the chair and closing his eyes — "you've got to win all the time. It's funny, how the public can be." ♣

Winnipeg's Jimmy Ball, far left, made the classic mistake of turning his head at the end of his race to check on his competition and narrowly missed winning an Olympic gold medal at the 1928 Olympic Games in Amsterdam, settling for a silver behind American Ray Barbuti in the men's 400m race. To attest to the closeness of the race, and to the appeal of the 100m Olympic champion, Ball inscribed on the photos he signed "... almost a Percy Williams finish."

1926

Hockey

Will U.S. Cash Cripple our Hockey?

by Charles H. Good
March 1, 1926

Can the backers of professional hockey in Canada hold their own against the money-bags of rich United States promoters or will Canadian hockey fans be forced year by year to see their stars disappear to shine in another firmament? That is the question which is worrying "pro" hockey fans.

For professional hockey is, first and last, a money-making affair. And, sad to say, our neighbours to the South possess more of that useful commodity, variously known as "jack" or "dough" or "mazuma" than we do. So, if hockey develops into a battle where the longest purse is bound to win, Canada's chances of retaining any star hockey experts will be very slim indeed.

It [organized hockey] has been going on for some time now but it is only in the last few years that it has developed into a real paying proposition in the eastern part of the country. The St. Pats, of Toronto, pack 'em in with but an indifferent team and the Canadiens and Maroons, of Montreal, play to capacity whenever they perform, no matter who their opponents may be. Ottawa misses very seldom, but there is grave danger that the strain of supporting a team of the calibre of the Senators, coupled with the long jumps entailing much extra expense, may at no late date compel the backers of the club to relinquish their franchise. This would be a national calamity, as Ottawa has bulked largely in the hockey world for these many years.

Here's the United States all worked up over the great puck chasing sport with Brooklyn, Philadelphia, not to speak of Chicago, Detroit and other sizeable cities ready to crash into the sport with both feet, in other words, all dressed up and nowhere to go. Signs are not lacking that those interested in the sport across the border are prepared to divorce themselves from their Canadian affiliations as soon as the time is ripe. Already there is some talk of the formation of a league composed of American cities alone.

And with all these cities hot after hockey, how long will Canada be able to hold its teams? As stated before, professional hockey is played for money and it is only logical to presume that star puck chasers will gravitate to the place where they can fatten their exchequers. This applies to clubs as well. Hamilton was frozen out; and what can happen to one can happen to all.

Time was when the fans yelled themselves into laryngitis, if that's the way you spell it, over players to whom $750 to $1,200 a season was big money. Them was the days that is no more. Progress and prices go hand in hand, and far be it from hockey to interfere with the laws of nature. Prices to-day in the NHL run from $2,000 up. They do say that Lionel Conacher coaxes the Pirates to the tune of $7,000, while Hap Day of St. Pats, former Varsity and Hamilton star, brings down a six and three ciphers. ♣

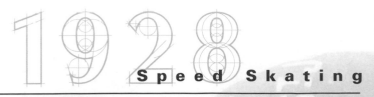

Speed Skating

A Skating Ace

by Louis Arthur Cunningham
March 15, 1928

Charles Gorman

Each year, about the time the championship skating meets are held, there appears in one or other of the big store-windows of Saint John's principal street a collection of cups, medals and trophies that would lead one to think the nation's athletes had pooled the symbols of their success. There you may see coveted cups and shields emblematic of the Mid-Atlantic Championship, the Canadian Indoor Championship, the United States Indoor, the International Indoor and Outdoor, the World's Championship — for speed skating — one man's achievements. Five world's records: the 440 yards, indoor and outdoor; the 220 yards, 1-6th mile and 75 yards indoors.

People crowd around to look: not very many. It's a thing taken for granted that the trophies should be there. If they were anywhere else they'd cause more excitement: they're so much a part of the Saint John that produced such skaters as Breen Duffy and Fred Logan, and proudly boasts that in it was born the man who brought this dazzling array of silver and bronze home with him — Charlie Gorman.

He's rather a taciturn seeming fellow, this Gorman. His face is forbidding and when, in the crux of a race, it's twisted into an angry, fighting scowl, it does succeed in intimidating his rivals. It's a square, dogged face, fit accompaniment for the sturdy build of his body. There's Youth in it, too — fighting, reckless Youth.

Gorman's a prize jokester. He dearly loves to 'kid' the crowd along and get them going. "Skating's a joke," he'll tell you. "If you're winning you go right ahead and win, making it look as if you were tearing your heart out; if you're losing, pick a nice soft snowbank, do a nose dive into it and get up swearing."

He will tell you that, but he never does it. He fights from start to finish and he's a hard loser, so hard that some are ready to call him a bad loser. But he's not that. To win a race means everything to him, he puts all he has into every event he enters.

He holds five world's records and all the championships available. At the Olympics he had everything to lose and relatively little to gain. But he went prepared to put his best into holding his crown.

When he left for St. Moritz, there was nothing of a send-off, no blare of bugles, roll of drums or cheering. He just went. He wouldn't say anything except the usual cry that he wasn't feeling in so good form. He wanted to be in Europe a few months before the races to get acclimated, to learn their methods thoroughly.

Four years ago, Gorman came back from the 1924 Olympics at Chamonix, defeated. But, as we look now at his career before and since that Olympiad, it seems clear that what he went through at Chamonix was the most significant factor in his development as a skater.

It was all new to him. Nervous and high strung by temperament, when the skaters lined up for the 500 metres he made three false starts. Finally, he got away better than Charles Jewtraw, his chief rival, the American International Champion, and took the lead, which he held, going at a terrific clip, until within twenty-five yards of the finish; then he crumpled up and Jewtraw, carried on by the furious pace Gorman set, flashed across the line, a winner in 44 seconds.

Gorman was badly undertrained, yet he entered the 5,000-metre race, which he could not finish.

The Olympic system of racing is vastly different from that followed in America. The skaters race against time, their thoughts not upon their speeding rivals, but upon a stop-watch.

This handicapped Gorman, as it did the Americans; and our method proved the undoing of Thunberg, the European Champion, when he appeared in America.

Canada

It was particularly hard on Gorman, for the element of personality is taken quite out of the race. Gorman's fighting instinct, his growling attitude, adopted for the game's sake towards other contenders, often has a psychological effect, especially upon the less seasoned skaters. But you can't frighten a stop-watch. It ticks inexorably.

But 1924 was Gorman's year. Less than a week after his return from Europe he went to Saranac Lake and fought through to win the United States National Amateur Outdoor Speed-Skating Championship with a total of ninety points. By way of good measure, he hung up a new world's record for the outdoor 440 yards — 36 and 3/5 seconds. By the end of February he was going great guns. At Lake Placid he won the International Championship from Francis Allen, of Chicago, in the last minute of the last race of the meet.

In February, 1926, skating at Saint John against the world's best, he won the world's championship, piling up a total of 140 points.

Clas Thunberg, the Finn, came to Canada for the meet, and Donovan and O'Neil Farrell,

Charles Gorman

a great field of entries. Thunberg was the Olympic champion. Only this year he captured the championship of Europe and he and Gorman met again at St. Moritz. Thunberg is a marvel but he was more handicapped by our style of racing than were the Canadian and American skaters by the European system.

The last event of that meet, the five mile race, was skated at twilight in a blizzard blast that cut to the bone. Gorman won it and the meet.

Frank Stack

Jack McCullogh

If a prophetic Moses had arisen to foretell the wonders that would be, he would have been howled down; but, as the subtitle-artist has it — came the winter of 1927, and on the frozen circuit epic events took place. The year is a unique record of straight success for the Canadian speed-skater.

Early in January, he won the Mid-Atlantic championship meet at Newburgh, scoring 110 out of a possible 120 points.

The next meet was at Detroit, the United States National Outdoor Championship. It was skated under difficulties of rough ice and unfavourable weather. Here Gorman tied for first place with Harry Nelson, scoring 80 points.

Early in February he went to Quebec, where he won the Canadian Indoor Championship, with a total of 120 points. It looked just too good to last and it was thought the great meets at Saranac and Lake Placid would give Gorman, now hailed as 'the fastest man in the world,' an upset. But at the International Championships, held at Saranac, Gorman broke the world's record for the 1-6th mile, and at the close of the meet he had piled up 140 points, leading the nearest contender by 30, and clipping a second off his old record of 36 3/5 for the 440, made at Lake Placid in 1924.

Then to Pittsburgh for the United States Indoor Championships. He took three firsts and the meet with a total of 150 points. In every event, except the three-mile, in which he did not start, he had the field.

That ended the circuit of 1927. Gorman had won every honour available in one season.

This year at the quaint old Swiss city of St. Moritz, Gorman met old friends and foemen. Thunberg was there, stronger and speedier than ever. O'Neil Farrell was there, Valentine Bialis, Jaffee and Eddie Murphy. He had fair time in which to work out on this side, though he passed back and forth several times between Saint John and Detroit before it was definitely known that he

would go with Logan and Ross Robinson to the Olympic winter sports. This time he arrived at St. Mortiz with the Americans, not ten days later, and he had with him staunch allies. He made no promises to anyone before leaving and would say nothing for the press. But to friends he again voiced the determination to win the 500-metre race, that once proved his Waterloo. ❦

Postscript — Shortly after this Maclean's article went to press a cable from St. Moritz announced that Gorman finished seventh in the Olympic 500-m race on February 13, 1928. Another skater fell in front of him and Gorman had to slow down to avoid him. Officials declined to allow Gorman a second chance to skate, and he subsequently withdrew from the 5,000 m race.

Early women speed skating champions, Leila Brooks (above), 1930, and Jean Wilson (top right), 1931.

Hilda's Olympic Memory

Hilda Strike, 1932

Even though Olympic judges and athletes take an oath to play fair, the Games are no stranger to controversy, whether brought on by circumstances, bending the rules, or even society's changing sensibilities. Consider the great Jim Thorpe, who in 1912 was stripped of his Olympic medals for having been paid as a summer minor-league player in an unrelated sport, medals which were reinstated years after his death. Or Canada's Sylvie Fréchette, who had to fight for two years to be rightly recognized as a gold medallist following a judge's error at the Barcelona Olympics in 1992.

Canadian sprinter Hilda Strike's story fits in the same category, although in her case the controversy didn't come to light until nearly 50 years after she won a silver medal at the 1932 Olympic Games in Los Angeles.

Hilda Strike raising her arms for an Olympic silver medal, 1932.

Born in Montreal on September 1, 1910, Hilda played many sports while growing up: softball, skating, swimming, badminton, volleyball, basketball and of course, running. Hilda was a sprinter and her best event was the 100 metres.

When Hilda arrived in Los Angeles, she came as Canadian champion in the 100m and Canada's female athlete of the year. Her teammates dubbed her "Skinny," because she only carried 105 pounds on a five-foot, four-inch frame.

Her tiny frame apparently had the experts fooled that week. No one seemed to believe "Skinny" really had those fast times in her. Given that the great Stella Walsh seemed to have a lock on the event, the race would be for the silver, between Marie Dollinger or Wilhelmina Von Brennan. No one figured on Hilda.

Silver medallist Hilda Strike, next to Poland's Stella Walsh.

Canada

The field in the final race was tough. Stella Walsh (born Stanislawa Walasiewicz) lived in the US but competed for Poland. She was the first woman to break 12 seconds in the 100m.

When the gun went off, Hilda leapt out of the blocks in a start so fast she made the others look anchored. In two strides she was a yard in front. By ten strides she was two yards ahead, and by twenty strides she had pulled even further ahead.

The women's 100m start at the 1932 Olympic Games in LA. Hilda Strike is in front, third from the right.

Skinny was flying down the line, and it looked like no one was going to catch her. At 50 yards, she was still ahead. The same at 60 yards. Then, finally, came the challenge, from the great Stella Walsh. At 80 yards Stella was on Hilda's heels. And by 95, she had caught her.

But Hilda wasn't about to give up. Reaching far, far down into her reserves, she came back with an additional burst of speed that brought her in line with Stella. But Stella answered, and reached the tape a foot ahead of Hilda.

For Hilda, the race marked a personal best — her time of 11.9 shaved a lot off her posted time as Canadian champ of 12.2 seconds.

The gold medallist and the silver medallist warmly shook hands on the track. The race was over. Hilda went on to pick up another silver medal in the 4 x 100m relay. She continued running, but never did beat Stella, although she always gave her a run for her money. In fact, later that year, Hilda and Stella raced again at the Canadian National Exhibition, and again the threat posed by Hilda forced the other sprinter into setting a new world record.

In time, Hilda married softball star Fred Sisson, retired from competitive running but continued to coach.

The story should end there, but it continues, in one of the most unusual postscripts in Olympic history.

In 1980, Stella Walsh was killed during a robbery. She was 69 years old. At the coroner's inquest, a cloud of controversy began to arise. Although the officials refused to discuss the situation, the coroner was having difficulty determining Stella Walsh's gender. It appeared that Stella was an anatomically correct male, which clearly called into question her eligibility to compete in women's events. Perhaps, according to the rules, Hilda should have received the gold medal after all.

When Hilda Strike was reached for comment, she was asked if she felt she deserved the gold, or if she would pursue the issue with the International Olympic Committee.

"No," Hilda replied, *"I don't think so. When we went out on the track that day, I accepted that field and raced against them. That was what happened that day. Eight of us ran; I came second."* ❦

Hilda Strike showing off her Olympic medals at her Hamilton home in 1980.

Track and Field

Phil Edwards

Few countries have benefited as Canada has from the sporting accomplishments of first generation immigrants. Sprinter Donovan Bailey and boxer Lennox Lewis, both Olympic gold medallists, are only two of many who have gone on to world renown. Early in the century it was middle-distance runner Phil Edwards who raced his way to fame and the Olympic medal podium for his adopted country.

Edwards came to Canada with his family in the 1920s from British Guyana, by way of New York. Even though the Edwards family came from an upper-class background (Phil's father was a respected magistrate), they still had to contend with the discrimination that the society of the time practised against black people. It was a time when the black population of Canada had shrunk to less than one percent and their lives were limited to jobs as railway porters for men and house cleaners for women.

Edwards had two goals in life — he wanted to compete in the Olympics, and become a doctor. British Guyana did not have an Olympic team and continuing his studies in New York would only allow for his career goal, so he moved to the nearest country with a British connection and ran for Canada in the 1928 games. He competed in three straight Olympics, compiling an unmatched competitive record.

Wearing Canada's uniform in 21 events from the 1928 Olympics in Amsterdam, through the depression-era Olympics of Los Angeles in 1932, and ultimately the infamous Nazi-organized games of Berlin in 1936, Phil Edwards was eliminated from further competition only once. That was in 1928 in the 400m semi-final after two first places in preceding heats. Every other time he advanced to the finals and ended his athletic career with five Olympic medals, all bronze. Although a small handful of Canadian athletes won four Olympic medals during the century, Edwards remained the only one to win five.

During his career he went from being an outsider to the leader of the Canadian track team and a man held in such high esteem that his teammates would at one point challenge accepted convention in the capital of the British Empire to support him.

Duncan McNaughton, Canada's high jump gold medallist in 1932 says, "Phil Edwards was one of my favourite people in life. One of the finest human beings I ever met. He studied medicine at McGill, had been Phi Betta Kappa at New York University, and put up a damn good show in every Olympics in which he competed." Margaret Lord, who chaperoned the 1936 Canadian team, declared, "He was wonderful man. And while times were different then and people of different races seldom mixed, he was welcomed in the best homes in Hamilton."

The 1928 Olympics were magnificent Games for Canadians, including double gold medallist Percy Williams from Vancouver, Saskatoon high jump gold medallist Ethel Catherwood, and Barrie,

Ontario's Fanny Rosenfeld (herself an immigrant from Russia), leader of the winning Canadian women's 4 x 100m relay team. Phil's third place medal as a member of the 4 x 400m relay team was almost an afterthought.

By the 1932 Olympics, though, his career was in full flight. He reached the finals in his three events, the 800m, 1500m, and 4 x 400m relay, and won bronze in each of them. There's no telling what he may have done with supportive coaching — in those days Canada's officials were appointed on the basis of administrative connection rather than specialist's knowledge.

"He was a natural," says James Worrall, who carried the Canadian flag in the 1936 Opening Ceremonies and competed in the 400m hurdles. "There was no one else in Canada who knew as much about middle-distance running as Phil. He had his own tactics and training methods. We called him the 'old rabbit.' He'd go out fast, take the lead, and try to hold on. His legs seemed disproportionately long for his body, and when he accelerated, his body seemed to slump, with his hip level going down two or three inches as he opened up his stride."

Edwards' character and athletic achievements had earned him not only respect but the captaincy of Canada's 1936 team. In Berlin the gold medal winning performances of American Jesse Owens challenged the racial theories of the host German Nazis but a more silent debt was owed to Edwards in the games' premier event, the 1500m.

Here the eventual winner, Jack Lovelock of New Zealand, found himself hopelessly boxed in early in the race. He appealed to Edwards and the gallant Canadian, perhaps sensing his own time had passed, let his opponent through. It may have been the difference in Lovelock's memorable victory as he outraced his American rival Glenn Cunningham.

In the 800m, Worrall painfully watched his good friend lose his final shot at gold. "There was a moment or two at the top of the final stretch where the American John Woodruff and Phil held the lead together. All I saw from my angle was what appeared to be one torso and four legs running under it, and then Woodruff pulled away." Edwards had to settle for his fifth and last bronze medal.

His teammates would have one last chance to salute their leader. On the way home Phil was refused entry to an exclusive Canadian-owned London hotel on Baker Street. The old ghost of segregation had raised its ugly head in the capital of an empire which included all races. Outraged, the more than 50 Canadian athletes who had already checked in immediately packed their bags and left with Phil in search of a more accommodating facility.

In his later years Dr. Edwards was renowned as an expert in tropical diseases. He took pride as an administrator in leading his first country of British Guyana (eventually known simply as Guyana) to the Olympics near the end of colonial rule.

He served Canada in World War II. Many years later his daughter Gwen learned of an incident from his military service which captures his essence: "I got a letter from someone who had served under him during the war who recalled how an army captain in Ontario was making life particularly difficult for some troops. 'Why are you pushing them so hard,' my father asked. The captain turned on him and asked why my dad was questioning his methods and then challenged him to a fight.

"Dad said no but he would race the fellow. The other guy perhaps not knowing of his background, agreed and said he'd go light on the men if he lost. Of course dad won. My father was always concerned with the welfare of the troops.

"At dad's funeral in 1971 people brought their doctor bills to pay. That was the esteem in which he was held."

In 1997 Phil Edwards was recognized with membership in Canada's Sports Hall of Fame. ❧

1937

Hockey

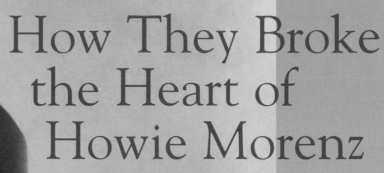

How They Broke the Heart of Howie Morenz

by Trent Frayne
October 15, 1953

As long as hockey lasts they'll be telling the legends about Howie Morenz: How he lived only for the game, for the fans at the Forum, how he died in tragedy and misery when the team he loved sold him down the river after a bad season.

Sixteen years have passed since Howie Morenz died on the floor of a hospital room in Montreal. There are some who believe this greatest of hockey players died of a broken heart.

Howie Morenz was more than the best hockey player that ever lived. He became a part of the nation's folklore, a symbol of a hockey era that is now only a memory, of a time when the ice heroes were a rough-hewn and sometimes hard drinking lot, fiercely loyal to their team. Even the smoke-filled rooms in which they played had a warmer look and smell than the antiseptic palaces of today. To the millworkers and tram drivers and off-duty cabbies who jammed the rush end of the Forum in Montreal and called themselves the Millionaires Morenz was a superhuman figure. Between periods they toasted him surreptitiously on homemade gin. Their battle cry, *"les Canadiens sont là!"* never reached such frenzy as when Morenz started winding up behind his own net with a queer little

1907

March 7, 1907

Owen "Bud" McCourt died the morning after he was hit on the head with a stick during a brawl in a Federal Amateur Hockey League game between Cornwall and Ottawa. He was the first recorded player to die from game-related injuries. Charles Masson was charged with manslaughter but acquitted at a trial. Prior to the incident "Bud" McCourt was tied for the league scoring title with 16 goals in eight games. Following his death, Cornwall withdrew from the Federal League. The game between Cornwall and Ottawa was actually a replay which was ordered after Ottawa protested McCourt's eligibility earlier in the season because he had played two games with Montreal Shamrocks of the Eastern Canada Amateur Hockey Association. McCourt's eligibility had already been conceded by the time the two teams took the ice. Therefore, the March 6th replay of Ottawa's February 15th loss to Cornwall was totally unnecessary.

bouncing jig that sent him hurtling down the ice in an exhilarating moment of excitement that reached its crescendo when he threw himself between the defencemen and crashed the puck past the goalkeeper.

For the twelve years he wore the uniform of the Canadiens Morenz was an idol. Since the bleak March night in 1937 when he died he has become a legend.

When Canadiens were hard-pressed it was usually Morenz who brought the hoarse roar from the Millionaires and the happy nods from the millions who followed his exploits by radio or through the newspapers. And Morenz did not have such modern advantages as the forward pass, the center red line and the seventy game schedule in which to pile up goals. During the fourteen seasons he played in the NHL the schedule progressively increased from twenty-four games to forty-eight. The two hundred and seventy goals he notched were scored in the equivalent of nine present seasons.

Morenz led the Canadiens to three Stanley Cups and won the Hart Trophy three times as the league's most valuable player. He took top scoring honours in two seasons and was among the five highest scorers in no fewer than eight seasons. But Howie's value lay not merely in the number of goals scored. He had a way of getting pay-off goals when the Canadiens needed them most. One night in 1930 the Chicago Blackhawks, with their superb goalkeeper, Charlie Gardiner, plus strong defensive tactics, held the Canadiens to a tie until ten minutes to two in the morning — the longest overtime game up to then. Finally Morenz barged past big Taffy Abel and beat Gardiner with the goal that eliminated Chicago from the Stanley Cup playoffs.

Morenz was the most sought-after player in the game. After one thrilling contest in New York in 1926 in which he scored the winning goal in overtime, the Rangers offered sixty thousand dollars for him. Montreal Maroons heard of the offer and bid seventy-five thousand. Leo Dandurand, owner of the Canadiens, declined both offers "Morenz," he said, "is beyond price."

Although young Morenz lived for hockey he apparently did not think he was good enough for the NHL. On a trip home from Montreal he stopped in Toronto to watch the professional St. Pats, ancestors of the Maple Leafs, play the Ottawa Senators. "You don't have to worry about me becoming a professional," he told his mother when he got home, "those fellows are far too good."

If he didn't have confidence in his ability to play professionally, the pro teams did. Charlie Querrie, of the Toronto St. Pats, offered him a thousand dollars to play in the team's five remaining games of the 1922-23 season. Dandurand offered him twenty-five hundred dollars for the twenty-four game season of 1923-24 and grew concerned when Lou Marsh, a referee and sports writer, telephoned that the St. Pats were hot after

Morenz. Canadiens dispatched Coach Cecil Hart to Stratford with a pocketful of cash.

When Stratford fans and officials heard about it they begged Morenz to reconsider. Letters of protest were sent to Dandurand and a minister wrote to a Toronto newspaper decrying the audacity of the Canadiens in "luring an under-age boy to the wicked city of Montreal."

At training camp in Grimsby, Ont. Morenz was tried out between Aurèle Joliat and Billy Boucher. Odie Cleghorn, the regular center, was never able to win his job back.

Though his personal glory grew, the team's success meant more to Morenz than his own. In a playoff against Boston he faced off in overtime against Cooney Weiland of the Bruins. The puck flew in the air as their sticks clashed. Weiland took a half-swing and bounced it into the Canadien net for the winning goal. At four o'clock next morning, Elmer Ferguson, Montreal sports writer, answered a knock on his hotel-room door and found Morenz there. "He was in complete despair" Ferguson recalls, "He'd been walking the streets since the game ended, berating himself for Weiland's goal."

His great shot made him the scourge of goalkeepers. "He could shoot harder than anybody I see nowadays," insists little Roy Worters, who played for the New York Americans. He recalls Morenz, who wore No. 7 on his uniform, as the fastest skater he ever saw. "When he'd wind up behind that net he wasn't No. 7," Worters says, "he was No. 777, just a blur."

Then came the day when Morenz was no longer a blur to his opponents, when the great strides became a fraction slower and the whizzing shot a shade less lethal. It didn't come quickly and it wasn't always perceptible but by the spring of 1933 Morenz had fallen to ninth place among the scorers and the Canadiens were lagging in the standings.

By the spring of 1934 Howie hadn't regained his form and his spirits hit a sickening bottom one night in the Forum when part of the Montreal crowd booed him. Cheers from the loyal Millionaires quickly drowned the boos but Leo Dandurand recalls that Morenz came to him after the game "sobbing like a child."

Dandurand faced one of the most difficult decisions of his life. The idea of selling Morenz to another team had been unthinkable during Howie's magnificent years. Yet Morenz was visibly slipping and the prospect of the volatile fans turning on a man who had meant so much to the Canadiens made Dandurand writhe. In the summer of 1934 he made his decision: he traded Morenz to Chicago.

But in Chicago things were scarcely better. He couldn't get along with Major Frederic McLaughlin, the rich and irascible Chicago owner of whom he later said, "He's a tough man to work for, always waiting to jump on a player who has an off night." After Canadiens beat the

Howie Morenz lies in state at the Montreal Forum, allowing thousands of fans to say goodbye to a fallen hero.

Hawks 2-1, McLaughlin stomped angrily into the dressing room. He stopped in front of Morenz, pointed a finger accusingly at him and charged him with being responsible for the defeat.

Through the next two games Morenz sat on the bench. Then he went to McLaughlin. "Could you sell me or trade me?" he asked. "I'm not helping you sitting on the bench, and I might be going stale." A few days later McLaughlin made a straight trade with the New York Rangers for a run-of-the-mill forward named Glenn Brydson.

In 1936 Cecil Hart, Morenz' great friend and coach for ten years who had been replaced by Newsy Lalonde the year Morenz was traded to Chicago, came back to the Canadiens. His first move was to buy back Morenz and recreate the famed Morenz-Joliat-Gagnon line. Morenz

was thirty-four but to the surprise of most hockey men he began to get back in stride immediately. Again in the beloved Forum, with the shrill cries of the Millionaires once more cascading down on him, Howie had compiled sixteen scoring points by Jan. 28. On that fateful night his skate caught in the boards as Chicago's Earl Siebert body-checked him. His left leg twisted under him and he broke three bones in the ankle and one in the leg.

It was the tragic climax of Morenz' career. After eleven years of success and adulation and two years of disillusion and dejection he'd started on the road back. Now, in a hospital bed with his leg in a plaster cast, came the realization that he was through.

After he'd been lying in bed for a month, pale and drawn and fretful, his nerves gave way. But, as he'd always done, he battled back and he still insisted to visitors that he'd be wearing No. 7 again next season, better than ever.

On the night on March 8, 1937, he couldn't stand his confinement any longer. Heaving his leg in its plaster cast off the bed he forced himself upright, took one

April, 1919

The influenza epidemic spread through North America and cancelled many events, including the final games of the 1919 Stanley Cup playoffs between the Seattle Metropolitans and the Montreal Canadiens. Five Montreal players were hospitalized and one, Joe Hall, died from the flu on April 19. "This has been the most peculiar series in the history of sport," said PCHA President Frank Patrick about the 1919 final. The games between the teams were tied at two, so no winner of the Cup was declared.

faltering step, then slowly crumpled to the floor. He was dead.

The death certificate said the cause was "a cardiac deficiency and acute excitement." Complicated perhaps by a broken heart. Many of his friends believed that drugs and alcohol helped weaken his once rugged constitution.

On March 11 Howie's body was placed at center ice in the Forum, and Canadien players formed an honour guard as thousands filed past. Fifteen thousand people moved slowly and silently into the Forum for the service and twenty-five thousand more with heads bared packed the streets outside. Thousands more lined the long route to the cemetery up the snow-covered slopes of Mount Royal. The casket was covered by a huge floral "7" Howie's uniform number. It was the final tribute of his teammates. No Canadien player ever again wore the number. ♣

HHOF

Teammate and friend Aurèle Joliat stares at the empty locker of Howie Morenz. Shortly afterward, the Habs retired Morenz's famous number 7 sweater.

HHOF

1918

HHOF

1925

November 28, 1925

Montreal Canadiens' netminder Georges Vezina, who played every Canadiens game for 15 years, was replaced by Al Lacroix when Vezina came down with tuberculosis. On March 26, 1926, Vezina died from the dreaded disease. The NHL immediately named its "Best Goalie Award" the Vezina Trophy in his honour.

HHOF

Allan Cup Battles

The Allan Cup is awarded to Canada's top amateur hockey team. The games are, and seemingly always have been, classic hockey battles.

The 1940-41 Allan Cup playoff series between two Nova Scotia teams — the Glace Bay Miners and the Sydney Millionaires — was no exception and has been dubbed "Canada's last Civil War." The Miners' Forum all but wore out the 78-rpm record of God Save The King in a futile attempt to restore order and quell riots on and off the ice. Sweepers were on constant stand-by to gather up toe rubbers, overshoes, fish heads and lumps of coal — and this just during the pre-game warm-up.

Jo-Jo Grabowski, an import who played with the handicap of the loss of an eye, was Glace Bay's playing coach. Martin MacDonald was the team manager and as shrewd a horse trader as ever came down a pike. He cobbled together the finest senior team money could buy and he winked at the league's four imports rule. Glace Bay had ten imports and Martin MacDonald said the six extras were as a result of "job transfers" — from non-existent firms in Quebec and Ontario.

The Glace Bay Miners were the toast of Eastern Canada — Charlie Phillips, Tiger Mackie, Boots Baird, Jim Dewey, Earl Newboldt, Vic Hannaberry, Pop Monson, Moe White, Irving MacGibbon and Fess Anderson. Sydney Millionaires also had a powerhouse line-up — Bill Dickey, Keith Langille, Jack Fritz, Mel Snowden, Ray Powell, Dick Kowcinak, Johnny McCreedy, Jack Atchison, Grant Hall, Vern Buckles and Bobby Walton.

Several — McCreedy, Walton, Dickie, Phillips and MacGibbon later went on to play in the six-team National Hockey League. Halifax sportscaster and columnist, Pat Connolly, said that on any given night the 1940-41 Miners or Millionaires would beat any of the teams in today's NHL.

The 1940-41 Glace Bay Miners had one weak link, though. Their goaltender was a 19-year old Prince Edward Island kid, Earle Boates, nicknamed, naturally, "Leaky" Boates. Miners' fans scoffed that he couldn't stop a beachball.

Martin MacDonald offered Boates $200 to join the Army before the playoffs but Boates wasn't buying. Next, the crafty manager gave him $100 and a train ticket to Montreal and told him to make himself scarce. He then solemnly told a Sydney sportswriter that Boates had enlisted in the Cape Breton Highlanders and "gone off to fight the Hun."

The Miners were then given permission to pick up Bill "Legs" Fraser whose team had been knocked out of playoff competition. Glace Bay swept the first three games of the final series by lop-sided scores. Sydney lodged a protest which went through the league and up to the Maritime and Canadian Amateur Hockey Associations. "Legs" Fraser was declared ineligible and Glace Bay's three wins were nullified.

All hell broke loose. Riots in the stands were like a Sunday School picnic compared with what happened next. Coal miners with pick axes and pan shovels barricaded the King's Highway between Sydney and Glace Bay. It was like a scene out of *Les Miserables* and the barricades weren't coming down until "Legs" Fraser was reinstated.

Restaurants in Glace Bay refused to serve anyone from Sydney. Sydney wholesalers could not bring their delivery trucks into Glace Bay. A priest in Glace Bay railed against injustice from his pulpit and told his flock that God was on the side of the Miners. Glace Bay Mayor Dan Willie Morrison, also president of District 26, United Mine Workers, fired off live rounds at Ottawa and the CAHA. He said he feared work stoppages and that coal shipments critical to the war effort would be cut off.

Cape Breton South MP, Clarie Gillis, rose in his Commons seat and denounced "the injustices perpetrated by the rich and powerful Sydney merchants on the working people of Glace Bay."

The tide was turning. The hockey grandees were beginning to have sober second thoughts. But, Earle "Leaky" Boates chose that moment to surface in Moncton and the first person he bumped into on the sidewalk was Frank Gallagher, President of the MAHA.

The jig was up. Martin MacDonald ordered Boates "to come home and bring my $100." Sydney put nine pucks behind Boates in a 9-1 shellacking. Glace Bay threw in the towel and defaulted the rest of the series.

The Millionaires then blasted their way past Hull Volants and Montreal Royals who had Pete Morin, Buddy O'Connor and Gerry Heffernan on

1908-09

The Ottawa Cliffsides were the very first team to win the new trophy for senior hockey supremacy — the Allan Cup — donated by Sir Montagu Allan of Montreal. They were also the first team to lose the challenge trophy — all in the same season. The Cliffsides defeated a Montreal squad for the Cup in the 1908-09 season. When the season was over and their skates were hung up, three weeks later, though, Queen's University challenged — and won. The Allan Cup spent all of three weeks in Ottawa before being taken to Kingston. It would not come back to Ottawa for 33 years when the Ottawa RCAF won it in 1942.

The Allan Cup

Canadian Men's Senior Hockey Championships

Year	Champions	Year	Champions	Year	Champions
1908	Ottawa Cliffsides	1939	Port Arthur	1971	Galt Hornets
1909	Kingston - Queen's University	1940	Kirkland Lake Blue Devils	1972	Spokane Jets
1910	Toronto St. Michael's	1941	Regina Rangers	1973	Orillia Terriers
1911	Winnipeg Victorias	1942	Ottawa RCAF	1974	Barrie Flyers
1912	Winnipeg Victorias	1943	Ottawa Commandos	1975	Thunder Bay Twins
1913	Winnipeg Hockey Club	1944	Quebec Aces	1976	Spokane Flyers
1914	Regina Victorias	1945	WW II - No Competition	1977	Brantford Alexanders
1915	Winnipeg Monarchs	1946	Calgary Stampeders	1978	Kimberley Dynamiters
1916	Winnipeg 61st Battalion	1947	Montreal Royals	1979	Petrolia Squires
1917	Toronto Dentals	1948	Edmonton Flyers	1980	Spokane Flyers
1918	Kitchener Hockey Club	1949	Ottawa Senators	1981	Petrolia Squires
1919	Hamilton Tigers	1950	Toronto Marlboros	1982	Cranbrook Royals
1920	Winnipeg Falcons	1951	Owen Sound Mercurys	1983	Cambridge Hornets
1921	University of Toronto	1952	Fort Francis Canadians	1984	Thunder Bay Twins
1922	Toronto Granites	1953	Kitchener-Waterloo Dutchmen	1985	Thunder Bay Twins
1923	Toronto Granites	1954	Penticton V's	1986	Cornerbrook Royals
1924	Sault Ste. Marie Greyhounds	1955	Kitchener-Waterloo Dutchmen	1987	Brantford Motts
1925	Port Arthur	1956	Vernon Canadians	1988	Thunder Bay Twins
1926	Port Arthur	1957	Whitby Dunlops	1989	Thunder Bay Twins
1927	Toronto Varsity Grads	1958	Belleville McFarlands	1990	Chomedy Laval Warriors
1928	University of Manitoba	1959	Whitby Dunlops	1991	Charlottetown Islanders
1929	Port Arthur	1960	Chatham Maroons	1992	Saint John Vitos
1930	Montreal AAA	1961	Galt Terriers	1993	Whitehorse Huskies
1931	Winnipeg Hockey Club	1962	Trail Smoke Eaters	1994	Warroad Lakers
1932	Toronto Nationals	1963	Windsor Bulldogs	1995	Warroad Lakers
1933	Moncton Hawks	1964	Winnipeg Maroons	1996	Warroad Lakers
1934	Moncton Hawks	1965	Sherbrooke Beavers	1997	Powell River Regals
1935	Halifax Wolverines	1966	Drumheller Miners	1998	Truro Bearcats
1936	Kimberley Dynamiters	1967	Drummondville Eagles	1999	Stony Plain Eagles
1937	Sudbury Tigers	1968	Victoriaville Tigers	2000	Powell River Regals
1938	Trail Smoke Eaters	1969	Galt Hornets		
		1970	Spokane Jets		

their roster for the right to meet the Western Canada champions for the Allan Cup. Sydney all but chased Regina out of the rink in winning the first two games of the best of five series, but Regina won the next three games and the Allan Cup.

The colourful "Legs" Fraser finally won his Allan Cup with the Ottawa Senators in 1947. He had gone on to glory with T.P. Gorman's powerhouse Senators' senior teams — alongside Larry Regan, Emile Dagenais, Dr. Bobby Copp, Jim McFadden, Lude Check, Ray Trainor, Stan Pratt, Billy Watson and Nils Tremblay. He passed away in Winnipeg in 1998 at the age of 76.

Earl "Leaky" Boates did join the Canadian Army and, after the war, he finally got to Montreal where the only person he knew was his old teammate from Verdun, Moe White. He managed a Montreal textile plant and died there in 1978.

More than 50 years later, the lone survivor of the Sydney Millionaires was Jack Fritz. The rest were all gone — born 50 years too early — else they would have been playing in the NHL. Locals said that on the anniversary of the 1940-41 Allan Cup series Jack Fritz put on his helmet and a blazer and laid a wreath at the bullpen entrance where the Sydney Forum once stood — and took the salute on behalf of his absent teammates. ❧

HHOF — James McCarthy

1948

Hughie Riopelle's greatest moment was not to be. The 20-year old Ottawa St. Pat's College hockey star, leading scorer in the Ottawa City Junior League with 24 goals and 24 assists in 24 games, was at the 1948 RCAF Flyers tryout camp playing on a line with Wally Halder and George Mara. "Our line was flying," when coach Frank Boucher called him in and abruptly and unexpectedly told him he was cut. Two years later, while playing senior hockey in England, Hughie was asked by the Flyers' Manager, Dr. "Sandy" Watson, if anyone ever told him why he was cut. No one had. The Athletic Director at St. Pat's did not want to lose his top scorer with playoffs coming up. He went to the Flyers' front office and threatened to make waves — to stir up bad press "if a second rate team without a hope in hell of winning took a kid out of school for three months to play hockey in Europe." Hughie Riopelle was cut and by the end of the century, 52 years later, still looked back with sadness that his greatest moment was snatched away from him by a manipulative college athletic official.

1958

On January 18, 1958, Willie O'Ree became the first black player to score a goal in the NHL, during his brief stint with the Boston Bruins in 1957-58 season. He had played senior hockey with the Quebec Aces and played his first NHL game on January 18, 1958 at the Montreal Forum. O'Ree played one more game as a Bruin, replacing an injured player, and then returned to the Aces. O'Ree recalled there was no mention of the historic feat of his goal in the local newspapers. "Nobody called me the 'Jackie Robinson of hockey' then but that's how I felt. Of course, Jackie had far worse things happen to him than I ever did, but there I was, in a place where no black man had ever been." "For two minutes afterwards, people in the Boston Garden just stood and cheered for me," O'Ree wrote in his autobiography. "It was amazing ... I knew the fans in Boston were on my side but I didn't know how much."

General Highlights

1928-1934

The Regina Roughriders made the trip east to play in the Grey Cup six times in this period — and lost every time. The club would not win the Cup until 1966, by which time it was known as the Saskatchewan Roughriders.

1936-1940

At a track meet in 1936, Canadian Eric Coy set the world record in the discus throw. Coy became the clear favourite for the upcoming 1940 Olympic Games, but of course the Games were never held because of WW II. His record throw would not be broken for 16 years.

1950

In the 1950 Stanley Cup playoffs, Detroit's Gordie Howe was skating across the ice to check Toronto's Ted Kennedy. When Kennedy stopped quickly to avoid the check, Howe crashed into the boards and was in hospital's critical care for the next 24 hours. None the worse for wear, the next year he went on to win the scoring title.

1953-1983

Toronto-based football teams often won championships in the first half of the century, but experienced a 30-year dry spell in the second half of the century.

1954

The 1954 Grey Cup is best remembered for Edmonton Eskimo Jackie Parker's heroic return of a Montreal fumble for a long touchdown run late in the game. But it was Eskimo centre Eagle Keys who, despite the pain of a broken leg sustained earlier in the game, came onto the field to snap the ball for the game-winning convert.

1955

In the 1955 Grey Cup game, quarterback Sam Etcheverry of the Montreal Alouettes passed for a record 508 yards — and still lost the game.

December 9, 1956

Trans Canada Flight #810 flying from Vancouver to Regina crashed into the side of Mount Sleese in the Rocky Mountains, killing 62 passengers and crew. On board were four players from the Saskatchewan Roughriders returning from the All Star Game: Mel Beckett, Mario DeMarco, Gordon Sturtridge and Ray Syrnyk, as well as Calvin Jones from the Winnipeg Blue Bombers. The families of Mel Beckett and Mario DeMarco donated a commemorative trophy to recognize the Most Outstanding Offensive Lineman in the West.

1949-1974

Jim Silver of the Vanderhoof Bears in BC's Intermediate A Cariboo League holds one longevity hockey record that even Gordie Howe didn't break. Silver played for the Bears for 25 consecutive years, from 1949 to 1974. When told by reporter Jim Kearney about his feat, the dry-witted Silver thought it over for a few seconds, then replied: "I must say, Gordie's had a bit more incentive than I've had."

Sam Etcheverry, 1950s.

HHOF — Turofsky Collection

December 12, 1933

Toronto played Boston in a game that got rough. King Clancy slammed Boston's star Eddie Shore into the boards; Shore got up to retaliate but mistakenly hit Toronto's Ace Bailey from behind. Bailey's head hit the ice hard and he was rushed to hospital in critical condition. He recovered his health, but never played again. Bailey and the Leafs considered suing Shore and the Bruins. Instead, a benefit game between a group of NHL All-Stars and the Maple Leafs was played on February 14, 1934 — with the proceeds going to cover Bailey's medical expenses. At the game, Bailey and Shore shook hands. "I know it was an accident," said Bailey that night, but many remained doubtful.

Shore is seen on the far left, next to Ace Bailey. That's Conn Smythe beside Bailey.

Jackie Robinson

All the Months in Canada Were Like That

In 1997, major league baseball honoured the 50th anniversary of Jackie Robinson breaking the league's colour barrier by making his National League debut with the Brooklyn Dodgers, decreeing that all of its teams would retire Robinson's playing number of 42.

When he joined the majors in 1947, however, it could be argued that Robinson had already overcome his greatest challenge — his entry into organized baseball the previous season, with the minor league Montreal Royals. But of all the furies Robinson faced in that first full year of peace following World War II, the least of them were with the people of Montreal themselves.

For example, when Robinson and his wife went apartment hunting, their landlady not only agreed to have them as tenants, but also insisted that they use her things. One has to transport oneself back to 1946 to understand the significance of that moment. At the end of the war blacks and whites in the United States were still segregated in separate divisions of the armed forces, the Red Cross recorded and distributed blood by the colour of its donor, and washrooms and drinking fountains were designated for racial use.

As far back as the 1880s some baseball leagues had tolerated integrated play before the objections of white players and fans reduced organized mainstream baseball to a whites-only game. Black people played on barnstorming teams and Negro League organizations allowed stars like Josh Gibson and Satchel Paige to earn a living in the 1930s and '40s.

By the end of World War II, however, the liberal press and political movement were actively organizing on behalf of civil rights for blacks, including the right to play baseball in the major leagues. These forces found unlikely allies in more conservative, entrepreneurial interests that argued for the same rights for more pragmatic reasons, recognizing the advantages of tapping into a new market of consumers and producers.

This uneasy coalition included Branch Rickey, general manger of the Brooklyn Dodgers, who represented the entrepreneurial camp, and Wendell Smith of the Pittsburgh Courier, part of the liberal press. Together they conspired to get Robinson into the Dodgers organization.

The Dodgers' chief farm team in Montreal seemed a likely spot to place Robinson, since an image had been created about Canada and more specifically Quebec which suggested that racism did not exist. It was of course a false picture, but there was at least a partial acceptance. It is a testament to Montrealers "so-what" attitude that the press conference in the fall of 1945 announcing his signing was not treated as a big deal.

The presence of black players wasn't altogether new to Montrealers. The Quebec Provincial League had welcomed black players and even an all-black team in the 1930s, a decade before organized baseball. In 1936, however, an exhibition game between an integrated Provincial League all-star team and the Montreal Royals scheduled for Montreal's Delorimier Stadium was cancelled at the last minute when several Royals players objected to the appearance of three black players.

For Robinson and his wife Rachel the journey to the Dodgers spring training camp in 1946 was their first major obstacle. Bumped off flights, delayed for up to 12 hours, and relegated to the back of buses, the Robinsons reached Florida ready to quit.

They didn't, and on March 4, 1946 Robinson made history by putting on a Royals uniform. He and a black pitcher John Wright became the first men of their race in the modern era to play for a team in organized mainstream baseball. Among their supporters was the Royals' French Canadian shortstop Stan Breard who asked Jackie to pose with him for a souvenir photo.

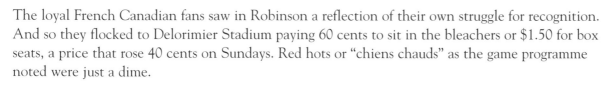
Montreal Royal Jackie Robinson sliding home in 1946.

Robinson experienced an undercurrent of rejection all season particularly while playing in American cities like Baltimore and Syracuse. Still his greatest supporters were his wife Rachel and the Montreal fans.

The loyal French Canadian fans saw in Robinson a reflection of their own struggle for recognition. And so they flocked to Delorimier Stadium paying 60 cents to sit in the bleachers or $1.50 for box seats, a price that rose 40 cents on Sundays. Red hots or "chiens chauds" as the game programme noted were just a dime.

Robinson became a city hero, appearing at charity benefits along with members of the Montreal Canadiens hockey team. He befriended the city's other pioneering athlete, Herbie Trawick of the Montreal Alouettes, the first black player in the Canadian Football League despite the hostile objections of Toronto and Ottawa.

Robinson stole 40 bases, second in the league to teammate Marvin Rackley, he hit .349, scored 113 runs and drove in 66 runs. In the process he endured taunts of such vociferousness that he required occasional breaks. He once told a coach that no one else could ever understand the pressure under which he had to play.

It got worse in the playoffs.

Reaching the Little World Series against the southern American city of Louisville, he endured a flood of prejudiced comments flowing from the stands. Black attendance was kept deliberately small and limited to specially designated areas. The Royals fell behind two games to one and returned home in confusion and doubt.

Montrealers responded by taking their own form of vengeance. They harangued the Louisville players causing Robinson to say, "I didn't approve of this kind of retaliation, but I felt a jubilant sense of gratitude for the way Canadians expressed their feelings."

The Royals rebounded to win three straight and take the Little World Series title. For his part Robinson was toasted as a hero. "It was probably the only day in history that a black man ran from a white mob with love instead of lynching on its mind," wrote Sam Martin.

When the crowd caught up to him he was serenaded in French with the cry, "Il a gagné ses épaulettes." ("He has earned his stripes.")

They were still singing in taverns throughout the city as Jackie and Rachel Robinson flew out of Montreal that night, but he later told Wendell Smith, "As the plane roared skyward and the lights of Montreal twinkled and winked in the distance, I took one last look at this great city where I had found so much happiness. I don't care if I ever get to the majors, I told myself. This is the city for me. This is paradise." ❦

1956

Hockey

The Year the Russians Took the Gold Away

by Malcolm Gray
February 14, 1994

Canada-Russia, 1956

In ice hockey, at least, Canada used to reign supreme, winning six of the first seven Olympic gold medals. But in Cortina d'Ampezzo, Italy in 1956, as the Cold War deepened, there was suddenly a new adversary: the Soviets, competing in their first Winter Games. Canada's amateur champions, the Kitchener-Waterloo Dutchmen, lost an early contest to the Americans, but still had a shot at the gold going into the final game of the round-robin tournament against the Soviets. "There was an emotional factor," recalls team manager Ernie Goman, now 79 and a retired insurance salesman in Kitchener, Ont. "We were receiving wires from home saying, 'You're the defenders of democracy' and 'You shouldn't set foot on Canadian soil unless you win.'"

In the big game, the Canadians just could not penetrate the solid Soviet defence. And when the Dutchmen lost 2-0, Canada's Olympic hockey dynasty came to an end. Afterward, recalls Goman, "half our players were crying."

Unlike Canada, Goman points out, the European countries were sending all-star teams. "Until the experience of 1956," he says, "there was still a feeling here in Canada that we could send any of our first-class amateur teams and win. We had our eyes opened." In Cortina, where the Canadians took bronze, Goman was also awarded an honourary Olympic gold medal for his contributions to hockey over the years. And he won a silver with the Dutchmen at the 1960 Games in Squaw Valley, Calif. After that, Canada began icing its own amateur all-star team. But since the NHL hoards the country's very best players, Goman says, the Olympic team is still not the best it could be. ♣

HHOF/NDE

1956

Cortina d'Ampezzo, Italy

Pairs figure skaters Frances Dafoe and Norris Bowden were disappointed in winning Olympic silver medals at Cortina, Italy in 1956. At the previous Games in Oslo the young pair had come a respectable fifth. They rapidly improved on that early result until 1954 when they won the World Championship, again in Oslo. They won again in 1955 in Vienna, beating out the local Austrian favourites in the process. Their expectations were high for 1956. They arrived early, skated in several exhibitions and were well prepared with no injuries to worry about. During the Olympic competition they skated well, and in the opinion of many observers (and not only the Canadian ones) they easily skated as well as the year before. Yet, by the smallest of fractions, the Austrian pair they had defeated the year before nudged ahead of them on the officials' cards. They had no need for disappointment, though, as their popular success at the World Championships helped carve the way for future skaters. When they retired after their Olympic competition, they were both elected to Canada's Sports Hall of Fame.

Mary Stewart, Canada's Swimming Star

Because the Olympic Games are held only every four years many athletes miss out on a chance at an Olympic medal if their peak performances happen to fall in the middle of that interval.

Mary Stewart of Vancouver falls into that category. She was the second of two Stewart sisters who dominated Canadian women's swimming in the mid-1950s and early 1960s. The older sister, Helen, won a gold medal in the 1955 Pan American games after winning a relay silver at the age of 15, in the Empire Games, in 1954. She had set the world record that the great Aussie swimmer Dawn Fraser, a three-time Olympic gold medallist, broke in 1956.

Mary's meteoric career began when she went to the Pan Am Games in 1959, at the age of 13, and joined her sister in winning a silver relay medal. She had already started a string of record breaking that saw her hold all Canadian freestyle records, up to 220 yards, by the time she was 14. She made the Olympic 100m freestyle final in Rome at the age of 14. Then, in winning at both Canadian and American national championships she set world records at 110 yards and 100m in the butterfly. She was the finest female butterfly swimmer in the world when she went to Perth, Australia, in 1962 for the British Empire Games and she did not disappoint. She took the gold in the 100m fly, added a bronze in the 100m freestyle and silvers in both the freestyle and medley relays. She won four more silver medals at the Pan Am Games in 1963.

Had the Olympics been held in 1962 or 1963, Mary would have been a strong medal contender. By the 1964 Tokyo Olympics, Mary was past her prime, even though it would be another two years before her records started to fall. Mary's mantle fell to a young Elaine Tanner, who was coached by Howard Firby, also Mary's coach.

Mary Stewart was in many ways Canada's first truly international swimming star. She was voted Canada's female athlete of the year in 1961 and 1962 by both the Amateur Athletic Union and the Canadian Press. ♣

Mary Stewart receiving the Velma Springstead Award as Canada's Athlete of the Year, 1961.

Lucy Wheeler Wins Canada's First Alpine Skiing Championship

Lucy Wheeler first made Canadian ski history with her bronze in the downhill at the 1956 Olympic Games in Cortina, Italy.

She had given Canadian skiing its first Olympic medal, but the racer from St. Jovite, Quebec, wanted more.

Two years later, she was at the 16th international alpine championships in Bad Gastein, Austria. The daughter of a resort owner in the Laurentians, Wheeler had been trying to win a world championship in international competition since she became a member of the Canadian alpine team in 1954. She distinguished herself by winning the famed Hahnenkamm races in Kitzbuhel, Austria, a week before she took the bronze in Cortina. But that magic world title still eluded her.

Bad Gastein did not start well for Wheeler. She placed 14th in the opening slalom event, held on Monday, February 3. Heartbroken, the 23-year-old told reporters after the race that she'd found the course to be as sticky as honey. But there was nothing to do but ready herself for the next event, the downhill, to be held two days later.

Wednesday dawned, and Wheeler was back on Graukogel Mountain. It was an overcast day, and a light snow was falling. She faced a difficult, technical course, composed of hard-pack snow, with the threat of ice in a few places. The run dropped 589 metres (1,931 feet) and needed 27 gates to guide the racers down. The field of 42 featured Europe's best, including the ever-dominant Austrians and Swiss.

But for Wheeler, the moment had clearly arrived. She zoomed downhill in 2:12.1, beating out Switzerland's Friedel Daenzer by .3 seconds. It was Daenzel who had edged ahead of Wheeler to take the silver at the 1956 Olympic Games. With that world title win, Wheeler gave Canada its biggest day ever in international ski competition.

Wheeler was ecstatic. "I can't believe it," she told reporters at the time. "I almost missed a gate up there in the run and I had to make an extra turn to get through it. My skis had just the right touch for this varying snow. I am so very happy."

Notably, Anne Heggtveit was racing alongside Lucy that week, placing eighth in the slalom and seventh in the downhill — the future Olympic gold medallist was already showing evidence of her great potential.

Lucy Wheeler with Ottawa Rough Rider Kaye Vaughan.

But the week wasn't over yet. Still to come was the giant slalom, scheduled for Saturday. The course was one-mile in length, with a drop of 407 metres (1,302 feet). As the race began, the course was soft and mushy throughout.

As the day progressed, though, the surface turned to hard-pack, and many of the top European skiers fell. Wheeler stayed on her feet and carved her way through the 55 gates in 1:54.6.

It was a time that none of the top racers could best, not even Daenzer, who was third at 1:55.4. Wheeler had won her second world title of the week.

Despite her stunning success, Wheeler had to settle for second place in the combined alpine, nosed out again by rival Daenzel. It was that 14th placing in the slalom that robbed Wheeler of the women's crown.

But Wheeler was anything but upset, saying at the time, "I had a wonderful run, but I almost skidded off the course about midway. I lost grip of my right pole and I had to make a grab for it — how lucky I am to have finished second in the combined."

In an almost unprecedented double win, Wheeler put Canada on the world ski map, and how. In the space of two days, Canada realized its first two global alpine skiing titles. ◆

Yvon Durelle and the Greatest Light-Heavyweight Title Fight Ever

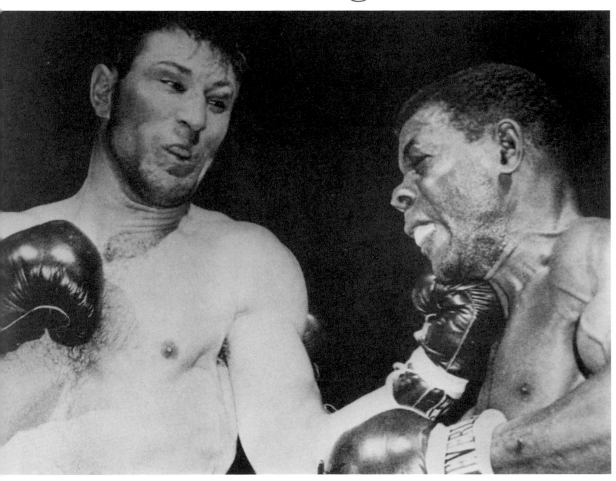

Ring historians and sportswriters describe the December, 1958, Yvon Durelle-Archie Moore light-heavyweight title bout as "the greatest light-heavyweight fight ever fought." It was fought before 8,848 spectators in the Montreal Forum and televised across North America. It became the sports story of the year in the year-end Canadian Press poll.

Archie Moore was the light-heavyweight champion of the world and the fight was his seventh title defence since he won the crown from Joey Maxim in 1952. Yvon Durelle, who went into the fight a 4-1 underdog, was described by Archie Moore in his autobiography: "some call him a rough club fighter without style or class." Moore was also quoted: "Marciano was a house wrecker, and he was, but it took a volley to get the job done. This guy (Durelle) — one punch."

Durelle was 29; Archie Moore was 45 "or thereabouts."

Yvon Durelle sent Moore to the canvas three times in the first round and the light-heavyweight championship of the world was in his grasp. Durelle had a mental lapse in that first round, though, forgetting that in a title fight the three knockdown rule did not apply.

Durelle had Moore in trouble in the fifth round and dropped him again but Moore was up again as referee Jack Sharkey counted nine. The aging "Mongoose" rallied and knocked Durelle to the canvas for a six count in the fifth round and a count of two in the seventh. Durelle was saved by the bell in the 10th round but absorbed a savage beating in the ninth and 10th rounds before Moore finished him off at the 49-second mark of the 11th round.

It was the most electrifying comeback in the history of boxing.

The venerable Archie Moore had fought nine world champions and seven members of the Boxing Hall of Fame. Durelle was the Canadian light-heavyweight champion from 1953 to 1957 and British Empire champion in 1957. In 1954 he fought Floyd Patterson, later world heavyweight champion, and floored him in the last round. Patterson was only saved by the bell.

Archie Moore scored 141 knockouts in 194 ring victories — more than anyone else in the history of boxing. He insisted on fighting in the heavyweight class and fought the likes of Marciano, Patterson, Muhammad Ali and Ezzard Charles.

Durelle was born in and remained in the northern New Brunswick fishing village of Baie Ste. Anne. His 20-year boxing career began in 1947 and brought him enough financial bounty to own four 45-foot fishing vessels and employ 17 men during the 1950s. The fishing business was always close to his heart.

That all went, and all that remained at the end of the century were his memories and his museum, a large room attached to his house displaying all his boxing memorabilia. A video tape of his 1958 fight with Archie Moore played non-stop. Yvon and his wife, Theresa, were always there to greet his fans and friends.

Yvon was named to the New Brunswick Hall of Fame in 1971, Canada's Sports Hall of Fame in 1975 and the Boxing Hall of Fame in 1989. ❧

Bob Hayward and Miss Supertest III

It wouldn't be too farfetched to compare Bob Hayward to Superman's alter ego Clark Kent — he was a mild-mannered and soft-spoken chicken farmer who transformed himself into the fastest boat driver in the world when he got behind the wheel of a hydroplane. Unlike Superman, though, Hayward's body was not invulnerable, and on September 10, 1961, his quest for speed killed him when the boat he was driving went out of control during a race on the Detroit River.

But for his love of engines, Hayward might have achieved only whatever fame awaits chicken farmers. As a boy growing up in Embro, Ontario, he loved racing boats with outboard motors. When he was old enough to get a driver's license, he graduated to cars. As a teenager, he put together a drag racing car that was once clocked at more than 200 km per hour. He worked as a farmer and a trucker until 1947, when Jim Thompson asked him to join his boat racing crew.

Thompson, who was president of the Supertest Petroleum Corporation, did most of the driving in the early years, with Hayward lending his expertise in fine-tuning the engines and doing some test driving. But by 1957, Hayward had worked his way permanently into the pilot's seat, and in his first year set a world speed record of 184 miles per hour (about 290 km/hr), driving Miss Supertest II.

In 1958, Thompson decided to make an attempt to become the first Canadian to win the Harmsworth Trophy, which since 1903 has symbolized world supremacy in power boat racing. At the time, American boats had taken the title for 39 years straight, which made some people take the Canadian challenge less seriously. Putting their knowledge and experience to work, Thompson, Hayward and the rest of the crew set to work designing and building the next generation of power boat. Launched in 1959, the new boat was christened Miss Supertest III.

Weighing about three tons, Miss Supertest III was heavier than most of her competitors but at least as fast. She was powered by a 2000 horsepower Rolls-Royce Griffon engine, a power plant also used in a number of aircraft. As the boat picked up speed, the hull rose to about 20 cm out of the water, supported only by the propeller spinning at 11,000 revolutions per minute, the rudder and two "sponsons" (strips of metal mounted at the front of the hull). At racing speed, only about 1.5 square feet of the boat contacted the water, the rest riding on a cushion of air.

Hayward and Miss Supertest III didn't disappoint the hopes of the design crew, winning the first race they entered on July 4, 1959 — the Detroit Memorial.

Less than two months later came the real challenge — the run for the Harmsworth, which consisted of three 45-mile races held over three days on the Detroit River. Hayward was up against the American champion, Maverick, driven by Bill Stead, to see who could navigate the triangular

Miss Supertest III

three-mile course the fastest. Hayward was an easy winner on the first day, but during the second race he misjudged a turn early on and never caught up. For the final race on August 27, Hayward decided to concentrate on timing. He took the lead at the start, and never relinquished it. Stead, in a vain attempt to catch Miss Supertest III, made the same mistake on a turn that Hayward had made in the second race. The Canadians sped on to the finish line and the Harmsworth trophy unmolested.

By virtue of being the defending champion, when it came time to defend the championship a year later, Hayward and Miss Supertest raced "at home" on Lake Ontario near Picton. The crew successfully defended their championship and followed up with a third straight title in 1961. That was the last race ever for Miss Supertest III.

Hayward's tragic death came when he was racing Miss Supertest II (Miss Supertest III was reserved for Harmsworth challenges) in the Silver Cup regatta on the Detroit River, a venue he was more than familiar with. Entering a turn at more than 200 km/hour, though, something went wrong. The hydroplane, which even under normal conditions maintained a tenuous connection with the water, became airborne and then flipped over, slamming Hayward against the water. The force of the crash broke his neck.

Soon after Hayward's death, Miss Supertest III was retired. Owner and designer Jim Thompson would only say that Hayward's death had accelerated a decision he was going to make anyway. The team had realized its goal of winning and defending the Harmsworth Trophy, he said at the time, and would derive little satisfaction under the circumstances from continuing to race. When she was retired, the magnificent boat had been raced just four times, winning every time.

Miss Supertest III's top speed was never known. Even though it would be easy to assume that Hayward was a daredevil considering his choice of sport, he was in fact a very careful man. Nobody knew better than him how quickly a hydroplane could go out of control, particularly if the water conditions featured long swells that could act as launching ramps for a boat. Accordingly, he never opened the throttle fully, winning races based on his driving ability as much as the technology he had at his disposal.

Along with Hayward and Thompson, Miss Supertest III was inducted into Canada's Sports Hall of Fame in 1960. There were only three other non-human entries into the Hall of Fame during the 20th century: The Bluenose schooner, Kentucky Derby winner Northern Dancer and show jumper Big Ben. ❧

1962

Canada's national team was no match for the competition most of the time during a 1962 tour of the United Kingdom, but did manage a hard-fought tie with the legendary Barbarians. Two weeks after Canada's tie with the Barbarians, though, the Wales Under-23 squad shut Canada out 23-0. Buzz Moore was again feted by his competitors and was carried off the Cardiff Arms pitch on the shoulders of his opponents as the band played and the crowd sang "Alouette."

Bruce Kidd won the 1962 Commonwealth Games gold medal in the six-mile run and was Canada's Athlete of the Year in 1961.

Crothers and Kidd

They probably didn't know it, but they were about to make a big contribution to Canadian sports history.

In 1960, two runners were warming up for a special race at the Canadian National Exhibition. One was Bruce Kidd, whose best distance was three miles, and the other was Bill Crothers, a specialist in the 800, be it yards or metres. Kidd wanted to break the four-minute-mile barrier, and Crothers was there to pace him.

Kidd didn't make it, missing by 2.2 seconds, but the competitive rivalry and friendship critical to developing a Canadian track presence did. Both runners were members of the East York Track Club, and trained under coach Fred Foot.

Kidd became a bona fide track star on January 15, 1961, when he won a two-mile indoor race in Boston in world record time. The track world was wowed, and he made headlines — because Kidd, by the way, was still a kid, a seventeen-year-old high school student in Toronto.

It wasn't just his age, although that was a big part of it. It was that he pulled this big move on the US indoor track circuit. Kidd, who later became well known as an advocate of athletes' rights, sport historian and a spokesperson against apartheid, was breaking down barriers even then. His exploits and results on the US indoor circuit showed others, including Crothers, that Canadians could compete at this level.

In so doing, he turned on a whole new generation: Kidd attracted youth to track at a time when the sport was virtually non-existent in Canada. Among other things, he is credited with inspiring the 1963 indoor track meet at Maple Leaf Gardens — the first to be held in 27 years.

Kidd's track career reached its apex the next year, when he won a gold medal in Perth, Australia at the 1962 British Empire and Commonwealth Games (later called simply the Commonwealth Games). He won the Lou Marsh Trophy, and was twice chosen by the Canadian Press as Canada's Male Athlete of the Year.

Things looked good for the 1964 Tokyo Olympics, but unfortunately when those Games rolled around Kidd was largely sidelined with injuries, not to mention having the flu. Luckily for Canada, Bill Crothers was hitting his stride by that time.

Racing against a field that included world record holder and defending Olympic champion Peter Snell of New Zealand, Crothers achieved Canada's best result in track from Tokyo, with a silver medal. It was Canada's first Olympic medal in track in 16 years. The top four runners in the race came in under the previous Olympic record.

Crothers' greatest moment was to come a year later, in a race that gave him his revenge against Snell. Undefeated since 1961, Snell had beaten Crothers in every one of their match-ups.

On June 10, 1965, Snell and Crothers competed against each other in an 880-yard feature race at the Toronto International Meet, held at Varsity Stadium. Close to 20,000 people were in the stands that day, on hand to witness two titans of track fight to the finish.

Crothers was clearly the underdog — Snell had beaten him only a month before at a meet in Los Angeles. His coach, Fred Foot, told him to stay on Snell's heels, because the New Zealanders knew how to get out of jams.

So Crothers did. But with 220 yards to go, Crothers, running right behind Snell, was getting boxed in by two other runners. When Snell started to break away, Crothers dipped through the gap between the two other runners before it could close, and went with Snell.

With 50 yards to go, Crothers saw the finish line and began to pour on the speed. And to the sound of a wild roar bursting from the hometown crowd, Crothers breasted the tape first. Hundreds mobbed Crothers as the crowd went wild. Even newspaper reporters, who were supposed to remain neutral, were dancing excitedly in the infield.

Everyone there knew they had just witnessed a pivotal moment in Canadian sports history. ❧

Bill Crothers winning an Olympic silver medal in the 800m, 1964 Tokyo. Crothers was Canada's Athlete of the Year in 1963.

Track and Field

Harry Jerome

Even looking only at his world records, Harry Winston Jerome was one of the greatest sprinters Canada has ever produced. From 1959, when at only 18 he ran his record-equalling 100 metres, through 1968, when he ran his final race at the Mexico City Olympics, he posted more world-class performances than any sprinter of his era. For four years in the 1960s he was co-holder of the world record in both the 100 metres (10 seconds flat) and the 100 yards (9.1 seconds).

Along the way he won gold at the 1966 Commonwealth Games and the 1967 Pan-American Games. But the gold he really wanted eluded him at three Olympic Games. His best was a bronze at Tokyo in 1964. This, however, was not defeat. It was triumph over near-impossible odds just to get there and compete.

Two years previously, at the 1962 Commonwealth Games in Perth, Australia, after he pulled up lame halfway through the 100 metres, there was some doubt he'd ever walk properly again, let alone race. He had torn the big muscle in the front of his left thigh; there was an indentation in which he could thrust his entire fist.

Following the injury in Perth, team officials kept him away from the press and bundled him onto the first available plane out of town. Only after he got back to Vancouver was the seriousness of the injury disclosed. Meanwhile, since there was no other information available, several journalists jumped to the conclusion that he had quit, an accusation that had its genesis in 1960 at the Rome Olympics. That same charge had been levelled at him in Rome when he staggered off the track halfway through his sprint semi-final. The problem was a pulled hamstring muscle, but since the then 19-year-old runner wouldn't talk to the media, the assumption was made that he had caved into race pressure and quit.

At that stage in his life, Jerome had what might justly be called a prickly personality. Communication was not one of his strengths. Rightly or wrongly, as a black man who grew up in the then almost totally white community of North Vancouver, he felt discriminated against. He put off many sportswriters and track and field officials, almost all of whom were white.

The surgeon who performed a long and difficult operation to repair his leg in 1962 encouraged him to start running once more at a time when Harry hoped for nothing more than to be able to walk again without a limp.

He took off all of 1963 while returning to the University of Oregon, where earlier he had won an athletic scholarship and eventually graduated with a master's degree in physical education. He started training again in the spring of 1964.

Only six months later, in September, he won his Olympic bronze. Bob Hayes of the United States won gold by equalling Jerome's world record of 10 seconds flat. Harry was $^{2}/_{10}$ths of a second back, equalling the time of silver medallist Enrique Figuerola of Cuba. The Cuban out-leaned the

Canadian at the tape in what otherwise looked like a dead heat.

The son of a railway porter, Jerome was born in Prince Albert, Saskatchewan in 1940, and was given his middle name of Winston in admiration of British Prime Minister Churchill and his dogged defiance of the German Air Force during the London blitz that year.

The family moved to North Vancouver when he was 12. At school, baseball became his game and he got into track almost accidentally. After seeing him run the base paths, the track coach at North Vancouver High convinced him he had a bigger future as a sprinter.

He soon proved the coach right, breaking Percy Williams' 31-year-old record for the 220 yards in his final Vancouver and District High School Championship meet in 1958. A year later, now enrolled at Oregon and running in a meet at Saskatoon, he equalled the world record of 10 seconds flat, set earlier that summer by Armin Hary of Germany.

He equalled his second world record two years after the Tokyo Games. In a 1966 meet in Edmonton, he matched Hayes' record of 9.1 seconds in the 100 yards sprint. It was a mark that stood until 1974. Jerome's final appearance on the world stage was in 1968 at Mexico City, where the Olympic track events were run for the first time on an artificial surface at an altitude of more than 2,000 metres.

Jerome was now a physical education teacher at Templeton High School in Vancouver and no longer training as intensively as before, but he still ran one of the best times of his career, — 10.1 seconds. But under these new conditions, it was only good enough for an unnoticed seventh place. American Jimmy Hines set a world record of 9.9 while winning gold.

Jerome retired, but continued to contribute to sport by working for the federal Fitness and Amateur Sports directorate and setting up cross-country sports clinics.

After several years with Sport Canada, he returned to British Columbia where he set up the Premier's Sports Awards program to encourage sport and fitness at the elementary school level.

On December 7, 1982, riding across Vancouver's Lions Gate Bridge as a passenger in a friend's car, he suffered a brain seizure and died on the way to hospital. Only 42, his sudden and tragic death came just a week after Percy Williams, Canada's double gold medal winner (100 and 200 metres) at the 1928 Olympics, committed suicide. ❧

1966

Boxing

Anatomy of a championship:

How Chuvalo Won by Losing

by John Robertson
May 14, 1966

Mitchell Chuvalo is only six years old, and is far too young to be reading the sports pages, or to understand why anyone would call his daddy a punching bag — and an unworthy one at that — before he fought Cassius Clay.

But Mitch was there that night in Maple Leaf Gardens, and he saw those devastating punches welt and disfigure his father's face and make the blood run in twin rivulets from his matted hair.

Perhaps it was cruel to expose Mitch to this, but I watched him squirm excitedly in his seat during the last round, and I heard him implore the referee to get out of the way, during one clinch, so his dad could sock this guy Clay a good one.

After the final bell, while thousands of grown men stood and applauded the unbelievable, almost-incredible courage of his father, Mitch tugged his mother's hand toward the corner of the ring where the trainers and seconds were ministering to the man he was so proud of, even in defeat.

George saw him and bent his head over the top rope so Mitch could reach up and grip both sides of the towel that encircled his sweaty, bewhiskered face. And there, in front of almost fourteen thousand people, they embraced, man to man.

Pride gushed from the boy's eyes, and for the first time that night, George Chuvalo gave way to his own emotions and blinked back tears.

Flanked by his manager, Irving Ungerman, and his trainer, Theo McWhorter, the man almost everyone had branded an unfit challenger ducked through the ropes and tottered wearily down the steps, into the beckoning arms of his pretty, redheaded wife Lynne. His mother, who had refused to even look at the ring for most of the evening, so she wouldn't have to see as well as hear those punches crunch against the face and body of her son, reached past Lynne and caressed the back of George's head with a hand that trembled more with relief than pride.

Referee Jack Silvers and the two judges had unanimously declared Clay (alias Muhammad Ali) the winner, and quite justly so. But to Mitchell, Lynne, Mrs. Chuvalo and thousands of others there that night, there was no loser. Even the men along press row who had been non-believers until George had battled and bled for fifteen rounds to win them over, flung down their pencils and cheered him at the end.

"The man's not human," one said of Chuvalo. "Clay must have hit him five hundred times. He never even flinched." A British voice said, "It was like watching a chap hanging on a pub door at closing time. But Chuvalo took it all, and he might just have saved boxing in the process."

This was a crow-eating time for the three hundred and sixty boxing reporters, most of whom had traveled with mixed feelings to Toronto to cover what many of them considered the biggest championship farce in the lurid history of heavyweight boxing.

Chuvalo had lost three of his last four major fights. His only impressive credential was that although he'd lost eleven of his forty-seven bouts, he'd never been knocked down. But this said more for his courage and stamina than for his ability.

Clay's image in the United States had deteriorated to the point where he had been forced by public opinion to take his title out of the country to defend it. It was bad enough, all along, to be associated with the Black Muslims, but he had really capped everything with his now-famous crack about his draft status: "I ain't got no quarrel with them Viet Congs."

At the same time, no one questioned Clay's fighting ability. He had knocked out eighteen opponents in twenty-two pro fights, and had humiliated two former world champions, Floyd Patterson and Sonny Liston.

So the fight shaped up as a fourth-rate affair, pitting a champion considered too unpopular to fight in his own country against a challenger who had been labeled an unworthy opponent by almost everybody. Sam Leitch of the London *Daily Mirror*, a leading British sports authority, took a cue from his editor and demanded a world boycott of the bout. Typical of United States press reaction was the barb tossed by columnist Arthur Daley of the *New York Times*. He told his readers, "They are charging $100 ringside here for a fight that isn't worth 30 cents." And sports editor Milt Dunnell of the *Toronto Star* had phoned his department all the way from Florida and ordered, "Don't even suggest in any of your advance stories that Chuvalo has a chance, because you and I both know he hasn't."

But on the fight night, Chuvalo was to punch holes in their pessimism. After a little-league buildup, he turned in a big-league performance. As I looked up through the ropes, 3,900 fans in the Gardens were shrieking with excitement as Chuvalo plodded out of his corner at the opening bell and took six punishing jabs before he landed a wild left hook to Clay's midsection. But then for round after round he kept doggedly carrying the fight to Clay, who stubbornly refused to back off,

throwing faster and often more telling punches at the Canadian champion. It seemed inevitable that Chuvalo would go down. But he absorbed the punishment unflinchingly for the full fifteen rounds. His face bled and rose in grotesque lumps, but even in the final moments Chuvalo was punching back. By the time the judges awarded the decision to Clay, Chuvalo had already won something Clay had lost long before, if he'd ever had it: the respect of everyone who saw or heard the fight.

The fight had been over for almost twenty minutes, and in the press room at Maple Leaf Gardens the reporters glanced irritably at their watches. They had deadlines to meet, and they were waiting for Chuvalo and Clay to emerge from their dressing rooms.

Chuvalo and his manager, Irving Ungerman, elbowed their way inside. George's nose was bent and swollen. His eyes were bluish slits, and a patch of skin was missing from his forehead. Many of the same men who had publicly labeled him as unworthy of a title shot, now looked sheepishly at him as he moved to the platform.

"Were you ever in trouble?" someone asked, incredulously.

"He never hurt me," said George, through swollen lips. "I'd like another crack at him. I feel I've earned it."

There were more questions. Yes, he thought Clay was the fastest heavyweight he'd ever fought; but, no, he didn't punch as hard as some others he'd fought. When the questions trailed off, Chuvalo excused himself and began moving slowly out of the room.

Chuvalo paused at the door, then turned back to face them. For the first time, his battered, impassive face was forming a grin. "Listen, you guys, you're all invited back to the Prince George Hotel. The party's on us."

A few minutes later Clay came in, flanked by three Muslim friends. He was wearing evening clothes in midnight blue, and he adjusted his bow tie as he hopped up on the platform. He was unmarked.

"I warned you," he said. "But you wouldn't listen. Chuvalo is the toughest man I've ever fought. Tougher'n Liston, Patterson, Jones and all the rest. His head is the hardest thing I've ever hit." As evidence, he held up his swollen fists.

When the interview was over, his bodyguards cleared the way for him through the throng: "Give him room. Give him a three-foot path…"

It was more than Chuvalo had given him all night. ♣

1968

January 13, 1968

Bill Masterton of the new Minnesota North Stars suffered massive brain injuries after his head hit the ice during a game and died two days later in hospital, never regaining consciousness. It was the only on-ice fatality for the NHL in the century. The NHL named a new award for perseverance and sportsmanship after Masterton.

1970

April 29, 1970

Following an off-ice fight with teammate Ron Stewart in New York, star goaltender Terry Sawchuk entered a local hospital with a stomach injury. Later, while waiting for an operation to remove his gall bladder, Sawchuk suffered a fatal heart attack. No charges were laid and the death was ruled an accident.

Terry Sawchuck

1967

The Toronto Maple Leafs baseball team won the AAA Minor League championship, then folded, ending a long tradition of baseball in Toronto.

1971

The Canadian Men's Archery Team came third in the World Championships, with Emmanuel Boucher setting a world record in the Double 30m.

1976

The Victoria Bate Construction Softball Team was the last "club side" to represent Canada at the World Softball Championships. At the 1976 Championships in New Zealand, only two matches remained to be played when bad weather conditions forced cancellation of the tournament. The winner of Canada versus New Zealand was supposed to play the USA for the championship, so officials of the International Softball Federation decided on three co-world champions.

December 11, 1970

Toronto Maple Leaf rookie Brian Spencer had an ominous NHL debut. As he was about to play his first NHL game against the Buffalo Sabres, his father Roy Spencer was on the west coast and naturally wanted to watch his son play. Unfortunately, the local CBC station was scheduled to show the Vancouver Canucks and not the Leafs game. Upset, Roy went to the CBC studio 70 miles away in Prince George to complain, carrying a gun. The police were called and Roy Spencer died in a subsequent shootout.

February 21, 1974

Former Maple Leaf star defenceman Tim Horton was enticed out of retirement by his old coach Punch Imlach, who was now coaching in Buffalo. He was having a good, solid, season, but following a game in Toronto Horton, aged 44, wrecked his sports car and was killed driving back to Buffalo from Toronto.

December 30, 1986

In a tragic accident, four Junior A players with the Swift Current Broncos were killed when the team bus lost control and crashed while travelling between games. Killed were Scott Kruger, Trent Kresse, Chris Mantyka and Jason Ruff.

November 28, 1971

Grey Cup

The Fumble. The Argonauts were playing the Calgary Stampeders in Vancouver's Empire Stadium. The unexpectedly low scoring game was played during a torrential rainstorm, with the Stampeders holding a slight lead in the final quarter. With less than two minutes to go, the Argonauts intercepted the ball inside the Calgary 20 yard line. Being cautious, the Argos decided to keep the ball on the ground and run down time before kicking a last minute and likely easy field goal to win the game. The plan went sour, as standout running back Leon McQuay took the ball, ran to his left, and fumbled the ball and the Grey Cup away.

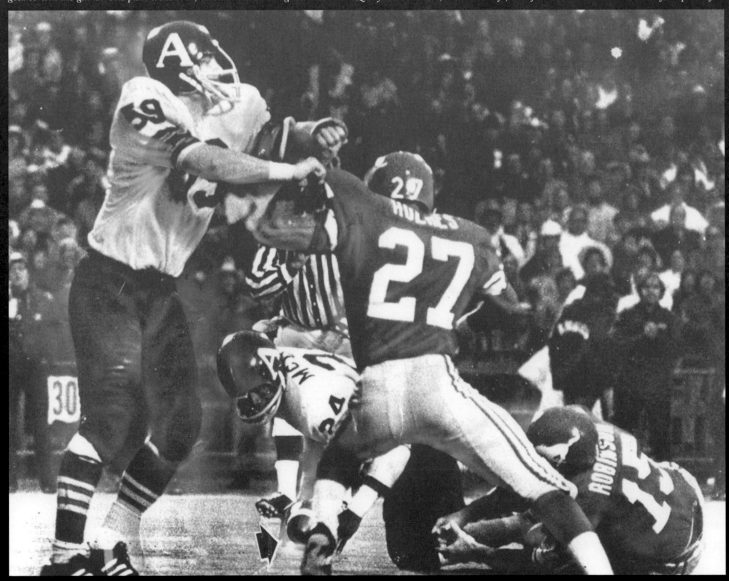

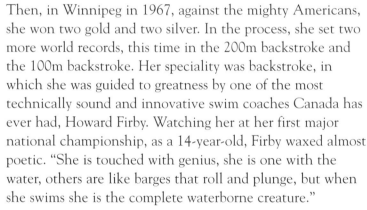

Elaine Tanner
Canada's "Mighty Mouse"

Being a favourite to medal at an Olympic Games can put an almost unbearable pressure on any athlete. Certainly it would have to be a tremendous weight for a 17-year-old. That was the position Elaine Tanner found herself in when she went to Mexico City for the 1968 Olympic Summer Games.

She was favoured in both the 100m and 200m backstroke, having beaten all the best swimmers in the world in the time leading up to the games. The previous two years had seen Canada's "Mighty Mouse" dominate women's swimming at the 1966 British Empire Games in Jamaica and the 1967 Pan Am Games in Winnipeg. In Jamaica she won an astounding seven medals — four gold and three silver. Her name also went in the books beside two world records: the 440 yd freestyle relay and the 220 yd butterfly. She won the Lou Marsh Trophy as Canada's outstanding athlete in 1966.

Then, in Winnipeg in 1967, against the mighty Americans, she won two gold and two silver. In the process, she set two more world records, this time in the 200m backstroke and the 100m backstroke. Her speciality was backstroke, in which she was guided to greatness by one of the most technically sound and innovative swim coaches Canada has ever had, Howard Firby. Watching her at her first major national championship, as a 14-year-old, Firby waxed almost poetic. "She is touched with genius, she is one with the water, others are like barges that roll and plunge, but when she swims she is the complete waterborne creature."

While Elaine toiled away perfecting her stroke in the pool in preparation for the 1968 Olympics, troubles were brewing elsewhere, long before she went to Mexico City. In a move that some called "a compromise" and others labelled purely political, a relatively unknown swim coach was named to lead Canada's Olympic swim team. Ted Thomas had little experience in international competition and was unknown to most of the swimmers on the team. They didn't know him or his ways but they knew he was not on the same training wavelength as any of them.

In those days the coaching staff was very limited, and since she was his only swimmer Elaine knew that Howard Firby would not be on the team. She hoped he would be able to help her by being in Mexico City, though. Before the Games, the team trained at high altitude in Banff, a great idea in theory, but in practice a mistake since the pool was an undersized hotel recreational facility. In the end they spent more time running than swimming, and swimmers, generally, aren't runners. So, the young people who arrived in Mexico City were confused and in many cases disheartened before starting their greatest challenge.

When they got there they found substandard accommodation on the ninth floor of their building, with an elevator that soon conked out, meaning a climb of nine stories. They were an unhappy group but for Elaine it was doubly upsetting as she was considered her country's main hope for a gold medal in any sport. The Americans were fully aware of her, since she had defeated their best backstrokers in both the 100m and 200m previously. So, in effect, they double-teamed her. Kaye Hall was entered in both events, but the 100m was her speciality. Lillian "Pokey" Watson was entered in only the 200m. Elaine, in contrast, had to swim relays as well as both backstrokes. Hall, from Tacoma, Washington had raced Elaine 25 times, starting when they were 12 years old, but had never beaten her. In the heats Elaine was the fastest, posting a new Olympic record of 1:07.4, two-tenths of a second better than Hall. But, in the final, Hall swam the race of her life, Elaine in lane four and Hall in five. Hall went out like a rocket and was ahead at 50m, fighting off Elaine's challenge to win in 1:06.2, a new world record. Elaine took silver with 1:06.7, the second fastest time ever. It was a great achievement, but for Elaine she felt like she had failed.

Three days later she had to try and erase that memory and concentrate on the 200m. Watson was fastest in the heats, at 2:29.4, but Elaine was a comfortable 2:30.9, second fastest. In the final Watson was in lane four, Elaine in five and Kaye Hall was in three. Tanner, who always liked to go out fast, was ahead at 50m in 32.83 and still led at the 100m mark, in 1:08.7. Then Watson turned it on. She had paced herself perfectly and she won the third leg to go ahead at the 150m mark. Elaine just couldn't catch her on the final leg. This was a new event in the Olympics and Watson set the record of 2:24.8. Elaine, at 2:27.4, held off Hall for silver.

Elaine also won bronze in the 4 x 100m freestyle relay, making it the greatest Olympic performance ever by a Canadian woman. Still, it was heartbreak for a confused teenager, who afterwards said that she was unable to focus on her race because she could only think about the 20 million Canadians who expected her to win. A lot of things had mitigated against her, but in her own eyes she had failed. At the press conference after the 100m backstroke she saw the assembled reporters, broke into tears and fled. When the Games were over, the spark was gone, and she retired from swimming soon after. She was only 18 but she called it a day. It was a sad day for Canadian swimming when it came time to say goodbye to a girl who, in three short years had written a new chapter in Canadian swimming history. ❧

Long-time Canadian swim coach Howard Firby helped guide Elaine Tanner's career.

Olympic bronze medallists in the women's 4 x 100m relay, 1968.

Bruce Robertson
and
Leslie Cliff

The pride of the Vancouver Dolphins

By the beginning of the 1970s, in the pride of the legacy of Elaine Tanner and Mary Stewart, the Dolphin Swim Club in Vancouver had become the most successful swim club in the country. With a strong, family supported organization that included family participation at all levels, the club was producing many of Canada's top international competitors.

Derek Snelling had come from England, to take over the coaching from Howard Firby and he was fortunate enough to find in his blossoming pack of stars two Vancouverites who were to do great things in Olympic, Pan Am and British Empire Games swimming: Bruce Robertson and Leslie Cliff, the leaders of the Dolphins from 1971 to 1975.

Though she was the younger by two years, Cliff had the earlier start in international competition. As a 15-year-old she went to Edinburgh for the 1970 British Empire and Commonwealth Games. But it was the next year, 1971, that she first rocked the swimming world. The mighty East German women's swimming machine hadn't yet been manufactured, and the Americans were the reigning world power. In Cali, Colombia, at the Pan Ams, the 16-year-old Cliff won three gold and two silver medals. She won golds in the 200m and 400m individual medleys, the events that were to be her specialty. Another gold came in the medley relay.

Then Canada went to Munich, for the 1972 Olympic Games. The Americans, led by Mark Spitz, and the Australian women, led by Shane Gould, were considered totally dominant. Cliff and Robertson, almost a two-person team, mounted a gallant challenge. Robertson swam to a silver medal, forcing Mark Spitz to set a world record and breaking the former world record himself in the 100m butterfly. Cliff took silver against a formidable field in the 400m IM, making it two silver medals for Canada. While most top nations had depth in their swim teams Canada did not — the two Vancouver swimmers were really a country's only hope. That meant they both had to swim a number of events, including relays. Cliff was the most versatile female swimmer at the games and Robertson, though he never discussed it, had battled asthma throughout his life. He put a positive spin on it, telling his mother that he thought coping with asthma had given him superior breath control.

Those swims at the Olympics foreshadowed great things to come for both of them. In 1973 Robertson took over from Spitz as the king of the butterfly by winning gold at the first-ever World Aquatic championships in Belgrade. He was named Canada's male athlete of the year. In 1974 Robertson and Cliff again led the Canadian team, this time a strong team with some depth, to the Commonwealth Games in Christchurch, New Zealand. There, Cliff capped a stellar career by taking gold in both 200m and 400m individual medleys. Robertson put on one of the greatest displays of swimming versatility in Commonwealth history by winning two gold, two silver and two bronze medals. Then, in 1975, he won three silver and two bronze at the Pan American Games in Mexico City.

Of the international medals won by Canadians from 1971-1975, the lion's share can be credited to the talents of Cliff and Robertson. ♣

1971

Legends Retire

Two of the NHL's all-time best and most-respected players retired at the end of the 1971 hockey season. At 44 Gordie Howe, left, ended his record 25-year career with the Detroit Red Wings as the league's career leader in many categories, including goals, assists and points. He would, of course, return to hockey with the WHA two years later and the NHL again in eight years. Meanwhile, Montreal's long-serving captain Jean Béliveau, right, also retired ... for good. Béliveau played with Montreal for 20 seasons, was on 10 Stanley Cup-winning teams, captained the Habs to five Stanley Cups and was a rare 500-goal and 1,000-point man in the NHL. "I took the right decision," he said at the time, "because at 40 you have to get closer to your family." In 1999 he would turn down the opportunity to be Canada's Governor General.

Nancy Garapick
and
Cheryl Gibson

Medals and question marks

Nancy Garapick, double Olympic bronze medallist in the 100m and 200m backstroke, 1976.

CSI/COA

Cheryl Gibson, 400m individual medley Olympic silver medallist, 1976.

CSI/COA

An Olympic swimming medal is a very elusive prize and certainly has been for Canadian swimmers through the years.

In terms of achievement the women have been somewhat more successful than the men in remedying this situation.

Elaine Tanner broke a drought of decades when she won two silver and a bronze in Mexico in 1968, Leslie Cliff and Donna Marie Gurr followed up in 1972 with silver and bronze medals respectively. There were high hopes for Canada, as host of the games, in 1976, in Montreal.

Canada

Nancy Garapick waves from podium, at the 1976 Olympic Games.

Two young women, of vastly different backgrounds, from different ends of the country, led the way for Canada. Nancy Garapick came from Halifax, certainly not a hotbed of Canadian swimming. Cheryl Gibson, on the other hand, came from Edmonton which had one of the strongest swimming programs in the country. Nancy was essentially a one-woman team, from the Trojans in Halifax, but thanks to amazing natural talent and an understanding and motivating coach named Nigel Kemp, she had emerged as one of Canada's outstanding swimmers. When she was just 13, in 1975, she broke the world record for the 200m backstroke. Her time of 2:16:33 surpassed the previous record held by East German Ulricka Richter, who later played a role in Nancy's story. Nancy swam freestyle and butterfly as well as backstroke, but it was in the backstroke, like Elaine Tanner eight years before, that she was a top hope for Canada. She had not set the world on fire in the Olympic trials, but she qualified with a third place finish in the 100m back and a second in the 200m. Nancy thrilled the country, which for the first time was getting complete television coverage of all the heats in swimming, by winning her heats in both the 100m and 200m. She set an Olympic record of 1:03:28 in the 100m. This was heady stuff, for a 14 year old to be ahead of the world's greatest including the American powerhouse! But strange things were happening in that Olympic pool, particularly in the women's finals. Nancy finished third in each final, beaten out by the East Germans who were just overpowering everyone. In the 100m final Nancy again went under the 1:04 mark, but was behind Richter and Treber. Richter's time was 1:01:83, an unheard of margin in the 100m.

Cheryl Gibson, meanwhile, was one of Canada's most versatile and durable swimmers. She competed in the butterfly and backstroke, and put together all four strokes in swimming's most gruelling race, the 400m individual medley. She actually defeated Garapick in the 100m backstroke in the Olympic trials and also won the 200m butterfly. Ironically, she was third at the trials, although she was the Canadian record holder in the 400m IM. At the Olympics she started rather slowly, or it seemed that way because others, particularly the East Germans, were going so fast. Cheryl easily beat her old Canadian record, but just made it into the final in the 400m IM. She had saved her best effort for that final and she swam her greatest race, a smashing new Canadian record of 4:48:11! But she was still second to Tauber of East German by almost 6 seconds, again an incredible margin.

At the time, suspicions were raised and rumours circulated that the powerful East German machine was fuelled partly by performance enhancing substances. The accusations were substantiated years later, although not always with respect to specific athletes. Also revealed were selection, coaching, and training techniques employed by the East German sport system, none of them against the rules, but which some felt were inappropriately harsh.

It's tempting to speculate about what would have happened had the East Germans not been such a dominant force. Nancy Garapick would have had two gold medals in the backstrokes and in the 100m backstroke it could have been a Canadian sweep, with Wendy Cook winning silver and Cheryl Gibson the bronze.

In the individual medley Gibson, "The Gibber" as she was known, would have won gold and very probably Becky Smith, also from Edmonton, would have won the silver. One can never be certain what "would have happened." Some view certain results from the Montreal Olympics and subsequent competitions as tarnished because of suspicions about drugs. On the positive side, reaction in Canada and other countries led to efforts to ensure swimming and other sports remain "clean." ❦

Greg Joy – Canada's Jump for Joy

Canadian Press CP

At the 1976 Montreal Olympics, Canadian athletes won no gold medals, the only host country to do so in the century. But on last day of competition, just when our spirits needed lifting, Greg Joy jumped into our hearts and our memories by defeating the American favourite and winning a silver medal.

During the mid-1970s, high jumper Dwight Stones was the world record holder and a seemingly unbeatable foe. By 1976, every jumper in the world knew Stones, watched him with awe and eagerly anticipated his performance at the Olympic Games.

"Every day in training it was 'I've got to beat Dwight. If I'm not doing it, Dwight is,'" said Joy after the competition. "Just before I left for the Olympics I was training in El Paso. I put the bar at 7' 4", the height I ended up jumping at the Games. I easily went over it three times and I said, 'Okay, I'm ready,'" he recalled.

When they got to Montreal, Joy and the rest of the jumpers were ready to compete, but Stones and several others felt the facilities were not quite as prepared as the athletes. They were right. The construction of many of the Games' facilities had been subject to untold delays, labour problems, and cost overruns, leading many to feel the central venues for the Games would not be ready in time.

Stones was a premier track and field athlete who was constantly being interviewed by the media about everything. Quite simply, he didn't like the shape the facilities were in, especially since he was forced to share a room with 12 other athletes. In blunt fashion, he told the media just that, in the process calling the organizers and the labour unions "rude."

Montrealers took the criticisms personally, feeling that he had called all French Canadians rude. That was not the case, but the damage was done. In the Olympic Stadium, the audience booed

Greg Joy

National Archives

Stones at every opportunity during the qualifying round. That first day, Stones did not help gather any sympathy as he blew kisses to the unsympathetic spectators. When he returned the second day wearing a t-shirt reading "I love French Canadians," it was too late.

Unlike most jumpers at the time, Stones made a very wide approach to the bar to gain speed before jumping. If conditions were right, he could soar. If it was wet, his take-off was slower and his jumps lower. On the final day of the Montreal Olympic Games, just when the high jump final was scheduled, it rained.

Stones was the first jumper in the final round. He easily cleared the bar at 2.18m. Canada's Greg Joy followed shortly thereafter, but needed three jumps to clear the height.

"I was actually sliding on the takeoff surface because I had little short pin spikes for dry surfaces. So after two attempts I checked my spikes and went 'oh man!' When I changed my spikes to longer ones, I easily cleared it on my third attempt," Joy explained later.

The bar was moved to 2.21m, with Stones and Joy clearing it with ease. But the rain was getting worse.

"I remember turning to my teammate and saying, if the rain stops this instant, I'm breaking the world record today, if it doesn't stop, that's the last height I'll clear," Stones told the media following the competition.

The rain only got harder.

"I remember going to the official and asking how hard it would have to rain for them to postpone this thing. And he looked at me and took the perfect comedic pause and said 'Harder than this,'" recalled Stones.

Like a good Boy Scout, though, Joy was ready for the rain. Being from Vancouver, he had practised jumping on a wet surface many times. With only four jumpers remaining in the competition, the bar was raised to 2.23m. Stones missed all three of his attempts. Joy missed once, then again. A hushed crowd and a nationwide television audience watched Joy prepare for his third attempt. He steadied his nerves, went to his start position, rocked seemingly for hours on his feet, made a clean approach to the bar and cleared the height. Shooting a triumphant arm in the air upon landing, Joy knew he had secured Canada's first high jump medal since 1932. He had beaten his archrival and the world record holder, Dwight Stones. But there was more work to be done, because Polish jumper Jacek Wszola had also cleared the height.

"I was so focused on beating Dwight. When I beat him my day was done. I just didn't have it in me any more."

Most people watching that day still think of Joy's performance as a victory, but he in fact finished with the silver medal after Wszola cleared 2.25m to win. On the way to the podium to get his bronze medal, Dwight Stones was booed. "No one deserves that at the Olympics," said Joy. "He was disappointed enough, but to get up in front of 70,000 people and get booed, it's just heartless."

Years later, Joy recalled his moment: "I happened to be in the right place at the right time. I'm proud of winning an Olympic medal, but the reaction to going over the bar in Montreal was disproportional to the accomplishment of the day. Every day of my life someone mentions that jump — and I finished second!" ♣

Toller Cranston

Genius. Iconoclastic. Outspoken. These are among the most frequent words used to describe Toller Cranston, the legendary Canadian men's figure skating champion. When he took to the ice, an audience was liable to jump up and cry, "Bravo! Bravo!" as if it were an opera house, not a skating arena.

Cranston, a skater and a painter, is widely credited with revolutionizing men's figure skating. Until the late 1960s, male figure skaters suffered from the "penguin syndrome." They held their heads erect and their backs rigid, and never, ever, used their arms in an expressive fashion.

Growing up in Kirkland Lake, a northern Ontario mining town known for producing tough hockey stars, Cranston decided to take up figure skating at the age of seven. And somewhere along the line, he also decided he wanted to skate like a dancer. He moved his arms and his body like a dancer, expressing himself and interpreting the music. He pioneered the style of skating that is the standard today.

It was not an easy road. Cranston had to fight hard for recognition by the skating establishment, and endured bitter disappointments along the way.

In 1968, he went to the Canadian championships in Vancouver, seeking a spot on the Olympic team. Still a teenager, he summoned a performance that left the audience marveling at his prowess. But in a piece of dubious judging, his marks ranged from two 5.9s to a 4.9. To his distress, and the audience's anger, he did not make the team. His moves were seen as effeminate, and few understood him.

One person who did understand was Ellen Burka, the famous coach who had guided her own daughter, Petra, to the World Championship in 1965. Burka told the impressionable young skater that he was doing the right thing, and that people just did not understand.

Seething with disappointment, Cranston began to lose the discipline necessary to become a top level skater. He was living in Montreal, studying at the École des Beaux-Arts, and practising when he could find ice time. But he was no longer really applying himself. Then one day, Cranston gave Burka a call. She took him under her wing, and helped him develop his full potential as a skater.

On paper, his greatest achievement was winning a bronze medal at the 1976 Olympic Winter Games in Innsbruck. He arrived in Innsbruck in trademark Cranston style: eschewing the official Olympic outfit, he wore a full-length sheared muskrat coat to his accreditation.

Cranston had to come from behind to secure a place on the podium, though. After the figures, never his strong suit, he stood far from the podium in seventh place. Ahead of him stood several strong contenders, including England's John Curry and Russian's Vladimir Kovalev.

But Cranston fought back in the short program, skating a brilliant routine that combined the best of his artistry with masterful technique. His performance earned him top marks and bumped him up to fifth place.

The short program was to be his peak performance. In the long, Cranston skated below his best, touching a hand to the ice during a triple toe loop. He also skipped a triple Salchow during a combination, although he threw one in later. Still he was strong enough to come second in the long program, and move up the third place to take the bronze.

The gold was won by John Curry, who skated brilliantly — Cranston-style — in the long program. Curry was not the only disciple — many of the young skaters at Innsbruck were already mimicking Cranston's artistry.

Ironically, Cranston, who is widely regarded as the most influential skater of his generation, was never rewarded with a world championship. He was the Canadian men's champion six times. At the 1974 World Championships in Munich, he became an instant legend with a freestyle skate that drew a prolonged standing ovation from the German audience, and won him a bronze medal. In part, Cranston's lack of success must be attributed to his Achilles' heel, the compulsory figures, which in those days still accounted for a great deal of the mark. While he did not achieve the gold medal on the world stage that he aspired to, he did achieve another, perhaps greater accomplishment: a legacy and influence that was still felt more than two decades later. ❦

Toller Cranston, right, receiving his Olympic bronze medal, 1976.

1978

Considered to be Canada's greatest male gymnast of the century, Philip Delesalle was honoured by the gymnastics world in 1992 when the move he introduced on the pommel horse was officially named the "Delesalle." He won five consecutive Canadian championships (1976-80), and won the gold medal as all-around gymnastics champion at the 1978 Commonwealth Games. He retired at the height of his career and was unable to realize his goal of Olympic gold when Canada did not attend the 1980 Moscow Olympics.

CSI

1977

Hockey

A Farewell to Greatness

by Robert Miller
Feb. 21, 1977

Number 4, Bobby Orr.

Late last month, in what was probably his last appearance as a professional hockey player, Bobby Orr was able to play only two shifts against the inept Vancouver Canucks. Power plays, of course. During the second, the puck skipped past him at the Vancouver blueline. Instinctively, he started to whirl and give chase. But he couldn't do it. Even a routine pivot was beyond the wounded knee. Orr winced, limped to the Chicago bench and sat, with buried heart, watching the game sputter along to a weary draw. The world's greatest hockey player — and who, really, can argue the point? Denis Potvin? — was through. Even Orr thought so. Washed up and perhaps even permanently crippled at the age of 28. "I can't go on like this," he said a day or so later, before leaving for Florida and writing off yet another National Hockey League season. No, Bobby. You can't. Neither can we.

It has been said far too often: Bobby Orr on one leg is better than most hockey players on two. Maybe he is. Certainly he is a better box office. But Bobby Orr was never just a hockey player. He was a virtuoso, an original, possibly a genius — and he had been those things since boyhood, skating his way from the ponds of Parry Sound to the great arenas of the continent. Glenn Gould can probably play a brilliant one-handed piano. Rudolf Nureyev can certainly dance a mean boogie. But would they? Should they? Why should Bobby Orr try to play one-legged hockey? Why should anyone — fan, owner, coach, teammate — demand it from him? Let him go now, away from the pain and the spotlight. Let him leave with his dignity and his millions. He has earned them. Let him leave us with the memories, with the knowledge that when we watched him we were watching a man/boy play our game at a level we had never realized it could reach.

Canadians have always made too much of hockey — and not enough. It is, as a friend of mine often says, our third official language. Well, Bobby Orr gave it a grammar and a new accent. He changed hockey, and our perception of it, in a way that no individual performer had ever changed a team sport before. The Russians, perplexed, called him a halfback, borrowing a football term to explain Orr's innovative approach. How else to explain a defenceman who won scoring championships? Ever practical, though, the Russians did not attempt to play in the "Boo-bie Orr" manner. They left that to the less gifted North American pros. The Russians knew what we all knew: there was only one Number 4. Anyway, when translated into Russian, Canada's third official language became ideologically correct: a collective pastime, played impersonally, impassively, efficiently. Orr, a capitalist, played it all by himself, even though he always let his teammates share in the fun, the exuberance, the rewards of the game. He made them better than they were, richer than they dreamed. In the good years, he absolutely dominated. There was nothing he couldn't do with a puck, a stick and a pair of skates. His fellow pros paid him the ultimate compliment: they never took their eyes off him when he was on the ice. Later, in their own practices, they would try to copy the things he did. The most talented would master some of Orr's moves. Orr would simply invent new ones that rendered the old ones obsolete, and take the game on to a higher level.

When he left Boston, home of the GOD BLESS ORR COUNTRY bumper sticker, Mayor Kevin White was able to say without blushing: "Bobby Orr has been to Boston the equivalent of a great natural or historic resource, like Paul Revere's house or the Bunker Hill monument." When he signed with the Blackhawks for three million dollars (not one cent of which he has accepted, because he doesn't feel he has earned it), The *New York Times* made him the subject of its "Man in the News" column, where normally statesmen and tycoons are profiled. Although the press in Canada faithfully chronicled his exploits, his agonies and his wretched medical luck, a strange resentment seemed to lurk between the lines. A Toronto newspaper poll coughed up his name as one of the world's biggest bores. How typically Canadian.

We have too few heroes in this country, just as the Americans have too many. We have a habit of chipping away at our heroes, digging for flaw, hauling them down and finally, enjoying their humiliation. Orr deserves better, but could be pardoned for doubting he'll get it. He has heard the boobirds of Maple Leaf Gardens. He has seen the anticipatory glint in the vulture's eye every time the knee went. He has read the injudicious (and until now, premature) obituaries. Denis Potvin, an excellent defenceman whose talent nearly matches his ego, has even dared to disparage Orr's work in the Canada Cup series last fall. Overpraised, grumped Potvin, who complained that his own efforts had been simultaneously under-appreciated. Wrong. I remember Orr, bad leg and all, taking on the world at half speed and still showing everyone, Potvin included, how it's done, how our game is played. Orr has endured it all — the boos, the bloodlust, the jealousy and the pain — without complaining, just as he has accepted the cheers and the honours and the fame and the money without gloating.

But how frustrating the past few seasons must have been. How infuriating for the body not to be able to obey the brain's commands. How depressing to watch lesser talents flash by, doing their best but not quite doing it right. How satisfying it would be to come back, just one more time, healthy, and win a scoring title or a Stanley Cup. It would be in Orr's nature to try. Al MacNeil, one of the four Team Canada coaches last fall, says he has never seen an athlete with as positive a mental attitude. "The guy is just fantastic, that's all."

Hockey fans everywhere, to say nothing of beleaguered franchise owners, naturally hope a medical miracle will occur. But if there is to be no miracle, if there is only to be a half-speed Orr, a one-legged wonder, then I hope the player will agree to leave well enough alone. The fans don't owe Orr anything but respect; he has always given them his very best. Orr doesn't owe the fans anything either, except maybe the right to remember the way he played our game. No one wants to see Orr tagged as a has-been. Let him surrender his mantle to Potvin, or more likely, Larry Robinson or Borje Salming. But don't let one of them tear it off his shoulders as he tries to hobble by. 🍁

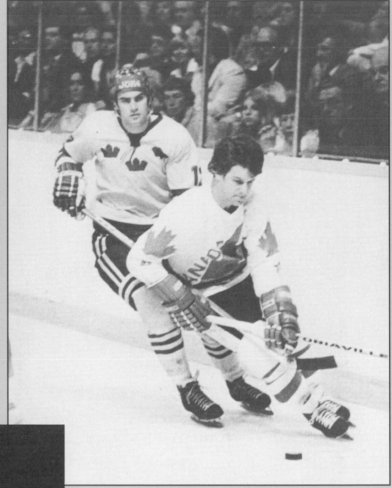

1976 Canada Cup.

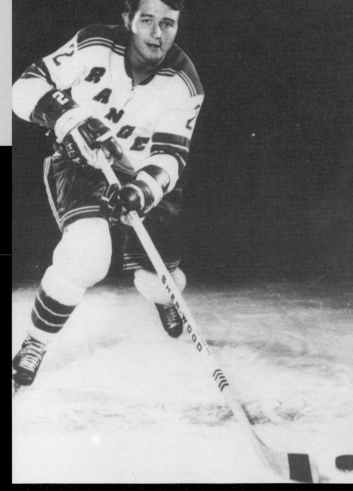

Brad Park, 1972

"I thought I just couldn't line up and shake hands with them [the *Bruins*] after the game [the 1972 *Stanley Cup* final]. I was all set to leave for our dressing room when I noticed Orr was the first in line. Because of my tremendous respect for him I changed my mind." — Brad Park quoted in the Hockey News, 1972.

Toronto native Brad Park was an outstanding defenceman for 17 years in the NHL. He never won the James Norris Trophy as the league's top defenceman, though, having the misfortune of being slightly overshadowed by two other all-time greats, first Bobby Orr, then Denis Potvin. He finished second in balloting six times.

Nonetheless, Park was five times named to the NHL's first All-Star team and twice to the second. He played his first seven and a half seasons with the New York Rangers before being traded to the Boston Bruins, where he played another seven and a half seasons before winding up in Detroit for two years. He was also a solid, valued, member of the Team Canada in the classic Canada-Russia Series of 1972

In 1,113 NHL games, Park scored 213 goals, assisted on another 683 for 896 points. He also earned 125 points (35 goals, 90 assists) in 161 playoff contests.

May 10, 1970. In one of the most timely hockey photos in the century, Bobby Orr is caught "flying through the air" just moments after scoring the Stanley Cup series-winning overtime goal against the St. Louis Blues. It didn't take long for his joy to show, either.

HHOF — Fred Keenan

Highlights

Orr Highlights

March 20, 1948

Robert Gordon Orr was born in Parry Sound, Ontario.

September 3, 1966

An outstanding junior player with the Oshawa Generals, Bobby signed his first professional hockey contract with the NHL's Boston Bruins, for a league-high $70,000. He would not disappoint, winning the Calder Trophy as the NHL's top rookie at the end of the 1966-67 season.

May 10, 1968

Bobby won his first of eight straight Norris trophies as the league's top defenceman, an NHL record.

March 15, 1969

Bobby recorded his 60th point of the season, an assist, surpassing the previous record for defencemen set by Pierre Pilote of Chicago in 1964-65.

March 20, 1969

Bobby celebrated his 21st birthday in style during a 5-5 tie between Chicago and the Bruins, scoring his 21st goal of the season and surpassing the defence-scoring record set by Flash Hollett during the 1944-45 season.

March 15, 1970

Bobby scored two goals and an assist in a 5-5 tie between the Bruins and Detroit and became the first defenceman in NHL history to score 100 points in a season.

March 22, 1970

Bobby scored two assists in a 5-0 Bruin victory over Minnesota, setting the season-assist total of 78 and breaking teammate's Phil Esposito's 1968 mark.

April 5, 1970

No one thought it was possible for a defenceman to win the Art Ross Trophy, until Bobby scored an assist in the last game of the season to become the NHL's leading scorer for the season.

May 8, 1970

Bobby became the first defenceman to win the Hart Trophy as the NHL's Most Valuable Player. This year he also received the Art Ross (scoring), Norris (defence) and Conn Smythe (playoff MVP) trophies to go with the Stanley Cup won by his Boston Bruins.

May 10, 1970

Bobby scored the Stanley Cup overtime winner against the St. Louis Blues in "flying" fashion.

May 4, 1972

Bobby passed the career playoff goal total for defencemen, netting his 17th goal in only 47 games. He surpassed the 16-goal total of Red Kelly set over 94 games.

May 5, 1972

Orr won the Hart Trophy for the third time in a row and the Norris for the fifth consecutive time, both NHL firsts.

May 11, 1972

Bobby scored the Stanley Cup-winning goal against the New York Rangers in a 3-0 victory.

September 4, 1972

Bobby could not play in the famed Canada-Russia Series because he was recovering from a serious knee operation; he was nonetheless named to the team and travelled with them throughout the series. Bobby made up for not playing in the series by being named the MVP in the first-ever Canada Cup, won by Canada in 1976.

December 21, 1972

In his 423rd game, Bobby set the career scoring record for defencemen by scoring his 541st point, an assist. He broke the mark Doug Harvey set over 1,113 games.

January 1, 1973

Bobby recorded six assists in a game against Vancouver, tying the defence record set by Babe Pratt (1944) and Pat Stapleton (1969).

November 15, 1973

Bobby scored three goals and four assists to become the first NHL defenceman to score seven points in a game, in a 10-2 victory over the New York Rangers.

November 17, 1973

Bobby again broke a scoring record belonging to Doug Harvey, scoring four assists in a game against Detroit to set the NHL career assist mark (456) for defencemen.

March 12, 1974

Bobby became the first player in NHL history to score 100 points or more in five consecutive seasons.

October 7, 1976

After signing with Chicago in the off-season as a free agent, Bobby scored a goal and an assist in his first game as a Blackhawk.

October 28, 1978

Bobby Orr scored the final goal of his NHL career against Detroit in a 7-2 loss.

November 8, 1978

"The day the music died, hockey style." Bobby Orr retired from hockey, his wounded knees too battered to continue.

June 12, 1979

At 31 years of age, Bobby Orr became the youngest player of the century elected the Hockey Hall of Fame.

Career Summary:

12	seasons (7 full)
657	games
270	goals
645	assists
915	points
74	playoff games
26	playoff goals
66	playoff assists
92	playoff points
1	Calder (Rookie) Trophy
8	Norris (Defence) Trophies
3	Hart (MVP) Trophies
2	Art Ross (Scoring) Trophies
2	Stanley Cups
2	Conn Smythe (Playoff MVP) Trophies
8	First Team All-Stars
1	Second Team All-Stars
1	Canada Cup (1976)
1	Canada Cup MVP (1976)

Gilles Villeneuve, from Bertierville, Quebec

1973-1976

Regarded as one of the finest and fastest drivers ever on the Formula One circuit, Gilles Villeneuve of Bertierville, Quebec, began by driving snowmobiles, winning the world snowmobile championships in 1974. He entered his first automobile race in 1973 and by 1976 he was completely dominating the Formula Atlantic series in North America. Villeneuve won a record nine of 10 Formula Atlantic races that year, subsequently receiving many offers to race with the faster and more famous Formula 1 teams in Europe. He initially signed on with McLaren, eventually joining up with the legendary Ferrari Racing Team. He would later remark: "If someone said to me that you can have three wishes, my first would have been to get into racing, my second to be in Formula 1, my third to drive for Ferrari…"

Gilles Villeneuve's family at his funeral.

Gilles Villeneuve taken by his pall bearers.

1979

The first of Villeneuve's six F1 wins came the next year, fittingly enough in Canada. His best F1 season was 1979, when he ended up second in the year-long championship to Ferrari teammate Jody Scheckter.

1979

"His signature race was not a first, but a second. At the 1979 French Grand Prix at Dijon, Jean-Pierre Jabouille was racing for Renault and posted the first win for a modern turbo car. Rene Arnoux was running well and looked to make it a Renault one-two finish. Villeneuve, however, asserted a wheel-banging, tire-boiling, duel with Arnoux that no witness to it is likely to forget. Villeneuve's insane insistence that his slower Ferrari could beat Arnoux's faster Renault was rewarded, and he finished just ahead of the Frenchman. It is probably safe to say that this was the most exciting race for second place in the history of motor racing." (Denis A. David, official Formula 1 biographer)

1982

Gilles Villeneuve crashed while practising for the Belgian Grand Prix in May of 1982, causing fatal injuries to Bertierville's world famous hero.

Gilles Villeneuve's funeral procession.

General Highlights

October 19, 1981

The most disappointing moment in the history of the Montreal Expos came during a one-game playoff to determine who advanced to post season play. The LA Dodgers' Rick Monday hit a home run off Expo pitching ace Steve Rogers to seal the LA victory and end Montreal's best-ever season.

Bob Molle (Wrestling)

Only 18 days after back surgery, Bob Molle won the silver medal in freestyle wrestling at the 1984 Olympic Games. He then played eight years with the Winnipeg Blue Bombers as an offensive guard and won the Grey Cup twice (1988 and 1990).

1980-89

For runner Lynn Williams, her most memorable event was her bronze medal performance at the 1989 World Cross Country Championships in Norway, since she considered cross country to be the purest, most competitive, form of middle distance running. Still, the public likely remembers her best for her performance in the 3000m at the 1984 Olympics in Los Angeles, where she ran to a bronze medal after the infamous Zola Budd - Mary Decker tumble.

1992

At the Indianapolis 500, Canadian Scott Goodyear came the closest ever to victory without winning, coming second by half a car length.

1980

Known as "El Perfecto," jockey Avelino Gomez won 4078 races, including four Queen's Plates (a record at that time). A firecracker with an unpredictable temper, Gomez also loved to react to the crowd's cheers or jeers. He regarded himself as an entertainer and clearly rejoiced when his antics aroused the crowd. Gomez died following a tragic three-horse accident during the running of the Canadian Oak Stakes at Woodbine in 1980.

The Firth Sisters

Cross-country skiing is considered one of the toughest sports in the world, demanding large amounts of strength, endurance, determination and coordination. It demands all of the energy an athlete can give, frequently under adverse weather conditions. It's no wonder then, that two of Canada's best skiers during the 1970s and 1980s hailed from 200 km north of the Arctic Circle, where harsh weather is a constant reality. Twin sisters Sharon and Shirley Firth dominated Canadian cross-country skiing for two decades. They represented Canada at four Olympic Games from 1972 to 1984, a feat which was only matched by legendary speed skater Gaétan Boucher.

The Firths learned how to ski thanks to the efforts of Father Jean Marie Mouchet, the local Roman Catholic priest who set up a program for area kids. With his help the girls' talent blossomed quickly. Growing up helping their father trap game, they came by their fierce competitiveness naturally. Once the news got out about Father Mouchet's efforts to teach kids to ski, the federal government helped too, setting up a program that would see the best skiers get extra help from Norwegian coach Bjorger Petterson.

The federal program gave the Firth sisters and others a ticket to see the world. By 1972, the group from the Mackenzie Delta was so strong that it provided seven of the nine members of the Olympic team. Shirley Firth almost didn't make it to Sapporo, Japan, for the Olympics, contracting an almost fatal case of hepatitis. The fighter in her overcame the disease, but she was too weak to be competitive. Sharon finished 26th in the 5 km classic style race, which still stood as a tie for the best-ever Canadian result at the end of the century.

Despite the fact that team officials at times expressed the desire to see new, young talent on the team, the Firths remained the top skiers in Canada through to 1984, when they retired after the Sarajevo Olympics. Their careers include a total of 48 Canadian championships.

National Archives/BCSHOF

Debbie Brill

As the 20th century ended, two amazing cases of long-term durability graced the Athletics Canada record book. Both involved high jumper Debbie Brill.

Both her Canadian record heights — 1.99 metres indoors, set in 1981, and 1.98 metres outdoors, set in 1984 — were still intact and under no threat. And the woman herself, who turned 47 on March 10, 2000, continued to compete and was indisputably the best masters jumper in the world.

Brill, who began competing in the Fraser Valley town of Haney when she was 13, also shared the distinction of helping develop and popularize a new style of jumping that eventually became universally accepted. In 1969 she was competing in a meet in Vancouver that also featured America's Dick Fosbury, 1968 Olympic gold medallist and inventor of the high jumping technique known as the "Fosbury Flop." The 16-year-old Brill noted his style and cried out: "Hey, look at that! He jumps just like me!"

It hadn't occurred to her that the American jumper was supposed to have been the sole discoverer of the biggest breakthrough in leaping over a bar from one foot since the scissors jump became passé. She had been doing it this way for a couple of years herself, having discovered — as did Fosbury — that if you don't mind landing on the back of your head, it's the most efficient way of gaining maximum altitude. She had coined her own name for her jumping style, calling it the "Brill Bend."

Thanks to her technique and her determination to win, Brill first became Canada's number one jumper that same year, at the age of only 16. She was still number one when she retired from open competition in 1987 at 34.

During more than 30 years of competition, her record includes at least one gold medal in every international event she entered except for the Olympics, the World Championships and the World University Games, where she won one silver in two appearances. She was named to the Canadian team for four Olympics from 1972-1984 (including the boycotted 1980 Moscow Olympics), four Commonwealth Games (1970 and 1978-86), two Pan American Games (1971 and 1979), and one World Championship (1983 — outdoor).

An eighth place finisher with a height of 1.82m at the 1972 Olympics in Munich, she improved both her abilities and her ranking over the next four years. Entering the Montreal Olympics in 1976, she held the Canadian record of 1.89m, and was ranked fourth in the world. Expectations were high that she would continue her upward trend and finish in the medals. Inexplicably, Brill and three other world class jumpers never even made it out of the qualifying round.

Despite her disappointment, Brill was not about to call it quits. Four years later, she was still at the height of her skills and ready to aim for the Olympic podium again, but fate intervened and

prevented her from redeeming her Montreal experience at the 1980 Moscow Olympics due to the Western boycott of those games. Still competing, she improved to fifth at the 1984 Olympics in Los Angeles with a jump of 1.94m.

Ironically, what may have been Brill's greatest triumph happened back in Montreal's Olympic Stadium, the scene of her crushing disappointment in 1976. During the second World Cup of track and field, she was part of a top-flight field of international high jumpers. She jumped like one inspired, and one by one her competitors went out. Finally it was down to two: Brill and Sara Simeoni of Italy. Both failed twice to clear 1.96m, and some thought Brill was about to succumb to the pressure. Going first on the third and final attempt, though, she sailed over, putting all the pressure on her Italian rival. Simeoni's final try knocked the bar off for a third time, and the gold medal belonged to Brill.

Interspersed with her Olympic appearances were numerous medals won in other international events, including two golds (1970 and 1982) and a silver (1986) in the Commonwealth Games, and one gold (1971) and a bronze (1979) in the Pan Am Games. Her "first" career effectively ended in 1987 when she underwent surgery to repair two damaged Achilles tendons.

Ten years later, at 44, she started masters competition, winning yet another Canadian championship and setting a world record of 1.75m, 15 centimetres above the existing global masters record.

Brill finished out the 20th century in style by winning the world masters meets in 1998 and 1999, equalling her newly established record against a field of 25 in Eugene, Oregon, and setting a new one, 1.76 metres, a year later in Gateshead, England.

Her masters career was interrupted briefly following her 1999 World Masters record jump at Gateshead. Trying for a leap of 1.80 metres after winning the gold, she broke her left foot. Nonetheless, she came back to win the 2000 North American Masters, held in Kamloops, with a leap of 1.65 metres.

Co-winner of the Bobbie Rosenfeld Award as Canada's Female Athlete of the Year in 1971, Brill was inducted into the Canadian Amateur Sports Hall of Fame (later renamed the Canadian Olympic Hall of Fame) in 1982 and a year later was named an Officer of the Order of Canada.

While she never won the ultimate prize — Olympic gold — for a decade and a half she was among the top half dozen women jumpers in the world. For world-class longevity, Canada has produced no other track and field athlete like her.

Nor anyone, for that matter, who has marched so independently to her own drummer. Early in her career she dropped out for the better part of two years to try the drug and hippie scene. She shocked people with a candid interview on sex and the single athlete. At the beginning of the 1980s she deliberately chose to become a single mother.

And, at the start of the new century — besides still jumping because "I enjoy it so much" — this mother of three and long ago hippie worked with her medical doctor husband, operating a Vancouver detox centre. In all respects she came full circle. ❦

Diane Jones Konihowski

Some of the most physically demanding challenges in track and field, let alone all of sport, have always been the combined events — the ten-event decathlon for men, and the five-event pentathlon, later replaced with the seven-event heptathlon, for women. Featuring a variety of running, jumping and throwing sections, the gruelling combined events require that athletes master a wide range of skills, rather than specializing in a single one. The physical requirements for each section are sometimes opposed too — for example, the strength and size that would make someone a good thrower might handicap them in a running race.

Enter Diane Jones Konihowski, whose superb all around athletic skills took her to the top of the Canadian and world stage in the pentathlon during the 1970s. First named to the national team as a high jumper and javelin thrower while only in Grade 10, the shining moment of her career was a record-shattering gold medal performance at the 1978 Commonwealth Games in Edmonton. Along the way, her other honours also included two Pan American Games gold medals.

Born in Vancouver and raised in Saskatoon, Jones Konihowski showed her wide range of athletic skills early. In 1967 she competed at the first ever Canada Games, playing on Saskatchewan's volleyball team. Two years later, she won gold in the pentathlon at the 1969 Canada Games.

Her skills developed steadily, and earned her a berth on the Olympic team in 1972 as the second ranked pentathlete in Canada. With personal bests in all five sections of the event, she placed 10th in Munich that year, and continued to climb the world ranks. She won gold at the 1975 Pan American Games, setting the stage for what many hoped would be a medal performance in front of a Canadian crowd at the 1976 Olympics in Montreal.

As with a number of other prominent Canadian athletes, she would be disappointed. Hosting the Olympics seemed to be more of a jinx than a help for several Canadian medal contenders, as Canada earned the dubious distinction of being the first host country to be shut out of gold medals. In fourth place with only the 200m left to run, which was probably her weakest event, Jones Konihowski had to settle for a sixth place finish overall.

Two years later, the world's eyes turned to Edmonton for the Commonwealth Games, and Jones Konihowski's name was again featured in discussions about possible medals. As one of Canada's top hopes, she was given the honour of being the final runner to carry in a baton bearing a message from Queen Elizabeth II during the Opening Ceremonies. She also escorted Prime Minister Pierre Trudeau on a tour of the athletes' village. In short, there were high expectations.

Just as Montreal seemed to have been a jinx a few years earlier, so Edmonton seemed to be a place where various athletes turned those disappointments into medals. Among them were swimmer Graham Smith and high jumper Debbie Brill, who, like Jones Konihowski, had disappointing results in 1976.

Leading up to the Commonwealth Games, Jones Konihowski had shed 20 pounds in an effort to improve her performance in the 800m (which had replaced the 200m since 1976), the long jump and the high jump. It was a calculated risk, because the change in focus also meant that her throwing ability would be diminished.

More than 30,000 fans crowded Commonwealth Stadium the day of the pentathlon competition. Jones Konihowski started the day well with a 13.85 second performance in the 100m hurdles and followed up with a 14.85m shot put, well below her personal best due to her lighter frame. Her weight loss strategy worked, though, because in the next section, the high jump, she cleared 1.88m, nearly 10 cm above her normal level. Her final jump set a Commonwealth record, and would have earned her a bronze medal in the open high jump event. She finished off with a 6.41m long jump and a personal best 2:12.1 in the 800m. Her final point total was 4768, more than 500 points better than her nearest competitor and shattering the previous Commonwealth record. More than 20 years later, that leap was still among the top 10 jumps ever recorded by Canadians.

But for a twist of fate, the defining moment of her career could have come two years later, on the Olympic stage rather than at the Commonwealth Games. Politics intervened, and Jones Konihowski, along with a number of other talented athletes of her generation, were left wondering "What if?" when Western nations boycotted the 1980 Olympics in Moscow. Ranked second in the world that year, she would certainly have been considered a medal contender. As it was, just two weeks after the Moscow Olympics she defeated a field of the world's top pentathletes (including all the Olympic medallists) at a meet in Detmold, West Germany.

She didn't agree with the boycott, and wasn't shy about sharing her opinion. She even considered defying the boycott and going to Moscow anyway, but backed down in the face of overwhelming criticism that even included death threats. Speaking to Terry Jones of the Edmonton Sun in 2000, she said she regretted not going through with her decision to compete. "I'll never know," she said. "Nothing can change that. But Moscow is so long ago. I had a great career." ❧

Marcel Jobin – "The Fool in Pyjamas"

National Archives/CSI

"In those days, when I went out training in my red track suit, people would harass me, children would throw rocks, and dogs snapped at my heels. It was Quebec during the 1960s, and I was the 'fool in pyjamas,'" remembers race walker Marcel Jobin sadly.

When he trained on the streets of St. Boniface, curious onlookers couldn't fathom what good could be accomplished by a man in a red track suit walking in such a funny way for kilometres on end, and so they jeered him with that unflattering epithet.

But this extraordinary athlete continued to walk. During his 17-year career, he was indisputably the best race walker in Canada, and during his best years challenged the top walkers in the world. Hailing from Quebec's Abitibi region, he won the Canadian championship in the 20 km walk 15 times, including 13 in a row.

His best performance over 20 km came in 1984, when he finished first in the Canadian Olympic team selection trials with a time of 1:24:08. It was a Canadian record that stood until 1991.

During his walking career, Jobin set nearly 100 Canadian records at various distances from 3 km up to 50 km. His international appearances featured two Olympic Games (including competing before partisan crowds at the Montreal Olympics in 1976), four Pan American Games and two Commonwealth Games.

After the 1984 Olympics in Los Angeles, he retired from competition without having won an Olympic medal, but the "fool in pyjamas" had succeeded in making the whole country more familiar with race walking. He also, by his own admission, succeeded in rising above the countless insults which had been inflicted on him in his home town because of his chosen sport.

In his book published at the height of this competitive career in 1980, he wrote, "How would you expect me at this point to be spontaneously friendly and smiling when, for more than 15 years, I have been subjected to daily insults? Imagine what an endurance runner who is at the limits of exhaustion might feel in the 18th or 19th kilometre of his training run if he suddenly gets treated like an idiot by four or five little urchins by the side of the road, or worse, by several contemptuous-looking old men."

After his retirement from competition, Jobin stopped race walking, but ran regularly for enjoyment. Even as he approached his 60s, he remained an athlete in his heart. ❧

1979

Canada's women's basketball team won a bronze medal at the World Championships. Sylvia Sweeney of Montreal was named the Most Valuable Player in the tournament.

HOCKEY 1984

The End of Flower Power in Montreal

by Hal Quinn
December 10, 1984

His tearful announcement shocked and saddened the hockey establishment and legions of fans. At age 33, Guy (The Flower) Lafleur retired last week, signaling the end of one of the game's most brilliant careers and marking the passing of another era in one of the most successful franchises in professional sports history. Few athletes in any sport could raise spectators out of their seats the way Lafleur did for 14 National Hockey League seasons. In the storied tradition of *les Habitants*, Lafleur was the French-Canadian superstar, inheriting the mantle from the legends who preceded him — Jean Béliveau, Maurice (Rocket) Richard and Howie Morenz. Fans from Montreal to Los Angeles chanted "Guy, Guy, Guy" each time he started on one of his thrilling rink-long rushes. Then the cheering stopped. This season Lafleur lost the masterful scoring touch. Suddenly, he was no longer the star, no longer the leader.

The Canadiens have won 22 Stanley Cups, and Lafleur's name is engraved four times on the NHL's championship trophy. But the Habs have not won the championship since 1979, and although Lafleur led the team in goals last season with 30 he was scoreless in his last 15 regular season and 12 playoff games. This year Lafleur had only two goals and three assists in 19 games. "Maybe I'm not as motivated as in my big years," *le demon blond* said last week. Those "big years" in the 1970s earned Lafleur a special place in the hearts of hockey fans and assured his place in hockey's Hall of Fame.

The native of Thurso, Que., was the dominant and most exciting player in the league over the past decade. After a brilliant junior career with the Quebec Remparts, Lafleur joined the Canadiens in 1971 and, in his first three seasons, scored 29, 28 and 21 goals. Then, in 1975 he blossomed and scored 53 times. For the next five seasons he scored 50 or more goals, won three scoring titles, the Hart trophy twice as the NHL's most outstanding player, the Conn Smythe trophy once as the most outstanding player in the playoffs, and he was an All-Star right winger six times. In 961 regular season games, Lafleur scored 518 goals and added 728 assists, making him ninth on the NHL all-time goal-scoring list and eighth on the total points list. ♦

Steve Bauer Puts Canadian Cyclists on the World Map

The fortunes of Canadian competitive cycling spent many years in obscurity before starting to climb out of the quagmire in the early 1970s. Led by riders like Jocelyn Lovell, Hugh Walton, Sylvia Burka and Karen Strong, the sport began a resurgence. These athletes acquitted themselves well in international competition, but more importantly they paved the way for the next generation of riders to reach the upper echelons.

Among the many bike racers they inspired was Steve Bauer of Fenwick, Ontario. Originally a hockey player, he eventually ascended both to the Olympic medal podium and came closer than most to one of the most coveted prizes in cycling — winning the prestigious Tour de France.

Developing his skills and reputation on the North American circuit, Bauer was considered a favourite in the 190-km 1984 Olympic road race in Los Angeles. As the race evolved, he found himself in the lead group with three Americans and two Norwegians. Unlike the others, Bauer had no teammates to support him, which meant the Canadian had no choice but to chase down any of the other riders who chose to break away.

With 20 km left, American Alexi Grewal decided to break. By the time the riders entered the final 15.8 km lap he had built up a 20-second lead. Then Bauer decided to make his move, and bridged the gap. The two spelled each other off at the front for the remainder of the lap to help conserve energy for the final sprint, when all bets would be off. Bauer seemed fresher than Grewal, and set the pace more so than the tired American. Rather than try to leave the American behind, though, he was confident that he would be able to outsprint him at the end. That decision would come back to haunt him, as Grewal narrowly beat him in the final sprint, winning by less than half a metre. Afterwards Bauer speculated that he had chosen too high a gear for the uphill sprint, leaving him the consolation prize of a silver medal.

Steve Bauer racing to the finish and getting an Olympic silver medal (far left) at the 1984 Olympic Games in LA.

Turning professional immediately after the Olympics, Bauer earned a spot on the French La Vie Claire Team. Despite his credentials, as a rookie his job was to ride in support of, and if necessary sacrifice himself for, the team's two stars — Bernard Hinault and Greg Lemond.

Not only did he perform his role well, he also surprised seasoned observers with his more than respectable results. For more than half of the Tour's three weeks of grueling daily grind, he wore the white jersey that symbolized the leading rookie. He eventually finished 10th, a remarkable achievement for a North American, let alone one new to European racing.

Bauer raced the Tour 11 more times, his high point coming in 1988. Winning the first stage, he was awarded the famed yellow jersey that signifies the Tour's overall leader. He was only the second Canadian ever to wear the yellow jersey. By this time Bauer was recognized as a star in his own right, and had riders to support him. He held the yellow jersey for five days, settling for 4th place by the end of the Tour. He again led the Tour in 1990, this time for 10 days.

Just before his retirement in 1996, he returned to the Olympics, which allowed professional riders to enter for the first time. He couldn't repeat his feat of 12 years earlier, though, finishing 41st. Later that year, he retired, ending a 20-year competitive career. ♣

Canada

1986

Alex Stieda Leads the Tour de France

The Tour de France is the ultimate bicycle race. Some call it the toughest sporting event in the world — some three weeks of racing an average of 160 km every day at speeds between 40 and 70 kilometres an hour. Just to be entered in the event was an honour for Alex Stieda, who in 1986 was the lone Canadian rider on the US-based 7-Eleven team, the first North American team to enter the Tour.

Rookies are not expected to excel in an event in which 30 percent of riders don't even finish. Still it was a dream come true for Stieda to be competing, and when he found himself in 20th place out of 200 riders after the initial stage, the dream got even better. The next day, he was able to break away during the 80-km stage and found himself not just winning that stage, but jumping into the overall lead of the Tour after the race. Along with that went the privilege of wearing the coveted yellow jersey — known throughout the cycling world as identifying the Tour's leader. Along with it also came media attention such as the young rider had never experienced.

Not unexpectedly, his hold on the yellow jersey was short-lived, but a veteran Dutch rider told Stieda to cherish the memory — he had accomplished what most cyclists only dream of. He also encouraged the Canadian to finish the Tour to prove that he was worthy of having worn the yellow jersey, if only for a day. Stieda did just that — finishing 120th out of the 132 that finished. ❧

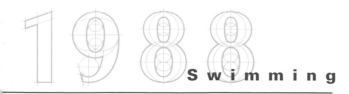

Sports Psychology, Victor Davis Style

Victor Davis "pushed and pulled" Canada to an Olympic silver medal in the 4 x 100m medley relay at the 1988 Olympic Games in Seoul.

CSI/COA

Team dynamics. What makes a team click? What is at work when a group of underdogs exceeds all expectations and comes up big? Just ask Mark Tewksbury.

The 100m-backstroke specialist was selected to represent Canada at the 1988 Olympics in Seoul, his first Olympic Games. He was 20 years old.

"I arrived, full of confidence, in an Olympic village with thousands of people who all have way more attitude than me," Tewksbury relates. "At 6' 2", I was shorter than many of the women. My confidence took a hit."

Then, on the day of his event, he looked around the pool and saw all the greats of swimming, including Olympic champions and world record holders, gathered together under one roof. By the time he stood in the ready room, Tewksbury was psyched out. He came fifth, and was happy with his placing, but his time was well behind the leaders. The question was, did he, or would he ever, belong on the podium?

The very next day, first thing in the morning, he was poolside again. He'd been selected to race the 4 x 100m medley relay, along with Sandy Goss, Tom Ponting and the late, great, and infamous competitor, Victor Davis. They had never worked as a team before, and they had to race that same night!

"I think it's safe to say there were also personality conflicts at work," says Tewksbury. "We weren't necessarily the best of friends, and we were all very different people. But we had this big challenge ahead, and we had to get along."

Like Tewksbury, Goss and Ponting had not reached the podium in the individual events. Goss and Ponting (along with Davis and Mike West) were members of Canada's silver medal 4 x 100m medley relay team in 1984, but their best result so far in Seoul was Ponting's fourth place in the 200m butterfly. Davis, on the other hand, was one of the great individual swimmers. He held the world record and was the 1984 Olympic champion in the 200m breaststroke. In Seoul, he had come fourth in the 100m breaststroke, but was only 3/10ths of a second away from the gold medal.

"On paper, the four swimmers who arrived at the pool that morning ranked about fourth or fifth in the relay," Tewksbury says. "Sandy, Tom and I all thought, 'Cool! Fifth!' Victor, however, had a different idea."

Davis had decided that the team could get in the medals. He was used to being on the podium and would not settle for anything less. The unofficial leader set to work on his teammates.

"Perhaps because he had already won medals, he could clearly see himself winning a medal. He kept saying, over and over, 'I think we can win a medal tonight. I think we can win a medal tonight.'"

"He was such a strong person, so focused, so intent, that you couldn't help but get caught up in his belief. He held his vision out for the rest of the team. By the end of the day, the three of us all shared Victor's vision. When we arrived at the pool that night, we went in believing we could get a medal."

Davis held them together throughout the event. When Tewksbury started to waver in the ready room, rubbing shoulders with a relay-size grouping of great swimmers, Davis would literally grab his head and pull him back into their group.

"When I looked away again, Victor grabbed my ear, stared me down, and said, 'You can look at those other guys all you want, but you have to swim the backstroke leg of this relay, and if you don't swim well, I will kill you.'"

By his own admission, that got Tewksbury focused.

Up first, Tewksbury did swim well, posting a faster time than he had in his own event. But he was still far behind the leading Americans and Russians.

Davis swam the next leg, the breaststroke. Ahead of Davis, in the next lane, the Russian breaststroke specialist took off fast. Davis hit the water after him, and kept behind him, establishing a strong, steady pace.

"After the turn, the Russian began to fade. Victor kept doing the same thing, which was this strong, steady pace. And he almost caught him — at the time, it was the fastest split ever recorded in a relay. Suddenly, we found ourselves fighting for silver."

Ponting did the butterfly, and kept the team in the running, staying right beside the Russian. Goss was up last, against a famous Russian who had never been beaten in 12 years of competition.

"Victor was on the deck by now, and he started screaming, 'Sandy, you can do it. You can do it.' I quickly joined in — but I'm thinking, 'Poor Sandy, this situation is brutal.'"

The Russian dove in, and Goss went after him a tenth of a second later. Goss stayed with the Russian throughout the first leg, and through the turn, until almost 75 metres of the 100 were over. Throughout it, Davis kept screaming like a maniac, along with Tewksbury.

"I don't know how Sandy did this, but he began to pick up his pace. He got even with the Russian, and in the last 10 metres, he surged past him. We won the silver."

"I saw that day that Victor was the real thing," says Tewksbury. "Through his belief in us, he raised the team to his level. He was an incredible leader." ❧

Figure Skating

Indelible Memories

1988 Olympic Silver Medallist
Brian Orser recalls the glory

by Brian Orser
December 2, 1991

The passers-by at Toronto's city hall square were treated to an unexpected performance. A photographer was using the rink in the area as a backdrop for a picture of Olympic double silver medallist and former world-champion figure skater Brian Orser. When the photo session ended, Orser put on his skates and took a turn on the ice — casually spinning and somersaulting with the compact elegance that carried him to eight Canadian men's titles between 1981 and 1988, in addition to his international honours. Orser is now skating professionally, and in an exclusive account for Maclean's, he recalled his own impressions of the tension- and hope-filled months that precede an appearance on the Olympic stage.

It seems incredible that four years have gone by since the Olympic Winter Games in Calgary, and that in less than three short months, our national teams will be battling for Olympic gold in Albertville, France. Just the thought of the tough competition that our athletes will soon face stirs my own deeply competitive instincts, sending a rush of adrenaline surging through my body. Looking ahead to the Games also brings back a flood of vivid memories from Calgary. I will never forget how my heart pounded when the huge crowd of 60,000 people in McMahon Stadium jumped to their feet and cheered wildly as I carried the Canadian flag into the opening ceremonies.

Nor can I erase the memory of how that warm reception quickly gave way to the mounting pressure to vanquish my archrival, Brian Boitano of the United States, and win the gold medal for all of Canada. In my mind's eye, I can still clearly see the tiny mistake in the triple jump that cost me the gold, but on the final day of the Games, my feeling of disappointment gave way to a sense of melancholy as the Olympic flame flickered and went out — a tumultuous week in my life was over.

It was not supposed to end the way it did. I was the world champion and had won the silver medal at the 1984 Olympic Games in Sarajevo, Yugoslavia. The whole country was eagerly anticipating a gold-medal performance in Calgary. When my name was finally called and I skated out onto the ice, the Olympic Saddledome seemed to be crackling with energy. Suddenly, there I was — Brian Orser, from small-town Ontario, completely alone in the middle of the rink in front of 20,000 people. I was saying to myself over and over, "This is it, this is the Olympics."

Then, the first strains of *The Bolt*, Russian composer Dmitri Shostakovich's epic composition celebrating the Russian Revolution, started, and for the next 4 1/2 minutes I was lost in a world of my own. I poured every ounce of concentration and energy I could muster into my routine, and when I landed my final triple jump, the Saddledome was vibrating with thunderous

CSI/COA

applause. Like the partisan throng, I felt that I had skated one of the best routines in my life and that the gold medal was mine. All that remained was for me to climb the podium and accept it. For the next couple of minutes, with the medal all but in my grasp, I was filled with a feeling of overwhelming joy. I finally knew what it felt like to win the gold.

Then came the crushing, gut-twisting letdown. I knew that Boitano had also skated exceptionally well, and then I got the signal that still burns in my memory today. The head official slowly raised two fingers in the air. It seemed impossible, but suddenly I was second, and my illusion of Olympic gold vanished into the cold Calgary night. With the whole country, if not the entire sporting world, watching me on television, I had to come back down to earth without showing my deep disappointment.

As I look back, I am still amazed that I could have soared so high and fallen so low in just a flicker of time. But as the months went by, I took solace in the fact that just to compete in the Olympic Games is a rare and wonderful experience. After all, only a handful of the world's top athletes ever get an opportunity to compete in the Games. And only a very few of them leave the Games with a medal.

And even though I was the reigning world champion at the time, I never thought for one second that winning the Olympic gold was going to be easy. In fact, my preparations for the Olympics actually began when I met with my coach and manager, Doug Leigh, in June, 1987, a full nine months before our Canadian team's entrance into McMahon Stadium. In our meeting, we discussed the upcoming Games and set a daunting goal: to win nothing less than the gold medal in Calgary.

Almost immediately, we set monthly, weekly and daily training goals, but to take the gold in Calgary, we knew that I would have to peak at the highest level of physical and mental training, almost on the very eve of the competition. To peak precisely at that point, however, required complete harmony among coach Leigh, my choreographer, Uschi Keszler, and myself.

CSI/COA

That is not easy to accomplish in an Olympic year. Demands from the media and the prestige of the Games not only increase the pressure on the athletes, but also create hundreds of distractions. The television networks, newspapers and magazines all wanted time for interviews, and I felt that as national and world champion, I had to accommodate everyone. But finally, Leigh intervened and literally locked the door of the Orillia, Ont., arena, where we were training, behind us.

But winning takes more than harmony and positive thinking. It also requires brute determination. And during the early summer of 1987, I stuck doggedly to the set plan. I started each day at 5 a.m. with a high-energy breakfast of organic food, including granola, oats, raisins, nuts, freshly squeezed orange juice and coffee. Then, I left for the Orillia arena for six hours of intense, uninterrupted training. In 1988, figure skating still contained a compulsory figures requirement, and I would spend the first two or three hours working on my highly demanding figures routine, tracing intricate patterns into the ice with my skates.

After three hours of work, I would eat another high-energy meal. That one usually consisted of what we called "power balls," home-made from protein powder, oats, almonds, peanut butter, nuts and brewer's yeast. Following that, I practised my actual Olympic routine for about three hours. I had my own apartment in Orillia, and when I arrived home, I would usually prepare a hearty meal of chicken or fish, along with fresh organically grown vegetables. But despite the heavy workload, my training was not over. In the evening, I would either head to the Orillia YMCA or back to the rink for an hour of weight training and running. Finally, at about 9 p.m. I would wind down by watching a movie video — and prepare to do it all over the next day. ♣

Brian Orser won Olympic silver medals in 1984 and 1988. He was the World Champion in 1987 and runner-up in 1983, 1984, 1985, 1986 and 1988.

Elizabeth Manley – Surprises, Smiles and Silver

In the lead-up to the 1988 Winter Olympics in Calgary, all eyes were focused on the "Battle of the Carmens." The contest in women's singles figure skating, according to the pundits, was between 1987 world champion Katarina Witt of East Germany and 1986 world champion Debi Thomas of the United States, who were both doing routines to the music of Carmen. As for Canadian skater Elizabeth Manley — well, she was more or less written off by the press as an inconsistent skater who would never manage to pull off a medal performance. Even her hometown press in Ottawa gave her scant attention.

But Manley was about to give the chattering classes a lesson in respect.

Given the general attitude, and the fact that she came down with a fierce flu just before the Games, it's a wonder that Manley even got on a plane. But board it she did, fighting a debilitating cold, strep throat, a fever and ear infections. Compounding her state of misery, the flight from Ottawa to Calgary was a milk run: leaving Ottawa, Manley stopped in Toronto, Thunder Bay, and Saskatoon, before finally arriving in Calgary on the verge of collapse.

By sticking to doctor's orders, her health improved a little each day. Still, her flu made a run-through of her program impossible. And so it is an equal wonder that Manley even showed up for figures in the Saddledome. To her delight and surprise, she pulled off fourth place in the first segment of the three-part competition, when she had been expecting to barely make the top ten.

Next up was the short program. Although on the mend, Manley still was not well enough to do a complete run-through at practice, and had to settle for a mental run-through. She was nervous, but she was determined to do the best she could under the circumstances. It turned out that that meant skating her best-ever short program. From the moment she stepped out on the ice, her nervousness completely disappeared and Manley was in control, landing all her requirement elements cleanly and with the grace of a champion. The crowd, mostly Canadian with a large American contingent, roared its approval.

CSI/COA

Manley moved up to third place, and now looked like a serious medal contender, depending on how the long program went. While she was delighted with her performance, she knew better than to get over-excited. The long program loomed ahead, and she took the day's rest between the two events to steady herself and mentally prepare for it.

She drew an excellent position for the long program, skating third after Katarina Witt. Witt's position had a disadvantage — the judges generally withhold top marks in case a later competitor gives a better skate. For Manley, skating after the German skater meant she would not have to mentally deal with the standing ovations from the many American fans for their skaters, which had rattled her nerves in the past. Debi Thomas, the top American skater, drew last position.

On the day of the long program, as was her habit, Manley did her laundry. She was in the common room at the Olympic Village, folding her clothes, watching the early skaters do their programs. The members of the Canadian bobsleigh team (one of whom Manley was dating at the time), who happened to be there, looked at Manley curiously. "Shouldn't you be there?" one of them finally asked. When she explained it was hours before she'd be competing, they gave her a sweatshirt, and told her to "have the strength of a four-man bob."

Perhaps it was the encouragement of the bobsledders. Perhaps all the attention and pressure showered on the two "Carmens" meant less stress for Manley. Whatever the reason, Elizabeth Manley was "on" that night in the Saddledome as she had never been before. She skated the performance of her life, reaching the pinnacle of her abilities at exactly the right moment.

CSI/COA

The excitement began when Manley landed a huge triple Lutz near the start of her program, sending shivers through the Saddledome crowd. That jump also delivered a message to the pundits that the contest, as all competitive events are, was still wide open. Drawing confidence from that first triple Lutz, Manley never once faltered, but grew in strength and confidence throughout the program. In all, Manley whipped off five triple jumps. She defeated the best in the world to win the long program outright and grab the silver medal overall. Witt won the gold, and Thomas had to settle for bronze.

For Canadians, the moment that will always be remembered is the sight of Manley, breathless after finishing her routine, leaping into the air, both weeping and laughing with unrestrained joy. As the crowd jumped to its feet with a roar, someone threw a cowboy hat on the ice. Manley quickly donned it, and leapt into the air again.

She hadn't even seen her marks. Nor had the crowd. She didn't know the colour of her medal. The celebration was about excellence, not winning. But still, it didn't hurt that the press conference room was jammed that night by media wanting to ask about her silver medal. ♣

1987

Track and Field

Life in the Fast Lane

by Tanya Christie
September 12, 1988

In less time than it takes to lace a pair of track shoes, his life changed forever. In 9.83 seconds, on the afternoon of Aug. 30, 1987, Benjamin Sinclair Johnson Jr., 26, ceased to be, in his own description, "just Ben." From the moment that the Canadian broke the tape at the World Track and Field Championships in Rome — completing the 100-m dash one-tenth of a second faster than any man had run the distance before — Ben Johnson was no longer just another athlete. He was not even simply Canada's best hope for a gold medal at the Seoul Summer Olympics. Ben Johnson was the world's fastest human.

On the track, he was the master of the clock. Away from it, time was no longer his own. An intensely private life was suddenly very public. As Johnson prepared for the Games, he reflected wryly on the past year. "I didn't know what it was going to be like," he said. "Now I'm successful and I'm paying for it."

Johnson has paid for that success in hours of photo sessions, days of handshakes and forced smiles, and months of disturbing newspaper headlines. With wealth and fame have come public scrutiny of his every move and motive. Indeed, the run in Rome itself became embroiled in controversy when the man who came second, American Carl Lewis, hinted that Johnson's speed was improved by drugs. Post-race tests disproved the allegation, but other problems were more difficult to dismiss. For months, an injured hamstring in his left thigh kept Johnson out of competition, but he was seldom out of the headlines.

And he is keenly aware that however fast he ran in Rome, and however quickly he runs in Seoul, someone will some day break his record. Olympic gold, on the other hand, endures. "The gold medal is something people remember," Johnson said. "It is something no one can ever take away from you." His days of being "just Ben" may be over, and his status as the world's fastest man may be fleeing, but in less than 10 seconds in Seoul, Johnson hopes to secure a place in sports history that neither Carl Lewis nor the clock can ever eclipse. ❧

CSI/COA

For a brief period in 1988, Ben Johnson was the undisputed fastest man in the world, and on September 24th he let rival Carl Lewis know it in Seoul. Days later, though, his world would crumble.

1988

The King of Seoul

October 3, 1998

In the brilliant sunshine of a warm Saturday afternoon in Seoul, Ben Johnson did what no man has ever done before, and few, beyond Johnson, thought humanly possibly. In a few unforgettable seconds, Johnson redefined man's ability to propel himself by the sheer power of body and will. Last week, on sport's grandest stage, the Summer Olympics, in sport's most elemental event, the 100-m sprint, the 26-year old Canadian toyed with the seven fastest men the rest of the human race had to offer and became the king of Seoul. The contest won, the gold medal secure, Johnson glanced over his left shoulder at his closest rival, American Carl Lewis, raised his right arm in a victory salute and glided over the finish line. Looking up from Lane 3, Lewis saw the clock and, like

Ben Johnson receiving his 1988 Olympic gold medal, which he would keep for just three days.

the 70,000 spectators in Olympic Stadium, he stared in disbelief. The clock read 9.79 seconds. The man who in Rome in August, 1987, became the first man ever to run 100m in 9.83 seconds, had suddenly broken the 9.8-second barrier. Just as quickly, Ben Johnson had entered another realm.

The voyage to the gold medal — and a new, world record — in the dash began amidst the hype of a worldwide television audience and the anticipation of athletes and spectators at the stadium. As the eight fastest men in the world limbered up, along the runway of the stadium's east side, Hristo Markov of Bulgaria and Igor Lapchine of the Soviet Union were competing for the triple-jump gold. At two pits at the south end, male high jumpers, hoping to qualify for the following day's finals, stretched between loping challenges to the bar. Finally, a hush descended over the crowd as the public address announcer requested "quiet at the start, please" of the men's 100-m final. As Lewis settled into the block in Lane 3 and Johnson spread his massive arms to the width of Lane 6 to take his signature position, the calm was but faint forewarning of the fury to follow.

When the starting gun sounded, Johnson — in brilliant red shorts and singlet top — erupted from the block. In Rome, his start was timed at 0.129 second off the block. In Seoul, it was 0.123 second. In the next few moments — the stadium infield quiet, the circling pigeons ignored — the audience, like a north-south wave, rose to its feet involuntarily, perhaps hoping to see more, yet knowing it would not understand.

Johnson reached the 50-m mark in 5.52 seconds, 0.13 second ahead of his longtime rival Lewis. The observers in the stadium knew that Lewis, even when he lost to Johnson in Rome, was the faster man over the final 50m of the dash. But not last Saturday. Johnson turned on what his coach, Charles Francis, calls the "second acceleration". As the metres blurred by, Johnson at 60m was 0.16 second ahead of Lewis. At the 80-m mark he was 0.17 second in front. From the gun, the race was never in doubt — just as Johnson had predicted weeks earlier when he said, "When the gun go, the race be over." As the roar from the stadium swelled with each step, Johnson — like a true Olympian — raised his right arm triumphantly. ◆

1988
Track and Field

The Steroid Scandal:

Was He Drugged? After the Games, Ben Johnson's Fight to Prove He Was 'Clean'

Bob Levin with Chris Wood and Hal Quinn in Seoul, John Bierman, Nora Underwood and Ann Finlayson in Toronto, Theresa Tedesco and Marc Clark in Ottawa, Martin Stuart-Huarle in Falmouth, and correspondents' reports

October 10, 1988

In the darkest hour of his life, Ben Johnson lay motionless on his hotel bed, clad in a white T-shirt and covered only by a sheet. He listened in stunned silence as Carol Anne Letheren, *chef de mission* of Canada's delegation to the Seoul Summer Games, repeated what he already knew: that a second test had confirmed the presence in his urine of traces of stanozolol, a banned anabolic steroid. It was 3:30 a.m., Sept. 27, and in the chill Asian dawn, Letheren had come to take back the Olympic gold medal that Johnson had captured just 62 hours earlier and that now lay on his bedside table, still attached to its red, white and blue ribbon. "Ben," she said, "we love you, but you're guilty."

He was a rocket, a role model, a national hero. He was the world's fastest human and, to Canadians, he was never Johnson, just Ben. In the glare of the Olympic spotlight, he had vanquished his American archrival Carl Lewis in a 100-m explosion of nearly superhuman speed, smashing his own world record in the process. But when the steroid scandal burst upon the world last week, Canadians, who had risen as one to applaud Johnson's triumph, doubled over in sickened disbelief, taking Johnson's humiliation as their own. Children wept openly. Many people clutched at faint hopes of some innocent explanation. Others branded Ben as a betrayer, a cheat. But as the week wore on, and as increasing attention turned to the role of the runner's entourage, more and more Canadians contended that Johnson was not a villain but a victim. "Part of the tragedy may be that Ben was not acting alone," said Roger Jackson, president of the Canadian Olympic Association. "If he was not, it would be unfair if the people around him do not pay the price, too."

Johnson's dramatic downfall — after winning *the* glamour event of the glittering Games — set off the worst scandal in Olympic history. It captured headlines around the globe and cast the world's eye into the shady corner of drugs in sport — and particularly on steroids, synthetic versions of the male hormone testosterone that are widely believed to boost strength and endurance. Nine other Olympians from six other nations also tested positive for banned substances. Still others dropped out of the competition. Nearly lost in the clamour were fine performances last week among those who *did* compete in the XXIV Olympiad. Among the Canadians,

"Ben, we love you, but you're guilty."

CSI/COA

synchronized swimmer Carolyn Waldo grabbed two gold medals — one in a solo performance and a second in a dual performance with Michelle Cameron — and decathlete Dave Steen surprisingly took a bronze; sailors Frank McLaughlin and John Millen also scored a bronze; and, on Sunday in Seoul, boxer Lennox Lewis won a gold medal.

But it was the story of the 26-year-old Johnson that continued to captivate the Canadian public — a story that was at once a mystery, a cautionary tale and, above all, a personal tragedy. The cast of characters includes Johnson's personal doctor, Mario Astaphan; his Virginia-based manager, Larry Heidebrecht; and his coach, Charlie Francis — an inner circle of handlers who came under widespread suspicion but vehemently proclaimed their innocence. "I can tell you unequivocally," Astaphan told *Maclean's*, "that the [steroid in Johnson's system] didn't come from me, from Charlie or any one of the entourage." In fact, Heidebrecht alleged darkly that some outsider may have spiked Johnson's water bottle. "This was something that happened in the warm-up area or in the testing area itself," he insisted. Johnson himself, in a letter published at week's end in the *Toronto Sun*, stated that "I have never knowingly taken illegal drugs nor have had illegal drugs administered to me."

Olympic laboratory officials, however, said that the steroid was plainly present and they dismissed claims of race-time sabotage. They maintained that the runner's urine profile indicated long-term steroid usage and that he had apparently stopped taking the drug several days or weeks before the Games. Robert Dugal, a Montreal scientist and a member of the International Olympic Committee's medical commission, said that unless Johnson was tricked, he was "careless, ill-advised or someone miscalculated."

The price of that error was punishingly clear. Not only did the 100-m gold go to American Carl Lewis, but the International Amateur Athletics Federation banned Johnson from its sanctioned competitions for two years. In Ottawa, Federal Sport Minister Jean Charest banned Johnson for life from Canada's national team and from Sport Canada funding — about $650 a month. But two days later, under an avalanche of opposition criticism in the Commons that Johnson had not been given a fair hearing, Charest softened, announcing a government inquiry into the affair and expressing the wistful hope that the gold medal might one day be returned. Still, Johnson's commercial contracts for everything from shoes to milk began to dry up, and the golden promise of millions more in endorsement dollars disappeared overnight — leaving the Jamaican immigrant with an uncertain future at best. Said his Canadian agent, Glen Calkins: "God is going to have to come out of the heavens to fix this one." 🍁

Ben and Charlie.

1989

Track and Field

The Steroid Scandal:

Testimony About Ben Johnson's Use of Banned Drugs Stunned the Sports World

by Ric Dolphin with Dianne Rinehart in Moscow, Peter Lewis in Brussels, William Lowther in Washington, Leigh Ogston in Montreal, John Howse in Calgary and Hal Quinn in Vancouver

March 13, 1989

The central figure in the drama that unfolded in a Toronto hearing room last week was a man who was not even present — Ben Johnson, the Canadian track star who was disqualified at last September's Olympic Games after traces of banned anabolic steroids were found in his urine. Testifying for three days before a federally appointed inquiry, track-and-field coach Charlie Francis said that he first encouraged Johnson to use steroids in 1981 and that, as far as he knew, Johnson had regularly used them up to the time of last summer's Olympics in Seoul, South Korea, As well, Francis said that 12 other leading Canadian runners who trained under him used the synthetic hormones. Then, he went on to paint a stunning picture of widespread — and steadily increasing — drug abuse by athletes around the world.

Francis claimed that in using steroids, the Canadian athletes were merely following the example of many top-ranking international track-and-field stars. He declared that as many as 80 per cent of the world's leading athletes may be using steroids to improve their athletic

Charlie Francis, Ben Johnson's coach.

Canadian Press CP

performance. "There are people who stand up there and claim, 'Oh, I did it clean, I just worked hard,'" declared Francis. "It just isn't true."

Francis's testimony before the inquiry under Mr. Justice Charles Dubin of the Ontario Supreme Court sent shock waves through the Canadian and international athletic communities and triggered intense debate about whether his estimate of the extent of steroid use among athletes was wildly exaggerated — or chillingly accurate. At the same time, his statement before the commission contradicted Johnson's own insistence after the Olympics that he never "knowingly" used steroids. Johnson, who refused to comment on Francis's statements last week, is expected to testify later this month. At the same time, Francis's meticulously detailed account of how and why his athletes turned to steroids aroused serious concerns about the role that the Canadian Track and Field Association (CTFA) and Sport Canada — the federal department that funds Canadian athletes — may have had in tacitly accepting the use of steroids.

The 12 hours of testimony by the 40-year-old Francis amounted to a far-ranging indictment of the Canadian and international sporting establishment. While his fiancée, Angela Coon, a 21-year-old university student and hurdler, watched, Francis told the inquiry that American and European athletic teams had been systematically using steroids since the 1964 Summer Olympics in Tokyo. He also claimed that a program of voluntary steroid testing set up by the US Olympic Committee in late 1983 was actually designed to help American athletes escape detection by drug tests at international competitions. As well, Francis said that the Soviets provide a similar checking system for their athletes.

Francis — without saying so specifically — appeared to accuse American track star Florence Griffith-Joyner of steroid use. He implied that "Flo-Jo" — who announced her retirement from sports three days before he took the stand — could not have set a world record in the 100-m women's event at Seoul without steroids. His allegation sparked a sharp denial in Los Angeles by Griffith-Joyner's agent, Gordon Baskin, who insisted that she "has never and will never use steroids."

Francis's accusations before a packed hearing room in a downtown Toronto office building also drew a strong response from the international athletic community. Some athletes and officials said that Francis had exposed a reality that had been concealed for too long. In Lausanne, Switzerland, Michele Verdier, an official with the International Olympic Committee, said that she was relieved that the conspiracy of silence had been broken. She added, "These revelations make it obvious we must tighten the screws ever harder against abuses." Said Sir Arthur Gold, chairman of the British Olympic Association, about Francis's revelations: "I may be shocked and saddened. But surprised? No. It tends to confirm what we all suspect."

In his testimony, Francis defended the decision to have Johnson use steroids. He said that in 1981, the sprinter was "on the threshold of breaking into international prominence." He added that "it's pretty clear that steroids are worth approximately a metre at the highest levels of sport." Johnson, said Francis, had to decide in effect whether to start one metre behind his competitors — "an unacceptable situation for a top-level athlete."

At one point, Francis displayed a graph of the women's 100-m world records between 1948 and 1988 and pointed to the world record of 10.49 seconds set last year by Griffith-Joyner — more than one-quarter of a second faster than the record 10.76 seconds in 1984. Without naming her, Francis questioned how, without

In the earlier days, Ben Johnson was still good enough to win an Olympic bronze medal in the 100m in LA, 1984.

the help of steroids, there could have been such dramatic improvement after decades of more gradual gains.

Francis's revelations raised the possibility that the process by which Canadian athletes are selected and subsidized during training may actually encourage steroid use. Under the carding system, only those Canadian athletes who attain international ranking in their sport can expect to be named to Canadian national teams and receive a monthly stipend (averaging about $650) from Sport Canada.

For his part, Andrzej Kulesza, the Montreal-based coach of the Canadian national weight-lifting team, said that the whole philosophy of sports in Canada must change. "It's a matter of approach," he said. "We are very ambitious people in Canada. We want to catch up to the rest of the world and we are taking shortcuts" — in the form of steroids. He added that Francis's estimate of steroid use in international athletics is probably exaggerated.

To others, last week's testimony underlined a basic flaw in the world of international sports that encourages adulation and financial rewards for a few stars, such as Ben Johnson, while obscuring the traditional motives of amateur sport. Said Ron Bowker, the Victoria, BC, coach of Canada's Olympic women's distance runners: "I abhor the thought that you have to play the game dirty to have a chance at a medal. What is coming out of this inquiry is a look at the values that we have all attached to sport — that winning is everything. We've got to rewrite the ethic of why we're in sport and what we want to achieve with it." ◆

1989

Track and Field

A day of reckoning:

Ben Johnson Admits That He Took Steroids

June 26, 1989

"Did you state publicly to the Canadian people,
'I'm innocent and I never took any banned substances?'"

"Yes, sir."

"Those statements were not true?"

"No, sir."

Toronto Star — E. Combs

The world had waited almost nine months for Ben Johnson's answers and, last week, he gave them under oath to a judge at a federal inquiry into drugs in sport. The sprinter's account differed markedly from his initial declarations last fall that he had not used banned anabolic steroids in capturing an Olympic gold medal in the 100-m dash at the Seoul Summer Games. The man who raised his arm in victory on Sept. 24 over his US rival Carl Lewis last week covered his eyes with his hand and admitted that he had cheated. Said Johnson in a halting voice, attempting to explain his deceit: "I lied, and I was ashamed for my family and friends and the kids who looked up to me and the Canadian athletes who want to be in my position."

Johnson dispelled any lingering illusions about his past familiarity with steroids during six hours on the witness stand at the federal judicial inquiry before Mr. Justice Charles Dubin of the Ontario Supreme Court. Appearing in turn confident and confused, eager and hesitant, the compact 27-year-old runner testified that he had — with the help of others, including his physician Jamie Astaphan — swallowed or injected five performance-enhancing banned substances during a seven-year period leading up to Seoul. ♣

The Dubin Inquiry

The Commission of Inquiry into the use of Drugs and Banned Practices Intended to Increase Athletic Performance, presided over by Justice Charles Dubin, was created in response to sprinter Ben Johnson's positive test for steroids at the 1988 Olympics in Seoul. From January 11, 1989 to October 3, 1989, the public hearings called 119 witnesses and accumulated more than 14,000 pages of testimony. More than 300 briefs and exhibits were received by the Commission. For the first time, hints and allegations about drug use in a variety of sports were confirmed, and in subsequent years countless changes were made to anti-doping efforts, including increased testing, more stringent sanctions and educational efforts.

In his final report, Justice Dubin attributed the use of banned substances to various factors, including an over-emphasis on winning, unrealistic expectations of athletes, changes in social mores, and the failure of sport organizations to take greater measures to prevent cheating. He wrote: "We cannot allow sport, which we expect to build character, to become a means of destroying it, encouraging hypocrisy and cynicism in athletes and other young people." Some of Commission's 70 specific recommendations included:

- The development of educational programs;
- Increased use of random, out-of-competition testing;
- Increased and standardized sanctions for those found guilty of using banned substances or practices;
- That Canadian sport organizations play a role in ensuring appropriate anti-doping standards both domestically and internationally;
- That sanctions should also apply to anyone found guilty of helping an athlete to use banned substances or practices;
- Establishment of consistent appeal and arbitration processes;
- Federal funding of sport that focuses on broad participation in sport — not just on elite sport. ♦

Canadian Press CP

The Honourable Charles L. Dubin.

1988
Hockey

The Great One Becomes a King

by Nora Underwood with Deborra Schug in Vancouver, Kerry Diotte and Erik Floren in Edmonton and Anne Gregor in Los Angeles

August 22, 1988

HHOF — Paul Bereswill

HHOF

HHOF

HHOF — Paul Bereswill

Tuesday, Aug. 9, 1988, is a day that few Canadian hockey fans will ever forget — the day the country lost its national hero, Wayne Gretzky, to the United States. Last week, in one of the biggest deals in sports history, Edmonton Oilers owner Peter Pocklington traded the 27-year-old centre and two other Oilers to the Los Angeles Kings and, in return, got two Kings players, three first-round draft choices over five years — and $18 million. The announcement touched off a wave of sadness and anger among Oilers fans, thousands of whom called the Oilers head office and radio phone-in shows to protest the move. So did many non-hockey fans, who see Gretzky as a modest and clean-living young man worthy of their respect. But at an emotional news conference in Edmonton that night, Gretzky said that the trade had been his decision. And he added, "For the benefit of Wayne Gretzky, my new wife and our expected child in the new year, it would be beneficial for everyone involved to let me play with the Los Angeles Kings."

But shortly after, three former Oilers stepped forward and told a different story — that Pocklington had forced Gretzky to leave Edmonton. Pocklington insisted that he had wanted Gretzky to continue playing for the Oilers. But late last week, the colourful entrepreneur lashed out at his former favourite son, saying that Gretzky had faked his tears at the Edmonton news conference. "Wayne has an ego the size of Manhattan," said Pocklington. "I understand that, though. If people had told me how great I was day in and day out for 10 years, I'm sure my ego would be a pretty generous size, too." And, although Gretzky maintained that the trade had been his idea, his new wife, US actress Janet Jones, placed the blame on Pocklington. She added, "Wayne wouldn't let Edmonton, fans, Canada and, most important, his teammates down without good reason. Pocklington is the reason Wayne is gone." Later, Pocklington issued a statement saying that his remarks about Gretzky's ego had been "totally out of context."

Former Oilers defenceman Paul Coffey also said that Gretzky was dismayed about leaving the team. Declared Coffey, who played for the Oilers from 1980 to 1987: "There's no bloody way he wanted to go [to Los Angeles]. He's a small-town guy." Coffey added that Gretzky was "just a piece of meat," sold by Pocklington at the height of his marketability.

The deal may, in fact, benefit everyone involved. Pocklington will receive Kings centre Jimmy Carson, left-winger Martin Gelinas, first-round draft picks in 1989, 1991 and 1993 and the $18 million. In addition, Gretzky is assured of a $1.8 million salary until 1992 and

possibly a share in any increase in the team's gate receipts, subject to negotiation. Along with Gretzky — who has set numerous scoring records over his nine-season National Hockey League career, has eight consecutive most-valuable-player awards and led the Oilers to Stanley Cup victory four times — the Kings get Oilers defenceman Marty McSorley and centre Mike Krushelnyski. After making the biggest deal in NHL history official, McNall said, "I've got to do something radical to sell hockey in LA, and there's no name in hockey like Wayne Gretzky."

If Gretzky had played out his contract with the Oilers — which was set to expire after the 1991-1992 season — he would have become a free agent. And the longer Pocklington had waited to sell Gretzky, the less money the Oilers would have received.

Indeed, Pocklington was clearly trying to save the Oilers from the fate that the New York Islanders suffered. Like the Oilers, that team also won four Stanley Cups, between 1980 and 1983, led to victory by Denis Potvin, Mike Bossy and Bryan Trottier. But now — with Potvin retired, Bossy injured and Trottier past his playing peak — the team has lost its primacy.

For the Kings, the trade is a good short-term gain, according to Quinn, and the club is taking the risk of cutting off its future to save the franchise now. "It's a star-oriented city," said Quinn. "Gretzky will have an effect on their team, and if he can make them winners, then it's going to be a tremendous move. I think they'll bring more people into their building — perhaps even sell it out — because of Gretzky."

On March 31, 1980, Peter Pocklington said of Gretzky: "There is no price on greatness. They'd have my head if I sold him." And what Pocklington's exact reasons were for ultimately taking that chance — and setting off one of the most controversial and emotional sports deals of the century — may never be known. Shortly after his verbal attack on his former star last week, Pocklington went on a fishing trip in the Arctic and did not plan to return for a week. But one thing is certain: at the Kings' first exhibition game in The Forum — scheduled for Sept. 28 — it will be standing room only. ◆

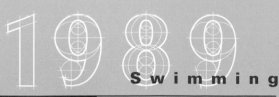

1989
S w i m m i n g

An untimely end:

Victor Davis's Controversial Life – and Death

by Barbara Wickens with Brenda O'Farrell in Montreal
November 27, 1989

Proud and unpredictable, Olympic medallist Victor Davis lived his life amid controversy. For some, Davis's accomplishments as a swimmer, including the gold medal he won for the 200-m breaststroke in a record 2:13.34 at the 1984 Los Angeles Olympics, were overshadowed by one temperamental act. At the 1982 British Commonwealth Games in Brisbane, Australia, while Queen Elizabeth II looked on, he kicked over a chair after Canada's medley relay team was disqualified on a technicality. Last week, Davis's death at the age of 25 was as controversial as his life. Davis died on Nov. 13 from massive brain injuries, 2 days after a car struck him outside a bar in a Montreal suburb at about 12:30 a.m. the previous Saturday. But following the accident, there were conflicting reports about what had happened — and controversy over police handling of the case.

In the early hours of Nov. 11, Davis and his girlfriend, Donna Clavel, 22, and another friend, Jennifer Watt, 21, left the bar and restaurant in the quiet suburb of Ste-Anne-de-Bellevue. Clavel said that when Davis went across the street to buy some orange juice, three men who had been drinking in the bar began shouting at her and Watt as they waited in his car. Clavel said that after Davis chased them away, the men drove a black 1989 Honda at Davis as he stood in the middle of the street. The impact threw him more than 30 feet, and he landed headfirst on a parked car. Said Clavel: "I don't know if they were playing chicken or what."

Jeffrey Boro, the lawyer representing the men in the Honda, gave a different version of the events. Boro said that two witnesses saw Davis throw a bottle at the windshield of his clients' car moments before it struck Davis. Boro suggested that the car may have swerved into Davis after the driver and his two passengers turned their heads to avoid being struck by breaking glass from the car windshield.

Following the Nov. 11 incident, police officers impounded the Honda. But a Montreal police spokesman said that the police did not ask the driver to take a Breathalyzer test because they had no reason to think that he had been drinking. By week's end, no charges had been laid in Davis's death. The swimmer's family hired Montreal criminal lawyer Raphael Schachter to monitor the investigation. Schachter said that criminal charges should be "a distinct possibility, at least."

Davis was a hard-driving competitor, and his maverick image resurfaced after he was charged with assault in 1983 following an altercation at a party held at his home in Waterloo, Ont. The charges were subsequently dismissed. Davis was named a member of the Order of Canada in 1985. After failing to qualify in the 200-m breaststroke event for the 1988 Seoul Olympics, Davis spurred the 4 x 100-m medley relay team to a silver medal with the fastest split for the breaststroke ever recorded, 1:00.9. Davis announced his retirement from competitive swimming last July 5, and founded a Montreal-based swimming pool safety company and placement service for lifeguards.

Following Davis's death, about 200 friends and associates gathered at Barry's Pointe-Claire home, where they toasted the athlete. Said Barry: "Victor was the greatest guy. He had the most incredible effect on those people he touched." Even in death, Davis touched his fans, who mourned the passing of a champion. ❧

CSI/COA

The Memorial Cup

Among the thousands of Canadian lives lost in World War I and other wars, there were many hockey players whose starring roles on championship teams were left to other people to fulfill. In 1919, the Ontario Hockey Association donated what was originally called the OHA Memorial Cup in remembrance of all the soldiers who died in that first global conflict.

By the end of the century, the Memorial Cup and its storied tradition represented 82 years of Junior Hockey supremacy. The Cup shaped the way Junior Hockey was played across the country. It was initially awarded to the national Junior Champions of Canada and, beginning in 1934, to the national Junior "A" Champions. In 1972, a round-robin tournament format featuring the champions of the Western, Quebec Major Junior and Ontario Hockey Leagues replaced the old play-down system to decide the champion. In the last 20 years of the century the host-city for the tournament was also invited to include a team, making it a four-team round robin.

The Cup went international in 1983 as the tournament was held outside Canada for the first time. The host team Portland Winter Hawks took home the title that year to become the first-ever non-Canadian winner.

Many future NHL stars played in Memorial Cup games and will attest that it was one of their proudest hockey moments. Yet, there were also many junior stars, players looking like sure NHL bets, who never played in such a bright spotlight again. ❧

Memorial Cup Winners

Year	Champions	Year	Champions	Year	Champions
1919	University of Toronto Schools	1947	Toronto St. Michael's	1974	Regina Patricias
1920	Toronto Canoe Club Paddlers	1948	Port Arthur West End Bruins	1975	Toronto Marlboros
1921	Winnipeg Falcons	1949	Montreal Royals	1976	Hamilton Fincups
1922	Fort William War Veterans	1950	Montreal Jr. Canadiens	1977	New Westminster Bruins
1923	University of Manitoba Bisons	1951	Barrie Flyers	1978	New Westminster Bruins
1924	Owen Sound Greys	1952	Guelph Biltmores	1979	Peterborough Petes
1925	Regina Pats	1953	Barrie Flyers	1980	Cornwall Royals
1926	Calgary Canadians	1954	St. Catharines TeePees	1981	Cornwall Royals
1927	Owen Sound Greys	1955	Toronto Marlboros	1982	Kitchener Rangers
1928	Regina Monarchs	1956	Toronto Marlboros	1983	Portland Winter Hawks
1929	Toronto Marlboros	1957	Flin Flon Bombers	1984	Ottawa 67's
1930	Regina Pats	1958	Ottawa-Hull Canadiens	1985	Prince Albert Raiders
1931	Winnipeg Elmwood Millionaires	1959	Winnipeg Braves	1986	Guelph Platers
1932	Sudbury Wolves	1960	St. Catharines TeePees	1987	Medicine Hat Tigers
1933	Newmarket Redmen	1961	Toronto St. Michael's	1988	Medicine Hat Tigers
1934	Toronto St. Michael's Majors	1962	Hamilton Red Wings	1989	Swift Current Broncos
1935	Winnipeg Monarchs	1963	Edmonton Oil Kings	1990	Oshawa Generals
1936	West Toronto Nationals	1964	Toronto Marlboros	1991	Spokane Chiefs
1937	Winnipeg Monarchs	1965	Niagara Falls Flyers	1992	Kamloops Blazers
1938	St. Boniface Seals	1966	Edmonton Oil Kings	1993	Sault St. Marie Greyhounds
1939	Oshawa Generals	1967	Toronto Marlboros	1994	Kamloops Blazers
1940	Oshawa Generals	1968	Niagara Falls Flyers	1995	Kamloops Blazers
1941	Winnipeg Rangers	1969	Montreal Jr. Canadiens	1996	Granby Predateurs
1942	Portage la Prairie Terriers	1970	Montreal Jr. Canadiens	1997	Hull Olympiques
1943	Winnipeg Rangers	1971	Quebec Remparts	1998	Portland Winter Hawks
1944	Oshawa Generals	1972	Cornwall Royals	1999	Ottawa 67's
1945	Toronto St. Michael's	1973	Toronto Marlboros	2000	Rimouski Oceanic
1946	Winnipeg Monarchs				

1992

Swimming

Unsinkable Sylvie

by Chris Wood in Barcelona with Mary Nemeth in Toronto
August 17, 1992

She swam, she would say later, "with all the emotion I had." To the soft strains of a gently lyrical soundtrack. Montreal's Sylvie Fréchette, wearing virginal white, adorned only with a discreet touch of lace, glided through an expressive synchronized swimming program that at times seemed tinged with melancholy. The poignant mood was fitting for a woman who, in order to compete at all, had to shake off the shock of a lifetime: the suicide of her boyfriend, Sylvain Lake, on the eve of the Olympics. If anyone deserved a fair shake at the Barcelona Games themselves, it was surely Fréchette. But although she outscored her sequined American rival, Kristen Babb-Sprague, in the final routine, she finished a fraction behind in the two-day event — the victim of a controversial judging error on the first day. Accepting her silver medal, the 25-year-old Fréchette demonstrated the same grace under adversity that she did in the water. Said the swimmer: "There was a mistake, but that is part of my sport. I cannot change anything. I did my very best."

For Canadians, what happened to Fréchette was one of the week's many frustrations. From the nagging hamstring injury to decathlete Michael Smith and the sudden fatigue of kayaker Renn Crichlow, to the missed jump of equestrian Ian Millar and his horse Big Ben, dashed medal hopes abounded. But Canadian athletes also grabbed final-week medals in track, wrestling, boxing and yachting. and in an Olympics dominated by the Unified Team and the United States,

the Canadians made their mark as well: the team's medal total of 18 is the country's best ever outside the 1984 Los Angeles Games, which were boycotted by the Communist bloc.

While Americans followed their basketball Dream Team's grab of Barcelona gold, for Canadians there was no second-week drama more powerful than that of the trouble-plagued Fréchette. Her grandfather had died in January. And less than a week before she was to leave for Spain, she discovered Lake's lifeless body in the carbon monoxide-filled townhouse that they shared in Laval, north of Montreal. In Barcelona, after giving one impromptu news conference, the synchronized swimmer retreated to the comparative privacy of the athletes' village and a closed training pool in order to concentrate on regaining her competitive focus.

By Aug. 5, as Fréchette began the first portion of the finals in her event — the execution of four figures drawn from synchro-swimming's repertoire of ballet-like movements — it was apparent that she had succeeded. On the first of the four, only American Babb-Sprague scored higher. Fréchette would later describe the second, called an albatross spin, as "the best figure of my life." At least four of the five judges, sitting in pulpit-like stands around the pool, plainly agreed: they punched scores of 9.2 or better into the small electronic keypads connected to the facility's scoring computer.

But at the fifth judging position, there was consternation. Brazilian judge Ana Maria da Silveira had also rated Fréchette's figure highly: later, the swimmer's coach, Julie Sauvé, said that da Silveira had told her that she intended to award a 9.7 — but instead struck keys registering an 8.7. Almost instantly, it appears, she tried to activate a device intended to allow her to recall a mistyped score. Swiss judge Marlis Haeberlis, whose position was next to da Silveira's, recounted: "She tried to correct it, and she couldn't make that recall thing work. Finally, because she was all excited, she pushed several buttons."

According to Haeberlis, the referee, American Judith McGowan, was too far away for da Silveira to call, and assistant referee Nakako Saito of Japan spoke such poor English that she failed to understand da Silveira's predicament. "By the time somebody got the referee," concluded Haeberlis, "the marks were already read." Competition rules state that once marks are disclosed publicly, they cannot be changed. McGowan ordered the lower mark to stand, and Fréchette ended the day in second place behind Babb-Sprague — the wife of Toronto Blue Jays backup catcher Ed Sprague.

The next afternoon, Fréchette returned to the pool determined to give her best. The uncorrected mark of the previous day, she said later, had "helped me a lot — I was so mad, so full of energy." What she did was score a 99.160, a full .120 higher than Babb-Sprague — but not quite enough to overcome the deficit that resulted from the mistaken mark. Effectively, her second-place fate had been sealed earlier in the day by a panel of 13 members of the so-called "bureau" of the International Amateur Swimming Federation (called FINA, the acronym for its name in French), that considered Canada's appeal.

Fréchette's case was contained in a written brief, while referee McGowan also submitted one. Astonishingly, however, the panel made no attempt to question da Silveira or anyone else directly involved in the previous day's mix-up. After more than an hour, by a vote of 11 to 2 (the two Canadian members voted against the majority), the jury upheld McGowan's original ruling. "We do not entertain issues of fact," explained FINA secretary Ross Wales, an American lawyer. Challenged to justify the panel's decision to read only written reports and not hear directly from any witnesses, Wales added blandly: "Hearsay is accepted."

Canada's team leader, Ken Read, called the ruling "obscene." And Fréchette, when asked in French whether she felt that she deserved the gold instead of the silver, laughed gently and replied, "*Dans mon coeur* (in my heart)." In Montreal, Fréchette's brother, 21-year-old Martin, declared: "She is better than a gold medallist. Here, in Quebec, she's a queen." ❧

Sylvie Fréchette shows her 1992 Olympic silver medal, before it turned to gold.

It took 16 months, but Sylvie Fréchette finally received the Olympic gold medal she had worked so hard to earn. In a nationally televised ceremony held at the Montreal Forum on December 15, 1993, IOC member in Canada Dick Pound presented her with the medal.

Pound had been one of the driving forces behind reversing the ruling made during the Games in Barcelona. The appeal was made on Sylvie's behalf by the Canadian Olympic Association to FINA, the international swimming federation. FINA agreed in October, 1993 to recommend that the International Olympic Committee award her a gold medal, and the IOC agreed two months later. There were two other occasions in Olympic history when a medal was awarded long after the Games had ended, but this was the first time the circumstances included the admission of a mistake in a judged sport.

Fréchette competed at one more Olympic Games, this time in the team event in Atlanta in 1996. The team won the silver medal.

Alan Eagleson – The Rise and Fall of the Eagle

Of all the characters that have walked across the history pages devoted to Canada's national sport, Alan Eagleson ranks among the most colourful and controversial. Credited with being the moving force behind finally forming the NHL Players Association in 1967 and getting the 1972 Canada-Russia Summit series off the ground, as well as being the agent for many star players, he became arguably the most powerful figure in organized hockey during the 1970s and 1980s. His fall from grace during the early '90s, following allegations of corruption and fraud, left his reputation in tatters, though.

Eagleson was extremely self-confident, tireless and energetic. Other words to describe him range from brash, loud, swaggering, blustering, a human battering ram, bullying, a wheeler-dealer and profane, to visionary, competent, committed and caring. People tended to either love him or hate him.

The Eagle's first forays into hockey came through his association with a number of Toronto Maple Leafs players during the early 1960s. Acting as lawyer and financial adviser, he became the trusted confidant of a number of Toronto players. Meanwhile, he was also building a network of friends in political circles, serving as an MPP and later becoming the President of the Ontario Progressive Conservatives.

His horizons expanded greatly when he was asked to represent a teenaged Bobby Orr in contract negotiations with the Boston Bruins. During a time when NHL owners observed labour practices that today would be considered at the very least draconian, Eagleson lined up a record contract for the player everyone knew would be the next superstar. Along the way, he became the first ever player agent representing NHL players.

As far as most hockey players were concerned, his reputation as a man they could trust to represent them was cemented by his close relationship with Orr (he also managed the young player's business affairs), coupled with his reported role in ending a dispute in 1966 between the AHL Springfield Indians' players and the team's legendary iron-fisted owner, Eddie Shore.

In early 1967, with the support of a number of players, Eagleson went to each NHL team and pitched the idea of a players' union with him at the helm. Although some players expressed reservations about a player agent also being the head of their union, they were hungry for someone to look after their collective interests. In the cocky young lawyer, who was never at a loss for colourful language, they saw someone they could relate to. The team owners, who had aggressively put down a similar attempt headed by Detroit Red Wings' star Ted Lindsay to organize the players a decade earlier, also saw Eagleson as someone they could do business with.

By 1972, Eagleson was well entrenched and became one of the key figures in the Canada-Russia "Series of the Century." Reports vary as to his level of influence in terms of bringing the series about in the first place, but his prominent role (through his position as Executive Director of the NHLPA) in ensuring the players' availability for that series and planning the subsequent Canada Cup series was indisputable. He sat on the Board of Directors of Hockey Canada for more than two decades after its formation in 1969, becoming its chief international negotiator. His extensive network of prominent friends also helped generate millions of dollars in sponsorship money.

Playing multiple roles as agent, union boss, personal financial adviser and international hockey mogul gradually made him one of the most powerful men in hockey, but also sowed the seeds of his eventual destruction. From the outside, it was frequently ambiguous whose interests he was acting in, and his reported refusals to supply information or justify his decisions didn't help. Allegations about conflicts of interest were only strengthened by the fact that his hockey jobs were regularly tied into a maze of family-owned or operated businesses.

His lavish lifestyle, which included substantial perks for his friends and family, led to accusations of mismanagement and corruption. Bobby Orr, for example, who completely trusted Eagleson to handle his business affairs, ended his playing days virtually penniless. Many players felt that there were two standards when they needed personal help from the NHLPA: one for Eagleson's personal clients and another for those who chose different agents. And, when it came to negotiating the players' collective bargaining agreement, many wondered how he could bargain effectively with owners whose cooperation he needed when it came time to sign up players for international tournaments. While conditions improved substantially over the years for players, issues such as restrictions on free agency remained effectively unchanged during Eagleson's tenure.

Even though disputes flared up periodically, the Eagle remained on his perch, seemingly impervious to any challenge. In 1991, though, Russ Conway, the sports editor of Lawrence, Massachusetts, *Eagle-Tribune*, published the first in a series of investigative reports on Eagleson that contained detailed allegations about hockey pensions, disability insurance, mismanagement of money, abuse of power, and more. While some accusations were directed at the NHL and the team owners, most of the fingers pointed squarely at the Eagle.

Over the next few years, more accusations flew, and the movement to dethrone him gained momentum. Legal investigations began in both Canada and the United States, and in early 1994, Eagleson was indicted in US federal court on more than 30 counts that included racketeering, fraud, embezzlement, obstruction of justice and receipt of kickbacks. The ensuing legal battle that took place on both sides of the border cost him dearly. He maintained his innocence throughout, but eventually the man who boasted that he never ran from a fight pleaded guilty to three of the charges and was sentenced to 18 months in jail, a $1-million fine and a year's probation. To add insult to injury, he was eventually disbarred from the Law Society of Upper Canada, ousted from the Canada's Sports Hall of Fame and the Hockey Hall of Fame, and stripped of his Order of Canada. He successfully avoided extradition during his legal battle, and served just over six months of his prison sentence at a minimum-security prison in Mimico, Ontario.

Opinions were divided on the merits of the charges and the appropriateness of the punishment. Many people, including a large group of former players, felt Eagleson's chickens had come home to roost. Others suggested that he was the victim of a miscarriage of justice. Former Supreme Court of Canada Justice Willard "Bud" Estey (formerly a director of Hockey Canada), for example, said he thought Eagleson pleaded guilty "because the Americans had him over a barrel." Frank Orr and Chrys Goyens, in their book *Blades on Ice*, said, "Whatever his indiscretions, they pale in comparison with his accomplishments over a quarter of a century." Former Maple Leafs' star Darryl Sittler adds, "I trusted Al's leadership and advice and I continue to have confidence in him."

Many former players, including some who had been speaking out for years, credited Conway with performing a public service in his exposé. In Conway's book *Game Misconduct*, Carl Brewer is quoted as saying, "We in hockey are grateful for it; Eagleson had to be stopped." Jean Ratelle added, "Without Russ Conway's unbelievable dedication, Alan Eagleson's betrayal of NHL players might never have been exposed." ♣

R o w i n g

Silken Laumann

CSI/COA

In the summer of 1991, Silken Laumann was at the top of her field. She was being hailed as the favourite to win the women's single sculls for the 1992 Barcelona Olympics.

Laumann had just completed a remarkable season. She was the overall winner in a series of six races for the World Cup. Then, in a single race in Vienna she was crowned world champion. She received honour after honour, including being named the Canadian Athlete of the Year.

In May 1992, with a little more than two months before the Barcelona Olympics, Laumann was competing in a pre-Olympic race in Essen, Germany. Before the race, tragedy struck.

"During my warmup this German boat came out of nowhere," she recalls. "It crashed right into my right leg, severing all the muscles, tendons and ligaments from midway up my right shin all the way to the ankle."

The initial medical report predicted she would never row again. A little later, it was determined that with rest and rehabilitation she would get back into competition. But the medical experts all agreed that the Barcelona Olympics, just two months away would not be a possibility. Laumann disagreed with the prognosis and set out to prove the doctors wrong.

"The first goal I set for myself was the Barcelona Olympics," she recalls. "I didn't know if it was possible. When I looked at the big open wound I sort of wondered if it was possible."

Rehabilitation and training pushed Laumann to new ends, both physically and mentally.

"The medal was bronze, but the moment was golden."

"There were many tears," recounts her coach, Mike Spracklen, "because Silken is an emotional person. But it was not the sort of sadness that 'I'm not going to make it,' but rather 'When am I going to make it?' She wanted to go to the Olympics, and no one was going to stop her from going."

Five weeks after the accident and one month before the Barcelona Games, Laumann announced that she was going to Barcelona. But she was not going to Barcelona to be just another competitor. Her priorities were set. She was going after one of the medals.

As the Games started, the world wondered whether the barely-healed leg would stand up to the rigours of competition. In the eyes of most, it was amazing that she was in Barcelona in the first place. She amazed the world again when, on August 2, 1992, she became one of the six finalists in the single sculls.

Throughout most of the final, Laumann trailed in fourth place behind Elisabeta Lipa of Romania, Annelies Bredael of Belgium and Anne Marden of the United States.

"With about 1,000 metres to go I thought I was going to die. I knew I couldn't win but I wanted one of the medals," said Laumann. "I said to myself, I'm not coming in fourth. Fourth is the worst possible position — to just miss a medal."

Laumann set her sights on America's Anne Marden in third place. Bit by bit, she moved up on the American. A few metres before the finish, she did it. Laumann had the bronze.

At the medal ceremony for the race, one columnist was already writing the lead paragraph to his story. The lead was: "Canada won four gold medals and one bronze in rowing at the Barcelona Olympics. Let the word go out that on this occasion Silken Laumann's bronze medal shines as brightly in the Barcelona sun as any of the gold." ❦

Atlanta, 1996

Postscript

Still looking for the elusive Olympic gold medal, Silken Laumann remained in rowing for four more years following her Barcelona experience. She won the single sculls gold medal at the 1995 Pan Am Games in Mar del Plata, Argentina, but later she and her women's-fours teammates were disqualified from their gold medal performance. Laumann had inadvertently taken the wrong over-the-counter cold medicine, which contained a banned substance, tested positive and the whole team had to return their medals. Laumann trained more intensely than ever in preparation for the single sculls at the 1996 Olympic Games in Atlanta. In a tough battle, she had to concede the final race of her long career to Ekaterina Khodovich of Belarus, settling for a silver herself.

1999

Motor Sports

Tragedy in the fast lane:

Family, Friends Mourn Greg Moore

by James Deacon
November 15, 1999

Speed kills, and Greg Moore knew it. The dashing British Columbian accepted the risks — of injury, disability, even death — that were part of driving racecars for a living. He wasn't cocky about it, nor was he convinced of some innate invincibility. He was simply an optimist. In the precociously calm manner in which he approached his life, the 24-year-old from Maple Ridge weighed racing's risks against his own considerable abilities and liked his odds. His training and experience enabled him to judge the limits of his car and of himself, and he had a rare talent — some of it learned, most of it innate — that allowed him to push those limits without overstretching himself. But no driver can control everything on the track. Moore said so himself just two days before his death. "You'll never be able to make race cars completely safe," he told reporters at California Speedway prior to last week's ill-fated Marlboro 500. "Things happen at speed."

For family, friends and fans, Moore's own philosophical words will have to suffice as an answer to why he died. By late last week, track officials still weren't sure exactly what did happen at 350 km/hr to cause the driver to lose control and crash horrifically into an exposed concrete barrier. Helio Castro-Neves, the driver immediately behind Moore on the 10th lap of the race, said it appeared the car simply hit a bump in the track, lifted a bit and started to spin. But that, critics charged, would not have proved fatal with better safety

Associated Press AP

precautions around the track, and some drivers wondered privately why the race was allowed to continue when it was clear Moore had been killed. Adrian Fernandez, the Mexican star who won the Marlboro race, was disconsolate. "This is a tragedy for all of us," he said, in tears. "The win doesn't mean anything."

Handsome, single and quick to smile, Moore was among the most popular drivers in one of North America's most popular sports. He dominated every series from kids' go-carts on up, and at times he seemed capable of doing the same on the top-ranked CART circuit for Player's Racing. At 20, after setting the record for most victories in a single season on the second-tier Indy Lights series, Moore was promoted to fill the Player's seat left vacant when Jacques Villeneuve signed to drive in Formula One. In 1997, at 22, Moore became the youngest driver ever to win a CART race, and for stretches of the past two seasons, he led the overall points race. On both occasions, he eventually fell back by year's end, but that, experts say, was due to the failings of the car, not of its driver.

His death angered many in the tight community of drivers. David Empringham, a racing instructor and former Player's teammate of Moore's, said gravel spillways and tire barriers used at many other tracks might have slowed Moore's spin through the infield and cushioned his crash against the exposed cement wall. "Hopefully," Empringham said, "this will make a lot of people sit down and take another look at how to make these things safer." There was sadness, too, particularly at a private funeral in Vancouver attended by many in the racing world, including Canadian stars Paul Tracy, Patrick Carpentier and Villeneuve, who flew from Europe when he heard the news. "Everyone knew he was a hell of a race car driver," fellow driver Jimmy Vasser told the 1,200 who attended the service, "but he was 10 times the human being."

Moore always marvelled at his own good fortune, to be paid so well for something he loved to do, and he was a champion autograph-signer for kids and fans alike. As a tribute to Moore's upbeat attitude, his father, Ric, said at a public memorial in Maple Ridge that given the chance, his son would tell mourners to "lighten up and have some fun. Remember me as I was, a regular guy who had a great job." That modesty was the quality fans and friends cited most often in notes pinned to bouquets left at the memorial. So it was fitting that, while he made his name as a great driver, Greg Moore will be remembered for being a great guy. ❧

Sport Promotion Network

1992

Four-time world figure skating champion Kurt Browning suffered injury, bad timing, poor luck and less than his usual stellar performances at the three Olympic Winter Games he competed at. His best performance was sixth in 1992.

1992

Chris Lori started out as a decathlete at the University of Windsor. In his quest to become an Olympic athlete, he switched sports in the early 1980s, becoming Canada's top bobsleigh driver in over 20 years. His success at World Cup competitions put Canada back on the bobsleighing map, and also fuelled his desire to win an Olympic medal. He almost made it, finishing an agonizingly close fourth by .32 seconds at the 1992 Olympic Winter Games in Albertville, France.

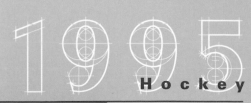

1995

H o c k e y

Death of the Nords

The Quebec franchise packs up for Denver

by James Deacon
June 5, 1995

The writing, in both languages, had been on the wall for years, so there was no surprise last week when the money-losing Québec Nordiques finally died. The wake was quiet in Quebec City, where the team began 23 years ago in the World Hockey Association before joining the National Hockey League in 1979. At a largely emotionless news conference, team president Marcel Aubut and the other shareholders — the Quebec Labour Federation pension fund, La Mutuelle insurance company, the Daishowa paper company and the Metro-Richelieu grocery store chain — announced that they had sold the franchise to COMSAT Entertainment group of Bethesda, Md., for $103 million. Aubut claimed that the team could not survive in the NHL's smallest market without a new publicly funded arena and ongoing government support. But Quebec Premier Jacques Parizeau instead offered to buy out Aubut and underwrite some team deficits for two years while the provincial government conducted a feasibility study on the arena. That, the owners decided, was not enough — and now the soon-to-be-renamed Nordiques are off to Denver.

The Nordiques were killed by a disease that afflicts many small-market teams — including the Winnipeg Jets who, a week before, narrowly escaped the same fate as the Nordiques when a proposed deal to move them to Minneapolis fell through. In Quebec, said Aubut, "The new realities of the hockey industry, the size of the Quebec City market and the absence of adequate government help sounded the knell of the Nordiques." Their revenues from advertising, TV and ticket sales did not cover skyrocketing payroll costs.

The NHL's governors will have to approve the sale and settle on a transfer fee to be paid to the league — possibly as high as $13 million. Even if that fee comes off the sale price, the vendors will make a handsome profit: they bought the team in 1988 for about $15 million. COMSAT, meanwhile, can be equally pleased with its end of the bargain. The company, which already owns a National Basketball Association franchise in Denver, plans to have both teams playing out of the city's McNichols Sports Arena until the new $130 million Pepsi Center is completed prior to the 1997-98 season. The Rocky Mountain City is getting not an expansion franchise but one of the league's most talented teams. "We're bringing winners into Denver," enthused COMSAT president Charlie Lyons. Quebec's loss, Colorado's gain. ❖

1995

Hockey

Out in the Cold

by James Deacon, with Donald MacGillivray
May 15, 1995

With their team down by one goal in the waning minutes of the season's final game last week, Winnipeg hockey fans stood and cheered, exhorting the home-town Jets to come back against the visiting Los Angeles Kings. It was an emotional and prolonged outpouring of support, prompted by the fact, that earlier in the day, last-ditch efforts to keep the money-losing team in the Manitoba capital appeared to have failed. As the seconds ticket away for both the game and the franchise, the 15,562 fans at the Winnipeg Arena changed their chant from "Go Jets go!" to "Save our Jets!" And when the game finally ended — the Jets lost 2-1 — the fans and players shared a teary send-off, a lingering parting of old friends. Later, players such as veteran centre Thomas Steen, who has been a Jet for all his 14 years in the National Hockey League, were too distraught to talk to reporters in the sombre locker-room. "There were a few wet eyes in our dressing room tonight," explained centre Randy Gilhen. "I don't think the guys realized until tonight how much the people really care."

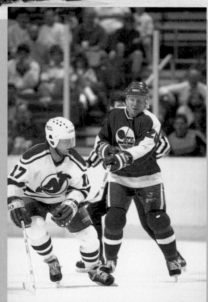

After 22 seasons, the Jet's history in Winnipeg came to an end last week. The team will soon by sold to another city — Minneapolis, Atlanta and even Hamilton are possible destinations. "I guess that's the next job at hand," said a disconsolate Barry Shenkarow, the team's president and majority owner, as he announced the demise. But the outcome, however devastating to the people of Winnipeg, was no surprise. Shenkarow had long warned that, without a publicly funded arena with luxury boxes and other revenue-generating amenities, the team would not be able to survive in the NHL. Although the city and provincial governments helped out financially, and a business group called the Manitoba Entertainment Complex pledged to buy the team and help raise funds to build a new arena, no one was willing to absorb the ongoing operating losses of the franchise. And the league, which has to approve any ownership changes, was not prepared to permit the sale to local buyers without that guarantee.

Shenkarow, who took control of the Jets just before they joined the NHL from the defunct World Hockey Association in 1979, said that operating costs, including skyrocketing payrolls, had simply outgrown the team's ability to generate revenue. "For a purely business transaction, the NHL is too big for Winnipeg," he said. "I think everybody knows that."

By failing to find a local buyer, he and his partners, including local governments, would profit handsomely if they were to sell to an American bidder. To keep the franchise in Winnipeg, they had agreed to sell the Jets to the MEC for $32 million, compared with the anticipated $90 million they can expect to get on the open market.

But that was little consolation in a city stripped of its team. "What was great for me and all my hockey-playing friends was that the NHL never seemed like a million miles away," said Gilhen, who grew up in Winnipeg. "It was something you could really relate to. It's a shame the kids here have to lose that." Among the fans who jammed the Arena and booed the American anthem when it was played before last week's final game, there was grief and a strong sense of loss. "I can't believe this is the last game in this arena," said Lissa Palamar, a 28-year-old physical education teacher. "We have awfully long winters here. Now what are we going to do?" ❖

HHOF — Paul Bereswill

HHOF — Paul Bereswill

1998
Hockey

Hockey Meltdown

by Bruce Wallace
March 2, 1998

The 1998 Olympic [men's] gold-medal hockey game had plenty in common with all those gold-medal games of the 1960s and 70s, except this time the Russians and the Czechs wore Nike. After all the hype and great expectations, a team of hustling but lead-handed Canadians was reduced to the supporting cast in what may qualify as the greatest hockey tournament ever staged. European teams swept the medals. Canada played gamely but unsuccessfully for bronze.

But prescience does not take away the sting. "The loss is devastating, the worst feeling in the world," Wayne Gretzky said in a near whisper after dropping the semi-final, 2-1, to the Czech Republic in a dramatic, ratchet-up-the-tension Olympic twist called the shootout. The Canadians were so crushed that they failed to regroup for the next day's bronze-medal game against Finland. The Finns won 3-2 in a game played in a funereal atmosphere at Nagano's Big Hat arena, where the normally boisterous crowd seemed to sense that polite, sympathetic clapping was more suitable for a consolation game. "Sure it would have been nice to go home with a medal," said Theo Fleury, leaving the Canadian dressing room for the last time, a day earlier than expected. "But we came here to win."

That is the conundrum now facing Canadian hockey: in a sport where international parity exists among half-a-dozen (if not more) elite teams, Canadian players and fans remain conditioned to expect only gold from those who wear the Maple Leaf. Canada's women's team tasted similar pressure when it fell 3-1 to the Americans in the final of the first-ever Olympic women's hockey tournament. Even the players seemed to regard the silver medals around their necks as symbols of failure. "We have a silver medal, but the fact is we lost the game," said Cassie Campbell, part of a Canadian team that dissolved into inconsolable sobs after losing. "It doesn't feel like we won anything."

The Canadian women's loss was just as heartbreaking. In the most important women's hockey game to date, a team that had won all four world championships came up flat. Their freewheeling third period was not enough to overcome a swifter — on this night — American squad. And just as men's team general manager Bobby Clarke has taken heat for his selection of players, women's coach

February, 1998 — Women's hockey entered the Olympic arena for the first time. Canada's six-time world champion women's hockey team lost its only significant game of the decade, the gold medal game to the USA.

CSI/COA — Scott Grant

CSI/COA — Scott Grant

CS/COA — Scott Grant

CSI/COA — Scott Grant

CSI/COA — Scott Grant

by a goal — watched video clips of their finest moments to the tune of *Simply the Best*. The move provoked sneers from critics. "It worked," retorted Miller, whose team went on to play their best period of hockey. "Yeah," said assistant coach Daniele Sauvageau wryly. "Maybe we should have played the video *earlier*."

Shannon Miller endured sniping for the handling of hers. Most attacks focused on the way she prepared her team for the Olympics, suggesting players were too high-strung and tight under her guidance.

Opponents like US captain Cammi Granato certainly thought the Canadians were tense. "They had all the pressure of holding off a team that has finally caught up to them in talent," said Granato. American coach Ben Smith handles his team in a fatherly manner, says Granato. He tells parables before a game. Canada's Miller, on the other hand, likes to keep her team in "the bubble," isolated from distractions like family, then "motivate the hell out of them" at the last minute, she says. The last minute for the Canadians came before a desperate third period when the team — down

Miller's players defended her to the hilt, suggesting that male hockey writers just don't like the women's game. But in the aftermath, the Canadians looked like crash survivors. Tears flowered freely hours after the game at a reception for players and their families. They talked of the importance of the Olympic journey, but it was still too soon to forget the dashed expectations.

"You'll wake up tomorrow and feel dead, completely drained," Clarke told a group of women, as they all sucked on cigars. "But in two or three days, you'll come back." Perhaps when the players and the nation come out of their funk, they will take a little pride in the way the world has embraced Canada's game. ♦

CSI/COA — Scott Grant

Highlights
Hockey Highlights

1994-1995

The NHL and the NHL Players Association were at loggerheads in their contract negotiations and the owners technically locked the players out of the arenas for months. It looked like the season would be scrapped. At literally the last moment, a deal was reached and the semblance of a season started January 20 with just 48 games scheduled per team — the shortest season since 1941.

July 28, 1994

Former NHL players won a lawsuit against the NHL over missed pension payments, forcing the NHL to pay the retired players over $40 million collectively.

May 25, 1995

The Quebec Nordiques were sold and moved to Colorado to become the Avalanche.

1996

As sometimes happens, Team Canada threw everything it had against the United States in the inaugural World Cup of Hockey, but were stonewalled by hot goaltender Mike Richter in a 2-1 loss.

CSI/COA — Scott Grant

Hockey

Blood Sport

by James Deacon with Michael Snider
March 6, 2000

It was probably inevitable that Marty McSorley and Donald Brashear were going to butt heads. They came from different backgrounds: Brashear was born in Bedford, Ind., but was abused by his father and was eventually sent by his mother, a Quebecer, to live with a foster family in Montreal; McSorley had a happy family life on his parents' farm in Cayuga, Ont. But in their hockey careers, they had much in common. Both were self-made, having earned their way to the National Hockey League as fighters before refining their talents to become useful, regular-shift players — Brashear as a forward, McSorley on defence. Since 1996, they fought practically every time they faced one another — five times in all. The last of those battles came last week, barely two minutes into the first period of a game between Brashear's Vancouver Canucks and McSorley's Boston Bruins. As usual, Brashear was the clear victor.

What was not predictable was how the next McSorley-versus-Brashear confrontation would conclude. The first-period beating burned McSorley, and he repeatedly tried to goad his foe into a rematch later in the game. Brashear wouldn't bite — why bother when his Canucks were building a solid 5-2 lead — but he did taunt the entire Bruins' bench with an exaggerated flex of muscles midway through the final period. That just seemed to make McSorley angrier. In the hockey fighters' code of honour, showboating is a cardinal sin and offenders must pay.

So, with less than a minute on the score-clock and Brashear already on the ice, McSorley jumped over the boards intending, he said later, to provoke another fight. But instead, in a grotesque lapse of character, McSorley skated up from behind and, with just 2.7 seconds left, clubbed Brashear in the right temple with a vicious two-handed slash of his stick. The Vancouver forward dropped like a felled tree. Making matters worse, his helmet slipped off just before impact, allowing his head to bounce sickeningly on the ice. McSorley was immediately besieged by several Canucks, while

Brashear — unconscious, his body twitching ominously, blood seeping out of his nose — was treated by emergency medical staff and carried away on a stretcher.

Miraculously, the 28-year-old Brashear soon regained consciousness and may be able to return to action in a matter of weeks, depending on how quickly he recovers from a severe concussion. Thanks to that durability, the National Hockey League dodged a deadly bullet in Vancouver last week. The force of McSorley's blow and the place on the head where it hit might have easily killed Brashear. Fans, officials and players all condemned the attack, and Vancouver police launched an investigation that could yet result in charges this week.

The league, meanwhile, suspended the 36-year-old McSorley for the Bruin's remaining 23 regular-season games and for the playoffs, should Boston qualify. That is the longest suspension in NHL history for an on-ice infraction — but not nearly long enough for many critics. "You've got to talk years with that kind of thing," said Dallas Stars forward Mike Modano, himself a victim of a now-infamous hit that kept him out for 10 days earlier this season.

In public-relations terms, the league plainly suffered a severe concussion, too. The attack was replayed endlessly on TV networks and Web sites all over North America, reinforcing among casual viewers — especially in the all-important US market — the stereotype depicted in the 1970s cult classic, *Slap Shot*, which portrayed hockey as a violent fringe sport more closely aligned with wrestling and roller derby than with baseball, basketball and football. "For the fan who maybe doesn't see this game a lot," said Anaheim Mighty Ducks star Paul Kariya, "this is what they are going to focus on and this is what the papers are going to push. For our league, this type of criticism is horrible."

There is no question that the NHL has made some effort to curb violence. It has changed rules, toughened suspensions and gone to a new two-referee system to dramatically reduce the number of fights and serious fouls in recent years. But the league still allows fighting, and while stick fouls such as McSorley's are rare, vicious cross-checks and slashes are not. Elbows to the head are still too common, as are hits from behind, which may be the most dangerous foul of all. The worst recent example occurred last October, when Anaheim defenceman Ruslan Salei sent Modano, at high speed, twisting headfirst into the boards.

Even Marty McSorley admits there is no excuse for what he did. "I got *way* too carried away," he said in his solemn post-game apology to Brashear. All he wanted to do, he said, was start a fight.

> **September 21, 1969**
>
> *The game was not meant to be this rough. During a pre-season game in Ottawa, Boston's Ted Green and St. Louis' Wayne Maki had a vicious and memorable stick-swinging duel, which resulted in a fractured skull for Green. Both players got suspended — Green for 13 days and Maki for 30, but Green missed the entire season due to the injury.*

As seen on a CTV Sportsnet television broadcast in March of 2000, Boston Bruin Marty McSorley is about to deliver a high stick to the head of Vancouver Canuck Donald Brashear. McSorley would be suspended for one year and face criminal charges.

Whatever, McSorley's senseless act may well be his last in the NHL. The Ontario farm boy has struggled in recent years to find employment in the NHL, and his current notoriety is not likely to help his cause even with two talent-poor expansion franchises joining the league next season. And without somewhere to play, McSorley will have little chance to redeem himself in the eyes of sports fans — or in his own.

It could have been a much happier ending. McSorley is the quintessential rags-to-riches hockey player. With only modest abilities, he offered to do his teams' dirty work as an enforcer, first in Pittsburgh and then, more gloriously, alongside Gretzky in Edmonton and Los Angeles. Though sheer hard work, McSorley became a solid player in the middle years of his career, playing key roles on the power-play and penalty-killing units. Soft-spoken and articulate, he took a keen interest in the business of the sport and became a vice-president with the NHL Players' Association.

But along the way, things took a turn for the worse. Feeling McSorley had lost a step and was becoming less proficient as a regular defenceman, his previous employers in San Jose and then Edmonton (his second stint there) began using him more in his original role, as a fighter.

One insider who has known McSorley for his entire career, and who asked to remain anonymous, says the tough guy probably stayed in the game too long. Enforcers are supposed to intimidate their counterparts on other teams, and when they are no longer able to do that, they either get out of the game or resort to ever more dangerous tactics. McSorley alluded to that possibility himself, saying ruefully: "I guess I'm trying to write cheques my body can't cash."

Still, it is misleading to view the McSorley-Brashear incident in isolation. Sure, Brashear was an antagonist and, certainly, McSorley must be held accountable for his actions and pay the highest price. But the coaches bear responsibility, too, for allowing those players on the ice at that time. They had fought before; there was bad blood; the game was already decided; the only possible outcome was fighting for fighting's sake — or worse.

But then, the NHL has its traditions. Just about every team holds at least two roster spots for so called tough guys. The league insists fighting is part of the game, and that it helps discourage other dangerous fouls. All evidence to the contrary: if fighting were really an essential part of the game, then the Russians and Swedes would be good at it. And if it discouraged serious fouls, then Chicago's Gary Suter would not have ended Kariya's season with Anaheim two years ago with a cross-check to the face. And Mike Stapleton of the Atlanta Thrashers would not have crunched his elbow jarringly into the face of Colorado's star centre, Peter Forsberg, just last week. And so on. And in the McSorley case, fighting was clearly part of what *led* to the brutal slashing.

The NHL is left with a contradiction. It suspends players for high sticking, boarding and elbowing fouls, but it tacitly condones bare-knuckle fighting by levying only five-minute penalties against players who drop their gloves. In a pre-season game in 1997, Ryan Vandenbusche of the New York Rangers knocked Toronto's Nick Kypreos unconscious with a single punch. Kypreos, like Brashear, fell to the ice, suffered a massive concussion and was forced to retire. Kypreos was a veteran tough guy who fought knowing the risks. But that incident demonstrated that fighting can be as dangerous as McSorley's stickwork, particularly since today's enforcers are bigger and better brawlers than they were a generation ago.

The league doesn't see it that way. During a conference call announcing McSorley's ban, Campbell said changing the rules on fighting was "not something we are concerned about." Market research reveals that while fans deplore dangerous stickwork, a high number — too many to risk losing, apparently — like fighting. "We have not got to the point," Campbell said, "where we say fights should be illegal." ❧

2000

McSorley found guilty

Almost eight months after striking Donald Brashear in the head with his stick during a game, Marty McSorley was found guilty of assault with a weapon. He received an 18-month conditional discharge, essentially a probationary period that would leave him with no permanent criminal record. It was the first conviction of an NHL player since 1988, when Dino Ciccarelli spent a day in jail and received a $1000 fine for a stick-swinging incident. While disagreeing with the verdict, McSorley chose not to appeal the case, saying he wanted to put the situation behind him.

Canoeing

Caroline Brunet – Victories and Disappointments

CSI/COA

When the 2000 Summer Olympics in Sydney closed, kayaker Caroline Brunet had won a silver medal in the 500m K-1 event. Most athletes in the world would be full of happiness with such an accomplishment. But for Caroline conquering everyone in the world except one was a failure, a cruel disappointment.

The athlete to whom everyone had conceded the gold medal had a difficult time in this Olympic race. The benefits of ten years of preparation were swept away in an instant by the uncontrollable variations in the weather that are often responsible for disrupting sporting events. On that day, the elements were raging. Athletes waited for hours in the dressing rooms before officials finally decided that the races would go on despite strong winds that were battering the Olympic canoeing basin. They were facing an immovable deadline, since it was already the last day of competition. Despite the pleas of the athletes to delay the race so they could challenge each others' talents and technique under normal conditions, the International Olympic Committee, the Organizing Committee and the International Federation refused to bend, and decreed that the races could not be held after Closing Ceremonies.

The final races were duly held, and history recorded that Josefa Idem Guerrini of Italy won the gold medal in the 500m K-1. Caroline finished second, seeing her dream slip away.

It was her fourth Olympic competition, and yet again she failed to reach her main goal — winning Olympic gold. In Seoul in 1988, she reached the semi-finals in the 500m K-1 and 500m K-4 while paddling in her first Olympics. At the Barcelona Olympics in 1992 she improved to seventh in the K-1 and sixth in the K-4.

Brunet then restructured her training program, moved to Denmark and enlisted former world champion Christian Frederickson as her coach. The changes paid off. In Atlanta in 1996, she won a silver medal, finishing just .2 seconds behind the gold medallist. But for Brunet, finishing so close and yet not winning the gold medal was a difficult pill to swallow.

Many athletes would be happy to have done their best and had a chance to participate in the Olympics. Brunet was never one to rest on her laurels, though, and always wanted to push herself further.

During the three years leading up to the Sydney Olympics, Brunet dominated all her competitors, winning eight of the nine World Championship gold medals that were up for grabs in K-1 events. In 1997, she finished first in the 200m, 500m and 1000m at the World Championships in Dartmouth, Nova Scotia. The next year in Szeged, Hungary, she again took the 200m and the 500m, and finished second in the 1000m. Then in 1999, it was triple gold again, this time in Milan, Italy.

By the time she got to Sydney, Brunet was clearly the favourite, her status emphasized by being chosen as the Canadian team flag bearer in the Opening Ceremonies. She had been training 30 hours a week, including 20 on the water and another 10 in the gym. At 31 years old, the perfectionist from Lac Beauport, Quebec, had put in so many hours of intense training that she said before the Sydney Olympics, "When I retire from competition, I'm never going back into a gym." Her demanding regimen didn't give her a moment's respite and left her exhausted. Her shoulders were sore, and her hips tired. Her solid 5' 8" frame had been mistreated, particularly in her lower back. Eighteen years after winning her first race at home in Lac Beauport at the age of 13, she was so close to her goal. Nevertheless, the forces of nature were unleashed, making things still more difficult for her.

CSI/COA

Brunet knew well that millions of strokes of her paddle had worn her away, and that the difference between gold and silver was infinitesimal. On May 29, 2000, she told Le Devoir report Mylène Moisan, "I train to win. All I can do is work on myself. I can't control my opponents, so I work on myself as much as possible."

Brunet was also aware that some of her opponents might have taken performance enhancing drugs. Kayaking is a physically demanding sport. She added to the reporter, "When I knew that I was racing against people who were using drugs, I knew what I was up against. I've been beaten that way before. It's possible to win clean, but it's harder. Personally, I don't want to win by cheating."

There were in fact questions raised about Guerrini of Italy, and other members of the Italian team, about drug use. Beating Brunet by .79 seconds in an event Brunet had won handily for several years, Guerrini later turned out to be one of 61 athletes identified by Italian journalists as having tested positive for banned substances before the Olympics.

But Brunet would not have wanted to get a gold medal after the Games. She told a Montreal Gazette reporter in December 2000, "For me, it would not have the same meaning if they gave me a gold medal today. There was one gold medal to win at the finish line, not one year, or two or three years later. Of course I would have hoped for a different ending, but I've moved on. I think people generally exaggerated my disappointment."

The winner of the Lou Marsh Trophy as Canada's top athlete in 1999 added, "I'm going to take a year off and see how much I miss competing. I need rest for my body to recover. Sometimes I think it will be easy to retire from competition. Other days, I'm not so sure. I have even thought about the 2004 Olympics in Athens, but that's so far away." ❧

Brunet Highlights

Caroline Brunet's K-1 Career Highlights

Olympic Games

2000 Sydney	Silver	K-1 500m
1996 Atlanta	Silver	K-1 500m
1992 Barcelona	7th	K-1 500m
1988 Seoul	13th	K-1 500m

World Championships

1999	Gold	K-1 500m, K-1 1000m
1998	Gold	K-1 500m, K-1 200m
1997	Gold	K-1 500m, K-1 200m, K-1 1000m

Canadian Championships

1991-1999	Gold	K-1 500m

Canada

2000

C u r l i n g

In Too Few Years,
a Life to Remember

by Bruce Wallace
March 13, 2000

If there was any sense that curling was not getting the respect it deserved at the 1998 Nagano Winter Olympics, Sandra Schmirler never let on. Tucked away in the snowy mountain resort of Karuizawa, 66 km southeast from the main action in Nagano, Schmirler and her Canadian teammates played with exuberance on the ice, and were enthusiastic boosters of the sport off it. After games, they would linger over beers to explain the sport they loved to curious foreign reporters and confused Japanese fans for whom curling was a chaos of ricocheting rocks.

Schmirler's forever friendly exterior masked the tremendous stress she carried within. It was not just the pressure to bring home gold for the hundreds of thousands of curling-mad Canadians, but the emotional burden of being 15 times zones away from her infant daughter Sara, who stayed at home in Regina with Schmirler's husband, Shannon England, a computer systems analyst. Publicly, she had a curt answer to those who asked about the separation. "I have a beautiful daughter and that's the most important thing," she'd say. Privately, it was tougher to cope. When three-month-old Joey Hart arrived in Karuizawa where his father, Richard, was playing for Canada's men's team, Schmirler burst into tears at her first sight of the baby.

It was clear in the tributes that followed her death from cancer at just 36 last week that Schmirler will be remembered as much for her devotion to friends and family as for her success on the world's curling sheets. And the Biggar, Sask., native's sporting achievements were substantial. She and her rink of Jan Betker, Joan

McCusker and Marcia Gudereit dominated the sport through the 1990s, winning three Canadian championships and three world titles to go with that first-ever Olympic gold. They did so with a style that declared they were just best friends out having a good time, almost amused that these wonderful things were happening to *them*.

The route to the top began in the flatlands of Biggar, where Schmirler and her two older sisters were introduced to curling by their parents, Shirley and Art. She was an all-around athlete, a good competitive swimmer, and she threw her first rocks on natural ice curling sheets flooded on the farm of her childhood friend Anita Silvernagle, who lived just outside of town. "Sandra was a fierce competitor — even as a kid she hated losing," recalled Silvernagle who skipped the rink with Schmirler playing third that won the 1981 Saskatchewan high-school championship. Silvernagle remained a lifelong friend, and described the sacrifices Schmirler made to climb to the top of her sport: the thousands of rocks thrown, the hours spent watching tapes of her delivery, the summer vacations sacrificed in order to have the time available to travel for winter competitions. "She gave up lots of things once she got that taste of winning," says Silvernagle.

As an adult, Schmirler curled out of Regina, where the competition even at the club level was always world-class. Her success made her famous in a sport that is the winter lifeblood of so many Canadian communities. "You could say curling is as much for the spirit as for the flesh," says the main character in Saskatchewan writer W.O. Mitchell's *The Black Bonspiel of Willie MacCrimmon*. That essence was apparent in Schmirler's emotional style: the hugs for teammates, the open joy in shots made. And when she showed up in Biggar for the annual rodeo days in the summer of 1998, she brought her gold medal and Olympic team jacket along, and let anyone who wanted try them on.

The cancer that claimed her was discovered in August, 1999, less than two months after the birth of her second daughter, Jenna, and only four months after her father died of cancer. Doctors attacked the tumour that was pressing on her esophagus with radiation and chemotherapy, but they were never able to determine the exact nature of the disease. While recovering from the treatments, she turned down countless requests for interviews and appearances, preferring to fight her battle privately, and spend every possible moment among loved ones, especially with her two little girls.

But as she began to feel better, she agreed to provide commentary on telecasts of the Canadian junior championship in Moncton last month. In a teary but brave news conference there, just three weeks before she died, an alternately funny and combative Schmirler declared her illness had made her see the world differently, and spoke of her wish to spend as much time with her family as possible. "I now know losing a curling game isn't the end of the world," she said. There are many, though, who say that Sandra Schmirler *never* lost sight of those things — family, friends, where you are from — that are most important in life. ♣

CSI/COA

Schmirler Highlights

Sandra Schmirler's Career Highlights

1993	Canadian Champion	World Champion
1994	Canadian Champion	World Champion
1997	Canadian Champion	World Champion
1998	Olympic Champion	

While everyone who competes in sport
strives to win, the top step of the podium
is reserved for a select few.
However, the feeling of pride and
celebration is shared by many,
whether it is a local minor hockey
tournament or a gold medal at the
Olympics. Often we celebrate winners as
national heroes, but we also see in them
a reflection of everyone's desire to be
their best, to strive for excellence, to win.
In Victory, we celebrate our homegrown
heroes and the moments
when they thrilled us all with their
exceptional achievements.

1937   1991
900   1962
1938   1992
902   1967
1940   1993
905   1971
1948   1994
909   1973
1950   1999
912   1976
1952   2000
915   1978
1954
928   1980
1955
930   1984
1956
935   1989
1957
936   1990
1960

Canada

Our
Century
in Sport

1900-2000

Chapter IV

Victory

**Team Canada '72
leader, Phil Esposito**

Brian Pickell

The Beginnings

On September 2, 1972, at 8:29 P.M. Eastern Standard Time, an American referee named Gordon Lee skated into the centre ice circle at the Montreal Forum and dropped a puck between a Canadian named Phil Esposito and a Soviet named Vladimir Petrov. In his 18 years as an amateur hockey official, Lee had presided at hundreds of game-opening faceoffs, more than he or anyone else could remember, but this one was different. This one he would remember for the rest of his life, and so would millions of Canadian hockey fans — because that simple act of dropping the puck between Esposito and Petrov started the clock on the greatest hockey series in history: Team Canada vs. the USSR National Team.

Between September 2 and September 28, 1972, Esposito and 34 of the best hockey players in Canada, all of them stars in the National Hockey League, played eight games against Petrov and 27 of the best players in the Union of Soviet Socialist Republics. Four games in Canada — in Montreal, Toronto, Winnipeg, Vancouver — and four games in Moscow. It had been 20 years since Canada had won an Olympic gold medal in hockey; 11 years since a Canadian team had won the world hockey championship. During that time, Soviet hockey teams had won three gold medals and were 10 times world champions. Still, we clung to the belief that ours were the best hockey players in the world. International rules had prevented us from sending our best players, our pros, to compete in the Olympics and world championships, even though the Soviets were amateurs only by strict definition. This then, the first meeting between our best and their best, a special exhibition series arranged by Hockey Canada, the Canadian Amateur Hockey Association and the Soviet Hockey Federation, would be a test. These eight games would tell the story. Which country really developed the finest hockey players, Canada or the USSR?

HHOF — Graphic Artists

in September 1972

But this was more than just a sporting event, because for Canadians, hockey is more than just a sport. It's our national game, a part of our culture, our history, our national identity. Hockey is the one thing about which we have always been able to say, "We are the best." The Soviets have their writers, their musicians, their scientists. Our heroes, with names like Morenz, Clancy, Conacher, Chabot, Schriner, Durnan, Bauer, Bentley, Howe and Béliveau, have been hockey players. Not that there haven't been other men in other fields just as worthy, but the hockey player, with his speed, his grace, his strength and his physical bearing has touched something that runs strong and deep in the Canadian consciousness. If the Soviets lost this series, they would lose no more than that, a hockey series. But for Canadians, haunted by the knowledge that the world doubted our superiority at the game we called our own, there was more at stake. To lose this series would be to lose face.

If ever Canada was a Main Street, it was on the night of September 2, as Team Canada and the Soviets faced off for the first time. Elsewhere in the world, even in the Soviet Union, sport enthusiasts were caught up in the excitement of the Olympic Games in Munich. But in Canada the struggle about to begin between these two hockey teams seemed a thousand times more important than what was happening anywhere. For 27 days Canadians would put aside cares of unemployment, inflation, the impending federal election and the war in the Middle East, engrossed in the hockey players who were setting out to defend something more Canadian than the maple leaf on their sweaters. In places as distant as Corner Brook and Prince Rupert and as different as Regina and Rimouski, in living rooms and bars, 12 million Canadians were huddled in front of television sets, watching as Esposito and Petrov took the series' first faceoff.

Petrov's stick was faster, beating Esposito's to the spot where Lee had dropped the puck and batting it toward the Team Canada goal. The series had begun. It would not be won until the last minute of the last game, and by that time, after the most exhilarating 480 minutes of hockey anyone can remember, Canadians would have learned far more than whether we were still the world's greatest hockey players. We would have learned humility, and we would have lost our complacency. ❦

(Reprinted from "27 Days in September," courtesy Canadian Hockey Association and Team Canada 1972)

Canada's Team of the Century

In a public opinion poll conducted by the Canadian Press at the end of 1999, Team Canada '72 was selected as Canada's *"Team of the Century."* Not surprisingly, the clear choice for the Canadian *"Sporting Moment of the Century,"* was Paul Henderson's series-winning goal with 34 seconds remaining.
Interestingly, team members received no payment for their participation in the Series and, in fact, received no formal recognition at all – no cup, no trophy, no bonuses. They did, of course, receive undying fame.
In December, 2000, Team Canada '72 was honoured by the Hockey Hall of Fame as the greatest team of the 20th Century. Almost every player from the team was present as the Hall unveiled a special monument depicting the Team's achievement. To cheers of the popular 1972 rallying cry, *"Nyet Nyet Soviet, Da Da Canada,"* the players greeted their many fans and accepted their due recognition.

HHOF

Coach Harry Sinden

Brian Pickell

H o c k e y

Views from the Bench

by Ron Ellis

Training camp – August 1972

The phone rang. The selection committee for Team Canada '72 called to invite me to participate in the Summit Series against the Soviet Union. Thirty-five players were being selected to take part in a training camp at Maple Leaf Gardens in Toronto

Brian Pickell

The series was what all Canada was waiting for and our professional players as well. The Soviets were perennial World Champions and Olympic Champions, but until now they had not faced our Canadian pros. Each player that attended the camp would participate in at least one of the eight games that would be played across Canada and in Moscow.

Before the first practice session, I looked over the lineup sheet. I was assigned to a line with Paul Henderson, my teammate in Toronto, and Bobby Clarke, the young leader of the Flyers. We were not the first line listed on the sheet, but, after the first day on the ice, we caught the attention of the coaching staff. Our unit stayed together for the entire series. Bobby Clarke was a younger version of Norm Ullman, who centred Paul and I on the Leafs. We did not have to make a lot of adjustments to our game. As well, all three of us played in both ends of the rink and this certainly helped to handle the Russian counter attacks.

All I know is that we were named to the starting lineup for game one in Montreal

The shock of game one

Brian Pickell

The tension was electrifying in the Montreal Forum. Prime Minister Trudeau dropped the puck in the opening ceremonies and the much-anticipated game was on. Esposito scored at the 30-second mark followed by a Henderson goal a few moments later. Just like everyone said, it will be a romp, right? Not so. I remember when we were up 2-0 Paul said to me on the bench after a tough shift, "This is going to be a long series." I gave him an affirmative nod mainly because of the pain I was feeling in my chest and legs. Even though we had jumped into an early lead, it was obvious that they were a match for us. The Russians tied the score before the period was over and went on to a convincing 7-3 win. Shock waves were felt from coast to coast. How could this happen? Our team was set back to say the least by the play of the talented, well-conditioned Soviet team. One player in particular caught my eye. His name was Valeri Kharlamov and his two goals in the second period set the tone for the rest of the game.

Getting even in game two

After a collision in the first game with an opponent, I woke up the next morning unable to move my neck. My first thought was maybe I wouldn't be able to play another game, as I couldn't shoot the puck. I told the training staff about my condition. They passed the info onto Coach Sinden. Harry asked me if I could take on the role of trying to shut down the dangerous Kharlamov. I wanted to stay in the lineup and took on the challenge for game two. The team played well in Toronto. We had to win. Going down two games to nil was out of the question. Two great goals for Canada come to mind. First a spectacular power play goal by Yvan Cournoyer on a neat setup from Brad Park as Yvan streaked around a defender and deftly deposited the puck in the net. The second was a short-handed goal by Peter Mahovlich who undressed a Soviet defender before deking Tretiak for the score. That goal made it a 3-1 game after Yakushev cut our 2-0 lead in half. We went on to tie the series with a 4-1 win. Kharlamov didn't score.

HHOF — Graphic Artists

Taking charge – almost

The Winnipeg game proved to be critical to the outcome of the series. If Team Canada could win this game and gain momentum for game four, the series would be well in hand.

With a little over six minutes remaining in the second period; we held a well-deserved 4-2 lead. By the end of the period it was tied 4-4 and that's how the game ended as there was no scoring in the third period. Tretiak was outstanding as he stopped 38 shots and was selected the player of the game for his team. We let the Soviets off the hook and we would soon pay the price.

Trying, but playing poorly

Our team did not play well in Vancouver. The effort was there but the results were not. Couple this with a Soviet team that knew if they could win in Vancouver, they would then have a stranglehold on the series. The final score was 5-3 in favour of the Soviets. After the four games in Canada, the Soviet's record was two wins, one loss and a tie.

Brian Pickell

This was the low point of the series and the low point of my hockey career. The Vancouver fans were frustrated as was all of Canada and this frustration was exhibited as they booed our team off the ice. The media called for our team to win all eight games by large scores. The fans believed the articles and broadcasts and when it wasn't happening, we got the brunt of it. I didn't blame the fans at this point of the series. Their frustration was justified. The unknown in the grand scheme of things was just how good the Soviets were and how well prepared they were for this series.

Phil's speech

Phil Esposito was our team leader from the first day of training camp. Espo is a competitor and he wanted to win this series and was willing to do anything to make it happen. He set the tone at our training camp and it was infectious. It was fitting that he scored the first goal of the series. Phil was the right guy to interview after the game in Vancouver. The players didn't see it live but we knew he would represent us well. Did he ever. When I first saw the interview I was blown away. Here was a player dripping in perspiration, frustrated and angry. He basically said two things. First that our guys were giving our best and second that the Soviets were a much better team than anyone in Canada could have imagined. He pointed out the main reason our guys were playing and that was because we were Canadian and wanted to represent our country. We were not playing for money.

Our pension fund was to receive part of the profits from the series and Phil made it clear that they could throw that out the window. Being Canadian and having an opportunity to take on the Big Bad Bear was our only motivation.

Becoming a team

Before heading to Moscow for the remaining games, we spent 10 days in Sweden. The time in Sweden would serve two purposes. First, Team Canada was supposed to be up in the series at this time with four lopsided wins and a few days in Sweden would be a little holiday. Secondly, the two scheduled games with the Swedish National Team would allow our players to familiarize themselves with the large international ice surface. *If the team had gone straight into Moscow after the demoralizing loss in Vancouver, I dare say the final outcome may have been different.*

In Sweden, we became a team. Remember now that we were 35 players from different NHL teams and some bad blood had built up over the years. Now we had to put egos and animosity on the back burner and prepare for the challenge of beating the Soviets in Moscow. The team practised hard and played two spirited games with the Swedes, taking three of four points. The team was going into Moscow with a new mindset.

The two Bobbys:

What difference would Orr and Hull have made in the series?

Bobby Hull would have been selected to the team in a heartbeat. However, he had just joined the Winnipeg Jets in the new World Hockey Association and this series had been negotiated with the NHL. He would have made a difference with his speed, strength and shot. As a matter of fact, he was in the audience during the game in Winnipeg and I know he was pulling for us. Let's not forget that Bobby is first of all a Canadian and proud of it. He represented the WHA in a similar series in 1974 and displayed his superior skills to the Soviets.

Bobby Orr of course was invited to training camp. Unfortunately, he was going through a time when he was recovering from more knee surgery. He gave it a valiant try and much against his will decided he was not fit enough to play. Bobby Orr, however, did not go home. He stayed with the team throughout the entire series in Canada and Russia. Bobby was a real inspiration to the team. Just having him around the dressing room passing on what he saw on the ice was invaluable. Bobby was able to play in the first Canada Cup in 1976 and was selected the MVP of the series and he also showed the Soviets skills they had never faced before. Even off the ice, he was a big part of our team. So much so, that all of us wanted his name on the monument that was unveiled for Canada's Team of the Century at the Hockey Hall of Fame in Toronto. Thankfully, he agreed.

Not having Hull or Orr in the lineup only added to the adversity Team Canada '72 overcame on the road to victory.

The games in Moscow: at first deceiving

Canadian fans, after having time to digest Phil's speech in Vancouver, made their own assessment of the series. When we arrived at the arena in Moscow, large mail sacks full of telegrams and cards were waiting for us. We taped them to the walls in the dressing rooms until we ran out of space. A new-look Team Canada took the play to the Soviets and built up a 4-1 lead by the 4:56 mark of the third period. Then the roof caved in. Our team made a couple of costly errors and also had some bad luck. However, the Soviets deserved full marks for scoring four unanswered goals in the third period with a marvelous display of hockey skills and skated to victory with a 5-4 win. They thought they had delivered the final fatal blow, but that was not the case. The team to a man knew we had controlled the Russians for most of the game and strongly felt we could do it again. A key factor at this time was that the 3,000 Canadian fans in Moscow gave us a standing ovation as we skated off the ice. They hadn't given up on us yet.

Brian Pickell

Brian Pickell

Games six and seven: the set up

Team Canada had to win the final three games in Moscow. A tie would give the Soviets the victory. The team was confident but all hockey fans know what can happen with a bouncing puck. No scoring in the first and the Soviets scored first early in the second period. It did not look good, but in true Canadian style, Dennis Hull, Cournoyer and Henderson scored within a minute and a half. Paul's goal stood up as the winner in a 3-2 victory. The longest two minutes of my life happened at the end of the third period. I took a holding penalty at the 17:39 mark. The guys killed it off and we were one step closer in our Canadian comeback.

The win in game six gave us a chance to get back in the series if we could win the seventh game. This time we scored the first goal. Guess who — our leader Espo capped off a power play marker. The Russians, true to their character, kept coming at us and went ahead 2-1. However, Espo responded again to see the first period end at two goals each. There was no scoring in the second period and the tension was building.

Rod Gilbert, who gave his all throughout the series, scored a key goal to give us the lead back early in the third period. We were holding Kharlamov off the score sheet, but their other star Yakushev scored his second of the game to tie it up. It was now time for Paul to score his second winning goal in two games. He would not allow himself to be denied as he beat three different Russian players and scored on Tretiak as he was falling to the ice. It was an incredible effort. The final minutes ticked off and we had now tied up the series.

Victory & relief: "we did it!"

Everything that could happen in a game happened in game eight:

The referee fiasco leads to early penalties and a 1-0 lead on another goal by Yakushev. The team played hard and we fought through a lot of adversity, however at the end of the second period we found ourselves trailing 5-3. How could this be happening? Every player has given so much to get us back in the series and now with one period left we had another mountain to climb. I will always remember the atmosphere in the dressing room between the second and third periods. I think most Canadian hockey fans would have understood if we had lost control of our emotions at this time. What I remember is a group of athletes that were composed and confident. It is a memory I will carry for a lifetime.

We knew we needed an early goal. Again our leader seemed to say, "follow me" and Phil scored that goal at the 2:27 mark of the third period. The action on the ice was intense and highly skilled. Both teams had numerous scoring chances and the goaltending of Dryden and Tretiak was superb. Finally after a lot of work by Espo, Cournoyer tallied to tie the score at 5-5 around mid-way through the third period. This is when our team, with Pete Mahovlich leading the way, rescued Al Eagleson from the Russian police and brought him back to our bench. The police had grabbed him when he approached

Brian Pickell

the timekeeper's box to ask why the red light had not gone on after Cournoyer's goal. Seeing a Canadian grabbed because of an unjust call seemed to help us dig even deeper. As one, the team rallied; we would not let down.

The last ten minutes of that game was the most exciting hockey of my career. Both teams played at such a high level it probably would have been fair if the score had remained a tie. However, word came to our bench that if the score remained tied, the Soviets were going to claim victory because of the differential in goals for and against. With this report, we seemed to be able to reach down for more energy and effort. After coming off the ice with about a minute left in the game, my teammate Paul stood up and called Peter Mahovlich off the ice. This is something you do not do in a game, particularly at the pro level. I think Peter wanted to give Paul another chance at a winning goal and he came off. Paul jumped over the boards and headed for the Russian goal. Cournoyer and Espo were working hard in the Russian end and finally Espo intercepted a pass and threw the puck at the net. Paul was right on the spot and on the second effort slid the puck into the net under Tretiak for a 6-5 lead. The team jumped all over Paul and everyone was saying, "We did it, we did it."

We still had 34 seconds to play. Coach Sinden showed some confidence in me as he sent me out to help kill off those final seconds. I will savour those moments after the victory forever. In the dressing room after the game, there was not a lot of celebration. Everyone was emotionally spent. There would be time to celebrate later.

Afterthoughts

When the plane lifted off the runway in Moscow, the team spontaneously broke out into a very spirited rendition of O Canada. Our first stop on the way home was in Montreal. Prime Minister Trudeau met us, along with 25,000 fans. We were put on fire trucks and driven around the tarmac to be greeted by the fans who were also singing O Canada in English and in French. It didn't seem to matter. Some of our players remained in Montreal and then we headed for Toronto where we were welcomed by 50,000 fans standing in the pouring rain at City Hall.

What a great day to be a Canadian

There was little time to celebrate as players reported to their respective training camps that were already in progress. In just a few days we would be facing each other in NHL league games. But, it would never be the same after what we went through together and the bond we formed in our own private war. Yes, we would play hard against each other but it would be with respect and admiration. I know for me, every time I played against Espo, Park, Clarke or Gilbert, there would always be smiles. As Espo said, "I went through war with these guys." We were a team, and the time and atmosphere of the day enabled all of Canada to gather with us. It is for that, I believe, that a 1999 Canadian Press poll named us Canada's "Team of the Century." I think we were, too.

I am so thankful for this experience not only for the impact it had had on my life, but also for the impact the series had on Canada as a nation. ♣

Henderson Scores for Canada!

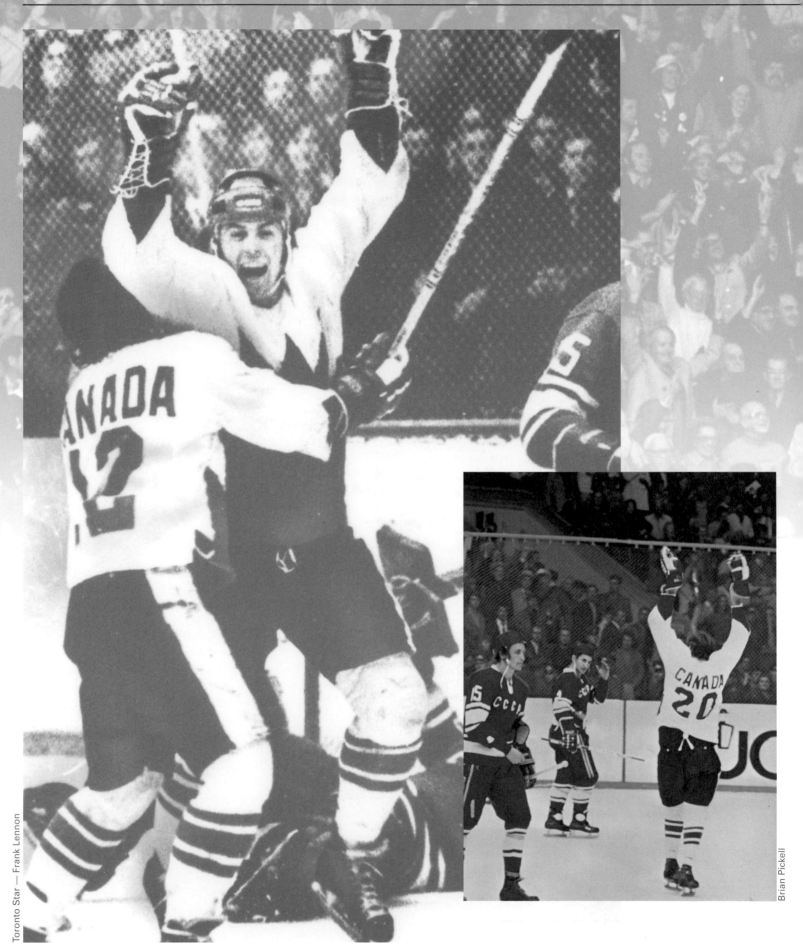

Toronto Star — Frank Lennon

Brian Pickell

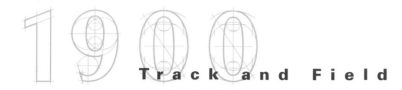

1900

Track and Field

The Unknown Olympian:

George Orton won his gold medal eight years before Canada even sent a team to the Games

by Tom Boreskie
September 4, 2000

On a sweltering July afternoon in 1900, George Orton, a stocky runner from Strathroy, Ont., stepped on a track in Paris to a smattering of cheers, mostly from American spectators. Having dominated North American middle-distance running for nearly a decade, Orton had come to Paris to compete in several events, including his specialty, the steeplechase, at the second — ever modern Olympic Games. It was Orton's day-he defeated Britain's Sidney Robinson by two seconds to become Canada's first-ever Olympic champion. But there was no celebration back in Canada, nor any hero's welcome when Orton sailed home. The reason? Orton achieved his distinction as a member of the United States squad because Canada didn't send a team to the 1900 Games.

One hundred years later, as 309 Canadian athletes prepare to compete at the Sydney Olympics next month, Orton's story is a tale of a very different time. Born in 1873, he became involved in athletics literally by accident. Temporarily paralyzed by a fall in childhood, he had overcome his handicap by running behind the family horse-drawn buggy, which had earned him the nickname "the boy who never walked." When his father, impressed with his son's speed, entered him in a local track meet, Orton won the half-mile and the mile. He continued to run while attending the University of Toronto and, later, the University of Pennsylvania in Philadelphia, where he won more American national championships than any previous athlete. That competitive record — and fairly relaxed rules

concerning US citizenship — earned Orton a spot on the American team. But he wasn't the only Canadian ringer wearing red, white and blue: he was joined by 800- and 1,500-m runner Alexander Grant of St. Mary's, Ont., his brother Dick, and Ronald MacDonald of Heatherton, N.S. MacDonald won the 1898 Boston Marathon, while Dick Grant was runner-up in 1899.

The athletics competition, which opened on Bastille Day, July 14, was marred by controversy. For a track, organizers had simply marked out a 500-m oval in the grass at a Paris horseracing circuit. To the athletes' amazement, the course had several dips and mounds, while its final straightaway ran slightly uphill through a grove of trees, causing spectators searching for a better view to leave their seats and inadvertently interfere with the competition.

The Americans arrived in Paris to find the finals of several events, including the 2,500-m steeplechase, had been scheduled for the next day, a Sunday, despite earlier assurances no Sunday competitions would be held. A number of US competitors boycotted for religious reasons, so in Orton's first event, the 400-m hurdles, only three runners answered the starter's call. Orton finished last, but that was good enough for the first medal ever by a Canadian at the Olympic Games.

Less than an hour later, he returned to the track for the steeplechase. The clear favourite, Orton was content to let others set the pace until the final lap. "About 300 yards from home," Orton later wrote in the *Philadelphia Inquirer*, "I seemed to realize that I was in the race for which I had come 4,000 miles." As the runners headed into the woods, Orton began his sprint and emerged from the trees with a sizeable lead. He won easily, collapsing across the line in world-record time.

Orton's Canadian teammates were less fortunate. Alex Grant was not able to adjust to the bizarre track conditions, while the marathoners, Dick Grant and MacDonald, struggled in grueling 39°C heat on a poorly supervised course routed through the streets of Paris. Both finished more than an hour behind the winner: MacDonald claimed the first three finishers had taken shortcuts, while Dick Grant unsuccessfully sued the International Olympic Committee, maintaining he was knocked down by a cyclist as he was about to overtake the leaders.

Soon after the Paris Games, Orton gave up competitive athletics to become track coach at the University of Pennsylvania and manager of the Penn Relays, the largest annual US collegiate track meet. He retired to New Hampshire where he lived until his death in 1958. Though a modest and unassuming man who considered himself only a "fair runner," he was revered in his adopted home. One Philadelphia sportswriter hailed him back then as the "premier American athlete of all time."

In Canada, however, Orton received no formal recognition for his Olympic victory during his lifetime. It was only in 1977, years after his citizenship came to public light, that he was inducted into his native country's Sports Hall of Fame. But even with that honour, Orton remains Canada's greatest unknown Olympian. ♣

Highlights

General Highlights

1900

At the start of the century George Dixon was the world featherweight boxing champion (and had been for most of the previous 10 years).

Eddie Connolly from St. John, New Brunswick, was the world welterweight boxing champion.

Toronto cyclist Archie McEachern won the world 25-mile cycling championships. Later in the year, and again in 1901, McEachern and his American partner shared the victory in the international paired six-day bicycle race in New York, and $1500.

1901

Canadian paddlers from Toronto and Montreal won every event in a series of canoe races held in Buffalo, New York, as part of a Pan American sports exhibition.

1904

Lou Scholes of Toronto won the prestigious Diamond Sculls race at Henley-on-Thames, England, setting a new course record in the process.

1905

M. Thompson of New Brunswick won her first of four straight Canadian Ladies' Golf Championships.

1906-08

Tommy Burns won the world heavyweight boxing title, defeating Marvin Hart in Los Angeles. Burns successfully defended the title 15 times, in sanctioned and exhibition bouts.

1907-14

Johnny Coloun of Toronto was declared the world bantamweight (also referred to as paperweight at the time) boxing champion, a title he held for seven years.

Johnny Coloun, 1907

John Scholes won the Canadian, US and British featherweight boxing titles to be declared the undisputed amateur featherweight world champion.

Etienne Desmarteau

The Irish-American Olympian John Flanagan eyed his superbly conditioned Canadian rival Etienne Desmarteau with considerable worry. Two years before, the strongman from Montreal had beaten him in the New York championships and now they were meeting again in the final of the 56-pound weight throw at the 1904 summer Olympics in St. Louis, the first games ever held in North America.

"Tell me sir," Flanagan asked, "I got three months off from the New York police but they're not paying me. How much time did your captain give you to come here?"

"You're better off than me monsieur," Desmarteau replied, "They told me I could go when I asked for two weeks, but don't count on having your job when you return."

"You Canadians do things in strange ways. We need all the time we can get to prepare for this throw."

Throwers did in fact need any edge they could get in the 56-pound event. The standard 16-pound hammer throw continues today as an Olympic challenge, but the 56-pound weight was contested only in these 1904 Games and then in 1920. The heavier stone took all of an athlete's concentration and mettle just to nudge it beyond 10 metres.

It was first day of September but already the games had been running two months. They would continue to nearly the end of November. Staged as a virtual sideshow to the St. Louis World's Fair, most events were dominated by Americans against the occasional Canadian or European. Among the outsiders was Toronto's George Lyon who beat a field of over 70 Americans to win the golfing gold, while a Canadian soccer team from Galt beat two American rivals for first place.

Canada hadn't sent a team to either of the first two Olympics, although at the 1900 games, George Orton, a former University of Toronto student and Canadian citizen won gold as part of the United States team. Historians on both sides of the border claim Orton's steeplechase medal as their own.

Pictures of Desmarteau show him to be extraordinarily fit and well proportioned. There was no huge gut, nor the deliberate movement which characterizes many contemporary big throwers. His ancestors had originally come to Quebec in 1757 and the original family patriarch was a blacksmith whose shop bore the image of two crossed hammers earning him the nickname of Des Marteaux. 150 years later the family tradition carried on in athletic competition.

Desmarteau was representing not only Canada but also the Montreal Amateur Athletic Association (MAAA), an organization that had deep roots in the city's sporting heritage.

He was born in Montreal in 1877 and was, at 6'1" and 225 lbs., the smallest of five brothers. A Montreal police captain spotted him working in a foundry owned by the Canadian Pacific Railway, and figured he was just what the police needed if they were to compete in sporting contests against rival forces in Toronto, Boston, and New York.

Joining the Montreal police was a stroke of good fortune for Etienne. Quebec had a tradition of great strong men, none more so than Louis Cyr, who once lifted a load of 4,100 pounds on a platform stretched across his back. These athletes depended on gate money appearances to earn a living, though, and this disqualified them from amateur events like the Olympic Games.

As a police officer, Desmarteau could not only afford the MAAA's annual fee of $10, but had a job which both encouraged his continuing fitness and supported his travel to competitions on behalf of the force. His athletic success owed much to his background as a football player, the sport that first got him into the MAAA in 1902.

When it came time for the Olympics two years later the club provided the then not inconsiderable sum of $600 to send him and four other club athletes, along with a trainer, to St. Louis.

Using both hands to grip a triangular bar which was attached to a large paving stone, Desmarteau would swing the weight taking just one turn within the nine-foot ring. Before throwing he focused on the three essentials of the throw — balance, strength, and timing. The weight took tremendous fortitude just to move and the act of actually swinging and throwing it required incredible concentration.

Even though the competition took place in late summer, the heat in St. Louis was oppressive. "Not sure I should have eaten so much," Flanagan groaned, and turning to his teammates he lowered his voice, "Boys I'm not feeling too well, one of you better show your stuff or that Canadian is going to beat all of us."

Desmarteau's 56-pound weight sailed from his outstretched arms and plunked into the sun-baked St. Louis turf 10.46 metres away. He smiled while John Flanagan and his teammates, the other five entrants besides Desmarteau, groaned. Only Flanagan with a 10.16 metre toss was close. James Mitchell, a veteran tosser who had set a hammer throw world record in 1892, was third.

In true Olympic spirit Flanagan and the others lifted Desmarteau on their shoulders and carried him around the field.

By winning, Etienne had denied the United States a sweep of the track and field gold medals. And so he returned to Montreal a hero. His job was quickly restored and a life of apparent fame awaited.

Life's cruel fate however imposed itself on the first Canadian to win a gold medal while competing for his home country. No one would have guessed that within a year of his triumphal 1904 Olympics Desmarteau would succumb to typhoid.

Years later a park was named after Canada's first undisputed gold medallist and he became one of five Canadians recognized on postage stamps saluting Canadian Olympians. ❧

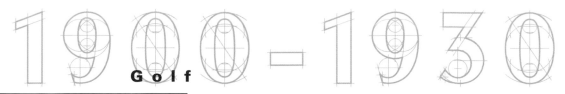

Golf

He Plays a Grand Game o' Gowf

By James A. Cowan
August 15, 1926

One day after he had finished a cricket match at the Rosedale ground, Toronto, George S. Lyon leaped a fence to a neighbouring golf course — he was in his thirty-ninth year — and, throwing away his bat, picked up a driver for the first time in his life. Next summer he went through to the semi-finals of the Canadian amateur golf championship. That's the kind of athlete he is!

He can properly be termed the dean of American golfers, and he is the most unique golfer in Canada, or in America, for that matter. There is no record of any other man taking up the game at the mature age of thirty-eight and then becoming an internationally-known wizard of the links, which is what Mr. Lyon did. Nearly three-score and ten, he is today the finest senior player on the continent, and if all the experts of any age who could be certain of defeating him today were gathered in one place, there would be no mob visible.

His greatest single triumph, perhaps, was the winning of the Olympic Cup at St. Louis twenty-two years ago. This is likely to remain the nearest thing to an actual world's amateur championship that any human being can attain. In this advanced age, the number of good golfers on the earth's greens is terrific and not even a Hercules with no other labours to perform could organize a tournament which would select the finest.

In the final at St. Louis, Mr. Lyon defeated Chandler Egan, then American amateur champion, by three up and two to play in a thirty-six hole match. That year, as Jess Sweetser's victory this season has recalled, was the last previous occasion on which an American carried off the British amateur title. Walter Travis had returned victorious from the Old Country only to be decisively beaten by Egan in the play for the American title. Egan, in turn, met his Waterloo when he tackled Mr. Lyon. The latter can never be induced to assert that he was a world's title-holder, but these are facts from the book and every man can draw his own conclusion.

It sounds highly reasonable to announce, then, that at the end of the 1904 season, a Canadian was sitting most definitely and unmistakably on the top of the heap.

The trophy which Mr. Lyon brought back from St. Louis as tangible evidence of the laurels he had won was a majestic creation which at the time, set a new record in the sporting world by reason of its all-round elaborateness.

Now it holds an important place among Mr. Lyon's collection of awards, not only because of the spectacular victory which brought it into his possession, but also because it represents, to him, the most gruelling week of golf he ever went through. He has since taken part in hundreds of contests but not one has equalled the Olympic matches so far as that aspect of the game is concerned.

On Monday, eighty-seven crack golfers stepped out for the qualifying round which eliminated all but thirty-two, and in this round Mr. Lyon was seventh. Each day, for the remainder of the week, he played a strenuous thirty-six holes against an opponent of international reputation. The Canadian star evidently believed in getting away to a smashing start for, in four of his five matches, he did the first hole of the course, which was 276 yards, in three.

Back in 1906 he made one of his most spectacular invasions of the United States when he went after the American title. He was runner-up for the championship and was only defeated after a spirited and thrilling match by Even Byers of Pittsburgh. Here and there, carefully preserved by ardent golfers, there are still to be found worn and yellow clippings from the American press in which can be detected a note of pained surprise that a Canadian should step in and come within an ace of taking away from that country one of its most cherished awards.

Among the gallery during the match with Byers was Alex Smith, the Scotch professional who won the open title in 1906 and again in 1910 and who is now at the Westchester-Biltmore Country Club. He viewed Mr. Lyon's play with continuous wonder. Many years later, along with Jerry Travers, he was visiting Canada and a match was arranged for the pair at the Toronto Golf Club against Mr. Lyons and George Cummings, the well-known professional. The visitors, renowned as they were, went down to defeat in the thirty-six hole match by two up and one to play.

"Mr. Lyon," said Smith, after it was over, with a rich Scotch accent which defies reproduction, "when I saw you playing against Byers in that American final, I said to myself and others, that with the Good Lord behind me and your luck, I could go out and lick any living man on the links. Yes, sir, at that time I thought your playing was a damn fluke. Now I realize that I was wrong. I am now here to declare that it was no fluke."

Smith had every reason to be led astray, since he had never seen Mr. Lyon play before he watched him in the American finals. The style of Canada's great golfer is weird and remarkable and an everlasting cause of amazement. It was once described by a learned gentleman of the American press as a cross between Maud Muller raking hay and a butcher killing a steer. The description is an exceedingly good one, except in one particular. It is not correct.

Mr. Lyon is, however, generally accused of playing championship golf by defying all the principles of the game, a paradoxical situation which has brought about a hundred mix-ups.

Mr. Lyon's style may not resemble the graceful collection of poses which we see exploited from time to time by the slow motion camera, but certainly it is both bold and aggressive.

He hits the ball with a glorious enthusiasm, walloping it firmly and heartily. Believing that the man who plays for safety is likely to be the loser, he enjoys taking chances and is one of the few people who appear to know accurately the dividing line between courageous playing and just plain foolhardiness.

Mr. Lyon jumped from the cricket pitch to the golf tee one October. The following summer he was entered in the matches for the Canadian Amateur Championship. He went right through to the semi-finals before any player was able to stop him, when he was defeated by the runner-up for the title.

The next year, 1898, he went at it again and won it handily. The finals in that season will go down in history because of the fact that Mr. Lyon defeated the runner-up, F. G. H. Patterson, a former champion of Cambridge, by twelve up and eleven to play.

This victory gave him temporary possession of the Aberdeen Cup and later in his career, when he won it three years in succession, the trophy, according to the rules in the deed of gift, became his in perpetuity.

Not one of the many who know him has ever hesitated to affirm that George S. Lyon has practically all the requirements not only of a great but also a tremendously popular athlete, barring, of course, the numerous arguments about his style on the links. As far as golf is concerned, he has been publicly referred to as Canada's grand old man of the game so often that the title is now as hackneyed as the title of a popular song.

But as a finishing and final touch to any picture of George S. Lyon, he should be seen at his golfing headquarters, the Lambton clubhouse, when he rises, at the request of everyone within shouting distance, to lead the assembled mob in the joyful rendering of an old-fashioned ballad.

He is certainly more than Canada's greatest golfer. He is the high priest of Canadian golf. ♣

1904-1930

George Lyon

In 1904 at St. Louis, George Lyon from Toronto's Rosedale Golf Club won the only Olympic gold medal of the century in golf. In 1907 he captured his third consecutive Canadian Amateur Championship (for the Aberdeen Cup), on his way to winning the Cup a record total of eight times in the century. He was equally successful as a senior, winning his first of six consecutive Senior Golf Championships in 1918. At the age of 72 in 1930, Lyon won his 10th, and final, Canadian Senior Championship.

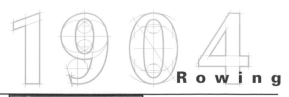

Lou Scholes

There was every likelihood that Lou Scholes would someday be a champion — it was just a matter of figuring out which sport he would take on to earn his crown. Being good at competing was simply in his blood. His father, for example, excelled at boxing, running and rowing. He was even better at snowshoeing, though, a sport in which he set world records. Young Lou's brother chose to focus on boxing, and won numerous amateur titles in both the featherweight and lightweight classes.

It took Lou a little longer to find his niche, but he eventually settled on rowing. With his family background, it was only natural that he chose not to rest on his laurels after winning some Canadian sculling titles. At the age of 21 he set sail for England to race in the Diamond Sculls at Henley, the most prestigious rowing title to be had.

Scholes' first attempt was unsuccessful — he was defeated in an early heat. Not one to be discouraged, he returned home determined to correct this miscarriage of justice. With his father's encouragement (or perhaps insistence), he took to the water again and the following year took both the Canadian and American sculling titles. A year later, in the summer of 1904, he was ready to take on the best in the world again.

Unlike his first outing at Henley, Scholes easily won his first heat by five lengths. It was the same story in the second heat — this time he was so far ahead that he deliberately slowed down in order not to embarrass his opponent. There was one more hurdle between Scholes and the final, but it was a big one. His semi-final opponent was the vaunted Oxford rower Jack Kelly, pegged by most as the one who would take the title that year.

Fate stepped in to give the Canadian rower a strategy to use against Kelly's speed and experience. A chance conversation with one of the race officials yielded the opinion that Kelly was unbeatable

over one mile, but might not have the staying power to keep up his pace for the extra 570 yards of the Henley course. Armed with this information, the Canadian contingent settled on a strategy that would see Scholes yielding the lead, yet keeping the Englishman in his sights for the first mile. Then he would go all out to see who had more stamina.

The race started as expected, with Kelly quick off the mark and building up a lead of two boat lengths. As the two approached the one-mile mark, the lead held, and many spectators considered the race to be won. Then Scholes' strategy went into high gear. While the English rower continued with his smooth, steady style, the challenger threw in a series of quick bursts that gradually closed the gap. Soon they were rowing head to head, in what people later called one of the finest races ever held on that historic course.

With about 100 yards to go, Scholes decided to risk everything on one last burst. Kelly tried his best to match the Canadian stroke for stroke, but with the finish line in sight he suddenly slumped over his oars, his body limp. Exhausted, Scholes crossed the line, not knowing at first whether or not he had won. Upon being told that he had, he rowed slowly over to his opponent's boat and helped revive Kelly by splashing water in his face. After pushing himself to a state of collapse, the Englishman still hadn't fully realized what was going on.

Since Scholes had defeated the pre-race favourite in one of the most exciting finishes ever, the final was almost an anti-climax. The next day, the refreshed Canadian easily beat a rower by the name of J. Clouette, shattering the course record by six seconds.

When the news flashed across the Atlantic that Scholes was bringing the coveted title back to Canada, he became the talk of the town in his native Toronto. The celebrations paled, though, beside the reception Scholes received three weeks later on his return home. He was welcomed with parades, banners and lavish gifts to commemorate his victory, the most remarkable of which was probably a large gold star with a laurel wreath superimposed on it, encrusted with diamonds and rubies. ❧

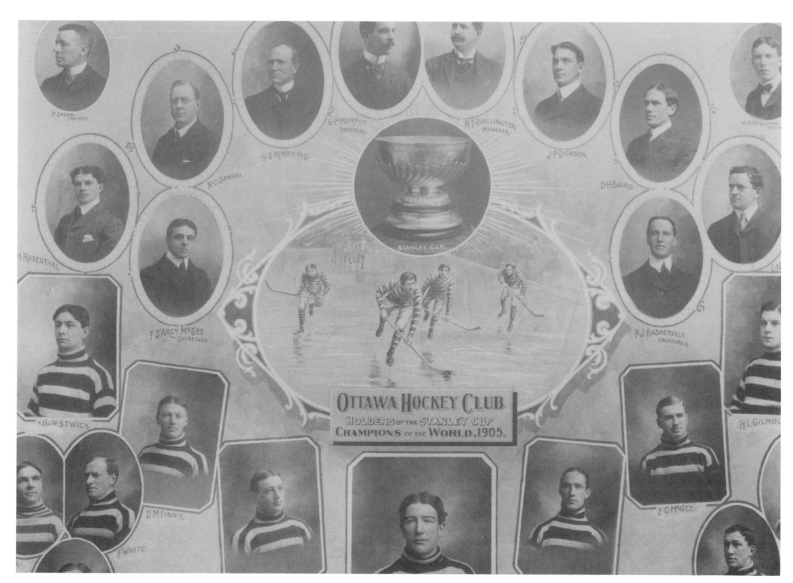

1903-1906 The Century's first hockey dynasty belonged to Ottawa's "Silver Seven" hockey club. Ottawa won the Cup in 1903 and beat all challenges for more than three years. In the process, the famed Silver Seven defeated teams from Rat Portage, Brandon, Trois Rivières, and Montreal's Victorias and Wanderers.

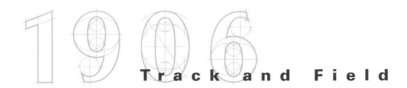

Track and Field

Canada's First Marathon Victory

by Arthur Flewitt
June 15, 1939

Thirty-three years ago Canada was electrified at the news that a Canadian, Billy Sherring, of Hamilton, Ontario, had won the outstanding athletic event at the Olympic Games held at Athens, Greece — the great Marathon race, run over the course reputed to have been traversed by the legendary Greek who carried news of victory on the battlefield from the plains of Marathon to Athens in 490 BC Few Canadians had even known that Canada had a handful of representatives at the games.

This gruelling race was run on May 1, 1906 on a day when the temperature was around 100 degrees. Sherring weighed 112 pounds before the race and ninety-eight pounds when it was completed. An extract from "Marathon Running" in the Spalding Athletic Library, 1909, reads:

"A Greek did not win the Marathon race, and for the good it would have done sport, it is too bad that a runner of that nationality did not carry off the honours. To be sure, we all give great credit to W. J. Sherring of Canada. He ran a plucky race and used great judgement throughout, and is entitled to all the glory that naturally goes with a victory in this, the most important race of the Olympic Games.

"As Sherring entered the Stadium he was met at the door by Prince George, who ran with him the entire length of the Stadium, applauding him vigorously. The 80,000 people within the Stadium were Greek sympathizers, but they took their cue from the sportsmanlike conduct of the Prince and cheered Sherring as no victor was ever cheered before in an athletic contest. The King and members of the Royal Family applauded him, and a large bouquet of flowers was sent to him by Queen Olga. As Sherring entered the marble arch doorway leading to the dressing room it was through a shower of roses that he went which certainly must have gratified the plucky victor.

"Frank, the American runner, and Sherring ran together for several miles of the journey, and at about the eighteenth mile, when Sherring was leaving Frank, he called out, 'Well good-by Billy', and off he went on his triumphal run."

Returning to Hamilton, Sherring was given a reception that was more than merely vocal. Not only was he presented with bonds of substantial value, but, because he was well qualified in other respects, he was assisted to a position as clerk in the Customs and Excise Department of the National Revenue. He never again competed in any big race, but he gave running exhibitions in almost every sizeable Canadian city as well as in the United States.

Today, after thirty-three years, Sherring is still in the Customs and Excise Department at Hamilton, holding now the position of senior clerk. He looks hale and hearty and physically fit to run another Marathon race. ❧

Hamilton's Billy Sherring being cheered by the Crown Prince of Greece en route to an Olympic gold medal in the marathon, 1906.

Tommy Burns, Canada's Heavyweight Champ

Tommy Burns was the only Canadian-born person ever to win the heavyweight boxing championship of the world during the century. He held the title from 1906 to 1908 and successfully defended it 11 times until he suffered a technical knock out in the 14th round before the fists of Jack Johnson in Sydney, Australia.

His 1908 knockout of challenger Jem Roche in Dublin in a minute and 28 seconds of the first round still stands as the shortest heavyweight title bout in history. In all, Tommy Burns won 46 professional bouts, 36 by knockouts, lost five and drew eight. At 5' 7" tall and only 175 pounds, his reach exceeded 74".

Tommy Burns was born Noah Brusso in a log house on a farm in Normanby Township, near Hanover, Ontario, in 1881. He was a superb but rough lacrosse and hockey player. A gifted all-round athlete, he lost a three-mile race to world champion speed skater, J.R. McCullough, by only one second when he was 17.

His first ring appearance was against a circus boxer who offered $5.00 to anyone who could last a round with him. Brusso knocked him out in less than a minute. He moved to Detroit where his professional boxing career began in 1900 when he was 19.

After only five pro bouts he was middleweight champion of Michigan. He knocked out an opponent in the first round and the loser was in a coma. Noah Brusso was arrested but charges were dropped when the fighter regained consciousness.

Brusso's mother heard the news and he promised her he would not fight again. Unable to fulfill that promise, he then changed his name from Noah Brusso to Tommy Burns and resumed his fight career. He knocked out another opponent who remained in a coma for three days. Burns and his corner handlers spent one night in jail.

Fighting as Tommy Burns, he lost a rare fight to Mike Shreck in Detroit in November, 1902, but did not lose again until world light heavyweight champion, Jack O'Brien, defeated him in Milwaukee in October, 1904 — 19 fights later. He lost one other fight in October, 1905, to T.J.

Sullivan in Los Angeles and the title fight against Jack Johnson on December 26, 1908.

In 1906, Jim Jeffries retired from the ring and the heavyweight title became vacant. Tommy Burns was a 17-1 underdog when he entered the ring against Marvin Hart for the title. The fight lasted 20 rounds, but Hart didn't land a punch for the first 14 rounds and the judges awarded Tommy Burns 18 of 20 rounds and the heavyweight championship of the world.

Burns' first two title defences were on the same night — March 28, 1906. He polished off two challengers — Jim O'Brien and Jim Walker — both in the first round. His toughest defences were against Philadelphia Jack O'Brien, world light heavyweight champion. They fought a 20-round draw on November 28, 1906, and Burns won a 20-round decision over O'Brien on May 8, 1907. His next eight title defences were all by knockouts — two in round one and three others in six rounds or less.

The winning streak ended in 1908 with challenger Jack Johnson, who stood six inches taller and weighed 30 pounds more than Burns when they met in Australia. Burns was knocked down in the first round and twice more before police stepped in and halted the fight in the 14th round. Johnson was badly hurt by Burns, who said that because the police and not the referee stopped the fight it should have been ruled a draw.

Canada's first World Heavyweight Champion, Tommy Burns, 1906.

After the fight, Johnson had to go to a hospital to have broken ribs taped up; Tommy Burns went to a racetrack.

Burns was denied a rematch with Johnson and fought only six more times. His last fight was on July 16, 1920, against Joe Beckett in London and Beckett knocked him out in the seventh round. It was the only time Tommy Burns went down for the count.

He lived a gypsy-like existence outside the ring. He owned a clothing store in Calgary; he promoted fights in Calgary in an attempt to find a "Great White Hope" to topple Jack Johnson from his heavyweight throne; he started up a health farm in California; he taught physical education to Canadian soldiers; he built a sports pub in London; and, owned a speakeasy in New York. In 1948 he was ordained as a minister of the Temple of Christ Healing.

Burns died from a heart attack in California in 1955 — penniless despite the fact the he had earned in excess of $200,000 in the ring and made small fortunes with his pub and speakeasy. Four mourners showed up for his burial. His grave was unmarked until 1961 when donations to the Canadian Olympic Boxing fund totalling $300 paid for a tombstone.

Tommy Burns was inducted into Canada's Sports Hall of Fame in 1955 and the International Boxing Hall of Fame in 1996. A plaque outside Hanover, Ontario, was unveiled in his memory in 1959. ❧

Bobby Kerr

The title of the World's Fastest Human has always been highly coveted, and the 1908 Olympics in London were no exception. With each successive Games, Olympic medals were becoming more prestigious. Canada's delegation in 1908 numbered 91 athletes, more than double the number that had gone to St. Louis four years earlier. Among them was the pride of Hamilton, sprinter Bobby Kerr.

Born in Ireland and moving to Canada as a boy, Kerr rose to sprinting prominence the old-fashioned way, paying his dues at the local and provincial levels before excelling at the national level. By the time he was ready to compete at the Olympics, he had reached the venerable age of 28, past the age that popular wisdom would consider ideal for events demanding quick reflexes and powerful bursts of speed.

Many observers did not credit Kerr with much of a chance in London, but in pre-Olympic competitions he began to prove them wrong. At a meet in Stamford Bridge, he captured two heats and the final of a 100 yard event in a single afternoon. He also captured both the 100 yard and 220 yard titles at the British championships just two weeks before the Olympics. Some naysayers persisted, but Kerr began to be seen as the man to beat in both the 100m and 200m Olympic races.

Competing in both sprint events meant a gruelling competition schedule, though. Kerr's Olympics started on July 20, with the heats for the 100m. He won his heat, clocking just a fifth of a second under the Olympic record. The next day, he won the semi-final in the same time, followed by winning his first 200m heat in the fastest time of the day. July 22 dawned with an even greater challenge: the 200m semi-final in the morning, followed by the 100m final in the afternoon. Facing fresh runners, Kerr came up short of the gold medal he had hoped for, as an unheralded South African runner named Reggie Walker came up to win. But for a controversial judging decision, the Canadian might still have had silver, since three of four judges placed him second. The referee sided with the lone judge who had placed American James Rector second, though, and Kerr was relegated to a bronze medal.

Of the six finalists who took to the track the next day for the 200m final, only Kerr had competed in the 100m, which meant he was again facing runners who were fresher than he was. It was his sixth race in three days. This time it didn't matter, though, as the durable Hamiltonian led the race right from the start. With two American runners hot on his heels, Kerr hung on to win the race by less than a foot.

Kerr returned home to a hero's welcome, as his adopted city celebrated his victory with praise, parades and gifts. The Hamilton Herald wrote, "He is the sort of citizen who, win or lose, will be a credit to his city and himself. He will leave sport better because of his participation in it." The Olympic champion continued to be active in sport after retiring from competition, acting as the captain of the 1928 Canadian Olympic team and the manager of the track and field athletes of the 1932 team. ❦

Walter Knox

Walter Knox was a 150-pound precision athletic machine whose incredible feats will likely never be matched. Despite showing absolutely no athletic promise as a youngster, things were different when he grew up. At a memorable meet in 1907 he won five Canadian championships — pole vault, shot put, discus, broad jump and 100-yard dash. In another meet in 1908 he competed against three world class record holders and beat all three in their specialties — Bobby Kerr, sprinter; Ed Archibald, pole vaulter; and Cal Bricker, broad jumper. In 1909 he equalled the world record in the 100-yard dash.

The crowning moment of Knox's career was in 1914, when he was pitted against British champion, F.R. Cramb for the equivalent of the decathlon championship of the world in Manchester. Knox finished first in six of the eight events.

He coached the Canadian Olympic team in the 1920 Antwerp Games and later served as head coach of the Ontario Athletic Commission. ♣

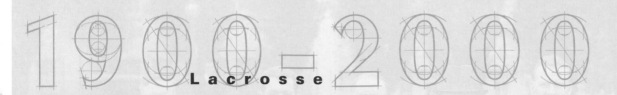

1900-2000
Lacrosse

Mann Cup
Senior Lacrosse Champions of Canada

Year	Champions
1910	Young Torontos, Toronto, Ontario
1911	Vancouver Athletic Club, Vancouver, BC
1912	Vancouver Athletic Club, Vancouver, BC
1913	Vancouver Athletic Club, Vancouver, BC
1914	Vancouver Athletic Club, Vancouver, BC
1915	Salmonbellies, New Westminster, BC
1916	Salmonbellies, New Westminster, BC
1917	Salmonbellies, New Westminster, BC
1918	Coughlans, Vancouver, BC
1919	Foundation Club, Vancouver, BC
1920	Salmonbellies, New Westminster, BC
1921	Salmonbellies, New Westminster, BC
1922	Salmonbellies, New Westminster, BC
1923	Salmonbellies, New Westminster, BC
1924	Salmonbellies, New Westminster, BC
1925	Salmonbellies, New Westminster, BC
1926	Westonmen, Weston, Ontario
1927	Salmonbellies, New Westminster, BC
1928	Emmets, Ottawa, Ontario
1929	Generals, Oshawa, Ontario
1930	Excelsiors, Brampton, Ontario
1931	Excelsiors, Brampton, Ontario
1932	Mountaineers, Mimico, Ontario
1933	Tigers, Hamilton, Ontario
1934	Terriers, Orillia, Ontario
1935	Terriers, Orillia, Ontario
1936	Terriers, Orillia, Ontario
1937	Salmonbellies, New Westminster, BC
1938	Athletics, St. Catharines, Ontario
1939	Adanacs, New Westminster, BC

Lally Patrick

Year	Champions	MVP (Mike Kelly Memorial Award)
1940	Athletics, St. Catharines, Ontario	
1941	Athletics, St. Catharines, Ontario	Blackie Black, Richmond Club, BC
1942	Combines, Mimico/Brampton, Ontario	Bert Large, Mimico/Brampton, Ontario
1943	Salmonbellies, New Westminster, BC	Bill Wilkes, Salmonbellies, New Westminster, BC
1944	Athletics, St. Catharines, Ontario	Ike Hildebrand, Salmonbellies, New Westminster, BC
1945	Burrards, Vancouver, BC	Frank Lee, Burrards, Vancouver, BC
1946	Athletics, St. Catharines, Ontario	Doug Favelle, Tigers, Hamilton, Ontario
1947	Adanacs, New Westminster, BC	Bob Lee, Adanacs, New Westminster, BC
1948	Tigers, Hamilton, Ontario	Doug Favelle, Tigers, Hamilton, Ontario
1949	Burrards, Vancouver, BC	Don Matheson, Burrards, Vancouver, BC
1950	Crescents, Owen Sound, Ontario	Lloyd Wooton, Crescents, Owen Sound, Ontario
1951	Timbermen, Peterborough, Ontario	Lloyd Wooton, Timbermen, Peterborough, Ontario
1952	Timbermen, Peterborough, Ontario	Lou Nickle, Timbermen, Peterborough, Ontario
1953	Timbermen, Peterborough, Ontario	Ross Powless, Timbermen, Peterborough, Ontario
1954	Timbermen, Peterborough, Ontario	Lloyd Wooton, Timbermen, Peterborough, Ontario

Ike Hildebrand

1955	Shamrocks, Victoria, BC	Geordie Johnson, Shamrocks, Victoria, BC
1956	Timbermen, Nanaimo, BC	Derry Davies, Timbermen, Nanaimo, BC
1957	Shamrocks, Victoria, BC	Jack Northup, Shamrocks, Victoria, BC
1958	Salmonbellies, New Westminster, BC	Norm McKay, Salmonbellies, New Westminster, BC
1959	O'Keefes, New Westminster, BC	Jack Bionda, O'Keefes, New Westminster, BC
1960	Sailors, Port Credit, Ontario	Dave Russell, Sailors, Port Credit, Ontario
1961	Burrards, Vancouver, BC	Bill Barbour, Burrards, Vancouver, BC
1962	O'Keefes, New Westminster, BC	Jack Bionda, O'Keefes, New Westminster, BC
1963	Carlings, Vancouver, BC	Gordon Gimple, Carlings, Vancouver, BC
1964	Carlings, Vancouver, BC	Bob Allen, Redmen, Brooklin, Ontario
1965	Salmonbellies, New Westminster, BC	Les Norman, Salmonbellies, New Westminster, BC
1966	Lakers, Peterborough, Ontario	John Davis, Lakers, Peterborough, Ontario
1967	Carlings, Vancouver, BC	John Davis, Lakers, Peterborough, Ontario
1968	Redmen, Brooklin, Ontario	John Cervi, Carlings, Vancouver, BC Joe Timchishem, Redmen, Brooklin, Ontario
1969	Redmen, Brooklin, Ontario	Bill Squires, Redmen, Brooklin, Ontario
1970	Salmonbellies, New Westminster, BC	Paul Parnell, Salmonbellies, New Westminster, BC
1971	Warriors, Brantford, Ontario	Bob McCready, Warriors, Brantford, Ontario
1972	Salmonbellies, New Westminster, BC	Paul Parnell, Salmonbellies, New Westminster, BC
1973	Lakers, Peterborough, Ontario	Pat Baker, Lakers, Peterborough, Ontario
1974	Salmonbellies, New Westminster, BC	Ken Winzoski, Salmonbellies, New Westminster, BC
1975	Burrards, Vancouver, BC	Ron Pinder, Burrards, Vancouver, BC
1976	Salmonbellies, New Westminster, BC	Dave Durante, New Westminster (Coquitlam), BC
1977	Burrards, Vancouver, BC	Doug Hayes, Burrards, Vancouver, BC Mike Smith, Burrards, Vancouver, BC
1978	Red Oaks, Peterborough, Ontario	Tim Barrie, Red Oaks, Peterborough, Ontario
1979	Shamrocks, Victoria, BC	Kevin Alexander, Shamrocks, Victoria, BC
1980	Excelsiors, Brampton, Ontario	Barry Maruk, Excelsiors, Brampton, Ontario
1981	Salmonbellies, New Westminster, BC	Wayne Goss, Salmonbellies, New Westminster, BC
1982	Lakers, Peterborough, Ontario	Jim Wasson, Lakers, Peterborough, Ontario
1983	Payless, Victoria, BC	John Crowther, Payless, Victoria, BC
1984	Lakers, Peterborough, Ontario	John Grant, Lakers, Peterborough, Ontario
1985	Redmen, Brooklin, Ontario	Wayne Colley, Redmen, Brooklin, Ontario
1986	Salmonbellies, New Westminster, BC	Geordie Dean, Salmonbellies, New Westminster, BC
1987	Redmen, Brooklin, Ontario	Eric Cowleson, Salmonbellies, New Westminster, BC
1988	Redmen, Brooklin, Ontario	Bill Thomas, Coquitlam Adanacs, BC
1989	Salmonbellies, New Westminster, BC	Ben Hieltjes, Salmonbellies, New Westminster, BC
1990	Redmen, Brooklin, Ontario	Paul Gait, Redmen, Brooklin, Ontario
1991	Salmonbellies, New Westminster, BC	Geordie Dean, Salmonbellies, New Westminster, BC
1992	Excelsiors, Brampton, Ontario	John Tavares, Excelsiors, Brampton, Ontario
1993	Excelsiors, Brampton, Ontario	John Tavares, Excelsiors, Brampton, Ontario
1994	Chiefs, Six Nations, Ontario	Darris Kilgour, Chiefs, Six Nations, Ontario
1995	Chiefs, Six Nations, Ontario	Paul Gait, Chiefs, Six Nations, Ontario
1996	Chiefs, Six Nations, Ontario	John Tavares, Chiefs, Six Nations, Ontario
1997	Shamrocks, Victoria, BC	Gary Gait, Shamrocks, Victoria, BC
1998	Excelsiors, Brampton, Ontario	
1999	Shamrocks, Victoria, BC	Paul & Gary Gait, Shamrocks, Victoria, B.C
2000	Redmen, Brooklin, Ontario	Nick Trudeau, Redmen, Brooklin, Ontario

William Fitzgerald

"Newsy" Lalonde

Minto Cup

Senior Lacrosse Champions of Canada

1901	Cup presented to Capitals of Ottawa who defeated Cornwall and lost to the Shamrocks of Montreal
1902	Montreal Shamrocks
1903	Montreal Shamrocks
1904	Montreal Shamrocks
1905	Montreal Shamrocks
1906	Ottawa Capitals
1907	Montreal Shamrocks
1908	New Westminster Salmonbellies

1909	New Westminster Salmonbellies
1910	New Westminster Salmonbellies
1911	Vancouver
1912	New Westminster Salmonbellies
1913	New Westminster Salmonbellies
1914 – 1918	War Years, no competition
1919 – 1934	The Cup remained with the New Westminster Club although in 1920, Vancouver claimed it after defeating the Salmonbellies.

Junior Lacrosse Champions of Canada

1937	Junior Terriers, Orillia, Ontario
1938	Mountaineer Juniors, Mimico, Ontario
1939	Junior Terriers, Orillia, Ontario
1940	Junior Terriers, Orillia, Ontario
1941 – 1946	War, no competition
1947	Junior Athletics, St. Catharines, Ontario
1948	Junior Burrards, Vancouver, BC
1949	Norburn Eagletime, Vancouver, BC
1950	Junior Athletics, St. Catharines, Ontario
1951	Mountaineers Juniors, Mimico, Ontario
1952	Excelsior Juniors, Brampton, Ontario
1953	Salmonacs, New Westminster, BC
1954	P.N.E. Indians, Vancouver, BC
1955	Monarchs, Long Branch, Ontario
1956	No. 177 Legionaires, Vancouver, BC
1957	Junior ABC's, Brampton, Ontario
1958	Junior ABC's, Brampton, Ontario
1959	Junior ABC's, Brampton, Ontario
1960	Junior Salmonbellies, New Westminster, BC
1961	Legionaires, Hastings, Ontario
1962	Shamrocks, Victoria, BC
1963	Green Gaels, Oshawa, Ontario
1964	Green Gaels, Oshawa, Ontario
1965	Green Gaels, Oshawa, Ontario
1966	Green Gaels, Oshawa, Ontario
1967	Green Gaels, Oshawa, Ontario
1968	Green Gaels, Oshawa, Ontario
1969	Green Gaels, Oshawa, Ontario
1970	Maple Leafs, Lakeshore, Ontario
1971	Road Runners, Richmond, BC

1972	P.C.O.'s, Peterborough, Ontario
1973	P.C.O.'s, Peterborough, Ontario
1974	P.C.O.'s, Peterborough, Ontario
1975	Gray Munros, Peterborough, Ontario
1976	Macdonalds, Victoria, BC
1977	Cablevision, Burnaby, BC
1978	Cablevision, Burnaby, BC
1979	Cablevision, Burnaby, BC
1980	Builders, Whitby, Ontario
1981	James Gang, Peterborough, Ontario
1982	James Gang, Peterborough, Ontario
1983	James Gang, Peterborough, Ontario
1984	Warriors, Whitby, Ontario
1985	Warriors, Whitby, Ontario
1986	Maulers, Peterborough, Ontario
1987	Maulers, Peterborough, Ontario
1988	Esquimalt Legion, BC
1989	Maulers, Peterborough, Ontario
1990	Athletics, St. Catharines, Ontario
1991	Athletics, St. Catharines, Ontario
1992	Arrows, Six Nations, Ontario
1993	Northmen, Orangeville, Ontario
1994	Salmonbellies, New Westminster, BC
1995	Northmen, Orangeville, Ontario
1996	Northmen, Orangeville, Ontario
1997	Warriors, Whitby, Ontario
1998	Lakers, Burnaby, British Columbia
1999	Warriors, Whitby, Ontario
2000	Lakers, Burnaby, British Columbia

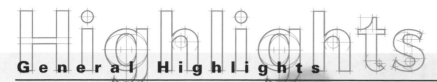
1907

Tom Longboat was often called "the greatest distance runner of them all." He won the 1907 Boston marathon by a wide margin, turned professional after the 1908 Olympics, won many races both in North America and Europe, and set the world record for the 15 miles.

1908-09

The Ottawa Cliffsides were the very first team to win the new trophy for senior hockey supremacy — the Allan Cup — donated by Sir Montagu Allan of Montreal. They were also the first team to lose the challenge trophy — all in the same season. The Cliffsides defeated a Montreal squad for the Cup in the 1908-09 season. When the season was over and their skates were hung up, three weeks later, though, Queen's University challenged — and won. The Allan Cup spent all of three weeks in Ottawa before being taken to Kingston. It would not come back to Ottawa for 33 years when the Ottawa RCAF won it in 1942.

1908

The New Westminster Salmonbellies won the Minto Cup in lacrosse for the first time, and held it every year but 1911 until 1934.

1909

Tom Longboat and Alfie Shrubb of England faced each other in the marathon "race of the century" at Madison Square Gardens in New York. Before over 12,000 spectators, Longboat would pass his rival for good during the 24th mile to win and be regarded as the world's best long distance runner.

1909

Canadians captured shooting's Kolapore Cup at Bisley for the ninth time and the MacKinnon Cup for the second.

1910

Canada won the coxless fours at the Royal Henley, with F. Carruthers, C. Allen, G. Aldous, and C. Riley teaming up for the victory. Canadians would also win the event in 1976, 1981 and 1987.

1915

Russel Wheeler of Montreal became the first Canadian to win both the indoor and outdoor world mass-start speed skating championships.

1919

Ada Mackenzie won her first of 10 National Amateur Championships. She also won some 27 other tournaments through 1950.

Lois Moyes Bickle

Lois Bickle won a record 10 Canadian international singles tennis titles (1906-1908, 1910, 1913, 1914, 1920-1922, 1924) and was an eight-time doubles champion.

Ada Mackenzie, 1919

KENORA THISTLES

The smallest town ever to win the coveted Stanley Cup was Kenora, Ontario. The population of Kenora at the time wouldn't even put a dent in the seating capacity of the old Maple Leaf Gardens.

The Kenora Thistles (the town was known as Rat Portage early in the century) were bridesmaids twice before they won the Stanley Cup in 1907. In 1903 and, again in 1905, the Thistles lost out to Ottawa's fabled Silver Seven hockey teams.

One of the stars of the 1907 Cup win was Arthur Howie (Art) Ross, the man who invented Art Ross nets and Art Ross pucks. He won one other Stanley Cup as a player with Montreal Wanderers. He scored 85 goals in 167 season games and six more in playoffs.

Art Ross is given much of the credit for establishing hockey as a major sport in Boston. He was Boston's coach and manager when the team joined the NHL in 1924 and coached the Bruins to three Stanley Cups between 1929 and 1941.

Two other prominent members of the 1907 Kenora Thistles were Harry Westwick and Alf Smith. Harry Westwick won three consecutive Stanley Cups with the Silver Seven and scored 24 goals in 13 games while playing with Ottawa in 1904-05. Alf Smith and his six brothers all had tryouts with Ottawa but only three could crack the star studded lineup. Smith won two Stanley Cups with Ottawa while playing on a line centred by Frank McGee. He also played on an Allan Cup winner with Ottawa in 1909. He was elected to the Hockey Hall of Fame in 1962.

George Hodgson – Canada's Best Swimmer Ever?

By 1912, the Olympic Games were growing in stature. With 28 nations in Stockholm that year, international competition was mounting. For Canada, George Hodgson's double gold wins in swimming served notice to the sporting world that Canada was a force to be reckoned with.

Life was certainly different back then. A self-taught swimmer, George learned his sport during summers at the family cottage and at the Montreal Amateur Athletic Association pool — the only pool in Montreal. Throughout his competitive career, George never had a coach.

Much later, talking about the times, George remarked that, "Compared with swimmers of today, we were slow-poke second raters...Now competitive swimming is a very serious sport. Swimmers benefit from rigid coaching. In my time, we swam for fun and coached ourselves. At Stockholm, the Canadian team actually didn't have an official coach."

Considering George's performance in the pool, it's tempting to wonder what he might have accomplished with a coach.

George's first win was in the 1500m freestyle, and it is safe to say that no Canadian will ever equal what George accomplished in this race. To begin with, his win earned Canada's first gold in Stockholm. He also managed to set three world records.

The official race was the 1500m, but beforehand, George told the judges he was going to continue on to race a full mile.

In the pool, he did the 1500m in a world record of 22 minutes flat. Incredibly, he blew away previous record holder Henry Taylor's time by 48.4 seconds. Even more incredibly, George was far from being spent. Touching the wall, George surged on to complete the full mile, eclipsing Thomas Battersby's world mile mark by 26.9 seconds. Along the way, he completed the first 1000 metres in 14:37.0 — yet another world record. While only the 1500m time was official, the greatness of his efforts rippled through the sporting world.

A few days later, George struck gold again, winning the 400m freestyle in a field of 28 competitors from 13 different countries. Again, he brought home not only a gold, but another world record at 5:24.4. In an incredible margin, he was 1.4 seconds ahead of Britain's John Hatfield, who won the silver with a time of 5:25.8. Australia's Harold Hardwick won the bronze in 5:31.2.

The win marked another momentous occasion: George become Canada's first-ever double gold medallist at the Olympic Games. With this win, he cemented his stature as one of Canada's great athletes.

Oddly, with two golds and three world records, George's wins were received with what can only be called modest fanfare. There was very little newspaper coverage leading up to the event — the paragraph or two devoted to George stands in sharp contrast to what Olympic hopefuls receive today. Even today, the name of the US athlete and native American Jim Thorpe resonates more strongly than does the name of George Hodgson.

Perhaps history will have the last word in George's story. All of his world records would hold for 12 years, until they were broken by Johnny Weismuller in the 1924 Olympic Games. And no Canadian swimmer would equal George's double golds until 1984 in Los Angeles, when Alex Baumann took golds in world record times. ❦

Canada's 1920 Olympic boxing team may have been the century's best. Nine Canadian boxers went to Antwerp and five returned with Olympic medals: one gold, two silver, and two bronze. Montreal welterweight Bert Schneider became the star of the team, winning Canada's first-ever Olympic boxing gold medal. Along with Schneider, Canada also claimed silver medals by bantamweight Chris Graham and middleweight Georges Prud'homme. Middleweight Moe Herscovitch and lightweight Chris Newton added a bronze medal each.

Johnny Miles, Marathon Man

When 19-year old Johnny Miles stepped up to the start line of the 1926 Boston Marathon the longest race he had ever run in before was only 10 miles. Sporting a red Maple Leaf on his jersey superimposed with "NS" for his home province of Nova Scotia, he nevertheless set new world and Boston Marathon records which stood until 1948.

Years later, a prominent Ottawa sport executive said, "Johnny was a natural athlete who had no access to elite coaching or training and didn't even own a pair of proper running shoes. Who knows? I think if he had had good coaching and good footwear he might have been capable of turning in a 2:10 marathon back in the 1920s."

In 1926 he ran against the world's best and won. He was actually already in the shower when Olympic world champion Albin Stenroos of Finland finished second four minutes behind him. Clarence DeMar, a seven time Boston Marathon winner, came in third.

The Boston Post's banner headline of April 20, 1926, proclaimed:

UNKNOWN KID SMASHES RECORD IN GREATEST OF ALL MARATHONS

After the race, the course was re-measured and found to be 176 yards short but Johnny Miles' Boston and world records stood.

The City of Boston was at the feet of the young runner from Florence, Cape Breton, whose job was delivering groceries for the local co-op store by horse and wagon. The Miles's family intended to take a train home the day after the race but ended up staying for a week of red carpets, police motorcycle escorts, receptions and media attention. Johnny Miles was given the key to the city of Boston.

Johnny's father, himself a gifted athlete, was a streetcar operator in Cardiff, Wales who came to Cape Breton in 1905 to "dig for the coal" in No. 1 Princess Mine in Florence. Johnny was born in Yorkshire, England, and when he was four months old his mother sailed for Canada to join her husband and begin a hardscrabble life in a coal mining company town.

When his father went off to fight in World War I, family finances were so tight that Johnny went to work in the coal mine at the age of only 11. Child labour laws had been temporarily suspended in Nova Scotia because of a manpower shortage. At first, he cleaned miners' lamps for 35 cents a day, later landing a better paying job underground as a "trapper," opening swinging doors to allow coal cars through. The presence of rats in the pit didn't scare him. He fed them scraps from his lunch pail. He reasoned that live rats scampering around meant there was no methane gas present.

He brought his unopened pay envelope home every Friday and gave it to his mother. His weekly allowance was 25 cents. Some weeks his mother had to ask him to give her back the 25 cents in order to buy groceries. He kept up his school studies at night.

Somehow Miles found time to run. While still in his teens he established both Nova Scotia and Maritime records for 10 miles and the Canadian record for five miles. After his 1926 Boston victory he set Ontario and Canadian records for 10,000 metres and was a marathon bronze medalist in the first ever British Empire Games in 1930.

Johnny Miles winning the 1926 Boston Marathon.

Johnny's final training exercise for his first marathon was a little unorthodox: he took a train 27 miles out of town and ran back home along the rail bed, through cold and slippery snow and slush wearing a 98 cent pair of sneakers. Two hours and 40 minutes later he was home. He was ready. The townspeople passed the hat and collected $300 — the equivalent of three months pay — to pay his Boston expenses.

The day before the race, Johnny and his father walked the entire length of the marathon course to familiarize him with landmarks and twists and turns in the route.

The length of a marathon course is 26 miles, 385 yards. The gruelling race is named after the 490 BC Battle of Marathon when Pheidippides ran 150 miles to Sparta in two days to bring news of a Greek victory over the Persians. Pheidippides reported: "Rejoice, we are victorious" and then fell dead. Introduced at the 1896 Athens Olympics, the course distance was extended to the current 26 miles, 385 yards, at the 1908 London Olympics so the finish line would be right in front of the Royal Box and King Edward VII.

Johnny Miles defended his Boston Marathon crown in 1927 but did not finish. He was forced to drop out after only six miles because his feet were bleeding badly. Soft tar was oozing into his running shoes from the super-heated asphalt in temperatures in the high 80s Fahrenheit.

He went back to Boston for the 1929 marathon and won again. Race organizers added 176 yards to the course and declared his winning time another world and Boston record. The great Clarence DeMar came in 9th.

He went back to Boston one more time in 1931 to defend his crown and finished a disappointing 10th. — 18 minutes behind the winner.

Johnny Miles ran for Canada in the 1928 Amsterdam and 1932 Los Angeles Olympics. Even though his times were respectable, he finished 16th and 14th. His biggest disappointment was in Amsterdam. He had been itching to run in the 10,000-metre race against Finnish legend Paavo Nurmi, but alas, Canada did not enter competitors in the race.

In 1983 he was inducted into the Order of Canada. At the time of his induction the teetotalling, non-smoking former Sunday School teacher was described as "a paradox of nobility and humility." Dr. John Williston, the founder of the New Glasgow marathon, said that people referred to Johnny Miles as "that beautiful person."

In 1967 be became a Member of Canada's Sports Hall of Fame and in 1980 a Member of Nova Scotia's Sports Heritage Hall of Fame.

Johnny Miles was a true amateur in every sense of the word. During his entire 15 year running career he never earned a single penny — victor's spoils or appearance money — for his remarkable feats. The winner of the most recent Boston Marathon enjoyed an $80,000 US payday. By contrast, Johnny Miles' biggest payday came when he was 17 and entered a three-mile race. One prize was a 98-pound bag of flour donated by a local merchant. The first runner to pass by the merchant's store at the mid-point of the race would win the flour. Johnny's mother needed the flour so he made sure he was first past the merchant's door. He finished that race in third place. But, he will forever be remembered for that first win in Boston in 1926. ❧

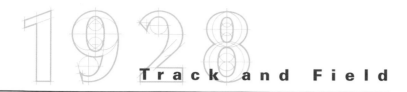
1928

Track and Field

How Percy Williams Swept the Olympic Sprints

by Ray Gardner
November 24, 1956

On July 30, 1928, in Amsterdam, Percy Williams, a runner who a few weeks before had won the sprints at the Vancouver high schools' sports day, startled the world by winning the hundred-metre event at the Olympic Games.

Two days later, Williams, just turned twenty and so light of build he was described as delicate, won the two-hundred-metre sprint to become the sensation of the ninth modern Olympiad.

Never before or since has any but a United States runner won both Olympic sprints, the classic events of the Games. Two United States runners had done it before: Archie Hahn, in 1904, and Ralph Craig, in 1912. Two have done it since: Eddie Tolan in 1932, and Jesse Owens, in 1936.

But only Percy Williams sprinted out of obscurity to do it. It was a triumph that stands today as Canada's brightest moment in Olympic Games history — perhaps in all the annals of Canadian Sport.

In Canada the victory inspired a national rejoicing that wasn't to subside until weeks later when Williams crossed the country in triumph, lionized in Quebec, Montreal, Hamilton, Toronto, Winnipeg, Calgary, and finally Vancouver.

Trained to a razor's edge, Williams weighed only 126 pounds, the lightest runner ever to win an Olympic sprint. After his victory in the 100, they said he'd never last out the grueling preliminary heats of the 200. In fact, the great Paddock declared that "it seemed impossible for that skinny little sprinter to do it." Yet in four days Williams ran eight races, winning six and placing second in two.

He did run faster races — in 1930 he set a new world's record of 10.3 seconds for the hundred metres — but he never won greater glory than in those four days at Amsterdam.

The first Canadian to reach Williams as he flung himself across the finish line in the two hundred metres was Bobby Kerr, of Hamilton, who himself had won the event at the 1908 Olympics. "Won't Granger be

pleased," Williams gasped. A few hours later he told the droves of reporters who sought him out, "Whatever I've done has been through my coach, Bob Granger."

Granger later commented that he had never seen worse style in a boy who could run like Williams did. "I think he violated every known principle of the running game," said the coach. "He ran with his arms glued to his sides. It actually made me tired to watch him."

From the summer of 1926 till the eve of the Olympics, Granger slaved over Williams to perfect his starting and running form.

Even so, Granger always maintained that his runner didn't master the correct arm movement in his starts until the day before the Games were to open.

At fifteen Percy had been stricken by rheumatic fever and, the doctors said, left with a damaged heart. He was even warned to avoid excitement. In any case, he was extremely light and far from robust.

In the spring and summer of 1927 and the spring of 1928, Granger kept Williams running — and winning — in every local meet. He ran what were, for a schoolboy, some remarkable times: 9.9 seconds for the hundred yards, 22 seconds for the two-twenty. In June 1928 he took his first stride toward Amsterdam by winning the British Columbia Olympic trials.

On June 5, a throng of track enthusiasts and relatives saw Percy and the other coast athletes off to Hamilton and the Canadian Olympic trials.

Broke, Granger was left behind. But two days later he was on his way east as a pantry boy on a CPR diner.

Percy Williams became the unexpected star of the Hamilton trials. Against a field of topnotch Canadian sprinters, most of them trained in American colleges, he won the 100 metres in 10.6 seconds, again equaling the Olympic record, and the 200 metres in 22 seconds.

The crossing was painful for Granger. He had counted on nine days at sea to perfect Percy's starts. Eventually he reached Amsterdam and, in Percy's room at the Holland Hotel, he drilled the youth in his starting. A mattress was placed against one wall, as a buffer, and Percy would take off from across the room. The management, not sharing Granger's obsession, objected. But nevertheless, it was there in the Holland Hotel, so Granger said, that the World's Fastest Human learned how to get off the mark in a hurry.

Percy Williams won his first heat easily, in 11 seconds, but was forced to run his fastest race of the Games,

10.6 seconds, to win his second heat and enter the semifinals. His diary entry showed extreme modesty:

July 29-My ideals of the Olympic Games are all shot. I always imagined it was a game of heroes. Well, I'm in the semifinals myself so it can't be so hot.

When they lined up for the hundred-metre final the young Canadian was dwarfed by the brawny Bob McAllister and Jack London, a two-hundred-pound British Negro. Frank Wykoff, George Lammers, of Germany, and Wilfred Legg, of South Africa, completed the field.

There were two false starts — first Legg broke, then Wykoff. The third start was perfect. Williams shot away with the gun, the rest on his heels. With thirty metres to go, Williams was still in front. Then London made a valiant effort to catch him but missed by a yard.

July 30-Well, well, well. So I'm supposed to be the World's 100M Champion. (Crushed apples.) No more fun in running now.

Now began two days of grueling running in the two hundred metres.

Williams wasn't conceded a chance against these fresh, more experienced and, off the record, faster runners. His best time, 22 seconds, was two-fifths of a second off their pace. What no one could know was that Granger's tactics and Williams' "gear shift" — a unique ability to change running styles while in full flight — would single out Borah and Koernig, one at a time, and kill them off.

When the two lined for the final of the two hundred metres, Williams faced Koernig and Jacob Schuller of Germany; John Fitzpatrick, a Canadian from Hamilton; Jackson Scholz, of the United States, the 1924 champion; and Walter Rangeley, of Great Britain.

Even before Amsterdam, Granger knew almost all there was to know about all the internationally known sprinters.

"Koernig is your man to beat," he told Williams, "He is a front runner — an inspirational runner — and if you come out of the curve even with him, or just ahead of him, you will kill his inspiration and win."

As they came out of the curve, Koernig and Williams were in the lead, running neck and neck. They ran that way until the last fifty metres. Thousands of Koernig's countrymen urged him on. Then Williams shifted gears, out of his flowing stride and into a blinding driving finish. For an instant the amazed Koernig seemed to hesitate. The skinny kid from Canada flashed by him and won by a yard over Rangeley, the Briton, who had come up fast to place second.

For the next three years Canada watched and marveled as the World's Fastest Human kept on running and winning. He set a new world's record of forty-five yards (4.9 seconds) and equalled three other world's records.

On August 9, 1930, Williams ran his fastest race, setting a new world's record of 10.3 seconds for the hundred metres. His Toronto mark was half a second faster than his winning time at Amsterdam, and would have been good enough to win in any of the four Olympics held since 1928.

The beginning of the end came on August 23, 1930, in the hundred-yard final of the British Empire Games. Williams was flying almost certainly to a new world's record, when with thirty-five yards to go, he pulled a muscle in his left thigh. In agony, he kept running, staggering out of his lane at the tape. He won in the remarkable time of 9.9 seconds — and then crumpled to the track. His leg was never right again.

The end came — as fame had come — at the Olympic Games. He ran third in two hundred-meter heats and then in the semi final, ran fourth and out to Eddie Tolan.

After that Williams stepped deliberately out of the limelight and devoted himself to business and to golf.

Looking back over the years, Percy tries to remember how he reacted to sudden fame. "I was just like any kid of twenty," he says. "I was simply bewildered by it all. I didn't like running. Oh, I was so glad to get out of it all." ❧

Percy Williams celebrates his 1928 100m and 200m sprint Olympic gold medals on his teammates' shoulders.

Canada

1920

Bert Schneider of Montreal won Olympic gold in welterweight boxing at the Olympic Games in Belgium. Canada also won two silver and two bronze medals in boxing.

Bert Schneider

1923

The Underwood Trophy, presented to the best team in women's basketball between US and Canada was first awarded. The Edmonton Grads held it for the next 17 years, until they were permanently given the trophy in 1940.

1924

The first Canadian Basketball Championships saw the Edmonton Grads winning the women's competition and the Raymond Union Jacks becoming the men's champions.

1924, 1928, 1932 and 1936

The Edmonton Grads were undefeated in exhibition basketball tournaments held at the Olympic Games in Paris, Amsterdam, Los Angeles, and Berlin.

1921, 1922 and 1923

Gladys Robinson of Toronto won the world indoor mass-start speed skating championships.

1924

D. Burke won the coveted King's prize at the Bisley shooting competitions.

1925

Vancouver's Percy Williams tied the 100m world record mark of 10.6 seconds.

1925

The Mann Cup became the annual national championship trophy for amateur lacrosse teams across the country, with contests alternating between east and west each year.

1925

For the first time, a Canadian women's track and field team went to an international sports competition, travelling to London, England.

1926

The Canadian Women's Athletic Federation was formed as part of the AAU of C.

Jack Delaney

1926

In boxing, Jack Delaney possessed an exceptional jab punch and a stiff right hand. He won the world light heavyweight boxing title in 15 rounds over Paul Berlinbach in Brooklyn. He relinquished the title in 1927 to try the heavyweight division but did not meet with nearly the same success.

1926

At the world mass-start speed skating championships in Saint John, New Brunswick, Leila Brooks won the women's world title and Charles Gorman won the men's. Brooks later set the world indoor mass-start mark in the half-mile.

Leila Brooks

1927

Albert "Frenchy" Belanger from Toronto first defeated Frankie Genaro of New York then Ernie Jarvis of England to win the world flyweight boxing championship. He would lose the title the next year. Belanger and Genaro would fight again for the title in 1930, this time with Genaro winning the crown.

Albert "Frenchy" Belanger

Edmonton Grads

1928

Rowing

Canada's Sculling Ace

by Aleck Sinclair
September 1, 1928

A blazing hot July day. The historic old Father Thames is a blaze of colour. Punts, launches, rowboats all are crowded with gaily bedecked figures, the men in blazers showing every conceivable combination of colours, the women in sports dresses equally as colourful and carrying brilliantly-hued parasols. It is the Henley Regatta and the most important race of this greatest of all regattas is being rowed — the race which shall finally determine the nation to whose representative the famous Diamond Sculls shall go.

At the finishing post are crowded the nobility and gentry — including royalty — of Great Britain, their eyes following with strained intentness the signals indicating the progress of two shells. In both of these shells are two young giants pulling with all the sweeping force which mighty muscles of back and leg alone can give. One of them draws rapidly ahead, the other tries frantically to increase the drive and speed of his strokes. In vain. The winner flashes by the post two full boat lengths ahead.

There is frantic enthusiasm. From out the first welcoming din of applause a huge voice booms:

"How was it, Joe?"

The oarsman rests easily on his sculls for a moment before replying. Then he looks up at his questioner a broad, rather lazy and quizzical smile on his handsome face.

"Great race," he pants. "He had me all out all the way."

This big fellow they call "Joe," is Joe Wright of Toronto, born in that city, of Canadian parents on both sides. And, be it said, young Joe chose those parents of his wisely. His father is the famous Joe Wright, Sr., in his day one of the greatest oarsmen known not only a singles sculler, but a sweep oar as well.

In 1915, when Joe junior was nine years old, Joe Wright, senior, went to the University of Pennsylvania as rowing coach

Joe Wright Jr., 1928 Diamond Sculls Champion

and left his son at school in Toronto, in charge of his married sister, Mrs. Walter Harris. When he returned in 1924, the famous coach found that his boy Joe had grown to such an extent that he was ready to take his place in the Argonaut Junior Eight. At once young Joe proved his quality. A junior oarsman, in his first year, the lusty young giant stroked his eight to victory at the Canadian Henley, held at St. Catharines, Ontario, and on the day following this race he stroked the same crew to victory, winning the Hanlan Memorial Trophy.

The following year Joe went with his father to Philadelphia, in which city Wright senior was acting as coach to the Penn. Rowing Athletic Club. Once again the young Canadian showed the stuff of which he was made. He rowed number six in the senior crew and this crew promptly took the National Championship of Canada into camp.

Not content with assisting at this triumph, Joe junior took to sculling the same year and won the junior, intermediate and senior singles at the American Henley, setting up new records for these three races. To crown all, he beat the most formidable sculler in America — if not all the world — the great Walter Hoover in the quarter mile single sculls race.

With a record such as this the critics, wise in matters aquatic, not unnaturally felt that they had in Toronto's Joe, a future winner of the Diamond Sculls, all to the honour and glory of the United States of America. But Wright, senior had other ideas. He may have agreed with the American critics that his lad had a chance to win the Diamond Sculls, but he had quite made up his mind that if this was going to happen the aforementioned honour was going to be Canada's. So he resigned his job as coach for the Penn. Athletic Club and returned to his native Toronto bringing his young stalwart with him.

In 1927 Joe made his sensational bid for the possession of the Diamond Sculls. Everyone who reads the daily papers knows what happened. Joe had his opponent, Lee — of Worcester College, Oxford, thoroughly beaten up to within ten feet of the winning post. Then in some inexplicable manner his oar got tangled up in a loose rope dangling from one of the boats which lined the course.

In this year of Our Lord, 1928, this amazing Joe Wright has met and vanquished his old enemy, Lee, and has brought back the Diamond Sculls to the country which had not had them in her possession since 1904 — the year in which Lou Scholes won them.

If you like to collect athlete's heights and weights here are Joe's: Height six-feet two inches. Weight, in training, around 180 pounds. Does the Diamond Sculls winner smoke? He does not. He tried it once, when he was very, very young, and decided that thereafter sport was good enough for him. If you have scrutinized the photos of the finishes of sculling and rowing matches you must have noticed that at the finish the oarsmen sat in their shell in a state of whole or partial collapse. Well, after young Joe raced Lee in the Diamond Sculls he walked briskly to the showers, took a little invigorating tingle and promptly marched down to the waterside and took his shell out of the water unaided.

Another evidence of his stamina is offered by the length of his inboard — the length of the oar from its outrigger to its end. In the case of Joe and his partner, Jack Guest, they both use more inboard than any other scullers in the world. It's very hard on the back, but it adds a whole lot to the propulsive power of the oar.

When this is published the results of the Olympics will show what luck Joe Wright has had. But regardless of good fortune or ill, there will be few who will deny that Wright, by virtue of his triumphs in all kinds of rowing events is, today, the greatest oarsman who ever sat in a shell. They can't take the Diamond Sculls away from him anyway. ❧

Diamond Sculls: Canadian Winners

Henley-on-Thames Royal Regatta

Year	Rower	Place
1904	Lou Scholes	Won
1927	Joe Wright Jr.	Finalist
1928	Joe Wright Jr.	Won
1929	Joe Wright Jr.	Finalist
1930	Jack Guest Sr.	Won
1931	Robert Pearce*	Won

* Pearce was a resident of Australia who immigrated to Canada in 1930

Four Diamond Sculls Champions: Joe Wright Jr., 1928; Jack Guest Sr., 1930; Lou Scholes, 1904; and Bobby Pearce, 1931.

1930

Jack of Diamonds

by Ted Reeve
September 1, 1930

When Jack Guest, of Toronto, swept his shell down the Thames to win the Diamond Sculls this year he successfully completed one of the longest voyages ever attempted in a motorless craft. Since setting out in quest of an oarsman's highest award, the young navigator has covered thousands of miles of water at thirty strokes to the minute. The story of his steady rise is set in a background of concentration, courage and calluses.

Five years ago our John was a gangling lad swinging desperately at the working end of a sweep oar. Today he is a big, powerful young man, holder not only of the Diamond Sculls but of the smoothest sculling style in the world. Given a good pair of blades and fairly level water, and Master Guest would make speed with a kitchen table. He has perfected his art, but to do so he has put in enough tugging toil to qualify as an honorary member of the Volga Barge Club.

It was 1927, while still holding down a seat in the Argo octette, that Jack showed enough in the solo flights to prove that he had a brighter rowing outlook ahead of him than the shoulder blades of a fellow member. That was the start. It has taken him four years to finish the journey, and in his painstaking progress he encountered enough bad breaks and backwash to swamp completely a less determined mariner.

He was ready. They knew that, and the only fear was that nervousness might again wreck the party, but it was a needless one. Trained to perfection, Guest could probably have become half hysterical and still set in thirty-four superb strokes every sixty seconds. There was no danger, however, for mentally as well as physically he arrived. Calmly, powerfully, he worked through the heats to the finals to meet the surprising German, Boetzelen, who had conquered Wright.

It was hardly a contest. The overeager European made a couple of false starts when he tried to stroke three ways at once, and then settled away to row a good race. Unfortunately for him, he would have needed an outboard motor and a set of sails to have held his own with Guest that sunny afternoon.

For half the route the dashing youth from the continent set his most terrific race, and then the big man from the Dominion, still rowing less strokes to the minute than his competitor, suddenly shot far into the lead, and in effortless rhythm increased the distance between the two shells until he flew across the finish line at least two hundred yards ahead of this second best oarsman at the Henley.

As he rested quietly on his blades, while a tremendous ovation rose from the picturesque regatta crowd on the banks of the beautiful course and the band played "O Canada," there must have passed before the mind of this twenty-four year old Canadian sculler a vista of the long cold spring days on the bleak Toronto waterfront, sweaty hours in the gym, and memories of exhaustion and spent efforts in other racing finishes on that same spot. And behind his calm exterior must have bubbled a lifting, glorious elation as he realized that already the cables were carrying the news of his achievement back home to his father.

Jack Guest Sr., 1930 Diamond Sculls Champion

Had the cool Canuck been pressed it is thought that he might have cut nineteen seconds off his time to equal the course record set by the immortal Kelly. As it was, he finished in eight minutes and twenty-nine seconds, which was well under par, and with no more trace of effort showing on his frame than if he had been on a brisk five-minute practice spin in a wheel chair.

Never has the success of a Canadian athlete met with more general satisfaction and enthusiasm. Those who knew Jack as a boy, when he was perfecting his form with a pair of tongs during the summer holidays on the Island ice route, could not have pulled harder in his support than the average reader who had followed his ever-increasing rowing ability only through the press, and yet admired the modest, clean-cut character that he has always displayed either in victory or defeat. ♣

Highlights

General Highlights

December 1, 1923
Records for the most points scored by a team in the Grey Cup, and the most lopsided Cup victory, were set when Queen's University beat Regina by a score of 54-0.

1927
The Canadians won the Kolapore Cup for the third consecutive year at the famed Bisley shooting competitions.

1928
Canada's first women's team entered the Olympic Games, six in track and field (Canada's "Matchless Six") and one in swimming. Five of the seven came home with gold medals.

1927
Seventeen year old George Young from Toronto won the prestigious 30-mile Catalina Swim and a $25,000 cheque, completing the course in 15 hours.

1927
Johnny Longden won his first horse race in 1927, en route to winning a record 6,032 races before retiring in 1966 to become a successful trainer.

1928
Joe Wright Jr. from Toronto won the prestigious Diamond Sculls race at Henley-on-Thames, England.

1929
The Regina Roughriders used the forward pass successfully all season, but the new play was not accepted into the Grey Cup Game until 1931.

1930
Jack Guest of Toronto won the prestigious Diamond Sculls race at Henley-on-Thames, England.

1931
Transplanted Australian Robert "Bobby" Pearce won the Diamond Sculls rowing out of the Leander Boat Club in Hamilton. At the time Pearce had already immigrated to Canada, although he still represented Australia in the Olympic Games.

1930
Badminton player Jack Purcell of Guelph, Ontario defeated four top-ranked British players who were touring Canada.

1930
The UBC Women's Team won the unofficial World Basketball Championships in Prague as part of the "Women's International Games."

Multiple Winners of Canadian Badminton Championships

Coke, E.F. Women's Singles National Champion: 1924 - 1926, 1928 - 1929. Women's Doubles National Champion: 1924 - 1928. Mixed Doubles National Champion: 1925

Mixed Doubles Canadian Open Champion: 1978
Clarkson, Wendy Women's Singles National Champion: 1976, Women's Singles Canadian Open Champion: 1976 - 1978. Mixed Doubles Canadian Champion: 1975, 1978 - 1979

Mixed Doubles Canadian Open Champion: 1990
Julien, Denyse Women's Singles National Champion: 1983, 1986 - 1988/89, 1991, 1994 - 1998. Women's Singles Canadian Open Champion: 1989. Women's Doubles National Champion: 1985-86, 1988/89, 1992 -1993, 1995, 1997. Women's Doubles Canadian Open Champion: 1985, 1990. Mixed Doubles National Champion: 1981, 1988/89, 1993, 1999

Miller, Jean Women's Singles National Champion: 1956, 1958, 1964. Women's Singles Canadian Open Champion: 1958 (combined competition) 1964 - 1965. Women's Doubles Canadian Open Champion: 1967. Mixed Doubles National Champion: 1960 - 1961 (combined competition)

Patrick, Anna (nee Keir) Women's Singles National Champion: 1932, 1934, 1937. Women's National Doubles Champion: 1937. Mixed Doubles National Champion: 1932, 1934, 1936 - 1937.

Shedd, Marjorie Women's Singles National Champion: 1953 - 1954, 1960, 1963. Canadian Open Champion: 1960 - 1962 (combined event), 1963. Women's Double National Champion: 1954 -1956, 1958, 1961 - 1966, 1969, 1971. Canadian Open Double's Champion: 1958, 1961 - 1962 (combined event with Nationals) 1963 - 1964. Mixed Doubles National Champion: 1956, 1958 (combined event), 1963 - 1964.

Walton, Dorothy Women's Singles National Champion: 1936, 1938, 1940

Women's Singles Canadian Open Champion: 1974
Youngberg, Jane Women's Singles National Champion: 1974, 1977 - 1978, 1981. Women's Doubles National Champion: 1974 - 1978, 1980. Women's Doubles Canadian Open Champion: 1974

Butler, Mike Men's Singles National Champion: 1983 - 1987. Mens Doubles National Champion: 1987. Mixed Doubles National Champion: 1984, 1986 - 1987

Grant, Doug Men's Singles National Champion: 1933-34, 1936

Macdonnell, W. Men's Singles National Champion: 1962 - 1967. Canadian Open Champion: 1962 (combined event with Nationals)

McTaggart, Dave F. Men's Singles National Champion: 1956 - 1958. Men's Singles Canadian Open Champion 1957 - 1958 (combined event with Nationals)

Paulson, Jamie Men's Singles National Champion: 1968 - 1969, 1973 - 1974. Men's Singles Canadian Open Champion: 1973 - 1974. Mens' Doubles National Champion: 1967 - 1970, 1973

Rollick, Bruce Men's Singles National Champion: 1970 - 1972, 1975 - 1976. Men's Singles Canadian Open Champion: 1968. Mixed Doubles National Champion: 1969, 1977

Samis, John Men's Singles National Champion: 1938, 1947, 1949.

Smythe, Don K. Men's Singles National Champion: 1952 - 1955. National Doubles Champion: 1952 - 1954, 1957 - 1958, Canadian Open (combined event with Nationals) 1957 - 1958

Wang, Wen Men's Singles National Champion: 1990, 1994, 1997

Birch, Richard (Dick) E. Men's Singles National Champion: 1937, 1939, 1948. Men's Doubles National Champion: 1951. Mixed Doubles National Champion: 1934, 1936 -1937, 1939 - 1940, 1947 - 1948, 1950, 1953

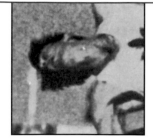

Duncan McNaughton

If ever the original spirit of the modern Olympics was at work, it was on a sunny summer day in the 1932 Olympic Games at Los Angeles, when British Columbia's Duncan McNaughton won gold in the high jump.

It was to be Canada's last Olympic gold in track and field for 60 years. Not until 1992 at Barcelona did Mark McKoy put Canada back on the gold standard with his win in the 110-metre hurdles. But McNaughton's win was unique in a manner seldom, if ever, seen in the competitive cauldron these Games have become.

Born in 1910, he was a student at Magee High School in Vancouver when Percy Williams won two gold medals in the 1928 Olympics at Amsterdam. Until then basketball was his sport of choice and, at 6-foot-4 1/2, he led Magee to the BC high school championship in 1929. He truly was the leader — captain, coach and leading scorer.

Inspired by Williams' success, he took up high jumping and really worked at it. Indeed, he sought and landed an athletic scholarship at the University of Southern California in 1930, becoming the first Canadian jumper to use the western roll at a time when the scissors jump was still the favoured way to get over the bar. Indeed, it was so new, that when he tried to use it in the first ever British Empire Games at Hamilton in 1930, he was disqualified. In a 1970s interview he said:

"I learned it from a Spalding athletic book. But I had a lot more to learn when I got to USC. I was a pretty green kid. The top jumper there was a fellow named Bob Van Osdel. He took me under his wing and spent a lot of time training me and helping in every way he could."

With Van Osdel's help, he smoothed out and perfected the western roll and, prior to the Olympics, won the California intercollegiate championship, setting a state record in the process. The year after the Games, he further proved himself by winning the US intercollegiate championship, the final competition of his career.

McNaughton was only named to the Canadian team because he happened to be going to school in LA He had to wage a one-man campaign by correspondence prior to the Games, trying to persuade officials in Canada that he should represent his country. Undeterred by the constant refusals of Canadian Olympic officials, he waited until the Canadian team arrived and then badgered them in person until they finally relented.

As for his Olympic win, he said:

"At the Olympics it turned out that we [McNaughton and Bob Van Osdel] were the final two competitors in the high jump. I missed a jump and he came over and told me what I was doing wrong. Then he gave a couple of tips on how to correct my mistake.

"I took his advice and made it over the bar. He failed in all three tries. And that's how I won the gold."

It wasn't quite that simple. There were 20 competitors in the field, including the American world record holder, at six feet, 8.5 inches, George Spitz. He was the odds-on favourite to win gold, but went out at six feet, four inches, leaving four — including McNaughton and Van Osdel — in the competition.

The other two went out at six feet, six inches. Three hours into the event, the weary finalists battled on for another hour. When they both failed to clear six feet, seven inches, the two approached the judges and suggested that first place be split between them. The offer was refused, the bar was lowered to six feet, 6.5 inches and both failed on three jumps at that height.

So back it went to six feet, six inches; then to six feet, 5 1/2 inches. McNaughton, utilizing the tips given him earlier, made it on the first jump. Van Osdel missed on all three attempts.

The two became lifelong friends. Indeed, Van Osdel was godfather to two of McNaughton's three daughters. What happened in the high jump competition and lasting friendship that ensued, say the purists, are what the Olympics are supposed to be all about.

Graduating from USC in geology, McNaughton went on to a distinguished career in that field. In the late 1930s, he worked for the Canadian Geological Survey, joined the Royal Canadian Air Force in 1941, and while a pilot with No. 405 (Pathfinder) Squadron, won the Distinguished Flying Cross and bar.

Following World War II, he returned to USC, where he earned his PhD in geology and taught for a while as an assistant professor before going to work for various US oil companies. Eventually he set up his own petroleum consulting business in Dallas.

Reflecting on his winning jump in that 1970s interview, he chuckled and said: "I'm pretty amazed at what they're doing now. Even appalled. What I did is just a pretty good high school jump now." ♣

1933

Boxing

Don't Call Me Baby Face

By Jimmy McLarnin as told to Ralph Allen
December 1, 1950
Part of a Five-part series

In a fight, it's the first hundred seconds that are the hardest. You're cold physically. Your muscles are a little stiff and your reactions are a little slow. You're unsettled mentally.

There is always a moment, just before the first bell rings, when you stare through the floodlights hanging above the ring, trying to pick out the people who are for you and the people who are against you. On some faces

you see more faith in you than is reasonable and on some you see more hostility than is called for.

You look back across the ring at the man you're going to be fighting and try to remember how you're going to fight him and how you have figured he's going to fight you. For an instant you draw nothing but a blank.

On May 29, 1933, I fought Young Corbett III for the welterweight championship of the world at Wrigley Field in Los Angeles. This was a very important fight for me. I had won 11 fights against world champions in various weight classes-some while they were champions and some after they ceased to be champions — but I had never held a title myself. I'd had to wait five years for my shot at the welterweight title and during the last two I'd been ranked unofficially as the best welterweight in the world. If I blew this one and had to wait another five years I knew I'd never get there.

Pop Foster, my manager, and I agreed that the first minute or two of the Corbett fight might be particularly critical. Corbett was a big man, as strong as a horse, with long arms and heavy shoulders. Besides, he was a southpaw and boxing a southpaw is like trying to read by a mirror. Everything — his leads, his crosses, his footwork — goes from right to left instead of left to right. I'd only fought one southpaw before, a good one named Lou Brouillard, and he'd beaten me.

"If you can make him open up, you'll win," Pop told me the day we signed for Corbett. "If you can't he may hug you to death."

We still didn't have a written guarantee, but it looked good. I floated down the aisle to the ring feeling as smug and lightheaded as a bride. I sat forward on my stool and looked across at Corbett. He looked pale and anxious — the way a fighter usually looks when he's up for his fight.

George Blake, the referee, waved us to the middle of the ring and gave the stock instructions ending with the stock phrase — "Go to your corners and come out fighting."

Corbett obeyed to the letter and with a vengeance. I hadn't taken two steps before he was on top of me, throwing his left hands — his best hand.

In the first minute it crashed past my arms half-a-dozen times and bounced against my ribs like a bucketful of hot rivets. His first charge pinned me against the ropes and as I tried to circle away he hooked another hard left to the head.

I couldn't find room to get away from him, much less to throw a punch at him.

These punches of his all hurt. I was glad he was throwing them, but I was by no means glad they were landing. Over the thud of his punches I heard the crowd roaring behind me the way a fight crowd always roars in a moment of climax. Finally I half knocked and half shoved him away with a left and when he stepped back I had a little room to move around.

Corbett had one bad habit. Pop and I had both noticed it the night we watched him win the title from Jackie Fields. When he hit to the body with his left he dropped his right a little. So when Corbett came in again I kept my hands high, showing him my ribs. As he brought the left in, his right came down and a piece of his jaw was suddenly open above the right glove, less than a foot from my left hand.

I was rolling toward him, ready to throw the left or hold it, depending on whether or not I saw a target. I let it go.

It was a good punch, one I'd been working on for nearly 15 years. Its arc started upward but at the last instant I turned my elbow and the fist corkscrewed and came in slightly downward. Corbett fell like a hinge on a spring.

His pants hit the floor first. Then his shoulders thumped back and he rolled over on his side.

I backed into a neutral corner for the count. Corbett was on one knee at four, blinking and shaking his head and he shoved himself to his feet at nine. I rushed out of the corner, feinted with a right and hit him another hard left on the jaw. He went down again, near the ropes. He grabbed the lower rope and dragged himself to his feet one strand at a time. He threw one arm over the top strand and turned his back to me.

As I moved past George Blake, the referee, I said: "You'd better stop it, Mr. Blake." Blake shook his head. I spun Corbett away from the ropes with another left and hit him two more lefts on the head. He went down again. This time Blake didn't count.

It was over in two minutes, 37 seconds, the shortest championship fight in the history of the welterweight division. 🍁

Highlights

General Highlights

1930

Leila Brooks won her third North American outdoor mass-start speed skating championship.

1931

Jean Wilson continued in Leila Brooks' footsteps, winning the North American mass-start women's speed skating championships.

1932

George Jost was the first alpine skier to use a low crouch style in competition and in so doing became the first Canadian to win a major European ski race at the Arlberg-Kandahar downhill race in Austria.

1932

A team from Manitoba won the 1932 Olympic Winter Games demonstration event in curling at Lake Placid.

1932

"Torchy" Peden won a star-studded six-day cycling race at Madison Square Garden in New York, one of 148 six-day races Peden would win in his career.

1931-33

St. Eugene Quebec's Lou Brouillard defeated "Young" Jack Thompson to win the world welterweight boxing championship. Brouillard would lose the title in 1932, and win it again in 1933. In 1933 he was also recognized as the world

middleweight champion. He lost both titles to Vince Dundee in Boston later that year.

1932

Ross "Sandy" Somerville's victory in the 1932 US Amateur was a first for a Canadian golfer. Between 1926 and 1931, Somerville captured six Canadian Amateurs and was a finalist on four other occasions. A gentleman golfer throughout his lifetime, Somerville served as president of the RCGA in 1957.

1933

Jack Purcell won the World Professional Badminton Championships in England, retaining the title year after year until after World War II.

1935

Leila Brooks won her final North American mass-start speed skating championship.

Francis "Frank" Amyot

The name "Amyot" was synonymous with canoeing excellence in the 1920s and '30s. In 1925 the four Amyot brothers placed first in all divisions — senior, intermediate and junior singles — at a meet in Carleton Place, Ontario.

The best known paddler in the family was Frank, who was the Canadian singles champion six times and captured Canada's only gold medal in the 1936 Berlin Olympic Games. Early in life, his ambition was to be a sculler but the $250.00 cost of a shell was beyond his means as a teenager. Not to be deterred from pursuing a competitive career, he abandoned his rowing plans and built his own canoe.

He was not built like a typical paddler. He was 6' 2", weighed 200 pounds (91 kg) and therefore needed an oversize canoe in order to accommodate his frame. Given his size, his stroke was also longer but less frequent than most. He used his paddling style as a strategic advantage by taking an early lead, then relying on his long stroke to give his opponents the demoralizing impression that he was paddling easily.

Amyot had more than a dozen years of competitive successes behind him when he was chosen in 1935 to be not just a competitor, but also the coach and manager of the Canadian Olympic team. Unfortunately, whether for lack of funds or lack of recognition, he and his fellow paddlers were offered no money to get to Berlin. He and his teammates, whom he described later as an "orphan outfit," even had trouble acquiring team uniforms. In order to make the trip to Germany, they had to rely on help from the Canadian Canoe Association, the Britannia Boat Club (Amyot's home club) and other donors.

In Berlin, he took an early lead in the 1000m, but Bohuslav Karlik of Czechoslovakia passed him with a scant 250m to go. One length behind but undaunted, Amyot responded with his own spurt of strong paddling and passed his Czech rival with 50m left. He won the race by more than four seconds, winning Canada's only gold medal at those Games. He received his medal from Adolf Hitler.

"The greatest thrill of my life came when I was called to stand on the pedestal while the Canadian ensign was run to the Olympic masthead, and Canada's national anthem was played," he told the Ottawa Journal later.

Amyot's triumphant return home was accompanied by a $1,000 purse from the City of Ottawa and admirers. In those days, such a gift could be enough to jeopardize his status as an amateur, but the Canadian Canoe Association refused to recognize any sanctions against him.

Before his Olympic triumph, Amyot was known as a hero for a different reason. In 1933 he had helped rescue three men in danger of being carried to their deaths in the Deschenes Rapids of the Ottawa River. Their canoe had capsized, and Amyot was the first to race to the rescue. With the three hanging onto his canoe, he battled the current single-handedly until more help arrived. ❦

1936 Olympic Champion, Francis Amyot

1940s

Track and Field

Marathon Champ

by Elmer W. Ferguson
June 1, 1940

He's twenty-six years old, his body is 133 pounds of steel, whalebone, rubber and heart. He's only five feet six inches in height; he has flashing eyes, dark-brown, almost black; his hair is as ebony as any raven's wing, has a wave as fetching as that of any movie star, and twice as natural; he has a John Barrymore profile, a Cary Grant fore-face.

That's Gérard Côté, who overnight became the 1940 athletic hero of Canada when, on Patriots' Day, April 19, he raced over the historic Boston marathon course faster than human feet and legs had ever covered that classic route before — 26 miles, 385 yards in 2 hours, 28 minutes, 28 seconds.

He earns a few dollars a week in the little city of St. Hyacinthe, near Montreal, as an agent for publications and newspapers; he has no club backing of any kind, his father being his only sponsor; he ran over 1,000 miles, mostly on roads rough with snow and ice, to prime his slim, sun-tanned body for the great test at Boston; he ran much of the time alone, in the dreary business of fitting heart, lungs and legs for battle against the cream of America's greatest distance runners; he had seventeen dollars in his pocket after travelling from Montreal to Boston by bus; at Boston he had no trainer, no athletic advice or help; he ran on his own experience and intuition and with this equipment he won the world's most famous long distance race, in a time faster than any human had ever pounded over the heartbreaking course.

That is Gérard Côté, the athlete who raced swiftly and smoothly away from the field, and won in a swirl of flashing smiles, waving hands, as old Boston thundered applause for the amazing feat of the little Habitant, who became the ninth Canadian to lead the field in this ancient race. Eleven wins for Canada in forty-four runnings.

Côté became a runner by accident. He rose to the peaks of greatness through his own indomitable will, by natural ability aided by the only very casual coaching, which eliminated early faults; by reading the works of great runners of the past, Paavo Nurmi and Arthur Newton, shrewdly adopting from these what he thought was best for himself in the matter of style, diet and training. His training motto, as he plods the roads is

"Three hours slow is better than two hours fast," and it was on this basis that he fitted his slim body to perform the historic feat he accomplished over the hilly Boston marathon course.

This new hero of French Canada, and indeed of the whole Dominion, has dabbled a bit in all sorts of athletics. He once skated in a roller derby, and won it. In baseball he plays third base or shortstop. In softball he's a pitcher with a fastball.

He's a hockey player and snowshoer in winter. He set a world mark of one hour three minutes for ten miles on snowshoes at Montreal last winter' a world record of fifty-two minutes for eight miles at the great St. Paul snowshoe reunion. He's a natural athlete, dynamic, highly vitalized, loves action in all his sports, is seldom out of competition.

In the beginning he wanted to be a fighter like Louis or Armstrong. To be a good fighter, a well-conditioned fighter, road-work is essential; long and tiresome hours of it. So boxing-bent, he went out and ran, and ran, and ran. And then he learned, as he trotted over the quiet streets of picturesque little St. Hyacinthe, that he could run, and run, and run without tiring.

"In the race," he said, "I knew myself. I knew what my body could do. I was never in distress. I felt good and strong. For here I was running on a perfect day, with conditions ten times better than those under which I trained. I was ready. I was fit. I knew myself."

On previous essays at winning the classic Boston race, Côté had been accompanied by trainers, friends, advisers. They all meant well, but in his enthusiasm he worked too hard in advance of the race, left his endurance and vitality and spark scattered over the long trail. One year he ran the whole route a couple of days before the race. When the race came, he could hardly raise a gallop.

This year he didn't put on a running shoe for three days before the race. He went to Boston absolutely alone, rode there by bus, arrived with just seventeen dollars in his pocket. A kindly hotelman with a deep-rooted love for athletics, Walter E. Seaver, had met Côté before, had taken a liking to the dynamic little Habitant, gave him a room and fed him well. Côté relaxed, went to the mark fresh, sped away, was never headed. In one spot, where

Gérard Côté, from St. Hyacinthe, Quebec, won the famed Boston Marathon in 1940, 1943, 1944 and 1948.

automobiles clogged the road, he had to dash off the pavement onto the sidewalk and battle his way through the throngs. But he kept running. The end was in sight. He didn't know he had run so fast, because he felt so fine and fresh. He knew he was far ahead, and so he slowed down a bit, waved at the roaring crowds, smiled his beaming smile for the cameras that clicked. For this kid is a natural showman. He trotted home with Tarzan Brown's "unbeatable" one-year-old record of 2.28.51 shattered, could have run it two minutes faster, says he'll do a 2.25 marathon next year.

And maybe he will. ❧

Basketball

"They're World Champions

by Frederick B. Watt
January 15, 1929

In 1914, J. Percy Page, principal of the Commercial High School in Edmonton, began to begrudge the breaking up of basketball teams turned out under his direction. Mr. Page was a basketball enthusiast and had formed a habit of producing winning school teams. So the first women's Commercial Graduates club was formed, composed of outstanding members of former school line-ups. In 1915 they won the Alberta championship on the formation of the provincial league, and they have won it every year since then.

With monotonous regularity the Grads, as they came to be known generally, knocked over everything that came their way. Dominion championships for women's basketball were unknown at that time and, as the eastern title was held in London in 1922, the first year that the Edmontonians cast their eyes toward a Canadian crown, it appeared that this unsatisfactory state of affairs was to continue indefinitely. The Shamrocks of London could offer no financial guarantee, and a little known aggregation had scant hope of raising funds in a hometown that was heavily supporting other sports. But the girls were keen about that Dominion playoff. Finally, with a little outside assistance, they dug down into their own pockets, made the long trip east and won the title.

They've held it ever since.

In 1924 came an even greater ambition. The world's title had been claimed by a United States team, but the Grads, even after whipping these claimants, were not satisfied that they were entitled to the honour, with the sport flourishing in Europe and the Strasbourg team claiming the championship on that side of the world. So they went to the now healthy club funds, sailed to Europe, showed the leading exponents of the game — including Strasbourg — how basketball should be played, and came home with the world's championship.

They still hold it, having defended the honour at Paris at the same time that Canada's 1928 Olympic team was covering itself with glory at Amsterdam.

Since 1914, 308 league, championship and exhibition games have been played against the leading teams of the American and European continents. The Grads have won 301 of them.

Edmonton Grads, 1928

Naturally this has not been accomplished by five girls alone. Of the team that went to Europe in 1924, not one, not even a substitute player, was on the 1928 line-up. In that lies the wonder of it all and in that lies the greatest tribute to Coach Page — that year after year a team dependent on a single school should be broken up, reorganized and still be able to more than hold its own with anything on this well-known globe. In the present team the old rule of allowing only Edmonton Commercial High School graduates to play was broken for the first time at the urging of the citizens who believed that the team should be civic rather than one representing a single institution. Gladys Fry, a University of Alberta graduate, the present centre, is the first girl to fill a regular berth on the team under the new ruling.

There are four stages to a Grad. A student on entering Commercial High School is given the opportunity of trying for the junior school team. By the time she has won a place she has been well sized up by Mr. Page. When she makes the proper weight, she has a chance for the senior line-up. Then, with graduation, or in her last year at school, a place on the Gradettes is hers to win. The Gradettes, younger sisters to the Grads, have the same taking ways in intermediate circles that the world's champions have in the senior group. Finally, if a young lady has basketball "it," there is a black and gold uniform that is known throughout the world waiting for her.

It is not unnatural that the finished Grad machine is well-nigh perfect. Coach Page is a student of human nature as well as an expert of tactics in the hoop pastime.

He knows his players closely from the time they have scarcely the strength to heave the ball against the backboard until they are able to ring up a perfect one-handed basket on the gallop four times out of five. The girls themselves have played together or watched each other play for years. They have been drilled as thoroughly as guardsmen, every play being carried out on signals that have never yet been solved by the opposition. Added to this, years of notable successes have built up the strongest sort of tradition. That, in itself, is a sixth player on the floor. It is not to be wondered at that there has been no stopping a line-up built and maintained with such skill and foresight.

It's the teamwork that does it. Player for player the Grads have run into many stars who were their match, and sometimes their superiors. They have never yet, however, had their spirit of co-operation equalled. On their way to Europe in 1928 they met an all-star team in Hamilton composed of picked players from that city and Toronto. There were some positively brilliant players on the Eastern team yet they were swamped 61 to 14. Individual excellence proved futile against well-knit team-work.

In the United States they take their basketball seriously. Big commercial institutions eager to bring their names before the public, finance teams of picked players so generously that in many cases the situation amounts almost to professionalism. The Grads have played forty-five games with the best of these. They lost three — all in a row. It occurred when the Canadians were on tour.

They were billed for ten games in eleven nights, the hours between encounters being almost entirely occupied by travelling. It was at the hands of their ancient foes, the Cleveland Favourite Knits, whom they had defeated originally for the old mythical world's championship, that they met their greatest loss. The American girls took three out of four close tussles from the fagged Canadians and promptly claimed all the honour the Grads held, although the series was billed for only the American title. The Grads debated the controversy a bit, then piped down and waited until the next international series brought the teams together again. Cleveland went down under a smothering defeat and the argument came to an abrupt conclusion.

The present regulars, as Mr. Page says, are as near perfection as would seem humanly possible. Margaret MacBurney, right forward, is without a doubt as fine a sharpshooter as the game has ever seen. Mildred McCormick, the other forward, handles the ball with an ability that is positively poetic. Both are small and

EDMONTON COMMERCIAL GRADS
1915 ══════════ /// ══════════ 1940

Front Row:- Sophie Brown, Kay MacRitchie, Jean Williamson, Mable Munton McCloy, Mr. Page, Mrs. Page, Etta Dann, Helen Northup, Betty Bawden.
Second Row: Babe Belanger McLean, Doris Neale Chapman, Margaret MacBurney, Millie McCormack Wilkie, Winnie Martin Tait, Harriet Hopkins. and Nellie Perry McIntosh, Mae Brown Webb, Mary Dunn Dickson.
Third Row: Helen Stone, Elsie Bennie Robson, Evelyn Coulson Cameron, Jessie Innes Maloney, Marguerite Bailey, Abie Scott Kennedy, Helen McIntosh Lees, Daisy Johnson, Gladys Fry Douglas, Edith Stone, Connie Smith McIntyre, Ethel Anderson Lovatt, Elizabeth Elrick Murray, Dorothy Johnson Sherlock.

elusive but solid enough to take the hardest punishment. Gladys Fry is built for the centre position and has filled perfectly the place vacated by the famous Connie Smith two years ago. Despite the fact that she holds down the hottest berth on the floor, she is the coolest person in the match from whistle to whistle. The defence for Kate Macrae and Elsie Bennie speaks for itself. No team has ever piled up a big score against the two husky, methodical custodians of the home cage. Miss Bennie, senior member of the line-up, captains the team.

It is not only the athletic ability of the girls which has won them the esteem of all comers. The moment the final whistle has blown, the players, who a moment before had been giving and taking hard knocks on the unyielding maple floor with the fortitude of rugby players, emerge as thoroughly feminine and entirely likeable young ladies. They are in constant demand at social functions and public gatherings. Best of all, conceit is unknown to them. They are, if anything, too self-effacing.

Two things have been constant in the changing scene of the Grad panorama — the team spirit and Coach Percy Page. Certainly, the man who has directed the destinies of the organization could not have achieved the same heights without some really remarkable players to work with, but it is equally certain that the finest collection of basketball players that could have been assembled would have been halted at a certain point had there been a different skipper at the helm. ♣

Highlights

Grads Highlights

1915-1940

The Grads were undefeated in Canadian championship play throughout their history.

Depending on the source, the Grads won between 502 and 524 games, losing only between 20-24. Regardless of the exact number, their record is unparalleled in sport history.

Over the course of their 25-year history, the Grads outscored their opponents by more than 2:1. In 1912, Percy Page originally accepted the coaching duties of the high school team that was the precursor of the Grads because he lost a coin toss with one of his colleagues.

James Naismith, the inventor of basketball, called the Grads "the finest team that ever stepped out on a basketball floor."

Grad's coach Percy Page announced in April, 1940, that the Grads basketball team would cease operations later that spring. Citing Page's older age, mounting pressures, as well as little desire to carry on the team without its long-serving coach, a motion to withdraw was made by the last Grad Captain, Etta Dunn, along with its last President, Daisy Johnson, a former Grad's star. Finally, it was decided that the last game for the Grads would be in June, 1940.

June 3-7, 1940 - Edmonton City Council passed a resolution of appreciation for the Grads and all they had done for the city over their 25-year reign, by virtue "of their unprecedented record in the world of amateur sport." Former Grads made their way back to Edmonton for the final series of games, the final hurrah, the final cheers. Their opponents in the best-of-three series were the Chicago Queen Anne Aces, a team they had played many times with their usual success. The first game was almost anti-climatic, as thousands of Edmontonians filled the arena to watch their team win easily 56-34. Two days later the Grads posted what was scheduled to be their final victory, defeating Chicago 45-38 to win the game and the series. It was decided, though, and agreed earnestly by the Chicago players, to allow the public one last chance to watch their Grads. It was a teary night on June 6, 1940, as the Grads hit the court for their final game. Memories were everywhere as former star players were introduced to start the game and then asked to join in with the 6,200 spectators. The Grads, fittingly, won their final match ever, 62-52.

The Underwood Trophy, emblematic of women's basketball supremacy, was presented to the Edmonton Grads for their permanent collection in 1940. In 25 years of competition, the Grads never lost possession of the trophy.

Captain
Angus Walters

Bluenose – First Lady of the Sea

Bluenose was royalty. She was a queen. She was the First Lady of the sea, renowned up and down the Atlantic seaboard. Despite her lineage, though, she took her final voyage to the bottom alone just before midnight on January 30, 1946. Her eight-man crew was spared as she was ground to splinters on a sharp coral reef off Haiti. The 143-foot long beauty with the narrow stern which once parted unforgiving waters with an awesome combination of grace, raw power and speed, was gone forever.

The era of sail was over. The economies of the fishing industry made Bluenose an antiquated throwback and she had been cast off to be sold as a tramp vessel to end her racing and fishing days hauling freight in the Caribbean.

Former Nova Scotia Premier and Senator Harold Connolly asked, "What in the world were we thinking of? When the mantle of time fell around her shoulders, we did not so much as honour her with an old age pension."

Teletype bells clattered in newsrooms around the world. A terse four-word bulletin said it all:

Bluenose Sunk Off Haiti

By 1942, Bluenose's long-serving skipper, Angus Walters, had been left with little choice but to relinquish his majority ownership share. His pockets weren't deep enough and he had already exhausted most of his savings in 1939 to satisfy Bluenose's debts and save her from the auctioneer's hammer. After a lifetime at sea, he "swallowed the anchor" and opened a dairy business on shore. The fishing industry, meanwhile, was on hold because of the menace from German U-boats during World War II.

Bluenose entered the world in 1921 because international yachtsmen were bickering over the America's Cup. Halifax newspaper publisher, Senator William H. Dennis, thundered from his editorial crows nest: "to hell with the America's Cup. Let's have a man's race, no schooner yachts but genuine fishing schooners."

Horror of horrors, in the very first race between Lunenburg and Gloucester schooners the American saltbanker "Esperanto" sailed home with the trophy and $4,000 in prize money.

Lunenburg's pride was wounded. Angus Walters and Halifax marine architect, William Roue, joined together to build the fastest fishing schooner afloat. She would be named Bluenose — a nickname derived from the blue coloured "calico" potatoes Maritimers grew.

Roue's radical approach was a low center of gravity and a minimum of ballast. A combination of revolutionary design and lucky accident gave her an unusual bow line that was given part of the credit for her speed. "What a nose that gave Old Stormalong," wrote Charles Rawlings in Maclean's Magazine years later. "With her big bowsprit jutting out of it she seemed to glower like an angry she-elephant." Angus Walters sold 350 shares in the schooner at $100 each.

Bluenose's masts were of Oregon pine. The rest of the craft was from Nova Scotia's forests - framing of spruce and oak, bottom planking of birch, rails and topside of oak and decks of pine. Smith and Rhuland Shipyard, Lunenburg,was commissioned to build her. The Duke of Devonshire, Canada's Governor General, made a special trip to Lunenburg to hammer in the first spike.

Bluenose was a true Lunenburg saltbanker except her masts were higher and her hull deeper. She carried 10,000 feet of sail.

On October 16, 1921, seven months after her March launching, Bluenose won her first race by 16 1/2 minutes over eight other vessels over a 40-mile course. She won the right to represent Canada against the American contender "Elsie." During the race, "Elsie" unfurled her ballooner and a 27-knot wind swept it away along with her foretopmast. In a gesture of sportsmanship, Angus Walters doused his ballooner. Bluenose crossed the finish line 13 minutes and 15 seconds ahead of "Elsie."

She was the new champion and would successfully defend her title against all challengers.

According to popular belief, Bluenose was never beaten. In fact, she lost heats to US schooners "Henry Ford" and "Gertrude L. Thebaud" but Bluenose was a money player and never lost a final for the International Fisherman's Cup. She often left US challengers so far behind the timers stopped timing.

In 1931 fish prices dropped and many 'bankers turned to rum running. But Bluenose's career took a different turn. In 1933 her skirts had their first taste of fresh water as she sailed into Chicago to represent Canada at the Century of Progress Exhibition. In 1935 she sailed for England for the Silver Jubilee of King George V and Queen Mary. Bluenose was at Spihead when the King reviewed the fleet and he presented Captain Walters with a mainsail from "Britannia."

Bluenose's racing days were over, though. Diesel engines and twin screws were installed and she returned to being a full-time fishing schooner. The typical Lunenburg saltbanker was built to last 10 years; Bluenose was 21 when her owners sold her off as a tramp.

She was the most famous fishing vessel afloat, but a campaign to preserve her as a national monument was becalmed.

In 1929, Bluenose under full sail appeared on a Canadian 50-cent stamp. In 1988 Captain Angus Walters and Bluenose appeared on a 37-cent stamp and in 1998 marine architect William Roue was honoured on a 45-cent stamp.

Another myth that has persisted for years is that the schooner on the Canadian 10-cent coin since 1937 is "Bluenose." It is not. The designer, Emanuel Hahn, was commissioned to produce a design of "a fishing vessel under sail." The Canadian Mint considers his design a composite.

Not a sliver remains of Bluenose in the waters off Haiti. There were rumours that some porcelain artifacts were the property of a resident of Les Cayes, Haiti, but Jim Tupper of the Lunenburg Fisheries Museum scoffs: "Hardly a month goes by when someone doesn't offer us a piece off Bluenose." Another skeptic adds: "Can you imagine a fishing schooner with her own crested china service?"

Defeat never rested in Bluenose's sail locker until she encountered a razor sharp reef off Ile Vache, Haiti. On her final voyage to the bottom a Union Jack waved proudly from her mainmast.

Both skipper Angus Walters and Bluenose were inducted into Canada's Sports Hall of Fame. Yet, despite her proud history, nothing of Bluenose remains or could be salvaged to remind Canadians and the world of her greatness. ✤

The Bluenose II was made on the exact scale and design of the original Bluenose, seen here in the 1980s.

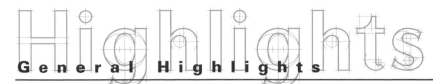

Highlights

1936-1939

Dorothy Walton started her domination of Canadian women's badminton, winning three national titles in three attempts, and made several challenges for the All-England Title.

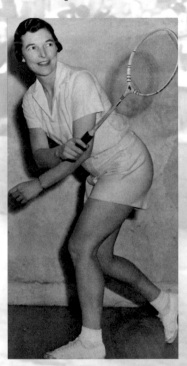

1936

The professional golf tour was really just beginning in 1936. This year it included a stop at Vancouver's old Shaughnessy course. BC's best amateur player at the time was young Kenny Black. His father was the longstanding pro at the course and Black knew the course well. He entered the tourney as an amateur. Just 24, he went out and shot a course record 63 in the final round to beat the likes of Byron Nelson and other big name stars to win the tournament. He was the first Canadian to win a US professional golf tour event. As an amateur, though, he was not eligible to collect the winner's share of the purse.

Jules Huot

One of the finest of all Quebec golf professionals, Jules Huot's victory at the 1937 General Brock Open marked the first time a Canadian professional had won a PGA tournament (Kenny Black won the 1936 Vancouver Jubilee Open as an amateur). Known as "le petit Jules" in Quebec, the diminutive player captured the CPGA Championship and the Quebec Open three times, won five Quebec PGA Championships and finished as low Canadian professional at the Canadian Open on two occasions.

1940

In the King's Plate in 1940, a horse named "Willie the Kid" won a purse of $6,720, which was the horse's only victory in his life.

1940

In 1940 the Canadian Basketball Championship was still a prestigious title, and the scoring star this year was 17-year old Norm Baker, playing for the champions, the Victoria Dominoes. Baker went on to lead the Dominoes

for years to come and in 1950 was voted Canada's Basketball Player of the half century.

1941

Kenny Lindsay of Vancouver won the world bantamweight boxing title.

1942-1943

George Woolf won the North American horse racing money title two years running.

1946

Jockey George Woolf, from Cardston, Alberta, twice led all North American jockeys in the 1940s in prize money, though not in wins. From 1927 through 1946, Woolf won 721 races. He was known as the "Iceman" during his racing days, cut tragically short when he fell in a race in 1946 and died from his injuries.

Famous and outgoing, Canadian jockey George Woolf is seen in the left photo on the equally famous *Whirlaway* at Suffolk Downs in 1942. Following a win on Pavot in 1940, he joined up with movie star Racquel Torres after a victory at Aqua Caliente, right.

1942

Horse Racing

Johnny Longden: The Greatest Horse I Ever Rode

By Johnny Longden with Trent Frayne
June 7, 1958
Part 2 of a five-part series

On a brisk spring morning in 1942 at the Belmont race track near New York I was galloping some two-year-old horses that belonged to a wealthy American owner named John D. Hertz. I'd taken two or three for a few turns around the track and then Don Cameron, who was Mr. Hertz's trainer, pointed to a rangy brown fellow being saddled by one of the grooms.

'Take him for a little ride, John,' Don said. 'I don't know much about him yet but his old man could run some.'

I've ridden some great horses in my thirty-one years of racing — Whirlaway and Noor and Swaps come quickly to mind — and I've also seen some great ones : Nashua and Citation, for example, the only thoroughbreds in the world ever to win a million dollars. But that early spring morning in 1942 was the day I first saw the greatest horse I ever rode or saw, that sleek brown two-year-old, Count Fleet, who turned out to have a mind of his own, a sense of humour and a chivalrous way with lady horses.

After I got on him outside the barn we walked out on the track and he just decided we'd go the wrong way. I couldn't change his mind, try as I did, so we galloped away clockwise instead of counter-clockwise as traffic runs on North American race tracks. This would have been fine if the track had been deserted but it wasn't. There were other jocks working other horses, and right away here were two of them heading straight for us. We went right between them in what could have been one hell of a collision.

I got that crazy colt to a stop and walked all the way back to the barn, leading him. I told Don Cameron that the colt was nuts, and to keep him away from me.

The next morning I was walking past the barn and Don called to me.

'Hey John,' he said, grinning. 'You want to work that crazy colt?'

'Not me, kid,' I said.

'Oh, come on. Nobody else will.'

So I said okay, and this time Count Fleet was kind enough to go where I wanted him to go and he even showed a fair turn of speed.

A couple of days later I heard that Mr. Hertz was offering the colt for sale, along with some other two-year-olds, at $4,500. So far there'd been no takers. I told Don I thought they ought to take the colt off the list. Whether my word influenced him or not I don't know, but Don suggested to Mr. Hertz that we keep the colt awhile and he came off the list.

Count Fleet wasn't an easy colt to teach. All he wanted to do was run and it didn't make any difference to him in what direction. I know one thing: on the day he was running I didn't ever have to reduce to ride him, because I couldn't sleep the night before for wondering what he'd think of next.

But I persevered with him. I'd talk to him. Eventually he got to know me. He wouldn't let anybody else on his back and it got so that I could do anything with him, mostly by talking to him and never ignoring him when I walked by his stall.

In his six races as a three-year-old, Count Fleet won on all kinds of track, fast and slow, wet and dry.

But I guess there is something different about the Kentucky Derby, probably because it's so highly publicized. It's one you sure want to win. I was a little worked up, I must confess, but not Count Fleet. In the paddock before the race, with the crowd buzzing and an electric excitement filling the air, he just stood there still as a stone while Don Cameron saddled him. He was completely relaxed. The other horses must have felt the excitement because you could see their muscles quivering.

The Count broke from the number-five gate and I took him to the top after a horse called Gold Shower tried to stay with him for about a quarter of a mile. He just kept galloping along, not extending himself, and nobody came up to challenge us. We came off the last turn a length ahead of Blue Swords and headed down the famous home stretch with speed in reserve, pulling steadily away and winning by a good three lengths.

In his next few races Count Fleet had even less trouble than he'd had in the Derby. He was a 1 to 7 favourite for the Preakness and he shot to the front like a skyrocket and drew farther and farther in front. He came swinging down the stretch with long hurtling effortless leaps and won by eight lengths. Wayne Wright, the jockey on the third-last horse, New Moon, grumbled afterward, 'Dammit, I couldn't even see the race.'

By the time we got to the Belmont Stakes, after winning the Withers, people were talking about no other horse. Count Fleet still had not been pressed so we still didn't know just what he could do flat out. I was convinced he could break every record in the book if a challenger would bring out his best.

Unfortunately, the Belmont Stakes on June 5 was not to be the day. The track was fast and the weather beautiful but we'd scared off the competition by this time. Only two horses from a long list of eligibles, Fairy Manhurst and Deseronto, went to the post against the Count and he won the mile-and-a-half race by what the chart-callers decided was twenty-five lengths, although it might even have been thirty. It was just no contest.

And though Count Fleet won as he pleased he didn't set a record. In the stretch he begain to shorten his stride as though limping slightly, and I suspected then that he'd kicked himself coming off the last turn. That must have been what happened because certainly no horse was close enough at any stage of the race to rough him.

Thus, when Mr. Hertz decided to retire Count Fleet, there never again was an opportunity to see what he could do if he extended himself. It's my personal opinion that he could have beaten any horse that ever ran. He could do everything — come up from behind or go right to the top or overcome a roughhousing — on any kind of a race track.

I often wish we could have gone all out just once with him — but as it is, he's done all right. One of his sons, Count Turn, won the Kentucky Derby in 1951 and that same year his progeny won purses worth $1,160,847 to make him the year's leading sire. Count Fleet was always a horse with a mind of his own. He was a big rough fellow but he never caused me any trouble. ❧

Barbara Ann Scott

Figure Skater Barbara Ann Scott has her Personal Priorities

She says her greatest personal moment was the day she married Tom King but her greatest moment in sport was in 1948 in St. Moritz when she won Canada's only gold medal ever in singles figure skating. After her victory, Ab Renaud and Reg Schroeter, forwards on the gold medal winning Ottawa RCAF Flyers hockey team, hoisted her on their shoulders and the triumphal photo was flashed around the world.

Interviewing Barbara Ann Scott-King about her incredible figure skating achievements is akin to trying to nail jelly to a wall. She is still so modest about the meteor's tail she blazed that she will deflect a question by answering: "Oh, you can get all that information from the Canadian Figure Skating Association."

She is the world's longest reigning monarch. She has been Queen of the Canadian figure skating world since she burst on the national scene in 1940, winning the Canadian Junior Championship when she was just 11 years old.

Barbara Ann Scott was and still is Canada's Sweetheart. During her skating prime she was everybody's choice for "The Girl Next Door." No one has ever come close to dislodging her from the throne she occupies through ability, grace and charm. Chatelaine magazine calls her "a female role model."

"The greatest moment of my life was my wedding day when I married Tom in 1955 and we have had 45 wonderful years together. My greatest moment in sport was at the Olympics in St. Moritz in 1948. I was on the dais in a blinding snowstorm. It was between periods of a hockey game. Eva Pawlik of Austria was runner-up with silver and Jeanette Altwegg of Great Britain won bronze."

"I was handed my gold medal in a case. They didn't put it around your neck on a ribbon in those days. Then, our flag was raised on the highest flagpole and our National Anthem was played. They played O Canada — so far away from home. It was the proudest moment of my life and the tears streamed down my cheeks."

Barbara Ann Scott, 1948, St Moritz

Canada

"That day, I skated free-style in the 13th position, not in the final group like they do today. There were 25 skaters so I was exactly in the middle."

Barbara Ann skated on ice that had been chopped up by a hockey game that same morning. Eight of nine judges gave her firsts.

The year before she had won the Canadian, North American, European and World championships, so she knew her competition. "In St. Moritz I skated against four national champions — England, Austria, Hungary and Czechoslovakia. We still keep in touch."

"In those days compulsory figures counted for 60 percent of your total marks." A magazine writer reported she was so far ahead after the compulsory figures she could have fallen down four times in the free-style and still won.

Olympic and World Champion Barbara Ann Scott with her coach, Sheldon Galbraith

Barbara Ann Scott came from a family of modest means and grew up in Ottawa. Her father, Clyde, was hit by machine gun fire and shrapnel on the European battlefield of St. Julien in April, 1915, and left for dead. A German search party moved his body and heard him groan. Two years after he had been given up for dead by his parents he came home to Ottawa. His war wounds hastened his premature death in 1941, though, and Barbara Ann and her mother had to make do on a very modest pension.

Barbara Ann began skating when she was seven. Skates and boots for growing feet were expensive, not to mention instructors' fees and travel expenses for competitions. Her mother knitted her skating costumes.

"I can remember when I was 10 years old being in New York being fitted for my first pair of Gustav Stanzione boots. They cost $25 a pair but they were the best boots money could buy then. Mr. Stanzione told my mother my foot wouldn't grow much more than a half-size thereafter. And they didn't. I also had a pair of Wilson blades from England and they cost $15. I wore them all through my amateur and professional skating careers."

In 1947, four dozen Ottawa friends raised $10,000 to send Barbara Ann, her mother and coach, Sheldon Galbraith, to the European championships in Davos, Switzerland, and the World championships in Stockholm. In winning the Worlds, six of the eight judges placed her first and two awarded her 6.0 — perfect scores.

In 1948, in Prague, she recorded the highest scores ever on a Prague rink and defeated 18 competitors from five countries for the European title. It was the last time a non-European would be allowed to compete for the European title.

Her training program was discipline, practice, more discipline and more practice. In Ottawa, she was up every morning at 7:00, made her bed, did the breakfast dishes, practised eight hours every day, studied under a tutor in late afternoons and was in bed by 8.30 p.m. every night.

She skated 11 miles every day just practising her school figures. She also pushed the limits of her sport — in 1942 she was the first woman to ever land a double Lutz jump in competition.

She was Canadian Junior champion at age 11 in 1940, Senior Champion in 1944, 1945, 1946 and 1948 and North American champion 1945-47. In 1947 and 1948 she won back-to-back European and World championships. In 1945, 1947 and 1948 she was awarded the Lou Marsh Trophy as Canada's most outstanding athlete.

1948 Olympic Winter Games, St. Moritz, Switzerland

Reliable Toy Company came out with a Barbara Ann Scott doll and every little girl in late 1940s Canada wanted one from Santa for Christmas. They sold like hotcakes for $5.95 each.

When she returned home to Ottawa from her gold medal performance in St. Moritz, 70,000 people — more than a third of the city's population — gathered to welcome her home. The Band of the Governor General's Foot Guard played "Let Me Call You Sweetheart" when her train arrived at downtown Union Station. The next day in Toronto another 70,000 people turned out to salute her.

She was invited to receptions at the White House and Buckingham Palace. She was, indeed, the "reigning Queen of the blades."

The only controversy Barbara Ann Scott was ever involved in was not of her doing — when the City of Ottawa tried to present her with the keys to a canary yellow Buick convertible. She could not accept the car because it would have cancelled out her amateur status.

"Of course, Avery Brundage (then President of the International Olympic Committee) was right. After all, I was still an amateur."

In 1948, at the age 19, she turned professional and performed in ice skating shows across Canada, the United States and England. In 1951 she replaced three-time Olympic champion Sonja Henie in Holiday Ice Revue. She formed the St. Lawrence Foundation to share part of her earnings from those shows with disabled children in Canada.

She retired from skating when she married Tom King in 1955. He was a former All-American college and National Basketball Association player who was Publicity Director for the Arthur M. Wirtz entertainment empire when he met Barbara Ann while promoting the Hollywood Ice Revue.

One of her few disappointments today is that the demands on female figure skaters are forcing them to place too much emphasis on athletic triple jumps at the expense of the artistic side of figure skating.

Despite all the honours and tributes that have been heaped on her, she said from her home in Chicago that the titles she is proudest of are "wife and Canadian citizen." ❦

1983   2000

1947

Barbara Ann Scott won the European singles figure skating title, as well as earning her and Canada's first-ever World Championship crown.

1948

Barbara Ann Scott won the Canadian, European, World and Olympic Figure Skating titles, becoming the first North American to win all these events in the same year. She also became the first Canadian figure skater to win an Olympic gold medal, and the first to win back-to-back world titles.

1948 RCAF Flyers

The 1948 Ottawa RCAF Flyers, gold medal winners in hockey at the St. Moritz Olympics, were a team that almost never was and probably never should have been.

The team was assembled at the very last minute because a stubborn Squadron Leader at RCAF Headquarters, Dr. Sandy Watson, refused to take "No" for an answer. Sandy Watson was stunned when he read in his morning paper that Canada would not be sending a hockey team to compete in 1948 — the first Winter Olympics to be held since 1936 (the 1940 and 1944 Games were cancelled because of World War II).

According to Canadian Amateur Hockey Association officials at the time, they were unable to find a strong senior team whose players could swear the Olympic Oath that they were true amateurs and not paid professional or semi-professional players.

With absolutely no mandate from the RCAF, Dr. Watson called George Dudley, secretary-manager of the CAHA, at his home in Midland, Ontario.

"Will an RCAF team be acceptable?"

"Yes, but you have 48 hours to advise the International Ice Hockey Federation."

Sandy Watson then went to work on the RCAF. He had no difficulty selling the idea to his immediate superior, Air Commodore Dave McFall. They then flew it past the Chief of the Air Staff, Air Marshal Wilf Curtis, the same day and he, in turn, sold Defence Minister Brooke Claxton. The Defence Minister phoned George Dudley, and Canada was in.

There was just one more hurdle. The RCAF didn't have a team, and the Olympics started in just three months. The fabled hockey Bouchers — father, George "Buck" and son, RCAF Sergeant Frank, were delegated to put a team together. Word went out to Air Force stations across Canada — "Send us your best for tryouts." A resulting 75 hopefuls showed up for tryout camp, most of whom were assessed as "pathetic."

The RCAF Flyers' first exhibition game before 6,000 fans in Ottawa's old Auditorium was against a mediocre McGill University team. The Flyers were thumped 7-0. In their second exhibition match, Bill Cowley's Army team from the Ottawa Senior League trounced them 6-2.

Sportswriters began loading live rounds in their rifles as the media went into a feeding frenzy. Critics insisted the Flyers be kept home. Others wanted Canada to withdraw completely from the Olympic hockey series. Still others wanted the Flyers replaced with a strong university team.

SOS calls went out to Walter Brown of the Boston Bruins, Conn Smythe of the Toronto Maple Leafs, Jack Adams of the Detroit Red Wings and Frank Selke of the Montreal Canadiens.

Frank Selke recommended Andre Laperrière, a 22-year old defenceman with the University of Montreal. Conn Smythe suggested two former University of Toronto stars, George Mara and Wally Halder. Next, Dr. Watson and Frank Boucher raided the 'Burgh team in the four-team Ottawa Senior League and signed up five players including Frank Dunster, formerly of the Oshawa Junior Generals, and high scoring forwards Ab Renaud and Reg Schroeter. The team roster was finally set. Or was it?

The Flyers finally won an exhibition game. They doubled a strong Belleville Intermediate team 8-4 and the newcomers accounted for six of the eight goals.

Just as a strengthened team was beginning to jell another roof caved in. The goaltender, Dick Ball, had a serious lung infection and could not pass the medical exam. George Mara and Wally Halder volunteered that the second best goaltender in all of Toronto (Walter "Turk" Broda was the best) was Toronto Transit Commission employee Murray Dowey.

A late night call to TTC Commissioner (later Mayor of Toronto) Allan Lamport by Sandy Watson resulted in a generous leave of absence for Murray Dowey. He was sworn in to the RCAF that same afternoon and fitted out with an ill-fitting uniform.

LEGENDS IN THEIR OWN TIME

Dr. Sandy Watson, left, Frank Boucher, André Laperrière and Ab Renaud, far right, are the only surviving members of the Royal Canadian Air Force Flyers hockey team, which won the gold medal at the Winter Olympics in 1948. The 1948 RCAF Flyers were voted the top military athletes of the 20th century by the Armed Forces. Milt Schmidt, second from right, the high-scoring Boston Bruins' great, represented the Bruins' 'Kraut line' that also included Woody Dumart and Bobby Bauer. Last night, the Canadian Armed Forces honoured their own in a glittering sports gala at the Congress Centre. See story on page A5.

JEAN LEVAC, THE OTTAWA CITIZEN

Pat MacAdam

50 years later the RCAF Flyers got together again, to celebrate again.

Sandy Watson recalls he "looked even worse than the original Sad Sack. He looked like a skinny bedraggled kid who had been dragged through a knot-hole."

On January 7, 1948, a team not given "a hope in hell of winning" was given a send-off by 500 relatives and fans at Ottawa's Union Station. The RCAF band played the Air Force March Past as they boarded a special Canadian Pacific coach bound for New York where they would board the Queen Mary.

In the next 80 days this rag-tag collection of "airmen" would travel 15,000 miles, play before 250,000 spectators, play 42 games, win 31, lose five, tie six and bring Olympic gold home to Canada. They would play all their games outdoors, in snowstorms, in rainstorms, in near blizzard conditions, in thin altitudes more than a mile above sea level, on slushy ice surfaces and on ice surfaces with foot high perimeter boards around them.

Canada

The United States hockey team was on the same ship as the Flyers. The Americans travelled top cabin; the Flyers went steerage. The Americans were kitted out in blazers, flannels, white shirts and ties; the Flyers wore baggy blue RCAF battle dress uniforms.

The Flyers left Canada with RCAF sweaters on their backs and basic RCAF monthly pay. Sandy Watson scrounged Tackaberry skates from CCM and 300 hockey sticks. The Flyers came home with one stick — the much taped over goalie stick Murray Dowey used while racking up five shutouts and allowing only five goals for a stingy 0.62 goals against average in eight Olympic hockey games.

Canada defeated Italy 21-1, Poland 15-0, Austria 12-0, the United States 12-3, Great Britain 3-0 and Sweden 3-1.

Wally Halder scored six goals against the US and George Mara potted four. George Mara had five goals and five assists against Italy. Every Flyer except Murray Dowey figured in the scoring in the 21-1 rout.

The Flyers won seven games and played Czechoslovakia to a scoreless tie to win gold.

Canada scored 69 times in their eight games. Wally Halder had 21 goals, George Mara scored 17 times, while Reg Schroeter scored an even dozen.

Adding to the celebratory mood, Flyer Hubie Brooks married his Danish war bride, Birth Grontved, in St. Moritz the day after their final game. (Hubie Brooks was one of only five Canadian airmen to win a Military Medal during World War II. He was shot down, captured, escaped, re-captured and escaped again to fight with partisans in the Carpathian mountains.) The Flyers' players formed a ceremonial arch of hockey sticks as the bride and groom left the church. Barbara Ann Scott, who won a gold medal in figure skating at St. Moritz, and Sandy Watson were Maid of Honour and Best Man.

When the Flyers departed for home a Prague newspaper saluted them: "Au revoir, Flyers, you are still our hockey masters; you taught us both hockey and sportsmanship."

The same team that left Ottawa amid criticism and doubt returned in triumph to a tumultuous welcome. Each player rode in his own separate Buick convertible through downtown Ottawa while the lunch hour crowd cheered. The parade ended at RCAF Headquarters and Sandy Watson handed the world championship hockey trophy (the Olympics doubled as the World Championship that year) over to Air Marshal Wilf Curtis. ✤

1948 RCAF Flyer, Olympic gold medallist and founder of the Olympic Trust of Canada, George Mara, in 1990

1948

Paradise Lost — Hughie Riopelle of Ottawa was a teenage hockey sensation attending St. Pat's College and was scheduled to join the 1948 RCAF Flyers for their Olympic quest. At the last minute it was decided not to take him because it would interfere with his schooling. The school's coach also did not want to lose the team's top scorer just before the playoffs.

Doug Hepburn

If Canadian sport ever needs the ultimate story of someone overcoming impossible odds to win a world championship, it need look no further than Doug Hepburn, the man who came from nowhere to win the 1953 world heavyweight weightlifting championship.

A native of Vancouver, he was born with a club foot and crossed eyes. As a child he had operations to correct both conditions, but the doctors botched the operation on his foot, leaving him with atrophied calf muscles and a permanently weak ankle.

Hepburn hated school. His classmates ridiculed him for his deformed leg and his scrawniness. In order to gain the strength and self-esteem he needed to stand up to the school bullies, he turned to weightlifting, an activity that soon became all-consuming. His school work suffered, so he quit school.

Everything Hepburn accomplished, he did on his own. A loner and self-taught, he went from 145 to an eventual 275 pounds. Early in his career he set a Canadian record when he pressed 300 pounds. Canadian weightlifting headquarters in Montreal wouldn't accept the record as legitimate because of all things, nobody there had heard of him.

He went to Los Angeles in 1949, where he won the US Championship by beating John Davis. Still, he wasn't invited to try out for Canada's next Olympic team. So, while he sat at home, John Davis, the man he'd beaten in LA, won the heavyweight gold medal at the 1952 Olympics.

The next year his weightlifting buddies in Vancouver went to work on his behalf. At a time when senior governments weren't investing as much as a dime in amateur sport, Doug gave ballpark exhibitions of strength while his friends passed the hat.

They managed to raise $1,377, just enough to get him to the world championships in Sweden and back. No coach. No trainer. Just Hepburn, the clothes on his back and a sprained ankle from a training accident. Then he went out and beat the best from 20 nations at Stockholm.

On the way home, waiting to get a plane seat out of London, he ran out of money. British weightlifters arranged another pass-the-hat show to keep him in food and lodging until he could get a flight to Canada. When he got home, he finally got some recognition. The Vancouver Sun held a banquet in his honour and he was named British Columbian of the year. Realizing that Hepburn would do well at the

1954 British Empire and Commonwealth Games, Vancouver's mayor offered him $150 a month to help him train. To preserve Doug's amateur status, he listed him as his personal bodyguard.

Hepburn won the gold medal at the Games, then tried to cash in on his fame in the wrestling ring. He hated the life, though, and started drinking to excess. In turn he became a lush, a hermit, a pop singer, a poet, philosopher and hippie. He liked to say in later life, when he was helping to operate a Vancouver gymnasium:

"In fact, I was the first of the hippies. I lapped the field and came back straight." ♣

Highlights

General Highlights

1949

The Toronto Tip Tops won the World Series Softball Championship with an 18-inning win over a team from Florida.

1949

Ken Watson of Manitoba became the first curler to win the Brier three times.

1949

Cliff Lumsdon of Toronto won his first of five world marathon swim championships during the Canadian National Exhibition 15-mile swim.

1950

Joe Primeau played for nine seasons with the Toronto Maple Leafs and centred the famous "Kid Line" with Charlie Conacher and Harvey "Busher" Jackson on his wings. He won the Lady Byng Trophy in 1932 and was named to the second All-Star team in 1934. Joe Primeau completed an unprecedented hat trick in 1951 when he coached the Leafs to a Stanley Cup, after coaching the Toronto St. Michael's Junior "A" team to a Memorial Cup in 1947 and Toronto Marlboros to an Allan Cup in 1950.

1951

Ernestine Russell won her first international gymnastics championship in 1951 at the age of 12; at 14 she was Canada's Female Athlete of the Year; and at 16 she won every event in the US Gymnastics Championships. Over the course of her career, she was Canadian champion seven times.

1951

Marlene Stewart (Streit) won her first Canadian Amateur Golf Championship, on her way to winning 22 Canadian Championships before the end of the century.

1951

Irene MacDonald, originally from Hamilton, won her first of 15 national diving titles between 1951 and 1961. MacDonald also won six US national titles between 1957 and 1960.

1951

Gilmour Boa won the King's prize at the Bisley shooting competitions.

1952

Marlene Stewart (Streit) won her first British Ladies Championship.

1953

Marjory Shedd won her first of six national badminton titles in Canada.

1954

A longtime professional at the Royal Montreal Golf Club, Pat Fletcher, became the last Canadian to win the Canadian Open Golf Championship in the century, although he didn't know it at the time. His victory in 1954 at Vancouver's Point Grey Golf and Country Club came on the heels of his CPGA Championship win in 1952 and three Saskatchewan Open victories in 1947, 1948 and 1951.

1954

Swimming

How Marilyn Swam the Lake

by June Callwood
November 1, 1954

The day that sixteen-year-old Marilyn Bell swam across Lake Ontario was a cold, sunny ninth of September. The small, tousle-haired Toronto schoolgirl swam forty miles from a log retaining wall in Youngstown, New York, to a slimy concrete breakwater off Sunnyside, Toronto's merry-go-round area, and thereby collected for herself whatever immortality awaits pioneer marathon swimmers, plus approximately $50,000 in contracts, prizes and gifts from Canadians who were moved by her courage.

No other human interest event in Canada since the Moose River mine disaster has stirred a reading and listening public so deeply and no other event has had such a bizarre and hectic setting for its drama.

At one point, with the girl's heavy, aching arms flogging the water between them, and her brain almost unconscious with exhaustion, a Canadian National Exhibition official and Marilyn's trainer engaged in a sharp, shouted debate over the most advantageous spot for her to land; at another point, Star and Telegram reporters pushed and connived for possession of the stretcher and ambulance that would carry the pale, shaking swimmer from the dock. Every now and then, rarely and wonderfully, someone showed real concern for Marilyn Bell.

Marilyn's swim had been planned by the Canadian National Exhibition sports committee as a crowd-drawing spectacle to demonstrate the prowess of Florence Chadwick, a 34-year-old American considered by many to be the world's greatest woman swimmer. The

CNE paid Miss Chadwick a $2,500 advance of the $10,000 she was to collect if she succeeded in swimming the lake.

Two Canadian swimmers, Winnie Roach Leuszler, 28, who had swum the English Channel three years before, and Marilyn Bell, 16, dove into the lake behind Miss Chadwick to demonstrate something or other to themselves and their friends. Neither expected any reward if she failed but Mrs. Leuszler had hopes that a large hat would be passed among CNE spectators if she succeeded. Marilyn Bell, who was the first woman to complete a 25-mile swim eight weeks before off Atlantic City, expected nothing.

The expenses of both Canadian swimmers, including a $700-a-day rental for the two boats to shepherd them across the lake, were being paid for by the Toronto Star, which could not fail to cause havoc on the other two Toronto papers, the arch rival Telegram and the morning Globe and Mail.

None of the imperfections in the drama of the race were evident around four o'clock in the afternoon of the day it happened, when Toronto learned that Marilyn was the only swimmer left in the lake. The highly vaunted Flo Chadwick had been pulled out of the water, sick and retching, at four-thirty in the morning; strong, heavily built Winnie Leuzler had quit in agony from cramps ten hours after her second start. A five-foot-one, 119 pound child was still swimming seventeen hours after entering the water at Youngstown, New York.

Offices began to empty and a traffic jam formed between downtown Toronto and the grandstand the CNE had built overlooking the lake. Radios everywhere were tuned to those stations which offered live coverage.

Seven miles out in the lake, across choppy water being blown almost parallel to the shore, Marilyn Bell was ready to quit for the fourth time. She was treading water, swimming two strokes and stopping to tread water again.

By now she had been in the water eighteen hours.

What Gus Ryder [Marilyn's coach] later called the crisis came around four in the morning, at almost the same time that Florence Chadwick quit swimming. Marilyn, exhausted from fighting the twelve-foot-high waves, stopped swimming and looked pleadingly at Ryder. "I'm cold, I'm numb," she called in her light child's voice.

"Marilyn," Ryder shouted back, "you've swum all night and that's really great. If you can do that you can do the rest. In another hour the sun will come up and it will be really nice." He fastened a paper cup into a ring at the end of a six-foot stick, poured corn syrup into the cup and passed it to the girl. She sipped the nourishing drink and tried not to cry. Ryder didn't offer to take her out of the water and after a moment she let the paper cup float away in the darkness and started swimming again.

As the sky lightened, everyone in the lifeboat was shocked by Marilyn's appearance. Her normally pretty and gay face was haggard, the muscles around her mouth slack and her eyes glassy. For more than an hour she had been swimming with her arms alone, dragging her legs motionless in the water behind her.

Ryder passed Marilyn more corn syrup, but her hand was shaking so much the cup spilled into the water. Next he passed her some liniment he had scooped out of a jar and dropped in a paper cup. Under his direction, she rolled over on her back and rubbed her legs with the liniment. She continued to cry.

"Swim over here, Marilyn," Ryder called. "We'll take you out".

The girl began to swim and Ryder watched her closely, noticing that her legs were moving again. "Pull away, Jack," he ordered. Jack Russell moved the throttle and the boat moved away from Marilyn. She kept on swimming, still crying.

"That's a bad sign," Ryder told Bryant softly. "If she keeps on crying, I'll have to take her out."

After a while she stopped crying and as the sun began to climb she was swimming strongly.

At 10.30 Ryder noticed Marilyn tiring again. He scribbled on a blackboard the news he'd been saving for such a crucial moment: "FLO IS OUT." Marilyn, delighted to learn she had outlasted the world's greatest woman swimmer, swam with renewed vigour.

In Toronto, CNE President Robert Saunders announced that since Florence Chadwick was out of the water, forfeiting $7,500, any swimmer who finished would get "a substantial amount of money."

Around four o'clock in the afternoon the Star boats heard the news on their radios that Winnie Leuzler was out of the water and that Saunders had announced Marilyn would get $7,500 — the balance of the Chadwick fee — if she finished.

It seemed doubtful, to everyone but Ryder, that she could finish. She had been in the water for seventeen hours and she hadn't slept in thirty-one hours.

Earlier it had struck Ryder and Bryant that Marilyn needed extra encouragement. They asked the Mona IV to locate Marilyn's best friend, a tow-headed member of the Lakeshore Club named Joan Cooke.

The summoning of Joan Cooke turned out to be a fine strategy. Towards five o'clock Marilyn began to falter again, clawing the water with no strength. Ryder asked Joan to jump in and swim beside Marilyn.

The splash of her dive woke Marilyn, who had been dozing again. She looked at her friend and laughed. "Don't touch her, Joan, you'll disqualify her," screamed Ryder. Joan nodded and called briskly to Marilyn, "Come on, let's go." Marilyn's stroke picked up and a tiny flutter of white water behind her showed that her feet were kicking. Joan stayed in the water a few minutes more, then climbed back in the Mipepa and wrapped herself in blankets.

At five o'clock Ryder pointed to the Toronto sky line and wrote on the blackboard, "WE ARE TAKING YOU STRAIGHT IN." In spite of this, Marilyn's stroke slowed from the sixty-four strokes per minute she maintained at her best to fifty strokes a minute. She stopped twice in two minutes, staring dazedly at the boats collecting from Toronto and Hamilton. The wind grew stiffer and colder and the waves pushed her west of the pink flares popping over the Exhibition.

At that moment, at 6.35, Marilyn stopped swimming and stood up, treading water.

"I'm tired," Marilyn wailed.

Ryder, not hearing, shouted "Fifteen minutes more, Marilyn. Come on!"

Like an obedient child, Marilyn put her face in the water and started swimming. At that point her conscious mind blanked out and she had the feeling she was far away, floating bodiless and light.

Once again she stopped and Ryder passed her the last of the eight pounds of corn syrup and the package of uncooked Pablum he had brought.

She became aware of a feeling that if she stopped again she would be finished. She never paused again.

Ryder turned on his flashlight. The darkness along the shore ahead turned out to be thousands of people, screaming unintelligibly. The Mipepa pulled aside and let Marilyn go in to the breakwater alone. She touched it with her left hand and stopped. It was six minutes after eight. She had been in the water 20 hours and 59 minutes.

Marilyn Bell can't remember touching the breakwater. When the lifeguards tried to pull her into one of their dinghies she was furious. "Let me go!" she cried. She thought they were trying to take her out of the water before she finished the swim.

Swim coach Gus Ryder is presented to HRH, The Queen Mother.

"She'll be the darling of the empire tonight," someone had predicted after the swim, "and forgotten tomorrow."

It didn't work out that way. The youth and smallness of the girl, the unexpectedness of her victory and the drama of the mile-by-mile radio and newspaper coverage caused a public reaction that most observers could compare only with Lindberg's flight across the Atlantic. ♣

In 1956, Cliff Lumsdon became the first person to swim the Straits of Juan de Fuca off Vancouver Island; he also won the 26-mile Atlantic City marathon. Later, Marilyn Bell became the first female to swim the Straits of Juan de Fuca.

Highlights

1955

The first televised Canadian Open golf tournament was won by a first-time PGA winner — Arnold Palmer, who shortly thereafter went on to golfing stardom.

1955

Al Balding's victory at the 1955 Mayfair Open was a first — no other Canadian had ever won a PGA Tour event in the United States. He finished sixth on the PGA Tour money list in 1957, the highest for any Canadian in the century. The Toronto native won the CPGA championship and CPGA Match Play Championship four times each. He was the individual low-scorer at the 1968 World Cup, where he teamed up with George Knudson to win the prestigious team event for Canada.

1956

Marlene Stewart (Streit) won the Canadian (again) and the United States Amateur Championships (first time for a Canadian woman) in the same year.

1957

Al Balding continued his winning ways, taking three PGA events in the year. Nick Weslock won his first of four Canadian Amateur Championships.

June 22, 1957

Canada's national soccer team's first appearance in World Cup qualifying play started off with a lopsided 5-1 win over the USA in Toronto.

1958

George Chuvalo won his first Canadian heavyweight boxing title in a career that lasted 20 years. Chuvalo would win and lose the Canadian title a few times along the way, finally relinquishing it for good in 1978. He also fought for the world title twice, losing to Ernie Terrell in 1965 and Muhammad Ali in 1966.

1958

Lucile Wheeler became the first Canadian to win a world alpine ski title by winning the downhill and giant slalom events at the World Championships at Bad Gastein, Germany.

1959

The Richardsons, led by skip Ernie Richardson, of Saskatchewan, won four Briers in five years, four Scotch Cups (forerunner of World Championship), five Provincial Championships, a Masters title, the Tournament of Champions and many "cashspiels" on their way to becoming one of the best curling teams in the world the entire century.

A long hitting former club pro from Vancouver, Stan Leonard, joined the PGA tour in the 1950s, and won three times, including the prestigious Tournament of Champions in 1958 in Las Vegas.

Golfer Al Balding of Toronto, 1955 Mayfair Open

The Boston Marathon – Canadian Champions

In the more than 100 years since it was first run, the Boston Marathon has been one of the most prestigious races in the world. Canadians started entering the race in 1900 and through the century won their fair share of these coveted titles, particularly early in the century. ❧

Highlights

Boston Marathon

1900

James Caffrey, Hamilton, Ontario
In the first year Canadians entered the Boston marathon, they ran away with the event. Canadians finished 1-2-3, with James Caffrey winning, Billy Sherring second and Frank Hughson third. Supposedly Sherring held the lead at the 15-mile mark and, thinking he had a larger lead than he had, sat down on some grass to rest a bit — Caffrey then promptly passed him for the lead.

1901

James Caffrey, Hamilton, Ontario
James Caffrey became the first repeat winner of the Boston Marathon.

1907

Tom Longboat, Hamilton, Ontario (6 Nations Reserve)
Famed long-distance runner Tom Longboat was only 19 at the time he made his only appearance in the Boston Marathon. He set a quick early pace and was leading the race in a tight duel with local favourite James Lee, when a freight train passing through blocked many runners behind them; only nine runners got by without interruption. Longboat continued his early fast pace and even in a late-race driving rain ran the fastest race on record.

1910

Fred Cameron, Nova Scotia
Fred Cameron had never run more than 10 miles in his life when he entered the Boston Marathon as a longshot. He took an early lead hoping to add distance between himself and his more experienced competitors. The tactic worked, as the Nova Scotian won the race.

1914

James Duffy, Hamilton, Ontario
Two Canadians put a stirring finish to one of the closest Boston marathons of the century. James Duffy from Hamilton and Montrealer Edouard Fabre changed leads at least four times in the final mile of the 42-mile run, with Duffy finally edging Fabre out by 14 seconds, the closest race on record.

1915

Edouard Fabre, Montreal
Fabre had come so close the year before at the Boston Marathon, and in 1915 he would not be denied his greatest victory. In blistering heat, Fabre kept with the leaders the whole race, while many others faltered, and took the lead in the last four miles. He hung on for his much anticipated victory.

1926

Johnny Miles, Sydney Mines, Nova Scotia
The presence of the reigning Olympic champion and three previous winners of the Boston Marathon in the field did not deter an unknown 19-year old delivery boy from Nova Scotia. Johnny Miles ran the race of his life, beating the more famed challengers and won the Boston Marathon in record time.

1929

Johnny Miles, Sydney Mines, Nova Scotia
This time he wasn't unknown, but it was still a surprise when Johnny Miles won his second Boston Marathon. After his 1926 win the young Nova Scotian had failed to complete either the 1927 or 1928 runs. Many thought he was a one-shot wonder until he again broke the race record, this time by four minutes.

1934

Dave Komonen, Timmins, Ontario
Dave Komenen was a Finnish-born cobbler living in Ontario's mining country. He made his own running shoes and ran away with the Boston Marathon, beating his nearest challenger by over four minutes.

1937

Walter Young, Quebec
Walter Young liked to race. In the winter he ran in snowshoes, in the summer in running shoes. He engaged in a see-saw duel with seven-time Boston Marathon runner-up John Kelley for 23 miles. Young finally took the lead for good and ended up winning by six minutes.

1940, 1943, 1944 and 1948

Gérard Côté, Quebec
Four times in the 1940s, Quebec's Gérard Côté ran away with the Boston Marathon title. In 1940 he won as a virtual unknown, defeating John Kelley. In 1943, he left his commando stint in the Canadian Army long enough to once again defeat John Kelley and win his second title. He won his third title in 1944 by only 60 yards, remarkably again over John Kelley, who must have built up some sort of angst about the Quebecker. Proving his earlier runs were not war-time flukes as some had suggested, Côté returned to the Boston Marathon in 1948 to stage another classic duel. Going "elbow to elbow" with Ted Vogel for 23 miles, Côté pulled away from the intense battle and won his fourth title.

1977

Jerome Drayton, Toronto
A record number of participants lined up for the 1977 Boston Marathon, and in the early going the crowded conditions forced Torontonian Jerome Drayton to run ahead of the pack and at a faster pace than he had planned. It worked, though, as Drayton took an early lead and won by 58 seconds over Veli Bally of Turkey. Drayton, third in the 1974 race, hooked up early in a duel with 1975 champion Bill Rodgers. However, as the 77-degree heat began to take its toll on Rodgers, Drayton pulled away and went on to defeat a record field of 2,810 in 2:14:46. This was Drayton's fifth Boston attempt as he became the first Canadian to win Boston since the 1948 triumph of Gérard Côté.

1980

Jacqueline Gareau, Quebec
Women and men start together at the Boston Marathon, and as several of the top men lead the runners through the course it is sometimes confusing to see just who is leading the women's division. Quebec's Jacqueline Gareau knew she led the other women most of the way. To her and most observers she was the apparent women's winner when she crossed the line in 2:34:28. One can only imagine her shock when she found another woman on the victory podium when she arrived. It was later revealed that Rosie Ruiz had entered the race just after Kenmore Square, three miles from the finish, and Gareau was rightfully awarded the title seven days later.

1984, 1986 and 1987

André Viger, Quebec
André Viger won his second of three Boston Marathon wheelchair titles in a world best time of 1:43:25. Viger's three victories in the most famous of marathons in North America seemed appropriate, since he was one of the pioneers of marathon racing for wheelchair athletes.

Canadian Winners of the Boston Marathon

Year	Athlete	Time	Event
1900	J.J. Caffrey	2:39:44.4	Men
1901	J.J. Caffrey	2:29:23.6	Men
1907	Tom Longboat	2:24:24	Men
1910	Fred L. Cameron	2:26:52.4	Men
1914	James Duffy	2:25:01.2	Men
1915	Edward Fabre	2:31:41.2	Men
1926	Johnny Miles	2:25:40.4	Men
1929	Johnny Miles	2:33:08.6	Men
1934	Dave Komonen	2:32:53.8	Men
1937	Walter Young	2:33:20	Men
1940	Gérard Côté	2:28:28.6	Men
1943	Gérard Côté	2:28:25.8	Men
1944	Gérard Côté	2:31:50.4	Men
1948	Gérard Côté	2:31:02	Men
1977	Jerome Drayton	2:14:46	Men
1980	Jacqueline Gareau	2:34:28	Women
1984	André Viger	2:05:20	Wheelchair
1986	André Viger	1:43:25	Wheelchair
1987	André Viger	1:55:42	Wheelchair

With its wide field and deep end zones, Canadian football became the haven for the forward pass during the 1950s, with quarterbacks the big stars. The salaries paid to the top players in Canada easily matched, and sometimes out-matched, those paid by American teams. As a result, many US college stars made their way to Canada.

Two such stars became the passing leaders of 1950s football in Canada: Jackie Parker and Sam Etcheverry.

Parker, also known as either "Ole Spaghetti Legs" or the "Fast Freight from Mississippi State," played defensive back, running back and quarterback for the Edmonton Eskimo powerhouse teams of 1954, 1955 and 1956, winning the Grey Cup each time over Etcheverry's Montreal Alouettes.

Sam "The Rifle" Etcheverry was a great passer in both the CFL and afterwards in the NFL, but as good as he was he never did win a professional championship as a player. By 1970, though, he was the head coach of the Grey Cup-winning Alouettes.

It wasn't only Americans who succeeded as quarterbacks in the '50s, as future Alberta Premier Don Getty led the 1956 Eskimos to the Grey Cup, using "Ole Spaghetti Legs" as his running back. ♣

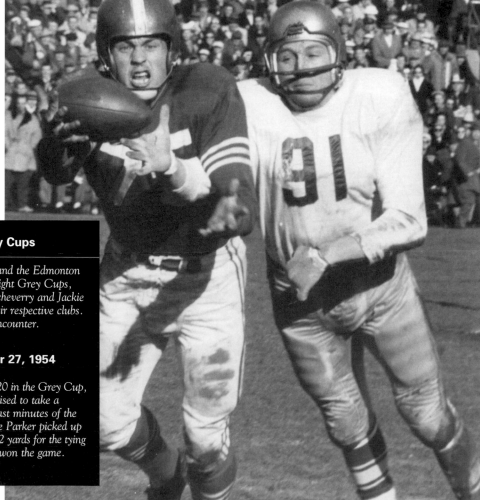

1954-1955-1956 Grey Cups

The Montreal Alouettes and the Edmonton Eskimos played three straight Grey Cups, with Sam "The Rifle" Etcheverry and Jackie Parker quarterbacking their respective clubs. The Eskimos won each encounter.

Grey Cup, November 27, 1954

With his team trailing 25-20 in the Grey Cup, and with the Alouettes poised to take a commanding lead in the last minutes of the Game, Edmonton's Jackie Parker picked up a fumble and returned it 92 yards for the tying touchdown. The convert won the game.

1961 Trail Smoke Eaters:

Canada's last world amateur hockey champions

The World Championship and Olympic hockey titles were regarded as Canadian possessions by divine right for much of the early part of the 20th century. Eventually, countries like Sweden, Czechoslovakia and the Soviet Union successfully challenged for the throne. From 1962 to the end of the century, European teams won all but two world titles, with the Soviet Union being particularly dominant.

Although it would later be recognized that Soviet hockey players were amateur in name only, in the 1950s and early 1960s Canada had not yet conceded that its amateur club teams were no match for the fast, disciplined Soviets. In a long-standing tradition, the Canadian Amateur Hockey Association invited the Chatham Maroons, Allan Cup champions of the year before, to represent the country at the 1961 World Championships in Geneva, Switzerland. Chatham opted for a Russian tour instead, which meant the lot fell to the runners-up in the Allan Cup, the Trail Smoke Eaters (who had also won the world title in 1939).

Coached by Bobby Kromm, the Smokies were backstopped by Seth Martin, who allowed only 11 goals in seven games on his way to being named the most valuable goaltender at the World Championships, a distinction he repeated in 1963, 1964 and 1966. On offence, former NHL player Jack McLeod led the way, winning the goal scoring title with 10 goals during the tournament.

The Canadians played tough, physical hockey, which sometimes had opposing teams crying foul. Nevertheless, they cruised through most of the tournament easily, defeating countries like West Germany and Finland 9-1 and 12-2 respectively. Only Czechoslovakia came close, battling the Smoke Eaters to a 1-1 tie.

At the time, there was no sudden-death playoff round in the tournament — the title was awarded to the team with the best round robin record. Canada's last game turned out to be against the Soviet Union, which had lost one game. Czechoslovakia, meanwhile, had already played its last game and finished the tournament undefeated. To become world champions, the Smoke Eaters not only had to beat the USSR (which would tie them with the Czechs in the standings), but win by at least three goals, since the title would go to the team with the better goal differential.

The game turned out to be an anti-climax. Still playing aggressive hockey, the Smokies ran up a 4-0 lead before the Soviet team got on the board mid-way through the third period. When the final buzzer sounded on that sunny March 12th in Geneva, the Smoke Eaters had vanquished the Soviets 5-1. Back in Canada, bragging rights were preserved for another year. Writing in the Vancouver Sun, Dick Beddoes said, "Trail's triumph proves Russian hockey is stuck on a plateau several fathoms below the Canadian level." Beddoes turned out to be wrong, though — it was the last World Championship ever won by a team of Canadian amateurs, while the Soviet Union won 18 times during the next three decades. It was not until 1994 that Canada won again, this time with professional players.

Soon after the Smoke Eaters victory, the CAHA decided to beef up Canada's international presence by icing all-star national teams, rather than club teams. It was the first step in a long evolution (both domestically and internationally) that eventually resulted in Canadian professional players being eligible to play at the World Championships and Olympics. ❧

Anne Heggtveit Wins Olympic Gold with a Record Margin

When dawn broke over Squaw Valley on February 26, 1960, it promised and delivered a stellar, sunny morning with clear blue skies.

Anne Heggtveit was up at 7 a.m. that day, squinting into the sun as she checked over the slalom course that she would shortly be racing. For her, the bright light was a good omen, at a time when any sign of change would be welcome.

The 21-year-old racer from Ottawa was not having a great Olympic Winter Games. A strong contender for the downhill and the giant slalom, she had to settle for 12th in both.

For Canada, the Olympic Games were half over, and we only had one gold, won by Barbara Wagner and Bob Paul in pairs figure skating. As if to add insult to injury, the hockey team, the Kitchener-Waterloo Dutchmen, was defeated by the United States, 2-1.

But up on Papoose mountain in the early morning light, Anne was feeling good. So good, she told her coach, Pepi Salvenmoser, "I've got a feeling this is it."

The slalom would be raced in two runs, the winner being the racer with the best combined time. Anne drew the second position. Thérèse Leduc of France drew first, and she ran the course in a very respectable 59.2 seconds. Then Heggtveit was off.

She tore down the 1,575 feet, winding and turning her way down the 53 gates. At the 10th gate, she misjudged her turn, stopping for a fraction of a second and losing precious time.

But she recovered, and continued to pound her way down the course, shaving the flags and giving her all. She crossed the line in 54 seconds flat.

It was a phenomenal run. Anne was so fast, the clockers reportedly did a double-take on their watches. But as second down the course, Anne had a long, nerve-wracking wait ahead of her.

One by one, the world's top skiers came flying down the hill. Betty Snite from the US followed right behind Anne, clocking in at 57.4, followed by racers from Austria, Germany, Switzerland, France, and Norway. But no one could touch Anne's time. The closest was the 15th skier, Marianne Jahn of Austria, who did it in 55.5.

Anne had taken the first run.

It was time for the second run down the hill, and the situation was quite clear. Short of disaster, Anne had secured herself a place in the medals. Her decision now was between turning in a conservative run to safeguard her position, or giving it her all and going for broke.

She went for it, attacking the sharply winding course, skidding a little at the third gate from the bottom, but never losing control. When she crossed the finish line the second time, the clock read 55.6.

"I used to have a bad habit of holding back in my second run," she recalled later. "But this time I didn't hold back at all. I knew that the other girls were good enough that I couldn't."

It was a good time — just one-tenth of a second behind the second fastest time of the first run. But again, Anne had to wait. She stood in the enclosure at the bottom of the hill, saying, "It's not finished yet." This time, her nerves were really stretched — the coveted gold was within her grasp, and each racer was threatening to knock her out of the top position. Betty Snite, of the US, finished faster at 55.5, but her combined time could not best Anne's. One by one, the others followed, and one by one, Anne held on to her lead. Finally, it came down again to Austria's Marianne Jahn.

As she came tearing down the course, the crowed oohed and aahed at her strength and speed. Then, two-thirds of the way down, Marianne fell down and tumbled. She recovered, but her time did not.

Anne had won the gold, and by an incredible margin of almost 3.3 seconds.

Her father, Halvor Heggtveit, remarked later in an interview that the hockey team's heartbreaking loss might have given Anne the ammunition she needed to do well for Canada. "I think it might have been the inspiration. It takes just some little thing to get them steamed up. I think, knowing Anne, that it would be just the type of thing that would make her grit her teeth a little harder."

Whatever the inspiration, it worked-and how. The brilliant runs this calm, intense skier ground out on Papoose mountain redeemed Canada and gave the team its second gold at Squaw Valley. Anne also made Canadian history — her win was Canada's first gold medal in skiing at the Olympic Games.

And the honours hardly stopped there. Since the Olympics doubled as the World Championships, the International Skiing Federation bestowed another two gold medals upon the Ottawa racer. She was named world champion for the slalom and, with best overall performance in all three events, for the women's alpine combined. These double golds marked yet another unprecedented honour for a Canadian skier.

Three golds in one day: it's little wonder that the name "Heggtveit" still inspires awe on the hills today. ❧

Figure Skating

Pairs Figure Skating

December 2, 1991

As teenagers, they were a study in contrasts: Robert Paul was as awkward and shy as Barbara Wagner was graceful and effervescent. But when the Toronto natives skated together, they moved in harmony. They first came together on the ice in 1952; over the next eight years they won five national, one North American and four world titles. With the 1960 Olympics looming, the pressure to bring home a gold medal was intense. Recalls Wagner: "If we had not won, I don't know whether I could have gone home."

Canadians' thirst for Olympic gold appeared to unnerve the skaters. As the critical event began, they seemed destined for disaster when, a minute into their routine, the record they were skating to skipped, throwing them out of step. Assuming that the judges had also noticed, Wagner and Paul stopped skating. As the record was reset, they regrouped — and turned in a gold-medal performance. Said Paul: "When it was over, I sat down and cried for a half-hour." ❧

Four-time World and 1960 Olympic Figure Skating Champions, Barbara Wagner and Bob Paul.

1963

Donald McPherson was the runner-up to Donald Jackson at the 1960, '61 and '62 Canadian Championships. In 1963 he became the first man to claim the Canadian, North American and World Senior Men's titles all in one year without having won any of them previously. Having just turned 18 years of age, he was the youngest man to win the world title.

1963

Marlene Stewart (Streit) won the Australian Women's Golf Championships, becoming the first person ever to win the national amateur golf championships of Canada, the US, Britain and Australia.

1964

Northern Dancer, owned by E.P. Taylor in Toronto, became the first Canadian-bred and owned horse to win the famed Kentucky Derby, doing so in a record time (2:00) that was only beaten by Secretariat (1973) during the rest of the century. Northern Dancer went on to win the Preakness (just missing the Belmont and the Triple Crown) and the Queen's Plate en route to being named Horse of the Year in both Canada and the USA. Northern Dancer was elected to Canada's Sports Hall of Fame in 1965.

1965

Figure skater Petra Burka was initially coached by her mother, the former Dutch champion Ellen Burka. In 1962, when Petra was 15 years old, she was the Canadian Junior Ladies Champion, and from 1964-1966 she was the reigning Senior Ladies Champion. She earned a bronze medal at the 1964 Olympic Games in Innsbruck. She had her career year in 1965 when she won the Canadian, North American and World figure skating titles. She was the first woman to complete a triple Salchow in world competition (1965), was chosen as Canada's Female Athlete of the Year in consecutive years, and twice won the Lou Marsh Trophy as Canada's Athlete of the Year.

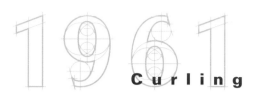

1961

C u r l i n g

Canada's World Champions of Curling

by Robert Metcalfe
January 7, 1961

One night in mid March, 1959, a Harry Lauder sort of Scot named Willie Young, captain of Scotland's champion curling team, sat hunched before a roaring fire in his farmhouse near Ayr. His florid face was grimly set and his glass of whisky was untouched.

His wife, busy with the supper dishes, became concerned for her normally cheerful and thirsty spouse. "Willie," she asked, "What's come over you? You're awful quiet tonight."

Willie stirred and sighed dejectedly. "Mrs. Young," he slowly replied. "I just don't know how I'm going to beat those fellows."

"Those fellows" were the Richardsons of Regina, Canada's curling champions and the first to play for the Scotch Cup and the world title in Scotland. Ernie, now 29, his brother Garnet, 27 and their cousin Arnold, 32, were carpenters in Regina; Wesley, 30, another cousin, was an instrument man at a Regina oil refinery. That day they had beaten Willie Young and his middle-aged team rather handily in the first of five games for the curling crown.

Mrs. Young told the Richardsons of Willie's dilemma shortly before they took him on in the second game. And Willie, who had lost only two of eighty games that season, never did find out how to beat the Richardsons. He lost the next four games as well. Said he, eyeing his aging crew: "Scotland will need younger players if we're to beat those fellows."

But Hughie Neilson, whose 1960 Scottish champions were all in their thirties, wasn't able to beat those fellows either. Like Willie Young, Neilson too lost five games to the Richardsons, and watched with chagrin as the upstarts from Canada again won the treasured cup and the curling title.

It was only the second year of the international contest and the cup was on its way back to Regina - bearing only the names of Ernie, Garnet, Arnold and Wesley Richardson. And wasn't curling a Scottish game? There was the rub. But Willie Young and Hughie Neilson had no need to feel alone with the problem of how to beat the Richardsons. The champions of nine Canadian provinces were wondering the same thing.

Just seven years ago the Richardsons, starting to curl for the fun of it, were bungling a game that Ernie as a youth had dismissed as a sport "for old men or muskrats" because it bored him.

The Richardsons introduced to Scotland a style developed in Saskatchewan where curlers aim at an enemy rock in the hope that their rock will knock it out of play and leave their own in a scoring position. It's a style that can easily be beaten if it's played erratically.

The Saskatchewan game beat the Scots, who lost even more convincingly when they tried to copy it in one match. The Richardsons countered by playing the Scots' conservative style, and won that game as well. This ability to curl equally well in draw or knockout style has made the Richardsons Canada's champions two years in a row. Theirs is only the third rink to accomplish the feat in thirty-one years of competition for the Macdonald Brier Tankard, which stands for the Canadian championship.

The Richardsons were favourites to win the 1960 Brier — a position they couldn't have hoped to reach only a few years before. Three of them, Ernie, Garnet and Arnold, began curling in 1953 with Norman Richardson, elder brother of Wes and a top curler at Regina's landlocked HMCS Queen, as skip. Norman skipped the rink for a year, though he winced at times as his green teammates slithered on the ice and their rocks sailed through the house — the target — and out of play.

"It was pretty funny," Garnet recalls. "We were sloppy. In the long run I guess we made it more by determination than ability."

The Richardsons curled only eighteen games that year and lost half of them. When Norman was posted the next year in Victoria (he skipped the Navy's championship rink in 1960), Wes Scott, a Regina carpenter, joined the team as lead and Ernie took over as a skip. Scott played two years with the team and his place was taken by Trevor Fisher, a Regina plumber. Wes Richardson didn't join the rink until 1958. "I got in on the gravy train," he says.

In 1960, the Scots hoped to beat the Canadians with Hughie Neilson, whose expert draw game, they were sure, would solve the Richardsons' knockout style. And in the first game at Ayr, Neilson gave them a run for their money.

The second game was played in Edinburgh, and the Richardsons began to aggravate a dour little Scot in the stands. Each time a Richardson rock banged a Neilson rock off the target, he growled: "That's nay curling."

On the fourth end, Neilson had two rocks on the target and one counted; four rocks sat in front of the target with only narrow openings, or ports, between them. Ernie skimmed his first rock through to the edge of the button and the complaining Scot fell silent.

When Ernie put his next rock through the narrow port and flush on the button, the Scot roared: "That is curling!" Neilson's team didn't recover.

Torontonian Bill Crothers stunned world record holder and Olympic champion Peter Snell in an 800m challenge race at Toronto's CNE grounds, outlasting Snell in the final stretch to hang on for the victory.

The Richardsons don't worry much about the Brier and Scotch Cup games; their toughest competitors are back home.

"When you're clear of Saskatchewan, the tension's off," says Ernie. "Then you can really relax and enjoy yourself."

On the ice, the Richardsons talk very little; they breeze through their games in two and a half hours or less. Eastern teams, they say, talk too much; their games last as long as four hours. Says Garnet: "The game's slow enough without wasting a lot of time talking out there." ♣

Ken Watson

Canadian Men's Curling Champions
The MacDonald Brier, 1927-1979

Year	Champion Skip	Team		Year	Champion Skip	Team	World Championsip Results
1927*	Murray Macneill	Nova Scotia		1955	Garnet Campbell	Saskatchewan	
1928	Gordon Hudson	Manitoba		1956	Billy Walsh	Manitoba	
1929	Gordon Hudson	Manitoba		1957	Matt Baldwin	Alberta	
1930	Howard Wood Sr.	Manitoba		1958	Matt Baldwin	Alberta	
1931	Bob Gourley	Manitoba		1959	Ernie Richardson	Saskatchewan	World Champions – Winner of Scotch Cup (precursor to World Championships)
1932	Jimmy Congalton	Manitoba		1960	Ernie Richardson	Saskatchewan	World Champions – Winner of Scotch Cup
1933	Cliff Manahan	Alberta		1961	Hec Gervais	Alberta	World Champions
1934	Leo Johnson	Manitoba		1962	Ernie Richardson	Saskatchewan	World Champions
1935	Gordon Campbell	Ontario		1963	Ernie Richardson	Saskatchewan	World Champions
1936	Ken Watson	Manitoba		1964	Lyall Dagg	British Columbia	World Champions
1937	Cliff Manahan	Alberta		1965	Terry Braunstein	Manitoba	2nd
1938	Ab Gowanlock	Manitoba		1966	Ron Northcott	Alberta	World Champions
1939	Bert Hall	Ontario		1967	Alf Phillips Jr.	Ontario	4th
1940	Howard Wood Sr.	Manitoba		1968	Ron Northcott	Alberta	World Champions
1941	Howard Palmer	Alberta		1969	Ron Northcott	Alberta	World Champions
1942	Ken Watson	Manitoba		1970	Don Duguid	Manitoba	World Champions
1946	Billy Rose	Alberta		1971	Don Duguid	Manitoba	World Champions
1947	Jimmy Welsh	Manitoba		1972	Orest Meleschuk	Manitoba	World Champions
1948	Frenchy D'Amour	British Columbia		1973	Harvey Mazinke	Saskatchewan	2nd
1949	Ken Watson	Manitoba		1974	Hec Gervais	Alberta	4th
1950	Tom Ramsay	Northern Ontario		1975	Bill Tetley	Northern Ontario	3rd
1951	Don Oyler	Nova Scotia		1976	Jack MacDuff	Newfoundland	9th
1952	Billy Walsh	Manitoba		1977	Jim Ursel	Quebec	2nd
1953	Ab Gowanlock	Manitoba		1978	Ed Lukowich	Alberta	3rd
1954	Matt Baldwin	Alberta		1979	Barry Fry	Manitoba	3rd

The Labatt Brier, 1980-2000

Year	Champion Skip	Team	World Championship Results
*1980	Rick Folk	Saskatchewan	World Champions
1981	Kerry Burtnyk	Manitoba	3rd
1982	Al Hackner	Northern Ontario	World Champions
1983	Ed Werenich	Ontario	World Champions
1984	Mike Riley	Manitoba	4th
1985	Al Hackner	Northern Ontario	World Champions
1986	Ed Lukowich	Alberta	World Champions
1987	Russ Howard	Ontario	World Champions
1988	Pat Ryan	Alberta	2nd
1989	Pat Ryan	Alberta	World Champions
1990	Ed Werenich	Ontario	World Champions
1991	Kevin Martin	Alberta	2nd
1992	Vic Peters	Manitoba	3rd
1993	Russ Howard	Ontario	World Champions
1994	Rick Folk	British Columbia	World Champions
1995	Kerry Burtnyk	Manitoba	World Champions
1996	Jeff Stoughton	Manitoba	World Champions
1997	Kevin Martin	Alberta	4th
1998	Wayne Middaugh	Ontario	World Champions
1999	Jeff Stoughton	Manitoba	2nd
2000	Greg McAulay	British Columbia	World Champions

* The Canadian Men's Championships were called the MacDonald Brier Championships from 1927 - 1979, and the Labatt Brier from 1980 - 2000.

Ron Northcott

Canadian Women's Curling Champions

Year	Champion Skip	Team	World Championships Results	Year	Champion Skip	Team	World Championships Results
1961*	Joyce McKee	Saskatchewan		1985	Linda Moore	British Columbia	World Champions
1962	Ina Hansen	British Columbia		1986	Marilyn Darte (Bodogh)	Ontario	World Champions
1963	Mabel DeWare	New Brunswick		1987	Pat Sanders	British Columbia	World Champions
1964	Ina Hansen	British Columbia		1988	Heather Houston	Ontario	2nd
1965	Peggy Casselman	Manitoba		1989	Heather Houston	Team Canada	World Champions
1966	Gail Lee	Alberta		1990	Alison Goring	Ontario	3rd
1967	Betty Duguid	Manitoba		1991	Julie Sutton	British Columbia	2nd
1968	Hazel Jamieson	Alberta		1992	Connie Laliberte	Manitoba	tied for 3rd
1969	Joyce McKee	Saskatchewan		1993	Sandra Peterson (Schmirler)	Saskatchewan	World Champions
1970	Dorenda Schoenhals	Saskatchewan		1994	Sandra Peterson (Schmirler)	Team Canada	World Champions
1971	Vera Pezer	Saskatchewan		1995	Connie Laliberte	Manitoba	2nd
*1972	Vera Pezer	Saskatchewan		1996	Marilyn Bodogh	Ontario	World Champions
1973	Vera Pezer	Saskatchewan		1997	Sandra Schmirler	Saskatchewan	World Champions
1974	Emily Farnham	Saskatchewan		1998	Cathy Borst	Alberta	3rd
1975	Lee Tobin	Quebec		1999	Colleen Jones	Nova Scotia	5th
1976	Lindsay Davie	British Columbia		2000	Kelley Law	British Columbia	World Champions
1977	Myrna McQuarie	Alberta					
1978	Cathy Pidzarko	Manitoba					
1979	Lindsay Sparkes (Davie)	British Columbia	3rd				
1980*	Marj Mitchell	Saskatchewan	World Champions				
1981	Susan Seitz	Alberta	2nd				
1982*	Collen Jones	Nova Scotia	5th				
1983	Penny LaRocque	Nova Scotia	3rd				
1984	Connie Laliberte	Manitoba	World Champions				

*The Canadian Women's Championships were called the Diamond "D" Championships from 1961 - 1971; the MacDonald Lassie from 1972 - 1979; the Canadian Ladies Curling Association Championship from 1980 - 1981; and the Scott Tournament of Hearts from 1982 to present date.

Team Ontario

Sandra Schmirler

Canadian Press CP

Donald Jackson

The first triple Lutz and a World Championship

Donald Jackson glided into the room on a late winter day in 2001, and, ever the professional, apologized for being a few minutes late. "It's been a bad snow day," he said. Normally he would have been at the rink at 6 a.m., but he was not teaching today.

Born on April 2, 1940, and working his way to the top of the figure skating world, Jackson remained a marvel nearly 40 years after winning his world championship. He was smoother than Fred Astaire on his feet, and just about everyday, rain, shine or snow, he was at the Minto Club rink in Ottawa, teaching and skating.

Throughout his life, Jackson counted himself a lucky man. Events bear witness to his good fortune. In 1961, he had been planning to fly to the World Championships on the same plane as the American team, because he was training in the US. A bronze medallist the year before at the Olympics, this was going to be his year. But he fell sick, and couldn't make the flight, so he decided he would fly with his fellow Canadians later that week. As he lay in bed, Jackson got the terrible news: the plane carrying the US team had crashed, leaving no survivors. In the face of that tragedy, said Jackson, he abandoned his own plans for the Worlds and went to funerals instead of skating events.

The next year he did go, and was crowned World Champion. With countless retellings and a book behind him, he was still excited to tell his story almost 40 years later. It's the story of the 1962 World Championships, of another Canadian skater pushing the envelope, of a performance that has been called one of the best in skating history…

By Donald Jackson

It was Friday, March 15, 1962, and I was at the World Championships, competing for the men's crown. I was about to go on the ice to do my free skating program.

I hadn't had an ideal time of it in Prague. I started off really well, scoring very high marks (for me, certainly) on my figures. I guess after doing so well on three of them my coach, Sheldon Galbraith, decided I should be okay on my own. No sooner did he leave than I went to do my fourth, and it didn't go well. At all. By the time I was done, I was 35 points behind Czechoslovakia's hometown favourite, Karol Divin, who so far was the clear leader in the competition.

The next day went better, with my fifth and sixth figures, and I only gave up 10 more points to Karol. But in total, I was a whopping 45 points behind him.

But I'd gotten lucky in the draw to decide the order in which we would skate the free program. Karol was 12th, I was 16th, and Alain Calmat, the European champion, was 18th.

I didn't watch Karol skate, because I didn't want anything to interfere with my preparation. That turned out to be a really good idea, because the judges gave Karol a whole set of 5.9s. If I'd seen those marks, I might have been telling a completely different story later.

I took to the ice to warm-up, and felt pretty smooth. So I tried a few practice jumps, and felt so good, I tried the triple Lutz. I had tried the jump countless times, but only landed it perfectly five times. I didn't put everything into it, but managed to land well, only touching my free foot down for balance. So I looked over at Mr. Galbraith (I always addressed my coaches this way) and flashed him a sign that said I was ready for it. So Mr. Galbraith gave me the thumbs up.

I went back to the locker area, where Mr. Galbraith and I waited out the final minutes. Just before I went back on the ice, I turned to him and asked, 'Is there a chance that I could pull up?'

Mr. Galbraith had seen Karol's scores, and knew that I would need perfect sixes in order to win. What he told me was, "Don, there's room at the top."

That was all I needed to know. I stepped out onto the ice.

The triple Lutz was first up. I think everyone in the audience knew that I had planned to try it, and they were all watching. The atmosphere was thick with tension. But I didn't think about it, and kept my focus on the steps need to complete the jump.

Skating across the ice, I built up speed, gaining more speed as I rounded the first corner. I pivoted backwards, and continued to gather momentum as I skated up the ice. As I reached my original starting point, I bent my right knee, bringing my body and my left leg way down, almost touching the ice. I straightened up, and swung my left leg down to touch the ice for takeoff. And then I was rising into the air, bringing my feet together, closing my arms into my chest, and spinning, spinning, spinning.

I did three revolutions and landed back on my left foot, with my arms spread out. The jump was clean. I had just landed the first triple Lutz in competition.

Well, I was feeling pretty good, but I knew it was important not to lose my focus. So I kept up the attack, including throwing in a triple Salchow. In all, I did 22 jumps in that performance: two triples, ten doubles, and ten singles.

When the marks came up, it was tremendous. Seven judges gave me perfect sixes!

With more skaters to come, I went into the dressing room. And then something happened that still touches me today. Karol came to see me. He shook my hand and said, "Don, I know it's close, but if I win, I'm going to give the gold medal to you. You skated the best tonight."

But I did win! All of it — the years of hard work, the financial hardships on the part of my family, the sacrifices my mother made so I could skate — had finally paid off. I was the men's World Champion!

Perhaps I could have won without the triple Lutz. I don't know. But I believe you have to take chances to win. But I do know that once I took the chance and landed that jump, there was no stopping me. ❧

Northern Dancer

First Canadian horse to win the Kentucky Derby

Northern Dancer was impatiently waiting for his groom, tossing his thick neck, and banging the side of his stall with a hoof. It was 2 a.m. on May 6, 1964. In approximately another 16 hours, the stocky Canadian stallion with the three white stockings and a striking white blaze would be running in the 90th Kentucky Derby, arguably the most famous and sought-after crown in thoroughbred racing. But for now, the Dancer wanted breakfast.

Finally, the oats arrived. The Dancer ate and drank for ten minutes, and then, satisfied, settled himself down in the straw and fell asleep.

Four hours later, his groom, Willie Brevard, woke the chestnut colt for a slow walk around the barn, to loosen his muscles. At 10 a.m., Brevard gave him more oats. At four that afternoon, his trainer, Horatio Luro, rubbed him down with an alcohol and water solution, which Luro believed would refresh the colt.

It was time to go to the track and saddle up.

Brevard took hold of the Dancer — a simple act executed with some caution, because the squirrelly Dancer liked to nip — and led him to the paddock beneath the grandstands. Some 100,000 spectators were already in the stands, watching as racing's greatest horses were saddled. At home in Canada, thousands were glued to their television sets, cheering for the homegrown hero.

At the Derby that day, the Dancer was the second favourite. The number one choice was Hill Rise, a champion coming off of eight straight victories. In fact, the famous jockey Willie Shoemaker had decided to ride Hill Rise, even though he had ridden the Dancer to two important victories previously. Said Shoemaker at the time, "I just think Hill Rise is a better horse."

So the Dancer was once again the "dark horse," unknown and underestimated. It had been like that since his birth. As a colt, he disappointed his handlers. He was a small, stocky horse in an industry that prizes stature. Far from detecting signs of greatness, those around him thought he looked unpromising. As a yearling Northern Dancer went up for auction at the Taylor farm, but no one made a bid. So owner E.P. Taylor, of the famed Windfields farm in Oshawa, decided to keep and train the small colt.

His training progressed, but recurring foot problems kept him from starting his racing career until August, 1963. He then won five of seven starts in Ontario, and none could dispute his obvious talents.

Riding the Dancer that day was Bill Hartack, a jockey known for controversial choices. In the paddock, Luro had a few final words with the jockey, advising him to hold back for three-quarters of the race and to make a move at the far turn. He also warned Hartack away from using the whip, for fear it would turn the chippy stallion sour.

Then, Hartack was up and off, parading up the track with the field to the starting gate. In the gate, the Dancer looked small. In horse terms, he measured 15.2 hands, putting him four inches shorter than Hill Rise, among others.

Northern Dancer accepting laurels

For the punishing mile and a quarter race, the field would go once past the grandstand, and then around again for a complete circuit of the one-mile rectangular track.

And then the horses were off, blazing past the grandstand in a big pack. As the field broke up, Hartack quickly settled the Dancer into sixth place.

But as they rounded the clubhouse turn, it became clear they were in trouble. Northern Dancer was running close the rail. Ahead of him was a wall of three horses, while Hill Rise, with the wily Shoemaker atop, was outside of him. The Dancer was boxed in.

Here Hartack made one of two crucial decisions. With a sudden burst, he brought the Dancer away from the rail, and the two quickly darted into a hole ahead of Hill Rise. Shoemaker was taken by surprise. He had clearly planned to keep them boxed in, but could not get his big horse moving in time to prevent the small horse's nimble escape.

The crowd roared excitedly. In his box on the first mezzanine, E.P. Taylor jumped up and thrust his fist into the air. Northern Dancer was on the move.

Rounding the final turn, the Dancer continued on the outside, passing the first three horses. There was a quarter of a mile to go, and the field was so close that the first six horses were only three lengths apart.

Here Hartack made his second major decision. Luro had said to not use the stick on the Dancer, but Hartack needed more to shore up the lead. So Hartack gambled, and gave the stallion a tap. The Dancer responded — by bounding ahead two lengths.

But Shoemaker and Hill Rise were now making their big move, as Hill Rise stretched out his long legs to close the gap. The two horses were now in a test of raw speed and endurance. They were a contrast in style. Hill Rise exemplified the classic flowing motion of the long-limbed thoroughbred. Northern Dancer ran with his head hung out in front, his big muscles straining, and his legs moving with quick short strides in a choppy, all-out motion.

Bit by bit, Hill Rise moved up. As the two thundered past a screaming crowd, Hill Rise reached the Dancer's flank, then girth, then shoulder, and finally his neck.

But Hill Rise was stopped there. The Dancer simply refused to be caught. Head out, running in the race of his life, Northern Dancer kept Hill Rise there, at his neck, and thundered past the wire in a record two minutes flat.

A Canadian-bred horse had won the Kentucky Derby for the first time. ❧

1964 Bobsleigh Team Wins Olympic Gold

Journalists covering the 1964 Winter Olympics in Innsbruck termed Canada's gold medal performance in the four-man bobsleigh event a "fluke" and dismissed the Canadian athletes as "playboys." The Canadian bobsleigh team had upset the favourite Italians and Austrians to win Canada's only gold medal of the Games.

In a sport where winning margins are calibrated in hundredths of seconds, the Canadian squad of Vic Emery, his brother John, Doug Anakin and Peter Kirby finished almost a full second ahead of runner-up Austria. The Italian sled was third — 2/100 of a second behind the Austrians.

Prior to arriving in Innsbruck, the Canadian four's practice starts were largely dry-land runs in a gymnasium and a few runs at North America's only bobsleigh run in Lake Placid, New York. The Italians and Austrians had been in Innsbruck for weeks. Vic Emery's squad had only four practice runs down the Innsbruck course.

In their first run in Olympic competition the Canadians destroyed the old course record but near the end of that first run an axle seized and "it became quite hair raising." Only by lurching their bodies in unison were they able to prevent being overturned on the final curve before the finish.

1964 Olympic Gold medallists: Vic Emery, John Emery, Doug Anakin, Peter Kirby

Vic Emery recalls: "After the first four-man heat in which we broke the record which was never broken afterwards, my teammates discovered that a rear axle had seized as we fairly caromed off the second last corner into the finishing straight. While I walked the run, my Italian mentor, Eugenio Monti, lying in third place at the time, called his mechanics over and by the time I reached the top for our second run, they had partially fixed it — good enough to get us down with the second fastest second heat and a substantial lead overall.

"Thinking back on Eugenio's totally unselfish gesture, sadly, I am afraid that such sportsmanship has long since left international competition.

"I came down with a tetanus reaction and barely got through the next day's heat before heading to the hospital. We were second in that heat and our lead was holding. We were fortunate that the championship was extended to three days because I recovered enough to once again pilot the fastest last heat giving us the title by a margin of one second. The next year in the World Championships we made that two seconds."

Nevertheless, the "playboy" label stuck and the myth continued to be exaggerated. They were "ski bums" from well-to-do families; they were in Innsbruck to party; they entered the bobsleigh competition as "a lark."

"Playboys?" Nothing could be further from the truth. The four Canadians were familiar faces on the Laurentian ski slopes, but this hardly qualified them as "ski bums." They were spirited but they had arrived for gold and nothing would deter them from their quest. At lunchtime after the day's sliding was over they would bring out their guitars and drink nothing more potent than milk before perhaps a little skiing with the Norwegian team to loosen up — to keep jangling nerves in check.

The Canadian team members were all superb, well-rounded, athletes.

Vic Emery was a graduate of the University of Western Ontario where he was a "Mustang" in swimming, wrestling and skiing. Before going to the Harvard Business School for his MBA, he flew off Canada's only aircraft carrier. He was also an Olympic level Finn sailor.

John Emery, who became a plastic surgeon living in California, had been an all-round athlete at Trinity College School and Queen's University as well as winning the Duke of Edinburgh Trophy for the best all-round athlete in the Royal Canadian Navy Reserve.

Doug Anakin, another Queen's graduate, was a top-flight skier, a mountain climber and an intercollegiate wrestling champion.

Peter Kirby graduated from Dartmouth and captained the Dartmouth 1956 ski team. He was Canadian junior alpine champion in 1951 and a member of the 1954 Canadian ski team at the world championships.

More than 30 years later, Vic Emery was still going strong. When contacted in March, 2000 for his reflections on the 1964 Olympics, he e-mailed back: "You have caught me in the back of beyond the Arctic circle in Swedish Lappland competing in the World Masters cross-country ski championships, prior to heading for Murmansk for the Russian ski marathon and then the Finnish Lapponia series before heading south."

Canadian Press CP

Canada's only other gold medal in the bobsleigh, in fact the only other bobsleigh medal of any colour, came at the last Winter Games of the century, at Nagano in 1998. Pierre Leuders and Dave MacEachern teamed up to win the gold medal in the two-man event. Leuders and MacEachern actually tied the Swiss team in the race, with both teams being awarded gold medals.

Celebrating their 1965 Bobsleigh World Championship.

In a sequel e-mail message, he was obviously not pleased with the "playboy" label: "I have just completed my last 50km of the season here in the Finnish Lapponia in just over three hours — good enough for fifth place in the open class in trench-like conditions underfoot. This followed an 'elite' Russian ski marathon of 50Km under atrocious conditions both weather-wise and underfoot. I won my age group to a fanfare complete with band — felt like '64 all over again. And my old team-mates are all equally active as we head towards our 70s."

"We were all rounded sportsmen who wanted to see how far we could go in a sport that didn't interfere with our careers. With only natural tracks, bobsledding had a short season then and gave us challenge, excitement and international camaraderie. It also seemed to suit me as a driver from my background of aerobatic flying in the Navy and so used to snow and ice in Canada's winter from car driving to ice hockey.

"We financed ourselves and took time off from our jobs (management, teaching, medicine) and we competed harder than we played — those who wrote or talk differently didn't know us from Adam, but they felt, from the victory party which was quite spectacular (Charlie Burns and Chuck Rathgeb threw the victory party in the Sport hotel in Igls and nobody got more than slightly hurt), that they had to make up stories. At the time, for two years with two Firsts in four-man and a Third and a Fourth in the twos, we were the best and it cannot be said that we wouldn't have been also in any different era, today included."

Vic Emery also dashes cold water on the suggestion he feuded with Canada's IOC member at the time, Sidney Dawes: "In fact, on my flight home he was on the same aircraft and offered me the chance to take over from him on the IOC which I refused because I felt that athletes should participate and not politic and we intended to defend our title the next year. Maybe I shouldn't have been so hasty on the IOC matter!"

The following year a team of Vic Emery, Peter Kirby, Michael Young and Gerald Presley captured the 1965 world four-man bobsleigh title in St. Moritz winning three of the four runs and defeating Italy by two seconds. In the previous week's two-man competition, Vic Emery and Michael Young took the Bronze medal despite the fact Vic Emery was still recovering from a shoulder separation suffered in a crash a few days before.

Their performances in St. Moritz in 1965 laid to rest, for all time, the charges by the skeptics that the gold medal at Innsbruck in 1964 was "a fluke." 🍁

Vic Emery "on top of the world," and still competing in 2000.

1967

Enjoying its international popularity, alpine skiing started a World Cup circuit featuring a number of races that led to an overall season-long championship. Canada's Nancy Greene won the first Overall World Cup Championship in 1967, and the second in 1968. Only Steve Podborski's 1982 World Cup downhill title came close to matching such season-long alpine supremacy by a Canadian.

1970

Betsy Clifford, at 16, became the youngest skier to win a World Cup race, winning the giant slalom world championship at Val Gardena, Italy.

1970

The men's crew from Ridley College in St. Catharines became the first Canadian crew to win the Royal Henley regatta in England. Ridley College crews would also win the coveted event in 1973, 1975, 1977, 1979, 1985, and 1986.

1972

A Canadian crew won the fours-with-cox event at the Royal Henley, a feat they repeated in 1981.

1973

Sandy Hawley became the first North American rider to record over 500 wins in one season, ending with 515.

1973

Vancouver native Bruce Robertson won the 100m butterfly at the first-ever World Swimming Championships.

1974

Lucelle Lessard of Loretteville Quebec won the World Women's Field Archery Championships, Olympic Division. She went on to place fifth at the Montreal Olympics in the same event.

At age 19, in her rookie year on the women's pro golf circuit, Oakville's Sandra Post won her first major golf tournament, and the first professional major ever won by a Canadian — the 1968 LPGA Championship.

1969

Dorothy Lidstone of Vancouver became the first Canadian to win the World Archery Championships. At the same event, the Canadian women's team came second.

1969

Majestic Prince, owned by Canadian Frank McMahon, won the Kentucky Derby and the Preakness.

1968- 1973

George Athans Jr. won every Canadian overall water ski championship between 1968 and when he retired in 1973. In 1971 he won the World Overall Water Ski Championships in Spain, repeating the feat a year later in San Francisco. In 1973, Athans won both the world overall and slalom titles in Bogota, Colombia.

Hungerford and Jackson

A golden pair in Tokyo

The alliance between the University of British Columbia and the Vancouver Rowing Club, under the coaching of Frank Read, produced some of the finest rowing performances in Canadian history during the late 1950s and early 1960s. Although Read left the scene in 1960, his legacy lived on for some time after. In fact, it led to Canada's only gold medal of the 1964 Tokyo Olympics, won by George Hungerford and Roger Jackson in the coxless pairs.

As happens from time to time in sport, Hungerford and Jackson's win was a case of the dark horse coming up from the outside to win. Not only were they not expected to win, but it was in many ways a surprise that they were in Tokyo in the first place. Through a series of misfortunes, their original Olympic plans to row in the more prestigious fours or eights had been dashed, replaced by what was considered the consolation prize of rowing in the pairs event.

In the tradition of the great UBC/Vancouver Rowing Club crews of the late 1950s and early 1960s, Hungerford and Jackson had banded together with their respective crews to share a house and eat, sleep and breathe rowing. Six months before the Olympics, Jackson was a member of a highly-regarded fours crew, and Hungerford rowed on the powerful eights crew.

Their days consisted of a morning workout starting at 5:30 a.m. and an afternoon workout at 5:30 p.m. In between, the athletes put in a full day's work as labourers. Their training left them with barely enough energy to climb the stairs up from the dock at the end of each session, but their speed, coordination and endurance improved steadily.

The first blow to Jackson's 1964 Olympic hopes came when one of the other members of the fours crew injured his back just before the Olympic trials. The spare who replaced him was just recovering from a similar injury, leaving the crew unable to qualify for the trip to Tokyo.

The UBC eights crew was selected, however, and the coach in turn named Jackson and Wayne Pretty, another member of the fours crew, as spares for the Olympic team. Unhappy at the thought of only being a spare, Jackson considered not going. But with the prospect of rowing in the Olympic pairs event as compensation, he changed his mind and set to work training with Pretty.

In August, two months before the Olympics, Hungerford came down with mononucleosis, and had to give up his seat in the eights to Pretty. Jackson was left without a partner until Hungerford recovered enough to train again in early September. The two turned out to be a perfect match — both weighed about 85 kg, while Hungerford stood 193 cm tall to Jackson's 195 cm. Even so, successful crews normally took years to develop the balanced rhythm that would enable them to react quickly to slight changes in each other's stroke. The Canadians had six weeks, and Hungerford still had to redevelop his strength.

To cope with the initial disparity in strength, they removed the rudder from their shell. That way they could tell right away if one rower was pulling less strongly than the other, since the boat would move in that direction. It also guaranteed that all the energy they had at their disposal went into moving the boat forward, rather than using the rudder to compensate for uneven handling.

At the Olympics, disaster almost struck in the first heat, as the Finnish boat started drifting into the Canadians' lane about three-quarters of the way through the 2000m race. If they were struck, they would be given another chance to row, but it was questionable how many hard races Hungerford had in him because of his illness. Jackson made a quick decision, and called for a sprint in order to avoid the Finns. What looked like an act of sportsmanship actually served to ensure that they conserved as much energy as possible for the final. The sprint also helped them win their heat.

When George Hungerford and Roger Jackson received their Olympic gold medals in 1964, no Canadian journalists were present.

The next day, the eights crew was eliminated from further competition, so any medal hopes in rowing rested on the pairs crew. Four days after winning their heat they were sitting at the start line for the final. Starting at 43 strokes per minute, they dropped that pace slightly as they pulled into the lead. At the halfway point, they remained in the lead, but anything could still happen. To guard their strength, Jackson had decided to maintain a steady pace throughout, rather than risk a finishing sprint.

At 1500m they were more than a boat length ahead, but the Dutch crew was beginning to pull up. As their rivals came closer and closer, Jackson had no choice but to call for a sprint with only 100m to go. Reaching into reserves that they thought didn't exist, the rowers strained for the finish line. Canadian and Dutch boats crossed within half a second of one another, but the Canadians had hung on for the gold.

Exhausted, the pair declined to give each other the traditional dunking in the waters of the Toda course.

Ironically, the craft Hungerford and Jackson used to win the race was borrowed from the University of Washington. It was no stranger to Olympic competition, though — Americans James Fifer and Duvall Hecht had used it to win the gold medal in the same event in 1956!

So unexpected was the victory that there were no Canadian journalists present to cover the story. They had all chosen to cover track and field events, where Harry Jerome and Bill Crothers were in the process of winning bronze (100m) and silver (800m) medals respectively. Once they heard about the medal, the media tried in vain to track Hungerford and Jackson down, who were calmly settling in for an early night's rest rather than going out on the town celebrating. It wasn't until the next morning that the media caught up with them in the athletes' village.

The Olympic gold medal earned them the Lou Marsh Trophy in 1964 as Canada's outstanding athletes. The pair only rowed together in another four events, and never matched the luster of their inaugural race. Although Jackson went on to race in the 1968 and 1972 Olympics (placing 11th in single sculls and 12th in the fours respectively), Hungerford retired from competition in the spring after the Tokyo Olympics. ❧

Hamilton Blows Away the Winnipeg Curse

CFHOF

Hamilton Ti-Cat quarterback and punter, Joe Zuger.

Playing in their eighth Grey Cup in nine years on 27 November 1965 in Toronto's Exhibition Stadium, the Hamilton Tiger Cats had reason to dread their sixth encounter in that period with Bud Grant's Winnipeg Blue Bombers. Four consecutive times the Bombers had beaten the Tabbies and Hamilton might have hoped for divine help.

What they got made this Cup final as memorable as previous mud and fog bowls in Toronto. A tremendous wind blew off nearby Lake Ontario, reaching up to 50 mph. Over 50 of the game's 60 minutes would be played in the east end of the field and in desperation the Bombers would surrender three safety touches rather than punt to Hamilton and give them favourable field position. At the time, a conceded safety allowed the punting team to retain possession on the 25-yard line.

"We knew that three safeties were calculated risks," said Grant, "but we couldn't let them have the ball by punting against that wind."

On one occasion when Bomber kicker Ed Ulmer did try to punt from his own 25, the ball got caught in the wind and drifted back towards him. The alert Tiger Cat defender John Barrow caught the ball in a tussle with Ulmer and ran it in for a touchdown.

Unbeknownst to most spectators and even some team officials, however, was the direction game officials had given to each coach prior to the game. Penalties for no yards would be waived if players were unable to avoid staying 10 yards from the punt because of the wind. Further, it was ruled that on such plays in which the wind played a major role the ball would automatically be ruled dead when caught by the punt returner. So Barrow's moment of glory was rescinded though Hamilton did take over at the point where he caught the ball.

"The officials really gave me the razzle-dazzle on that play," Barrow said later, "I wasn't even sure of my ground so I backed off."

Going into the fourth quarter the Tiger Cats had built a 22-13 lead thanks in part to kicker Joe Zuger's ability to evade Bomber tacklers who seemed to have pinned him back on his own 35 after the snap had sailed over his head. Not only did Zuger get away but Winnipeg surrendered a single point off his punt.

In the fourth, with the wind at their back the Bombers were stymied by Hamilton's superb defensive unit led by the game's eventual most valuable player John Barrow. Finally Hamilton had overcome the Bomber curse and that of their brilliant leader Bud Grant who would later move to the National Football League's Minnesota Vikings.

This great Hamilton team would have one more kick at Grey Cup glory two years later when they celebrated Canada's centennial by easily beating the defending champion Saskatchewan Roughriders and their future Hall of Fame quarterback Ron Lancaster. Lancaster again wound up on the losing end against Hamilton, 13-10, in the 1972 Grey Cup. A generation later Lancaster, now on Hamilton's side, would coach the Tiger Cats to Grey Cup victory in 1999. ♣

The Hamilton Tiger Cats and the Winnipeg Blue Bombers faced each other in seven of 12 Grey Cups from 1953-65, with the Bombers winning four cups. In 1965, though, it was the Ti-Cats' turn. Here they are seen on both offence (below) and defence (above) winning the 1965 Grey Cup.

Canada

Our
Century
in Sport

H o c k e y

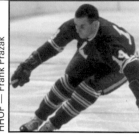

HHOF — Frank Prazak

Davey Keon and the 1967 Leafs

The day my big brother brought home the Stanley Cup

by Christena Keon-Sirsly

HHOF — Graphic Artists

We Keons hail from Rouyn-Noranda, Quebec, where our father worked in the mines. While everyone calls my brother Davey, the family has always called him David. During Centennial Year in 1967, when he was at the height of his career and the Maple Leafs and the Canadiens played for the Stanley Cup, I know many people thought my brother was this homegrown Toronto WASP. In fact, we were Catholic, from Quebec. It was an interesting and exciting time to be sure.

While our father was not into sports, David got into hockey through a second cousin of the family, Todd Sloan, who had played for the Leafs in the '50s. David, and my other brother Jim, played for the Noranda Club, because we lived in the English part of this twin town.

HHOF — Graphic Artists

Naturally, a famous rivalry existed between the two clubs, the French Rouyn and the English Noranda. Interestingly, during his whole hockey career my brother grew up playing against another future NHL player, Jacques Lapérièrre, who played for the Rouyn club. Meanwhile, Jacques' father worked with ours in the mines. Who would have guessed that in 1967, Jacques would be playing for the Canadiens against David and the Leafs for the Stanley Cup.

At 14, David was noticed by a local Leaf scout, Vince Thompson. Mother let David go to Toronto to play for the St. Mike's team on the condition that he finish high school with good marks. David promised he would, and off he went. Even there, he took some of his hometown rivalry with him, because Jacques Lapérrière played his Junior A hockey with the Montreal Junior Canadiens.

Father David Bauer, who later founded Canada's national teams in the 1960s, coached David at St. Mikes. He taught David how to check, reasoning that "at that size, he'll have to know how to check and how to get the puck from bigger guys." His coaching paid off big-time.

For a hockey player, my brother was small, at 5'8" and 160 pounds. But David had speed, a lot of speed, and could move the puck down the ice quickly. He was a good playmaker, as most centres are, but he was also so quick. He was only 20 years old when he tried out for the Leafs in 1960, and surprised a lot of people by making the team right away, scoring his first NHL goal on October 9, 1960. He went on to score 20 goals his rookie year and won the Calder Trophy as the NHL's best rookie to boot. Being my brother and such a gentleman, in his career he also received the Lady Byng Trophy twice. My parents were so thrilled at that. But the biggest thrill for us Keons was the 1967 Conn Smythe Trophy.

The Leafs were a great team during the early and mid 1960s, and 1967 may have been their best year. It was the Centennial year, and what better theatrics than to have archrivals Montreal and

Toronto vying for the Stanley Cup. Who would have thought that the star for the English speaking team would be a little centre from Quebec!

The feeling in Rouyn-Noranda went like this: everyone wanted Montreal to win, of course, preferably in four straight games with Jacques being the star. Ideally, people wanted Montreal to win each game 5-1, with David getting the one.

Our neighbourhood at home was, of course, cheering for David and the Toronto Maple Leafs. It seemed like the whole neighbourhood would to come over to watch David play — we'd gotten a TV just so we could watch him play, so I have always thanked David for that too.

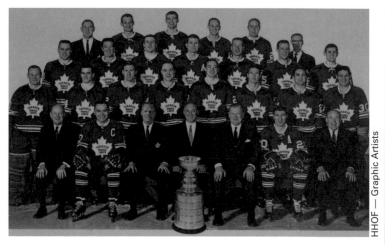

HHOF — Frank Prazak

My father was very proud of his son, and very nervous during his games. He had this nervous habit of putting a log on the fire whenever David came on the ice. I tell you, during that series you never felt such a warm place.

The playoffs unfortunately were around Easter that year, and Father was not thrilled. The Saturday night game would coincide with Mass, and our long-winded priest, Father Caulfield, made us miss even more of the game. But the good priest mentioned David during his sermon and wished him Godspeed. It must have worked, because that was the night David got three goals.

The Leafs won the series in six games, with several key goals from my brother. They say David always played his best during playoffs, and he held the Leafs' record for most playoff goals, with 32, until Wendel Clark broke it in 1996. In the final game, David scored a pair of short-handed goals. Not only did he help bring home the Stanley Cup, but he won the Conn Smythe for MVP.

In Rouyn-Noranda, people were upset that the Canadiens had lost, but they were all genuinely happy for David. I think they were even more happy because the Canadiens bounced back to win the Cup the next year and many more times after that. And, well, Toronto never did win again in the century. ♣

HHOF — Frank Prazak

1967

The 1967 Toronto Maple Leafs were the oldest team to win the Stanley Cup in the century. The Leafs had three players (Johnny Bower, Red Kelly and Allan Stanley) in their 40s and another nine in their 30s. The team averaged 31.4 years of age. Perhaps due to their advanced age, the team struggled during the regular season and almost didn't make the playoffs. But with three earlier Cup victories already in the 60s, coach "Punch" Imlach put faith in his veterans, stating: "Hockey is an old man's game in the head — where it matters." The Leafs shattered the hopes of the first place Chicago Blackhawks before dethroning the two-time defending Cup champions from Montreal in the finals.

HHOF — Graphic Artists

Equestrian Team Brings Home Gold as the 1968 Games Close

It's not over until it's over, the saying goes. And if there's one lesson Canadians learned from the 1968 Olympic Games in Mexico, it's that one.

Sunday, October 27 marked the last day of the 1968 Olympic Games in Mexico. Most of the Canadian team had already gone home, with very few medals to show — three silvers and one bronze, all won by swimmers, and not one gold. Newspapers had pronounced Elaine Tanner's silver medal on October 26 in the 200m backstroke as Canada's "last hope for a gold medal." Canada had come up empty-handed in track and field, rowing, gymnastics, sailing and every other sport. The media made dark pronouncements about Canada's showing, and spirits around the country were correspondingly low.

In a final sign of defeat, the Canadian team's chef de mission Howard Radford had left on Saturday night, even though the equestrian event, Grand Prix jumping, was still to come the next day.

Fortunately, the crowds didn't throw in the towel. Over 80,000 spectators jammed the Estadio Olimpico to watch the day-long final event under the hot Mexican sun. The Grand Prix jumping course had 14 obstacles, with 17 jumps in total, including a 15-foot jump over water. The goal was to complete the course with the fewest penalties, within the time limit. Each rider and horse had to do the course twice. The team with the lowest combined total would win.

Each country put in a team of three riders and their mounts — riding for Canada that day were Jim Day on Canadian Club, Jim Elder on The Immigrant, and Tom Gayford on Big Dee.

The usual suspects were favoured to win: Britain, West Germany, France or the US The Canadian team was not one of the favourites. But they had been labelled the "dark horse" entry by a West German publication (presumably with pun intended). In the horse world, such a nod speaks volumes. The spirits of the Canadian team were buoyed.

"At least, they know we exist," the understated Jim Elder remarked at the time.

The Canadian equestrian team had struggled for that international recognition. For years, they had been hampered by a "horse drain." No sooner would they finish training a world-class jumper, than the horse would get sold to the foreign teams for big prices.

But around 1964, the horse owners and the Canadian team made a commitment to hold on to the horses. The goal was to build a strong team for the 1967 Pan American Games, and of course, the 1968 Olympic Games.

Their efforts had paid off. In 1967, Jim Day won the individual gold medal at the Pan Am Games, while the team had made an excellent third place showing.

Even so, when compared with the 14 other teams sent to Mexico to compete, the Canadian team's horses were by far the youngest and least experienced. Both Big Dee and Canadian Club were failed racehorses, bought off the track for a few hundred dollars. The Immigrant and Big Dee were only in their first year of major competition. And The Immigrant was the type of mount that demanded an excellent rider. The young, ornery six-year old liked to kick his heels out after every jump — a habit that leads to knocking rails down and racking up penalty points.

During the first round, Jim Day and Canadian Club turned in an excellent 18-point round, while Tom and Big Dee delivered a very respectable 22.25. Then it was time for Jim Elder, who atop the fractious The Immigrant collected a mere 9.5 penalty points, a mark bested only by Britain's David Broome.

At the end of the first round, Britain was in the lead, holding a 48 to 49.5 edge on Canada. Then, the heavily favoured teams began to self-destruct. First, Britain's Marion Coakes was eliminated when she was thrown by her mount, Stoller, who refused a jump. France then took the lead, until Jean-Pierre d'Oriola blew his second round and racked up 29.5 points.

The "dark horse" team, however, did not succumb to pressure. Jim Day and Canadian Club had another 18-point ride, while Tom and Big Dee bettered their first round with 17.25 penalty points.

At last, it was time for Jim Elder and The Immigrant. The pressure was mounting. The Canadians were now clearly in the lead. Could the fractious green horse and the 34-year old rider put in another solid ride?

The answer was yes. The horse and rider collected only 18 points, giving the team the lowest score at 102 combined penalty points. Canada had won the gold!

With the odds against them, the Canadian team won by turning in five solid performances plus one brilliant ride in a sport where consistency is the key to success.

Across the country, as the news broke over Sunday night and Monday morning, the victory was hailed with delight. The Canadian equestrian team's gold medal eased the sting of disappointment, as the newspapers trumpeted Canada's "golden ending." ♣

Golf

One Perfect Shot – George Knudson

**Adapted from files and Maclean's: "Making Shots in the Dark"
By Hal Quinn, Sept 24, 1979**

Golf can't be taught, it can only be learned. Ben Hogan

Years ago, when good golf balls cost a buck, green fees were single digit and George Knudson was a regular on the PGA Tour, the bespectacled student of the game became interested in blind golfers. Knudson wondered if he, one of the greatest practitioners of the golf swing that the game has ever known, could hit the ball blindfolded. At first, he couldn't; after eight days he could. Knudson learned a lesson then that he shares now.

It was that search for perfection that brought Knudson to the tee a decade ago wearing a blindfold. The experience gave him the key to the golf swing and the focal point of a revolutionary approach to teaching golf which Knudson introduced this summer. The golf swing is one of the most elusive and ephemeral things in all sport, something that visits the average player for moments, sometimes hours, only to depart, unannounced. Knudson found the key with his eyes closed. "It's balance. If you're a little off, swinging with your eyes closed, you can topple over, eyes open, you mis-hit the shot."

As far back as he can remember, George Knudson wanted to be a golfer. As a youngster in Winnipeg he practiced with an intensity that sometimes left his hands so raw he couldn't compete. ("Throughout my career, I'd rather practise than play.") Lacking the physique of a natural long-ball hitter, Knudson became a technician. "From the beginning, I thought of my body as a machine, studying the moving parts, analyzing what each should do to make the perfect golf swing." While on the PGA Tour (eight victories, $527,371 earned) fellow golfers would pause to watch the Knudson swing. In all the years, all the thousands of shots on the practice tees and real ones, the perfect swing came once. "It was

in Tokyo in 1966, a five iron shot that I wanted to move from right to left, with the wind blowing left to right. When I put the swing on it, I knew it was perfect. It was something that I had worked towards all my life. My whole body felt like it was going to explode."

"That was the full bolt. I've hit one perfect shot in my life, and that's one more than most." ❧

George Knudson

George Knudson possessed one of the finest, purest, golf swings of all time. He was one of Canada's top PGA Tour professionals in the century, and likely Canada's best-ever touring pro, racking up 19 victories between 1961 and 1976 (including winning eight PGA tournaments in his 11 years on that tour — tops for Canadians in the century). Knudson won his first pro tournament in his first year on the PGA Tour — the Coral Gables Open. He would win the individual title at the 1966 World Cup in Tokyo and join with Al Balding to win the 1968 World Cup of Golf in Rome. His best year on the PGA Tour was likely 1968 when he won back-to-back events: the Tucson and Phoenix Opens. Knudson came in a heartbreaking second in the prestigious 1969 Masters Golf Tournament in Augusta, Georgia, missing a birdie putt on the 72nd hole by less than an inch that would have tied him with the winner, George Archer. At home, Knudson captured the CPGA Championship five times and was low Canadian professional at the Canadian Open on five other occasions. He followed his successful playing career with a successful career teaching golf. At 50 he decided to start playing the Senior PGA Tour in the US, but developed lung cancer and passed away shortly thereafter.

Career Highlights:
- 1961 Coral Gables Open Champion
- 1963 Portland Open Champion
- 1964 Fresno Open Champion
- 1967 New Orleans Open Champion
- 1966 World Cup - Individual Title
- 1968 Phoenix Open Champion
- 1968 Tucson Open Champion
- 1972 Robinson Open Champion
- 1972 Kaiser International Open Champion
- 1968 Won the World Cup with Al Balding
- 1969 Second, Masters Golf Tournament, Augusta, Georgia
- 1963 Low Canadian professional in the Canadian Open
- 1970 Low Canadian professional in the Canadian Open
- 1972 Low Canadian professional in the Canadian Open
- 1975 Low Canadian professional in the Canadian Open
- 1977 Low Canadian professional in the Canadian Open
- 1964 Canadian Professional Golfers Association Champion
- 1967 Canadian Professional Golfers Association Champion
- 1968 Canadian Professional Golfers Association Champion
- 1976 Canadian Professional Golfers Association Champion
- 1977 Canadian Professional Golfers Association Champion
- 1966 Winner of the Millar Trophy
- 1955 Canadian Junior Champion

"A million dollar swing and a 10-cent putter."

Golfing great Jack Nicklaus commenting on George Knudson in the 1960s.

Karen Magnussen – World Champion

Vancouver's Karen Magnussen was the Canadian junior figure skating champion in 1965 and senior national champion five times between 1968 and 1973. She won the championship crown for the last North American Championships in 1971. She captured the hearts of the skating world with a brilliant free skate performance at the 1972 Olympic Winter Games in Sapporo, Japan, that earned her the silver medal, Canada's only medal of the Games. She is most remembered, though, for winning the 1973 World Figure Skating Championship in Bratislava, Czechoslovakia.

In 1969 she had watched the world figure skating championships in Colorado Springs from a wheelchair — both her legs were in casts. Magnussen had gone to Colorado intending to skate, but she found she was suffering such pain that a doctor was called in. He quickly discovered stress fractures in both her legs. She had to forget the skating, get better and most importantly for her recovery — get her legs in casts. She had just turned 17, and had been practising seven hours a day, 42 hours a week, for 40 weeks a year since she was 12. Magnussen didn't only skate while growing up, she also did ballet and ran the roads, constantly building up her legs. Ultimately, the constant strain on the legs caused a series of vertical cracks — stress fractures. The only real prescription was rest: she spent a month in the wheelchair with the casts on, another month or more on crutches, and for the first time in a long while, she actually spent three straight months not on the ice. She remembered: "It was frustrating. Especially after all the hard training.
I suddenly went from seven hours a day to nothing. It's amazing how your muscles almost go to putty." By the summer's end though, she was back to full training and getting firm once again.

The next spring Magnussen had it all back as she defended her Canadian Championship and came third in the Worlds. By the 1971-72 season, she was prepared for her biggest tests. She moved up one notch in the ranking, getting silver medals at both the 1972 Olympics and World Championships. Then it all came together in 1973.

Skating confidently in Bratislava, Czechoslovakia, Karen Magnussen became the World Champion. British journalist Clive James noted: *"In the compulsories Janet Lynn had mucked up her double jump and left Karen Magnussen too far ahead to catch. With the competitive element eliminated, the spirit of the art was free to flourish and Magnussen turned in an absolute face-freezer — a display of dramatic power that ran like cold fury on silver rails, propelled by one continuous friction-free impulse from her eloquently stacked center section."*

On her return to Canada, Karen Magnussen received a hero's welcome (on her 21st birthday no less), a dinner with Prime Minister Pierre Trudeau, had a local North Vancouver rink named after her, and launched a Foundation in her name to support up-and-coming skaters. Having conquered the world, Karen Magnussen then turned professional with the Ice Capades and ultimately to coaching. ♣

Cindy Nicholas, First Woman to Cross the Channel Twice

On September 8, 1977, Cindy Nicholas made world history when she became the first woman to not only swim back and forth across the English Channel, but to do so in record time.

The previous record for the 43-mile double-crossing was 30 hours, set by American Jon Erikson in 1975. Nicholas smashed that record, cutting more than 10 hours by completing the crossing in 19 hours and 55 minutes.

The Scarborough, Ontario native expected a cold swim, but not one that would make her bleed. Leaving Shakespeare Beach, off Dover, she reached Cap Gris Nez off the French coast in 8 hours and 58 minutes. As required by the Channel Swim Association, she immediately turned around. But as she tried to leave, she was hit by five-foot waves, which threw her back on the rocks several times. She was left with bleeding scrapes and bruises.

Bloodied, but unbowed, the 20-year-old marathon swimmer conquered the waves and bravely soldiered on, completing the second leg in 10 hours and 57 minutes.

In the only disappointment of her swim, Nicholas narrowly missed setting a world record for the Dover-to-France leg by two minutes. But she was not too upset.

"The record wasn't really the important thing," said Nicholas at the time. "It mattered more to me that no woman had ever done this before. A time is something that can be beaten. This can't be taken away." ❧

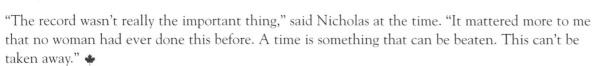

1927

On January 16, 1927, 17-year old George Young of Toronto defeated 102 of the world's best swimmers in the $25,000 Wrigley Marathon. He was the only contender to cross the 20-mile channel between Santa Contalins Island off the coast of California, and Point Vincente on the main land.

Alpine Skiing

Ken Read's First World Cup Victory

Ken Read, unofficial leader of the Crazy Canucks, first put on a pair of skis at the age of three. By the time he was eight, he was racing competitively. In 1974, at the age of 19, he joined the skiing elite, racing in his first World Cup season. The very next season, Read made Canadian sports history when he won Canada's first-ever World Cup race at Val d'Isère, also becoming the youngest male to ever win a World Cup downhill — a record that remained throughout the century. Here is Ken Read's story of the win, in his own words.

By Ken Read

In December, 1975, I checked into the Kandahar Hotel at Val d'Isère with the rest of my teammates from the Canadian men's ski team. We were feeling really good about the season that lay ahead. We'd posted promising results in the pre-Olympic season and the weather and snow co-operated for an excellent autumn training period.

There was even more good news. For once, our suppliers were also paying us more attention. We were well aware that to win at the elite level, you need the technical advantage of the best gear, the best skis, the best wax, and the best serviceman to choose and wax your skis. You don't get this treatment unless you're doing well. We Canucks had been steadily clawing our way to the top.

It wasn't just our style on the slopes that was different from the Europeans. Despite the fact that alpine ski racing is an individual sport, we worked as a team sharing information, strategies, and resources. Within our team of five — Dave Irwin, Dave Murray, Jim Hunter, Steve Podborski and myself - we were in Europe on a shoestring — there really wasn't much choice but to stick together. Most of us were away from our families for months at a time, and so the ski team became a family.

I know it wasn't like this on other national teams. On the Austrian and Swiss teams, for example, competition was so stiff a racer would never dream of sharing information — it would cost him his place.

I also know that while we had slowly earned the respect of the Europeans, the Canadian men were not really perceived as a serious threat to win on the downhill circuit. We were about to give notice.

To a certain extent, luck was with me at Val d'Isère. I'd jokingly predicted that in my first race amongst the world elite (the top 15) I would get number one (not a preferred start position) and finish first. The evening before, our coach, Scotty Henderson, returned from the team captains' meeting and threw my start bib across the room — "Number One — Just as you called it," said Scotty. Little did I dream what was in store. The conditions were difficult that year — there was only a thin layer of snow covering the course. Racers were nervous about Collumbin's bump, named, as is not unusual in downhill, for the racer who had ended his career there. One of Switzerland's greats, Roland Collumbin, had broken his back during training at the bump earlier in the week — the exact same place where he had broken his back the year before! The mighty mountain had begun to exact its toll.

My training runs during the week had gone by without incident. I had finished 10th, 12th and 15th, an improvement over last year, but nothing to indicate anything unusual. My teammates were also showing improvement over last year, but there was literally no indication of what was about to happen.

Sunday, December 7, 1975 dawned bright and clear. The temperature was a little warmer than forecast. My morning warm-up went uneventfully. My turns were crisp and clean and I felt relaxed and confident on my skis. I was enjoying myself, so much so, that I took too much time. This, coupled with an unexpected breakdown of the lift while I was some 100 yards from the top, forced me to scramble, so I had to hike it to the start. By the time I got there, the race start was 10 minutes away. I had no time for my usual pre-race routine, but I had no time to get nervous either. I whipped off my outer clothes, put on my race number, adjusted my bindings, and headed to the starting gate.

Then I was off. I let my skis glide freely through the upper reaches of the Oreiller-Killy piste, rapidly gaining speed towards the fearsome Collumbin's bump, which catapulted me some 50 metres. My focus was immediately back to the track. The line flowed easily as I rolled through the open section of the tower turns and meadow. Interestingly, the line I was taking was far from the track established by the forerunners.

But now the compression loomed — a deep depression followed immediately by a jump shrouded in dark shade. This test had exacted its toll on racers during training. Extending through the compression, I stayed on line and at the right moment, relaxed and let gravity do the work. I soared through the air, and then landed in a less than graceful manner, but on my feet and tucking for the finish. All that remained was the Schuss d'arrivee — a high-speed tuck through grinding bumps, my forte. I came in at 2:04.97. Considerably faster than any training times that week, but slower than Franz Klammer's record-breaking 2:03.19 set the year before.

Then came the nail-biting. That is the absolute downside of drawing first. Dave Irwin, who had drawn fourth position, skied well, but foundered slightly at the compression, which cost him. Next came Olympic Champion Bernhard Russi who posted the fastest split times yet. I thought the ski Gods were about to set the world right. But the compression was proving to be a worthy test and Russi, unbelievably, lost it at the bottom, and ended up placing second, two thirds of a second behind me.

A glimmer of hope began to emerge. I began to realize that my time might stand. But the "Kaiser" — Franz Klammer — had yet to ski. The Austrian great had drawn 14th, and I was convinced that he would quickly dispel my dreams of glory. When Klammer hit the course, the journalists and photographers got ready for the victory scrum.

At the final interval timer, Klammer was four-tenths of a second behind me. Would I squeak the win out, I began to wonder? Then, he experienced some minor trouble at the compression, but quickly got back on track. I eyed the clock. It was going to be close, indeed.

Then, an unexpected turn of events occurred. With less than 150 metres to go Klammer crashed. He was out.

My arms shot up in jubilation, checked a moment later, somewhat sheepishly, out of concern for my fellow competitor. Was Klammer okay? He was down, but fortunately unhurt.

I had won!

And to boot, it was a Canadian triumph, Irwin was fourth, Hunter was ninth, Podborski was 10th, and Murray 13th. Canada dominated the standings. It was an incredible placing, and the Europeans were shocked. To them, the outsiders had stormed the gates and stolen the holy grail of ski racing — a World Cup Downhill. Serge Lang, Father and Founder of the World Cup coined the phrase "Crazy Canucks" after this race to describe our passionate, determined attack. The signal was clear: we Canucks were a force to be reckoned with. ❧

Canadian Winners at Kitzbuhel, Austria

Year	Event	Athlete
1980	Downhill	Ken Read
1981	Downhill	Steve Podborski
1982	Downhill	Steve Podborski
1983	Downhill	Todd Brooker
1957	Downhill	Lucile Wheeler
1957	Combination	Lucile Wheeler

1976

Alpine Skiing

Just as Things Looked Hopeless, Kathy Saved the Day

by Michael Posner
February 23, 1976

The flags were coming down on Innsbruck's Marie Theresien Strasse, and the athletes had departed. The XII Winter Olympiad — conducted without incident, but not without surprise — was over.

But Canadians everywhere were saluting the most productive performance by a Canadian team in years, including a frankly unexpected gold medal in the women's giant slalom by 18-year-old Kathy Kreiner.

Kreiner, a native of Timmins, Ontario, zipped down the treacherous slopes of the Axamer Lizum in the unbeatable time of one minute, 29.13 seconds — thereby depriving West Germany's Rosi Mittermaier of the chance to become the first women's triple-gold medallist in alpine skiing. Kreiner's margin of victory over Mittermaier was a mere one-eighth of a second. "I would have liked to have seen Rosi win," the tall (five-foot-seven), angular Kathy said afterward, "but I'm not unhappy that I won." Then, after sipping victory champagne, she spoke to her father, Hal, a general practitioner in Timmins. "I'm looking out the window at the hill where it all began," Dr. Kreiner told his daughter. He was referring to the tiny, 350-foot slope on which Kathy and her sister, Laurie, 22, also on the Olympic team, had first skied. Said Kathy later: "It didn't sound like my father somehow. It sounded like he was in tears."

The delight that followed Kreiner's victory was at least equal to the surprise. Few Canadian fans were present for her performance and of more than a dozen Canadian news reporters in Innsbruck only one (from Canadian Press) was on hand. Even alpine ski manager Luc Dubois chose to stay in the Olympic village and supervise packing for the trip home. "Frankly," he said, "I didn't think they'd finish in the top 15." Based on the women's performances in earlier events, one could hardly blame him. Canada's highest placing in the downhill event — won by Rosi Mittermaier — was nineteenth (Laurie Kreiner), and only one Canadian woman managed to even complete the difficult slalom course (Laurie again, finishing in the last third, far behind winner Mittermaier). Interviewed after her disappointing twenty-second place finish in the

downhill, temperamental Betsy Clifford was asked if the Canadian public — supporters of the national ski team — might react unfavourably to the results. "(Obscenity) the Canadian public," cooed Betsy. "We're doing the best we can."

Clearly, their best was not good enough, until Kreiner's swoop down the three-quarter-mile Axamer course. She was the first starter, a decided advantage on the bumpy, icy slope. "The giant slalom is a race for technique," said Nancy Greene Raine, winner of the same event at the Winter Games at Grenoble in 1968. "You need finesse, and Kathy has it. She doesn't attack a course, she finesses it — she's a very technically exact skier. By skiing first, she was able to do her thing before the course became chatterboxed [rutted]." Kreiner agreed: "It's easier to hang on in that kind of snow. All along I felt that I could do well. I didn't go out to win a medal. I was just going out to do my best, but I knew my best might be a medal."

Appearing at the daily news conference for medal winners, Kreiner, wearing borrowed clothes (her own had been shipped home early to avoid excess

baggage charges), stuck out a playful tongue at Nancy Greene Raine, who shouted: "Way to go, Kather!" But it was a full five minutes before assembled newsmen were able to move their attention from the dimpled Miss Mittermaier, 25, easily and deservedly the most popular woman athlete in Europe this winter. (A fan gave Rosi flowers after the race, and she promptly presented them to Kathy.) Kreiner answered questions with her customary reticence, seemingly embarrassed by the endless flash of cameras and flow of questions on how she had slept and what she ate for breakfast. (She slept well, and had Austrian rolls and orange juice.) CTV staff erected a KREINER + CANADA = GOLD sign, executive producer Johnny Esaw launched a chorus of *For She's A Jolly Good Fellow*, and Nancy Greene Raine told Kathy, "You're the queen now. It's all yours." ❧

Innsbruck, 1976

"My most memorable Olympic moment is being the only Canadian in the finish area when Kathy Kreiner won her gold in Innsbruck (1976). The moment was special because Kathy and I had strategized in the morning at breakfast. She did what she could and won. It was great to be a small part of her winning." - Jim Hunter, Canadian Alpine Olympian

Tony Gabriel and "the Catch"

Grey Cup Game, 1976, CNE Stadium

It seems like it should have happened more often, but it hasn't. Only once has the Grey Cup Game been won on a last-minute, game-winning touchdown reception. It happened in 1976 as Ottawa and Saskatchewan battled for Lord Grey's trophy. Anyone who saw the historic play, who saw the hearts of Saskatchewan players and fans break, refers to it simply as "The Catch."

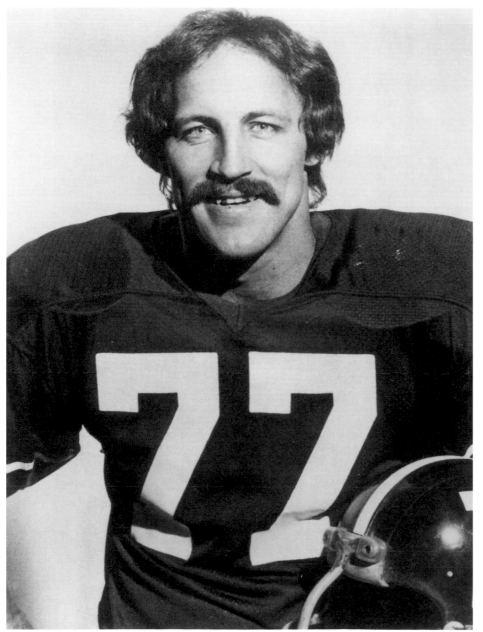

The powerful Saskatchewan Roughriders were expected to be in command of the game all day, but inexplicably were not. Yet even after spotting Ottawa an early 10-0 lead, thanks to an electrifying punt return for a touchdown by Bill Hatanaka, Saskatchewan's Ron Lancaster, a senior icon of Canadian football, had his team on the brink of victory. Leading 20-16 in the final minutes, the western Roughies held off a goal-line stand by Ottawa. Victory seemed secured. But, unable to keep the ball to run out the clock, the western Roughies were forced to punt the ball out of harm's way - or so they thought.

With 44 seconds left, Ottawa's quarterback Tom Clements went to work. In short order he managed to get the ball to the Saskatchewan 24, which was close, but not close enough. Ignoring a play sent in from his coach, Clements called one of his favourite passing plays — a "tight end flag." This called for his tight end to run from the far side of the field, down into the end zone and towards the corner flag. And, with a mere 20 seconds remaining in the fourth quarter, the whole stadium and millions watching on TV knew who the pass would have to go to in order to end the dream of Lancaster, the players and the rest of Saskatchewan: tight end Tony Gabriel.

"As I watched him [Clements] released a perfect pass that headed right for me." Gabriel said afterwards. "Mentally I had my fingers crossed; 'Let nothing distract me' I prayed ... I drifted in the direction of the ball, reached over and plucked it from the air. Gary Kuzyk who had come downfield on the pattern said he saw my face as I fingered the ball: 'Gabber, your eyes were six feet wide open!' ... Had I dropped the ball I would have kept on running, right out of the end-zone, all the way back to Ottawa and would have retired from football."

It was no surprise where the ball went. Gabriel was the 1976 CFL reception leader with 72 catches and was the only CFL receiver to get over 1000 yards. In addition to the "The Catch," Gabriel had already caught seven passes for 124 yards during the game. But clearly it was that final historic grab which confirmed his Grey Cup MVP award. It was also Ottawa's last Grey Cup victory of the century.

For Gabriel it was a reward well earned, but it wasn't the first time in his stellar career that he had come up with last-minute heroics in the Grey Cup against Saskatchewan. His first taste of the Cup happened in 1972 playing for his hometown Hamilton Tiger Cats in his second CFL season.

With the favoured Tiger-Cats tied at 10 with the Roughriders, and less than 90 seconds remaining in the game, Gabriel had not yet caught a pass. For the rest of the game, though, he shone. Starting at their own 15, Hamilton relied on three successive completions to Gabriel, and then one to Garney Henley, to take them into field goal range. With seven seconds on the clock, place-kicker Ian Sunter kicked the Grey Cup winning field goal.

Tony Gabriel received his highest personal honour in 1978, winning the Schenley as the Most Valuable Player in the CFL. No Canadian had won it since Ottawa's Russ Jackson had in 1969. And no Canadian did again in the century.

Tony Gabriel was inducted into the Canadian Football Hall of Fame in August, 1984. ♣

Tony Gabriel Highlights

2 Grey Cup Victories	1972 (Hamilton), 1976 (Ottawa)
1 Grey Cup Finalist	1981 (Ottawa)
Most Valuable Canadian Player	1976 Grey Cup
CFL Most Outstanding Player	1978
CFL Most Outstanding Canadian Player	1974, '76, '77, '78,
All-Canadian CFL All-Star	1972, '74, '75, '76, '77, '78, '79, '80

General Highlights

December 22, 1976

Canada was not thought to have a strong soccer squad this year, but ended up surprising tournament officials with a solid 3-0 victory over the USA in a World Cup playoff match in Port-au-Prince, Haiti.

1976

At the world championships in Norway, Sylvia Burka became the first Canadian to win the overall speed skating championship.

1976

Greg Athans, younger brother of world water ski champion George and son of Commonwealth Games gold medal diver George Sr., won the world professional freestyle skiing championships.

1976

Jockey Sandy Hawley won his fourth North American riding title in six years.

1977

Greg Carter won the World Badminton Championships played in Sweden.

1977

4000 people came to Burnaby's Swangard Stadium in 1977 to see Canada register its first international rugby victory, in its inaugural match against the USA. As of 2000, Canada had 20 wins and one draw from 29 international matches against the USA.

Doug Sturrock

1975

Ken Read of Calgary became the first Canadian, and North American, male to win a World Cup race, winning the downhill at Val d'Isère. Two weeks later, Dave Irwin of Thunder Bay won at Schladming.

1978

Cathy Graham Sherk had perhaps the finest year of amateur golf this century in winning the Ontario, Canadian, North-South, the United States Amateur and World Amateur Golf Championships. In response, Golf Digest named her the world's top Women's Amateur.

1974

Susan Nattrass from Edmonton established a world record in winning the women's world trapshooting championships in Switzerland (143/150).

1975

Nattrass again won the women's world trapshooting championship with a new record (188/200), this time in Munich. Fellow Edmontonian John Primrose won the world championship at the men's competition (197/200).

1976

Before 1984, there were no separate women's shooting events at the Olympics, but some events were open to both men and women. In Montreal, Susan Nattrass became the first female trapshooter to compete at the Olympic Games.

1978

For the fourth consecutive year, Susan Nattrass won the women's world trapshooting championships, scoring a record 195/200, bettering her own previous record by three.

BCSHOF

1979

Soccer has always been highly popular in BC In 1979 the Vancouver Whitecaps of the North American Soccer League won the league championship, and over 100,000 fans turned out for the team victory party in Robson Square.

1980

Canadians Bruce Ford and Patrick Walter from the Victoria Rowing Club won the double sculls at the Royal Henley regatta in England. Canadians next won in 1992.

1980

BC's Jean Gordon won the Women's World Cup of ten-pin bowling.

1980

Dan Halldorson and Jim Nelford teamed up to win the World Cup of Golf.

May 4, 1983

Sunny's Halo, owned by Toronto stockbroker David Foster, became only the second Canadian horse in history to win the Kentucky Derby. After a series of indifferent results in the time leading up to the "Run for the Roses," trainer David Cross Jr. discovered that stress fractures were virtually crippling the horse. A prolonged rest period in sunny California was just what the doctor ordered, helping Sunny's Halo gallop to a two-length victory in the Derby.

1984

Lisa Buscombe won the World Women's Field Archery Championships, Olympic Division.

August 3, 1984

Beating Cameroon 3-1 in Cambridge, Massachusetts, Canada qualified for the quarter-finals of the 1984 Olympic Games.

August 25, 1985

With a 1-0 win over a strong Honduran team in Tegucigalpa, Canada set the stage for Canada's World Cup qualification a few weeks later in St. John's. After winning 2-1 in St. John's on September 14, Canada qualified for the World Cup of Soccer finals for the only time in the century. Canada went to the World Cup, but did not manage a point, or a goal.

1985

The Toronto's Blue Jays won the American League pennant for the first time.

1985

Dave Barr, this time teamed up with Dan Halldorson, won the World Cup of Golf for Canada again. Later in the year, Barr narrowly missed out on winning the United States Open, exchanging the lead several times and ultimately finishing second by a stroke to Andy North.

1986

Canada won the World Amateur Golf Team Championship.

1986

Trevor Berbick wasn't born there, but he learned most of his boxing growing up in Nova Scotia. In 1986 he won the WBA version of the Heavyweight boxing title from Pinklon Thomas in Las Vegas. He would lose the title later in the year to Mike Tyson.

1987

Cliff Thorburn of Toronto (via Victoria) became the World Snooker Champion.

1987-88

Winnipeg's "Golden Boy" Donny Lalonde became the WBA light heavyweight boxing champion, defeating Eddie Davis for the title in November, 1987. He lost the title to the legendary "Sugar" Ray Leonard in November, 1988.

February 4, 1982

CSI/COA

23-year old skier Gerry Sorensen became the first Canadian since Nancy Greene in 1968 to win the Alpine World Ski Championship. Her victory earned her the Canadian Press Athlete of the Year award and many other accolades. Two weeks before the worlds, she had won World Cup downhills on consecutive days, so her World Championship run was not unexpected. What was unexpected was her career in the first place. Most skiers tend to make the national team by the age of 20, with the few remaining spots usually reserved for up-and-coming skiers. The slow start to Gerry's career was due to injuries, though, not a lack of talent. She was also fortunate that national women's coach Currie Chapman gave her a belated chance. During the 1980-81 season, Gerry was the oldest skier on the women's team, and the only rookie. By the end of the year, she was also its best skier. Said Chapman: "We usually place our skiers on a four-year program once they join the national team. By the fourth year you hope the girl will be among the first 15 seeds and in contention for a World Cup win. Gerry accomplished four years' work in one. It was just amazing."

National Archives

Graham Smith Swims to Commonwealth Glory

Most of us know the Commonwealth Games as the "Friendly Games." For swimmer Graham Smith, the 1978 Edmonton Games were closer to the "Family Games." For one, Edmonton was his hometown. For another, his mother officiated, older brother George presented medals, sister Becky competed, while sister Susan and brother Scott volunteered.

Finally, if that wasn't enough, the pool where the 20-year-old Smith swam was named after his father, Dr. Don Smith.

At the 1976 Olympic Games, Smith had set himself the goal of winning a medal for his father, who was seriously ill with cancer. Sadly, he came up short and had to settle for two fourth-place finishes. It was up to sister Becky, also a competitor, to win two bronze medals for their father, in the 400m individual medley and the 4 x 100m freestyle relay. Later that year, Dr. Smith passed away.

Smith bit down his disappointment, and went back to training. In the spring of 1978, he went to Thunder Bay to meet with his coach, Don Talbot, and prepare for the summer. There, he embarked on what he has described as the most strenuous training he had ever experienced.

The summer arrived, and so did the Commonwealth Games. Smith was in peak form and ready to redeem himself, but the pressure was on, to put it mildly. He was in his hometown, his family was all around, and of course, he was swimming in the pool named after his father. To boot, the facility stood about half a mile from where Smith grew up and went to school. Smith would either respond, or succumb to the pressure.

As the results attest, Smith was in no mood to crack. In one of the most incredible sweeps of all time, the Edmonton native won gold medals in six events: the 200m and 400m individual medleys, the 100m and 200m breaststrokes, the 4 x 100m freestyle relay and the 4 x 100m medley relay. In one day alone, he won two golds — swimming the 200-metre individual medley in the afternoon, followed by the 200m backstroke.

And as if six golds were not enough, he set or helped to set five Games records.

For Smith, these were now the Golden Family Games. It was only fitting that as a member of Canada's swimming nobility that one of his medals, for the 100m backstroke, was presented by none other than Prince Andrew.

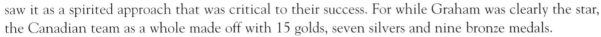

"Winning in front of a hometown crowd, and in the pool named for my father, was a real high," Smith said at the time. "The family support was very important. Whenever I needed a helpful push, it was there."

As Smith racked up gold after gold, much was being made about the displays of Canadian patriotism during the competition. Throughout the Games, the swim team did chants, built up rivalries, and pushed themselves in every way. The home crowd quickly got caught in the spirit, and roared with approval at each race.

Some found it to be excessive patriotism. Others, including Smith, saw it as a spirited approach that was critical to their success. For while Graham was clearly the star, the Canadian team as a whole made off with 15 golds, seven silvers and nine bronze medals.

By the end of the competition, the media were also speculating about Smith's chances at the upcoming World Championships. When he won the 200m individual medley event at the worlds in a record time of 2:03.65, beating out three other world record holders, the talk then turned to his medal potential at the 1980 Olympic Games in Moscow. With a host of world records, six Commonwealth golds and many other honours, Smith seemed to be poised for a sweep in the Olympic pool.

In one of those twists in history, politics entered the sports arena. Canada joined many other nations in boycotting the Moscow Olympic Games in protest of the Soviet Union's military activities in Afghanistan. If any single athlete lost as a result, surely it was Graham Smith. The 1980 Olympics would have been his for the taking.

Adding to this, scheduling changes implemented since that time have assured no athlete will ever win that many golds.

In hindsight, given how history has unfolded, the political action taken in 1980 seems overblown. For Graham Smith, 1978 would remain his exceptional year.

To be sure, it was a year that would comfort any athlete. Smith was named co-winner of the Lou Marsh Trophy, together with Ken Read, as Canada's athletes of the year. He also got to write a page in sports history, and one of the most glorious chapters in Commonwealth Games history. ❧

National Archives

Graham Smith was Canada's best swimmer of the 1970s. He amassed an incredible career total of 56 gold, 23 silver and eight bronze medals at various international events. He established 17 Canadian, three Commonwealth and two world records.

At the 1978 Commonwealth Games in Edmonton, in a pool named after his father, he won a record six gold medals. The highlight of his career came three weeks later in the world swimming championships in West Berlin. He won the gold medal, and became the world champion, in the 200m Individual Medley, shattering the world record by 3/4 of a second. Smith retired in 1982 to coach future Canadian champions, and was elected to Canada's Sports Hall of Fame.

Motor Sport

Villeneuve Triumphs at Monaco North

by Michael McHugh
October 23, 1978

It was like the old days of Expo 67. Huge crowds all excited and all going in the same direction. Packed subway trains released their cargo of spectators on Ile Notre-Dame. Instead of pavilions, they had come to see the spectacle of Grand Prix car racing. Already the air was full of screaming engines upshifting and downshifting their gears through the corners, bright colors traversing the visual field. The cars moved with the speed of cannon shells. Somehow the helmeted figures inside were controlling these mobile rocket-sleds. The air was filled with swirling scents of racing oil. Big-time auto racing had hit Montreal, the new Monaco of the North.

The sleek black Lotus-79 of Jean-Pierre Jarier made the fastest time in the qualifying races. The Lotus car incorporates an inverted wing design for its body, a design first used in the Second World War on the wing of the Mosquito aircraft; the faster the car goes, the more suction effect develops beneath the car to pull it down, giving greater traction in the corners.

Jody Scheckter was second in qualification, driving the WR-5 Walter Wolf car. His driving style suited the sliding and slippery conditions of the track. Third fastest was Gilles Villeneuve of Berthierville, Quebec, in his Ferrari 312 T-3. A Canadian car and a Canadian driver both in the top three, the debut of the new Grand Prix circuit Ile. Notre-Dame was off to a flying start.

Montreal is a city of flair and exuberance. Witness the way the Olympics were pulled off despite the difficulties and pundits. And with an eye on the upcoming municipal elections, what better way than for Mayor Jean Drapeau to peacock his way into public attention by staging a premiere sporting event, the Grand Prix of Canada. He jumped at the opportunity when presented to him by Grand Prix du Canada Inc., an umbrella company of Labatt Breweries.

Prime Minister Trudeau landed in his white Jet Ranger helicopter, with a great flourish, to start the race. The cars made one warm-up lap before arriving at their staggered grid positions and the engines reached a frenzy as the starting light was given by Trudeau. The pack of cars swarmed toward the first chicane and after one lap, Villeneuve had been passed by Alan Jones. In the back of Villeneuve's mind were his instructions to go easy on the first 15 laps to allow his tires to warm up.

The order was Jarier pulling away from a small train made up of Jones, Scheckter and Villeneuve. Alan Jones began to have one of his rear tires go flat and on the 20th lap of the 70-lap race he was passed by Villeneuve. At the last hairpin turn of the course the fans were out-yelling the noise of the cars. "Go, Gilles, go," they chanted. Coming into the turn the two cars were side by side, Villeneuve suddenly accelerated, then applied maximum force to his brakes. He slid in front of the Wolf car and now was occupying second position. Recalling the incident later he quipped, "Yeah, I really had to grit my teeth on that one."

Meanwhile Jarier's Lotus had built up an immense lead of over 30 seconds. Suddenly on the 48th lap, Jarier pitted his car. The gearbox had ruptured an oil seal; he had driven his car too hard. His day was over. Just then Villeneuve passed by the pits and glanced quickly at his pit signal.

A shiver went up his spine. He realized that he was leading the race. As he circled the twisting course around the perimeter of the island he kept saying to himself, "Ferrari is the best car, Ferrari is the best car." He began to get anxious. He recalls the experience; "Those were the longest laps of my life. I kept hearing extra noises from the car." Controlling his steering wheel, gearshift and brake pedal, he talked himself deeper into concentration. "My car won't break now, it will never break." He was pacing himself; the pain in his back from the constant brusque movements and over 2,000 gear changes had vanished. He was aware, out of the corner of his eye, of the partisan crowd waving him on.

As the bright red Ferrari made its last lap, it was swept along by a wave of outstretched hands. When Villeneuve crossed the finish line he flung both his hands in the air in jubilation. He had won his first Grand Prix. A Canadian champion appears to be in the making. ❧

Prime Minister Pierre Trudeau, right, congratulates Gilles Villeneuve on his Canadian Grand Prix victory October 8, 1978. Villeneuve became the first Canadian to win a Formula One race, driving his Ferrari to victory in Montreal. Mayor Jean Drapeau looks on in the background.

Gilles Villeneuve Formula 1 Victories

Year	Race	Location
1978	Circuit Ile Notre-Dame	Montreal
1979	Kyalami	South Africa
	Long Beach	United States - West
	Watkins Glen	United States - East
1981	Monte Carlo	Monaco
	Jarama	Spain

The Vanier Cup

Governors General of Canada had a healthy tradition of supporting sport throughout the century. The most visible manner, of course, was the donation of trophies bearing their names, trophies that became synonymous with excellence in certain sports and Canadian tradition, notably the Grey Cup and the Stanley Cup.

Likewise, the Vanier Cup was created in 1965 when His Excellency Georges Vanier, then Governor General of Canada, granted permission to name the trophy awarded to the winner of the annual Canadian College Bowl the *Vanier Cup*.

For the first two years, the Canadian College Bowl was an invitational event featuring two top university football teams selected by a national panel. The first winner of the trophy was the University of Toronto Blues who, by coincidence, were also the first winners of the *Grey Cup* in 1909.

In 1967, the *Canadian College Bowl* was declared the national football championship of the CIAU and included Atlantic and Western Canada semi-final playoffs to determine the finalists for the Championship. The Vanier Cup was awarded to the winners.

In 1982, the name of the *Canadian College Bowl* game was changed to *The Vanier Cup*, Canada's University Football Championship. ♣

VANIER CUP RESULTS

Year	Champions:		Finalists:	
2000	University of Ottawa	42	Regina Rams	39
1999	Laval University	14	Saint Mary's University	10
1998	University of Saskatchewan	24	Concordia University	17
1997	University of British Columbia	39	University of Ottawa	23
1996	University of Saskatchewan	31	St. Francis Xavier University	12
1995	University of Calgary	54	University of Western Ontario	24
1994	University of Western Ontario	50	University of Saskatchewan	40 (OT)
1993	University of Toronto	37	University of Calgary	34
1992	Queen's University	31	St. Mary's University	0
1991	Wilfrid Laurier University	25	Mount Allison University	18
1990	University of Saskatchewan	24	St. Mary's University	21
1989	University of Western Ontario	35	University of Saskatchewan	10
1988	University of Calgary	52	St. Mary's University	23
1987	McGill University	47	University of British Columbia	11
1986	University of British Columbia	25	University of Western Ontario	23
1985	University of Calgary	25	University of Western Ontario	6
1984	University of Guelph	22	Mount Allison University	13
1983	University of Calgary	31	Queen's University	21
1982	University of British Columbia	39	University of Western Ontario	14
1981	Acadia University	18	University of Alberta	12
1980	University of Alberta	40	University of Ottawa	21
1979	Acadia University	34	University of Western Ontario	12
1978	Queen's University	16	University of British Columbia	3
1977	University of Western Ontario	48	Acadia University	15
1976	University of Western Ontario	29	Acadia University	13
1975	University of Ottawa	14	University of Calgary	9
1974	University of Western Ontario	19	University of Toronto	15
1973	St. Mary's University	14	McGill University	6
1972	University of Alberta	20	Waterloo Lutheran University	7
1971	University of Western Ontario	15	University of Alberta	14
1970	University of Manitoba	38	University of Ottawa	11
1969	University of Manitoba	24	McGill University	15
1968	Queen's University	42	Waterloo Lutheran University	14
1967	University of Alberta	10	McMaster University	9

Art Martin

Being There...

**By Tim Wardrop, Defensive Back / Punter, Queen's Golden Gaels,
1978 Vanier Cup Champions**

Wrapped up in a simple game, played by two university teams and 80 (almost) grown men, is an event which includes tremendous history, school spirit, camaraderie, and a lifetime of great memories for the participants. As I view the athletes of today, I realize what a tremendous difference there is between those for whom sport is a livelihood, and those of us who, as student-athletes, competed for the pure enjoyment of the game. To this day, I can watch the Vanier Cup (indeed any Canadian University football game) and get that same positive feeling from seeing well-rounded individuals working as a team to achieve the highest of goals.

Simply put, the Vanier Cup was an incredible experience. To play in a national championship, in front of a throng of frenzied fans and a national television audience was certainly a major part of that experience, but it was really much, much more.

We had earned the right to meet the UBC Thunderbirds in the final by beating St. Francis Xavier the previous week in the Atlantic Bowl in Halifax. Given the tremendous respect we held for each of the other teams in the Atlantic and Western Bowls, we clearly felt we were the underdogs (due in no small part to our consistently being ranked behind the other three remaining teams). With our victory over the X-Men came an overwhelming sense of responsibility: we were now in "the big game." As our coach, Doug Hargreaves, so aptly put it, you seldom have a chance to prove you are NOT #2, and now we had our opportunity. All the renowned Queen's spirit and tradition, all those who had played for past Golden Gaels teams, all our fellow students and Queen's alumni ... they were counting on us to represent them well.

College Bowl week in Toronto was a whirlwind of activities: the All-Canadian Dinner, Kick-off Luncheons, a pep-rally at Toronto City Hall, press interviews ... and sandwiched in between were practices, chalk talks, physiotherapy, calls to friends and family and an attempt (!) to keep up with studies.

Art Martin

The game? It was almost anti-climactic. For those who played, it was a defensive struggle, won by special teams and good fortune, rather than the clear dominance of any team (the contest was so close, CBC had set up their cameras for post-game interviews in the wrong dressing room). But the 10,000 fans packed into a cold and damp Varsity Stadium, shouting over the sound of the Queen's Band, made us feel like it was the game of a lifetime. Looking back, there were many life lessons taught within the context of the event (too many to mention here), and I know I am much better off for the experience. And when I show my children the video of the game, they see me in a different way — as a young adult, playing with the enthusiasm of a child, and briefly experiencing the thrill of being in the limelight. ♣

Editor's note: *At the end of the century, Tim still held two punting records for the Vanier Cup: most punts (15) and fortunately for him, most yards (610).*

Steve Podborski, King of the Mountains

Val d'Isère. Garmisch-Partenkirchen. Kitzbuhel. Val Gardena. For the downhill skier, these are more than just place names. They conjure up images of race courses carved out of mountain slopes so steep that the average person would hesitate to negotiate them on bare ground, let alone when they are covered with ice and snow. This is the stage for the glamourous and demanding World Cup ski circuit, where every year the world's best take each other on in the most basic of sport challenges: the first one to ski down the mountain wins. But, since each mountain offers unique challenges, it isn't enough to win on just one mountain in order to be considered the best in the world. Some courses are technically demanding, testing the skier's instinct and reaction time; others favour good gliders or those with superior endurance. You have to prove yourself consistent enough and adaptable enough throughout the gruelling World Cup season.

The privilege of being called the *King of the Mountains* has traditionally been claimed by skiers who grew up within spitting distance of the Alps. But with the arrival on the scene in the mid-1970s of the "Crazy Canucks," so named because of their aggressive style of attacking the mountain, it became only a matter of time before the Europeans would have to concede defeat. Finally, on a late winter day in March, 1982, Canadian Steve Podborski took home the honours, the first North American man, indeed the first non-European, ever to win the overall World Cup title.

Podborski had been heart-wrenchingly close the year before. He had won three races in a row in the 10-race season, and led the standings going into the last two races of the year in Aspen, Colorado. A disappointing finish by Podborski in the first race and two strong efforts by Austrian Harti Weirather meant that the Canadian lost the title by a scant 28/100ths of a second on the final day of the 1981 season.

Disappointing as it was to see the title slip through his fingers, Podborski knew without a doubt that with a little more hard work, it was in his grasp. The first couple of races of the 1981-82 season were not auspicious, though. Fourth place finishes at Val d'Isère and Val Gardena put him behind his pace of the previous season. He entered the next event in Crans-Montana, Switzerland determined to do better. Despite falling in the training run, he served notice that he was a force to be reckoned with by winning on race day.

The next stop on the circuit was Kitzbuhel, Austria, where two races were scheduled down the famed Hahnenkamm — probably the most revered and feared race course in the world. For every skier who has skied down that mountain to glory, many more have failed. The course is unforgiving to say the least, and winning on it requires every ounce of skill a skier can muster. Losing control at speeds that can exceed 140km/hour does more than put a skier out of the race — it can be life-threatening. The extreme technical demands were a good fit with the aggressive style of the Crazy Canucks, though. Podborski did more than stay on his feet through the first run down the Hahnenkamm — he finished with the second best time of the day, beaten only by archrival Harti Weirather. The next day the battle against the mountain was on again, and this time Podborski prevailed, ascending to the top of the podium for the second time that season.

Speaking to Maclean's Magazine, Podborski described what went through his head during a race: "The only thing I want to do when I'm going fast is go faster. You don't think, there is no thought process required in ski racing. You react like an animal. At the finish you can turn on the real world again, and start talking again. During the race you see only the things that are absolute necessities to maintain life."

A month later, Podborski won his third race of the season in Garmisch-Partenkirchen, Germany, and followed up with another second place on home turf in Whistler, BC This meant going into the last two races in Aspen with exactly the same scenario as the previous year. Podborski led the standings, and only Weirather had a mathematical chance of catching him. This time, though, Weirather was unable to repeat his last-minute charge and was forced to concede victory to the Canadian. Podborski finished the season with three wins, two seconds, and two fourths, never finishing out of the top 15.

As well as being the pinnacle of Podborski's career, the World Cup title was the pinnacle of the whole Crazy Canuck era. Starting in the mid-1970s Canadian team officials decided to concentrate their energies on downhill events. Podborski's teammates — skiers like Dave Irwin, Dave Murray,

"Jungle" Jim Hunter, and Ken Read — launched an assault on Europe's ski hills that very quickly drew attention to a group of skiers who attacked every race with death-defying determination. Read was the first Canadian to win a World Cup downhill race and came within a hair's breadth of winning the World Cup title himself in 1980, only to have it snatched away in the last race of the year, just as Podborski did in 1981.

Podborski entered international competition a few years after the other Crazy Canucks. Following the lead of his teammates, particularly his close friend Ken Read, he improved steadily. A bronze medal at the 1980 Olympics in Lake Placid solidified his claim to be considered among the world's best. One of his fellow skiers paid him the compliment in 1981 of calling him the best technical skier in the world, a sentiment echoed by journalists. All knew that the personable young man from Toronto with a diamond-tipped stud in one ear would one day be crowned *King of the Hill*. ♣

Gaétan Boucher Wins Double Gold

"Three medals were waiting for me in Sarajevo. Those Games were the best moment in my career."

Those are the words speed skater Gaétan Boucher used to describe his unprecedented three-medal haul at the 1984 Olympic Winter Games in Sarajevo. By winning two gold and one bronze medal in a sport traditionally dominated by Europeans, he accomplished what no Canadian had done before in ANY individual winter sport.

CSI/COA

Even before the Olympics, the 1983-84 season was already a great success for Boucher. In the months leading up to the Olympics, he had established his dominance over his competition at a number of international meets, and he arrived in Sarajevo as one of the favourites.

His first race of the Games was the 500m, speed skating's shortest event. He was expected to do well in this test of pure sprinting power, but not dominate. The resulting bronze medal in that event proved that his confidence was well-founded, and set the stage for his specialty: the 1000m. Conditions were less than perfect in a pollution-plagued city, but nevertheless he skated with what reporter James Christie of *The Globe and Mail* called "strides that sent ice crystals dancing off his skate blades." Driving through the finish line in a time of 1:15.80, he beat his closest competitor by more than eight-tenths of a second, a huge margin in a sport that measures times to the hundredth of a second. Three days later, he met the challenge again, winning his second gold of the games in the grueling 1500m by almost half a second.

Boucher became a national hero overnight, but the season wasn't over yet. Only weeks after the Olympic torch was extinguished in Sarajevo, he proved his mettle again by finishing first overall at the World Sprint Championships in Trondheim, Norway.

The 26-year-old's accomplishments were extraordinary for several reasons. Canada was not known as a powerhouse of speed skating, except in the then-fledgling short track events. Other Canadians had acquitted themselves well in previous Olympics, notably Boucher's teammate Cathy Priestner (silver, 1976); Gordon Audley, (bronze, 1952); Alex Hurd; (silver and bronze, 1932); William Logan; (double bronze, 1932); and Frank Stack, (bronze, 1932), but none had ascended to the same heights as this young man from Ste. Foy, Quebec.

Because of the relative obscurity of speed skating in Canada, adequate training facilities were scarce. For most of Boucher's career, the choice was to practice in rinks designed for playing hockey, or to live abroad to take advantage of artificial ice ovals in Europe. By necessity, most Canadian speed skaters competed in both long track and short track, in contrast to the specialization that happened later. It was while training in a hockey rink a scant 11 months before the Sarajevo Olympics that his chance of even getting to those games took a dramatic turn for the worse. While negotiating one of the tight turns that make short track racing an exciting spectator sport, Boucher lost his footing and crashed into the boards. As he lay on the ice and later in a hospital bed, the reality of what his badly-broken ankle might do to his career began to sink in. Fortunately surgery was able to fix his injuries, and the forced layoff actually gave him a much-needed psychological break from a sport that requires a high degree of mental energy in the quest for the perfect skating technique.

The layoff also enabled him to come to terms with one of his toughest competitors: himself. His career had been dogged by an inability to come through in some major competitions, probably due to a nagging lack of confidence. It was a different Boucher that flew into Sarajevo in February of 1984, though — this time he was entering competition knowing he was the best and determined to prove it to the world. The Canadian team shared his confidence, choosing him as the team's flag bearer for the Opening Ceremonies.

Like many young Canadians, Boucher started playing hockey at an early age, and given his athletic prowess would likely have excelled. As fate would have it, though, he went to the local speed skating club with the aim of improving his skating for hockey, and liked it so much that he decided to stay.

Boucher drew national attention to speed skating, contributing greatly to the success of future generations of skaters. It was very fitting that one of the only two artificial ice speed skating ovals in Canada, located in Ste. Foy, Quebec, was christened in his honour. His exploits, combined with holding the 1988 Winter Olympics in Calgary, helped instill the confidence in many other skaters that they had what it takes to ascend to the top level of the podium.

His international career spanned four Winter Olympics, and included winning two world short track championships, an Olympic silver medal in the 1000m at the 1980 Winter Olympics, and setting a world record in the 1000m. Many other honours are his also: World Cup and World

CSI/COA

Gaétan Boucher, Canada's most decorated winter Olympian of the century.

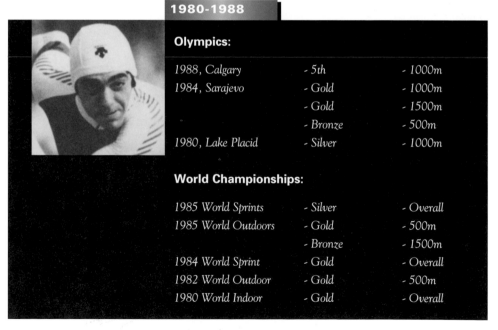

1980-1988

Olympics:

1988, Calgary	- 5th	- 1000m
1984, Sarajevo	- Gold	- 1000m
	- Gold	- 1500m
	- Bronze	- 500m
1980, Lake Placid	- Silver	- 1000m

World Championships:

1985 World Sprints	- Silver	- Overall
1985 World Outdoors	- Gold	- 500m
	- Bronze	- 1500m
1984 World Sprint	- Gold	- Overall
1982 World Outdoor	- Gold	- 500m
1980 World Indoor	- Gold	- Overall

Championship medals too numerous to list; Canadian Junior Athlete of the Year in 1980; Canada's Outstanding Athlete of the Year (Lou Marsh Trophy) in 1984; Officer of the Order of Canada in 1984; inducted into Canada's Sports Hall of Fame in 1984; and four-time recipient of the Mérite sportif québecois.

Despite recurring injuries, Boucher continued competing until 1988, when he bid his competitive career adieu on home ice at the Calgary Olympics. Racing in his fourth Olympics, he narrowly missed bringing home yet another medal by finishing fifth in his signature event, the 1000m. Skating in front of a supportive home crowd, it was a fitting way to end almost two decades of competition.

Gaétan Boucher's career was long and successful, but it will always be remembered for hitting its peak in 1984 in Sarajevo. ❦

Alwyn Morris and Hugh Fisher

At first glance, Alwyn Morris and Hugh Fisher didn't look particularly well matched to paddle a kayak together. Fisher, 183 cm tall and fair-haired, grew up in suburban Vancouver, while Morris, nearly 10 cm shorter and a full-blooded Mohawk, hailed from the Kahnawake Mohawk community near Montreal. But the two became friends soon after Morris joined the national team in 1977. When they were paired up for the K-2 event in 1982, they showed a natural chemistry that few pairs have. After winning a silver medal in the 1982 world championships, the pair was considered a gold medal threat for the 1984 Olympics in Los Angeles. The enormous pressure generated from high expectations took its toll in their first race, the 500m. Mistakes early in the race cost them the lead, and they settled for a bronze medal. Less tense, but more determined, Morris and Fisher arrived at the start of the 1000m with gold on their minds. The German pair jumped out to a quick lead at the start, but the Canadians were confident that their rivals would fade over the full distance. Paddling strongly, they gradually ate up the distance between the two boats, took the lead and never looked back. On the podium, Morris held aloft an eagle's feather, a traditional native symbol of lifeforce, honour and courage. It was also in honour of Morris's grandfather, who had a profound influence on his sport career but died before seeing his grandson receive the ultimate prize. ♦

Canadian Canoe Champions

Canadian Senior World Sprint Champions

Year	Athlete	Event		Location	
1991	Renn Crichlow	MK-1	500m	Paris	France
1995	Marie-Josée Gibeau, Corrina Kennedy	WK-2	200m	Duisburg	Germany
1995	Caroline Brunet, Alison Herst, Klari MacAskill, Corrina Kennedy	WK-4	200m	Duisburg	Germany
1997	Caroline Brunet	WK-1	200m	Dartmouth	Canada
1997	Caroline Brunet	WK-1	500m	Dartmouth	Canada
1997	Caroline Brunet	WK-1	1000m	Dartmouth	Canada
1998	Karen Furneaux , Marie-Josée Gibeau-Ouimet	WK-2	200m	Szeged	Hungary
1998	Caroline Brunet	WK-1	200m	Szeged	Hungary
1998	Caroline Brunet	WK-1	500m	Szeged	Hungary
1998	Steve Giles	MC-1	1000m	Szeged	Hungary
1999	Caroline Brunet	WK-1	1000m	Milan	Italy
1999	Caroline Brunet	WK-1	500m	Milan	Italy
1999	Caroline Brunet	WK-1	200m	Milan	Italy
1999	Karen Furneaux, Liza Racine, Carrie Lightbound, Marie-Josée Gibeau-Ouimet	WK-4	500m	Milan	Italy
1999	Steve Giles	MC-1	500m	Milan	Italy

Canadian Olympic Gold Medallists in Sprint Canoeing

Year	Athlete	Event		Location	
1924	Roy Nurse	MC-1*		Paris	France
1924	Sandy Lindsay, Harry Greenshields	MC-2*		Paris	France
1924	Sandy Lindsay, Harry Greenshields, Roy Nurse, George Duncan	MC-4*		Paris	France
1936	Francis Amyot	MC-1	1000m	Berlin	Germany
1984	Larry Cain	MC-1	500m	LA	USA
1984	Hugh Fisher, Alwyn Morris	MK-2	1000m	LA	USA

Canadian Slalom Canoe World Champions

Year	Athlete	Event		Location	
1999	David Ford	K1		LaSeu d'Urgell	Spain

* Demonstration Sport

Baumann, Davis and Ottenbrite Lead the Way With Gold in Los Angeles

Alex Baumann

Victor Davis

Anne Ottenbrite

For Canada, the 1984 Los Angeles Olympic Games went a long way towards redeeming its previous performance. At the 1976 Montreal Olympics, Canada suffered the humiliation of being the first host nation unable to win gold. But in 1984, Canada won 10 gold, 17 silver and 16 bronze medals.

In an incredible effort, the Canadian swim team was responsible for four gold, three silver and three bronze. Leading the way were Alex Baumann, Victor Davis and Anne Ottenbrite.

Baumann was under particular pressure at the Games. He was the world record holder in the 200m and 400m individual medleys, and he'd been chosen as Canada's flag bearer in the opening ceremonies. In addition to the competitive pressure, Baumann was also racing under the shadow of recently losing his father to cancer, and his brother to suicide.

Many fine athletes have collapsed under similar pressure. Baumann's preliminary heat in the 400m IM, held on the morning of Monday, July 30, would tell his tale. With the hot California sun beating down, and a warm wind whipping up the pool, Baumann dove into the water and touched the wall four minutes and 22.46 seconds later, setting an Olympic record. Almost eight hours later, Baumann was back in the pool, outstroking Brazil's Ricardo Prado to set a new world and Olympic record of 4:17:41.

Five days later, Baumann was poolside again, for the 200m IM. The competition was fierce. As the early morning smog enveloped Los Angeles, 11 swimmers broke the 14-year-old Olympic record during the preliminary heats. In the final race that night, Baumann blew away all records with a time of 2:01:42. Baumann's double golds were especially sweet — no Canadian swimmer had won gold in the pool since George Hodgson won two at the 1912 Stockholm Games.

Then there was Victor Davis. Emotional and temperamental, Davis was notorious for an incident at the 1982 Brisbane Commonwealth Games. When his gold-medal-winning 4 x 100m medley relay team was disqualified, Davis had a temper tantrum, kicking a chair and sending towels, plants and trash flying — all in the presence of Queen Elizabeth II.

Anne Otttenbrite, 1984

Alex Baumann, 1984

With his reputation signed, sealed and delivered, Davis arrived in Los Angeles and continued to churn the waters, Davis-style. Placing second in the 100m breaststroke, Davis punched the water in frustration. Clearly, he felt he had lost the gold, not won the silver. Pulling himself from the pool, Davis strode to the warm down pool and immediately dived in, staying underwater for a full length, far away from the rousing ovation being given to Steve Lundquist, the US winner.

Davis had one more serious shot at gold, in the 200m breaststroke held four days later. As the reigning world record holder, with a time of 2:14.58, Davis knew he'd have to post that kind of time again. The feisty, fiery competitor set a blistering pace that left his opponents grappling with his wake. He touched the wall at 2:13.34, an incredible 1.24 seconds faster than his previous time. Canada's "bad boy" of swimming had finally won the gold he so coveted.

Anne Ottenbrite was another story altogether. That the 18-year-old swimmer made it to the University of Southern California pool in one piece seems to be a victory in itself. Two months before the Games, the accident-prone swimmer dislocated her right knee while trying on high heels. Arriving in Los Angeles, she then suffered mild whiplash in a traffic accident and strained a thigh muscle while zealously playing a video game.

Unlike Davis or Baumann, Ottenbrite had been billed as a bronze-medal contender. Her victory in the 200m breaststroke came about 45 minutes after Baumann won his first gold, and was, by her own admission, spurred on by his success. And, like Baumann, her win took on special meaning - it was the first gold medal in swimming won by a Canadian woman since the modern Games begin in Athens in 1896.

Three nights later, Ottenbrite picked up a silver in the 100m breaststroke, coming from sixth place to second in a thrilling finish. She finished her Games off with a bronze medal in the 4 x 100m medley relay, swimming the breaststroke leg.

Some critics pointed to the Eastern bloc boycott of the 1984 Olympics as the dominant reason for Canada's success, an argument that has some validity. In swimming and in various other sports, however, one could just as easily speculate that Eastern bloc domination was due to a certain nasty problem that was just beginning to raise its ugly head: steroid abuse.

In the final analysis, no one can dispute that Baumann's and Davis's gold medals are above question - both were world record holders going into the Games. Certainly, Canada's ongoing achievements at the Olympics and world championships are proof enough that nothing should tarnish the golden glow of the 1984 Olympic swim team. ❧

Victor Davis, 1984

Sylvie Bernier's Big Jump

"There was nothing in the world that could compare with what I was feeling. All the tears and all the crying were forgotten — it was worth the trouble. Those 12 years of training 25 or 30 hours a week were not too much to pay for such a joy." That's how diver Sylvie Bernier described her feelings about her gold-medal performance at the 1984 Olympics in Los Angeles to La Presse reporter Réjean Tremblay.

Right after going through doping control after her event, she launched herself towards her parents and two close friends. She jumped into the arms of her closest friend, Suzanne Francoeur, knocking both of them to the ground, laughing and crying at the same time.

Moments later, she told the reporter, "This is the biggest moment of my life. I have been preparing myself mentally for the last month. I rehearsed my dives in my mind, and saw the image of the Canadian flag being raised, with me on the podium. I'm exhausted — the stress is awful. When I came to meet the media and asked for a glass of water, I thought I was going to faint."

Bernier had just won the gold medal on the three metre springboard with 530.70 points, just 3.2 points ahead of her American rival Kelly McCormick. Another American, Christine Seufert, took third place with 517.62 points. It was the first Olympic gold medal ever won by a Canadian diver. It was also the first time a francophone athlete had won a summer gold medal since shooter Georges Généreux at the 1956 Olympics in Melbourne, and the first time ever a female athlete from Quebec had won Olympic gold.

Bernier was born in Ste. Foy in 1964. She started diving with a local club when she was nine, then joined the Laval University Club in 1976. In the following years, she established her presence on the provincial and national scene.

In 1977, she won the gold medal in her age group at the national championships. From 1978 to 1983, she took part in more than 30 major competitions in Europe, the Americas and Canada. During those years she won 10 gold medals, six silver medals and five bronze. Out of 31 competitions, she stood on the podium 21 times.

In 1983 alone, she collected five gold medals — two at the national championships, one at the Can-Am-Mex International Championships, another at a US Invitational meet and a final one at an International meet in East Germany.

For her final preparation for the Los Angeles Olympics, she joined the Club Aquatique Montréal Olympique (CAMO) in 1982, to work with well-known coach Donald Dion.

CSI/COA

Despite all her previous honours, on that Monday in August, 1984, Bernier had her eye on just one thing: fulfilling her dream as a young girl to someday win the Olympic gold medal on the three-metre springboard. After the qualifying round, she stood in third place. Putting her extraordinary steadiness and ingrained precision to good use, she doubled her concentration before executing the dive that could make the difference — her two-and-a-half somersault front pike.

She nailed the dive perfectly. It was the sixth of a series of 10, and assured her of the gold medal.

The next day she said, "I didn't know I was in first place. In competition I never look at the scoreboard, even to know my own marks. I don't want to know how the others are doing. When I get out of the water, I go back to listening to my walkman while I walk around. Yesterday I was listening to Flashdance."

Bernier was named Canada's Female Athlete of the Year in 1984 and the following year was made a member of the Order of Canada. After retiring as an athlete, she found new ways of contributing and staying involved with sport, particularly in the area of communication. ❦

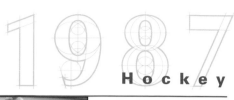

Hockey

Team Canada:
Greatest Show on Ice

by Hal Quinn
September 28, 1987

The towel around his neck was soaked with perspiration and champagne. From the ceiling in the Team Canada dressing room, spray from shaken Labatt's beer cans dripped steadily, pausing only briefly on his brow before joining the stream of sweat running off his chin into his saturated jersey. Minutes earlier Mario Lemieux had snapped a perfect shot — his 11th goal of the Canada Cup tournament — past Soviet goaltender Sergei Mylnikov. That goal, with one minute and 26 seconds remaining in the third period of the final game of the tournament, proved to be the exquisitely fine difference between the world's two best hockey teams in three of the greatest hockey games every played. Amid the bedlam that followed Canada's 6-5 victory over the Soviet Union in the decisive third game last week, Pittsburgh Penguin Lemieux reflected for a moment and said: "All the players in this room have to go back to their NHL teams, and they are not 'the best teams in the world.' We have to realize that and start all over again."

But as quickly as the Canadian NHL stars staked their claim to world hockey supremacy, their reign ended. Even as champagne corks ricocheted around their dressing room at Hamilton's Copps Coliseum, the realization set in that the team — together for 44 days in August and September — would never be together again. They had survived a 6-5 overtime loss to the Soviets in Game One, after recovering from a three-goal deficit. They had lost the lead twice in Game Two, before winning 6-5 in the second overtime period in perhaps the single best hockey game ever played.

And in the final game, they had stormed back, after trailing 3-0, to lead, tie and then win the Cup on Lemieux's goal. Said Edmonton Oiler left-winger Glenn Anderson, who recovered from a knee injury in training camp to play a key role in the Canadian triumph: "This is a better feeling than winning the Stanley Cup, but it's sad too. You don't know how good these people are until you play with them. The individuals become a team, and it will be sad to see them leave."

The six-nation Canada Cup will not be challenged again until 1992, and few from this year's edition will likely be chosen to represent the nation's hockey heritage. The 1987 team that disbanded last week was unique. It was a group of NHL superstars who, at head

HHOF — Paul Bereswill

The Soviets, at least their assistant coach and spokesman Igor Dmitriev, believed it. Declared Dmitriev: "With 17,000 Canadians in the arena hoping for them and with a Canadian referee [Don Koharski], they could not lose." The next encounter between the world's two hockey powers will likely be staged more equitably — four games in North America and four in the Soviet Union-in 1990.

The undisputed star of Team Canada and the tournament, Gretzky, has said he would like to finish his professional career with another similar series. Said Canada Cup chairman Alan Eagleson: "If Wayne wants an eight-game series with the Soviets in 1990, we will do it. The game of hockey owes it to him." Until then, hockey fans will savour the memories of watching three of the best games ever played. ❧

HHOF — Doug MacLennan

coach Mike Keenan's direction accepted supporting roles to the world's best player — Wayne Gretzky, who led all tournament scorers with three goals and 18 assists in nine games. They were also playing in the shadow of 21-year-old Lemieux, potentially the game's best scorer, who in addition to his 11 goals collected seven assists. Said Keenan, after pairing wits with Soviet coach Viktor Tikhonov — line-change for line-change — for more than 215 minutes of the swiftly paced hockey: "When you make a team like this, with thoroughbreds, you don't have the balanced personnel you would have on an NHL team. We had to establish roles for players who had never had those roles before."

Among those accepting unfamiliar roles harassing the skilled Soviet attackers was centre Dale Hawerchuk who has averaged more than 100 points in the past four NHL seasons with the Winnipeg Jets. The group also included St. Louis Blues Doug Gilmour, who scored 42 goals last season, and Mark Messier, who collected 107 points in the regular season before helping the Oilers win the Stanley Cup. Said Hawerchuk, who scored Canada's fifth goal in the final game, assisted on the fourth and won the face-off that set up the winner: "Something about falling behind brought out the best in this team." Added Gilmour, who earned more playing time as the tournament progressed: "Just being involved with this calibre of players is scary." Said Messier: "The offence of both teams was so tremendous that the defence couldn't shut everybody down. Three 6-5 games, it's just unbelievable."

HHOF — Wayne Arnold

Three images, one result. Mario Lemieux's goal to win the 1987 Canada Cup seen from in front, up high and on the scoreboard.

The Canada Cup

1976-1991

The original 1976 Canada Cup trophy was designed by Rolf Huecking of Carling-O'Keefe and cast in 100 percent Canadian nickel. The concept was the brainchild of Johnny McCreedy, the CEO and Chairman of INCO, and Alan Eagleson. Considerable difficulties were experienced casting and finishing the somewhat flawed three-feet high trophy and it was completed just days before the 1976 tournament. It was presented to Hockey Canada and placed on permanent display at Rideau Hall, the Governor General's Ottawa residence.

Johnny McCreedy

In addition to his involvement with the Canada Cup, McCreedy had a connection with a number of other famous trophies. He bore the unique distinction of playing on teams that won the Allan Cup (twice), the Memorial Cup and the Stanley Cup (twice). He threw in a World Championship title in 1939 just for good measure. One of his Stanley Cup titles came in 1942, when the Toronto Maple Leafs staged their famous rally to win the Cup after being down three games to zero against Detroit. McCreedy set up the winning goal.

Over time, the heavy nickel trophy began to deteriorate, showing evidence of cracking and surface flaws. INCO decided to quietly offer Hockey Canada a replacement replica cast from the original design with a more user-friendly nickel alloy. It was completed on August 30, 1981.

The matter of the replica became public knowledge when the Toronto Sun staged a "guess the weight of the Canada Cup contest" (it weighed 73 pounds) and INCO had to 'fess up. The replica was presented by INCO for display at the Hockey Hall of Fame.

After five tournaments, the Canada Cup was replaced in 1996 as the prize for world hockey supremacy with the World Cup of Hockey. The new trophy was designed by American Aaron Brode and is of hollowed aluminum polished in chrome. The tournament's logo appears in red and blue at the top symbolic of a hockey rink's red and blue lines. The trophy resides permanently in the Hockey Hall of Fame in Toronto.

On the ice, Team Canada won the tournament four of five times, coming second in 1981. Not surprisingly, the records for most appearances (4), most career points (77) and most points one Cup (21) are held by Wayne Gretzky. ❦

Canada Cup Results for Team Canada

Year	Wins	Losses	Ties	GF	GA	Final Result
1976	6	1	x	33	10	CHAMPIONS 2 of 3 from Czechoslovakia 6-0; 5-4 (OT)
1981	5	1	1	37	22	SECOND lost sudden-death final to USSR 8-1
1984	5	2	1	37	27	CHAMPIONS 2 of 3 from Sweden 5-2; 6-5
1987	6	1	2	41	32	CHAMPIONS 2 of 3 from USSR 6-5 (OT); 5-6 (OT); 6-5
1991	7	x	1	36	14	CHAMPIONS 2 of 3 from USA 4-1; 4-2

HHOF

Vicki Keith's 1988 Summer Holidays

At 6:01 a.m. on August 30, 1988, marathon swimmer Vicki Keith pulled herself out of Lake Ontario, vomiting, hallucinating, yet still triumphant.

The 27-year-old had just completed the final leg of a world-record setting marathon swim-crossing all five Great Lakes in one summer. And she did it all for charity, raising $300,000 towards an aquatic wing at Variety Village, a sports centre for children with disabilities in Scarborough, Ontario.

Keith began her odyssey on July 2, tackling Lake Erie. She had planned a double crossing, but 20 hours into her swim, and only 6.4 kilometres from finishing the second leg, she had to be pulled from the lake, beaten by powerful currents.

In 1986, just three years after being named to the national equestrian team, Gail Greenough became the first woman and the first North American to win the World Show Jumping Championships. Held every four years, the championships require the four finalists to ride one another's horses as well as their own. She was a finalist for Canada's Athlete of the Year in 1986, and was awarded the Order of Canada. Taking a break during the 1990s, Greenough's competitive career continued after the end of the century.

Undaunted, the Kingston, Ontario resident went on to tackle her next goal, and 17 days later, became the first person to conquer Lake Huron, crossing a 77-kilometre stretch in 47 hours.

On July 28, she emerged from Lake Michigan, the first amateur to cross that lake. A rough swim, she braved bad weather to finish the 72-kilometre crossing in 53 hours.

Lake Superior fell to the plucky marathon swimmer on August 15. The coldest of the five lakes, its temperature dropped to about 13 degrees Celsius. It was the only venture that made her nervous. The day before tackling the 35-kilometre stretch, she walked down to the beach, and after seeing the cliffs and the waves, she felt awed. The next day, during her swim, she saw a shipwreck beneath her. "I swam away as fast as I could," said Keith. "It was like looking down on a grave."

Aside from her fears, the Lake Superior swim was calm, and acted as a warm-up for her final leg, Lake Ontario.

It was a grueling swim, in part because of Keith's determination to keep on setting world records. For the first 38 of the total 51 kilometres, she did the taxing butterfly stroke, beating her own 1985 world record for butterfly swimming.

Then, 16 hours into the swim, Keith began to feel ill. Vomiting and hallucinating, she nonetheless continued to swim, but altered her course. After 23 hours and 38 minutes, she reached dry land, four miles away from her original destination at Toronto's Canadian National Exhibition Grounds. Despite her sickness, Keith did the crossing 10 hours faster than she had anticipated.

As she reached land, the swimmer who says that she was always the last to be picked for teams in schools sports secured her place in sports history and the world record books. ❦

Synchronized Swimming

CSI/COA

Winning Gold in Seoul

by Michelle Cameron

The Olympic Games are exciting, both to watch and to participate in. My swimming partner Carolyn Waldo and I witnessed some of this excitement in Calgary during the Winter Games. Witnessing this during the time leading up to the 1988 Olympics in Seoul, while we were still training, made it all more real for us. For us, the experience helped us see the Games and feel the excitement. On our first visit to Seoul we got to go on the site where we were going to be swimming. The pool was still a hole in the ground, so we stood at the edge and visualized what it would be like swimming there. Then we had a pre-Olympic meet in June against all of our main competitors (the Games were in September), so we had a good test run.

CSI/COA

We won the pre-Olympic meet, but the competition was a little too close for comfort. When we came back we decided to make some revisions to our routine, changing a few things so that we were displaying our strengths instead of looking at what our competitors were doing and trying to out-do them.

We weren't competing until the second week of the Games, so after the Opening Ceremonies (where Carolyn carried Canada's flag leading in all the athletes) we went to a little village about two hours away to train and stay focused. There was absolutely no heating in the pool, and by the time we got out after training we couldn't move because we were so frozen. It turned out to be a good thing, though, because when we got back to the Games the pool there seemed warm to us, and cold to everyone else.

Ben Johnson's 100m race took place a few days after we got back. It was so exciting to see him win — the Canadian building in the Olympic Village sounded like a rocket was going to take off with all the excitement when he won our first gold medal. The next morning, though, we were walking down to breakfast, and a camera crew came up to me and someone asked, "Did you hear about Ben Johnson?" That was how we heard that he had tested positive.

From that point on it was more challenging. Carolyn and I were already favoured, but there was a lot more pressure on after that, because we were the next hope for a gold medal. After a while the constant questions about whether or not we felt the pressure were starting to get to us. We held the world championship title already, so there was an expectation that we would win. When we trained and swam, we always visualized winning. Our coach Debbie Muir was incredible that way. Still, when Ben was disqualified it really tested us.

The compulsory figures, which were marked individually, were held two days before our freestyle routines and would count for half our total mark. During the first half of the figures all these things were going through my mind. The amount of media there was overwhelming. I wasn't swimming like I needed to and was ranked only about fourth after the morning. I went back to the Village and just wanted to go to sleep and wake up to a new morning and start over again. But I couldn't. The first figure in the afternoon was the most difficult one of the competition. When I trained, though, I always took the things that were the most difficult and worked so hard that I was the best at

CSI/COA

them. For that figure I went out and was so focused that I got the highest mark on it and got back into the game. Carolyn and I finished the compulsories with a lead over the Josephson twins from the United States, our main competitors.

Carolyn won the gold medal in the solo before our duet competition, relieving some of the pressure to win the "next gold," but I wouldn't touch her medal until we had won our own. Seeing it gave me a sense of "We're next," but I didn't want to count my chickens before they hatched.

During the finals, the Josephson twins (we called them the "Js") were swimming fifth and we were swimming eighth. We were always neck-and-neck in competitions, and it got closer every time. In years past I had never watched their routine, but this time I did, and thought, "That was really good." I didn't want Carolyn to know I was nervous, but the pressure was starting to build. The Js got four perfect tens out of the seven judges.

During our warmup we always jumped up and down to relax our muscles, then shook out each other's hands and arms. After that we had a quirky habit of putting our index fingers together and giving each other a quick "Bzzz" to make sure we were on the same wavelength. When we opened up the doors to go out it seemed like half the Koreans were waving Canadian flags, which gave us a great feeling.

As we got into the pose to start our routine, I looked over into the stands, and from a sea of Canadian flags and faces, I caught one set of eyes before we entered the pool. It was my Mom, out of 10,000 people there. It was very calming and very settling.

I felt much better once we were in the water, because we knew exactly what we were doing. Our routine was incredibly hard. About 70% of it was under water. Our opening sequence was almost a minute under water and included a lot of double leg manoeuvres and spins. The rest of the routine stayed at that level of difficulty — there was never a part where we had more breathing room. Still, it seemed like it went by so fast. Our last length is a fast piece of music, and I thought, "This is the home stretch." I heard the tape later of the TV commentator saying that we weren't even tired at this point, but all I remember is that I couldn't feel my legs. But because of the way we had trained, we knew that we could do it.

We had never told anyone, even each other, but we both knew we were retiring after the Olympics and that this was our last swim together. I didn't really watch the marks coming up — I just looked at the part of the scoreboard that showed our placing. It was a great feeling to see first place coming up. We were the Olympic Champions.

We were whisked off to get our track suits for the awards ceremony. When we came out of the door, we saw my family with a huge Canadian flag, which was the first time I had seen them since our arrival. It was great to hear the Canadian anthem and it made us both feel so proud. It was a good thing the medal weighed as much as it did, because it was the only thing keeping me on the podium.

I have a little Olympic ring that our manager had made for us in Seoul. I look at it every once in a while and realize what I'm capable of doing. When I was a kid I hated the water and was the least likely athlete. I was a really sick kid, but sport and nutrition changed my life. Now, when I speak at schools, I talk to kids about the choices they make and that we're capable of doing so much if we give ourselves a chance. ❧

Ian Millar and Big Ben Jump into History

CSI/COA

Show jumping rarely gets much play in the sports section. The rich and rarefied atmosphere of the sport has always made it seem too inaccessible to the average Canadian. But that all changed when Ian Millar and Big Ben broke into the show-jumping circuit. Canadians warmed immediately to the big bay gelding and his rider, and took the pair into their hearts.

When Ian and Big Ben made sports history, winning two World Cups back to back in 1988 and 1989, they were celebrated as heroes.

And heroic they were. In any sport, it would be rare indeed to consider a World Cup win as a warm-up exercise. But the pair's 1988 World Cup win was exactly that: prep work for the main event, the 1989 World Cup.

The World Cup is show jumping's most coveted indoor title. In reality, Ian and Big Ben's 1988 coup in Gothenburg, Sweden, was remarkable enough. The media trumpeted the win as proof of Canada's winning formula, for it was Canada's second title after Mario Deslauriers and his mount, Aramis, won in 1984. Reporters also cooed over Ian's bonus prize, a brand-new Volvo.

For their part, Ian and Big Ben struggled during parts of the four-day event, despite having taken the lead. Big Ben had a few uncharacteristic knockdowns — knocking down a rail on a jump — which had Ian worried. But by the end of the day, on Sunday April 10, 1988, the 12-year-old gelding and his rider were accepting congratulations from Princess Anne and listening to the strains of O Canada soar across the arena. It is doubtful they expected to repeat this experience.

Fast-forward one year. It was Wednesday, April 12, 1989, in Tampa, Florida. A whole new chapter in Canadian and world show jumping history was about to be written.

The first competition of the World Cup was the speed class, with five seconds added for every knockdown of a rail. Rider after rider suffered knockdowns, racking up the time. Finally, there were a few clean rides, each edging the next out by a few seconds.

By the time Ian and Big Ben cantered out onto the course, the pressure was mounting. No one, however, had yet been under 60 seconds. The Canadian rider saw the opportunity, and his horse responded. Together, they posted a clean round in 58.39 that proved untouchable. Rodney Jenkins, on Playback, came the closest with a clean round in 60.98.

The second phase of the competition, a timed-second jump-off class, was held on Friday evening, giving the horses a day of rest. In the event, only the clean rounds advance to a jump-off.

The order of competitors was reversed from the Wednesday event, which meant Rodney and Playback came out before Ian and Big Ben. While the US rider proved he was definitely in the competition, making only four faults on the first round, he did not qualify to advance.

For his part, Ian could have held back during the jump-off, and gone the "safe" route to maintain his lead. But that would have been giving second best, and that was not what he and Big Ben were about.

The pair went in, incurred four faults, but posted a solid time of 30.13. They won the second round.

Finally, it was Sunday, the day of the third and final phase, a two-round jumping competition. Following the second phase, the total scores are converted to penalty points. The leader gets zero, and all others are pro-rated after. The order is determined by standings, with the leader going last.

Princess Anne, in attendance at the final event, was impressed by the duo but wisely circumspect, remarking that it did not take much, at this level of competition, to make a mistake.

The pressure was on by the time Ian and Big Ben cantered out. Yes, they had zero points going in, but no horse and rider had ever successfully defended their title.

The pair almost succumbed to the pressure. At the second fence, Big Ben hit a rail, knocking it loudly, but it held. The tight spot behind them, they soared over the rest of the jumps and turned in a fault-free performance.

CSI/COA

Again, it was Rodney Jenkins and Playback who were edging ever closer. Heading into the second round of the final phase, Ian and Big Ben had a one "rail" lead, or four jumping faults over their chief rivals.

As the horse and riders tore up the course, the lead held by the Canadians become clear. Ian and Big Ben would win even if they knocked two rails down and racked up time faults. But the pair were not content with just winning: they had sports history on their mind.

The near-capacity crowd of 8,000 hushed in anticipation as Ian and Big Ben entered the arena. The fans were not disappointed. Big Ben jumped clean. As the pair sailed to the finish, the crowd jumped to its feet and roared in approval. They had just witnessed sports history.

Big Ben and Ian Millar became the only horse and rider to ever win back-to-back World Cups, and to do so in a sweep of all three competitions in the event. Ian was the first rider to have the title on two consecutive occasions; Big Ben the only horse to win the Cup twice, let alone consecutively.

As his ever-humble rider, Ian Millar, remarked after event, "You've got to understand that all I did was escort this horse around the courses. The hero is Big Ben."

Big Ben. What a good name for a Canadian hero. There is something very Canadian about it, evoking simple, hard-working greatness.

On Friday, December 10, 1999, at the age of 23, the gelding suffered a painful attack of colic, an extremely serious malady in horses. Ian was called back from a trip to Toronto to his farm in Perth, Ontario, to be with Big Ben. Early the next morning, Big Ben was euthanized.

The big horse with the big heart was mourned across the country. ❧

Lennox Lewis Wins One for Canada

By the time he had become heavyweight champion of the world in 1999, Lennox Lewis claimed in his heart "to have always been British even though I was very proud to represent Canada in two Olympics."

Canadians might wince at those words but it was certainly a fair exchange. Lewis's gold medal victory in the super-heavyweight boxing competition on the last day of the 1988 Seoul Olympic Games came at a time when Canadians were reeling from Ben Johnson's disqualification for steroid use after apparently winning the 100m sprint in world record time.

Born in London, England in 1965 to parents of Jamaican origin, Lewis had moved with his mother to Kitchener, Ontario a decade later. As a teenager in Kitchener he won many amateur boxing championships, eventually earning the right to represent Canada in the 1984 Olympics in Los Angeles. He was eliminated early, but planned for a second Olympic outing.

Lewis continued to grow in size and reputation, but the competition would be stiffer in 1988, with the return of Eastern bloc athletes who had boycotted the 1984 Games. Compounding the challenge was a freak accident in June when he broke the tip of his right thumb knocking out an American opponent.

CSI/COA

"It was actually a blessing in disguise," Lewis said. "It made me use my left jab more than before. I now use my left hand most of the time and the right for finishing off."

Adding to the pressure on Lewis was the Johnson affair. It threatened the harmony of the entire Canadian Olympic team with some, including Lewis, sympathizing with Johnson while others did their best to distance themselves from the situation.

"At first people were proud to call him Canadian but when the drugs thing came out they went back to calling him a Jamaican," Lewis said. "Taking an illegal substance was wrong but it left a bad taste with me the way people turned on him. He should have received much more support."

Lewis kept such thoughts to himself as he entered the ring for his gold medal match with the American Riddick Bowe.

Round One was a frustrating one for Lewis's supporters as the Canadian tried to match Bowe's inside, close range slugging.

Lewis's coach Adrian Teodorescu was furious. As Lewis returned to his corner the message was blunt. "What the hell are you doing?" Teodorescu raged. "Go out and fight him and knock him out. Stay away and use your long right hand."

It was just the wake up call Lewis needed as he landed five blows that resulted in a standing eight count to the bewildered American. They resumed boxing and Lewis caught Bowe with a looping right and then a quick left. The referee stopped the fight and Canada had won its first Olympic gold medal in boxing since Lefty Gwynne's bantamweight victory in 1932.

He dedicated the victory to his mother back in Kitchener as the whole country celebrated. After his success in Seoul, Lewis moved back to England and resumed a British identity as he fought towards an eventual world heavyweight title encounter with Evander Holyfield. Canadians will always treasure his timely gold medal for Canada in Seoul. ❧

CSI/COA

Lennox Lewis, 1988 Olympic Champion.

Canadian Professional Boxing World Champions

Division	Athlete	Reign	Title Note
Paperweight	Johnny Coulon	1908 - 1910	Undisputed
Flyweight	Frenchy Belanger	1927 - 1928	NBA
115 pound	Johnny Coulon	1910	Undisputed
Bantamweight	Johnny Coulon	1910 - 1914	World Title
Featherweight	George Dixon	1898 - 1900	Undisputed
	Jackie Callura	1943	NBA
Welterweight	Edddie Connolly	1900	Undisputed
	Lou Brouillard	1931 - 1932	Undisputed
	Jimmy McLarnin	1933 - 1934, 1934 - 1935	Undisputed
Middleweight	Lou Brouillard	1933	New York World Title
Light-heavyweight	Jack Delaney	1926 - 1927 (relinquished)	Undisputed
	Don Lalonde	1987 - 1988	WBC
Heavyweight	Tommy Burns	1906 - 1908	Undisputed
	Trevor Berbick	1986	WBC
	Lennox Lewis*	1992, 1994 - 2000 (plus)	WBC, Undisputed

*Lennox Lewis grew up in Kitchener, Ontario, and won a gold medal for Canada at the 1988 Olympics, he then turned professional in England in 1989.

Canada's Olympic Boxing Gold

Bantamweight	Horace Gwynne	1932, Los Angeles	Gold
Welterweight	Bert Schneider	1920, Antwerp	Gold
Super Heavyweight	Lennox Lewis	1988, Seoul	Gold

The Kurt and Elvis Show

For skating fans, it was a golden age. Few will ever forget the glory and the drama delivered by Kurt Browning and Elvis Stojko during the early 1990s. They held the world in their grasp every time they stepped out onto the ice. Pitted against each other by the media, yet these two titans of skating were friends first, who drew on their competitive rivalry to push each other to the top.

But push and play off each other they did. To begin with, two skaters could not have been more different in style.

Hailing from Caroline, Alberta, Browning was the seasoned veteran, a lively, engaging showman who set the rafters shaking with his powerful performances. Browning was a doubly blessed skater, a rare blend of technical and artistic skills. When Browning hit the ice, all who watched were swept up in the sheer joy of skating — and so this actor and athlete won audiences, judges, and media the world over.

Stojko was the young athletic contender, who climbed up the ranks in the shadow of Kurt Browning. He relished the challenge of competition from the start of his career. Stojko is recognized as a master technician, amazing all with the perfection of his jumps and earning the nickname, "The Terminator" from Browning. His macho, kung-fu skating style ushered in a new era in skating.

The prelude

The build-up to the main event began as early as the 1988 World Championships. Brian Orser was the reigning king of Canadian figure skating, but in his first appearance at the worlds, Browning made a name for himself by landing the world's first ever quadruple toe loop in competition.

The next year, Browning permanently won the hearts of Canadians with his first world title at the World Championships in Paris. He made history with a second world title at the 1990 World Championships in Halifax, becoming the first Canadian to win back-to-back titles.

Meanwhile, Stojko was inching into what was now Kurt's undisputed territory. In his first appearance at the worlds in 1990, the 17-year-old prodigy from Richmond Hill, Ontario, finished a very respectable ninth place. His coach, Doug Leigh, pronounced at the time, "He's an excellent technician. He's a skater to be reckoned with."

Kurt Browning

Elvis Stojko

In 1991, Browning won his third world title in a row, for a golden hat trick. To win, the skater who landed the first quadruple in competition unleashed a series of dazzling, dangerous moves, making history with three triple-triple jumps in his long program.

At the same event, however, Stojko moved up to sixth — and he also made history by landing the world's first quadruple-double combination jump.

While the ice still clearly belonged to Browning, Stojko was making his presence felt.

Tragic flaws revealed

All heroes must face their demons, and at the 1992 Albertville Olympic Games, both Browning and Stojko met theirs head-on.

When Browning was "on," he was unstoppable. Going into the 1992 Albertville Olympic Winter Games, all eyes were on Browning. He was a veritable shoe-in for a medal, most likely the gold.

But it was not in the cards. Under the intense pressure of the Olympics, the attending hype of the world media, and beset with a back injury, Browning cracked. He fell on a triple Axel in the short program and, visibly shaken, he never recovered. The three-time world champion ended up sixth. The charmer who breezed through competitions and shrugged off the pressure revealed that he was not as unflappable as he seemed.

Stojko was also at Albertville, shielded from the intense media scrutiny and the expectations of a nation by Browning's presence. Yet Stojko faced his own adversity, and was denied the chance to turn Browning's shocking placing to his advantage. In a sport that prizes tall, graceful elegance, his short, powerful, compact presence on the ice was not one to automatically draw the favour of the judges. Inexplicably, Stojko dropped from sixth to seventh midway through the event after skating well, while higher-ranked skaters were stumbling and falling around him. In an article for *Maclean's* magazine (Feb. 24, 1992), Brian Orser wrote, "And on a night when the skating was certainly not great, the judging was even worse than the skating...Canada's Elvis Stojko, who finished seventh — he was completely robbed. He pulled out a performance that was worthy of the Olympics. It was the perfect example of rising to the occasion. It was also poor judging."

The judging notwithstanding, Stojko proved he could skate at the highest level. It would be his last competition in the shadow of Kurt Browning.

Dress rehearsal

A month and a half after his humiliating sixth place finish at the Olympics, Browning was lacing up his skates at the World Championships in Oakland, California.

He was not one to brood, preferring to shake off his losses. After his long program, Browning said he put it behind him, as quickly as possible. "I went out that night, partied with my family and friends, went skiing the next day, went to a hockey game the next night."

Yet he clearly had a thing or two to prove in Oakland — and prove himself he did. Browning pulled his act together and skated his way to silver.

Hot on his heels, Elvis took the bronze, not yet able to surpass his friend, but finally able to impress the judges with his abilities. And he did it in his own, inimitable, martial-arts-inspired, techno-pop way. The up-and-comer stepped out from the shadows and into the limelight.

Elvis in action

Kurt skating

CSI/COA

CSI/COA

When Viktor Petrenko, who won the men's title that year, turned pro later that year, all eyes were on Kurt and Elvis for the 1993 crown. The subjects of intense speculation, the two were headed for an all-Canadian showdown at the World Championships in Prague, the Czech Republic.

The main event

The hype began at the 1993 Canadian nationals. The men's final, held in the 17,125-seat Copps Coliseum in Hamilton, was sold out. The pair did not disappoint — the judges gave them virtually the same marks, with Browning narrowly edging out Stojko. The stage was set for Prague.

Despite the attending media frenzy, the two steadfastly remained friends. "We'll compete against the rest of the world," said Stojko before leaving for Prague. "We'll cheer each other on."

Even so, these friends and rivals were still each counting on the other to push him ahead.

Stojko made no bones about that fact that his goal in Prague was to put pressure on Browning. But when he took to the ice on the day the short program, he went too far, and made two surprising technical mistakes in his short program. Stojko, being the type of skater who cannot rely on artistic marks to pull him up, was fifth.

Browning, on the other hand, skated a solid short program and stood first. Tellingly, however, he was upset when "The Terminator" fell back: "Having Elvis fifth, which was an incredible surprise, hurt me a little because I had been relying on a big fight with him to push me hard. The competition is what good skaters live for and when Elvis dropped back, I had to recalibrate my thinking."

Stojko faced a steep climb, and had to regroup quickly. Between him and Browning stood three skaters, including Russian skater Alexei Urmanov and American Mark Mitchell, who was second after the short.

One of the people he turned to was Donald Jackson, who won Canada's first men's world title in 1962. Jackson told Stojko that when he won the men's title in 1962, he too had placed fifth after the short, but came back to win with a powerful free skate.

Canadian Innovators

Canadian male skaters have taken home a lot of medals from international figure skating events, but they have also given back to the sport. Donald Jackson gave the world its first triple Lutz in 1962. Brian Orser and Vern Taylor share the honours for introducing the triple Axel. Taylor landed the first triple Axel at the World Championships in 1978 while Orser was nicknamed Mr. Triple Axel for perfecting the jump during his years at the top. Kurt Browning landed the first quadruple toe loop, among other dazzling new moves. But technical wizardry reached its zenith with Elvis Stojko, who landed the first quadruple-double combination in 1991, and the first quadruple-triple combination in 1997.

Then there is the artistry. With his dynamic, iconoclastic skating style, Toller Cranston revolutionized the sport in the 1970s. An actor as much as a skater, Browning immortalized the role of Bogie. And with the dirt-biking, kung fu master Stojko hitting the ice in black leather and metal studs, a whole new era of macho, athletic skating was unleashed.

Stojko took to these words to heart, for in what would be immortalized as a true, gritty, Elvis-style comeback, Stojko unleashed an extraordinary free skate, the most difficult routine of the whole event. He landed every one of his eight triples, including a difficult triple Axel-triple toe loop, with grace and ease.

If Browning's defence was to shrug off the pressure philosophically, Stojko's was to simply block it out. "I just could not think about the No. 5 standing and where I might go from there. What I had to do was skate the best program I could do and see what happened," he said at the time.

And what happened? Stojko jumped over three skaters into second place. In case the world had any doubts, Stojko had spoken: he would not choke, ever.

But he could not catch Browning. This was the year that Browning brought Humphrey Bogart to the ice, in a routine based on the film, *Casablanca*. The actor on blades, Browning delivered four and a half minutes of theatre on ice. Dressed in a white dinner jacket and black tie, he swept up audiences, judges and media alike with his elegant characterization of Bogie. It was almost as if he threw in the triple Axels for good measure.

CSI/COA

1987-1997

Ten Years at the Top (and counting)

Men's titles at the World Championship:
1987 – *Brian Orser*
1989 – *Kurt Browning*
1990 – *Kurt Browning*
1991 – *Kurt Browning*
1993 – *Kurt Browning*
1994 – *Elvis Stojko*
1995 – *Elvis Stojko*
1997 – *Elvis Stojko*

Not at the top, but still on the podium …

Olympics	World Championships
1984 – *Brian Orser, silver*	1976 – *Toller Cranston, bronze*
1988 – *Brian Orser, silver*	1983 – *Brian Orser, bronze*
1994 – *Elvis Stojko, silver*	1984 – *Brian Orser, silver*
1998 – *Elvis Stojko, silver*	1985 – *Brian Orser, silver*
	1986 – *Brian Orser, silver*
	1988 – *Brian Orser, silver*
	1992 – *Kurt Browning, silver*
	1993 – *Elvis Stojko, silver*
	1999 – *Elvis Stojko, silver*

It would be gold for Browning, and silver for Stojko, in an unprecedented one-two Canadian knockout.

When Stojko stepped up to the podium, the two shared a long, warm handshake. In a memorable statement that summed up their friendship, Stojko said, "Having Kurt say how happy he was to have me there beside him and to know how much he meant it because he's a great friend first, and a competitor later, was something really special to me."

Epilogue

Even after winning an unprecedented fourth title, Browning said that despite his injuries, he was geared up to keep going, largely because Stojko wouldn't let him stop.

But it was not to happen. At the Canadian Nationals in January 1994, the heir became king when Stojko won gold. In front of a hometown crowd in Edmonton, Browning skated poorly, and had to settle for silver.

One month later at the Lillehammer Olympic Winter Games, Browning's Achilles heel resurfaced. His short program was a disaster. But this time, Browning gamely came back with a strong free skate in the long program, finishing fifth overall. In his final statement as an amateur, Browning went out with a flourish and four World Championships, and on to a lucrative professional career.

Stojko won the Olympic silver in Lillehammer, but again, the whispers of bad judging resurfaced. Gold medal winner Urmanov, a solid skater in his own right, had fallen in the long, while Stojko skated cleanly and confidently.

Finally, at the 1994 World Championships in April, Stojko took his rightful place on the top step of the podium. In the next four years, he won two more golds and two silver at the World Championships, as well as one more Olympic silver. Despite struggling with injuries, as of 2000 Elvis was not ready to leave the building just yet, continuing to push the figure skating envelope with his unique combination of tenacity, strength and skill. ❧

Brian Orser, waiting.

1905-2000

Canadian National Figure Skating Champions

Year	Men	Women	Pairs	Dance
1905	Ormond Haycock	Anne Ewan	Katherine & Ormond Haycock	
1906	Ormond Haycock	Aimee Haycock	Katherine & Ormond Haycock	
1907	Minto Club burned down			
1908	Ormond Haycock	Aimee Haycock	Aimee & Ormond Haycock	
1909	Not Held			
1910	D.H. Nelles	Iris Mudge	Lady Evelyn Grey & Ormond Haycock	Lady Evelyn Grey & Dudly Oliver (Senior Waltz)
1911	Ormond Haycock	Lady Evelyn Grey	Lady Evelyn Grey & Ormond Haycock	
1912	D.H. Nelles	Eleanor Kingsford	Eleanor Kingsford & Douglas Nelles	
1913	Phil Crysler	Eleanor Kingsford	Muriel Burrows & Gordon McLennan	
1914	Norman Scott	Muriel Maunsell	Jeanne Chevalier & Norman Scott	
1915 - 1919	Cancelled due to World War I			
1920	Norman Scott	Jeanne Chevalier	Alden Godwin & Douglas Nelles	
1921	Duncan Hodgson	Jeanne Chevalier	Beatrice MacDougall & Allan Howard	
1922	Duncan Hodgson	Dorothy Jenkins	Alden Godwin & Major A.C. Maclennan	
1923	Melville Rogers	Dorothy Jenkins	Majorie Annabel & Duncan Hodgson	
1924	John Z. Machado	Constance Wilson	Elizabeth Blair & John Machado	
1925	Melville Rogers	Cecil Smith	Gladys & Melville Rogers	
1926	Melville Rogers	Cecil Smith	Constance Wilson & Errol Morson	
1927	Melville Rogers	Constance Wilson	Marion McDougall & Chauncy Bangs	
1928	Melville Rogers	Margot Barclay	Marion McDougall & Chauncy Bangs	
1929	Montgomery Wilson	Constance Wilson	Constance & Montgomery Wilson	
1930	Montgomery Wilson	Constance Wilson	Constance & Montgomery Wilson	
1931	Montgomery Wilson	Constance Wilson	Frances Claudet & Chauncy Bangs	
1932	Montgomery Wilson	Constance Samuel	Constance Samuel & Montgomery Wilson	
1933	Montgomery Wilson	Constance Samuel	Constance Samuel & Montgomery Wilson	
1934	Montgomery Wilson	Constance Samuel	Constance Samuel & Montgomery Wilson	
1935	Montgomery Wilson	Constance Samuel	Louise Bertram & Stewart Reburn	
1936	Osbourne Colson	Fleanor O' Meara	Veronica Clarke & Ralph McCreath	Mr & Mrs Don Cruickshank (Waltz); Veronica Clarke & Jack Eastwood (Tenstep)
1937	Osbourne Colson	Dorothy Caley	Veronica Clarke & Ralph McCreath	Mr & Mrs Don Cruickshank (Waltz); Veronica Clarke & Jack Eastwood (Tenstep)
1938	Montgomery Wilson	Eleanor O' Meara	Veronica Clarke & Ralph McCreath	Janet & Fraser Sweatman (Waltz); Veronica Clarke & Jack Eastwood (Tenstep)
1939	Montgomery Wilson	Mary Rose Thacker	Norah McCarthy & Ralph McCreath	Mr & Mrs Don Cruickshank (Waltz); Janet Clarke & Fraser Sweatman (Tenstep)
1940	Ralph McCreath	Norah McCarthy	Norah McCarthy & Ralph McCreath	Mr & Mrs Don Cruickshank (Waltz); Mrs Elmore Davis & Melville Rogers (Tenstep)
1941	Ralph McCreath	Mary Rose Thacker	Eleanor O'Meara & Ralph McCreath	Helen Malcolm & FKJ Geisler (Waltz); Norah McCarthy & Sandy McKechnie (Tenstep)
1942	Michael Kirby	Mary Rose Thacker	Eleanor O'Meara & Sandy McKechnie	Eleanor O'Meara & Sandy McKechnie (Waltz) Evelyn Rogers & McCollough (Tenstep)
1943	Competitions Cancelled due to WW II			
1944	Cancelled	Barbara Ann Scott	Cancelled	Cancelled
1945		Barbara Ann Scott	Olga Bernyk & Alex Fulton	Gloria Lillico & William de Nance Jr. (Schumaker) (Waltz); Olga Bernyk & Alex Fulton (Tenstep)
1946	Ralph McCreath	Barbara Ann Scott	Joyce Perkins & Wallace Distelmeyer	Gloria Lillico & William de Nance Jr. (Schumaker) (Waltz); Marnie Brereton & Richard McLaughlin (Tenstep)
1947	Norris Bowden	Marilyn Ruth Take	Suzanne Morrow & Wallace Distelmeyer	Margret Roberts & Bruce Hyland
1948	Wallace Distelmeyer	Barbara Ann Scott	Suzanne Morrow & Wallace Distelmeyer	Suzanne Morrow & Wallace Distelmeyer
1949	Roger Wickson	Suzanne Morrow	Marlene Smith & Donald Gilchrist	Joyce Perkins & Bruce Hyland (Silver Dance/Waltz); Pierrette Paquin & Donald Tobin (Foxtrot & Fourteenstep)
1950	Roger Wickson	Suzanne Morrow	Marlene Smith & Donald Gilchrist	Frances Dafoe & Norris Bowden (Waltz); Joy Forsyth & William DeNance Jr., (Foxtrot & Fourteenstep) Pierrette Paquin & Donald Tobin (Silver Dance)
1951	Peter Firstbrook	Suzanne Morrow	Jane Kirby & Donald Tobin	Pierrette Paquin & Donald Tobin (Silver) Mary Trimble & David Ross (Tenstep); Frances Dafoe & Norris Bowden (Waltz)

Brasseur and Eisler

Toller Cranston

Year				
1952	Peter Firstbrook	Marlene Smith	Frances Dafoe & Norris Bowden	Frances Dafoe & Norris Bowden
1953	Peter Firstbrook	Barbara Gratton	Frances Dafoe & Norris Bowden	Frances Abbott & David Ross
1954	Charles Snelling	Barbara Gratton	Frances Dafoe & Norris Bowden	Geraldine Fenton & William McLachlan
1955	Charles Snelling	Carole Pachl	Frances Dafoe & Norris Bowden	Lindis Johnston & Jeffrey Johnston
1956	Charles Snelling	Carole Pachl	Barbara Wagner & Robert Paul	Geraldine Fenton & William McLachlan
1957	Charles Snelling	Carole Pachl	Barbara Wagner & Robert Paul	Geraldine Fenton & William McLachlan
1958	Charles Snelling	Margaret Crosland	Barbara Bourne & Tom Monypenny	Geraldine Fenton & William McLachlan
1959	Donald Jackson	Margaret Crosland	Barbara Wagner & Robert Paul	Geraldine Fenton & William McLachlan
1960	Donald Jackson	Wendy Griner	Barbara Wagner & Robert Paul	Mary Jane Lennie & Karl Benzing
1961	Donald Jackson	Wendy Griner	Maria & Otto Jelinek	Virginia Thompson & William McLachlan
1962	Donald Jackson	Wendy Griner	Maria & Otto Jelinek	Virginia Thompson & William McLachlan
1963	Donald McPherson	Wendy Griner	Debbie Wilkes & Guy Revell	Paulette Doan & Kenneth Ormsby
1964	Charles Snelling	Petra Burka	Debbie Wilkes & Guy Revell	Paulette Doan & Kenneth Ormsby
1965	Donald Knight	Petra Burka	Susan & Paul Huehnergard	Carole Forrest & Kevin Lethbridge
1966	Donald Knight	Petra Burka	Susan & Paul Huehnergard	Carole Forrest & Kevin Lethbridge
1967	Donald Knight	Valerie Jones	Betty & John McKilligan	Joni Graham & Don Phillips
1968	Jay Humphry	Karen Magnussen	Betty & John McKilligan	Joni Graham & Don Phillips
1969	Jay Humphry	Linda Carbonetto	Anna Forder & Richard Stephens	Donna Taylor & Bruce Lennie
1970	David McGillivray	Karen Magnussen	Sandra & Val Bezic	Mary Church & David Sutton
1971	Toller Cranston	Karen Magnussen	Sandra & Val Bezic	Louise Lind & Barry Soper
1972	Toller Cranston	Karen Magnussen	Sandra & Val Bezic	Louise Lind & Barry Soper
1973	Toller Cranston	Karen Magnussen	Sandra & Val Bezic	Louise Lind & Barry Soper
1974	Toller Cranston	Linda Nightingale	Sandra & Val Bezic	Louise Lind & Barry Soper
1975	Toller Cranston	Linda Nightingale	Candy Jones & Don Fraser	Barbara Berezowski & David Porter
1976	Toller Cranston	Linda Nightingale	Candy Jones & Don Fraser	Barbara Berezowski & David Porter
1977	Ron Shaver	Linda Nightingale	Cheri & Dennis Pinner	Susan Carscallen & Eric Gillies
1978	Brian Pockar	Heather Kemkaran	Sherri Baier & Robin Cowan	Lorna Wighton & John Dowding
1979	Brian Pockar	Janet Morissey	Barbara Underhill & Paul Martini	Lorna Wighton & John Dowding
1980	Brian Pockar	Heather Kemkaran	Barbara Underhill & Paul Martini	Lorna Wighton & John Dowding
1981	Brian Orser	Tracey Wainman	Barbara Underhill & Paul Martini	Marie McNeil & Robert McCall
1982	Brian Orser	Kay Thomson	Barbara Underhill & Paul Martini	Tracy Wilson & Robert McCall
1983	Brian Orser	Kay Thomson	Barbara Underhill & Paul Martini	Tracy Wilson & Robert McCall
1984	Brian Orser	Kay Thomson	Kathy Matousek & Lloyd Eisler	Tracy Wilson & Robert McCall
1985	Brian Orser	Elizabeth Manley	Cynthia Coull & Mark Rowsom	Tracy Wilson & Robert McCall
1986	Brian Orser	Tracey Wainman	Cynthia Coull & Mark Rowsom	Tracy Wilson & Robert McCall
1987	Brian Orser	Elizabeth Manley	Cynthia Coull & Mark Rowsom	Tracy Wilson & Robert McCall
1988	Brian Orser	Elizabeth Manley	Christine Hough & Doug Landret	Tracy Wilson & Robert McCall
1989	Kurt Browning	Karen Preston	Isabelle Brasseur & Lloyd Eisler	Karen & Rod Garossino
1990	Kurt Browning	Lisa Sargeant	Cindy Landry & Lyndon Johnston	Joanne Borlase & Martin Smith
1991	Kurt Browning	Josée Chouinard	Isabelle Brasseur & Lloyd Eisler	Michelle McDonald & Martin Smith
1992	Michael Slipchuk	Karen Preston	Isabelle Brasseur & Lloyd Eisler	Jaqueline Petr & Mark Janoshak
1993	Kurt Browning	Josée Chouinard	Isabelle Brasseur & Lloyd Eisler	Shae-Lynn Bourne & Victor Kraatz
1994	Elvis Stojko	Josée Chouinard	Isabelle Brasseur & Lloyd Eisler	Shae-Lynn Bourne & Victor Kraatz
1995	Sebastien Britten	Netty Kim	Michelle Menzies & Jean-Michel Bombardier	Shae-Lynn Bourne & Victor Kraatz
1996	Elvis Stojko	Jennifer Robinson	Michelle Menzies & Jean-Michel Bombardier	Shae-Lynn Bourne & Victor Kraatz
1997	Elvis Stojko	Susan Humphreys	Marie-Claude Savard-Gagnon & Luc Bradet	Shae-Lynn Bourne & Victor Kraatz
1998	Elvis Stojko	Angela Derochie	Kristy Sargeant & Kris Wirz	Shae-Lynn Bourne & Victor Kraatz
1999	Elvis Stojko	Jennifer Robinson	Kristy Sargeant & Kris Wirz	Shae-Lynn Bourne & Victor Kraatz
2000	Elvis Stojko	Jennifer Robinson	Jamie Salé & David Pelletier	Marie-France Dubreuil & Patrice Lauzon

CSI/COA

Elizabeth Manley

Canadian Winners of World & Olympic Figure Skating Championships

World Champions

Men

1962	Donald Jackson
1963	Donald McPherson
1987	Brian Orser
1989	Kurt Browning
1990	Kurt Browning
1991	Kurt Browning
1993	Kurt Browning (2nd Elvis Stojko)
1994	Elvis Stojko
1995	Elvis Stojko
1997	Elvis Stojko

Women

1947	Barbara Ann Scott
1948	Barbara Ann Scott
1965	Petra Burka
1973	Karen Magnussen

Pairs

1954	Frances Dafoe & Norris Bowden
1955	Frances Dafoe & Norris Bowden
1957	Barbara Wagner & Robert Paul
1958	Barbara Wagner & Robert Paul
1959	Barbara Wagner & Robert Paul
1960	Barbara Wagner & Robert Paul
1962	Maria & Otto Jelinek
1984	Barbara Underhill & Paul Martini
1993	Isabelle Brasseur & Lloyd Eisler

Olympic Champions

| 1948 - | Barbara Ann Scott |
| | Women's Singles |

| 1960 - | Barbara Wagner & Robert Paul |
| | Pairs |

Barbara Ann Scott

Dafoe and Bowden

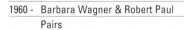

Maria & Otto Jelinek

The MacTier Cup

Rugby Canada

The MacTier Cup ranks among Canada's oldest sporting trophies. It was donated in 1922 by Montreal stockbroker A.D. MacTier as a challenge cup for supremacy in senior rugby in Eastern Canada. In its first three years of existence it was won by teams from Montreal and for the next four years by the University of New Brunswick.

But, for the next 12 years, until 1940, it was won by teams of coal miners from Glace Bay, Nova Scotia. A team from No. 11 Colliery won it in 1933. In 1930 Glace Bay Caledonias played Montreal Amateur Athletic Association to a draw and both teams' names are engraved on the cup. For the other 10 of those 12 years Glace Bay Caledonias had sole and undisputed possession.

Glace Bay's home field was South Street Park, a grassless expanse of compacted brown soil and rocks. The perimeter of the playing surface was bounded by a cinder running track. Visiting teams regularly complained about the skinned playing field and the gritty track. The tough coal miners were unbeatable.

In 1941, St. Francis Xavier University won the trophy and competition was suspended during the war years. The two-foot high solid silver trophy gleamed in St. F.X.'s trophy case until 1953, when St. F.X. changed over to Canadian football and rugby was dropped from the athletic program. A team from Glace Bay challenged St. F.X. for the MacTier Cup. The university ignored the challenge because it was unable to field a rugby squad. In response, a trio of rugby players from Glace Bay drove the 130 miles to Antigonish, removed the Cup from the trophy case, claimed it for the Caledonias and drove it home to Glace Bay.

The driver of the "getaway car" was Donald MacInnis, a player and later a coach of the Caledonias, and who four short years later became a long-serving Member of Parliament for Cape Breton South.

The MacTier Cup was taken to the Glace Bay Miners' Museum, not far from South Street Park, and housed there in a place of honour. Years later rumours persisted that the trophy had been lost when fire destroyed the museum building. Yet somehow, the MacTier Cup ended up back in the St. F.X. trophy case only to be liberated again, this time by University of New Brunswick students in 1963.

The trophy was restored by Rugby Canada in 1995, it appears to be none the worse for wear, tear and travel with only one visible "ding" in it. ◆

1990s

Women's Hockey

Equality on Ice: Women Hockey Players Win a World Profile

by D'Arcy Jenish with Sharon Doyle Driedger and Bruce Garrioch
April 2, 1990

The West German women managed just 12 shots on the Canadian net, and the Swedes only three. In return, the Canadians blasted 119 shots at their weaker European opponents in two games and outscored them by 32 goals to one. Despite the mismatches and lopsided scores, organizers of the first Women's World Ice Hockey Championship, held last week in Ottawa, expressed pleasure about a new profile for a little-known brand of the game. The Sports Network (TSN) televised four games nationally and about 85 journalists from six countries were accredited to cover the tournament.

Organizers said that their next objective is to get women's hockey accepted as part of the 1994 Winter Olympics in Lillehammer, Norway. Said Frances Rider, president of the Ontario Women's Hockey Association: "We're very confident it will be in the Olympics. It's long overdue."

After the decisive victories over Sweden and West Germany, most observers expected the Canadian women, who wore garish pink-and-white uniforms bearing stylized maple leafs, to advance to the championship game on March 25. Among the eight nations taking part, the US and Finnish teams were the tournament's other powerhouses. Although those three teams were far superior to their rivals, organizers said that holding a world championship should convince more women that hockey is not just a men's game, and that it will give current players an objective to strive for. Said Rider: "Up until now, there has been no elite international competition for women playing hockey."

Building women's hockey as an organized sport has been a slow process, even in Canada. The first national championship for women was held in 1982, and five years later the Ontario association hosted an international tournament in Toronto for six countries. As a result, the International Ice Hockey Federation sanctioned a women's world championship and, at a tournament last year, Sweden, Finland, Norway, West Germany and Switzerland earned the right to attend the Ottawa championship. The Canadian and US teams were selected on the basis of training camps attended by the best players in both countries. Japan agreed to represent Asia after China decided not to send a team.

CSI/COA

CSI/COA

In some of the other countries competing at the world championship, women's hockey is far less developed than it is in Canada because of lack of ice time and interest in the sport. There are only about 600 female players in Sweden, all in a single league. After Canada defeated Japan 18-0, team captain Tamami Nishida explained that there are only 30 to 40 women's teams in Japan, including five in Tokyo. Said Nishida: "We knew we couldn't beat Canada. They're not only fast and strong, they know hockey."

In some cases, that speed, strength and knowledge of the game result from years of playing and practising. Canadian forward Vicky Sunohara, a 20-year-old Scarborough, Ont., native, said that her father introduced her to the game at the age of 2 and enrolled her in a boys league when she was 5. Defenceman Judy Diduck, a 24-year-old Edmonton resident, said that she played road hockey with neighborhood boys for years, including her brother, Gerald, now a defenceman for the New York Islanders.

As female hockey players become more skilled, comparisons between the abilities of men and women are inevitable. The Canadian Amateur Hockey Association's Harold Lewis, who has been associated with the game for 50 years, said that many female players are quick, agile skaters and good stickhandlers. In most cases, they cannot shoot the puck as hard as men because they have less upper-body strength. But, in last week's tournament, the Canadian

women showed that they can play a tough brand of hockey. Their match against Sweden included several thunderous collisions and 21 minor penalties for such infractions as boarding, roughing and high-sticking. Indeed, whether the players are male or female, hockey is a game of speed, agility and emotion. With more exposure for the game, the world gradually is getting in on the secret. ♥

CSI/COA

CSI

Kerrin Lee-Gartner and Kate Pace – Queens of the Slopes

In the months leading up to the 1992 Olympic Winter Games in Albertville, France, it seemed like the glory days of the crazy Canucks were long over, replaced by the crashing Canucks.

Ken Read, one of the leaders of the Crazy Canucks during the late '70s and early '80s, was openly critical of the alpine team, calling their World Cup results an embarrassment. At the Games, it seemed he was terribly, terribly right. One by one, the medal hopes on the men's team crashed. Edi Podivinsky caught an edge, crashed and injured himself, while Cary Mullen, Brian Stemmle and Rob Crossan all wiped out.

As for the women's team, well, it was so beset with injuries that only two racers were entered in the downhill race: Kerrin Lee-Gartner and Michelle McKendry. A native of Rossland, BC, Lee-Gartner grew up just two doors down from Nancy Greene, Canada's skiing heroine of the '60s. While the strongest Canadian contender, Lee-Gartner had never won a World Cup race, her best placing being a third. And throughout her eight-year career she had been besieged with injuries.

It's not surprising, then, that pre-race analysis made little or no mention of Lee-Gartner, even though she posted the 3rd fastest practice run. Race day was Saturday, February 15, on a hill called "Roc de Fer" (the "Iron Rock") in the town of Meribel, one of the toughest women's downhill courses ever. Icy and treacherous, the run claimed many victims in the week leading up. The racers nicknamed one killer jump on the course "Noodles," because that's what they looked like after attempting it. A few skiers even pulled out, claiming it was too difficult.

But Lee-Gartner was not intimidated. "The approach I took was all or nothing," she recounted at the time. "I was going for the podium no matter what!" Her confidence was also boosted by a dream she'd had more than a year earlier, during which she heard an announcer (speaking French) introducing her as a gold medallist.

CSI/COA

Kerrin Lee-Gartner (middle), Olympic Champion, 1992.

Canada

Lee-Gartner raced 12th out of the 15 in the top seed. Racing ahead of her were skiing greats, like Germany's Katja Seizinger and Austria's Petra Kronberger. At every timing interval of the upper portion of the course, Lee-Gartner posted the second-best split times behind Seizinger. She won the race on the bottom of the course, a steep, winding pitch. When she zoomed across the finish line, the 10,000 spectators were stunned into silence by her time of 1:52.55, beating Seizinger by .12 seconds.

She cheered in delight, and then checked herself as the toughest part began: 19 other skiers had yet to race. Two skiers came within less than one tenth of a second, but in the end no one was able to beat her time, and Lee-Gartner began to celebrate the second best day of her life (the best was her wedding day to Austrian coach Max Gartner). Kerrin Lee-Gartner had won Canada's first Olympic gold in downhill skiing. No one, not even those crazy Canucks, had achieved that.

Kate Pace, World Champion, 1993.

Lee-Gartner's gold boosted the alpine team, and the Canadian team in general. It also boosted the hopes of an up-and-coming skier, Kate Pace-Lindsay.

Pace-Lindsay first made the national team in 1988, when double Olympic bronze medallist Karen Percy was still around. While she was always a solid skier with great potential, it's almost as if Kerrin Lee-Gartner's gold was a catalyst for Pace, driving her to her greatest skiing achievements.

The pride of North Bay, Ontario, Kate Pace-Lindsay had the kind of season in 1993-1994 that most skiers just dream about. She won two golds on the World Cup circuit, and picked up a few other colours for good measure. If not in the top five, she was surely to be found in the top ten. Pace-Lindsay was on top of the world.

Those who boast about their athletic prowess sometimes say they could win with one hand tied behind their back. At the 1993 World Championships, Pace-Lindsay came pretty close to accomplishing just that, having broken her wrist shortly before the event. In a cast and using a modified ski pole, she flashed down the course in Morioko-Shizukuishi, Japan, to win the championship. The win was pure determination and athletic prowess, and pure Kate Pace-Lindsay.

At the 1994 Lillehammer Olympic Winter Games, Pace-Lindsay was a strong contender for gold, but had to settle for fifth. The field included defending Olympic downhill champion Lee-Gartner, who came in 19th. No doubt Pace-Lindsay was disappointed, but she had her spectacular world championship win in 1993 to comfort herself with.

When asked who was the most impressive athlete he had ever met, Olympic 100m gold medallist Donovan Bailey answered, "Kate Pace-Lindsay." Her husband, Mark Lindsay, happens to be Bailey's personal physiotherapist.

Lee-Gartner and Pace-Lindsay — two of Canada's most renowned Queens of the slopes. ❦

Olympic Gold ...
"Go Now!"

by Mark Tewksbury

The day was August 7, 1991, one year before the 1992 Barcelona Olympics. I was feeling pretty good. I'd set a world record two years before, and as I prepped for a meet in Edmonton, my confidence was up. I was clearly seeing gold.

I was ranked second in the world in my event, the 100m backstroke. My arch nemesis, the American Jeff Rouse, was ranked first, but he had only beaten me by 6/100ths of a second six months earlier at the World Championships. As I stood in the pool (we backstrokers don't dive, but start from the pool), I felt this race was very much a warm-up for the Olympics.

I will never forget hearing the roar of the crowd at the end of that race. My stomach fell because I knew they were not cheering for me. Rouse had swum a time of 53.93, beaten me by 1.2 seconds, and demolished the world record.

I was devastated for days after. How on earth could I best that? It had taken me most of my national team career — seven years — to shave 1.2 seconds off my time. How would I accomplish the same in one year?

I sat back and re-examined my life. Clearly, at six hours a day, there was no more time available to be spent in the pool. I could do some work on my weak areas — my start and my turn — but I couldn't physically train for more hours in the day.

Perhaps, like Victor Davis had shown me all those years ago, what I needed was to believe in myself. One major move was to add the help of a strong psychological coach, just to work on my mental focus and attitude. That year was a real rollercoaster ride, between doubt and belief. Some days I totally believed in myself; and others I was plagued with doubts.

One key step that I took was to travel to Barcelona in March, six months before the Games would start. I needed to visualize the city and the pool, so that when July rolled around, it would seem very familiar. I managed to sneak into the pool area, and I stood up on the number 4 platform, visualized the crowd, and waved — much to the amusement of the construction workers overhead. Then, I stepped off, and went back to where I thought the ready-room would be, only to re-emerge and step up on the number 5 platform (you never know where you're going to qualify!). At that point, Spanish security caught up with me and kicked me out. But my mission was accomplished — I had my vision.

Because I knew I would be competing on a Thursday, I began to do something fun every Thursday, like go to dinner or catch a movie. Eventually, I woke up on Thursdays feeling excited about the day. My mental edge was building.

Finally, the Barcelona Games arrived. I wanted to see what the competition looked like, so I went to see the 200m breaststroke the day before my event. There was a Spaniard in that event, who'd also be in mine. Just before the event started, I heard this giant roar — the King and Queen of Spain had just arrived to watch him swim. Talk about pressure!

The Spaniard won. He was there in the ready room the next day, joking and laughing until he heard the King and Queen were there again. Then he became very quiet and very focused.

We had a tough final. The top four finalists — I was second behind Jeff — had finished one after another, each 1/10 of a second slower than the previous one. Basically, it was anyone's race.

Mark Tewksbury reacts to his winning time at the 1992 Olympic Games.

I was working hard to stay focused, which was hard with such an excited crowd. When 10,000 Spaniards cheered for Lopez-Zubero, I thought to myself, "They're cheering for me! They're cheering for me!" When the marshal blew the whistle to get ready, I jumped in the water and went straight to the bottom. The water is very cold, but silent. I stood on the bottom of the pool and I thought, "This is it."

I surfaced, placed my hands on the walls, and before I knew it, I was swimming.

I knew I'd have to be patient. I was a slow starter, and the Americans were very fast. I knew my only chance was to try to catch them on the second lap.

I kept a strong pace for the first 50 metres. After the turn, I glided underneath the water, surfaced and thought, "GO NOW, GO NOW, GO NOW. "

So I began to pick up my pace. I could see some swimmers behind me, but not Jeff. I knew he was in the lane next to me — and then I felt him, or more like I felt the splash of his feet at my head. "That's not good," I thought, but I dug in.

I'm stroking, and stroking. Slowly, that splash moved down past my head to my shoulders, waist, and knees. Then, I couldn't see the splash anymore. And when I pull my arm up and over at 10 metres, I see his hand, just ahead of mine. With five metres to go, I pull even.

At two metres, I have two strokes left. I stroke as hard as I can with my right arm, and with my left I lunge for the wall.

Grasping the wall, I look up at the scoreboard. I couldn't exhale. It was that intense. Then, my name flashed up first. I totally freaked out. It meant I had won this race!

Then my time flashed up: 53.98. I had shaved off the 1.2 seconds that had seemed so impossible only a year before.

Then, it hit me, and I almost went into a state of shock. After years of training, my dream had come true. I hadn't just won a race, I had won the gold medal at the Olympic Games. ❧

Mark Tewksbury, 1992 Olympic Champion.

CSI/COA

Kathleen Heddle and Marnie McBean.

Bonanza in Banyoles

Banyoles, site of the rowing course for the 1992 Olympics, was geographically removed by some 124 km from downtown Barcelona, but that didn't stop it from being home to some of the more dramatic action of the games. The Canadian team in particular made waves (literally and figuratively) by carrying off more gold medals than any other country, and coming second in total medals to the perennial powerhouse German team.

CSI/COA

Men's 8

CSI/COA

Heddle, right, and McBean.

Women's 4

Rowing through severe pain from a severe leg injury sustained just weeks before, single sculler Silken Laumann still managed to come up with bronze in Banyoles.

The women's team led the way, as crew after crew made it into the finals. By the time the water had calmed down again, they had made no less than three trips to the top step of the podium. The coxless fours crew started the ball rolling, followed by the coxless pairs and then the eights. The men's eights added a fourth gold, while Silken Laumann earned a bronze in single sculls with an odds-defying effort just 10 weeks after a devastating leg injury.

The five medals earned by Canada's rowers on August 1st and 2nd, 1992 was easily the best two-day performance of the century for a country not widely known for its rowing prowess. ♣

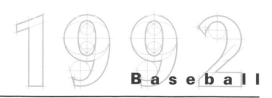

Devon White makes the catch of the Series.

Toronto Star

1992

Baseball

Baseball Heaven

World Series Victory: 'No one can ever take this away from us'

by Bob Levin
November 2, 1992

There are moments that swell the heart, race the mind, stir the soul. They blaze by in all their dizzying technicolour glory, bombarding the senses even as the brain is storing away memories, recording them like a video machine for later viewing.

Eight days, six baseball games — that is all it was. But it was so much more. Never mind that the first World Series on Canadian soil was played on shiny Astroturf, under a steel roof. Never mind that the paid gladiators who packed SkyDome with flag-waving Canadians were

all Americans, Puerto Ricans or Dominicans. For one stunning week, a game played with a stitched ball and a wood bat managed to unite Canadians from coast to coast even as the constitutional referendum was dividing them. More than 11 million of them tuned into some contests, and non-Torontonians did not even seem to mind that the centre of their televised attention, puffed up with pride, was hated Hogtown. And in the nation's largest city, the Blue Jays' 4-2 Series triumph over the

Toronto Star — J. Goode

Showing a lack of cultural awareness at the first World Series game involving a Canadian-based team, Canada's flag was flown upside down in Atlanta. Canada got the last laugh, though, as the World series went north of the border for the first time.

Toronto Star / M. Slaughter

The Blue Jays celebrate their first World Series victory.

Opening Introductions at the first World Series game played in Canada.

Atlanta Braves, wrapped up in gut-twisting style down in Dixie, sent a half million people pouring into the streets in a world-class frenzy. "When the final out registered, the city roared," marvelled 44-year-old Toronto police Insp. Gary Grant, watching over the dancing, singing throngs. "I must have high-fived 2,500 people by now — my arm will be on the disabled list tomorrow."

For all the intensity of the Series, baseball remains a kid's game, and the best-loved players showed an infectious enthusiasm. Take Joe Carter's Game 3 homer, which flew into the left-field press box, off one reporter's hands and into those of George Grande, a St. Louis Cardinals broadcaster who was doing radio reports on the Series. After the Jays' win that night, Grande, who has known Carter for years, found him in the clubhouse video room, going over his at-bats. Recounted Grande: "I said, 'Boy, that must feel great to hit a World Series home run.' He said, 'Yeah, it's great, it gave us the lead.' I said, 'Too bad you didn't get the ball.' And he said, 'Yeah, but I still have the thrill, I'll always have the memory.' And then I took the ball out and held it up and his eyes got big as saucers and he said, '*No.*' And I said, '*Yeah.*' And he said, 'This is the ball?' And I said, 'Here, it's yours,' and the look on his face was just amazing." ❦

Joe Carter gets the last out, 1992 World Series.

Yonge Street World Series Celebrations, 1992.

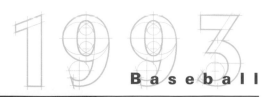

Baseball

Jumping for Joy:

What happened in Toronto late on the night of Oct. 23, 1993, is a moment for the ages

by Bob Levin
November 1, 1993

The moment will play forever. It will play whenever anyone shows World Series highlights, and it will play in the minds of millions of Canadians who saw it live at SkyDome or on television and knew they had just witnessed something very special. Joe Carter swings. The ball flashes off his bat. The crowd rises as one, sucking in a collective breath, disbelieving, then explodes as the sphere disappears over the left-field fence. Carter, watching as he runs, springs into the air, bounding around the bases like a crazed kid, shouting up into the roof where fireworks burst on almost too-perfect cue, his teammates burying him at home plate in a multi-player

Canadian Press CP

Joe Carter watches his game and World Series-winning home run in the bottom of the ninth inning as the Blue Jays beat the Philadelphia Phillies 6-4 to clinch their second consecutive Championship, October 24, 1993, in Toronto.

Toronto Star — J. Goode

pileup. The film isn't grainy or in black-and-white; the players don't wear quaintly baggy pants. But make no mistake: what happened in Toronto late on the night of Oct. 23, 1993, making the Blue Jays World Series champions for the second year running, is one for the ages.

That is partly because of the *way* it happened. In a sport that loves its lore, Carter's come-from-behind blast, completing a 4-2 Series triumph over the resilient Philadelphia Phillies, was only the second time that a Series had ended on a ninth-inning, game-winning home run (the first, by Pittsburgh's Bill Mazeroski, beat the New York Yankees in the seventh game in 1960). Then there is the magnitude of the accomplishment: repeating as champions (the 1978 Yankees were the last to do it) is the baseball equivalent of winning back-to-back Oscars, Nobel Prizes, provincial lotteries. And it is especially remarkable for an expansion team in just its 17th season — one that lost a dozen players from its Series-winning side of 1992. "I didn't think it could be any better than last year," said Jays' president Paul Beeston as the celebrations wound down in the Jays' clubhouse. "But it is — we're very, very proud and we'll savor this for quite awhile."

The Jays, meanwhile, had undergone a radical image change, which goes to show what World Series rings can do. "You don't hear anything anymore about what the team didn't do in the past," Carter said outside the batting cage before Game 2. "We won last year, and that's it." In fact, the American media had transformed them from the Blow Jays — widely ridiculed for not winning the big ones — into a club envied, even *hated*, for winning too much. They were called cocky, aristocratic, princely. But on the field, they proved they could get as down-and-dirty as the Phillies, especially in the bizarre, rain-soaked, run-filled Game 4 that swung momentum the Jays' way-another one for the Series' highlight film.

But it is the last image that will be remembered best. Even in the first electric minutes after Carter's Game 6 homer, the fast-forward age had turned the footage into an instant classic. Over and over, it played on the SkyDome Jumbotron as thousands of fans stayed to savor the moment. They whooped, they exchanged high fives, they roared at the announcement of the Jay's Paul Molitor as the Series' Most Valuable Player. But it was Carter who had supplied the magic. "The way they won, it was so dramatic," said Todd Levy, a 32-year-old physician from Thornhill, Ont. "It might never happen again in our lifetime." The real Joe Carter was making his way across the field, beaming but oddly diminished. The *other* Joe was still circling the bases, still jumping, jumping, a joy for all time. ❦

Joe Carter, 1993 World Series hero.

Toronto Star — P. Power

Myriam Bédard, Canada's Biathlon Queen

The setting was pure fairy tale - a quintessentially beautiful mountain town, built into a hillside and overlooking the largest lake in Norway, the land of mythic trolls. The winter weather seemed to have been scripted, prompting countless superlatives from journalists covering the 1994 Winter Olympics in Lillehammer. Added to the mix were thousands of Norwegian fans whose enthusiasm for sport was such that they cheered for all competitors, regardless of nationality.

Against this backdrop, Myriam Bédard added her unique chapter to Olympic and Canadian sports history by winning two gold medals in biathlon. Both were dramatic — the first because the margin of victory was so large, the other because the margin of victory was excruciatingly small in this demanding sport combining cross-country skiing with target shooting.

Bédard's rise to the ranks of the world's elite biathletes took more than the average amount of talent and determination. No Canadian had ever stood on the Olympic podium in a biathlon event. Indeed, until 1992, the best ever Olympic finish by a Canadian in an individual race was 33rd place. Bédard, who didn't start competing in biathlon until age 16, would change all that. From the time she joined the national team in 1987, she began a steady rise to the top.

During the three years leading up to the Lillehammer Olympics Bédard moved inexorably closer to the ultimate prize. She finished second in the overall World Cup standings in 1991. At the 1992 Winter Olympics in Albertville, France, where women's biathlon events made their Olympic debut, she earned her first medal, a bronze. The following year came gold and silver medals at the World Championships and another second place finish in the overall World Cup standings.

By the time she got to the 1994 Winter Olympics, Bédard was considered a favourite, placing more pressure on her to win. In typical fashion, though, she used her ability to focus mentally to shut out distracting influences. Her first race was the 15 km, which includes four shooting sessions of five shots each. The challenge in this sport is to ski as quickly as possible, then immediately try to slow the body's rhythm in order to shoot accurately. Time is of the essence, but shooting too quickly can be devastating, since each missed shot results in a time penalty. Having had problems earlier in the year with her shooting, Bédard deliberately took her time. In the end, she missed two targets — a two-minute penalty. Her closest rival had also missed two, however, and the eventual bronze medallist had missed three. Bédard took the gold and the Olympic Champion honours by an incredibly large margin of 46 seconds.

Winning her first race took much of the pressure off for the next event — the 7.5 km race. A much more relaxed Bédard was one of the last competitors to start. For the first two laps of the

Myriam Bédard, combining skiing and shooting to win Olympic honours for Canada.

Canada

course she skied quickly, and shot perfectly in the first of two rounds. A second gold medal looked like a real possibility. The second round of shooting seemed to dash those hopes, though, as two shots went wide of the mark. Each miss forced Bédard to ski a 150m penalty loop, and she entered the final 2.5 km lap more than 10 seconds behind the leaders. Spurred on by the crowd, which included her parents, she somehow found the reserves to pick up her pace. As coaches called out her split times, she knew she was gaining, she knew she had an opportunity to do something special, and put all her effort into the final uphill stretch. Totally spent, she crossed the finish line and slumped over, winning the race by a scant 1.1 seconds. She became Olympic Champion for the second time that week.

Incredibly, Bédard's second gold was won on a pair of mismatched skis. She was so relaxed before the race that she accidentally picked up one ski that had been properly waxed and set up for the 7.5 km sprint, while the other was meant for the 15 km event. Although Bédard had noticed a discrepancy in the way the two skis glided during the race, the cause was not discovered until after history had been made. A proud Canadian Olympic team named her as its flag-bearer during the Closing Ceremonies.

Myriam Bédard's first Olympic medal was a bronze at the 1992 Albertville Games.

As with many stories of extraordinary victories, Bédard's was not without controversy. She decided early in her international career to decline training with the rest of the Canadian team, opting instead to train on her own with the help of a European "mystery coach" whose identity she would not divulge. Officially she was listed as self-coached. Her insistence that this solitary path made her a better athlete inevitably led to conflicts with Canadian officials, and even jeopardized her status as a team member at one point. Bédard ultimately stuck to her guns, so-to-speak, confident that the route to success lay in the gruelling training regimen prepared by her coach and in having European technicians perform the crucial job of waxing and preparing her skis.

The other controversy erupted just after her first gold medal, this one seeming for a while to threaten the legitimacy of her victory in the 15 km race. A TV commentator alleged that the targets used in the competition were faulty and that several shots taken by Bédard's competitors that had registered as missed shots were actually hits. The accusation was backed up by digitally-enhanced video tape that showed shadows appearing on the targets that the commentator interpreted as direct hits. If the allegations were true, there were two other athletes who could be the legitimate winners, and Bédard would lose the gold. A proven technical failure would also make for a major Olympic scandal. Within hours, though, various officials responded, pointing out that bullets striking the perimeter of the targets could shatter, and that part of the bullet could then deflect to the centre of the target, but with insufficient force to register a hit. During the race, targets were also monitored by coaches with binoculars and none of the competitors had raised any concerns following the race. Whew!

A golden moment for Myriam Bédard in Lillehammer, 1994.

Ultimately, Bédard's victory stood untarnished. Back in Canada, her fame combined with her ability to be an articulate speaker and her winning smile put her in demand as a motivational speaker and spokesperson. Later in 1994 the first woman to win two Winter Olympic gold medals was also the unanimous choice for the Lou Marsh Trophy, awarded to Canada's Outstanding Athlete of the Year. ❧

Jean-Luc Brassard

CSI/COA

With his good looks, big grin and refreshing, low-key attitude, Jean-Luc Brassard became the media darling of the 1994 Winter Olympics in Lillehammer, Norway. Oh, and winning a gold in the freestyle skiing moguls event didn't hurt either.

Brassard's easygoing nature perfectly captured the joyous abandon of his hotdogging sport, which was still new to the Olympic Games and relatively new to the world at large (moguls was officially accepted onto the Olympic program in 1992, and aerials joined it in 1994). In the moguls run, competitors groove down the run with rap and rock music blasting, hitting two "airs," or jumps, along the way.

A native of Grand Île, Quebec, Brassard delivered a clutch performance on the mogul hill right when it counted to snag the gold. While he made it seem easy, it wasn't all going his way in the time leading up to the Games.

Brassard had dominated moguls skiing during the 1993 season, when his arch rival and 1992 Olympic champion, Edgar Grospiron, was out with a knee injury. An intimidating presence, Grospiron was back in full force for the 1994 season. By his own admission, the return of Grospiron shook Brassard.

"I was thinking about Edgar maybe every five minutes," Brassard said at the time. "I was the world champion from the start of the season, but I was always very nervous, always very impressed with Edgar."

And so for Brassard, the 1994 season got off to a shaky start. While he began to turn his luck around after Christmas, he was still not on solid ground. In the final pre-Olympic race in Salen, Sweden, he finished fourth, and felt his confidence ebbing. So much so, that when Brassard arrived in Lillehammer, the Montreal papers reported he was not feeling up to par, much to the concern of his parents. As a result, the Brassards decided, on the spur of the moment, to travel to Lillehammer to be with their son.

The arrival of his parents boosted Brassard's spirits. He also began to feel his confidence return during the training runs on the Norwegian course high over the picturesque town of Lillehammer. As he tested the course out during the week, he began to like it more and more. His confidence grew-to the point that Brassard came first in the preliminaries.

Over 10,000 people were on the hill on the day of the final run, lined up along the sides to watch the competitors strut their stuff. They were not disappointed.

CSI/COA

Jean-Luc Brassard's trademark Iron Cross-Cossack.

Because he had won the preliminaries, Brassard was the last to go. It was a strong omen that when Brassard took his position at the start, the sun broke through the clouds and lit up the entire run.

At the starter's signal — which in freestyle is a rooster's crow — Brassard began his descent. Sporting fluorescent yellow knee patches, so the judges could better see his leg position, Brassard geared down the moguls, his knees moving up and down like pistons in a race car.

His airs were huge and dynamic. By the second air — his trademark Iron Cross-Cossack combination — the crowd began to go wild. In this jump, Brassard flung both legs behind him, crossed his skis, and then whipped both legs in front of him into a split. His execution of this very difficult manoeuvre was perfect.

By the time he reached the bottom, the noise and jubilation of the crowd was deafening. Brassard was mobbed by media and well-wishers — even before his victory was posted, everyone knew they had witnessed the gold medal run.

And indeed they had. While several others posted slightly faster times than his, Brassard delivered technically perfect turns and jumps in a sport where good technique not only gets you down the hill faster, but counts for a significant part of the score. Grospiron had to settle for third with 26.64 points. Russian Sergei Shupletsov won the silver with 26.90 points. Well ahead of both, Brassard received a total of 27.24 points.

Not bad for a kid who, incidentally, hated the sport when his parents first took him. ♣

Donovan Bailey

Olympic Gold Medallist,
100m Sprint and 4 x 100m Relay

The year was 1996. The moment was the Centennial Olympics in Atlanta, when Donovan Bailey took the giant Canadian flag from the white-haired woman sitting in the front row. As he wrapped himself in it and proceeded to jog his victory lap around Olympic Stadium, no eyes were left dry in the stands or at home.

Donovan Bailey starting his way to immortality in Atlanta.

Bailey had won the 100m sprint in world record time. He was the fastest man in the world, and he won that title in what many called the fastest field ever to line up for the event in the history of track.

There were many moments leading up to that one. From the time the eight runners first took their position on the track, the tension was palpable.

The race began with a series of dramatic, nail-biting moments. The 1992 Olympic champion, England's Linford Christie, broke out in a false start. Then Trinidad's Ato Boldon did. Then, in a career-damaging move, Christie had another. With two false starts, he was disqualified. As the crowd held its breath, Christie refused to leave, gesturing angrily at officials, but to no avail. The champion was dethroned.

Finally, for the fourth time that day, the runners took their positions in the starting blocks, the gun went, and they were off.

All Canadians had their eyes trained on the man in the white jersey, but it did not look good. Even on this day of all days, his start was a typical Bailey start: slow.

At 40 metres, something began to happen, as Bailey, powering down his lane, began to pass the field. By 60 metres, he was in control, passing Boldon, who placed third, and Namibia's Frankie Fredericks, who placed second. There was no stopping Bailey. He won in 9.84 seconds, slicing .01 seconds off Leroy Burrell's June 7, 1994 world record.

For Canada, it was an emotional moment, one of glory and of redemption. The spectre of Ben Johnson's 1988 positive drug test that had cast a dark shadow over Canadian track and field was banished. In place stood a new national hero, a role model for all Canadians who was a success on and off the track. ❧

Men's 4x100m relay. The only regret the men's 4x100m relay team had after winning the Olympic gold medal was in celebrating a bit early and not setting a world record. Robert Esmie started the race and followed the message he had shaved on his head, "Blast Off." Glenroy Gilbert took the baton second and raced a personal best down the backstretch, where he handed it to a waiting Bruny Surin. Surin had the reputation of being able to run the corners best, and when he handed the baton to anchor Donavan Bailey, Canada was in the lead to stay. In a state of exhilaration, Bailey raised his arms in celebration with about 15m still to run. They won the gold but missed the world record by .29 of a second.

The smile says it all as Donovan Bailey wins the Olympic 100m in world record time.

Donovan Bailey, 1996 Olympic Champion and Fastest Man in the World.

Kathleen Heddle and Marnie McBean – Canada's most decorated Olympians

For Canada, the 1996 Atlanta Olympic Games yielded a golden harvest, indeed. If the exploits by sprinter Donovan Bailey and his teammates on the track brought Canadians to their feet, the performance of the rowing team once again established Canada as the force to be reckoned with. With a medal count matched only by Australia, a team with 10 times the budget, Canada's Olympic rowing team were the best in the world, powering their way to six medals — one gold, four silver and a bronze.

In terms of total accomplishments, Canada's rowing crews had no equal. Of Canada's 10 entries, eight made it the finals and no team placed below seventh. Of those stellar crews, no rowers shone brighter than Kathleen Heddle and Marnie McBean.

In one of sport's most demanding disciplines, McBean and Heddle were a study in smooth, unified power. The pair were already the talk of the sports world at the 1992 Olympic Games in Barcelona for bringing home two gold medals in the women's straight pair and the women's eight.

They were also a study in contrasts. Throughout their career, the two were noted for the polar differences in their personalities: the vivacious McBean would do all the talking, while the reserved Heddle would remain silent.

When they won their third gold at the 1996 Olympic Games in Atlanta and later added a bronze to their collection, the dynamic duo reached a new plateau. Only a tiny handful of Canadians had stood on the Olympic podium three times, let alone four, and none had won more than two gold medals until Heddle and McBean.

Becoming two of Canada's most decorated Olympians was not something they set out deliberately to do, though. After they performed in Barcelona, Heddle retired, heading back to school in Vancouver to finish her degree in psychology, and then got a job tracking subscriptions for a magazine. McBean, on the other hand, wasn't ready to quit. She landed corporate sponsorships and was promoting, among other things, shampoo and milk. She also created the *Fund for Olympic Rowers' Survival* by knocking on corporate doors.

McBean tried her hand at single sculls, but had to settle for second, unable to unseat rival Silken Laumann for the right to represent Canada. She hungered for more, and in 1994, convinced Heddle to come out of retirement.

But instead of picking up where they left off as the gold-medal-winning crew in the straight pair, they decided to tackle double sculls. In the straight pair, each rower has one oar, while in double sculls, each rower has two oars. The technique, strategy and responsibilities are significantly different from the straight pair.

McBean, as the bow sculler, sat at the front of the shell with her back closest to the finish line. It was her job to steer the boat by adjusting, ever so slightly, the pulling power of one hand or another. As the stroke sculler, Heddle set the pace, easing or cranking up the strokes depending on the position of the other boats in the race.

Heddle was known for setting a blistering pace — and it was McBean's job to keep up and keep the boat moving straight ahead.

As the Atlanta Games approached, pundits saw Heddle and McBean as potential winners, but cited their teammates, Wendy Wiebe and Colleen Miller rowing in the lightweight double sculls event, as the best gold-medal hope, in rowing and even on the entire Olympic team. And, in terms of media attention, all rowers stood in the shadow of Silken Laumann, a popular favourite since her remarkable comeback in 1992.

McBean and Heddle were about to change that.

When the gun went off for the women's double sculls final at Lake Lanier in Gainesville, Georgia, McBean and Heddle surged ahead immediately. By pulling hard off the start, they built a narrow lead over their main competitors, the Chinese and Dutch boats. Heddle set the pace, and they quickly settled into the race. But it was not easy going. Throughout, their slim lead was under constant attack, mostly from the Chinese.

"It felt as if we were moments away from having nothing left," McBean said. "The crowd was going crazy and I'm thinking, 'Where's the finish line?'"

But their strength and flawless rhythm were not to be matched that day. Heddle and McBean were an unstoppable force, powering across the finish line without giving way. Completely spent, they collapsed, drenched in sweat and gasping for breath. Eventually, they weakly lifted their heads towards the stands, where the crowd was going crazy. Without checking the scoreboard, they knew they'd won. Heddle fell back, holding McBean's hand, still trying to catch her breath.

The race left even McBean speechless: "I couldn't catch my breath, let alone say anything."

After the awards ceremony, McBean and Heddle were leaving to go ready themselves for their next event, the quadruple sculls, in which they would win a bronze. They'd just made Canadian history, a reporter told them. Had they planned it? "No," they answered. "We didn't even realize it until you told us." ❧

1996

Kathleen Heddle and Marnie McBean earned their third career gold medal in Atlanta — the most Olympic golds by any Canadian in the century. (The pair had won gold in Barcelona in pairs and as part of the women's eight crew.) This time in double sculls (each pulling on two oars), Heddle and McBean took an early lead and held it throughout the race, after challenges by both the Chinese and Dutch teams. In the end it was a clear win, but as McBean observed "I felt like we were just hanging on out there."

General Highlights

1991

Canada won the Team event at the 1991 World Water Ski Championships, and would win it again in 1993 and 1999. In less than 50 years, water skiing grew from a cottage industry to an international and Pan American Games sport. Canada has long been recognized as a world leader, and over the years Canadian skiers earned 12 World Championship gold medals:
* Charles Blackwell (1955)
* George Athans (1971, 1973)
* Pat Messner (1979)
* Joel McClintock (1979)
* Judy McClintock (1985)
* Beth Leboff (1992)
* Kim de Macedo (1993)
* Judy Messner (1995)
* Jeremy Kovak (1997)
* Jaret Llewellyn (1997, 1999).

1993

Myriam Bédard won the Biathlon World Sprint Championships.

1992-94

The University of Winnipeg Wesman Women's basketball team captured the country's attention by tying the North American record for most consecutive wins with 88. During this span the team defeated 30 different opponents and won two successive CIAU championships.

1992-95

Canada's rugby team continued its winning ways in the early 1990s by beating England and Wales in 1993 and France in 1994. As was the case throughout this decade, the goal-kicking of Gareth Rees helped Canada secure many of its points. In 1994, for instance, playing against France in Nepean, Ontario, Rees kicked six penalty goals to account for all of Canada's points in its 18-12 win.

Doug Sturrock

1993

Before 28,000 people at historic Cardiff Arms Park, Canada's National Rugby Team trailed Wales 24-19 when Al Charron finished off a brilliant stretch of continuous play to tie the score at 24-24. In a rare celebratory moment in sport, after making the winning conversion Gareth Rees turned to face his father Alan sitting in the stands, raising his arms as the whistle sounded to end the game 26-24 for Canada. At the time, the victory shocked all of Wales, where reaction may have been similar to what Canadians would have felt if Wales had beaten Canada in hockey.

1999

Mike Weir of Bright's Grove, Ontario, won the new PGA event in Vancouver, the Air Canada Championship.

2000

Mike Weir won his second and most lucrative PGA Tour event, the Tour Championship, in Spain.

February 20, 2000

In Federation Cup soccer play in San Diego, Mexico led most of the game 1-0, Canada then scored a late goal to send the match into extra time. Canada shocked heavily favoured Mexico, and likely themselves, in getting another goal to win 2-1 and advance to the Cup finals — where they won again.

February 24, 2000

Canada defeated Trinidad and Tobago 1-0 in a Federation Cup match in Los Angeles. The win against a traditionally superior team put Canada in the Federation Cup finals.

February 27, 2000

Though ranked 85th in the world, the Canadian National Soccer team defeated heavy favourite Colombia 2-0 to win the 2000 Football Confederation Gold Cup, symbolizing North and Central American soccer supremacy.

CSA

2000

One of the more memorable basketball moments of the year was the surprisingly strong performance by Canada's men's team at the Sydney Olympic Games. Canada was competing in its first Olympic competitions in 12 years and ended up beating supposedly superior teams from Australia and Russia as well as the vaunted Yugoslavian team en route to a 5-2 record. The team, led by NBA star Steve Nash, grabbed the nation's attention, though it lost to France in the quarter-finals.

Doug Sturrock

Associated Press AP

Canada's Triple Crown

Canada's rich horse racing history includes many famed courses, races and its own Triple Crown. Only six horses managed to win the three races making up the Canada's Triple Crown: the Queen's Plate, the Prince of Wales Stakes, and the Breeders' Stakes.

New Providence (1959) — *New Providence* finished first in a five-horse field by 1 1/2 lengths in the Breeders' Stakes, with Avelino Gomez in the saddle. The son of *Bull Page* became the first to sweep the series, which started with the Queen's Plate, followed by the Prince of Wales Stakes. The owner was Windfields Farm and the trainer was Pete McCann.

Caneboro (1963) — Another Triple Crown for Windfields Farm, this time with American veteran Manuel Ycaza riding *Caneboro* and winning by 4 3/4 lengths in 2:31 1/5 on a firm course. It was trainer Pete McCann's third Breeders' Stakes victory (he won with *Blue Light* in 1961) and second Triple Crown.

With Approval (1989) — *With Approval* became the third winner of Canada's Triple Crown, with a 7 1/2-length Breeders' Stakes win in 2:29 on a firm course under jockey Don Seymour for Kinghaven Farm. The victory was worth $199,160, but also earned a $1-million bonus for winning all three races. It was to be the first of three Triple Crown championships horses trained by Roger Attfield. *With Approval* went on to be named Canada's Horse of the Year.

Izvestia (1990) — Another Seymour-Kinghaven-Attfield combination resulted in another Horse of the Year award. *Izvestia* won by 8 1/2 lengths in 2:33 2/5 on a soft course for the Breeders' Stakes win. The winning purse was $183,900, but a $1-million bonus for sweeping the series made it another fine year for the champions.

Dance Smartly (1991) — Jockey Pat Day completed the series sweep with an eight-length romp on a wet or yielding turf course in 2:31 2/5. *Dance Smartly*, owned by Ernie Samuel's Sam-Son Farm and trained by Jim Day, paid $2.60 in winning the Breeders' Stakes. The victory was worth $182,140. It was the last year that a $1-million bonus went to the Triple Crown champion. *Dance Smartly* won a number of other major stakes in her career, including a Breeder's Cup race, and eventually wound up as Horse of the Year in 1991. She was the leading Canadian money-winner in the century.

Peteski (1993) — It was win number three for Attfield. *Peteski*, owned by Earle Mack of New York, won by six lengths in a four-horse field and paid $2.20. The Breeders' Stakes win was worth $137,550 and led to Horse of the Year honours. ❦

Motor Sport

The Canadian King: Jacques Villeneuve Seizes Formula One's Throne

by Barry Came
November 10, 1997

They sat down together for a quiet beer in the end, once their season-long struggle finally came to a close in a single, spectacular moment at a tight corner called Dry Sack. It was Michael Schumacher who took the initiative, showing up with his wife on the doorstep of Jacques Villeneuve's trailer. By then, the stands were deserted, the paddocks still, at the Circuito de Jerez in southern Spain. And that suited Schumacher fine. For the straitlaced German, who drives for Italy's Team Ferrari in the traveling road show known as Formula One racing, had a difficult task to perform. He had come to acknowledge defeat, no small matter for a proud, even arrogant man who has long been regarded as the sport's reigning monarch. But there is a new sovereign in Formula One now. And for the first time in the circuit's celebrated history, the king is Canadian.

Villeneuve, in only his second F1 season, captured the 1997 world driver's championship in the most dramatic fashion, surviving a brutal, seemingly deliberate attempt by Schumacher to force him off the track and out of contention for the title. It happened two-thirds of the way through the 69-lap European Grand Prix, staged on Oct. 26 amid the dry hills and olive-clad valleys of Andalusia. After trailing Schumacher from the start, Villeneuve finally saw an opportunity to pass on the 48th lap of the race at Dry Sack, a sharp, right-hand turn. The German's scarlet Ferrari took a wide line into the curve and Villeneuve, at the wheel of his Renault-powered Williams, darted up the inside, pulling ahead. And suddenly, in full view of an estimated worldwide TV audience of 350 million, Schumacher lurched right, driving his Ferrari into the side of the Williams, forcing Villeneuve's vehicle into the air. "He hit me really, really hard," said Villeneuve after the race. "We banged wheels and my car jumped off the ground. I really felt the crash had broken something."

For Schumacher, it was a disastrous gamble. The German had entered the European Grand Prix, the last of the season's 16 races, with a one-point lead in the drivers' standings over the 26-year-old from St-Jean-sur-Richelieu in Quebec. He needed only to finish the competition in Spain ahead of Villeneuve to secure his third world championship. But when he collided with the Canadian, he drove himself out of the race. After bouncing off Villeneuve's Williams, Schumacher's Ferrari slewed sideways into a gravel trap and stuck fast. And as he sat, rear wheels spinning ineffectually in a cloud of dust, he watched helplessly as Villeneuve barreled down the track on his way to the title.

Even then, it was no sure thing. There were still 21 laps to go and Villeneuve's vehicle had been damaged in the collision. "My car felt very strange," Villeneuve later recalled, "especially in the right-hand corners, and the rear end was not stable at all. I was pushing hard for a few laps, then slowing down because the tires were heating up in a very strange way." Still, Villeneuve nursed his Williams along, gradually losing ground to a clutch of pursuers. Finnish driver Mika Hakkinen and Scotland's David Coulthard, both in Mercedes-Benz-powered McLarens, steadily narrowed the gap until they overtook Villeneuve on the last lap. "I saw Mika closing on me," Villeneuve recounted, "and I did not want to get into a big fight and David was also close so I let them through."

Villeneuve's third-place finish, however, was good enough. It allowed the Quebecer to pick up four points, giving him 81 for the season and a three-point victory over Schumacher. And with that, Villeneuve not only became the first Canadian to capture a Formula One driver's championship but also the first driver of any nationality to hold the top three titles in international motor car racing — the F1, the CART IndyCar and the Indianapolis 500 championships.

It did not take long for Villeneuve to celebrate his triumph in Spain. On returning to the paddock at the Jerez circuit, he was hoisted aloft by ecstatic Williams team mechanics, all sporting fluorescent yellow wigs in emulation of the young driver's crop of peroxide-blond hair. That marked the opening stages of a gigantic party that began in Jerez and later moved on to an all-night

Associated Press AP

disco in nearby Cadiz down on the Atlantic coast. It was a bleary-eyed Villeneuve, pleading for sleep, who appeared the following day for 3$^1/_2$ hours of live television, beamed worldwide. Nowhere were those broadcasts more avidly followed than in Quebec, where they were picked up and retransmitted repeatedly by three of the province's television networks.

Canadian motor sport officials anticipate less tangible benefits as well. "Villeneuve's victory is certainly going to raise the profile of the sport in this country," predicted Ralph Luciw, chairman of the board of governors of the soon-to-be-inaugurated Canadian Motorsport Hall of Fame in Toronto. Even though the facility, located on the ground floor of a downtown Toronto office building, will not be officially opened until Nov. 18, Luciw reported that a steady stream of curious passers-by have been dropping in since Villeneuve's triumph. "It's sparked an awful lot of interest," he said. "And we hope to spark it further by arranging to have one of Villeneuve's cars on display in the near future."

Villeneuve, meanwhile, is poised to cash in heavily on his triumph. Craig Pollock, the driver's Swiss-based manager, refused to disclose Villeneuve's annual take, but he is believed to have earned, in salary and endorsements, around $10 million this year. And Pollock did concede that "Jacques' value has now shot up considerably, particularly in terms of endorsements."

Just as important, the Canadian driver's achievement may finally lay to rest many of the doubts that have persisted about him in racing circles, engendered in large part by his dyed blond hair, his penchant for rumpled grunge dress and, not least, his candour. Villeneuve, in fact, now finds that he has traded places in more ways than one with his archrival Schumacher as a direct result of the race in Spain. It is the well-groomed Schumacher who has

suddenly become the sport's bad boy. The German driver is scheduled to explain his actions at the Dry Sack corner before an extraordinary meeting of the sport's governing body, the FIA, in Paris on Nov. 11. Schumacher conceded last week that he "made a mistake" while stopping short of an outright apology. "It's part of the game," he said. "But I didn't try to foul." If the FIA decides otherwise, the German would face a multimillion-dollar fine as well as a multiple suspension, likely for three races, next season. And if that happens, it is going to be even more difficult to unseat the brash young Canadian who now occupies Formula One's throne. ☙

Jacques Villeneuve Formula 1 Victories

Year	Race	Location
1996	Nurbergring	Luxembourg
	Silverstone	Britain
	Hungaroring	Hungary
	Estoril	Portugal
1997	Interlagos	Brazil
	Buenos Aires	Argentina
	Barcelona	Spain
	Silverstone	Britain
	Hungaroring	Hungary
	Zeltweg	Austria
	Nurbergring	Luxembourg

1997 Formula 1 World Champion

Associated Press AP

1998

Speedskating

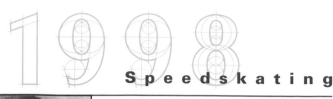

High-Speed Dream Team

by James Deacon
February 23, 1998

Tomomi Okazaki had just finished posting the fastest time of the day at the M-Wave in Nagano, but as she passed by stands full of adoring fans, she held her finger to her lips, asking for quiet. Trying to direct the crowd's attention to the featured race of the day, Okazaki pointed back towards the start line, where Canada's Catriona LeMay Doan and Susan Auch were getting set for the last pairing of the two-day sprint final. The audience responded and, for a second, there was quiet inside the cavernous M-Wave, all eyes on the two women in red and black awaiting the gun. They didn't disappoint. Pitted against one another because they were the top skaters in the previous day's heats, LeMay Doan and Auch blasted through the first 100m on their way to the fastest 500-m pairing ever clocked in Olympic women's competition. LeMay Doan crossed first, beating Auch by a mere three-tenths of a second. "What a great race," a breathless but thrilled LeMay Doan said afterward. "Susan really pushed me."

For the Canadians who were lucky enough to be there, the colours of Valentine's Day will from here on be gold and silver. LeMay Doan and Auch came into the race saddled with huge expectations — they finished the World Cup season ranked first and second, respectively, in the 500m. "I felt really nervous," said Auch, who also captured silver at the Lillehammer Games in 1994. "But I have done well under pressure before, and that gave me confidence." Auch jumped into an early lead and forced LeMay Doan into overdrive. "I had to tell myself that I was the strongest skater out there," LeMay Doan said, "and trust that I could make up the ground on the back stretch."

What a week at the races, and what a show of strength from what has suddenly become the dominant team on the Canadian Winter Olympics roster. No matter how well they do, the men's and women's hockey

World and Olympic Champion, Catriona Le May Doan.

CSI/COA

teams can muster only two medals. In five days, the long-track speed-skating team grabbed one gold, two silver and a bronze, and there were prospects for more this week. LeMay Doan holds the world record in the women's 1,000m and was entered in the 1,500. Among the short-track skaters, sprinters Isabelle Charest and Marc Gagnon were contenders in four events.

Jeremy Wotherspoon and Kevin Overland started it all early last week by capturing silver and bronze in a thrilling 500-m men's long-track competition, won by local hero Hiroyaso Shimizu. Two more Canadians, Sylvain Bouchard and Patrick Bouchard (no relation), finished right behind Overland, giving Canada four of the top five spots. But in the 1,000m on Sunday, Wotherspoon, a tall, slender 21-year-old from Red Deer, Alta., who holds the world record in the event, had a disappointing skate and the Canadians finished out of the medals.

Despite the grim overcast and cold drizzle in Nagano, it was all sweetness and light inside the spectacular M-Wave. There were the usual nationalist rivalries among the more than 10,000 who ringed the oval — the stands at a speed-skating competition are nothing if not tribal. The Dutch in their neon-orange outfits, the Japanese in blue-and-white, Germans, Poles and clumps of red-and-white Canucks waved flags, blew horns, sang songs and cheered their racers. But everyone applauded good performances, no matter the skater's nationality, and LeMay Doan crossed the finish line to a thunderous ovation that followed her around the oval as she flashed her million-watt smile. More personally, she was congratulated while coasting down the backstretch by her husband, Bart, a rodeo bull rider who drives the Zamboni at the Calgary Oval.

LeMay Doan and Auch are each other's toughest rivals, but it is a friendly rivalry. They credit sprint coach

Skating star Catriona Le May Doan in action at Nagano, 1998.

Derrick Auch — Susan's brother — with promoting a team ethic that has eased whatever tensions have arisen. A lawyer who put off joining a Calgary firm so he could continue coaching the sprinters through Nagano, Derrick, 30, has an easygoing manner, and even in the minutes before the gold-medal race, he had the skaters loose and laughing. He says it helps both skaters to be able to train regularly with their fastest competition. And before taking their stances at the starting line, the two skaters wished each other luck. "I was genuinely happy to see her win," Auch said, "to see her arms raised when she crossed the line."

Thanks to their success in the past two World Cup seasons, LeMay Doan, Auch and Wotherspoon were well-known in the speed-skating world, especially in the sport's European hotbeds — Holland, Norway and Germany. "Canada has always had one or two good skaters," says Mette Bugge, who covers the sport for the Norwegian newspaper *Aftenposten*. "But now it is a full team, and Canada is becoming one of the big speed-skating countries."

The revolutionary clap skate, with its hinged toe, has enabled all competitors to go faster. But it is Calgary's Olympic Oval, a legacy of the 1988 Games, that is the biggest reason for the Canadians' remarkable rise. It is the fastest ice in the world, which helps skaters learn to cope with higher speeds. And it is open 10 months a year, far more than most European tracks (The Viking Ship arena built for the Lillehammer Games is open only 60 days a year because of the high cost of maintaining the ice).

At Nagano's Holland House, a bar-restaurant near the M-Wave that provides a little home cooking for rabid Dutch fans, Egon Boesten says his 15-year-old son, Jan, is on the Dutch junior team and wants to attend school in Calgary so he can train at the Olympic Oval. "Everyone wants to go to Canada," Boesten says.

Watching the medal bonanza last week, Gaétan Boucher wondered what might have been. He was Canada's hero at the Sarajevo Games in 1984, winning two golds and a bronze. But at the time there was no indoor oval — he had to train in Europe.

The skaters don't expect their Nagano success to spur construction of ovals in every neighbourhood, but they hoped their medals have some impact. "It'd be nice to see lots of little kids signing up at clubs next year," Susan Auch said. LeMay Doan wasn't thinking about next year — she had more immediate concerns. "Now I can relax a bit," she said, threading her way through a gauntlet of reporters. "Then it'll be time to get ready for the next race." ♣

1994–1998

Susan Auch won back-to-back Olympic silver medals in 1994 and 1998. Before she competed in Nagano she told reporters, "I had a dream that I was standing on the podium listening to O Canada." After Catriona Le May Doan's gold medal performance nudged her out again from the top spot, she added; "I just always thought the music would be for me."

Celebrating gold in Nagano, Catriona Le May Doan.

Ross Rebagliati

First-ever Olympic snowboard champion

Nearly two decades after the original "Crazy Canucks" took the European alpine skiing community by storm, a new generation made its way to the 1998 Olympics in Nagano with the same agenda in mind. This time it was snowboarders who were taking to the slopes in a brand new event, though, trying to both bring home gold and to prove to the world that what had been seen as a radical fringe sport deserved a permanent spot on the Olympic program.

Canadian snowboarders had notched up some good results leading up to the Nagano Olympics, and were considered serious medal threats in the men's giant slalom and in both the men's and women's halfpipe events. Even though he had finished third in the overall World Cup standings two years earlier, Ross Rebagliati was considered less of a medal threat than teammate Mark Fawcett. Rebagliati had struggled earlier in the 1997-98 season, even starting to wonder at one point how long he would continue competing on the international circuit.

After the first of two runs, it didn't look promising. Rebagliati finished eighth, not exactly a disappointment, but a long way from the medals. Proving the depth of the Canadian squad, the lead was actually held by another of the new breed of Crazy Canucks — Jasey Anderson.

The second run came close to being postponed, as wind, fog and snow rolled in after only five skiers had completed their runs. After a 20-minute delay, the races resumed, and it was a revitalized Rebagliati who stood in the starting gate. "I knew what I had to do here," he told reporters later. "I'd rather have no time than a slow time. I had to go for it."

Canadian Press CP

That all-out, throw caution to the winds approach had been the trademark that earned the original Crazy Canucks their nickname, and it stood Rebagliati in good stead too. By the time all the skiers had finished, he had the second-best time in the second run, good enough for the overall gold medal. Fawcett, meanwhile, had fallen on his second run, while Anderson's time dropped him back to 16th place.

A jubilant Rebagliati was on top of the world. His name was suddenly known across Canada, and he reveled in the crowd's attention. It was to be a short-lived celebration, though, as the drug-testing laboratory was in the process of analyzing Rebagliati's urine sample. Soon the news was flashed around the world: the lab had found traces of marijuana in his system.

Canada

Lloyd Langlois

The scene was a painful reminder of what had happened in Seoul 10 years earlier when Ben Johnson was stripped of his gold medal after testing positive for steroids. Rebagliati instantly went from hero to cheat in some people's eyes. Japanese police even detained him for questioning under that country's strict drug laws.

While admitting that he had smoked marijuana, Rebagliati said he had quit more than a year ago, and that its presence in his blood came from second-hand smoke inhaled at parties that he had attended in his home town of Whistler, BC Canadian team officials and many members of the public also came to his defence, arguing that if anything the drug would have a negative impact on performance and that it was questionable to even be testing for it in the context of this competition.

History did not repeat itself this time, as Rebagliati's ordeal had a different ending than Johnson's. An arbitration panel agreed with his appeal of the disqualification, handing him back that historic first-ever Olympic snowboarding medal. The celebrations continued, albeit on a somewhat more subdued note. ❦

Philippe Laroche

Freestyle Skiing World Cup Wins

Men						
Year	Athlete	Event		1986	Yves Laroche	Aerials*
1980	Greg Athans	Moguls*		1987	Jean-Marc Rozon	Aerials*
1980	John Eaves	Aerials*		1989	Chris Simboli	Combined
1980	Greg Athans	Combined*		1989	Chris Simboli	Overall
1980	Greg Athans	Overall		1991	Philippe Laroche	Aerials
1981	Jean Corriveau	Aerials*		1992	Philippe Laroche	Aerials
1982	Craig Clow	Aerials		1993	Jean-Luc Brassard	Moguls*
1983	Bill Keenan	Moguls		1993	Lloyd Langlois	Aerials
1983	Alain Laroche	Combined		1994	Philippe Laroche	Aerials*
1983	Peter Judge	Overall*		1994	David Belhumeur	Combined
1984	Yves Laroche	Aerials*		1996	Jean-Luc Brassard	Moguls
1984	Alain Laroche	Combined		1997	Jean-Luc Brassard	Moguls*
1984	Alain Laroche	Overall		1997	Nicolas Fontaine	Aerials
1985	Lloyd Langlois	Aerials*		1997	Toben Sutherland	Combined
1985	Alain Laroche	Combined*		1997	Darcy Downs	Overall
1985	Alain Laroche	Overall		1998	Nicolas Fontaine	Aerials*
1986	Anna Fraser	Aerials*		1999	Nicolas Fontaine	Aerials

Overall World Cup Standings Winners

Women						
Year	Athlete	Event		1983	Marie-Claude Asselin	Combined
1980	Lauralee Bowie	Aerials		1985	Meredith Gardner	Aerials
1980	Stephanie Sloan	Combined		1993	Katherina Kubenk	Combined
1980	Stephanie Sloan	Overall*		1993	Katherina Kubenk	Overall
1981	Marie-Claude Asselin	Aerials*		1996	Katherina Kubenk	Overall
1981	Marie-Claude Asselin	Combined*		1997	Veronica Brenner	Aerials
1981	Marie-Claude Asselin	Overall*			* Other Canadian medallist(s) in same event	
1982	Marie-Claude Asselin	Aerials				
1982	Marie-Claude Asselin	Combined		1997	Canada	Nations World Cup
1982	Marie-Claude Asselin	Overall		1998	Canada	Nations World Cup
1983	Marie-Claude Asselin	Aerials		2000	Canada	Nations World Cup

Philippe Laroche

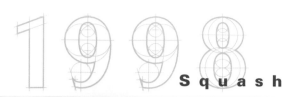

Becoming a World Champion

by Jonathon Power

The most memorable moment of my squash career is winning the World Open Championships in 1998 in Qatar. Graham Ryding (the 2nd ranked player in Canada and one of the top 15 in the world), myself, my coach and a couple of guys who were filming a documentary arrived there together in December of 1998. We had a little Canadian posse, which was rare for me at a tournament because I'd been traveling on my own for so long. It was nice to have a bit of support in doing this when I was so far away from home.

It was a standard World Open draw — the top 64 guys in the world. I wasn't one of the top two seeds, but I certainly knew I had a chance to win. The court also suited my playing style to a "T", which is a very fast, very aggressive attacking style of squash.

I ended up having to play Graham Ryding in one of the early rounds, which was a really nerve-wracking match for me, having to play the guy you train with every day — your best buddy. That added an extra stress to the tournament.

I played really well, and breezed through to the final. Basically that whole year only myself and one other guy had won any tournaments. Peter Nicol from Scotland, who at the time was the number one in the world and I were just going back and forth. We had exchanged victories — I'd lost to him in the Commonwealth Games and a few other tournaments and I had beaten him in a few tournaments. It was a pretty important match, my first World Open final.

We played a long, hard-fought game, probably one of our best matches ever. There was a point in the third game when I knew I would win the match. We played this crazy point, where I had him doing corners, and he was running and running, picking up every ball. This rally went on for what seemed like ages, and he was just hanging on. Finally I played a simple shot to the back of the court and he didn't run for it — his legs just collapsed from under him. At that point I knew I had broken him, physically and mentally.

After that I tried to build on the momentum and keep my nerves out of the way. Because it was the World Open final he just hung on, longer than I expected him to even after that rally. He was just a fraction off the pace but he was still hanging tough — he wouldn't give me anything for free.

As of December, 2000, Power's rivalry with Peter Nicol continued unabated. Since the 1998 World Open, one or the other has held the world's number one ranking. Power's win at the YMG Capital Squash Classic on December 1, 2000 evened their career records against each other at 11 wins each.

Getting the world number one ranking was everything I'd ever worked for. I had dedicated myself to playing squash full time since I was 12 years old. So that was the crowning moment, when I won the World Championships and became number one in the world.

I knew from an early age that I wanted to be a professional athlete. We grew up on military bases all over Canada and my dad ran the gyms. I went to the gym every day when I was a little kid and played sports with my father, my brother and anyone who was around. At the base in Prince Edward Island they had a couple of squash courts and my dad was getting hooked on this game. He would take us to the gym and we'd hit the ball around with him and it started from there. Then we started playing junior tournaments and traveling around. My brother and sister played too, and we became a bit of a squash family.

My dad was my first coach. He committed himself to learning everything he could about the game. At the age of 12 he made me decide between basketball, tennis, golf and squash as to what I was going to do for the rest of my life. I chose squash, and then he decided he would send me over to England to train with Ramat Khan, the world champion's coach for the summer. I had this opportunity because I was the top kid in North America and one of the top kids in the world.

I improved dramatically over that summer. Khan was definitely an influential coach. Although it was for a short period of time it inspired me to play the professional game.

My father knew what it took to become a top professional athlete. He had the foresight to get me over to Europe and to compete as much as I could, playing all different types of players. I had to learn how to lose and learn how to win, and work hard all the time.

We often fought, especially as a teenager, but deep down he knew I really wanted it. He knew when to back off and when to push. It wasn't easy by any stretch of the imagination. But just as I was getting down on myself when things weren't going well, something would click, or something good would happen that would inspire me.

Nobody had done anything like this in Canada, which definitely made it harder for me. The normal thing people do is go to university and then get a job, but I just wanted to be a pro squash player. I left school at a young age and moved to Europe. I was very focused and had my goals laid out from a very young age.

Even though I am one of the two top-ranked players in the world, I don't get that much recognition for it in Canada. Squash is a tough sell in Canada, which I find odd because there are so many people who play, especially in urban centres. But it's been getting a lot of good press lately and it's really turned the corner. When people think about it, it reminds them of their college days, because that's when a lot of people learn to play the game.

I just want to get it in the media and pump it up over the next five years while I'm playing professionally. I'm confident squash will take off in Canada. Even when I stop competing, I want to have a hand in the sport. Squash has given me a lot over the years and I'd like to give something back. ❧

Canadian Press CP

Simon Whitfield, Canada's Golden Triathlete

Going to the 2000 Olympics in Sydney was a bit like going home for Simon Whitfield, and after he emerged victorious from the first ever Olympic men's triathlon race, he felt even more at home. A dual Canadian/Australian citizen, he had spent half of his time Down Under preparing for his sport's Olympic debut. Even though his world ranking of 21st seemed to make him a long shot, he also knew that the way he had been racing in pre-Olympic events gave him a realistic shot at the medal podium.

Associated Press AP

When the gun sounded, Whitfield and 51 other competitors dove into Sydney Harbour for the swimming portion of the race — 1.5 km through chilly ocean water. With more of an athletic background in running, he emerged from the water in 28th place, but well within striking distance of the leaders of the tightly-bunched pack. By the time he raced through the transition zone to start the 40-km cycle he was only 38 seconds behind Australian Craig Walton, the race leader at that point.

The cycling course took the triathletes six times around a 6.6 km circuit through downtown Sydney, with spectators lining the route. Using the experience and strength gained from his eight years in the sport, Whitfield gradually moved his way up through the pack. At one point he was in ninth place, only nine seconds behind the leader. On the fifth lap, though, he lost ground, dropping 28 seconds off the pace. Then, with only a kilometre to go, he came inches from disaster. A rider ahead of him miscalculated, causing a crash that took down a number of riders. A similar incident in the women's triathlon event had cost Canada dearly, as medal favourite Carol Montgomery (ranked third in the world) was put out of contention when she crashed. Fortunately, the story in the men's race was different. Whitfield didn't go down in the crash, but had to come to a complete stop in order to avoid it. By the time he resumed his ride and entered the transition zone, he was back in 27th place, 66 seconds behind the leader.

A lightning-fast change gained him two seconds and three places as he started the 10-km run for the finish line. Known as a strong runner who can gain a lot of ground on the final leg, he began his assault, this time chasing leader Olivier Marceau of France. By the 5-km mark he looked ready to challenge for a medal, running strongly in fourth place, while Marceau's 22-second lead was fading.

High over city streets, the aerial cameras showed his steady progress best to Canadians watching on television. Hopes that he would challenge for a bronze medal gradually turned to a seemingly certain silver as he inexorably reeled in two more runners (including the now-spent Marceau).

Finally, the hunt for the gold medal was down to two: Whitfield and Stephan Vuckovic of Germany, a long-time friend of Whitfield's. Ironically, the two had jokingly argued in the past about which one was the stronger sprinter. Vuckovic made his move early, and it looked like Whitfield didn't have it in him to respond. But with less than 500 metres to go on the final downhill stretch, he unleashed his own sprint, speeding by the German who had to content himself with silver. The ecstatic Canadian raised his arms in celebration and literally sprang through the finishing tape as he hit the finish line.

It was Canada's first gold medal of the 2000 Olympics, all the sweeter for the fact that several Canadian medal hopefuls had disappointing results the day before. Despite his dual citizenship and the fact that he attended school for four years not far from the scene of his gold medal performance, Whitfield was adamant that he only wanted to race for Canada. "I'm Canadian through and through," he said. ❦

Canadian Press/COA

Leading in the Canadian Olympic team in Sydney, 2000, was reigning canoe World Champion Caroline Brunet.

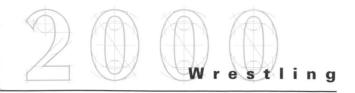
The Long Route to Olympic Gold

by Daniel Igali

CSI/COA

I cannot pinpoint when I started wrestling. In my tribe, the Ijaw tribe in Nigeria, wrestling is part of our culture, like hockey is to Canada. I therefore grew up knowing how to wrestle, although in Nigeria, it was a traditional Nigerian folk style of wrestling.

I grew up among five girls, (I have five other sisters on my mother' side) and a variety of other brothers and sisters (by my father's other wives). There are 21 children at the moment (a complete soccer team with reserves if you include my mothers and father). I therefore did not have a shortage of wrestling partners and was notorious for having a different school uniform every month as I was always wrestling around and getting my uniforms torn.

My family was poor, and we had to share everything. We had to line up for our turn to brush our teeth, and four of us shared one bed. We didn't always have enough food for three meals a day, but you got used to it.

When I was ten, a wrestling Olympian, Appah Macauley, had just returned from the 1984 Olympics in Los Angeles. He told us about hard work and wrestling with the white man. He told us he flew on a plane to get to Los Angeles and that it was the best experience he had ever had. That was enough reason, I thought, to have a few wrestling matches with friends on the grass. Too bad the uniform got torn, but that was the first step to get to the Olympics.

I did not start freestyle wrestling until 1990, which also happened to be my first national championships. I was fortunate enough to win it on my first try. I competed in my first African Championships in 1993 and became the African Champion at 62 kg the following year.

I clearly remember a fateful day in 1992 at the Murtala Mohammed airport in Lagos, Nigeria during a proposed Olympic qualifying trip. I was ready to claim one of three spots at the African Greco Roman Championship in Senegal to qualify for the Olympics in Barcelona. I had been in a training camp for two months, preparing for this big event, and I was ready, but at the airport they suddenly told us that there was no money. "Go back home," they said.

While being an African Champion was nice, my wrestling didn't really take off until I came to Canada in 1994 for the Commonwealth Games (where I finished 11th overall). The political situation in Nigeria was very volatile and my aims of studying alongside sports were becoming impossible. So after the Games, I decided to stay in Canada. It was the most difficult decision I ever had to make. My family back home was extremely upset, and so was I, but there were many people in Canada who befriended me and made it easier.

I remember those days washing dishes, picking berries, working construction, and working graveyard shifts as a security guard. Would I become a rich man now? Would companies sponsor a kid from the fresh water swamps of Bayelsa State, Nigeria if I won a gold medal? Don't expect a cent, I thought. Be content with whatever you get. After all, you have done well for a kid from the gutters.

The turning point in my career came after I lost to Terry Steiner in the final match of the 1996 Clansman international tournament. I was leading 7-1 with less than a minute to go and ended up giving up six points and lost the match in over time. After this match, I vowed never to be embarrassed in that way again. With the help of my coaches I immediately changed my training regimen and went on to place fourth at the 1998 World Championships. I also placed second at the 1998 World Cup (which I felt I should have won), and in 1999 became the world champion. It was going to be a tough road to become the next Olympic champion, but I believed the gods were on my side.

My greatest inspiration in Canada was my host mother, Maureen Matheny, who opened her home to me and reminded me of my mother in Nigeria. Maureen died of cancer five days after I won the World Championship. I have a lot of respect for her and she'll continue to be one my greatest inspirations. She, like the gods, was with me in Sydney.

2000 Olympic Wrestling Champion Daniel Igali showing the world the colours of his adopted land.

It had been my dream to be an Olympian since I was ten. Once the competition began nine days after the Opening Ceremonies, I realized my biggest aim in life: to step on a wrestling mat in Sydney and have my first match as an Olympian. Anything else that happened would be a bonus.

I was in great spirits and couldn't wait for the whistle to blow. I was also very nervous, but not because I was afraid of getting beaten. Nelson Mandela puts it best. "Our deepest fear is not that we are incapable, our deepest fear is that we are powerful beyond measure."

My first match was against an Iranian. It went in my favour, but it was too close for comfort. I looked forward to my second match against a Cuban, which I won 3-1 in overtime. Then came the semi-final, against the American Lincoln McIlravy, who I had fought five times before. I had won twice, including at the 1999 World Championships. This match went to overtime too, but in the end I beat him.

Before the gold medal match against the Russian my coach Dave Mckay came over to discuss strategy, but I waved him away. I was not in any mood for strategy. The strategy would take care of itself when the whistle blew. No, I cannot lose, I thought. I didn't have that word in my vocabulary at that point. I remember McIlravy coming up to me in the change room and saying, "You are the best athlete I have ever wrestled against. Good luck. Win the gold."

The rest is history. I did the celebratory jog around the maple leaf and sealed the gold medal with a kiss. It was all about making a complete circle, I told reporters after. I had been in Canada for six years, and had finally arrived exactly where I wanted to be. When I climbed the podium for the medal ceremony, the tears refused to stop. It was awesome to win the gold medal for Canada.

The best thing the Olympics did was showcase wrestling to the Canadian people. I saw so many kids who want to be Olympic wrestlers. I genuinely enjoy talking to the kids. I can talk to them about wrestling but I can also tell them about my life experiences. Canadians have so much, and people don't always appreciate it.

I have enjoyed my opportunity to be in the spotlight. Even my pet fish tends to treat me with greater respect now. I get a feeling, he knows that WE DID IT! ❧

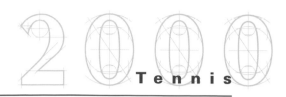

2000

T e n n i s

The Canucks
Who Knocked the "Woodies"

by Andrew Phillips
October 9, 2000

"How did it happen?" the Australian host asked. Mark Woodforde and Todd Woodbridge — renowned Down Under as "the Woodies" — were being grilled on how they managed to lose their final match as the world's most successful tennis doubles team. And how, the host went on, could they let it go to "a couple of no-name Canadians"?

The "no-names" in question — actually Daniel Nestor of Toronto and Sébastien Lareau of Montreal — whipped the legendary Woodies soundly to win gold, Canada's first-ever Olympic medal in tennis. And to do it on the Australian duo's home court, amid inevitable choruses of "Aussie! Aussie! Aussie! Oi! Oi! Oi!" made the victory even sweeter. "It's nice to send them off with a loss," said Nestor, "especially in front of their home crowd, and especially the way we did it."

The way they did it was convincing. After a shaky opening set, the Canadians took three straight to win. Nestor dominated, especially with a booming serve that hit 194 km/h during a match that ground on for two hours and 43 minutes. Woodforde and Woodbridge, with an unparalleled doubles record of 61 world titles over a decade together, had to settle for a silver. It was their last match: at 35, Woodforde is retiring from tennis.

Sadly for Canadian tennis, though, the Nestor-Lareau partnership is unlikely to be lasting. Both Nestor, 28, and Lareau, 27 dumped other doubles partners about a year ago to play with each other. Lareau asked Nestor to team up during a tournament in Shanghai. "I was a little surprised," Nestor recalled, "but when I thought about it, it made sense." Nestor is a left-hander with the bigger serve; Lareau is a rightie who is stronger at the net. "We don't really have any weaknesses," Nestor said. But despite their Sydney success, both said they will focus on their singles game and team up only for key matches, including next year's grand slams.

The victory was special for Nestor, too, because it marked his comeback from delicate surgery on his left shoulder. "I know a lot of players who never really recover from that, who can never hit as hard as they did," he said. "I was worried." But he started playing again in May — and showed last week he is as good as ever. As for Lareau, winning gold for his country was "the highlight of my career, a magic moment." ❦

Canadian Press CP

Queen's Plate Winners
Race held at Old Woodbine over 1 1/4 mile

Year	Winning Horse	Owner	Jockey	Time
1900*	Dalmoor	J. E. Seagram	Lewis	2:14
1901	John Ruskin	J. E. Seagram	Vititoe	2:18
1902	Lyddite	Wm. Hendrie	Wainwright	2:15
1903	Thessalon	N. Dyment	Castro	2:15
1904	Sapper	N. Dyment	J. Walsh	2:12
1905	Inferno	J. E. Seagram	H. Phillips	2:12
1906	Slaughter	J. E. Seagram	Treubel	2:11.3
1907	Kelvin	T. Ambrose Woods	Foley	2:12.3
1908	Seismic	J. E. Seagram	Fairbrother	2:11
1909	Shimonese	Valley Farm Stable	Gilbert	2:10.2
1910	Parmer	Valley Farm Stable	J. Wilson	2:12.2
1911	St. Bass	H. Giddings	E. Dugan	2:08.4
1912	Heresy	Brookdale Stable	Small	2:11
1913	Hearts of Oak	H. Giddings	J. Wilson	2:09.1
1914	Bee Hive	H. Giddings	G. Burns	2:10.3
1915	Tartarean	C. Millar	H. Watts	2:09.1
1916	Mandarin	J. E. Seagram	A. Pickens	2:12
1917	Belle Mahone	J. E. Seagram	F. Robinson	2:08.4
1918	Springside	G. M. Hendrie	L. Mink	2:08.4
1919	Ladder of Light	G. W. Beardmore	L. Lyke	2:09.2
1920	St. Paul	H. Giddings	R. Romanelli	2:09
1921	Herendesy	Brookdale Stable	J. Butwell	2:10
1922	South Shore	Thorncliffe Stable	K. Parrington	2:12
1923	Flowerful	Seagram Stable	T. Wilson	2:11

Race held at Old Woodbine over 1 1/8 mile

Year	Winning Horse	Owner	Jockey	Time
1924**	Maternal Pride	H.S. Wilson	G. Walls	1:57.3
1925	Fairbank	J. C. Fletcher	C. Lang	1:56.2
1926	Haplite	Seagram Stable	H. Erickson	1:59.3
1927	Troutlet	R. H. New	F. Horn	1:55.4
1928	Young Kitty	Seagram Stable	L. Pichon	1:57
1929	Shorelint	Thorncliffe Stable	J. D. Mooney	1:57.3
1930	Aymond	R. H. New	H. Little	1:57.1
1931	Froth Blower	R. W. R. Cowie	F. Mann	1:59.1
1932	Queensway	R. W. R. Cowie	F. Mann	1:55.1
1933	King O'Connor	Seagram Stable	E. Legere	1:56.2
1934	Horometer	R.S. McLaughlin	F. Mann	1:54.1
1935	Sally Fuller	E. F. Seagram	H. Lindberg	1:55.2
1936	Monsweep	H. C. Hatch	D. Brammer	1:55
1937	Goldlure	H. C. Hatch	S. Young	1:55.2
1938	Bunty Lawless	W. F. Morrissey	J. W. Bailey	1:54.2
1939	Archworth	G. C. McCullagh	S. D. Birley	1:54.2
1940	Willie the Kid	M. A. Kane	R. Nash	1:55.4
1941	Budpath	H. C. Hatch	R. Watson	1:56.4
1942	Ten to Ace	H. Giddings	C. W. Smith	1:57.4
1943	Paolita	C. H. Hemstead	P. Remillard	2:02.3
1944	Acara	H. C. Hatch	R. Watson	1:54.4
1945	Uttermost	H. C. Hatch	R. Watson	1:53.4
1946	Kingarvie	Parkwood Stable	J. Dewhust	1:55.3
1947	Moldy	Parkwood Stable	C. MacDonald	1:54.1
1948	Last Mark	J. G. Fair	H. R. Bailey	1:52
1949	Epic	E. P. Taylor	C. Rogers	1:52.1
1950	McGill	V. Sheridan	C. Rogers	1:52.2
1951	Major Factor	E. P. Taylor	A. Bavington	1:53
1952	Epigram	Three V's Stable	G. Robillard	1:58.3
1953	Canadiana	E. P. Taylor	E. Arcaro	1:52.1
1954	Collisteo	Bur-Fit Stable	C. Rogers	1:52
1955	Ace Marine	L. Mahoney	G. Walker	1:52.2

Race Venue changed to New Woodbine

Year	Winning Horse	Owner	Jockey	Time
1956***	Canadian Champ	W. R. Beasley	D. Stevenson	1:55

Race Distance changed to 1 1/4 mile

Year	Winning Horse	Owner	Jockey	Time
1957****	Lyndon Cay	E. P. Taylor	A. Gomez	2:02.3
1958	Caledon Beau	C. Smythe	A. Coy	2:04.1
1959	New Providence	E. P. Taylor	R. Ussery	2:04.4
1960	Victoria Park	Windfields Farm	A. Gomez	2:02
1961	Blue Light	K. R. Marshall	H. Dittfach	2:05
1962	Flaming Page	Windfields Farm	J. Fitzsimmons	2:04.3
1963	Canebora	Windfields Farm	M. Ycaza	2:04
1964	Northern Dancer	Windfields Farm	W. Hartack	2:02.1
1965	Whistling Sea	Oliver Ranches	T. Inouye	2:03.4
1966	Titled Hero	P. K. Marshall	A. Gomez	2:03.3
1967	Jammed Lovely	C. Smythe	J. Fitzsimmons	2:03
1968	Merger	Golden West Farm	W. Harris	2:05.2
1969	Jumpin Joseph	Warren Beasely	A. Gomez	2:04.1
1970	Almoner	Parkview Stable	S. Hawley	2:04.4
1971	Kennedy Road	Mrs. A. Stollery	S. Hawley	2:03
1972	Victoria Song	Green Hills Farm	R. Platts	2:03.1
1973	Royal Chocolate	Stafford Farm	T. Colangelo	2:08.1
1974	Amber Herod	Stafford Farm	R. Platts	2:09.1
1975	L'Enjoleur	J. L. Levesque	S. Hawley	2:02.3
1976	Norcliffe	Norcliffe Stables	J. Fell	2:05
1977	Sound Reason	Stafford Farm	R. Platts	2:06.3
1978	Regal Embrace	Windfields Farm	S. Hawley	2:02
1979	Steady Growth	Kinghaven Farm	B. Swatuk	2:06.3
1980	Driving Home	CFCW Racing Stable	W. Parsons	2:04.1
1981	Fiddle Dancer Boy	J. B. W. Carmichael	D. Clark	2:04.4
1982	Son of Briartic	Paddockhurst Stable	P. Souter	2:04.3
1983	Bompago	Carl Cardella & Partners	L. Attard	2:04.1
1984	Key to the Moon	B. K. Y. Stable	R. Platts	2:03.4
1985	La Lorgnette	Windfields Farm	D. Clark	2:04.3
1986	Golden Choice	R. Sanderson	V. Bracciale Jr.	2:07.1
1987	Market Control	Kinghaven Farm	K. Skinner	2:03.3
1988	Regal Intention	Sam-Son Farm	J. Lauzon	2:06.1
1989	With Approval	Kinghaven Farm	D. Seymour	2:03
1990	Izvestia	Kinghaven Farm	D. Seymour	2:01.4
1991	Dance Smartly	Sam-Son Farm	P. Day	2:03.2
1992	Alydeed	Kinghaven Farm	C. Perret	2:04.3
1993	Peteski	E. I. Mack	C. Perret	2:04.1
1994	Basqueian	F. Stronach	J. Lauzon	2:03.2
1995	Regal Discovery	No. 1 Stable	T. Kabel	2:03.4
1996	Victor Cooley	Windways Farm	E. Ramsammy	2:03.4
1997	Awesome Again	F. Stronach	M. Smith	2:04.1
1998	Archers Bay	Eugene Melnyk & R. Bristow Farm	K. Desormeaux	2:02.1
1999	Woodcarver	G. Schickedanz	M. Walls	2:03.13
2000	Scatter the Gold	Sam-Son Farm	T. Kabel	2:05.53

*Race held at Old Woodbine over a distance of 1 1/4 mile

** Race changes to a distance of 1 1/8 mile

*** Race venue is moved to New Woodbine

**** Race distance is changed to 1 1/4 mile

Lorie Kane, from PEI

Golfer Lorie Kane was the runaway choice for the 2000 Bobbie Rosenfeld Award as Canada's female athlete of the year. Kane, who also won the award in 1997 and was runner-up to speed skater Catriona Le May Doan in 1998, started her stellar year slowly, her two second place finishes bringing to nine the times in her career that she had come second without a single victory. "But for some reason in August I really turned things around and started playing some great golf."

She went to St. Louis for the Michelob Light Classic in early August and recalled a woman telling her: "This is your week." How did Kane respond? "I looked at her right in the eye and I said, 'Yes it is and I'm the only one who could do something about it.' And I simply went on and won."

Associated Press AP

Kane won the tournament by three strokes. The joy of winning was shared by her fellow pros, who doused her with beer at the 18th hole. "For some of those girls to change plane tickets and reservations to stay with me and to celebrate with me really meant a lot," Kane said. "The beer shower was a lot of fun. I don't think I've worn that outfit since. I don't know that I ever will."

After her win, Kane gave part of the credit to something very Canadian — hockey. She watched a press conference with Mark Messier when he rejoined the New York Rangers. She said seeing a successful hockey player like Mark put things into perspective helped her focus more as well.

Her August success continued, with fall victories at the New Albany Golf Classic and the Mizuno Open. "In a 10-week run, I won three times and finished in the top 10 about eight times," Kane said. "It's just been a fantastic run." Kane finished the season fifth on the LPGA money winnings list with $929,189 US.

Associated Press AP

Kane, an Islander through and through, credited the support network in her home province for giving her the grounding to handle success. "It was easy for me to leave and find success on the road and the LPGA Tour because I know when I come home, I'm Lorie, I'm still the same Lorie. People might see me a little bit differently as someone they see on TV and I'm a little more recognized but I still am Lorie Kane from Charlottetown, Prince Edward Island." ❧

Associated Press AP

Mike Weir and the Reign in Spain

By the end of the century, the major professional golf tours around the globe hosted championship tournaments, each counting as part of the respective tour's season. Only the top players from each tour qualified. Four of these World Golf Championship tournaments were held in 2000, one of them at the famed and quirky Valderamma Golf course in Sotogrande, Spain, the *American Express Championship*. By the time the final putt was sunk, the laurels, not to mention the $1,000,000 first prize, belonged to Canadian Mike Weir.

"It's a huge win, a world championship," Weir beamed enthusiastically afterwards.

Weir, who hailed from Bright's Grove (near Sarnia), Ontario, was eight strokes off the pace heading into the third round on the weekend. He could have been closer to the front, save for a double bogey suffered on the treacherous Hole 17. The layout of the hole was controversial, and confounded the players all week long. Time after time the world's best golfers hit apparently safe shots onto the green, only to see the ball spin back into the pond surrounding the front of the green. During the second round on Friday, Weir himself hit two balls into the water, leaving him eight behind the leaders.

Weir badly needed to gain some momentum on the weekend, and he got just that, first shooting a tournament-low 65 on Saturday, followed by a 69 on Sunday. "There were so many players with a chance to win, my plan was to just try to keep hitting the ball solid," he noted after Sunday's round.

His low round on Saturday put Weir in a position to challenge on Sunday, but the players all still had to get by Hole 17. Playing in the final pairing, Weir first watched World Number 1 Tiger Woods hit a near-perfect shot onto the 17th green, only to see it and his chances of victory fall back into the pond. Then four-time major winner Nick Price did the same. Five players had held or shared the lead during Sunday's final round, but heading into 17 Mike Weir was the only one who remained atop the leader board.

On Friday, Weir had figured he was only about one or two inches away from a perfect shot on 17, only to end up with that double bogey. He couldn't afford to do the same thing on Sunday. Clinging to a two-stroke lead, he played safe, laid up one shot and hit his approach to the back of the green. He still faced a steep, winding, slippery down hill chip, a shot that nearly went in. He tapped in the ball for par, parred the final hole as well and won the tournament by two shots over Lee Westwood of England.

"The 17th hole is a very difficult hole, a controversial hole," Weir said. "But it adds to the flavour of this event and this golf course." It was Weir's second PGA victory, but a much more significant one than winning the Air Canada Championship in Vancouver the year before. With the win he earned due respect from all sources for being a top player, not to mention the money. "Three years ago I was playing when $100,000 Canadian was the total purse. To win $1,000,000 American is far and above what I ever dreamed," he said after accepting his trophy as the *American Express World Championship* winner. ✤

Associated Press AP

Canada

A Century of Grey Cups

1909-1929

UNIVERSITY OF TORONTO | 26 | 1909 | PARKDALE CANOE CLUB | 6

Led by Hugh Gall and Smirle Lawson, the University of Toronto captured the first ever Grey Cup Game, and Varsity's first of three consecutive Cups. On a bleak December day, 3,800 spectators turned out at Rosedale Field in Toronto to watch Varsity's Gall run and kick his team to victory. Gall's eight singles in the game remained a record throughout the century. U of T won 26-6.

UNIVERSITY OF TORONTO | 16 | 1910 | HAMILTON TIGERS | 7

Hugh Gall repeated his dominance of the previous year, running and kicking his team to its second straight championship, this time 16-7 over the Hamilton Tigers. Mid-game, when the momentum seemed to change to Hamilton, Gall changed his kicking strategy and started running with the ball more – and setting up the winning touchdowns for his teammates Red Dixon and Jack Maynard.

UNIVERSITY OF TORONTO | 14 | 1911 | TORONTO ARGONAUTS | 7

The Varsity running game again proved to be the catalyst in its 14-7 Grey Cup victory. Jack Maynard scored another touchdown for the defending champions, but the star of the game was Toronto quarterback Peter Thompson who constantly fooled the Argonaut defenders with fakes (known as the "hidden ball" effect) and timely passes to Maynard and other runners.

HAMILTON ALERTS | 11 | 1912 | TORONTO ARGONAUTS | 4

Finally, a different team won the Grey Cup, and even a different city – Hamilton beating the Toronto Argonauts 11-4. Interestingly, the game was almost not played because the attendant looking after the ball had locked it away to be safe and then left for home. The game was delayed by an hour, and the organizers had to pay the City of Hamilton $1.75 to replace the lock they broke to retrieve the ball. The star of the game was Hamilton's Norman Leckie.

HAMILTON TIGERS | 44 | 1913 | PARKDALE CANOE CLUB | 2

A powerful Tigers team defended Hamilton's honour for the Grey Cup and predictably trounced the Parkdale team 44-2. The Tigers were a force all year and had been expected to win by a lot. Former Varsity star Hugh Gall scored the only 2 points for Parkdale, while Art Wilson and Ross Craig led the charge for Hamilton and accounted for 25 points between them.

TORONTO ARGONAUTS | 14 | 1914 | UNIVERSITY OF TORONTO | 2

Two teams from Toronto battled for the Cup this year, with the underdog Argonauts winning their first championship of the century 14-2. Jack O'Connor's accurate kicking proved to be the key to the Argo victory, constantly keeping the Varsity defenders at bay and often out of position.

HAMILTON TIGERS | 13 | 1915 | TORONTO ROWING & ATHLETIC ASSOCIATION | 7

Sometimes games are remembered for something other than the score, and this was one of them. Although the Tigers prevailed 13-7 and certainly appeared to be the better of the two teams, the officiating of former U of T star Red Dixon was severely criticized. Many of Dixon's calls, especially close calls involving scoring plays, were awarded to Hamilton. After the game the home crowd chanted "Three cheers for Reddy Dixon — the best player on the Tiger team." Police were called in to disperse the near riotous crowd after the final whistle. Dixon's refereeing almost made one overlook the actual game, where Hamilton's Sam Manson shone.

1916-1919 NO GREY CUP GAMES DUE TO WORLD WAR I

In 1916-17 organized football was not played because of Canadians' commitment to the war efforts. In 1918 and 1919 the play resumed, but there was little public interest "in pursuing playoffs or anything else to celebrate at this time." There would be no Grey Cup during this time.

UNIVERSITY OF TORONTO | 16 | 1920 | TORONTO ARGONAUTS | 3

With the war behind them, the Varsity squad received many players returning from overseas and the stacked team proved victorious over the Argos 16-3. Although he didn't score in the game, the player who made dazzling runs throughout was Varsity's Joe Breen. Future gridiron legend Harry Batstone made his Grey Cup debut with the Argos.

OTTAWA SENATORS 2 4 — 1925 — **WINNIPEG TAMMANY TIGERS** 1

Ottawa played host to its first Grey Cup, with the hometown Senators defeating the western champs from Winnipeg convincingly, 24-1. Ottawa, which broke Queen's 26-game unbeaten string to advance to the final, and then beat the Tigers for the Cup, were led by the strong efforts of half back Charlie Connell and quarterback Charlie Lynch.

OTTAWA SENATORS 1 0 — 1926 — **UNIVERSITY OF TORONTO** 7

Showing everyone that the previous year was no fluke, the Senators won their second straight Cup, 10-7 over the University of Toronto. Regina had won the western final, but decided not to make the trip east because of the lateness of the season, making the eastern final the Grey Cup game. Joe Miller of Ottawa was the star of the game providing the offensive spark for the Senators by scoring five of the 10 points.

BALMY BEACH 9 — 1927 — **HAMILTON TIGERS** 6

For the second year in a row the eastern finalists played for the Grey Cup, as the western champions again decided not to travel east. The Cup game itself received rave reviews, however, as the underdog ORFU-champion Beach squad defeated the powerful Big Four champion from Hamilton, 9-6. Beach's Mansell Moore was the star of the game, constantly getting good yardage on his runs and punt returns, providing Beach with continual advantageous field position.

HAMILTON TIGERS 3 0 — 1928 — **REGINA ROUGHRIDERS** 0

The west was finally represented again in the Grey Cup, this time by the Regina Roughriders, albeit in a 30-0 loss to the Hamilton Tigers. The Tigers' Hawley "Huck" Welch proved to be the dominant player of the game, consistently out-kicking his western counterpart. Frank Leadley, having graduated from Queen's, also starred for the Tigers in the game.

HAMILTON TIGERS 1 4 — 1929 — **REGINA ROUGHRIDERS** 3

Quite simply, football was being played differently in the west than the east in 1929. The west used the forward pass while the east did not. In the first Grey Cup featuring the forward pass (for the first half of the game only), Hamilton defeated the Roughriders for the second year in a row, this time 14-3. "Huck" Welch was again the star of the game, but by far the most exciting plays came from the forward passing plays of Regina (who, unlike Hamilton, had used the play during the year). It didn't help them on the scoreboard though.

TORONTO ARGONAUTS 2 3 — 1921 — **EDMONTON ESKIMOS** 0

A major rule change saw the elimination of the centre scrum, removing the two players previously used solely for protecting the "heel-back." This changed the number of players on the field from 14 to 12. Western teams also began competing for the Dominion's Championship this year, much to the chagrin of their eastern counterparts. The Edmonton Eskimos became the first western team to challenge for the Cup and faced the favoured eastern champions. The Argonauts prevailed convincingly 23-0, showcasing their new star and eventual Athlete of the Half Century, Lionel Conacher.

QUEEN'S UNIVERSITY 1 3 — 1922 — **EDMONTON ELKS** 1

Kingston played host to its only Grey Cup game of the century, with the home team Queen's University Golden Gaels winning its first of three straight Grey Cups. Queen's legends Harry Batstone and Frank "Pep" Leadley ran and passed their way to a 13-1 victory over Edmonton.

QUEEN'S UNIVERSITY 5 4 — 1923 — **REGINA ROUGHRIDERS** 0

54-0. It didn't get any worse, or better, than this - depending on which side of the cheering you stood. Queen's players "Pep" Leadley and Harry Batstone were once again stellar in leading the Golden Gaels to the most convincing victory of the century. Rumours ran rampant that Queen's ran up the score to protest playing against a weak western team in the first week of December – right before exams. Leadley and Batstone became heroes. Writing in the Manitoba Free Press, W.J. Finlay said that Queen's "...uncorked their daring end runs and long passes at full speed, faked kicks, and then ran the ball back ... and gave an exhibition of skill with their hands and feet that western rugby had never seen."

QUEEN'S UNIVERSITY 1 1 — 1924 — **BALMY BEACH** 3

The Queen's Golden Gaels became the last university team to be crowned Grey Cup Champions, defeating Balmy Beach 11-3 on November 29. The date is important. Queen's went through the season undefeated and announced they would not play in a Grey Cup played in December because it would be too close to exams. A game against the western champion Winnipeg Victorias was scheduled. But, the players in Winnipeg and the managers of the team could not agree on travel arrangements and, in the end, the management refused the players permission to travel to the game. The Balmy Beach – Queen's game for the eastern championship was then declared to be for the Grey Cup. When Winnipeg finally relented and agreed to travel east, the Canadian Rugby Union said "too late" for Queen's had already won the game, "locked up their equipment" and, presumably, were studying for exams.

1930-1944

BALMY BEACH | 1930 | REGINA ROUGHRIDERS
1 1 | | 6

The Roughriders again traveled east to play for the Grey Cup and again were on the losing end of the final score, this time 11-6 against Balmy Beach. The score was getting less lopsided, though, which proved that the western game was improving. This year, the forward pass was banned because only one team had used it during the season (a very pro-eastern bias since it was the Beach squad which did not use the play). Future columnist Ted "the Moaner" Reeve proved to be the star. Seeing limited action because of a sore shoulder, Reeve made two game-saving tackles and one blocked punt in the fourth quarter to preserve the Beach victory.

MONTREAL WINGED WHEELERS | 1931 | REGINA ROUGHRIDERS
2 2 | | 0

The forward pass was allowed for the entire game and it was Warren Stevens of the Montreal Winged Wheelers who threw the first touchdown pass in Grey Cup history, en route to a 22-0 victory over, again, the Regina Roughriders. The forward pass made the game exciting for the fans, but the real game-winning excitement came at half time. The day of the game was icy and the field was getting very slippery; the players would need different footwear. Regina had ordered special shoes just in case, but they hadn't arrived in time. Or so they had thought. Apparently, the shoes were delivered to the Montreal dressing room at half time, whereupon the Winged Wheelers put them on and easily won the second half.

HAMILTON TIGERS | 1932 | REGINA ROUGHRIDERS
2 5 | | 6

Regina made its fifth consecutive trip east for the Grey Cup, and registered their fifth straight defeat, this time to Hamilton 25-6. The Tigers' Brian Timmis and Dave Sprague combined for a powerful running attack, gaining over 200 yards on the ground between them and, more importantly, keeping the ball in Hamilton's possession and not Regina's passing attack. The westerners were once again no match for their eastern rivals.

TORONTO ARGONAUTS | 1933 | SARNIA IMPERIALS
4 | | 3

A new playoff format saw the west playing the ORFU Champion and the winner playing for the Grey Cup against the Big Four Champions. This "extra" game did not help the Winnipeg team and they lost an exciting semi final to the Argonauts. The Argos then turned around the next week to defeat Sarnia in their first appearance in the Cup in a very defensive 4-3 struggle. Ab Box was the star of the game with many open-field game-saving tackles preventing the Imperials from generating any solid offence.

SARNIA IMPERIALS | 1934 | REGINA ROUGHRIDERS
2 0 | | 1 2

In their seventh Grey Cup final, and sixth in seven years, the Roughriders still couldn't manage a win, going down to the Sarnia Imperials 20-12. The Roughies weren't blown away though, putting up a tough fight against a squad made up of virtually the same players that lost the Grey Cup a year previously. Sarnia's Ormond Beach was the game star, running and tackling "all over the field."

WINNIPEG WINNIPEGERS | 1935 | HAMILTON TIGERS
1 8 | | 1 2

The west finally won the Grey Cup! In a thrilling and shocking ending to the gridiron season, the western representative Winnipeg 'Pegs beat the eastern Hamilton squad 18-12. The eastern press and the administrators chastised the west for their use of American imports, but it was in fact legal to play anyone who played for the team during the year. As a result, Fritz Hanson became etched in Winnipeg lore as the hero of the first Grey Cup taken west. Returning kicks and running the ball for over 300 yards, Hanson showed both speed and finesse that Hamilton just could not stop. The west was ecstatic, the east...was not.

SARNIA IMPERIALS | 1936 | OTTAWA ROUGH RIDERS
2 6 | | 2 0

So unhappy was the east with Winnipeg's victory the previous year that the CRU instituted a confusing rule in which only Americans resident in Canada on January 1 could play for any team. Western officials were so upset they refused to send their champion squad (Regina again) to defend the Grey Cup title. Instead, the eastern final was for the Cup, with Sarnia prevailing over Ottawa 26-20. Sarnia's winning efforts, especially those of Hugh "Bummer" Stirling, were overshadowed by the spectre of Ottawa's quarterback. In 1929 George Morrison had been suspended from football for life by the CRU for his role in a very rough game. Although no one actually witnessed him doing any direct harm, he was the captain of the team and he was punished. "Life" ended up meaning six years and Morrison returned to lead Ottawa to the Grey Cup, albeit in a losing cause.

TORONTO ARGONAUTS — 1937 — WINNIPEG BLUE BOMBERS

4 | 1937 | **3**

Winnipeg travelled east to play the Argos, and in losing 4-3 showed that the best team on the field does not always win. The Blue Bombers, as they were now called, had a few chances to break the game wide open early on, but key fumbles on their part stopped any momentum. Fritz Hanson, star of their 1935 victory, played well but ended up fumbling a punt early on. Toronto pounced on the loose ball and three plays later scored the winning field goal.

TORONTO ARGONAUTS — 1938 — WINNIPEG BLUE BOMBERS

3 0 | 1938 | **7**

This was Red Storey's "15 minutes of fame" long before the phrase became popular. It was a very close, defensive, game until Storey broke loose in the fourth quarter. The seldom used back noticed the Bombers were double teaming one of his teammates, so when Storey got the ball on an end run, he just took off in the other direction for a 28-yard touchdown run. Then when the Bombers got the ball, Storey (still on the field and playing defence in the two-way days) intercepted a Winnipeg pass and ran in for his second touchdown. Two long runs by Storey, one of 100 yards, set up another Argo touchdown. Then just to put the game out of reach, Storey scored his third touchdown of the quarter on a running play very similar to his first touchdown, securing a 30-7 Argo victory. In his own words, Storey noted that "...all told, I ran something like 190 yards in 12 minutes..."

WINNIPEG BLUE BOMBERS — 1939 — OTTAWA ROUGH RIDERS

8 | 1939 | **7**

Now the tables turned for Winnipeg. Ottawa had had a superb year, scoring 207 points and allowing only 51 in 12 games. The Rough Riders were the clear favourites, but no one mentioned that to the 1935 star, Fritz Hanson. Again, Hanson's ability to run back punts and gain extra yards rushing wide with "blinding speed and agility" gave the game to Winnipeg 8-7. Hanson ended up with 126 yards rushing, and even threw the Bombers only completed pass.

OTTAWA ROUGH RIDERS — 1940 — BALMY BEACH

8 + 12 = 20 | 1940 | **2 + 5 = 7**

Another rule dispute meant the Grey Cup was again an all-eastern competition. And, for the only time ever, the game was decided on a two-game total point basis. Ottawa actually won both games, 8-2 and 12-5, for a Cup-winning score of 20-7. The first game was played in a blizzard and it seemed amazing that any scoring was done. Ottawa's Dave Sprague, playing on a severely injured leg, was the star of the game with a fourth quarter running display that seemed impervious to the weather conditions.

WINNIPEG BLUE BOMBERS — 1941 — OTTAWA ROUGH RIDERS

1 8 | 1941 | **1 6**

The west returned to challenge for the Grey Cup and that meant Winnipeg's Fritz Hanson again leading the way. Several Ottawa players had retired at the end of their 1940 victory, including Dave Sprague, but it did not prevent the team from winning the eastern final. Often-used Hanson ended as the game's star, for the third time, making several key runs when it looked like the Bombers could be losing yardage. Nearing the end of the game, Winnipeg failed in a third down try and Ottawa was given ideal field position to win with a field goal. Their attempt from inside the 20 went wide, however, and the Bombers hung on for victory, 18-16.

TORONTO RCAF HURRICANES — 1942 — WINNIPEG RCAF BOMBERS

8 | 1942 | **5**

In the middle of World War II it looked like play for the Grey Cup would be suspended as it had been during World War I. Then the military got an idea – since the game was gaining importance across the country and since both watching and playing it meant much for morale, it was decided that the armed forces would develop teams of their own and challenge for the Cup. For the next three years, military teams provided for some very exciting Cup games.

In 1942, thousands of Canadians listened to the Grey Cup broadcast on their radios, and almost 13,000 showed up at Varsity Stadium in Toronto to watch the RCAF from Toronto defeat the RCAF from Winnipeg, 8-5. Fans, players and media alike were highly praised for trying to restore some "normalcy" to life, even if that meant cheering for military-based teams. There were many stars in the actual game, including Toronto's Bill Stukus who valiantly tried to establish his accurate passing game. It was a cold day though, so the Hurricanes had to rely on Don Crowe's running to squeak their way to victory.

HAMILTON FLYING WILDCATS — 1943 — WINNIPEG RCAF BOMBERS

2 3 | 1943 | **1 4**

The Wildcats were coached by former Hamilton star Brian Timmis, who noted: "This title is a title that has been won by the armed services, and the people who gave them the arms to fight with. On my Hamilton team are airmen, sailors, war workers and army reserves, all doing a job for peace." The Wildcats won 23-14, due in large part to Joe Krol whose accurate passing and deft tackling seemed to stymie the Bombers all afternoon. The Bomber's Ches McCance, appearing in his sixth Cup, had a superb day running the ball, even in a loss.

MONTREAL ST. HYACINTHE NAVY — 1944 — HAMILTON FLYING WILDCATS

7 | 1944 | **6**

For the last time in the century the Grey Cup was an all-eastern affair. This time it was because of the war efforts in the west, though, not because of any rule squabbling. For the first time a team from the QRFU was represented in the Cup as the St. Hyacinthe-Donnacona base Navy crew challenged for the Cup after a surprisingly successful season. Joe Krol again led Hamilton and had the Wildcats tied at 6 with just less than three minutes to play. The Navy men got the ball back, carried it down the field, and with little time left kicked the ball into the end zone in an attempt to win the game by a single point. Hamilton, though, read the play well and had someone in the end zone to get the ball. Unable to run it out, Hamilton's Gord Miller kicked the ball back out. The navy recovered and marched the ball to the Wildcat 15. From there the Navy easily kicked their single point rouge in the next play and won the Grey Cup, 7-6.

1 9 4 5 - 1 9 5 7

TORONTO ARGONAUTS		WINNIPEG BLUE BOMBERS
3 5	**1945**	**0**

The first post WW II Grey Cup saw the Argos' Joe "King" Krol start a charge that would lead Toronto to five titles in eight years. This year his passing, running, kicking and tackling (being one of several two-way players) led to two touchdowns and a convert en route to a 35-0 Cup win over Winnipeg. Former Argo player and coach Annis Stukus stated that, "Krol did everything except play the National Anthem on a piccolo."

TORONTO ARGONAUTS		WINNIPEG BLUE BOMBERS
2 8	**1946**	**6**

Toronto and Winnipeg met for the second year in a row, and again the Argos were one-side victors, 28-6. This is the year made famous by the Argo "Gold Dust Twins," as Joe Krol and Royal Copeland dominated the game and the season. Krol passed for three touchdowns, scored one himself and kicked three converts on his way to establishing stardom for himself and his team. Copeland's speed, runs and pass catching were a thrill to witness.

TORONTO ARGONAUTS		WINNIPEG BLUE BOMBERS
1 0	**1947**	**9**

The Bombers were getting closer, but for the third year in a row the western champs from Winnipeg lost to the Argos, this time by the close score of 10-9. Winnipeg led 9-1 at half time and looked like they were to win the game, when some unlucky bounces occurred. First, in the third quarter two Bomber defenders collided allowing Royal Copeland to catch an easy pass from Joe Krol to narrow the score. Then in the fourth quarter, Winnipeg faked a kick, threw a pass to a wide-open Johnny Reagan who swiveled his way into the end zone for an apparent touchdown. Alas, Referee Hec Creighton ruled that Reagan was not over the line of scrimmage when he initially caught the pass (as was the rule in those days) and the play was nullified.... much to the horror of the Bomber players and coaches. Toronto then scored two more singles to tie the score and with less than a minute to go the Argos stopped an ill-fated Winnipeg third down gamble. The ensuing turnover gave Toronto ideal field possession from which to kick the winning point.

CALGARY STAMPEDERS		OTTAWA ROUGH RIDERS
1 2	**1948**	**7**

Grey Cup week was born this year. Singing, dancing and drinking Calgarians swarmed Toronto during the week of the game in a never before seen display of civic pride and enthusiasm. The festivities Calgary brought would begin a tradition during Grey Cup week that would last through the century. During the actual game, won by Calgary 12-7 over Ottawa, two unusual plays tipped the scales toward Calgary. In the first half Calgary had possession at the Ottawa 20. After a play, the Stampeder players entered their huddle, except Normie Hill. Hill stayed lying down on the ground near the sideline. When the ball was snapped, the unnoticed and undefended Hill jumped up and ran towards the end zone to catch the go-ahead touchdown pass. Then, later in the second half, Ottawa ran a running play. Thinking the play was dead because of an incomplete pass, Ottawa went to huddle. An alert Woody Strode calmly picked up the "loose" ball and ran towards the goal where he was stopped at the 15. On the next play Calgary scored. Ottawa players afterwards explained they had thought the ball was dead, when in fact it was a forward lateral behind the line of scrimmage and not a forward pass past the line of scrimmage. A small mistake, perhaps, but it cost Ottawa the Grey Cup. The Stampeder fans, needless to say, went wild on their way back to Calgary.

MONTREAL ALOUETTES		CALGARY STAMPEDERS
2 8	**1949**	**1 5**

Calgary returned as the western Champions this year, only to be dethroned by the Alouettes, 28-15. The field, as would be the case for the next few years, was awful, muddy and wet. The momentum in the game seemed to change with a referee's call, or rather, with a "Judge of Play" call (an off-field referee). Head Referee Hec Creighton did not make a call on a Calgary interception of a long Montreal pass. The Judge of Play, Jimmy Simpson, rushed onto the field to indicate the Montreal receiver had been interfered with and the interception should not stand. The Als kept the ball, the momentum and eventually won the Cup.

TORONTO ARGONAUTS		WINNIPEG BLUE BOMBERS
1 3	**1950**	**0**

This game was later christened the Mud Bowl. Toronto, led by Joe Krol again, defeated Winnipeg 13-0 in a game remembered more for the playing conditions than the scoring. The field was the worst ever, with mud and water everywhere. There were puddles at least six inches deep in places and it made the game very sloppy to say the least. At one point Winnipeg's "Buddy" Tinsley lay motionless face-down in a puddle. Referee Hec Creighton rolled the big lineman over and Tinsley remained still; the fans gasped, thinking he had drowned. He had not. Fortunately, as Tinsley stated afterwards, he was not "motionless" just "mad" and did not feel like moving.

OTTAWA ROUGH RIDERS

2 1 — **1951** — **1 4** — SASKATCHEWAN ROUGHRIDERS

Saskatchewan entered the game with a number of injuries and a suspension of one of its top players, Bob Sandberg. The western Roughies gave a good fight, but ultimately lost to the eastern Rough Riders, 21-14. The game was played on an excellent field for a change and it was close until Ottawa broke it open with a long gain. Ottawa's quarterback, Tom O'Malley, gave a great fake hand off to Benny MacDonnell leaving Howie Turner wide open for a pass from O'Malley. The play resulted in a 68-yard gain and an Ottawa score which Saskatchewan never recovered from.

TORONTO ARGONAUTS

2 1 — **1952** — **1 1** — EDMONTON ESKIMOS

In the first live television broadcast of a Grey Cup game, the screens went blank for 29 minutes as a repairman had to climb above Varsity Stadium to fix the antenna. Edmonton scored early on a run by Normie Kwong, only to see the Argos bounce back and take the lead. In the fourth quarter (seen on television after the repair) it looked like the Eskimos were coming in for the go-ahead score. Instead, Edmonton fumbled the ball on the Argo 17 and Toronto recovered. On the next play, game star Nobby Wirkowski found Zeke O'Connor wide open for the game-clinching touchdown. The Argos went on to win 21-11. This was the final Grey Cup for the Argos' Joe Krol.

HAMILTON TIGER CATS

1 2 — **1953** — **6** — WINNIPEG BLUE BOMBERS

The favoured Hamilton squad defeated the Bombers, 12-6, in a surprisingly close game. The "play of the game" occurred right at the end when Winnipeg was crowding in for the tying score. Bomber quarterback Jack Jacobs saw two receivers open for a long gain, Tom Casey and Neill Armstrong. Jacobs opted for Casey as did the Hamilton defender Lou Kusserow. Timing his hit perfectly (or illegally if you're from Winnipeg), Kusserow knocked Casey out of the way of the reception, ensuring Hamilton's victory.

EDMONTON ESKIMOS

2 6 — **1954** — **2 5** — MONTREAL ALOUETTES

Edmonton's Jackie "Spaghetti Legs" Parker and Montreal's Sam "the Rifle" Etcheverry would be the football stars of the west and east respectively for the next three years and meet in the Grey Cup each time. This year, Edmonton won with a strong fourth quarter effort, 26-25, and on one of the most controversial turnovers in Grey Cup history. Moving in for the game-clinching score, Montreal had the ball on the Edmonton 10-yard line. Als' halfback Chuck Hunsinger was rolling left when it was apparent he was to be stopped for a loss. Rather than lose ground, Hunsinger either tried to toss the ball away, lateral it, or plain fumbled the ball. Regardless, the ball lay on the ground for what must have seemed like an eternity for Hunsinger. Not sure of the call, an alert Jackie Parker scooped it up and ran 95 yards for the winning touchdown. After the game, a tearful Hunsinger swore he meant to pass the ball and therefore the play should have ended. Referee Hap Shouldice disagreed, however, enabling the Eskimos to capture the Grey Cup.

EDMONTON ESKIMOS

3 4 — **1955** — **1 9** — MONTREAL ALOUETTES

In a game played in Vancouver's new Empire Stadium, this was the first Grey Cup played west of Ontario. And, in the second of three consecutive wins over Montreal, Edmonton won 34-19. There were three stars of the game and, unfortunately for Montreal, two of them were from Edmonton. Normie Kwong of the Eskimos made gains all day and rushed for a record 145 yards and two touchdowns. Meanwhile, the Als' Sam Etcheverry had a splendid day passing for an incredible 508 yards, and still lost the game. As well as Jackie Parker played on offence, directing the solid Eskimo attack all day, he was even better on defence this day, knocking down several key passes.

EDMONTON ESKIMOS

5 0 — **1956** — **2 7** — MONTREAL ALOUETTES

For the third year in a row, the Eskimos were victorious over the Alouettes, this time in a second half runaway, 50-27. In the third quarter, with the game tied, Montreal fumbled a punt on their own 20. Two plays later Edmonton was in the lead for good. Shaken by the sudden turn of events, the Als lost the ball three more times in the next few minutes, two on interceptions and another on a fumble. Each time the Eskimos scored. Then in a last ditch effort to keep the score close, Montreal was stopped on a third down gamble, leading to the final Eskimo touchdown by Jackie Parker. Future Alberta Premier Don Getty quarterbacked the Eskimos solidly all day and scored two touchdowns.

HAMILTON TIGER CATS

3 2 — **1957** — **7** — WINNIPEG BLUE BOMBERS

Hamilton started an 11-year defensive domination of the league, that would see them going to the Grey Cup nine times. In the first of their epic battles with Winnipeg, the Tiger Cats defeated the Blue Bombers, 32-7. Hamilton carried the play all day, but it is not their solid defence which is remembered in the game — it was the act of a spectator. The star of the game was clearly the Ti-Cat's Ray "Bibbles" Bawel, who was superb offensively and defensively all day. Running down the sidelines to an apparent touchdown, Bawel was literally tripped by a spectator who sneaked onto the field. Not knowing what to do, Referee Paul Dojack gave Hamilton the ball half way to the goal line from where the infraction took place. Cookie Gilchrist scored on the next play, but the conclusion of the game was already known. Rumours flew around as to who the "tripper" was for some time, and years later Ontario Justice David Humphrey admitted that as a young lawyer it was he who tripped Bawel and slipped anonymously back into the crowd.

1958 - 1967

WINNIPEG BLUE BOMBERS	1958	HAMILTON TIGER CATS
3 5		2 8

In the first year of the new Canadian Football League (CFL), the Bernie Faloney-led Hamilton team was expected to repeat as champions. Jim Van Pelt of Winnipeg had other plans, though. Van Pelt passed 17 times, ran the ball four times for 28 yards, caught a return pass for 20 yards, and was also responsible for kicking the team's field goals and converts. The turning point may have taken place with eight seconds to go in the first half. Rather than run out the clock, Hamilton tried to punt, but the snap went over punter Cam Fraser's head, into the end zone and into Winnipeg's hands for a go-ahead touchdown. Hamilton was also over-concerned by a call to eject Ralph Goldston when he punched Leo Lewis. The ejection seemed to distract the players and they made costly mistakes. Winnipeg won 35-28.

WINNIPEG BLUE BOMBERS	1959	HAMILTON TIGER CATS
2 1		7

For the third straight time Hamilton and Winnipeg met for the Grey Cup. Hamilton held the lead for most of the day in a defensive first three quarters. It looked early on like Hamilton's Vince Scott had blocked a Bomber punt and fallen on it in the end zone for a touchdown, but he did not have control as he and the ball slid out of the end zone. Hamilton was given a single only, and could not hold on to their slight lead. The pressure put on the Ti-Cat defence from spending so much time on the field began to show, and Winnipeg scored 18 fourth quarter points to win 21-7.

OTTAWA ROUGH RIDERS	1960	EDMONTON ESKIMOS
1 6		6

In a game controlled by the larger Ottawa team, the Rough Riders took the Grey Cup 16-6 over Edmonton and Jackie Parker. The player of the game was Ron Stewart for his repeated timely and long punt returns and his overall solid play. The Riders' Lou Bruce also made a number of timely tackles and jarring hits. One such hit was on a punt. Bruce hit the punt returner on the Eskimo two-yard line so hard and so perfectly timed that the ball was fumbled — and Ottawa's Kaye Vaughan recovered in the end zone for his only career touchdown. The game is also remembered for the fact that it didn't actually end. With 41 seconds still to go, the fans started to spill onto the field. Just when Ottawa quarterback Russ Jackson was to run a play to run out the clock, a fan picked up the ball and started running away with it. The crowd loved it and stormed the field; after which Commissioner Sydney Halter ruled the game over.

WINNIPEG BLUE BOMBERS	1961	HAMILTON TIGER CATS
2 1		1 4

The only overtime Grey Cup of the century was played in Toronto, December 2, 1961, between Winnipeg and Hamilton. The Ti-Cats were in the lead most of the game, starting early with a 90-yard touchdown pass and run from Bernie Faloney to Paul Dekker. Winnipeg made it 7-1 by the end of the first quarter. In the final minute of the first half, Hamilton had the ball on Winnipeg's one-yard line, but couldn't score. Instead, on the last play of the half, Faloney fumbled and Winnipeg recovered, squandering a great chance for Hamilton to control the rest of the game. The Bombers got a field goal to get within three in the third quarter, only to see Hamilton score another touchdown on another long pass and run play. The Bombers got another field goal to end the third quarter 14-7 for Hamilton. Nearing the end of regulation time, Winnipeg's Kenny Ploen lost 20 yards on a crucial play inside the Hamilton 10 yard line. This must have either sparked Winnipeg or made the Ti-Cats overconfident, as on the next play Ploen hit his receiver for a 33-yard gain with the ball inside the five. The Bombers scored on the next play, and converted, sending the game into two 10-minute overtime halves. Only one scoring drive was needed for Winnipeg. Ploen directed an 80-yard march against the tired Hamilton defence in the second overtime half. From the Ti-Cat 20, Ploen looked for Ernie Pitts in the end zone, but finding him covered, took off for the end zone himself to score the only overtime touchdown in the Grey Cup during the century. Winnipeg won, 21-14.

WINNIPEG BLUE BOMBERS	1962	HAMILTON TIGER CATS
2 8		2 7

This classic later became known simply as the Fog Bowl. In a see-saw battle, the Winnipeg Blue Bombers again defeated the Hamilton Tiger Cats to win the only game to take two days and the first to be completed on a Sunday, 28-27. For all intents and purposes this was a tied game. Whenever one team scored, the other would come back to do the same. Hamilton's Garney Henley scored first on a 74-yard gallop through the Bomber defenders, but the Tabbies then missed the single point convert. Winnipeg followed up immediately with an 83-yard Bomber drive and Leo Lewis touchdown. The game continued back and forth all day until the fourth quarter, with Winnipeg hanging on to a one-point lead. By then the fog from Lake Ontario had drifted in and become so thick you could not see the scoreboard. Commissioner Halter decided to postpone the final 10 minutes of play until the next day. Try as they might, the Ti-Cats could not get the final point the next day and ended up on the losing end of the score ... by one point.

HAMILTON TIGER CATS | 2 1 | 1963 | BC LIONS | 1 0

The BC Lions. made their first trip to the Grey Cup, albeit on the losing end of a 21-10 game to the Hamilton Tiger Cats. BC was led by its star, Willie Fleming, who would have to have a great day for his team to win. Early in the second quarter, however, with Hamilton nursing a 7-0 lead on a pass from Bernie Faloney to Willie Bethea, Fleming's day would end. Carrying the ball up the sidelines, Fleming was "kind of" tackled by Hamilton's Gene Ceppetelli. Yet, because he hadn't gone down, and because the whistle hadn't blown, Angelo "King Kong" Mosca of the Ti-Cats also got in on the tackle. Many considered Mosca's tackle a late hit and his devastating blow crippled Fleming, who had to leave for the rest of the game. With him went BC's chances for the Grey Cup. CFL Commissioner Sydney Halter ended the debate, stating that it was a close call and best left to the judgement of the on-field officials who ruled it an innocent hit. The tackle was analyzed for years, and depending on who you were cheering for there were arguments on both sides of the equation. Fleming himself said he couldn't remember the tackle. Mosca repeated that he hadn't heard the whistle and therefore Fleming was fair game. Photos of the play seem to side with Mosca - who would hear about the hit the rest of his CFL career.

BC LIONS | 3 4 | 1964 | HAMILTON TIGER CATS | 2 4

Revenge would be sweet, as BC returned to meet Hamilton in the Grey Cup again. This time BC made sure to bring a full team and not just Willie Fleming, and they outperformed the Tiger Cats to avenge the previous year loss, 34-24. BC's Fleming and Joe Kapp were the offensive stars of the day, giving the Lions an early lead which they never relinquished. The Ti-Cat's Bernie Faloney managed to keep his team in the game for the most part, passing for 239 yards and two touchdowns as well as rushing 57 yards himself. A poorly-attempted lateral to end the third quarter, resulting in a Hamilton fumble and BC recovery, dashed any comeback hopes for Hamilton.

HAMILTON TIGER CATS | 2 2 | 1965 | WINNIPEG BLUE BOMBERS | 1 6

Weather again was a major factor in the "Wind Bowl." A strong wind coming across Lake Ontario did not make ideal playing conditions at Toronto's CNE Stadium for the Grey Cup between Hamilton and Winnipeg. Kicking would prove pivotal to the eventual winners. So strong was the wind at the outset that, starting with the wind at their backs, Hamilton scored a single on the opening kick off. Playing against a ferocious Ti-Cat defence, and not moving the ball at all against the wind, Winnipeg Coach Bud Grant decided it was better to give up three safeties for six points rather than make short punts and face the possibility of Hamilton scoring three touchdowns for 21 and putting the game out of reach. The decision proved crucial as Hamilton ended up winning the game by six points, 22-16. John Barrow of Hamilton's defence was the clear MVP, but it was a Joe Zuger Tiger Cat single that was the game highlight. Zuger watched in horror when a third down, third quarter, snap sailed over his head. Intending only to get the ball and make a quick punt "for something," Zuger retrieved the ball on his own 35 and heaved the punt all the way into Winnipeg's end zone for Hamilton's final point of the game.

SASKATCHEWAN ROUGHRIDERS | 2 9 | 1966 | OTTAWA ROUGH RIDERS | 1 4

Finally, after years of producing top quality football teams from Regina, after appearing in nine Cups, Saskatchewan gave their fans something to cheer about, defeating Ottawa 29-14 to win the Roughriders their first Cup. League MVP Russ Jackson was no match this day for the "Little General" from the west, Ron Lancaster. When Lancaster wasn't throwing or scrambling with the ball for long gains, he was handing off to the most powerful short-yardage running backs of the century, George Reed. Reed ended up with 133 yards rushing. Together, Reed and Lancaster provided little opportunity for Ottawa's offence to be on the field, keeping possession for Saskatchewan time after time.

HAMILTON TIGER CATS | 2 4 | 1967 | SASKATCHEWAN ROUGHRIDERS | 1

In honour of Canada's 100th birthday, the Centennial Year Grey Cup was played in the nation's capital. Try as they might, Saskatchewan's Lancaster and Reed could not duplicate their heroics of the year before and failed to gain much ground at all against a superbly conditioned Hamilton defence. Quarterback Joe Zuger led Hamilton to their first touchdown on the opening drive of the game. On the return possession, it looked like the Roughies were going in for a score, but Ed Buchanan dropped what looked like a sure touchdown pass. They settled for a single. That was it for the Rider offence as they would not get close to scoring again. Meanwhile, the much maligned Zuger executed his play selection ideally, scored one touchdown, threw for another and kicked three singles to deservedly win the game's MVP Award. The Ti-Cats won 24-1.

1968-1977

OTTAWA ROUGH RIDERS		1968	CALGARY STAMPEDERS	
2	4		2	1

Ottawa's Russ Jackson and Vic Washington led the Rough Riders to a close 24-21 Grey Cup victory over the Stampeders. Calgary was missing its top runner and would need to rely on its passing attack, led by Peter Liske. It almost worked. Trailing 14-11 early in the fourth quarter and on their own 30, Ottawa set up in a new formation. Washington was the lone running back and everyone else was spread out wide. On the snap, Jackson lateraled the ball to Washington — who dropped it. What could have been the winning turning point for Calgary turned out to be their worst nightmare as the ball miraculously bounced right back into Washington's arms without him missing a stride. The Calgary defenders hesitated for a second, giving Washington enough space to speed down the field for an 80-yard touchdown run. Ottawa held the lead the rest of the game and won the Cup.

CALGARY STAMPEDERS		1971	TORONTO ARGONAUTS	
1	4		1	1

The first Grey Cup on artificial turf was exciting. Played during a downpour at Vancouver's Empire Stadium, Calgary (which had not won since 1948) and Toronto (not having won since 1952) met for the championship. The swift Argos were led by Joe Theisman and Leon "X-Ray" McQuay and seemed a threat each time they touched the ball. The rain and the staunch Calgary defence, led by middle linebacker Wayne Harris, managed to keep the Argos at bay for most of the game. Then it happened. With just over three minutes left to play, and with Calgary leading 14-11, the Argos Dick Thornton intercepted a Calgary pass at midfield and returned it to the Stamps' 11 yard line. On the next play, Theisman handed the ball to McQuay to run around the left end, a play he was successful on all year. Seeing the play cut-off, McQuay tried to cut back and in the process slipped and, depending on the source, either dropped the ball or landed first and fumbled. In any case, the Stampeders recovered to end the threat. Yet, Calgary couldn't get their offence moving and were forced again to punt the ball to the Argos, giving them one last chance to mount a comeback. But they never got the chance. Calgary punted towards the sidelines and as the ball bounced along the ground, a seemingly alert Harry Abofs of the Argos kicked the ball safely out of bounds. But, according to the rules of the day, any kick out of bounds meant a change of possession — Calgary would get to keep the ball. This time they kept it and ran out the clock to win, 14-11.

OTTAWA ROUGH RIDERS		1969	SASKATCHEWAN ROUGHRIDERS	
2	9		1	1

Russ Jackson's swan song turned out perfectly for him, but not for Saskatchewan. Having announced his retirement before the playoffs, Jackson played superbly all game, masterminding a passing and ground attack that Saskatchewan just could not match. The eastern Rough Riders defeated the western Roughriders, 29-11. Perhaps Jackson's best attribute on this day was his scrambling ability. Time and time again it looked like the Roughrider defenders had Jackson trapped behind the line, only to see the elusive quarterback break free to either throw a pass or run for a first down. He ended the day and his final CFL game with 254 yards passing, four touchdowns and no interceptions, the game's MVP Award and the Grey Cup. He then became a teacher and principal.

MONTREAL ALOUETTES		1970	CALGARY STAMPEDERS	
2	3		1	0

Calgary had defeated Edmonton in the western final on the last play of the game and were expected to carry this momentum with them in the Grey Cup. It didn't work, however, as the third placed Alouettes controlled the game most of the day to win 23-10. One of the more memorable plays was a Moses Denson 10-yard touchdown run in the first quarter for the Als. Seemingly tackled behind the line of scrimmage for a loss by the Stamps' Terry Wilson, Denson refused to go down, broke Wilson's tackle attempt and literally carried two others into the end zone. Als quarterback, Sonny Wade, was at his best in directing the Als to victory.

HAMILTON TIGER CATS		1972	SASKATCHEWAN ROUGHRIDERS	
1	3		1	0

Grey Cups have often been exciting and often the winner was decided with a last minute kick - as was the case in 1972. The first half saw Hamilton gain a 10-point advantage from an Ian Sunter field goal and a controversial Dave Fleming touchdown catch from rookie quarterback Chuck Ealey (Fleming caught his pass deep in the corner of the endzone, and could have been out of bounds). The Roughies came back to score 10 points of their own before the end of the half to tie the game. The second half was a defensive struggle, until late in the game. Saskatchewan made an interception near mid-field and were poised to score, but the Hamilton defence held firm. The Ti-Cats received the subsequent punt at their own 15 with 1:21 left in the fourth quarter. Three consecutive passes to rookie tight end Tony Gabriel put Hamilton in Saskatchewan territory. Ealey then found veteran and that year's CFL MVP Garney Henley open at the Roughie's 26 yard line, where Henley made a superb one-handed catch to put Hamilton in scoring range. With only 13 seconds on the clock, Ti-Cat coach Jerry Williams said to place kicker Ian Sunter "Go in there and do your best; if you miss we'll beat them in overtime." The pressure off, Sunter kicked the ball through the uprights for a 13-10 winning score and the Grey Cup for Hamilton.

OTTAWA ROUGH RIDERS — 1973 — EDMONTON ESKIMOS
22 — 18

Ottawa won an electrifying Eastern Final and Edmonton came from behind in the last minute of the West's Final to reach the Grey Cup in 1973. Both teams came with solid defences and opportunistic offences. Edmonton scored a touchdown on its first possession, after the Rider's Wayne Smith levelled Eskimo quarterback Tom Wilkinson. Not deterred, Ottawa's quarterback Ric Cassatta engineered two scoring drives of his own, one with a third-down gamble, to put Ottawa in the lead at half time. Mid-way through the third quarter Ottawa's Jim Evenson scored on a bull-like three-yard plunge to keep Ottawa in control. The Esks would score again, but not until the last minute to keep the score a respectable 22-18 in favour of Ottawa.

MONTREAL ALOUETTES — 1974 — EDMONTON ESKIMOS
20 — 7

Montreal's vaunted offence made them favourites for the game, but it seemed like a wet and windy Empire Stadium field might make the game interesting. It didn't though. The "Ordinary Superstar" Johnny Rogers and quarterback Sonny Wade led the Als to a relatively easy-looking 20-7 victory over the Eskimos. Wade came in early in the second quarter to replace starter Jimmy Jones and seemed not to notice the wet weather. Rogers, though not registering spectacular statistics in the game, drew lots of attention towards him and away from his teammates to make it that much easier for Wade. Alouette kicker Don Sweet added 14 points from his foot and Junior Ah You and the Als defence controlled the Eskimo offence all day.

EDMONTON ESKIMOS — 1975 — MONTREAL ALOUETTES
9 — 8

It was -25 degrees at game time in Calgary's McMahon Stadium and the play on the field showed how cold it was. No touchdowns were scored as the appropriately named Eskimos defeated the Alouettes 9-8. In a kicking duel, Edmonton's Dave Cutler out-kicked Montreal's Don Sweet to win the Outstanding Canadian Award for the game. Sweet had a chance to put the Als in the lead in the final minute, attempting a very reachable 16-yard field goal. The snap and hold though were not clean and Sweet had to try to kick the ball from its side, not its end. His wide attempt gave the Als a single, which wasn't enough. The Eskimos held on for the win.

OTTAWA ROUGH RIDERS — 1976 — SASKATCHEWAN ROUGHRIDERS
23 — 20

One of the more exciting finishes to a Grey Cup occurred at Toronto's re-configured CNE grounds. The grounds had been changed to adapt to the new Blue Jays baseball team, the field drawn almost sideways to the stands, and the lakeside seats were not the best for seeing the action. Nonetheless, the game was played and the Roughriders, as expected, seemed to be in control for most of the game. Yet, despite Ron Lancaster completing 22 of 35 passes for 263 yards and two touchdowns, they had not put the game away with any timely scoring and seemed to rest on their small lead. Ottawa's quarterback Tom Clements would make the westerners pay for that lapse. Clements, with just over a minute left in the game, engineered the Rough Riders into scoring position and with 20 seconds left in the game heaved a pass deep into the Saskatchewan end zone where a surprisingly open Tony Gabriel made "the catch." The Rough Riders upset the Roughriders 23-20.

CFHOF

MONTREAL ALOUETTES — 1977 — EDMONTON ESKIMOS
41 — 6

This game came to be called the Staple Bowl. The day before the Grey Cup a heavy snowfall fell in Montreal, wreaking havoc on the Olympic Stadium grounds crew and leaving the field soaking overnight. In the early hours of the day of the game, the temperature dropped quickly, literally freezing the field. Realizing footing would be crucial to the game, players on both teams tried everything from broomball shoes to tennis shoes. The Montreal players, led by one inspiring player, found the best solution — putting staples through the bottom of their shoes to gain traction on the frozen artificial turf. Although the Als' Don Sweet kicked a record-setting six field goals in the game, and quarterback Sonny Wade made excellent plays and punted extremely well, it is hard to imagine that they would have had the same opportunity if both teams used staples. Montreal won in a "walk," 41-6. Of course, weather would not have played a factor if the stadium's roof had been finished on schedule in 1976.

CFHOF

1978-1988

EDMONTON ESKIMOS — 2 0 — 1978 — MONTREAL ALOUETTES — 1 3

The Edmonton Eskimo dynasty begins. For five consecutive years the Eskimos would win the west and beat each eastern foe to win the Grey Cup, an unparalleled success in the century. In 1978 the Esks were seeking revenge against the Alouettes, and got it, winning 20-13. The star of the game was Edmonton's portly quarterback, Tom Wilkinson, who kept using short passes and timely rushes to tire the Montreal defence. The highlight of the game was a fake field goal by the Eskimos in the third quarter. Tom Scott received a perfectly timed lateral from the holder Wilkinson, as the kicker Dave Cutler pretended to kick, and ran for a first down. The Esks scored shortly thereafter, never looking back.

EDMONTON ESKIMOS — 1 7 — 1979 — MONTREAL ALOUETTES — 9

For the third year running the Alouettes and Eskimos played for the Grey Cup. And, even though Montreal had the stars, it was Edmonton which won the game, 17-9. The offensive star of the game came from the losing Montreal side. David Green seemed to be the only part of the offence working, but work he did, netting 142 yards rushing on 21 carries and 30 yards on four receptions for the Als. The defensive star also come from Montreal, with Tom Cousineau being the reason the clearly superior Eskimos did not run up a bigger score.

EDMONTON ESKIMOS — 4 8 — 1980 — HAMILTON TIGER CATS — 1 0

Hamilton scratched and clawed its way to get the Grey Cup, and seemed to have little energy left for the actual game. Edmonton put the game out of reach early, getting a field goal and touchdown on their first two drives. Ti-Cat kicker Bernie Ruoff made it close for a bit with two field goals but then the rout was on — with Eskimo quarterback Warren Moon leading the onslaught en route to a 48-10 victory. Moon ended up with 398 yards passing, 71 yards rushing, three touchdowns and a resume with which to go to the NFL and star there the rest of the '80s.

EDMONTON ESKIMOS — 2 6 — 1981 — OTTAWA ROUGH RIDERS — 2 3

The 14-2 Eskimos easily won both the regular season and western playoffs to appear in their fifth straight Grey Cup. The Rough Riders, though, went 5-11 and barely won the eastern playoffs. It was supposed to be a blow-out for Edmonton, and Ottawa entered the game as at least 22-point underdogs. Led by the game's star, J.C. Watts, Ottawa almost pulled off one of the greatest upsets of the century. The Ottawa offence opened the scoring on their first drive and continued to put unprecedented pressure on Edmonton's defence. The Rough Rider defence, meanwhile, was not allowing Warren Moon and the vaunted Edmonton attack any opportunities. Ottawa jumped to a 20-0 lead, with Edmonton only getting a single point in the first half. The Eskimos scored on their first series in the second half, then scored again shortly thereafter following an inopportune turnover for Ottawa on its own three-yard line. The Riders countered with a field goal, but then the Eskimos came back to score another touchdown and tied the game on a two-point convert. Time was short and could have been on Ottawa's side, except for a very controversial (and wrong according to Ottawa fans) offensive pass interference call on a Tony Gabriel reception. What looked like a sure ball-possession play to put the team in scoring position turned into a no-gain and forced the Riders to punt the ball. In the last 30 seconds, the Eskimos then manoeuvred the ball close enough for Dave Cutler to kick the winning field goal as time ran out - the Esks won, 26-23.

EDMONTON ESKIMOS — 3 2 — 1982 — TORONTO ARGONAUTS — 1 6

Showing they were one of the best dynasties in the century, Edmonton won the Grey Cup for a record fifth consecutive time, this time over the Argonauts 32-16. The game's outcome was never really in question, as the Esks were led by game star Warren Moon. Moon ended the game with 319 yards in 21 completions and was the game's leading rusher with 91 yards. On defence, Dave Fennell was as dominating as Moon was on offence and was named the defensive star of the game. Following the game it was announced that Moon and coach Hugh Campbell were leaving Edmonton and heading for the NFL. The dynasty ended.

The Century Plaza Hotel was host to the Grey Cup whenever the games were played in Vancouver.

TORONTO ARGONAUTS 1 8 — 1983 — BC LIONS 1 7

For the rest of Canada it was a beautiful jinx; for Toronto an eternity. After waiting 31 years, the Argos finally won another Grey Cup, coming from behind to beat the Lions to win 18-17. Early in the game BC quarterback Roy Dewalt threw a perfect over-the-shoulder pass to "Swervin Mervin" Fernandez for a 60-yard touchdown. The Argos followed up with their own touchdown drive, ending in a 14-yard pass from Condredge Holloway to Cedric Minter. By the end of the half, though, BC would score 10 more points to lead 17-7. There would be no more scoring for the Lions, though. The game's star didn't even play until the second half, when Joe Barnes replaced Holloway as the Argo quarterback. Barnes changed the way the Argos attacked the Lion defence and threw for 175 yards and ran for another 36 in just that half. The Argos gained momentum and kept BC at bay to win by a point.

WINNIPEG BLUE BOMBERS 4 7 — 1984 — HAMILTON TIGER CATS 1 7

On a frozen field in Edmonton, it was thought that the strength of the Ti-Cat defence could keep the Bombers from scoring. It looked good for Hamilton as they jumped out to a 14-0 lead, and for a moment it appeared as though they could pull off the upset. It didn't happen, though, as Blue Bomber quarterback Tom Clements apparently didn't know the field was slow, and led Winnipeg to an easy 47-17 victory. After the early lead, Hamilton could do no right and Winnipeg no wrong. Clements ended the game with 281 passing yards on 20 completions, and was voted the game's star.

BC LIONS 3 7 — 1985 — HAMILTON TIGER CATS 2 4

Hamilton was looking for revenge for its 1984 defeat, but they wouldn't get it this year, losing 37-24 to a determined and explosive BC team. This time it was the west which started early, as BC jumped into a 13-0 lead. Hamilton did not fall down, though, and came back to take a brief 14-13 lead. BC scored early in the second half and seemed to take control of the game on one play. On his own 44, BC quarterback Roy Dewalt passed towards Jim Sandusky, that might have been incomplete but for Ti-Cat Paul Bennett getting his hand up to block the pass....and deflect it right into Sandusky's waiting arms. Sandusky then raced the rest of the way to the end zone to seal the Lions' Grey Cup victory.

HAMILTON TIGER CATS 3 9 — 1986 — EDMONTON ESKIMOS 1 5

Hamilton got to its third consecutive Grey Cup the hard way. Playing a two-game total-point eastern final, the Ti-Cats were well behind the Argos after the first game. Quarterback Mike Kerrigan, though, led Hamilton's 59-56 total-point comeback victory over Toronto and then carried this momentum right into the Grey Cup. Facing a favoured Edmonton squad, Hamilton never let the Eskimos get on track, forcing turnovers and jumping at every offensive opportunity The 39-15 final score flattered the losing Eskimos. Kerrigan ended with 304 yards passing and two touchdowns and was the game star. Paul Osbaldiston booted 21 points for Hamilton to be named top Canadian.

EDMONTON ESKIMOS 3 8 — 1987 — TORONTO ARGONAUTS 3 6

The 75th Grey Cup game was a thrilling, two-way, high-scoring finale, ending with the Eskimos out-pointing the Argonauts 38-36. It seemed every time one team would score a field goal or a touchdown, the other would come back to match it. Edmonton got the first touchdown on an electrifying 115-yard record return of a missed field goal. The teams then traded field goals until Toronto had its own long touchdown on a 61-yard pass and run play to Gill Fenerty. The scoring kept coming for both sides until Toronto held the lead, 36-35, with about two minutes remaining. Quarterback Danny Barrett led the Lions into scoring position with 45 seconds left, when Jerry Kauric kicked the game-winning field goal.

WINNIPEG BLUE BOMBERS 2 2 — 1988 — BC LIONS 2 1

Since the demise of the Montreal franchise, the Blue Bombers were asked to play in the east division. It took a couple of years, but the inevitable happened; two apparently western teams played for the Grey Cup. BC was back again, and for the second year straight they would provide fans with an exciting, close game. This time, though, the Lions would lose, 22-21, to Winnipeg. The game was close all day, with the turning point being a failed third down gamble by BC in the third quarter. On their own 21, the Lions thought they had a yard to go for a first down, when in fact it was closer to two yards. The quarterback sneak failed, Winnipeg took over on downs and scored to take the lead three plays later. Winnipeg receiver James Murphy was the Bomber star, catching five passes for 165 yards and scoring the only Bomber touchdown.

CFHOF

Toronto Star — J. Maher

1 9 8 9 - 2 0 0 0

SASKATCHEWAN ROUGHRIDERS
4 3

1989

HAMILTON TIGER CATS
4 0

In the greatest, most thrilling, Grey Cup game of the century, the third-place Roughriders defeated Hamilton 43-40. Hamilton took an early lead, then in the second quarter the teams exploded for five touchdowns between them, ending the half with Hamilton in the lead 27-22. The teams exchanged field goals early in the third quarter. With Ti-Cat kicker Paul Osbaldiston back to punt, the intended snap went over his head and into the Ti-Cat end zone, where the Roughies scored a safety. Saskatchewan quickly thereafter followed up with a touchdown to gain momentum. The teams traded field goals again, then Dave Ridgway added another three-pointer to make it 40-33 for the Roughies with less than two minutes to go. Led by Mike Kerrigan, the Ti-Cats marched down the field, using up most of the clock, and engineered a 75-yard touchdown drive, culminated with a third down 15-yard touchdown pass to a spinning, diving, Tony Champion. When Osbaldiston kicked the convert to make it 40-40, it looked like the second overtime in Grey Cup history was about to take place. However, there was just enough time left for the Roughriders to make one more march up the field, enabling Ridgway to kick his 33-yard Grey Cup winning field goal on the last play of the game.

WINNIPEG BLUE BOMBERS
5 0

1990

EDMONTON ESKIMOS
1 1

Going against Canadian geography, Winnipeg again represented the east in the Grey Cup, and demolished Edmonton, 50-11. The Bomber defence, led by linebacker Greg Battle, established its superiority early in the game and kept the Eskimo attack off balance throughout the game. Meanwhile, Winnipeg's quarterback Tom Burgess engineered a solid first half performance, leading the Bombers to a 10-4 half-time lead. Burgess and his teammates could do no wrong in the second half. First Battle returned a 32-yard interception for a touchdown, then Burgess and Perry Tuttle hooked up on a 55-yard pass-and-run, and the rout was on. Battle and Burgess, who ended up with 286 yards passing and three touchdowns, were the joint stars of the game.

TORONTO ARGONAUTS
3 6

1991

CALGARY STAMPEDERS
2 1

Hollywood and Hockey met the Grey Cup this year, with entertainer John Candy and NHL Superstar Wayne Gretzky joining the Argo ownership ranks with Bruce McNall. The new ownership tried to entertain fans as much as play football, and this year they did both. They signed high-profile Raghib "Rocket" Ismail fresh from the US college ranks, and the price paid off in the Grey Cup as "Rocket" would end up with 261 all-purpose yards and a touchdown on an electrifying 87-yard punt return in the third quarter. On the ensuing kick-off, the Stampeders lost whatever chance they may still have had when they fumbled the kickoff and the Argos scored again shortly thereafter. Toronto hung on to win the Cup 36-21. Interestingly, the unofficial star of the game came in a losing cause, as Calgary quarterback Danny Barrett set Grey Cup records with 34 completions in 56 pass attempts.

CALGARY STAMPEDERS
2 4

1992

WINNIPEG BLUE BOMBERS
1 0

In a game featuring two of the greatest quarterbacks to play in the CFL, Calgary's Doug Flutie outgunned Winnipeg's Matt Dunnigan, 24-10. Flutie, the season's league MVP, started things off early for the Stampeders, completing a 40-yard pass on the opening play of the game. Before the end of the first quarter, Flutie connected with Dave Sapunjis for a 35-yard touchdown pass. Flutie's scrambling, passing and running illustrated just how well his style of play was suited to the CFL — he ended up passing for 480 yards and two touchdowns on 33 completions, and rushed for another 20 yards.

EDMONTON ESKIMOS
3 3

1993

WINNIPEG BLUE BOMBERS
2 3

The Eskimos upset the Doug Flutie-led Calgary Stampeders in the western final, and Winnipeg once again emerged from the east to advance to its fourth Grey Cup in six years. The Blue Bombers seemed on the defensive from the start, especially after an early blocked punt was recovered by the Esks on the Winnipeg four-yard line. Edmonton scored on the next play. On the ensuing kickoff, disaster struck again when the Bomber returner fumbled on his own 26 yard line. Four plays later, Eskimo quarterback Damon Allen threw a touchdown pass into the endzone for Jim Sandusky. On the next series of plays, Winnipeg was intercepted, leading to another Eskimo score, this time a Sean Fleming field goal. Very quickly it was 17-0 for the Eskimos. Early in the second quarter, this lead increased to 21-0. Winnipeg got things going by the end of the half to trail 24-10, but it was just too much to make up as Edmonton won the game, 33-23. The Canadian player of the game was Eskimo kicker and UBC graduate Sean Fleming, who booted six field goals, two converts and a single.

BC LIONS
2 6

1994

BALTIMORE FOOTBALL CLUB
2 3

In an effort to generate needed revenue, a new incarnation of the CFL saw American-based franchises vying for Lord Grey's Cup. What seemed like a good idea at first, would turn sour in the next few years. But for this game at least, national pride was on the line as a US-based team challenged for the Cup for the first time ever. The Baltimore Football Club (not named yet, pending permission to use the old Baltimore "Colts" name, ultimately denied) were the favourites, largely as a result of being allowed to play an all-American team, whereas the Lions (and all Canadian-based teams) were still required to use 18 Canadian players on their roster. It all made for a glorious us-vs.-them grudge match, and resulted in one of the most-watched Grey Cups of all time. The game itself was close throughout, with both clubs exchanging the lead several times. After Baltimore had tied the score late in the fourth quarter, BC marched down the field to the Baltimore 37. From there it was assumed that Vancouver native and the century's CFL scoring leader, Lui Passaglia, would kick the go-ahead field goal. But he missed, sending a shiver across the Lions' bench, and likely across all of Canada. Baltimore, though, was still hemmed in its own end and two plays later was forced to punt the ball back to the Lions. Once again, BC moved the ball into field goal range, and on the last play of the game, Passaglia had the opportunity to redeem his just-missed scoring chance. The kick was good, and BC won 26-23.

Canada

BALTIMORE STALLIONS **3 7** | **1995** | **CALGARY STAMPEDERS** **2 0**

This year it happened. The newly-named Stallions faced the Stampeders in an historic match - for the only time in the century the Grey Cup was awarded to a team based outside of Canada as the Stallions defeated the Stampeders, 37-20. Doug Flutie and Jeff Garcia, each destined to return to the NFL, shared the quarterback duties for Calgary in the Grey Cup game. Neither could generate enough offence against a powerful Stallions squad. Tracy Ham on the other hand, could. The Baltimore pivot would pass for 213 yards and run for 24 en route to being named the game's MVP.

TORONTO ARGONAUTS **4 3** | **1996** | **EDMONTON ESKIMOS** **3 7**

Baltimore did not really get a chance to defend its Grey Cup. Other US-based clubs in the CFL folded and the return of the NFL to Baltimore encouraged the Stallions to relocate, essentially reviving the defunct Montreal Alouettes franchise. But it was the Argonauts who would represent the east, riding the arm of the newly-acquired Doug Flutie through the regular season and the playoffs to face Danny McManus and the Eskimos in Hamilton. A snowstorm the day of the game blanketed the field white and wet by game time, leading many to think the game would bc low scoring. It was anything but. Edmonton started the scoring with a safety and a thrilling, 65-yard, shoestring catch by Eddie Brown to take an early 9-0 lead. Not to be outdone, the Argos' Jimmy "the Jet" Cunningham then returned a punt 80 yards to narrow the score. The two teams then traded touchdown drives and field goals, with Toronto adding another touchdown late in the first half to lead 27-23. The Argos scored first in the third quarter and seemed to put the game out of reach with a 40-yard interception for a touchdown off a tipped McManus pass. The Eskimos did not quit, though, and staged a mini-comeback to narrow the score. But it was not enough, as the Argos won the game and Cup, 43-37.

TORONTO ARGONAUTS **4 7** | **1997** | **SASKATCHEWAN ROUGHRIDERS** **2 3**

Toronto's Doug Flutie passed for 352 yards, threw for three touchdowns, ran for another, won his third Grey Cup MVP Award, and led the Argonauts to their second straight Cup victory, this time 47-23 over Saskatchewan. The Argos looked in control for most of the game, while the Roughies, who had finished third in the west, looked happy to be in the game at all. The highlight of the game may have been Adrian Smith's 95-yard kickoff return to start the second half, effectively killing any dreams the Roughies had of making a comeback in the game. Paul Massotti caught six passes for 102 yards and was named top Canadian in the game. Massotti also received the MVP car in a very generous offer from Flutie.

CALGARY STAMPEDERS **2 6** | **1998** | **HAMILTON TIGER CATS** **2 4**

There is nothing like last minute heroics to win a national championship, or to lose, and that's how the '98 Grey Cup Game ended. Hamilton scored a touchdown late in the fourth quarter to lead by one point, 24-23. With just enough time to get the ball back and try to get in scoring position, the Stampeders did just that. Then, with no time left on the clock, Calgary's Mark McLoughlin booted a 35-yard field goal to win the Cup 26-24. For the Ti-Cats it was heartbreaking, and reminiscent of their own last-second victory of just the week before over Montreal. It was the Stamps second victory in four years, this time led by quarterback Jeff Garcia and receiver Allan Pitts.

HAMILTON TIGER CATS **3 2** | **1999** | **CALGARY STAMPEDERS** **2 1**

Revenge is sweet. Redeeming their loss to Calgary the year before, Hamilton's Danny McManus and Darren Flutie showed why they were such a feared passing tandem. McManus was the game MVP and completed 22 passes for 347 yards on the day, throwing two touchdown passes, each to Flutie. Flutie ended with six receptions and 109 yards in addition to his two touchdowns. Although the game was never out of reach for Calgary, Hamilton seemed to control the game from the outset and were never seriously threatened for the lead after the second quarter. Paul Osbaldiston booted three field goals, three converts and two singles for the Tabbies, en route to a 32-21 victory.

BC LIONS **2 8** | **2000** | **MONTREAL ALOUETTES** **2 6**

Fittingly, the final Grey Cup of the century witnessed a classic finish, with the BC Lions outlasting the Montreal Alouettes, 28-26. And, even though it may not have been Lui Passaglia's greatest game, it turned out to be his greatest CFL moment. The 46-year old living legend kicked balls for the Lions for 25 years, and had become the CFL's leading scorer in the century. He served notice that he would retire after the game, regardless of the outcome. Then, with 1:25 left on the clock, Passaglia's 29-yard field goal proved to be the winning points for the Lions' fourth Grey Cup win. The kick made up for a dreadful first half, when Lui hit just one of four attempts. "It made it interesting, but we also knew how to finish it lately, so that's the key," said Passaglia in a quote that summed up both his game and his career. The Lions had overcome a sluggish start to the season and a coaching change en route to become the first team in CFL history to win the Cup after finishing the regular season with a losing record (8-10). Running back Robert Drummond was the game's MVP, and Sean Millington the top Canadian, collectively running 260 yards and scoring three touchdowns.

The Grey Cup
Champions 1909-2000

Year	Field	Game City	Champion	Score	Finalist	Score
1909	Rosedale Field	Toronto	University of Toronto	26	Parkdale Canoe Club	6
1910	Hamilton Cricket Grounds	Hamilton	University of Toronto	16	Hamilton Tigers	7
1911	Varsity Stadium	Toronto	University of Toronto	14	Toronto Argonauts	7
1912	Hamilton Cricket Grounds	Hamilton	Hamilton Alerts	11	Toronto Argonauts	4
1913	Hamilton Cricket Grounds	Hamilton	Hamilton Tigers	44	Parkdale Canoe Club	2
1914	Varsity Stadium	Toronto	Toronto Argonauts	14	University of Toronto	2
1915	Varsity Stadium	Toronto	Hamilton Tigers	13	Toronto Rowing and Athletic Association	7
1916-1919 No Games						
1920	Varsity Stadium	Toronto	University of Toronto	16	Toronto Argonauts	3
1921	Varsity Stadium	Toronto	Toronto Argonauts	23	Edmonton Eskimos	0
1922	Richardson Stadium	Kingston	Queen's University	13	Edmonton Elks	1
1923	Varsity Stadium	Toronto	Queen's University	54	Regina Roughriders	0
1924	Varsity Stadium	Toronto	Queen's University	11	Balmy Beach	3
1925	Lansdowne Park	Ottawa	Ottawa Senators	24	Winnipeg Tammany Tigers	1
1926	Varsity Stadium	Toronto	Ottawa Senators	10	University of Toronto	7
1927	Varsity Stadium	Toronto	Balmy Beach	9	Hamilton Tigers	6
1928	AAA Grounds	Hamilton	Hamilton Tigers	30	Regina Roughriders	0
1929	AAA Grounds	Hamilton	Hamilton Tigers	14	Regina Roughriders	3
1930	Varsity Stadium	Toronto	Balmy Beach	11	Regina Roughriders	6
1931	Molson Stadium	Montreal	Montreal A.A.A. (Winged Wheelers)	22	Regina Roughriders	0
1932	AAA Grounds	Hamilton	Hamilton Tigers	25	Regina Roughriders	6
1933	Davis Field	Sarnia	Toronto Argonauts	4	Sarnia Imperials	3
1934	Varsity Stadium	Toronto	Sarnia Imperials	20	Regina Roughriders	12
1935	AAA Grounds	Hamilton	Winnipeg 'Pegs	18	Hamilton Tigers	12
1936	Varsity Stadium	Toronto	Sarnia Imperials	26	Ottawa Rough Riders	20
1937	Varsity Stadium	Toronto	Toronto Argonauts	4	Winnipeg Blue Bombers	3
1938	Varsity Stadium	Toronto	Toronto Argonauts	30	Winnipeg Blue Bombers	7
1939	Lansdowne Park	Ottawa	Winnipeg Blue Bombers	8	Ottawa Rough Riders	7
1940	Varsity Stadium	Toronto	Ottawa Rough Riders	8	Balmy Beach	2
	Lansdowne Park	Ottawa	Ottawa Rough Riders	12	Balmy Beach	5
1941	Varsity Stadium	Toronto	Winnipeg Blue Bombers	18	Ottawa Rough Riders	16
1942	Varsity Stadium	Toronto	Toronto RCAF Hurricanes	8	Winnipeg RCAF Bombers	5
1943	Varsity Stadium	Toronto	Hamilton Flying Wildcats	23	Winnipeg RCAF Bombers	14
1944	Civic Stadium	Hamilton	Montreal St. H-D Navy Combines	7	Hamilton Wildcats	6
1945	Varsity Stadium	Toronto	Toronto Argonauts	35	Winnipeg Blue Bombers	0
1946	Varsity Stadium	Toronto	Toronto Argonauts	28	Winnipeg Blue Bombers	6
1947	Varsity Stadium	Toronto	Toronto Argonauts	10	Winnipeg Blue Bombers	9
1948	Varsity Stadium	Toronto	Calgary Stampeders	12	Ottawa Rough Riders	7
1949	Varsity Stadium	Toronto	Montreal Alouettes	28	Calgary Stampeders	15
1950	Varsity Stadium	Toronto	Toronto Argonauts	13	Winnipeg Blue Bombers	0
1951	Varsity Stadium	Toronto	Ottawa Rough Riders	21	Saskatchewan Roughriders	14
1952	Varsity Stadium	Toronto	Toronto Argonauts	21	Edmonton Eskimos	11
1953	Varsity Stadium	Toronto	Hamilton Tiger Cats	12	Winnipeg Blue Bombers	6
1954	Varsity Stadium	Toronto	Edmonton Eskimos	26	Montreal Alouettes	25
1955	Empire Stadium	Vancouver	Edmonton Eskimos	34	Montreal Alouettes	19
1956	Varsity Stadium	Toronto	Edmonton Eskimos	50	Montreal Alouettes	27

1957	Varsity Stadium	Toronto	Hamilton Tiger Cats	32	Winnipeg Blue Bombers	7
1958	Empire Stadium	Vancouver	Winnipeg Blue Bombers	35	Hamilton Tiger Cats	28
1959	Exhibition Stadium	Toronto	Winnipeg Blue Bombers	21	Hamilton Tiger Cats	7
1960	Empire Stadium	Vancouver	Ottawa Rough Riders	16	Edmonton Eskimos	6
1961	Exhibition Stadium	Toronto	Winnipeg Blue Bombers	21	Hamilton Tiger Cats	14
1962	Exhibition Stadium	Toronto	Winnipeg Blue Bombers	28	Hamilton Tiger Cats	27
1963	Empire Stadium	Vancouver	Hamilton Tiger Cats	21	BC Lions	10
1964	Exhibition Stadium	Toronto	BC Lions	34	Hamilton Tiger Cats	24
1965	Exhibition Stadium	Toronto	Hamilton Tiger Cats	22	Winnipeg Blue Bombers	16
1966	Empire Stadium	Vancouver	Saskatchewan Roughriders	29	Ottawa Rough Riders	14
1967	Lansdowne Park	Ottawa	Hamilton Tiger Cats	24	Saskatchewan Roughriders	1
1968	Exhibition Stadium	Toronto	Ottawa Rough Riders	24	Calgary Stampeders	21
1969	Autostade	Montreal	Ottawa Rough Riders	29	Saskatchewan Roughriders	11
1970	Exhibition Stadium	Toronto	Montreal Alouettes	23	Calgary Stampeders	10
1971	Empire Stadium	Vancouver	Calgary Stampeders	14	Toronto Argonauts	11
1972	Ivor Wynne Stadium	Hamilton	Hamilton Tiger Cats	13	Saskatchewan Roughriders	10
1973	Exhibition Stadium	Toronto	Ottawa Rough Riders	22	Edmonton Eskimos	18
1974	Empire Stadium	Vancouver	Montreal Alouettes	20	Edmonton Eskimos	7
1975	McMahon Stadium	Calgary	Edmonton Eskimos	9	Montreal Alouettes	8
1976	Exhibition Stadium	Toronto	Ottawa Rough Riders	23	Saskatchewan Roughriders	20
1977	Olympic Stadium	Montreal	Montreal Alouettes	41	Edmonton Eskimos	6
1978	Exhibition Stadium	Toronto	Edmonton Eskimos	20	Montreal Alouettes	13
1979	Olympic Stadium	Montreal	Edmonton Eskimos	17	Montreal Alouettes	9
1980	Exhibition Stadium	Toronto	Edmonton Eskimos	48	Hamilton Tiger Cats	10
1981	Olympic Stadium	Montreal	Edmonton Eskimos	26	Ottawa Rough Riders	23
1982	Exhibition Stadium	Toronto	Edmonton Eskimos	32	Toronto Argonauts	16
1983	BC Place	Vancouver	Toronto Argonauts	18	BC Lions	17
1984	Commonwealth Stadium	Edmonton	Winnipeg Blue Bombers	47	Hamilton Tiger Cats	17
1985	Olympic Stadium	Montreal	BC Lions	37	Hamilton Tiger Cats	24
1986	BC Place	Vancouver	Hamilton Tiger Cats	39	Edmonton Eskimos	15
1987	BC Place	Vancouver	Edmonton Eskimos	38	Toronto Argonauts	36
1988	Lansdowne Park	Ottawa	Winnipeg Blue Bombers	22	BC Lions	21
1989	SkyDome	Toronto	Saskatchewan Roughriders	43	Hamilton Tiger Cats	40
1990	BC Place	Vancouver	Winnipeg Blue Bombers	50	Edmonton Eskimos	11
1991	Winnipeg Stadium	Winnipeg	Toronto Argonauts	36	Calgary Stampeders	21
1992	SkyDome	Toronto	Calgary Stampeders	24	Winnipeg Blue Bombers	10
1993	McMahon Stadium	Calgary	Edmonton Eskimos	33	Winnipeg Blue Bombers	23
1994	BC Place	Vancouver	BC Lions	26	Baltimore	23
1995	Taylor Field	Regina	Baltimore Stallions	37	Calgary Stampeders	20
1996	Ivor Wynne Stadium	Hamilton	Toronto Argonauts	43	Edmonton Eskimos	37
1997	Commonwealth Stadium	Edmonton	Toronto Argonauts	47	Saskatchewan Roughriders	23
1998	Winnipeg Stadium	Winnipeg	Calgary Stampeders	26	Hamilton Tiger Cats	24
1999	BC Place	Vancouver	Hamilton Tiger Cats	32	Hamilton Tiger Cats	21
2000	McMahon Stadium	Calgary	BC Lions	28	Montreal Allouettes	26

A Century of Stanley Cups

1899-1913

The Challenge Series Years

1899-1900   MONTREAL SHAMROCKS over WINNIPEG VICTORIAS

The century began with goal "nets" in place for the first time, replacing two sticks stuck in the ice. The Montreal Shamrocks defeated the challengers from Winnipeg 2 games to 1. The emergence of the professional hockey player was front and centre as the westerners were alleged to be enticing players with cash incentives. The Shamrocks later outscored a team challenging from Halifax to keep the Cup.

1900-1901   WINNIPEG VICTORIAS over MONTREAL SHAMROCKS

Winnipeg gained a measure of revenge from the previous year's defeat as they triumphed over the Shamrocks in two straight games. While Winnipeg was crowned the Stanley Cup Champion, they may not have been the best team in Canada in 1901. The Ottawa Silver Seven stormed through their regular season without a defeat and, considering that honour enough, did not offer a challenge for the Cup. Winnipeg would also beat a challenge from Toronto to keep the Cup in the west.

1901-1902   MONTREAL A.A.A. over WINNIPEG VICTORIAS

Montreal triumphed in three games versus the rugged westerners. After winning the first game and tying up the second game late in the third period to force overtime, the Montrealers clearly had momentum on their side. However it was a Saturday, and as midnight struck the mayor of Westmount halted the game to observe the Sabbath. Hockey was not yet the official religion of Quebec. The Montreal A.A.A., also known as the "Winged Wheelers," would beat Winnipeg again early in 1903 to retain the Cup.

1902-1903   OTTAWA SILVER SEVEN over RAT PORTAGE (KENORA)

As the winners of the Canadian Amateur Hockey League (CAHL) title, Ottawa beat out Montreal for the rights to play the Cup and was forced to play a challenge series against Rat Portage just two months after Montreal had last won the Cup. The games, played in mid March, were poorly attended and justifiably so; the only excitement on the slush that passed for the playing surface was when the puck was lost through a hole in the ice.

1903-1904   OTTAWA SILVER SEVEN over NUMEROUS CHALLENGERS

Winners of the Cup in March 1903, the Ottawa "Silver Seven" would win nine consecutive challenges for the Cup, and keep it in their possession until December 1906. This year they again beat Rat Portage as well as the Montreal Victorias. Ottawa and Montreal then forfeited a series because the teams could not agree on where to play the games. Ottawa then beat a team from Brandon to keep the Cup in the nation's Capital.

1904-1905   OTTAWA SILVER SEVEN over DAWSON CITY

This series was witness to many records that will probably never be broken. It saw the youngest goalie, 17-year-old Albert Forrest from Trois Rivières as well as the most goals scored by an individual in one game. Frank McGee scored 14 goals in Game 2 of the series after the Dawson City team proclaimed him as "not so hot" after only scoring one goal in Game 1. Ottawa easily beat the challengers from the North.

1905-1906   OTTAWA SILVER SEVEN over RAT PORTAGE THISTLES

This series was played in March, just two months after the Dawson City series was contested. The Silver Seven battered their smaller, quicker opponents from Northern Ontario. One player from Rat Portage, Bill McGimsie, succumbed to exhaustion and injury and lay prone along the goal line. For his efforts McGimsie received a five-minute penalty for goal obstruction. Ottawa kept the Cup then, but lost it to the Montreal Wanderers later in 1906.

1906-1907   MONTREAL WANDERERS over OTTAWA SILVER SEVEN
KENORA THISTLES over MONTREAL WANDERERS
MONTREAL WANDERERS over KENORA THISTLES
MONTREAL over NEW GLASGOW

The Wanderers ended the reign of the Ottawa team with a thrilling win, which saw the emergence of the Silver Fox, Lester Patrick as a genuine star. In the space of two months the Montreal team beat Ottawa, lost a challenge to Kenora and then regained the Cup in a rematch. Montreal also beat challengers from New Glasgow that year.

1907-1908 MONTREAL WANDERERS over
OTTAWA, WINNIPEG & TORONTO

The Montreal team defeated challengers from Ottawa and Winnipeg before facing a Toronto team and their young star player, Newsy Lalonde. Even with the future Hall-of-Famer, Toronto could not defeat the Wanderers, losing the one-game challenge 6-4.

1908 MONTREAL WANDERERS over
EDMONTON

Montreal defended the Cup for the fourth time in the calendar year. The series was truly the end of an era as the Wanderers beat an Edmonton team that featured only a single player who had actually played for the Edmonton club during the regular season. Buying players became the norm and assembling the best team money could buy could attain the Stanley Cup.

1908-1909 OTTAWA SENATORS over MONTREAL, GALT,
EDMONTON & ALMOST WINNIPEG

Because of a rule change, the winners of the ECHA (Eastern Canada Hockey Association) would automatically receive the Cup this year. Ottawa won the Cup with its 10-2 regular season record bettering Montreal's 9-3 record. Ottawa then defeated Galt (15-4) in an "exhibition." Winnipeg hoped to challenge, but arrangements couldn't be made in time. Ottawa then faced Edmonton and won 21-11 in a total-goal series to keep the Cup at the end of the season.

1909-1910 MONTREAL WANDERERS over
BERLIN (KITCHENER)

The establishment of the National Hockey Association (NHA - the successor to the CAHL and the precursor of the NHL), led to the Sens giving up the Cup to the Montreal Wanderers, who won the inaugural NHA regular season, and, at the time, the Stanley Cup. Montreal successfully defended against Berlin of the Ontario League, 7-3 in a one game challenge.

1910-1911 OTTAWA SENATORS over
PORT ARTHUR

The Ottawa team won the NHA and with it the Stanley Cup, defending their title against challenges from Galt (of the Ontario Professional Hockey League) and Port Arthur (the winners of the newly formed New Ontario League). This year saw the game change from two halves to the current three-period playing format.

1911-1912 QUEBEC BULLDOGS over
MONCTON VICTORIAS

The Quebec team were winners of the NHA, the League's new O'Brien Trophy and the Stanley Cup. In March, the Maritime Champions from Moncton challenged Quebec for the Stanley Cup, only to lose both games as the Bulldogs' Jack McDonald scored 9 goals.

1912-1913 QUEBEC BULLDOGS over
SYDNEY (But not Victoria)

Quebec took first place in the NHA and with this title the Cup, as Joe Malone led the league with 43 goals in 20 games. Sydney challenged for the Cup, and Malone again exploded, scoring 9 goals in Game 1 en route to an easy 20-5 two-game total score victory. The Bulldogs subsequently lost to a team from Victoria of the newly formed Pacific Coast Hockey Association, 2 games to 1. As it was only an "exhibition series," the Bulldogs retained the Cup.

1913-1926

The East vs. West Challenges

HHOF

1913-1914 TORONTO BLUESHIRTS over MONTREAL & VICTORIA

The outbreak of war overshadowed Toronto winning the NHA title over the Montreal Canadiens, 6-2, in a total-goals playoff. The NHA reached an agreement with the PCHA on a Stanley Cup series format. Toronto won the subsequent defence of the Cup in three straight games in the best-of-five series over Victoria, the Pacific Coast champions.

1914-1915 VANCOUVER MILLIONAIRES over OTTAWA SENATORS

After winning a playoff round against the Wanderers, the Sens travelled west to face the Millionaires on artificial ice. It was a meeting of two teams who played two different sets of rules: the western teams used seven men while eastern rules called for six players. It didn't matter to Vancouver as they won the Cup in convincing fashion, winning in three straight games and outscoring Ottawa 26 to 8.

1915-1916 MONTREAL CANADIENS over PORTLAND ROSEBUDS

This series marked the first time an American-based team contested for the Cup. The Rosebuds almost attained the unthinkable but for the heroics of the Canadiens' goalkeeper, Georges Vezina, nicknamed the "Chicoutimi Cucumber" for his coolness under pressure. Vezina backstopped Montreal to a hard fought five-game series win and the first of many Stanley Cups this century for the Canadiens.

1916-1917 SEATTLE METROPOLITANS over MONTREAL CANADIENS

World War I depleted the rosters of many teams. The unthinkable did occur in 1917 as the Seattle-based team, the PCHA Champions, defeated defending Stanley Cup and NHA Champions Montreal in four games.

1917-1918 TORONTO ARENAS over MONTREAL CANADIENS & SEATTLE

The NHA was dissolved and the National Hockey League (NHL) emerged, purely to rid the NHA of Toronto Blueshirts' owner, the abrasive Teddy Livingstone. The new League saw a new team in Toronto, the Arenas, beat the Canadiens, 10-7 in two games. Montreal's Joe Malone scored 44 goals in a 22 game regular season, thus becoming the League's first all-time leader in goals scored. On March 30, Toronto became the first NHL Stanley Cup Champion, defeating Seattle 3 games to 2.

1918-1919 NO DECISION

The Stanley Cup Finals, a gruelling event at the best of times, was compounded by the influenza epidemic sweeping North America. The series was tied at two games each with one tie, when five Canadien players and Manager George Kennedy were hospitalized. Joe Hall of Montreal succumbed to the disease five days later, on April 5. The series was never finished.

1919-1920 OTTAWA SENATORS over SEATTLE METROPOLITANS

Ottawa breezed through the NHL's regular season and faced PCHA Champion Seattle in the finals. After three games on outdoor slush the series was transferred to Toronto, the only indoor arena in Eastern Canada at the time. No matter, the Sens took the Cup in five games.

1920-1921 OTTAWA SENATORS over VANCOUVER MILLIONAIRES

Ottawa travelled west to Vancouver and triumphed in a hard fought five game series. Jack Darragh scored the tying and winning goals in Game 5 and promptly retired, going out on top of the world.

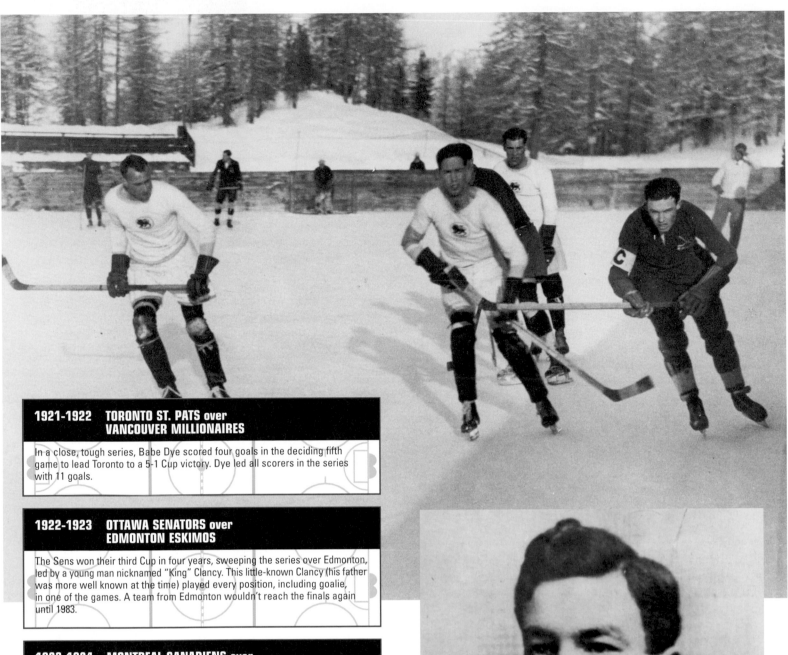

1921-1922 TORONTO ST. PATS over VANCOUVER MILLIONAIRES

In a close, tough series, Babe Dye scored four goals in the deciding fifth game to lead Toronto to a 5-1 Cup victory. Dye led all scorers in the series with 11 goals.

1922-1923 OTTAWA SENATORS over EDMONTON ESKIMOS

The Sens won their third Cup in four years, sweeping the series over Edmonton, led by a young man nicknamed "King" Clancy. This little-known Clancy (his father was more well known at the time) played every position, including goalie, in one of the games. A team from Edmonton wouldn't reach the finals again until 1983.

1923-1924 MONTREAL CANADIENS over CALGARY TIGERS

The series featured a Canadiens rookie from Stratford, Ontario, named Howie Morenz. The "Stratford Streak," Morenz was enticed to play for the Habs by owner Leo Dandurand, who went to Morenz's house and put his year's salary in cash on the table. It paid off as Morenz led Montreal to victories over the Vancouver and Calgary, scoring six goals in seven games.

1924-1925 VICTORIA COUGARS over MONTREAL CANADIENS

Victoria of the new WCHL became the last club outside the NHL to win the Cup by defeating the NHL's Montreal Canadiens 3 games to 1. Hamilton was supposed to have been the NHL representative, but its players went on strike after signing contracts for 22 games and playing 30, so Montreal took their place. It marked the end of the Hamilton Tigers franchise, which was sold to become the New York Americans. Hamilton did not get another team in the century.

1925-1926 MONTREAL MAROONS over VICTORIA COUGARS

The Maroons won the Cup on the strength of Nels Stewart's six goals in four games. This marked the last time for East-West challenges as the Western League folded after the Cup playoffs. Dunc Munro of Montreal became the first player to have won the Memorial, Allan and Stanley Cups.

HHOF

1926-2000

The NHL Takes Over

1926-1927 OTTAWA SENATORS over BOSTON BRUINS

The NHL assumed exclusive control of the Stanley Cup after the 1926 season and the demise of the Western Hockey League (successor to the WCHA). The NHL was now comprised of a Canadian and an American Division, each with five teams. The winners of each national division played off for the Cup. Ottawa defeated Boston in four games to claim their final Stanley Cup of the century. The series included the final tie game in Stanley Cup play; sudden-death overtime started in 1927-28.

1927-1928 NEW YORK RANGERS over MONTREAL MAROONS

The Rangers were led to the Cup by a most unlikely hero. At the ripe age of 44, Coach Lester Patrick suited up in goal after an injury to starter Lorne Chabot and allowed only one goal in two periods of work. The Rangers won their first Cup 3 games to 2.

1928-1929 BOSTON BRUINS over NEW YORK RANGERS

A new format saw cross-divisional match-ups in the playoffs. This became the year of the goalie as George Hainsworth of the Montreal Canadiens had 22 shutouts in the 44-game regular season. Not to be outdone, Boston goalie, Cecil "Tiny" Thompson, had three shutouts in five playoff games to lead the Bruins to the Stanley Cup.

1929-1930 MONTREAL CANADIENS over BOSTON BRUINS

The Canadiens defeated a powerful Boston club that lost only five times in the regular season and never back-to-back games. Even though finishing the season 26 points behind, Montreal defeated the Bruins in two straight when it counted most, with Howie Morenz scoring the winning goal.

1930-1931 MONTREAL CANADIENS over CHICAGO BLACKHAWKS

Montreal won its second straight Cup. In the semi-final against Boston, Bruins' coach Art Ross pulled a stunt not seen before, pulling his goalie to try to even the score for the Bruins. The Canadiens, dumbfounded, nonetheless held off the hard-charging Bruin attack and went on to defeat Chicago in the final.

1931-1932 TORONTO MAPLE LEAFS over NEW YORK RANGERS

The Leafs, led by the famous "Kid Line" of Busher Jackson, Charlie Conacher and Joe Primeau, won the Cup in dominant fashion. Three straight wins over the New York Rangers and the Cup was brought to Conn Smythe's Maple Leaf Gardens in its first year of existence. Interestingly, New York's games were moved to Boston because the circus had temporarily taken over the Rangers home in Madison Square Garden.

1932-1933 NEW YORK RANGERS over TORONTO MAPLE LEAFS

The Maple Leafs were no match for the powerful Rangers, especially after having won the right to challenge for the Cup only hours before the first game of the finals. The deciding game between Toronto and Boston had gone into six overtime periods, ending only when Toronto sub Ken Doraty finally beat the Bruins' "Tiny" Thompson. The Rangers won the finals easily, with Bill Cook getting the first ever overtime Cup-winning goal.

1933-1934 CHICAGO BLACKHAWKS over DETROIT RED WINGS

Chicago was led by its future Hall-of-Fame goaltender, Chuck Gardiner. Gardiner lost only one game out of eight playoff games that year, including posting a shutout in the double-overtime final game. Tragically, just two months after winning the Cup, Gardiner died in Winnipeg after suffering from a chronic tonsil infection.

1934-1935 MONTREAL MAROONS over TORONTO MAPLE LEAFS

The Toronto Maple Leafs were led by King Clancy and the incomparable "Kid Line." To make matters worse for Montreal, the Leafs had acquired three-time Vezina winner George Hainsworth to work the pipes. Toronto was virtually guaranteed the Cup, but someone forgot to tell Alex Connell. The Maroons goalie was almost unbeatable and the Maroons triumphed in three straight games, after which Connell left the game for good.

1935-1936 DETROIT RED WINGS over TORONTO MAPLE LEAFS

Detroit captured the Cup in four games (3-1) over the Toronto Maple Leafs. The Red Wings appeared to be a team of destiny after winning the longest playoff game in the Century, 177 minutes, in the semi-finals over the Montreal Maroons.

1936-1937 DETROIT RED WINGS over NEW YORK RANGERS

Detroit won its second straight Cup, defeating the Rangers 3 games to 2. It did not look good for the Red Wings early on as their starting goalie, Normie Smith, was injured in the opening game. Back-up goalie Earl Robertson entered the series and stood on his head, recording two shutouts en route to victory.

1937-1938 CHICAGO BLACKHAWKS over TORONTO MAPLE LEAFS

The Blackhawks did not look like champions when the playoffs began, finishing the regular season 30 points behind the Bruins. At the outset of the finals in Toronto, the Hawks' starting goalie, Mike Karakas, broke his toe and could not play. Their backup, Paul Goodman, was nowhere to be found. Alfie Moore, a minor leaguer living in Toronto and unable to get a ticket to the game, was seated in a nearby pub. Quickly pressed into service, Moore defeated the Leafs 3-1 and the Hawks went on to win the Cup in four games with their regular goalie, Karakas, back in net.

1938-1939 BOSTON BRUINS over TORONTO MAPLE LEAFS

Boston won their first Cup in 10 years riding the hot goaltending of rookie Frank Brimsek. They were a team of destiny as they won five overtime games in the semi-finals and finals. Mel "Sudden Death" Hill scored three overtime winners, including the semi-final clincher. The Bruins beat the Leafs 4-1 in the final.

1939-1940 NEW YORK RANGERS over TORONTO MAPLE LEAFS

The Rangers won their third Cup and their final one for the next 54 years. The Cup Final featured three overtime games, all won by the Rangers, including the deciding game won by a Bryan Hextall goal. The final four games were played in Toronto; the circus again taking over the Rangers' Madison Square Garden home.

Montreal looked poised to win a second straight title until Maurice Richard, frustrated by the constant barrage of sticks, shoulders and elbows from the Leafs, took a match penalty and was suspended for one game. Toronto took control of the series and won in six games.

1947-1948 TORONTO MAPLE LEAFS over DETROIT RED WINGS

The Leafs won their second Cup of three in a row by sweeping the Detroit Red Wings. Detroit's vaunted Production Line of Sid Abel, Ted Lindsay and Gordie Howe was limited to one point in the series by a stifling Leafs defence. The Leafs' Syl Apps retired after hoisting the Cup.

1940-1941 BOSTON BRUINS over DETROIT RED WINGS

The Bruins completed a four-game sweep of the Detroit Red Wings, after defeating the Maple Leafs in seven tight games in the semi-finals. The Boston fans were ecstatic, especially with the play of outstanding goalie Frank Brimsek. Yet the supportive Bruins fans would have to wait 29 seasons to cheer another Stanley Cup championship team from Beantown.

1948-1949 TORONTO MAPLE LEAFS over DETROIT RED WINGS

The Leafs became the first NHL team to win three straight Cups, as they rebounded from a fourth-place regular season finish to lose only one game en route to the title.

1941-1942 TORONTO MAPLE LEAFS over DETROIT RED WINGS

Things did not look good for the Leafs as they lost the first three games of the series to Detroit. Accomplishing the unthinkable, the Leafs bounced back and won the next four. Stories of this comeback would echo in dressing rooms as coaches exhorted their teams to keep working hard and not give up and "Remember the '42 Leafs!"

1949-1950 DETROIT RED WINGS over NEW YORK RANGERS

The Red Wings won the Cup in the second overtime of the seventh game against the New York Rangers without their best player, Gordie Howe. Howe was injured in the semi-finals against Toronto after crashing into the boards with a sickening crunch. Howe required a 90-minute operation to relieve pressure on his skull. New York again was forced to play its home games on the road... because the circus was in town.

1942-1943 DETROIT RED WINGS over BOSTON BRUINS

History would not repeat itself as the Wings, again up 3 games to 0, shutout the Bruins in game four. The season was marred by World War II as close to 90 NHLers served in the Armed Forces in some capacity.

1943-1944 MONTREAL CANADIENS over CHICAGO BLACKHAWKS

Les Canadiens won the Cup with relative ease. With the formidable Bill Durnan in goal and "the Rocket" leading the way up front, several individual and team records fell in the wake of the Canadiens, the most dominating being eight straight wins en route to the Championship. The most spectacular though was Richard scoring all five goals in a 5-1 semi-final victory over Toronto, and being named all three stars in the game.

1944-1945 TORONTO MAPLE LEAFS over DETROIT RED WINGS

With Maurice Richard scoring 50 goals in 50 games the Canadiens were heavy favourites to repeat as champs. Frank "Ulcers" McCool had other plans as the Leafs goalie backstopped them to the Cup. Detroit won three games in a row for the second time, but did not win the Cup - earning the dubious distinction of being the only team to do this not just once in the finals, but twice.

1945-1946 MONTREAL CANADIENS over BOSTON BRUINS

Montreal, the regular season champions, won their second Cup in three years, only losing one game in their playoff run. "Rocket" Richard scored his first of six overtime winners. Toronto, the previous year's champion failed to make the playoffs.

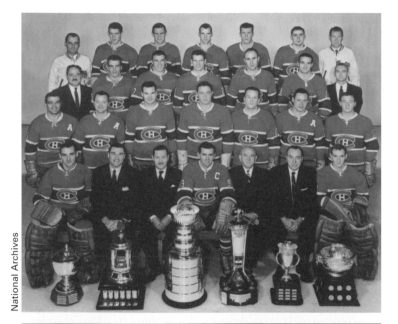

1950-1951   TORONTO MAPLE LEAFS over
MONTREAL CANADIENS

Bill Barilko scored the winning goal in overtime versus Montreal to win the Cup in a thrilling five game series in which every game went to overtime. On a fishing trip later that summer, Barilko's plane disappeared and his remains were not found until 1962, the next time the Leafs won the Stanley Cup.

1951-1952   DETROIT RED WINGS over
MONTREAL CANADIENS

Terry Sawchuk propelled the Wings to the Cup with an astounding 0.63 goals against average in eight straight wins in the playoffs, including four shutouts. He didn't allow a goal on home ice throughout the playoffs.

1952-53   MONTREAL CANADIENS over
BOSTON BRUINS

The Montreal Canadiens won the Cup in six games versus Boston. Rookie Jacques Plante recorded his first playoff shutout and Elmer Lach scored a goal in overtime that neither he nor Boston goalie, Sugar Jim Henry, saw go in the net.

1953-1954   DETROIT RED WINGS over
MONTREAL CANADIENS

Detroit won the Cup over Montreal in a hard fought seven game series. The winning overtime goal was another fluke, as Tony Leswick's seemingly harmless wrister from the point deflected off Doug Harvey's glove and into the Habs' net.

1954-1955   DETROIT RED WINGS over
MONTREAL CANADIENS

Detroit won their second straight Stanley Cup and Gordie Howe scored a then-record 20 playoff points. However, the "Rocket" was the bigger story, as he was suspended from the final games of the regular season and the entire playoffs by NHL president Clarence Campbell, after striking a linesman. His suspension incited a riot in Montreal, which caused over $30,000 dollars in damage and led to almost 100 arrests.

1955-1956   MONTREAL CANADIENS over
DETROIT RED WINGS

Toe Blake became only the third man to captain and coach a Stanley Cup Champion as he made the jump from player to coach look easy, winning the Cup in his first year of coaching. Jean Béliveau emerged as a big-time star scoring 12 playoff goals, seven in the five-game final.@

1956-1957   MONTREAL CANADIENS over
BOSTON BRUINS

Montreal won its second straight Cup, in five games over the Boston Bruins. Montreal's lethal power play during the season and the playoffs forced a rule change. Before the change, a penalized player was required to serve the full two minutes for a minor penalty regardless of how many goals a team scored.

1957-1958   MONTREAL CANADIENS over
BOSTON BRUINS

The Canadiens triumphed again over the Bruins for the Cup, this time in six games. The series highlight was "Rocket" Richard's 18th career playoff game-winning goal, in overtime of Game 5.

1958-1959   MONTREAL CANADIENS over
TORONTO MAPLE LEAFS

The Canadiens broke the record of consecutive Stanley Cups that they shared with Toronto by winning their fourth straight. Many counted the Habs out as they were without the services of Jean Béliveau and Maurice Richard at various times. The Canadiens showed they were a team for the ages as they overcame these setbacks and defeated the Leafs in five games.

1959-1960   MONTREAL CANADIENS over
TORONTO MAPLE LEAFS

Montreal won a record fifth straight Cup by winning eight straight playoff games over the Chicago Blackhawks and Toronto Maple Leafs. General Manager Frank Selke called them the "greatest hockey team ever assembled." The goal that Maurice Richard scored with an assist from his brother, Henri, in the third game would be his last in the NHL as he retired after the season.

HHJF

1960-1961   CHICAGO BLACKHAWKS over DETROIT RED WINGS

The Blackhawks used their sheer physical size to pound their smaller opponents, Montreal and Detroit, on the way to their first Cup win since 1937-1938. Bobby Hull was the standout player for Chicago, leading the Blackhawks over Detroit in six games.

1961-1962   TORONTO MAPLE LEAFS over CHICAGO BLACKHAWKS

The Leafs unseated Chicago as Stanley Cup champs in six games. However, they almost had no Cup to carry around the ice as a Montreal fan attempted to steal the Cup by smashing the trophy case in Chicago. Dick Duff fired the Cup-winning goal.

1962-1963   TORONTO MAPLE LEAFS over DETROIT RED WINGS

A supposedly 39-year-old Johnny Bower shut out Montreal's vaunted offence twice in a five game semi-final. The Leafs then beat the Red Wings in five, proving Coach "Punch" Imlach's pre-playoff prediction.

1963-1964   TORONTO MAPLE LEAFS over DETROIT RED WINGS

Bobby Baun returned from the dressing room and scored the game winning goal of Game 6 on a broken leg. Game 7 was anticlimactic with the Leafs winning 4-0 over Detroit. New Leaf Andy Bathgate won the only Cup in his stellar career.

1964-1965   MONTREAL CANADIENS over CHICAGO BLACKHAWKS

Jean Béliveau was unstoppable as he picked up 16 points and the first Conn Smythe Trophy, emblematic of the Most Valuable Player in the playoffs. Montreal defeated Chicago in seven games in a series in which the goalies, Gump Worsley for Montreal and Glenn Hall for Chicago, were incredible.

1965-1966   MONTREAL CANADIENS over DETROIT RED WINGS

The Canadiens came back from losing two games at home to beat Detroit in six games. In Game 3, Jean Béliveau scored on a memorable deke on an until-then-unbeatable Roger Crozier in goal. Crozier lost the Cup, but became the first player from a losing team to win the Conn Smythe Trophy as the MVP. The Habs' Henri Richard scored a very controversial Cup-winning goal after sliding into Crozier and the Detroit net.

1966-1967   TORONTO MAPLE LEAFS over MONTREAL CANADIENS

Dave Keon was the Conn Smythe hero as the Leafs won the last Leafs-Canadiens final series of the century, fittingly in Canada's Centennial Year. Keon was all over the ice, killing penalties and scoring goals, including two short-handed tallies in the deciding game. The Leafs rode the spectacular goaltending tandem of Terry Sawchuk and Johnny Bower en route to the Cup. Along the way they upset regular season champs, Chicago and heavily-favoured Montreal.

1967-1968   MONTREAL CANADIENS over ST. LOUIS BLUES

In the expansion year (the NHL went from 6 to 12 teams), Montreal was in last place at Christmas. They turned it around and went on a 16 game winning streak after the New Year, to take first place. Obviously peaking at the right time, the Habs lost but one playoff game and took the Cup in four straight against the expansion Blues, giving coach Toe Blake his eighth and final Stanley Cup. Blues' Scotty Bowman was in his first final as a head coach - it wouldn't be his last.

1968-1969   MONTREAL CANADIENS over ST. LOUIS BLUES

Montreal again swept the expansion St. Louis Blues, giving Habs Coach Claude Ruel his first Cup in his first season. The Canadiens' Serge Savard was the first defenceman to win the Conn Smythe as MVP.

1969-1970   BOSTON BRUINS over ST. LOUIS BLUES

Bobby Orr's overtime goal, portrayed in one of the most famous hockey photos of all time, completed the sweep of the Blues and brought Boston their first championship since 1941. Both Montreal and Toronto had missed the playoffs. Orr won his first Conn Smythe.

1970-1971   MONTREAL CANADIENS over CHICAGO BLACKHAWKS

Montreal won it 20th Stanley Cup behind the superb net minding of the unflappable Ken Dryden, who almost single handily defeated the regular season champion Bruins in the opening round. Dryden played all 20 playoff games, winning 12, including a 3-2 win in Game 7 in the finals, and picked up the Conn Smythe for his efforts. Henri Richard battled with Habs coach Al MacNeil over playing time, but was around to net the tying and Cup-winning goals.

1971-1972 BOSTON BRUINS over NEW YORK RANGERS

The Dynamic Duo of Esposito and Orr combined for 48 points in the playoffs as Boston won its second Cup in three years. Ranger captain Jean Ratelle ruefully noted the difference in the two teams: "They had Bobby Orr and we didn't." Orr won the Conn Smythe again.

1972-1973 MONTREAL CANADIENS over CHICAGO BLACKHAWKS

The "Pocket Rocket," Henri Richard, won his century-leading 11th Stanley Cup title as the Canadiens defeated the Blackhawks in six games. Conn Smythe winner Yvan Cornoyer led all scorers with 25 playoff points, including 15 goals. This time, Scotty Bowman was coaching the Habs to record his first Cup victory as coach.

1973-1974 PHILADELPHIA FLYERS over BOSTON BRUINS

The "Broadstreet Bullies" became the first expansion team to win Lord Stanley's prize. Bernie Parent shut down Bobby Orr and the Bruins, including a 1-0 win in the deciding game, on his way to claiming the Conn Smythe trophy. The Flyers' strategy of "tiring" Orr seemed to work.

1974-1975 PHILADELPHIA FLYERS over BUFFALO SABRES

The Flyers won their second straight title by defeating the Buffalo Sabres in a six-game series that had to be halted so that fog could be cleared from the ice surface in Buffalo. Parent shone through the fog to win another Conn Smythe trophy.

1975-1976 MONTREAL CANADIENS over PHILADELPHIA FLYERS

The quick and skillfull Canadiens overcame the intimidation tactics of the Flyers and thwarted their hopes of a third straight title. The Flyers' Reggie Leach lit up the scoreboard with 19 goals in 16 playoff games and was rewarded with the Conn Smythe in a losing cause.

1976-1977 MONTREAL CANADIENS over BOSTON BRUINS

The Canadiens continued their regular season dominance by blowing through the playoffs with a 12-2 record, including a series final sweep of the Boston Bruins. "Le Démon Blond" Guy Lafleur broke through to win the Conn Smythe with 26 playoff points.

1977-1978 MONTREAL CANADIENS over BOSTON BRUINS

Guy Lafleur and Larry Robinson were key components of the seemingly unstoppable Canadiens as they won their third straight Cup in six games over Boston. The word "dynasty" did not seem out of place when describing this edition of the Flying Frenchmen.

1978-1979 MONTREAL CANADIENS over NEW YORK RANGERS

Don Cherry's Bruins were ousted in the semi-finals by the powerful Habs when, with a one-goal lead with little over two minutes remaining in Game 7, they took a too many men on the ice penalty. The Canadiens' "Flower," Guy Lafleur, scored on the ensuing power play and the Habs went on to win in overtime. Montreal won the Cup Final in five; Bowman got his fifth Cup ring; Cherry got fired.

1979-1980 NEW YORK ISLANDERS over PHILADELPHIA FLYERS

Down 4-2 in the 3rd period in Game 6, the Flyers came back to force overtime. Nonetheless, after years of coming close, Bob Nystrom's overtime winner over the Flyers began the Islanders dynasty of the early '80s

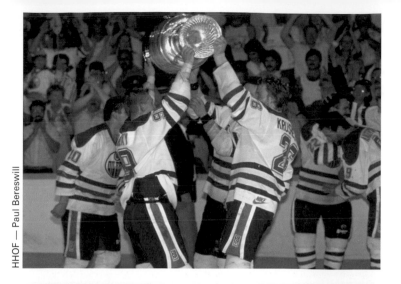

1980-1981 NEW YORK ISLANDERS over MINNESOTA NORTH STARS

Mike Bossy averaged nearly two points per game in the playoffs as the Isles defeated Minnesota in a five-game final. Bossy ended up with a then-record 35 points in 18 games to win the Conn Smythe Trophy.

1981-1982 NEW YORK ISLANDERS over VANCOUVER CANUCKS

The Islanders swept "King Richard" (goaltender Richard Brodeur) and the upstart Vancouver Canucks to win their third straight Stanley Cup. In a move designed to re-ignite divisional rivalries, the playoff format was changed from ranking the top 16 teams overall to advancing the top four in each division. This backfired as only two teams in the Campbell Conference had winning records. The Canucks recorded a losing season record (30-33-17) before staging a remarkable playoff run behind Brodeur's hot goaltending.

1982-1983 NEW YORK ISLANDERS over EDMONTON OILERS

Comparisons between the great Montreal Canadiens of the 1950s and the Islanders began as New York won its fourth straight championship. Edmonton outscored opponents 74-33 in earlier rounds, before being swept in four games in the final. Islander goalie and Conn Smythe winner Billy Smith was unbeatable in the net; Wayne Gretzky was held scoreless in his first final.

1983-1984 EDMONTON OILERS over NEW YORK ISLANDERS

The overpowering offence of Gretzky, Kurri, Coffey, Anderson and Conn Smythe winner, Mark Messier, proved insurmountable for the New York Islanders as they went down in a five game series. Including playoffs, Gretzky scored 100 goals on the season. He and the Oilers were just starting their dominance.

1984-1985 EDMONTON OILERS over PHILADELPHIA FLYERS

Records were smashed on the Oilers road to Stanley Cup victory. Wayne Gretzky got 47 points in the playoffs, including 30 assists while helping Jari Kurri notch four playoff hat-tricks. The Oilers won their second straight Cup, in five games over Philly.

1985-1986 MONTREAL CANADIENS over CALGARY FLAMES

Edmonton's seemingly inevitable road to the Cup was shut down when Oiler Steve Smith accidentally banked the puck off goalie Grant Fuhr and into his own net in Game 7 of the Smythe Division finals against the cross-province rival Calgary Flames. A 20-year-old Patrick Roy led Montreal and ten other Hab rookies to the Cup with a miserly goals-against-average of 1.92. The Habs won the final in five games.

1986-1987 EDMONTON OILERS over PHILADELPHIA FLYERS

Ron Hextall did his absolute best to stop the Oiler juggernaut, forcing the mighty Oilers to seven games. The Flyers came up just short as the Oilers won their third Cup in four years. Hextall received the Conn Smythe trophy for his efforts, even though he virtually attacked a few Oilers with his stick in the final game.

1987-1988 EDMONTON OILERS over BOSTON BRUINS

Amateur refs were used and the lights went out on the Bruins in a wacky year for the NHL. In the Wales Conference final between the Bruins and the Devils, New Jersey coach Jim Schoenfeld called referee Don Koharski "a fat pig" and was suspended by the League. Schoenfeld received a court injunction to coach but the referees union refused to work the game. A power failure in the Boston Garden in Game 3 of the finals between the Bruins and Oilers seemed fitting for the Bruins as they went down in four straight to Edmonton after the lights came back on.

1988-1989 CALGARY FLAMES over MONTREAL CANADIENS

The Oilers were dethroned by the recently-traded Wayne Gretzky and his new team, the LA Kings. The Kings then lost to the Flames. Calgary won the last all-Canadian final of the century over the Montreal Canadiens in six games. In a fitting end to a solid career, 500-goal scorer Lanny McDonald scored his final goal in the Cup-clinching game in Montreal. The Flames became the only visiting team to ever win the Cup at the Montreal Forum.

1989-1990 EDMONTON OILERS over BOSTON BRUINS

The Oilers proved they could win without "The Great One." Former Bruin goalie Bill Ranford came back to haunt his old team and win the Conn Smythe after backstopping the Oilers to a five game series victory over Boston. Edmonton's Petr Klima ended Game 1 at 15:13 of the third overtime period.

1990-1991 PITTSBURGH PENGUINS over MINNESOTA NORTH STARS

A back injury that forced Mario Lemieux to miss 50 games in the regular season could not hold him back from scoring 44 points in the playoffs, the second-highest in the century, and leading Pittsburgh to its first Stanley Cup. The North Stars were the first No. 16 seed to reach the final. That didn't help them in Game 6, losing 8-0 and the Cup to the Pens.

1991-1992 PITTSBURGH PENGUINS over CHICAGO BLACKHAWKS

Pittsburgh won the Cup for fallen coach "Badger" Bob Johnson who had succumbed to cancer earlier that year, and was replaced by Scotty Bowman. Mario Lemieux was his usual incredible self in the playoffs and won his second-straight Conn Smythe trophy, joining former Flyer-great Bernie Parent as the only men to win back-to-back honours in the century.

1992-1993 MONTREAL CANADIENS over LOS ANGELES KINGS

Montreal won an unprecedented 24th Stanley Cup title, this time over the Los Angeles Kings and Wayne Gretzky. It was the Kings' first final, and Gretzky's last. The final was marked by Marty McSorley's "too big a curve" penalty as the Kings were leading in Game 2. Montreal scored on the ensuing powerplay and never looked back, winning that game and the next three. Montreal, led by Patrick Roy in net, was unstoppable in overtime, winning 10 of 10 overtime games in the playoffs including three in the finals.

1993-1994 NEW YORK RANGERS over VANCOUVER CANUCKS

Led by 16 goal-scorer Pavel Bure, Vancouver took the favoured Rangers to Game 7 in the finals. Mark Messier guaranteed a Cup win and then delivered as Lord Stanley returned to NYC for the first time since 1939-1940, a 54-year drought.

1994-1995 NEW JERSEY DEVILS over DETROIT RED WINGS

After a lockout-shortened season of 48 games, the Devils won the Cup in what many call boring fashion, as they clogged up the neutral zone with a "trap," and ousted the Red Wings in four straight games.

1995-1996 COLORADO AVALANCHE over FLORIDA PANTHERS

The Quebec Nordiques moved to Colorado after the 1995 season and the transplanted Avalanche became the first team to win the Cup in the first season in a new city. Along the way, Colorado put an end to Detroit's season as the heavily-favoured Wings, losers of only 13 games in the regular season, fell in six games. Patrick Roy left Montreal in mid-season to anchor another Cup-winning team.

1996-1997 DETROIT RED WINGS over PHILADELPHIA FLYERS

Detroit broke a 42-year jinx as they ousted the Flyers in four straight games. The celebrations were short-lived, as six days after the Cup win a limousine carrying defencemen Vladimir Konstantinov and Viacheslav Fetisov and team masseur Sergei Mnatsakanov crashed, injuring all three, and ending Konstantinov's career. Wings goalie Mike Vernon won the Conn Smythe. Scotty Bowman was behind the bench, winning the Cup with his third team (Montreal, Pittsburgh, Detroit).

1997-1998 DETROIT RED WINGS over WASHINGTON CAPITALS

The Red Wings won their second straight Cup in a four-game sweep. Led by Conn Smythe winner and team captain Steve Yzerman, the Wings handed coach Scotty Bowman his record-tying eighth Stanley Cup victory. Bowman joined former Montreal legend Toe Blake as the only two to accomplish this feat.

1998-1999 DALLAS STARS over BUFFALO SABRES

Dallas defeated the Buffalo Sabres and Dominik Hasek on Brett Hull's triple overtime goal in Game 6. Huge controversy surrounded the goal as video reply showed Hull's skate to be in the crease, technically negating the goal. Hull was deemed to have control of the puck, the goal stood and the Stars won.

1999-2000 NEW JERSEY DEVILS over DALLAS STARS

The Devils run to the Cup took an unusual path when they fired coach Robbie Ftorek near the end of the regular season. With former Montreal great and Conn Smythe winner Larry Robinson behind the bench, the Devils won their second Stanley Cup over the defending champions.

HHOF — Paul Bereswill

The Stanley Cup Champions

The Challenge Series Years

Year	Team Name
1900	Montreal Shamrocks
1901	Winnipeg Victorias
1902	Winnipeg Victorias & Montreal AAA
1903	Montreal AAA & Ottawa Silver Seven
1904	Ottawa Silver Seven
1905	Ottawa Silver Seven
1906	Ottawa Silver Seven & Montreal Wanderers
1907	Kenora Thistles & Montreal Wanderers
1908	Montreal Wanderers
1909	Montreal Wanderers & Ottawa Senators
1910	Ottawa Senators & Montreal Wanderers
1911	Ottawa Senators
1912	Quebec Bulldogs
1913	Quebec Bulldogs
1914	Toronto Blueshirts

The East vs. West Challenges

1915	Vancouver Millionaires
1916	Montreal Canadiens
1917	Seattle Metropolitans
1918	Toronto Arenas
1919	NO DECISION - FLU EPIDEMIC
1920	Ottawa Senators
1921	Ottawa Senators
1922	Toronto St. Pats
1923	Ottawa Senators
1924	Montreal Canadiens
1925	Victoria Cougars
1926	Montreal Maroons

The NHL Takes Over

1927	Ottawa Senators
1928	New York Rangers
1929	Boston Bruins
1930	Montreal Canadiens
1931	Montreal Canadiens
1932	Toronto Maple Leafs
1933	New York Rangers
1934	Chicago Blackhawks
1935	Montreal Maroons
1936	Detroit Red Wings
1937	Detroit Red Wings
1938	Chicago Blackhawks
1939	Boston Bruins
1940	New York Rangers
1941	Boston Bruins
1942	Toronto Maple Leafs
1943	Detroit Red Wings
1944	Montreal Canadiens
1945	Toronto Maple Leafs
1946	Montreal Canadiens
1947	Toronto Maple Leafs
1948	Toronto Maple Leafs

Year	Team Name
1949	Toronto Maple Leafs
1950	Detroit Red Wings
1951	Toronto Maple Leafs
1952	Detroit Red Wings
1953	Montreal Canadiens
1954	Detroit Red Wings
1955	Detroit Red Wings
1956	Montreal Canadiens
1957	Montreal Canadiens
1958	Montreal Canadiens
1959	Montreal Canadiens
1960	Montreal Canadiens
1961	Chicago Blackhawks
1962	Toronto Maple Leafs
1963	Toronto Maple Leafs
1964	Toronto Maple Leafs
1965	Montreal Canadiens
1966	Montreal Canadiens
1967	Toronto Maple Leafs
1968	Montreal Canadiens
1969	Montreal Canadiens
1970	Boston Bruins
1971	Montreal Canadiens
1972	Boston Bruins
1973	Montreal Canadiens
1974	Philadelphia Flyers
1975	Philadelphia Flyers
1976	Montreal Canadiens
1977	Montreal Canadiens
1978	Montreal Canadiens
1979	Montreal Canadiens
1980	New York Islanders
1981	New York Islanders
1982	New York Islanders
1983	New York Islanders
1984	Edmonton Oilers
1985	Edmonton Oilers
1986	Montreal Canadiens
1987	Edmonton Oilers
1988	Edmonton Oilers
1989	Calgary Flames
1990	Edmonton Oilers
1991	Pittsburgh Penguins
1992	Pittsburgh Penguins
1993	Montreal Canadiens
1994	New York Rangers
1995	New Jersey Devils
1996	Colorado Avalanche
1997	Detroit Red Wings
1998	Detroit Red Wings
1999	Dallas Stars
2000	New Jersey Devils

Canada Our Century in Sport

CSI/COA

HHOF — Paul Bereswill

HHOF

Index

Date Due